Environmental Law

Environmental Law

John and Sharron McEldowney

Longman
is an imprint of

Harlow, England • London • New York • Boston • San Francisco • Toronto
Sydney • Tokyo • Singapore • Hong Kong • Seoul • Taipei • New Delhi
Cape Town • Madrid • Mexico City • Amsterdam • Munich • Paris • Milan

In memory of Ivor

Pearson Education Limited
Edinburgh Gate
Harlow
Essex CM20 2JE
England

and Associated Companies throughout the world

Visit us on the World Wide Web at:
www.pearsoned.co.uk

First published 2010

ISBN: 978-1-4058-4050-7

British Library Cataloguing-in-Publication Data
A catalogue record for this book is available from the British Library

Library of Congress Cataloging-in-Publication Data
McEldowney, John F.
  Environmental law / John and Sharron McEldowney.
    p. cm.
  Includes index.
  ISBN 978-1-4058-4050-7 (pbk.)
  1. Environmental law – England. 2. Environmental law – Wales. I. McEldowney, Sharron.
II. Title.
  KD3372.M2835 2010
  344.4204'6—dc22

                                                    2010006215

10 9 8 7 6 5 4 3 2 1
14 13 12 11 10

Typeset in 9/12.5 Giovanni by 35
Printed and bound by Henry Ling Ltd., at the Dorset Press, Dorchester, Dorset

Contents

Visit the *Environmental Law* mylawchamber site at **www.mylawchamber.co.uk/mceldowney** to access valuable learning material.

FOR STUDENTS
Companion website support
- Use the key issue checklists and practice exam-style questions with answer guidance to test yourself on each topic throughout the course.
- Use the updates to major changes in the law to make sure you are ahead of the game by knowing the latest developments.
- Use the live weblinks to help you read more widely around the subject, and really impress your lecturers.

Guided tour

How can I focus my learning to get the most out of my study?

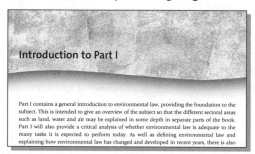

Introduction to Part I

Part I contains a general introduction to environmental law, providing the foundation to the subject. This is intended to give an overview of the subject so that the different sectoral areas such as land, water and air may be explained in some depth in separate parts of the book. Part I will also provide a critical analysis of whether environmental law is adequate to the many tasks it is expected to perform today. As well as defining environmental law and explaining how environmental law has changed and developed in recent years, there is also

The **Part introductions** give a broad overview on the major topics you'll be covering in the chapters ahead. **Chapter introductions** will further outline the major themes and concepts you'll be covering.

Conclusions

International environmental law is at the apex of global responses to environmental protection. At present it provides impressive coverage of many of the major areas where environmental protection is most acutely needed. The examples are numerous: perhaps the most momentous for our future is found in attempts to draw together an international response to global warming and climate change. In managing scientific advances with potentially substantial economic and environmental consequences, for example in the area of biotechnology, then international law on world trade is central. Even given impressive successes such as control of ozone depletion, there are a large number of shortcomings in international environmental law.

- The context, complexity and technical nature of international environmental law gives rise to ambiguity and uncertainty.
- International environmental law operates too often with a fundamental lack of clear objectives or priorities.
- There is an untidy relationship between the theory and practice of international environ-

Chapter conclusions will draw together the key issues and themes covered in each chapter.

Will difficult concepts in law be presented in a manageable way?

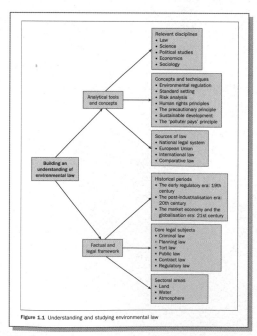

Figure 1.1 Understanding and studying environmental law

Diagrams are used to explain complex concepts and processes encountered in the study of environmental law.

Table 2.1 United Kingdom environmental taxes[2]

Transport taxes	Overview	Receipts
Fuel duty	Used on diesel and petrol	£23.35 bn
Vehicle excise duty	Variable tax on vehicle use	£4.81 bn
VAT on fuel duty	Used on fuel as well as pre-tax price of fuel	£4.09 bn
Company car tax	Estimated income value of a company car and fuel	£2.71 bn
Air passenger duty	Per passenger tax on flights from UK	£0.90 bn
Energy taxes	*Overview*	*Receipts*
VAT on domestic fuel	Applies to domestic fuel reduced rate of VAT	£0.88 bn
Climate change levy	Tax on energy use	£0.75 bn
Renewables obligation	Certificates for renewable energy sources	n/a
Resources taxes	*Overview*	*Receipts*
Landfill tax	Tax on waste	£0.73 bn
Aggregates levy	Tax on rock/mineral extractions	£0.33 bn
Water abstraction charges	Charged by the Environment Agency	£0.13 bn estimate
Emissions trading	*Overview*	*Receipts*
UK	UK emission trading scheme 2002–6	n/a
EU	CO_2 emissions	n/a

n/a-data not available.

Tables of key facts and statistics illustrate how environmental law and policy operates in practice.

Will there be examples I can use to place the law in context?

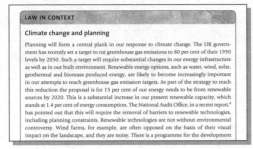

LAW IN CONTEXT

Climate change and planning

Planning will form a central plank in our response to climate change. The UK government has recently set a target to cut greenhouse gas emissions to 80 per cent of their 1990 levels by 2050. Such a target will require substantial changes in our energy infrastructure as well as in our built environment. Renewable energy options, such as water, wind, solar, geothermal and biomass produced energy, are likely to become increasingly important in our attempts to reach greenhouse gas emission targets. As part of the strategy to reach this reduction the proposal is for 15 per cent of our energy needs to be from renewable sources by 2020. This is a substantial increase in our present renewable capacity, which stands at 1.4 per cent of energy consumption. The National Audit Office, in a recent report,[8] has pointed out that this will require the removal of barriers to renewable technologies, including planning constraints. Renewable technologies are not without environmental controversy. Wind farms, for example, are often opposed on the basis of their visual impact on the landscape, and they are noisy. There is a programme for the development

CASE STUDY

Bathing Water Directive

There are a number of distinctive features about the EC Bathing Water Directive. First the directive was phased in over a period of time: two years to bring their laws into line with the directive and 10 years to bring the standards of bathing water into conformity with the directive. Secondly, the requirements of the directive can be waived where there are exceptional circumstances such as bad weather. For example, heavy rain can overwhelm a treatment works, resulting in poorly treated effluent being discharged into water. In recent years heavy rainfall has washed enteric micro-organisms arising from farm animals on agricultural land into sea water, resulting in a decline in water quality. In the past, the United Kingdom found it difficult to comply with the directive. In 1989 25 per cent of the designated bathing waters failed to reach even the minimum standards of the directive. Over the past 20 years our record has improved substantially. Past complaints that the United Kingdom failed to take adequate measures to ensure the quality of bathing waters at various resorts were upheld in *Commission v United Kingdom* (See: ENDS Report 222, p. 47, July 1993 Case C-56/90). The United Kingdom had

Law in Context boxes offer analysis of the issues affecting environmental law, such as the outbreaks of BSE and foot-and-mouth disease, environmental developments at an international level and activities of pressure groups, providing you with a deeper understanding of how the law you're learning actually works in practice.

Case study boxes appear throughout to heighten your awareness of key cases, legislation and environmental policy, providing you with the relevant detail you need.

Where can I find out more about topics in the book for my coursework?

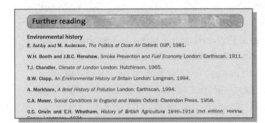

Further reading

Environmental history

E. Ashby and M. Anderson, *The Politics of Clean Air* Oxford: OUP, 1081.

W.H. Booth and J.B.C. Renshaw, *Smoke Prevention and Fuel Economy* London: Earthscan, 1911.

T.J. Chandler, *Climate of London* London: Hutchinson, 1965.

B.W. Clapp, *An Environmental History of Britain* London: Longman, 1994.

A. Markham, *A Brief History of Pollution* London: Earthscan, 1994.

C.A. Moser, *Social Conditions in England and Wales* Oxford: Clarendon Press, 1958.

O.S. Orwin and E.H. Whetham, *History of British Agriculture 1846–1914* 2nd edition, Harlow,

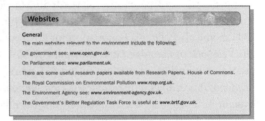

Websites

General

The main websites relevant to the environment include the following:

On government see: **www.open.gov.uk.**

On Parliament see: **www.parliament.uk.**

There are some useful research papers available from Research Papers, House of Commons.

The Royal Commission on Environmental Pollution **www.rcep.org.uk.**

The Environment Agency see: **www.environment-agency.gov.uk.**

The Government's Better Regulation Task Force is useful at: **www.brtf.gov.uk.**

Each chapter ends with **Further reading** to direct you to further resources available, allowing you to delve deeper into the subject.

Weblinks can be used in addition to this to find out where interesting and relevant further reading is available on the web.

Visit the *Environmental Law, first edition* **mylawchamber** site at **www.mylawchamber.co.uk/mceldowney** to access valuable learning material. Use the key issue checklists and practice exam questions to test yourself on each topic throughout the course. The site includes updates to major changes in the law to make sure you are ahead of the game, and weblinks to help you read more widely around the subject.

Acknowledgements

We are grateful to many people and institutions who have contributed to the writing of this book; at the University of Warwick Julio Faundez, Hugh Beale, Wyn Grant, and Thomas Perroud, and at the University of Paris – Sorbonne Professor Gerard Marcou; and at the University of Westminster Jane Lewis and Bob Scott. The University of Warwick provided a period of study leave that helped lay the foundations of this book, and the University of Westminster provided a period of study leave that helped with the completion of the book.

We have drawn from some of our previously published work, but in a significantly amended and updated form. These are Jacqueline Mackinnon and Paul Havemann's edited edition of John McEldowney's lectures while a New Zealand Foundation Distinguished Visiting Fellow 'Modernizing Britain: Public Law and Challenges to Parliament' published by the Centre for New Zealand Jurisprudence, 2001 and 'Human Rights, the Courts and the Environment – The Decision of the House of Lords in *Marcic* v *Thames Water Utilities Ltd.*' *The Yearbook of European Environmental Law* Vol. 5 (2005) pp. 93–110; Sharron McEldowney's articles on 'EU Chemicals Policy – a Foundation for Environmental Protection or a Missed Opportunity?' in *The Yearbook of European Environmental Law* Vol. 4, pp. 85–116, and 'A case study in environmental risk and its assessment in the BSE epidemic: Lessons for the future' in *Anglo-Japanese Academy Proceedings of the Conference on National, Regional and Global Transition: A Common Agenda for Anglo-Japanese relations in the Twenty-First Century*, pp. 305–312, ICCLP Publication, University of Tokyo, Japan.

Publisher's acknowledgements

We are grateful to the following for permission to reproduce copyright material:

Table 2.1 adapted from *The IFS Green Budget* IFS (2007) 192–4, Copyright Institute for Fiscal Studies; Table 14.1 adapted from *Renewable Energy: Options for Scrutiny*, National Audit Office (2008) 9

In some instances we have been unable to trace the owners of copyright material, and we would appreciate any information that would enable us to do so.

Table of cases

Table of statutes

Non-UK statutes

Table of statutory instruments

Table of international treaties and conventions

Table of European legislation

Part I

Fundamentals of environmental law

Introduction to Part I

Part I contains a general introduction to environmental law, providing the foundation to the subject. This is intended to give an overview of the subject so that the different sectoral areas such as land, water and air may be explained in some depth in separate parts of the book. Part I will also provide a critical analysis of whether environmental law is adequate to the many tasks it is expected to perform today. As well as defining environmental law and explaining how environmental law has changed and developed in recent years, there is also an explanation of the various sources of environmental law. In particular, we will take time to explain European environmental law and international environmental law, since their substantial influences have come to shape environmental law within the United Kingdom. Indeed, EU environmental law contributes an additional dimension by bringing a civil law tradition and legal thinking to the common law tradition of the United Kingdom. The converse is also true and it is important to recognise the many ways by which the common law approach has significant influence over the development of EU environmental law. There is a healthy dialogue evolving between legal systems that makes a fascinating study in its own right. Undoubtedly national interests are often challenged by external influence, which inevitably creates tensions. External pressures require careful adaptation to the needs of the UK and a thoughtful filtering into UK domestic law and the way we define legal problems. The environmental law of the UK may be viewed as overly reactive, not necessarily accommodating European law enthusiastically or easily. Adapt it must, however, because the context of UK environmental law today has an internationalist and European colour.

There is a further confounding element to environmental law and regulation that asks thorny questions of any jurisdiction. The problem is simple to state but much more difficult to manage. The goal posts keep moving. Our recognition and understanding of environmental problems are in constant flux, and solutions to environmental hazards and risks are, therefore, in need of constant updating. This continual need for change places considerable strains on regulatory systems, including that of the United Kingdom.

There has been a discernible trend towards 'green politics' topping the political and legal agenda in many European countries. In contrast, the spread of environmentalism has been patchy in the UK. Green politics have been largely dissipated across the UK's main political parties. There is no single effective voice for green issues, leaving the environmental agenda vulnerable to the pragmatism of the main political parties. Environmental initiatives may not take precedence and, indeed, may come a poor second against the plethora of traditional competing demands that drive the political parties and the government of the day. Nonetheless the politics of the environment in Europe has come to shape that in the UK through its influence on the EU.

The recent history of the UK holds considerable significance for our environmental law. The UK was one of the first major economies to nationalise its main water and energy sectors, including gas, electricity and coal in the 1940s. It was also the first to privatise the main water and energy utilities in the 1990s. Regulation has been central in the years since privatisation, which has required a more complex and technical regulatory system than at first assumed. The regulation of the privatised utility companies has proved important for the environment and deserves careful consideration.

There are a number of themes and specific topics that form the approach to environmental law in this book. The focus is on understanding the law and regulation but based on acknowledging that environmental problems are defined by their social, scientific and political context. The public's perceptions about science and law as well as politicians' policy choices also have great influence on environmental law. This is a wider discourse than simply studying 'black letter' legal topics. As environmental agendas are constantly changing it is not surprising that perceptions shift and with them environmental law and its development. The recent global financial crisis has served to underline how economies are interdependent and require global as well as national solutions. There is a growing movement in favour of corporate social responsibility that locates the environment and sustainable development firmly within finance and business.

Part I covers topics crucial to understanding environmental law, including the role of institutions, the setting of environmental standards and the general approach taken to regulation that is relevant to pollution control and prevention. Human rights are also important, with questions of governance and the role of civil society intertwined. There are several themes worthy of identification from the outset. Public interest in the environment, particularly climate change and energy use, sits uneasily with a consumer society. The citizen as consumer and energy user is often in opposition to the successful application of recycling strategies and adoption of green energy. Popular culture and the technical details of environmental law are an uneasy mixture of public perceptions and specialist understanding. While law is central to the management of the environment, it is the social, economic and political debates that determine what laws are passed and whether they are enforced. Environmental law is there to protect the environment and human well-being as well as to proactively engage in the preservation of ecosystems. It is also called upon to regulate and prevent our excesses and mistakes for future generations and this makes for an uneasy social and political context. This is a challenge that environmental law must meet.

1 A general introduction to environmental law

Introduction

Environmental law has become increasingly important and relevant to the general study of law. It has also become more and more important to other disciplines. Today, both lawyers and scientists engage across traditional subject boundaries to consider and attempt to tackle environmental problems. This comes at a time when environmental concerns have greater prominence on the political agenda of the early twenty-first century. High oil prices and reports on the impacts of climate change have placed the protection of the environment and finite resources as key to the future of the planet. Importantly, the focus on climate change is no longer only driven by government and activists but it forms an agenda for industry and commerce.[1] There is a growing recognition that our impacts on the earth have global health, resource and environmental consequences that will substantially influence the strength of economies and social stability. Sustainable development is a foundational concept in environmental law and draws together these disparate impacts. It engages with the market economy and social development while prioritising the protection of the environment for future generations.

There is no doubt that the environment has a growing relevance in the lives of most citizens. Home owners are uncomfortably aware of the need to provide good insulation as fuel costs rise. All new homes offered for sale must have Home Information Packs (HIPS), which include an energy performance certificate and form part of the drive to save energy and reduce carbon emissions. Major companies, concerned about the environment have called on governments to tackle climate change commensurate with maintaining a stable economy and market values. Recently the Stern Report, written by Sir Nicholas Stern, a leading economist and academic, has argued that climate change must be addressed urgently, as the economic costs of neglecting to do so are, in effect, equivalent to two major economic depressions.[2] The most recent scientific evidence and analysis of climate change have underpinned the international negotiations at the 2009 Copenhagen Conference to contain greenhouse gas emissions. International action has also focused on the destruction of the ozone layer in the upper atmosphere by human-made chemicals. The lifestyles of those in developed nations seem

---

[1] See E. Fisher, B. Lange, E. Scotford, C. Carlane, 'Maturity and methodology: starting a debate about environmental law scholarship' (2009) *Journal of Environmental Law* 213.

[2] Sir Nicholas Stern, *The Economics of Climate Change* HM Treasury, London: Stationery Office, 2006.

to be in conflict with responses to climate change. This is underscored by the social and economic desirability of cheap flights and the resultant more frequent use of planes, causing greater environmental harm. The public's attention has also been drawn to an array of other pollution problems from noise to motor vehicle fumes. Waste and its control are also high on the political agenda and there is considerable public debate about limiting packaging and adopting effective recycling strategies. Local authorities have taken a lead role in recycling strategies, including providing separate collection facilities for paper and other recycled items. The recent car scrappage scheme is intended to take older and less fuel efficient cars off the road and allow the purchase of new models that are more fuel efficient.

Since nineteenth-century industrialisation, science and scientific discoveries have provided the basis for many changes in society. Science and technology have often been the starting point for commercial development and consequent economic growth, and have substantially influenced the way we live. Indeed, it is difficult to think of any part of modern-day life un-affected by science. The generally high regard that science is held in by society is a product of this: the way science has influenced almost every aspect of our lives and well-being. Yet, our use of scientific and technological advance has contributed in large part to our often damaging impact on the world. Still the general public have come to expect that science will deliver advances and there are now demands for science to provide solutions to our environmental woes. It may be possible to solve problems such as poor energy efficiency in our housing, costly electricity and over-reliance on fossil fuels through scientific advances. Historical developments in tackling environmental pollution were, indeed, often science-led. Set against this, however, is a mounting scepticism about science being able to offer remedies and public doubts about the capability of science to diagnose and effectively describe environmental harm. This is partly due to a general disillusionment about scientific methodology and the empirical method of collecting data. As a consequence, there is growing scepticism that scientific evaluation can effectively or, indeed, should inform law. There is a general questioning about the hierarchy that science may impose on how data is to be evaluated and interpreted.[3] Despite these doubts, the fact remains that science is the most appropriate tool available to provide basic information on what is harmful and is important in helping to set standards. In examining environmental impacts science works within probabilities not certainty and must offer this uncertainty as part of the debate on action. Public debate about the environment is important so that choices and options are fully discussed. Political parties and government must engage with different institutions which provide the key settings for this environmental debate. The twenty-first century undoubtedly marks an important time for environmental law because the variety of rules and policy options may help create a more sustainable environment. The high cost of energy is, perhaps, a real opportunity to engage with the public about environmental responsibility and debates on sustainability.

Defining environmental law

The question of how to define environmental law is not as simple as it may at first appear. In fact, there are quite divergent approaches to how it should be defined and understood. Some writers see environmental law as providing a lead in the definition and analysis of

---

[3] J. Holder, 'New age: rediscovering natural law' (2000) 53 *Current Legal Problems* 151.

environmental problems. The law is regarded as a safeguard against being unduly influenced by scientists and scientific analysis. This may be a reaction against a scientific approach to the environment and giving undue weight to science and scientific knowledge in environmental protection (see above). It is felt that public debate and democratic institutions should shape the law and that this is preferable to giving scientists and scientific data too much authority. The approach we take in this book is to consider environmental problems in their social and legal context.

The debate over how to define environmental law is useful because differing approaches give a clearer insight into the way the environment may be protected and how best to design, draft and implement effective environmental laws. Defining a problem is one way of ensuring that the law is adequate and proportionate and it is on this basis that the law may be critically appraised and examined. Consequently environmental law may be more narrowly defined simply to mean the various laws that are applied to the environment. Legal definitions of environmental law are even narrower. The Environmental Protection Act 1990 defines the environment to consist of

> all or any, of the following media, namely the air, water and land; and the medium of air includes the air within buildings and the air within other natural or man-made structures above or below the ground.

This describes the focus of most environmental law. The creation of institutions to monitor and regulate the environment is another way of defining the areas covered by environmental law. For example section 4 of the Environment Act 1995 created an Environment Agency for England and Wales and for Scotland the Scottish Environment Protection Agency. General environmental and recreational duties are provided under the 1995 Act and are devolved on both agencies. Responsibilities for the environment are defined in terms of pollution control and include a Code of Practice, which covers the agencies' environmental and recreational duties. Ministers may give the new agencies guidance 'towards the objective of achieving sustainable development' (see section 4(3) of the Environment Act 1995). The term sustainable development is helpfully explained by the 1997 World Commission on Environment and Development (the Brundtland Commission) as 'development that meets the needs of the present without compromising the ability of future generations to meet their own needs'. The acceptance of the concept of sustainable development has dominated much thinking on environmental law.

Another way to describe environmental law is to concentrate on the harm caused to the environment by human activity. Pollution by humans may harm the environment, and the focus of pollution laws is to protect the environment by limiting or preventing human activity that may be deleterious to the environment. The Environmental Protection Act 1990 defines pollution as

> the release into any environmental medium from any process of substances which are capable of causing harm to man or any other living organisms supported by the environment.

In fact, this definition of the scope of environmental law lacks precision or clear boundaries, but inevitably relies on scientific assessment. The lack of precision is partly due to the difficulties faced by scientists in establishing environmental damage or harm. Indeed, it is impossible for scientists to prove a negative: that a substance will not cause harm under any circumstances. There is always potential for the unpredictable, unforeseen effect.

A useful definition of the environment linked specifically to economic activity and businesses is provided in the Environmental Management Standard ISO 14001. This refers to the

surroundings in which an organisation operates, including air, water, land, natural resources, flora, fauna, humans and their interrelation.

This brings together everything that goes to make up our world, while focusing attention on locality specific to an organisation working within the confines of environmental law.

As well as defining environmental law and what we mean by the environment, it is also useful to examine critically different aspects of the legal system and to review some substantive areas of law. In this way we can assess whether the general law and different areas of substantive law can contribute to improving and protecting the environment.

Applying criminal law to the environment raises a number of questions. How far should environmental law make use of the criminal law to set sanctions to deter and prevent lawbreakers? To what extent do criminal sanctions provide a satisfactory way to regulate the environment? The development of environmental crimes, covering acts or omissions that harm the environment, broadens the scope of environmental law and brings to the fore the role of different regulatory agencies in law enforcement. This poses the question of whether preventing environmental crimes is the best way forward in developing strategies for environmental protection. The recent inquiry by Professor Richard MacRory, a leading environmental lawyer, considers the role of criminal penalties in this field.[4]

The use of private law, in particular tort law, for environmental protection also raises questions. How far can negligence and nuisance afford a sound basis for environmental liability? Can action in negligence and nuisance provide adequate compensation for environmental harm and contribute to the prevention of the environmental damage? There is, in fact, a range of different mechanisms available which provide incentives to prevent environmental harm. The use of insurance, for example, is one important device.

Allied with private property rights is the role of town and country planning, environmental impact assessment and the use of compulsory purchase powers. Protecting the environment does not simply relate to pollution and waste but more generally to conservation and landscape preservation. The ecological costs of society in this context need to be assessed and carefully weighed against development. Planning law has the uneasy task of facing counterbalancing arguments. A market economy needs to grow and develop and planning law must remain flexible enough to accommodate commercial and private sector developments. Large-scale planning decisions over major projects, however, are often the subject of intense conflict with the environment at the centre of contested values about law and society. Large electricity-generating stations, airports, motorways and large infrastructure developments are just some of the examples where planning and environmental law directly face the difficult challenge set by sustainable development, mentioned above.

Environmental law also involves the issue of how public law rights are applied. The Human Rights Act 1998 incorporates the European Convention on Human Rights (ECHR) into the UK law and provides an additional layer of rights to the pre-existing common law and statutory arrangements. The 1998 Act has great significance as the Act has helped to

---

[4] R. MacRory, *Regulatory Justice: Making Sanctions Effective* London: Cabinet Office, 2006.

create a culture of rights in the United Kingdom through the increased use of judicial review to question the legality of public decision-making. It is also possible that many different forms of environmental harm may be protected on a rights basis enforceable by the courts. This remains open to a case-by-case approach by the courts.

The application of substantive legal principle to environmental problems invites further consideration of how the environment is regulated as a whole. There are many institutions and bodies involved in the process of regulating and scrutinising environmental problems. These vary considerably in the range and scope of their role, and it useful to provide some examples of the often complicated nature of the arrangements. In England and Wales, the Environment Agency checks on waste management and the illegal disposal or treatment of waste. It also has responsibilities for granting water abstraction licences (taking water from lakes or rivers or ground water), and for ensuring that anyone who causes or knowingly permits the entry of polluting matter into controlled waters is taken to court. Local authorities are responsible for air pollution and its control, including air pollution under the Clean Air Act 1993. Contaminated land is a joint responsibility of local authorities and the Environment Agency. Statutory nuisances fall under local authority jurisdiction and industrial pollution control is a joint responsibility between local authority and the Environment Agency. Hazardous substances and major accident hazard sites fall under the jurisdiction of the Health and Safety Executive and the Environment Agency. There are specific responsibilities concerning drinking water quality that are within the remit of the Drinking Water Inspectorate and the Secretary of State. In terms of the utilities such as electricity and gas, Ofgem has the role of overseeing competition and pricing. The Forestry Commission is responsible for forestry matters. Genetically modified organisms are regulated by the Health and Safety Executive and the Secretary of State. Finally, environmental taxes fall under the jurisdiction of HM Revenue and Customs.

Regulating the environment is undoubtedly an essential element of environmental law and these examples serve as a useful illustration of the intricate and complex regulatory structure that applies to the environment. Regulating the environment, however, is not simply a matter of applying the traditional command and control systems of regulation. It includes setting targets and providing incentives; in short it involves adopting a wide range of techniques. Many techniques applied to the environment today involve economic and fiscal instruments such as taxation as well as the traditional legal regulation of the environment.[5] Setting standards and ensuring their application is also frequently used to protect and, indeed, improve the environment. Public bodies, by using different types of rules, guidance and procedures, attempt to control and set boundaries on the activities of companies and individuals in the context of the environment. How to achieve effective environmental control is a major issue which involves an evaluation of the scope of criminal sanctions as well as the use of economic instruments. There is also a growing recognition of the value of civil sanctions and their application to environmental polluters.[6]

---

[5] See: Neil Gunningham, 'Environment law, regulation and governance: shifting architectures' (2009) *Journal of Environmental Law* 179.

[6] See: Defra, *Consultation on fairer and better environmental enforcement* London: Defra, 2009, ENDS Report 415, August 2009.

Why study environmental law?

There are good reasons to study environmental law. The range and diversity of environmental laws provides an intriguing mixture of law, rules and regulations together with the use of economic and social instruments. Environmental problems transcend national boundaries so that environmental law is not only found in national laws but also in European and international law. This makes environmental law interesting to a wide range of lawyers beyond the boundaries set by the study of a traditional legal system. Environmental law is also comparative. Different legal systems and cultures address environment protection in different ways and this has influenced the way environmental law has developed. Environmental problems are defined through science, political systems and society. The nineteenth century addressed problems arising from the industrial revolution through laws on pollution. The twenty-first century has seen a growing recognition that financial and corporate Britain has an important role in adopting environmentally friendly approaches. Large businesses such as high street retail stores have also realised the need to adopt environmental policies.[7] This makes the subject intriguing in terms of theoretical and practical legal approaches to environmental law. In writing about environmental law it is inevitably necessary to address the subject from the perspective of the twenty-first century. Lessons gained from history, however, are invaluable and worthy of study since they help to trace the evolution and the likely future of environmental law.

Students of environmental law, then, require a grasp of many law subjects. Integrating the study of these different elements of the law is a fascinating and demanding task. Environmental law sets us new challenges for the understanding of law. It is not only lawyers who may be interested in studying environmental law. The citizen may perceive environmental law as providing a convenient set of additional arguments to challenge government decision-making and to advance the protection of the environment. Citizenship participation in decision-making on subjects that affect the environment has grown over recent years and has become increasingly important. Pressure groups, such as Friends of the Earth, Greenpeace, and the World Development Movement, may see environmental law as worthy of study in order to build a case for or against a new development or project. Consequently environmental lobbying has become a high-stakes lottery of winners and losers. The activities of pressure groups have heightened public awareness of environmental matters. Lawyers and regulators may see the environment as needing protection, and environmental law is an important way forward. Environmental law offers new horizons in the field of jurisprudence and legal study. Addressing environmental problems engages new techniques and methods and, as we shall see, many of these are at the boundaries of law, science and regulation.

Environmental law

Environmental law will specifically engage undergraduate and postgraduate law students with an exposition and analysis of environmental law. There is also a wide range of students drawn from diverse disciplines such as science, politics, sociology and economics who find law and legal regulation of the environment an area of interest. There are policy advisers and

---

[7] Benjamin Richardson, 'Climate finance and its governance: moving to a low carbon economy through socially responsible financing' (2009) *International and Comparative Law Quarterly* 597.

organisations, both private and public, who require an understanding of environmental law. It is hoped that this book will provide a thought-provoking study of environmental law for these groups as well.

Principles and ideas in environmental law

As we have seen, environmental law is the law relating to the protection of the environment. There are many historical stages that go to make up modern environmental law; in fact few other legal subjects have undergone the transformation found in environmental law. This is largely because environmental law has developed in response to environmental problems. Industrialisation and economic development go side by side with scientific discoveries, which have led to enormous changes in society and in the way the environment is affected. The transformation of environmental law is also a reflection of a period of twenty-first century modernisation and the impact of globalisation on the market economies of the world. It should not be overlooked that each century has made its own unique contribution to environmental law. This has important implications for the different approaches to protecting the environment. Overall environmental law is not consolidated into a single code and students of environmental law face a quite daunting task in discovering the relevant law applicable to an environmental problem. Environmental law is found in an assortment of legislation and court decisions. It is also to be found in EU directives and regulations and cases decided by the European Court of Justice as a result of the United Kingdom's membership of the European Union. As environmental problems do not recognise national boundaries, there are many international treaties relevant to setting standards and protecting the environment.

Just as the sources of environmental law are diffuse, so the shaping of environmental policy and ultimately the law are the product of diverse pressures. These influences include new scientific and technological developments and the work of scientists in evaluating what is harmful to humankind and the environment. Scientific influence is clear from the period in the eighteenth and nineteenth centuries when law relating to public health and pollution control began. The common law developed from decisions made by judges, and many of the earliest common law cases helped in development of the law of property as well as private law, particularly tort law and nuisance law. Such laws were heavily weighted in favour of property and land ownership considerations. As a consequence, environmental law is inevitably controversial. Protecting the environment unavoidably involves regulating or interfering with the rights of ordinary citizens so that society as a whole may benefit. Environmental law is also moulded by theoretical analysis and the work of economists and political scientists. There are, also, a number of specific principles that guide and influence the shape and form of environmental law. These are sustainable development, the 'polluter pays' principle, and the precautionary principle. They are as follows:

1. The principle of sustainable development.[8] This principle sets the agenda for the future by attempting to ensure that environmental harm is controlled and environmental resources are protected. This involves attempting to reconcile the conflicting demands of economic

[8] Sustainable development was first defined in terms of social, economic and environmental criteria by the World Commission on Environmental Development (the Brundtland Commission) in *Our Common Future* (the Brundtland Report, 1987).

and social development against environmental and resource protection. It ensures that the benefits of any development outweigh its costs including environmental costs.

2. The principle of 'polluter pays'.[9] This principle is currently much in vogue. It asserts that the polluter should pay for any costs that arise from harm to the environment, or ill health or injury to individuals caused by pollution. The law has developed a number of strategies to implement this principle. One example is the landfill tax where polluters have to pay charges for waste disposal.

3. The 'precautionary principle'.[10] This principle means that the absence of scientific proof for a risk of environmental harm is not a sufficient reason for failing to take preventative action. In recent years it has largely been interpreted in terms of risk assessment. On example is in the area of genetically modified organisms (GMOs) where the European Union has adopted a precautionary approach to GM crops in the light of the scientific evidence and the scientific uncertainty of the time.

The three principles will be discussed in more detail in Chapter 2.

The changing shape of environmental law

The development of legal responses to the protection and enhancement of the environment is ongoing and makes environmental law a vibrant area of study. It is worthwhile at the outset to provide a few recent examples, interrelated initiatives and policies, that will serve to illustrate the variety and extent of change relevant to environmental law. The Planning and Compulsory Purchase Act 2004 provides reforms to the planning law system with an immediate impact on how the environment is planned and protected. Environmental Impact Assessment (EIA) has become a key consideration in development projects. It has the potential to substantially increase environmental information on and provide an enhanced role for the protection of the environment in infrastructure developments. The Human Rights Act 1998 has increased the role of judicial review and has the potential to augment the way environmental rights are protected. There are also signs of an increase in the activities of pressure groups, particularly in the use of judicial review. Changes in the way central government departments and local government are organised are likely to have an impact on the way we protect the environment. The Sustainable Communities Act 2007 provides for the sustainability of local communities. The 2007 Act includes requirements for energy conservation; for improvements in the transport system to take account of sustainability and for a decrease in emissions of greenhouse gases. Many of the regulatory agencies that are responsible for the utilities have been reformed into a system of 'meta-regulation'. Targets and outputs are set and the agencies have been provided with new powers that place emphasis on environmental protection. The environment agencies have been considerably strengthened at national and at European levels opening further channels to protect the environment.

---

[9] This principle originated from the UN Conference on the Human Environment held in Stockholm (1972). The principle is embedded in Article 130r(2) of the Treaty Establishing the European Community 1957 (as amended).

[10] First found as 'Vorsorgemassnahmen' in the Bremen Declaration of the First International Conference on the Protection of the North Sea. The principle now has a broader definition and is embedded in Article 130r(2) the European Union Treaty 1957.

There is a plethora of new scientific developments that set challenges for environmental regulation, for example in the expanding field of genetically modified organisms, in chemical synthesis and in nanotechnology. Unexpected events such as the outbreak of BSE and foot-and-mouth disease not only have implications for the food and agricultural industry but have made substantial demands on environmental regulatory systems and continue to influence environmental protection.

Environmental matters at an international level have frequently been controversial, including the failure of the USA to ratify the Kyoto Protocol on climate change. Recently the Bali Conference, concluded in early December 2007, again brought hard bargaining and near deadlock in responding to global change. The hard-won outcomes from the Bali Conference are as follows:[11]

- Policy-makers from over 180 countries discussed the next stages in forming an environmental agreement on what cuts are required in greenhouse gases.

- It was agreed to form a road map for the next two years to achieve a successor to the Kyoto Protocol of 11 December 1997.

- There was to be a major environmental conference leading to a new Climate Treaty in Copenhagen in 2009. This conference did not bring about a new treaty and made little advance in new measures to tackle climate change.

- There was an agreement that poorer countries should be rewarded for protecting forests and businesses should be able to trade carbon allowances.

It was hoped that developed countries would reach agreement to reduce carbon emissions by between 25 per cent to 40 per cent below levels by the year 2020. At the time this was opposed by the USA but since the inauguration of President Obama in 2009 the USA has adopted a new acceptance of the need for targets and mechanisms to embrace climate change.

The international effort to reduce the production and use of chemicals involved in ozone depletion has been a marked success. Unfortunately, it is now evident that some of the chemicals used as replacements for CFCs may themselves contribute to the problem. Agreements on controlling ozone depletion must evolve to account for this threat. There is an international effort, as well as action at national and EU level, to control use of industrial chemicals; in particular there is growing concern over a diverse range of chemicals acting as endocrine disruptors or hormone mimics, which may cause reproductive changes in humans as well as wildlife. In the European arena there is a change in focus from an emphasis on control and prevention of environmental harm towards a more concerted effort to apply the principle of sustainable development. The societal and economic context of the environment is thus increasingly recognised. There has, also, been a renewed emphasis on the precautionary principle, but with an attempt not only to include scientific consideration in risk assessment but to embed social issues as well. There is, importantly, increased recognition of the significance of the environment in the EU Reform Treaty. There are many economic advances that underpin new techniques adopted by environmental law and influencing its development. Environmental law is changing and growing and it is important that this book attempts to provide a likely road map for the future. This may take unexpected turns beyond those few outlined above and include consideration of the role of government, the burdens of regulation and the need to avoid excessive costs while complying with regulation.

[11] See: *guardian.co.uk/environment*.

How to study environmental law

Environmental law is built on the foundations of many legal categories, changing ideas and different concepts. While it is today a distinct specialist subject, it draws from various traditional areas of law that have been adapted as they are applied to environmental problems.

Private and public law are intertwined. Thus the building blocks of environmental law are to be found through a study of tort, particularly nuisance (including statutory nuisance) and negligence, contract law through agreed environmental standards, criminal law, the law of property and planning law, including aspects of public law, judicial review and, recently, human rights under the Human Rights Act 1998 are relevant and important. In the nineteenth century the development of regulatory law through inspectorates and inquiries began.

Today environmental law may be usefully studied through knowledge of institutions in terms of their role and relevance for environmental law and regulation. Institutions are useful sources of information and data. There are many public institutions and agencies that are important in this context and deserve mention here, as they will be referred to throughout the book, and include the Department of the Environment, Food and Rural Affairs (Defra), the Environment Agency and the Health and Safety Executive. There is also local as well as central government involvement in the environment. Uniquely, the Royal Commission on Environmental Pollution stands as a permanent body with responsibility to advise the government on environmental matters. As well as providing sources of information and advice, the regulatory bodies have many statutory duties and obligations. Rights and duties are often a theme in any discussion on the effectiveness of environmental law.

There are practical ways of familiarising yourself with environmental law: through the main law journals, websites and reading the key cases and statutes. One tip is that complex legislation is easily accessible through the House of Commons website, which provides access to Explanatory Notes and information. The House of Commons Research Papers are also a valuable source of material and are available from the House of Commons website.

There is yet another layer of complexity in the study of environmental law within the United Kingdom. Environmental problems can often be focused on a locality and are appropriately considered in the context of local issues. Since 1998, there has been devolved government to the regions: Scotland, Wales and Northern Ireland within the UK. This requires separate consideration of the law that is applicable within the jurisdiction of each devolved institution.

As mentioned, above, at the other extreme environmental law commonly extends beyond national boundaries. In the modern world of trade and globalisation, protecting the environment requires international action. International environmental law has given rise to important developments, most notably the Stockholm Conference (1972), the Rio Conference (1992) and the Bali Conference (2007). The Copenhagen Conference in 2009 has provided an agenda for the future discussion of the environment that has significant implications for the nature of our planet. A study of international environmental law is therefore a crucial part of understanding environmental law and allows useful examination of fundamental concepts and ideas.

European environmental law, through our membership of the European Community and today the European Union, is immensely important. As well as providing the basic rules for the market economy of the 27 member states, there are environmental standards that are directly enforceable across all these member states. Environmental law is inexorably linked to environmental policies and a general strategy to deliver economic and environmental principles that are sustainable. The interdependence between economic development and the environment is pivotal to the future of the member states. Knowledge of EU law is thus inevitably an important part of studying environmental law. The treaties, including the newly signed Reform Treaty 2007,[12] provide the basis for the development of environmental law within the EU. The role of the European Court of Justice and the contribution of the case law of the European Community to environmental law is also noteworthy and should be understood.

Environmental law may be studied from contemporary, historical or theoretical perspectives. One fascinating aspect is that the English common law has built up legal expertise on remedies and legal process that may be used to protect the environment. Indeed, these were often manipulated by lawyers and legal advisers to give redress for environmental wrongs. By the late 1970s, and the adaptation of European Community law into the English legal system, it became clear that the whole focus of environmental law was changing. The new direction was concentrated on preventing environmental harm rather than relying on the law of pollution and its control. This, together with the adaptation of the core legal categories such as tort, property and planning law, meant that environmental law began to gain cohesion through distinct values and concepts. In part this came from setting standards and providing codified and enforceable preventative measures. Underpinning the new environmental law was a much closer identification with scientific values, assessment and standards and with their application through law and legal mechanisms. Environmental law drew much closer to the techniques involving the use of economic instruments, setting targets and assessing risk. The basic framework was formed from the different sectoral areas of environmental law covering land, air and water. Environmental law has, therefore, now become more complex, technical and intricate than at any time in its history. At the same time it lacks coherence and there are few coalescing points that provide a way to understand the detail of environmental law and afford an easy basis for analysis. This is the daunting task faced by judges, lawyers and the private and public sectors when confronted with interpreting and understanding environmental law. The challenges of studying environmental law are further underlined by the need to address ambiguous and complex rules in the context of the social, economic and scientific context of their application. This makes it a necessity to read widely in the subject to understand the theoretical as well as practical context in which the legal rules work.

The question of how to approach this task requires some guidance as well as a road map of how to engage with environmental problems. A schematic approach to the study of environmental law is set out in Figure 1.1. The structural building blocks of the development of environmental law must be understood as part of the contemporary scene. Case law analysis needs to be combined with statutory interpretation, as much of environmental law is found in statutory formulations that resemble the codification that was promoted in the nineteenth century but has never been achieved. Environmental law is to be found in the sectoral treatment of the main substantive areas of land, water and air, but understanding the sectoral application of environmental law requires an understanding of how environmental law has developed and its state of transition.

---

[12] Once ratified, the Reform Treaty is expected to change the title to the Treaty Establishing the European Community (TEC). It will be known as the Treaty on the Functioning of the European Union (TFEU); the process of ratification by the member states will take some time.

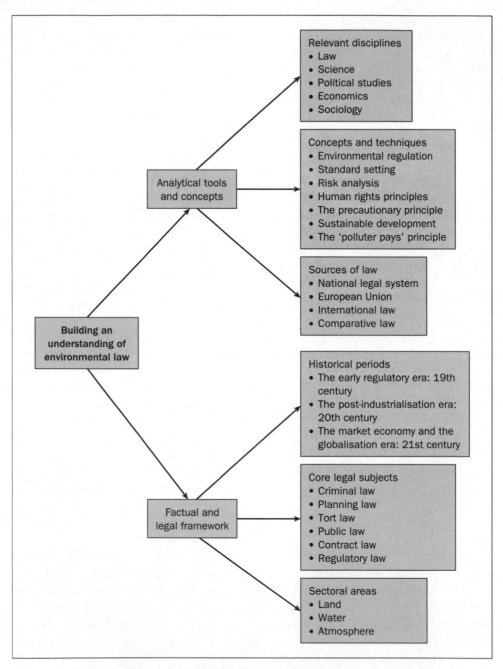

Figure 1.1 Understanding and studying environmental law

Further reading

General background: thematic and analytical

There is an enormous breadth to the writing on environmental law today that crosses many disciplines. This selection of the relevant literature is based on providing the reader with different perspectives that allow an analysis of the main contemporary issues in environmental law. General background reading must include historical as well as economic and legal analysis of environmental law. It must also address the environment today with a contemporary focus on the main issues. Included in our reading list are some books that help locate environmental law in a wider context of economic literature.

R. Attfield, *The Ethics of the Global Environment* Edinburgh: Edinburgh University Press, 1999.

S. Bell and D. McGillivray, *Environmental Law* Oxford: Oxford University Press, 2008.

D. Delaney, *Law and Nature* Cambridge: Cambridge University Press, 2003.

G. Harris, *Seeking Sustainability in an Age of Complexity* Cambridge: Cambridge University Press, 2007.

J. Holder and M. Lee, *Environmental Protection, Law and Policy* second edition Cambridge: Cambridge University Press, 2007.

C. Klonk, *Science and the Perception of Nature* Yale: Yale University Press, 1996.

M. Lee, *EU Environmental Law: Challenges, Change and Decision Making* Oxford: Hart Publishing, 2005.

R. Macrory (ed.), *Principles of European Environmental Law* London: Europa, 2004.

R. Macrory, *Regulatory Justice: Making Sanctions Effective* London: Cabinet Office, 2006.

J. Mcneill, *Something New Under the Sun: An Environmental History of the Twentieth Century* London: Penguin, 2000.

M. Redclift and G. Woodgate (eds), *The International Handbook of Environmental Sociology* London: Edward Elgar Press, 1997.

B.J. Richardson and S. Wood (eds), *Environmental Law and Sustainability* Oxford: Hart Publishing, 2006.

P.P. Rogers, K.F. Jalal and J.A. Boyd, *An Introduction to Sustainable Development* London: Earthscan, 2008.

R.W. Rycroft and D.E. Kash, *The Complexity Challenge: Technological Innovation for the 21st Century* London: Pinter, 1999.

Royal Commission on Environmental Pollution, 21st Report, *Setting Environmental Standards* Cm 4053 London, 1998.

N. Stern, *The Economics of Climate Change* London: HM Treasury, 2006.

C.R. Sustein, *Risk and Reason: Safety, Law and the Environment* Cambridge: Cambridge University Press, 2002.

Introductory and background reading

E.J. Evans, *The Forging of the Modern State: Early Industrial Britain 1783–1870* London: Longman, 1996.

T. **Jewell and J. Steele** (eds), *Law in Environmental Decision Making* Oxford: Clarendon Press, 1998.

A. **Markham**, *A Brief History of Pollution* London: Earthscan, 1994.

C. **Miller**, *Environmental Rights* London: Routledge, 1998.

R. **Porter**, *Enlightenment: Britain and the Creation of the Modern World* London: Penguin Books, 2000.

D. **Wilkinson**, *Environment and Law* London: Routledge, 2002.

Websites

General

The main websites relevant to the environment include the following:

On government see: ***www.open.gov.uk***.

On Parliament see: ***www.parliament.uk***.

There are some useful research papers available from Research Papers, House of Commons.

The Royal Commission on Environmental Pollution ***www.rcep.org.uk***.

The Environment Agency see: ***www.environment-agency.gov.uk***.

The Government's Better Regulation Task Force is useful at: ***www.brtf.gov.uk***.

International and European

Using internet resources such as ***http://www.ecplex.org***, it is possible to find useful sources.

The European Environmental Law Homepage is useful: ***http://www.eel.nl***.

There is an International Environmental Law Research Guide: ***http://www.ll.georgetown.edu/intl/guides/environment/***.

The World Conservation Union, founded in 1948 is also useful: ***http://www.icun.org/themes/law/***.

The United Nations Environmental Programme (UNEP): ***http://www.unep.org***.

There are also a variety of organisations as follows: ***www.wto.org*** and ***www.worldtradelaw.net***.

The OECD: ***www.oecd.org***.

Europe and European Union matters are covered at: ***www.europa.eu.int/eur-lex/en/index/html***.

Visit **http://www.mylawchamber.co.uk/mceldowney**
to access key issue checklists and practice exam
questions to test yourself on this chapter.

---

2 Themes and issues: environmental law in transition

Introduction

The twenty-first century finds environmental law in transition. This is perhaps unsurprising: our environmental impacts and environmental knowledge are never static and continually invite new solutions. In fact, until relatively recently environmental law was ill-defined: indeed it was often not treated as a subject in its own right. Today the importance of environmental law is well recognised beyond the legal community alone. Environmental law is seen as relevant to scientists, policy-makers and economists. It is studied by law students, the general public and forms the work of both practitioners and academics. Even so it is a subject that still lacks coherence as it is formed from many different parts. It is also exceptionally technical and the technical part of environmental law creates a formidable challenge. This could hardly be otherwise, given the many sources of environmental law – some statutory, some derived from European law or some based on international treaties. Environmental law also draws heavily on the case law developed through centuries of judicial decisions, which have often filled in gaps here and there or adjusted rules and concepts to fit new circumstances that were not entirely recognised earlier in the creation of legal rules. Even contemporary environmental law is often pragmatic in having to adjust to new science or changes in policy. In general the common law has resisted large-scale codification whereby the entire law on a given subject is to be found in a single codified statute. There are many instances, however, where statutory arrangements represent comprehensive and detailed codes in all but name. For example the law relating to contaminated land is to be found mainly in the Environmental Protection Act 1990. Even this codification, however, is supplemented by numerous amendments and adjustments to take account of new developments.

The sources and history of environmental law form the basis of this chapter. A historical perspective will help to show how environmental law is in an incessant state of evolution and continually adjusts to new developments. It also serves to illustrate the complex and technical skills that are necessary to interpret and apply environmental law correctly. Enforcing environmental law has always been somewhat unpredictable and one challenge facing policy development today is how to address past mistakes. Failures to prevent pollution or environmental harm may be the result of weak laws or weak enforcement or both. There is a perpetual optimism among law makers that new regulations or rules will inevitably lead to improvement. The reality may be more pessimistic and only a few successes can be counted in the application of environmental law. Many environmental law obligations are poorly regulated or enforced in Britain today, with the exception of European law.

Policy-makers appear to have learned some of the lessons from the past and there is a prevailing attitude that economic instruments (Table 2.1) are as likely to gain success as the application of more formal legal rules. This point is recognised in the use of economic instruments or the use of civil penalties as well as criminal fines.[1]

The reality is that most developed countries, including Britain, and key developing countries hesitate to introduce effective environmental laws that are likely to inhibit economic growth. One example of this reluctance is seen in controlling the emissions of carbon dioxide, which are closely linked to economic growth and drive climate change. Global climate change is one of the major environmental problems set to dominate the social and economic landscape of the twenty-first century, setting a major challenge for many countries to reduce carbon emissions (Table 2.2). We face hard political choices if environmental law and policy in this and other areas are to be effective.

Table 2.1 United Kingdom environmental taxes[2]

Transport taxes	Overview	Receipts
Fuel duty	Used on diesel and petrol	£23.35 bn
Vehichle excise duty	Variable tax on vehicle use	£4.81 bn
VAT on fuel duty	Used on fuel as well as pre-tax price of fuel	£4.09 bn
Company car tax	Estimated income value of a company car and fuel	£2.71 bn
Air passenger duty	Per passenger tax on flights from UK	£0.90 bn
Energy taxes	Overview	Receipts
VAT on domestic fuel	Applies to domestic fuel reduced rate of VAT	£0.88 bn
Climate change levy	Tax on energy use	£0.75 bn
Renewables obligation	Certificates for renewable energy sources	n/a
Resources taxes	Overview	Receipts
Landfill tax	Tax on waste	£0.73 bn
Aggregates levy	Tax on rock/mineral extractions	£0.33 bn
Water abstraction charges	Charged by the Environment Agency	£0.13 bn estimate
Emissions trading	Overview	Receipts
UK	UK emission trading scheme 2002–6	n/a
EU	CO_2 emissions	n/a

n/a-data not available.

[1] A good overview of environmental taxes is Andrew Leicester, *The UK Tax System and the Environment* Institute of Fiscal Studies, 2006 and Barbara E. Bell, 'Environmental taxation' (2008) *VAT Digest* 1.
[2] Data taken from: IFS, *The IFS Green Budget January 2007* London: IFS, 2007, pp. 192–4.

Table 2.2 Largest emitters of carbon dioxide[3] (tonnes, m, 2003)

1	United States	4,816.2
2	China	4,143.5
3	Russia	1,493.0
4	India	1,273.2
5	Japan	1,231.3
6	Germany	805.0
7	Ukraine	684.0
8	United Kingdom	569.1
9	Canada	565.5
10	South Korea	455.9

Historical foundations

The common law is the source of many principles found in environmental law today. It provided pre-existing forms of action and legal method that could be adapted into usable forms of redress to tackle environmental problems. It is even possible to trace the beginnings of environmental law as far as back as medieval times.[4] Eighteenth-century actions in nuisance and trespass formed the basis for environmental protection. The case law explored the boundaries of trespass and property law, particularly in the context of fishing rights. Public nuisance as a tort developed to the extent that it allowed the occupier of land to use and enjoy land free from any unreasonable interference. In its public form, public nuisance extended to an act or omission that is part of a legal duty and where the effect was to endanger the life, health, property or morals of the public. In such circumstances a public nuisance could be tried as a criminal offence as well as give liability in damages as a civil wrong. In its private form, the tort of nuisance could be used to address liability for physical damage to the adjoining land of a neighbour. This remains the case today. There were set boundaries on the limits of such liability. The prerequisite of liability was the unreasonable use of land, which was dependant on many variables. These included the nature and duration of the nuisance and the intention or purpose of the individual's action. The main emphasis and preoccupation of the law was individualistic rather than for the collective good.

The early regulatory era: nineteenth century

Industrialisation in the nineteenth century marked an important point in the development of environmental law. Private law principles found in tort through nuisance and negligence shifted from being predominantly focused on claims based on individual rights to claims that addressed the common good and consequently to compensation for injury to the person or damage to property. There was a high moral order and Victorian standards of propriety were

---

[3] Data taken from *The Economist Pocket World in Figures 2008* edition London: 2008.

[4] See: G. Williams and B.Hepple, *Foundations of the Law of Torts* London edition, 1964 and D. Ibbetson, 'The tort of negligence in the common law in the nineteenth and twentieth centuries' in Mark Lunney and Ken Oliphant, *Tort Law* Oxford: Oxford University Press, 2000, p. 12.

met by the adoption of rules that gave rise to liability insurance. This provided private property rights with additional protection. It was also a period of statutory intervention aimed at creating an environment necessary for the building of new towns and cities. There were a number of landmark legislative interventions worthy of mention. Standards in public health and housing were addressed under the Public Health Act 1875 that formed the beginning of the modern law on public health. The Alkali Acts of 1863 and 1868, including the Alkali etc. Works Regulation Act 1906, provided the basis for control of the heavy chemical industry. The Alkali Acts established the first ever inspectorate. It is noteworthy that many of the main public health provisions with an environmental impact were applicable at local level. There was a plethora of different local authorities, boards and other local bodies charged with various duties and responsibilities relevant to the environment. Legislation also included the Rivers (Prevention of Pollution) Act 1876. This set the standards for much anti-pollution legislation and applied criminal sanctions to support the 'best practicable means' of pollution control. Criminal prosecutions were rare but the possibility of their use was a threat held over any polluter.

The existence of regulatory systems of inspection and control laid the foundations of modern environmental law. The operation of environmental law from this time was formed around a new inspectorate that provided a 'command control' system of regulation (meaning that regulation left a degree of autonomy with the body being regulated with little direct oversight of its effectiveness), largely dependent on a degree of self-enforcement. There was a perceived necessity for a 'light touch' since the state, on behalf of public welfare, applied standards and enforceable regulation that interfered substantially with the private property rights of the new industrial companies and corporations. This interference extended to hours of work and eventually standards of employment. Inspection and light touch regulation came to form a coherent system of public health. The Public Health Act 1875 addressed the question of disease control and the setting of local sanitary controls. Outbreaks of typhoid and cholera alerted the authorities to the problems of unregulated housing and overcrowding. At the end of the nineteenth century, the beginning of a new era was marked by the Housing, Town and Planning etc. Act 1909. This consolidated many local and private Acts and created in embryo a new system of town and country planning in Britain. Two world wars intervened before the Town and Country Planning Act 1947 instituted a modern system of planning law based around the original idea of green fields surrounding cities and towns. The idea was to inhibit cities from expanding into open countryside. Setting boundaries around towns and cities remains a feature of the landscape today. The over-populated slums required more radical solutions and were addressed through new towns together with radically changed architecture to provide liveable space. Many of the environmental controls were locally based rather than centrally delivered. This empowered local authorities and both informal and formal community groups to make their own planning choices, but subject to overarching guidance from central government.[5] Local authorities expanded their powers and remit to address water pollution, and regulation of the local rivers and catchments (see the River Boards Act 1948).

The nineteenth century was also a period of judicial developments in the area of tort law. The changing social, economic and political developments in society were reflected in the

---

[5] Central government guidance is in the form of Planning Policy Guidance Notes (PPGs) These are gradually being replaced by Planning Policy Statements.

way tort law grew in importance.[6] The expansion of the law of nuisance to include the amenity value of land embraced aspects of the land's enjoyment. Things affixed to the land such as trees and crops were included while the amenity value of the land included protection from interference through sound, smell and vibrations. This gave rise to the potential for environmental protection when the conduct of the defendant amounted to an unreasonable use of land and this caused unreasonable interference with the claimant's land. The test of reasonableness grew from the determination to see the ordinary person's perception of the use of the land and probably reflected the role of the jury in civil cases prevalent in the nineteenth century.

Some landmark decisions are worthy of brief discussion. In *Bamford* v *Turnley*[7] the plaintiff complained that the defendant burning bricks on his land was unreasonable because of the resulting smoke and smell. The plaintiff's case was accepted. How did the court choose between what was reasonable and unreasonable? One way was to consider whether or not there was a public benefit that justified a reasonable interference in rights of the landowner. In the case the decision was based around the issue of what constituted a public benefit. The answer, according to Baron Bramwell in the Court of Exchequer Chamber, was that the test of public benefit was not conclusive of a case. Thus it may be for the public's benefit that railways should run, the gain of having the railway was sufficient to compensate the loss occasioned by the use of the land required for its site. This, however, should not interfere with the principle that there should be compensation where the railway caused harm. The nineteenth-century case law fitted environmental damage[8] into the compensation culture prevalent at the time. It was, as some commentators have noted, based on a crude cost–benefit analysis. Interestingly, this has an earlier resonance as is illustrated in the case of *Jones* v *Powell* in 1629[9]. In this case the Court of King's Bench were uncertain and divided over the principle of whether compensation was payable because fumes, smoke and other contamination from a brew house caused interference with a neighbouring property, including damage to the plaintiff's papers. Brewed ale was regarded as a higher social benefit than drinking water and the public's benefit was greater than the individual detriment suffered by the plaintiff when drinking water was contaminated. How far, however, public benefit could excuse dangerous or injurious activity was far from clear. The changing judicial attitudes were apparent in another decision in 1865 *Tipping* v *St Helen's Smelting Co*,[10] often regarded as a major breakthrough in the development of environmental law. The plaintiff bought some property, but several months later the defendant began the operation of a smelter works on property situated a mile and a half from the plaintiff's land. Fumes and damage to the defendant's property formed the basis of the defendant's claim. The jury found for the plaintiff and this finding was later upheld by the House of Lords. An injunction was granted, but this only prevented the factory from committing a nuisance. Eventually the factory was closed and moved a few miles. The decision had a limited impact on the general environment. Although the case demonstrated the potential for common law remedies to be applied to environmental problems, it also

---

[6] A.W.B. Simpson, 'Victorian judges and the problem of social cost: *Tipping* v *St Helen's Smelting Company* (1865)' in *Leading Cases in the Common Law* Oxford: OUP, 1995, pp. 164–7.

[7] (1862) 3 B & S 66, 122 ER 27.

[8] See: Pontin 'Tort law and Victorian government growth: the historiographical significance of tort in the shadow of chemical pollution and factory safety regulation' (1998) 18 OJLS 661.

[9] (1628) Hut 135; Palm 536.

[10] (1865) LR 1 Ch App 66.

illustrated the restrictive nature of the remedy on offer.[11] Moreover, there was a great deal of confusion over the exact principle applicable in the case.

Lord Westbury in the House of Lords approached the problem raised by *Tipping*, by focusing on the activities of a neighbour that gave rise to material injury to property. He distinguished cases of material injury from those which may cause 'sensible personal discomfort'. The latter appeared to offer some defence to landowners whose neighbours had to put up with some inconvenience that was necessary for the trade or business to be carried on. The distinction drawn by Lord Westbury is not entirely clear as there are many circumstances where 'sensible personal discomfort' may amount to material injury to property. The point of importance is that the locality where the material injury occurs is relevant and perhaps the real distinction was the type of damage to property. Here physical damage might be distinguished from economic loss. The latter only became the basis of tort liability much later in the history of environmental law.[12]

Taking the locality into account was a way of mitigating compensation claims but not as immunity against any claim. The suitability of an area and its environment was tantamount to the judicial acceptance that environmental considerations were related to the market development of an area and also acceptance of industrialisation as a necessity of Victorian progress. Within the boundaries of the locality there were some stricter rules and no one had an absolute right to make noise on their own land.[13] The courts were reluctant to express principles beyond the narrowest extension of the concept of interference with property. Cases were decided on the slimmest of margins[14] based on the concept of the legality of use of property. There were often moral judgements made on the fault or otherwise of the parties. The approach to fault liability had limitations, particularly with respect to the proof of intention or malice.

The courts came to adopt an alternative approach, holding that an occupier would be liable for the escape of a dangerous thing in the course of the non-natural use of the land. This rule came from the landmark decision of *Rylands* v *Fletcher*[15] that provided in certain defined circumstances the application of strict liability. *Rylands* v *Fletcher* was an important decision in the development of pollution control. The rule applies when persons, for their own purposes, bring on to the land and maintain there anything which is likely to do mischief should it escape. Potentially there is liability for all damage which is the natural consequence of the escape. The use of the land must be 'non-natural', which refers to the use of land that is out of the ordinary and unusual. The implication is that the bringing of something on to the land that has a special use increases the danger to the public. The rule was narrowly interpreted and extended to physical injury rather than to economic loss. The absence of proof of fault gave the rule particular relevance to environmental law when motive and intent might otherwise prove difficult to find. Adjusting and amending the common law to fit the changing circumstances of environmental pollution gave rise to applying cases such

[11] Simpson, *Victorian Law and the Industrial Spirit* London Selden Society 1995.
[12] *Hunter* v *Canary Wharf Ltd* [1997] AC 655.
[13] *Allen* v *Flood* [1898] AC 1.
[14] See: *Christie* v *Davey* [1893] 1 Ch 316 upholding the claim on behalf of the plaintiff who occupied a house and played, practised and taught music, against the defendant who complained and made noises on the partywall in response to the music.
[15] (1868) LR 3 HL 330.

as *Rylands* v *Fletcher* but with some caution. The natural use of the land included the force of nature for which there was no liability. It was only for the non-natural use that there was liability. The principle of *Rylands* v *Fletcher* seems to have arisen because in the late 1860s there were a number of reservoir failures, the most notable in March 1864 at the Bradfield Reservoir owned by Sheffield Waterworks Company.[16] Reservoir failures often led to landslides and water escaping on to adjoining property causing loss of life and injury to animals and damage to property.

Both legislative and judicial contributions to the development of an embryonic system of environmental law were supplemented by the actions of many voluntary and private organisations. For example, the work of the Coal Smoke Abatement Society, founded in 1880 and amalgamated in 1924 with other similar societies to form the National Smoke Abatement Society, was centred on the serious problem of smoke from burning coal. One leading writer in this field, Professor Clapp, neatly explained the problems of domestic heating in the context of environmental pollution:

> In 1881–5 the earliest years for which records exist, central London in the two winter months of December and January saw little more than one-sixth of the bright sunshine enjoyed in four small country towns.[17]

The cause was the industrial and domestic use of coal. Viewed from continental Europe, England seemed strangely connected to the open coal fire.

> Estimates of the heat loss from the open fire varied from seven-eighths to nine-tenths, and it was no wonder that a German chemist scornfully dismissed the English open fire as a system of chimney heating.[18]

There was also the work of the various statistical societies. The collation of statistical information on the environment was of long standing.[19] It was partly as a response to the commitment in running the British Empire, but was also related to the interdisciplinary studies that facilitated the running of empire. The early nineteenth century saw the establishment of a number of different statistical societies including the British Association for the Advancement of Science, formed in Cambridge in 1833; and the London Statistical Society, subsequently renamed the Royal Statistical Society, which was founded in March 1834. Similar societies appeared in Manchester, Dublin and Belfast. The House of Commons became the focal point of their activities. By providing information on the cause of crime, poverty and unemployment, the statistical societies contributed to parliamentary debates and inquiries. The 1842 Parliamentary Report on the Sanitary Condition of the Labouring Population of Great Britain came about because of the many deaths in the major cholera outbreak of 1831–2 when 32,000 lives were lost, representing a significant proportion of the adult working population. Statistical data pointed to overcrowding and poor sanitation as key determinants of the outbreak. The data appeared to support the miasma theory of the

---

[16] See: Francis Newark, 'The boundaries of nuisance' (1949) 65 LQR 480; Simpson, 'Bursting reservoirs and Victorian tort law: *Rylands and Horrocks* v *Fletcher* (1868)' in Simpson, *Leading Cases in the Common Law* Oxford: Oxford University Press, 1995.

[17] B.W. Clapp, *An Environmental History of Britain* London: Longman Pearson, 1994 p. 14. The four towns were Oxford, Cambridge, Marlbrough and Geldeston.

[18] Clapp, *op. cit.*, p. 17.

[19] See William Petty (1623–87) and John Graunt (1620–47) two of the founders of the study of statistics.

cause and effect of disease. The miasma theory was based on the belief that the removal of all putrefying and decomposing matter would succeed in the removal of disease. Thus, by purging the external environment of refuse and organic matter public health would be protected. The Nuisance Removal Acts and the Public Health Act 1848 came about through parliamentary lobbying on sanitary conditions.

Generally at this time the emphasis of environmental lobbying was linked to improvements in public health. These efforts were both national and international efforts. The Board of Trade established a Statistical Department in 1832 and many other government ministries devoted considerable efforts to the collection of statistical data. The Registration Act 1836 provided for the establishment of a national General Register Office to index, collate and record returns on births, deaths and marriages. Legislation that resulted from the work of statistical study included the Sewage Utilisation Act 1865 and the Sanitary Act 1866 that resulted in improvements to sewage control. The adulteration of food and food quality was addressed by the Adulteration of Food and Drugs Act 1872 and the Sale of Food and Drugs Act 1875. These are good examples of the type of regulatory body that was in place and gave Britain a reputation for strong legislation in this field. Many of the responsibilities for enforcement lay with local bodies, which gave rise to an even more sophisticated system of inspection, audit and reporting of the state of the environment.

The system described above undoubtedly lacked coherence and symmetry, but its advantages should not be overlooked. It operated on the basis that once specific public health or pollution problems had been identified, they could be targeted and remedied through the development of specific laws. The Victorians faced a considerable challenge at the time. The rapid industrialisation did not only affect the environment but also prompted hurried building of new towns and cities. This cannot be overlooked in understanding the responses to public health and environmental problems and evaluating their worth. Despite the complexity and growing diversity of responses to the environment, the foundations of environmental law were undoubtedly established by the end of the nineteenth century. Lessons learnt in the nineteenth century still have resonance today. This point will be explored later in Chapters 6 and 7 when the current system of environmental regulation is examined showing how the historical basis of regulation had a relevance in building environmental law. It was realised that data was needed to identify the causes of environmental problems and to provide a suitable environmental response. There was recognition that designing strategies to protect the environment was a multidisciplinary task. The industrial and economic development at the time was, of course, led by an emphasis on science and scientific discovery. Ironically, the new science that helped create the industrial revolution and its attendant problems was not particularly effective at providing a basis for environmental protection. There was one clear and important focus of concern and activity that emerged during the nineteenth century. Human squalor, particularly arising from the living and working conditions of industrial workers, was identified as the main rationale and justification for environmental protection. The response was originally a reaction to individual pollution problems after they had occurred and were recognised. This ultimately gave rise to a consideration of how best to prevent the pollution in the first place. There were, however, no simple solutions for the prevention of environmental harm and this ambition took longer to address than had perhaps been anticipated. In fact, for most of the last century Britain's environmental law struggled to come to terms not only with the outcomes of the industrial revolution but also with a new era of post-industrialisation, economic growth and globalisation.

The post-industrialisation era: the twentieth century

The two world wars that preoccupied the first half of the twentieth century created a lasting legacy for Britain and Europe. In the case of Britain, it also signalled the end of empire and a general industrial decline. In the early part of the twentieth century the focus for environmental law expanded and diversified. Industrial and urban expansion continued at the beginning of the century placing new pressures on the environment and public health. The number of alkali works reached 1,000, with a total of 1,500 processes registered. This was to double by 1974. In 1906 oil refineries and tinplate works came within the jurisdiction of the Alkali Inspectorate. Cement manufacturing was added in 1935. An even wider extension of the work of the alkali inspectors came with the significant Clean Air Act 1956. This Act was a response to unprecedented pollution from smoke and fumes.

The history of fog in London, together with its associated increased mortality from respiratory disease, stretches back to the seventeenth century. Cold weather provides ideal conditions for fog and during the mid-twentieth century London saw severe winter fogs. The years of 1945 at the end of the Second World War and 1948 were particularly bad, with a significant increase in deaths due to the fogs. It was commonly assumed that nearly 60 per cent of the working population was affected through either premature deaths or illness. The worst fog recorded was in 1952; particularly high concentrations of sulphur dioxide were measured. The effects of such poor air quality were far-reaching and devastating, causing a large number of deaths. Individual families often suffered disproportionate loss. The fact that London, the centre of the country's commercial life, was so badly affected focused public opinion on an age-old problem. The initial result was a series of enquiries led by the Ministry of Health. Finally, however, an intense public outcry and parliamentary debate forced the setting up of a full-scale enquiry under the chairmanship of Sir Hugh Beaver. The recommendations of the enquiry mirrored those associated with clean drinking water a decade before, namely that every effort should be made to restore clean air and prevent pollution. A fundamental aim from the enquiry was to reduce smoke emissions in populated areas by up to 80 per cent within 15 years. The Beaver Committee was not aware of the potential for smoke pollution to cause acid rain or contribute to global warming, but the committee was conscious that preventing pollution was a better option than having to deal with the consequences of polluted air. Industry started to tackle the problems identified by the Beaver Committee while the Alkali Inspectorate pressed for additional controls on grit and particulates, and over-emissions from steel and iron works. In the late 1960s and 70s the introduction of smoke-free zones saw the use of smokeless coal; in fact domestic fires began to be phased out anyway because of the introduction of gas central heating. Other energy sources such as oil were competitively priced in comparison to coal and were used for electricity generation. Oil also overtook solid fuel as a heating fuel in the 1970s. This period also saw the introduction of nuclear power stations for the production of electricity.

Environmental problems were also addressed in other ways. The Alkali and Clean Air Inspectorate were incorporated into the Health and Safety Executive when it was established in 1974. This gave rise to a multi-purpose agency that had safety at work as a major part of its remit. The Wildlife and Countryside Act 1981 provided a consolidation of nature conservation and protection for wildlife, flora and fauna. The Act was modified in 2000 with the Countryside and Rights of Way Act 2000, which gave public access to many areas of private land.

Planning law became an important means to both regulate and set priorities for land use. In rebuilding war-damaged Britain, the 1947 Town and Country Planning Act set a framework that has endured to this day. A major part of the planning system is to set enforceable limits on development around towns and cities. It was the 1947 Act that settled the adoption of a 'green belt' in which there could be no permitted development. The Act also set the agenda for a unified system of planning throughout the country that allowed the urban environment to be controlled, subject to central government guidance, by local planning decisions reached on a wide discretionary basis. The 1947 Act replaced the inadequate Housing, Town and Country Planning etc. Act 1909 and was a remarkable achievement. It was one of the first comprehensive systems of planning law. In fact, Britain led the way in the form that the 1947 Act adopted in placing local community-based planning under central direction. Public participation in the planning system was also an important element. The early years of planning under the 1947 Act serve to illustrate that there was a consensus over the role and direction planning should take. Citizen participation in the planning system came through the fact that planning decisions were made at a local level and citizens at a local level actively engaged with the planning process. The state was a major stakeholder in developments and as a developer became instrumental in the location and size of new towns and cities. The ideology of municipal socialism made local housing the mainstay of planning land use and amenity issues. So successful was the 1947 Act that it has retained its significance even up to the present day. It was consolidated under the Town and Country Planning Act 1990 with further changes under the Planning and Compensation Act 1991.

Planning and the environment make uneasy bedfellows. It is clear that much planning has environmental significance, but the impact on the environment was not initially directly part of the planning process. The integration of environmental matters into planning was rather ad hoc and took some time, since the 1947 Act was mainly centred on social objectives and community planning. Three different strategies introduced the environment into the determination of planning matters.

- First, the planning inquiry was adopted and used to meet the needs of planning large-scale projects. The planning inquiries into the grant of planning permission for the third London Airport and Sizewell B, a nuclear electricity generating plant, serve to illustrate the consideration of environmental matters as part of the overall planning objectives.

- The second strategy relates to the operation of development plans. These are locally based plans that assess planning needs and provide a road map for future planning decisions.

- The third strategy came about through membership of the European Community in 1972. This relates to the introduction of environmental impact assessment (EIA) as a material consideration in whether or not to grant planning permission. The process of embedding EIA began after the 1985 EIA Directive (85/337/EEC) and continues today under the 2001 Strategic Environmental Assessment (SEA) Directive (2001/42/EC).

There are a number of regulations used to implement the system of environmental assessment in United Kingdom law. In addition to the planning legislation, there were significant changes in the United Kingdom's approach to the environment. The Department of the Environment was set up in 1970, which signified the growing importance of the environment in ministerial policy-making. Membership of the European Community in 1972 provided a new source of vitality and direction for environmental policy and its implementation within the UK. This was an important period for environmental policy-making. Outside the planning field but with a potential direct influence on how planning is construed and analysed, international developments began to shape how the environment was perceived globally. In the same year as entry into the European Community, the United Nations Stockholm Conference was held marking the first major international conference on global development. It led, a year later, to the European Community's Environmental Action Programme, which marked an important moment in the future of the environmental policy within the European Commission and among member states.

In England and Wales a major step forward was taken with the Control of Pollution Act 1974. Its aims were both to consolidate and to provide some coherence to pollution control. This was the first Act to provide for water and waste disposal to be dealt with together. The 1974 Act also ensured that sources of pollution were not dealt with individually, but rather that they were regulated in context through a holistic treatment of the environment. Although air pollution remained outside the legislative framework of the 1974 Act, the Act coincided with the idea of the 'polluter pays' principle. This principle requires polluters to take responsibility for any harm their pollution may cause. Air pollution came under the Environmental Protection Act 1990, which also amended provisions on waste disposal and the regulation of genetically modified organisms.

Planned development related to the environment is another theme that comes out of legislation in the late twentieth century. The Government White Paper, *This Common Inheritance*[20] is worthy of note, because it interrelates forward planning and the protection of the environment. It gave rise to some significant environmental legislation, including the Pollution Prevention and Control Act 1999. This Act details controls on industrial processes, using a system of permits and adopts the philosophy of the White Paper through an integrated approach to pollution control. In addition, the 1980s saw the privatisation of many of the utilities including water, gas and electricity. This raised significant environmental issues that were addressed in a raft of legislation that included the privatisation of the main utilities. In the context of water utilities, for example, the Water Resources Act 1991 contains details of the law on water-pollution control and the protection of water resources. The 1991 Act was later revised in the Water Act 2003. The Water Industry Act 1991 relates to the management of water supply and sewerage, and regulates the various water companies. The significance of the environment for the utilities, the need for greater surveillance of the utilities, gave rise to the need for a new agency with a specific environmental focus. The United Kingdom created an Environment Agency in 1995 under the Environment Act 1995. The Act also addressed issues relating to liability for contaminated land. The Environment Agency assumed responsibility for integrated pollution control, waste regulation, water pollution and radioactive substances.

There were also a number of highly significant international developments towards the end of the twentieth century that had considerable significance for and impact on the environment. The first Ozone Treaty was agreed in 1985. This treaty began to tackle the problem of ozone depletion in the upper atmosphere, particularly over Antartica, caused primarily by human-made chemicals and resulting in substantial health and environmental risks. The 1985 Ozone Treaty also began the process of addressing climate change. Two years later the

---

[20] Cm 1200, 1990.

Brundtland Report[21] was published detailing how environmental problems might be addressed through the application of the principles of sustainable development. Environmental policy became an integral part of the European Community under the 1987 Single European Act. A year later the Intergovernmental Panel on Climate Change was established and, in 1992, this was followed by the United Nations Conference held at Rio that concluded major treaties on climate change and biodiversity. There are a number of noteworthy events that have given rise to environmental protection. The 1997 Kyoto Protocol to the 1992 UN Climate Change Convention provided a framework for steps to limit carbon emissions. The ratification of the Kyoto Protocol is complicated by the requirement that at least 55 parties, including a list of all Organisation of Economic Cooperation and Development (OECD) states responsible for 55 per cent of the total carbon dioxide emissions, must ratify the protocol. Despite the fact that many countries ratified the agreement, including the European Union for its member states, this still fell short of the requirements for ratification. The United States at that time refused to ratify the protocol because of concerns of setting too heavy a burden on US industry. Later this failure became the subject of intense discussion in 2007 at the Bali conference. This ultimately resulted in an agreement to take the Kyoto Protocol forward through fresh negotiation to a new international agreement. Since the election of President Obama in 2008 the United States has become more attracted to the Kyoto Protocol and has moved away from its resistance to international agreements. The Copenhagen Conference in November 2009 once more considered future climate change. The agenda included setting out measurable and enforceable CO_2 targets, but these were not agreed.[22]

Judicial activism and human rights

The courts have also contributed indirectly to the development of environmental law. It is clear that the use of private law principles in cases such as *Rylands* v *Fletcher* have been modified to tackle environmental issues. Moreover, the growth in negligence cases related to environmental matters has also defined the remit of the law. Liability, for example, for the pollution of groundwater may give rise to an action for negligence, nuisance or under *Rylands* v *Fletcher* (1868) LR 3 HL 330. Adapting the need for environmental protection through such principles offers an attractive way of developing environmental law. There are an interesting range of possibilities:

- Negligence arises from a failure to exercise the care demanded in the circumstances. A plaintiff must show that he is owed a duty of care, that the duty has been breached and that any harm suffered is due to the breach of the duty that the plaintiff is owed. Damages may be awarded on proof that the harm caused was foreseeable by the defendant.

- Nuisance is an interference with an occupier's use or enjoyment of land where there has been substantial injury to property or personal discomfort.

- The rule in *Rylands* v *Fletcher* is where a landowner is strictly liable for the consequences of escapes from his property and where the landowner is engaged in a 'non-natural' use of his land. The term 'non-natural' use has never been clearly defined. (See above.)

---

[21] *Our Common Future* New York: United Nations, 1987.
[22] See Chapter 1 for a summary of the potential for agreement after Bali.

A discussion on how the three grounds apply in cases involving water pollution can be found the landmark decision made by the House of Lords in *Cambridge Water Co Ltd* v *Eastern Counties Leather plc* [1994] 2 WLR 53. This case has had a significant influence on future developments in this area of law and this is likely to continue into the future. This case saw the House of Lords place restrictions on the availability of liability for past or historic pollution.

The facts of the case are that Eastern Counties Leather plc had manufactured leather at their works in Sawston, Cambridgeshire since 1879. The processes used organochlorine chemicals, specifically trichloroethene, until the mid-1960s, followed by perchlorethene. In the 1970s scientific evidence emerged that both chemicals were a possible threat to health. In the 1980s the European Community and the World Health Organisation set drinking water standards that only permitted very low quantities of these compounds (see: 80/778/EEC and DoE Circular 20/82; also: Water Supply (Water Quality) Regulations 1989, SI 1989 1147). The EC Drinking Water Directive expects that wholesome water should contain no more than 1 µg per litre organochlorines, in the specific case of tetrachlorethene and perchlorethene the maximum admissible concentration was to be 10 µg per litre. The impact of these standards on the Cambridge Water Company was considerable. The water company had been extracting groundwater from the area of Sawston through bore holes, and by the mid-1980s perchlorethene concentrations in the groundwater were found to be between 70 and 170 µg per litre. As a result of the new EC standards the water company found it impossible to continue using the extracted groundwater as a source of drinking water. As a consequence the water company moved its bore holes to an unpolluted zone and built a new plant at the cost of nearly £1 million. The Cambridge Water Company sought an injunction and damages from Eastern Leather who they alleged caused the pollution. The perclorethene was used by this company to degrease pelts and had been stored on site in drums. It was assumed that either the drums had leaked or there had been accidental spillage allowing organochlorine to leach into groundwater. The legal basis of the claim was in negligence, nuisance and the rule in *Rylands* v *Fletcher*.[23]

The case raises an important question concerning historic pollution. Should there be liability for acts done in the past on the basis of present-day knowledge and standards? Many sites across the country have been contaminated by past industrial activity, making liability for this historic pollution an important question, with potentially great financial significance to commercial and industrial organisations today. It is useful to pause to consider historic pollution in its scientific context. The standards that apply to drinking water today and the scientific evidence about the harmful effects of the chemicals were not available at the time the pollution began. There is very often a delay in scientific understanding of the impact of chemicals on health and the environment. More often than not problems related to human health become clear first, while the effect of compounds in the environment often remain unclear for prolonged periods. This is particularly the case at ecosystem level where changes can take years to become apparent. The impact may only develop after a threshold concentration is reached in the environment or after accumulation by living organisms. The assessment of 'safe' environmental concentrations of chemicals is still largely based on predictions from ecotoxicology studies on single selected species. These may subsequently prove to give an inaccurate prediction of the potential impact for other species, communities and ecosystems. Thus, even though the prescribed techniques at present have been applied to

---

[23] *Rylands* v *Fletcher* (1868) LR 3 HL 330.

determining safe environmental loads, they may subsequently prove invalid. Should businesses be held responsible where they have followed current best practice and any future problems remain unknown?

The High Court dismissed the action against Eastern Leather on the grounds that Eastern Leather could not reasonably have foreseen that the chemicals used in their processes could cause harm. Cambridge Water appealed to the Court of Appeal relying on the rule in *Rylands* v *Fletcher*. There was no appeal made against the High Court's ruling on nuisance and negligence. However, the Court of Appeal upheld Cambridge Water's case against Eastern Leather. The Court of Appeal followed the case of *Ballard* v *Tomlinson*[24] (1885), where a brewery successfully sued for contamination of its groundwater taken from its own well. The groundwater had been contaminated by a neighbour's discharge of sewerage. The Court of Appeal accepted that Eastern Leather had interfered with a natural right (the water company's ownership of the boreholes and various riparian rights that accrue) and that liability was therefore strict. The water company had shown that the pollution was caused by Eastern Leather and this was sufficient grounds for damages.

On appeal to the House of Lords the nature of liability was considered in relation to the claims made in respect of both nuisance and the rule in *Rylands* v *Fletcher*. Lord Goff delivered the speech of the whole House and held that there was no rule of law imposing liability for unforeseeable damage simply because the right affected was a natural right. The House of Lords held that some degree of foresight of risk is required to be proven, even in circumstances where there might be strict liability and in cases where past activities are the subject of present-day litigation. Eastern Leather's appeal was granted on the reasoning that at the time they made use of the chemicals they could not have foreseen the harm caused by the chemicals. As a result Eastern Leather could not be liable in damages[25] (see: *The Wagon Mound (No. 2)* [1967] 1 AC 617 upheld by Lord Goff in the *Cambridge Water* case).

The decision is of major significance. The House of Lords appears to have limited the effects of imposing strict liability through *Rylands* v *Fletcher*. This is particularly important in contaminated land cases. Foreseeability of harm is now regarded as a prerequisite for the recovery of damages in nuisance and in *Rylands* v *Fletcher*. The House of Lords' decision brought some relief to the concerns of commercial enterprises that arose from the Court of Appeal's decision because of the threat of the imposition of strict liability for historic pollution. A number of conclusions may be drawn from the *Cambridge Water* case:

(a) Historic pollution or retrospective liability, that is liability for past acts, is now made more difficult to prove because foreseeability is a requirement of both *Rylands* v *Fletcher* and nuisance liability. A prerequisite of liability is the foreseeability of damage of the relevant type if there was an escape from the land of things likely to do mischief.

(b) The House of Lords has accepted that liability in nuisance and in *Rylands* v *Fletcher* is based on strict liability (where fault need not be proven). *Rylands* v *Fletcher* did not create liability any more strict than the liability for nuisance. Strict liability renders the defendant liable where there is an escape occurring in the course of the non-natural use of the land, notwithstanding that all due care had been exercised to prevent the escape from occurring.

[24] (1865) 29 Ch D 114.
[25] *The Wagon Mound (No. 2)* [1967] 1 AC 617.

(c) The definition of 'non-natural' used in *Rylands* v *Fletcher* is sufficient to cover the storage of substantial quantities of chemicals on industrial premises. In *Cambridge Water* the House of Lords held that Eastern Leather's use of the land for the storage of chemicals was almost a classic case of 'non-natural' use. No further definition of what 'non-natural' included was attempted but it was accepted that the creation of an industrial estate and employment was not a natural use of the land. Lord Goff explained: 'I myself, however, do not feel able to accept that the creation of employment as such even in a small industrial complex is sufficient of itself to establish a particular use as constituting a natural or ordinary use of the land' (see: [1994] 1 All ER 53 at p. 79e).

(d) The House of Lords has sought to remove the differences between nuisance and *Rylands* v *Fletcher*. Nuisance is moved closer to the law of negligence, which reflects a continuing trend in liability during this century.[26] The House of Lords appears to be adopting principles from the law of negligence and applying them in the law of nuisance and the rule in *Rylands* v *Fletcher*. If this assumption proves to be valid then some fundamental issues are set to be questioned. Why should strict liability be retained at all under the rule in *Rylands* v *Fletcher*? *Cambridge Water* may be the start of a remarkable shift in civil liability whereby negligence becomes the main heading of liability for harm. Foreseeability becomes the crucial issue in determining damages. The aftermath of the decision led to the National Rivers Authority (now the Environment Agency) to undertake a clean-up programme for the contaminated groundwater.[27]

The post-Second World War period resulted in a new-found judicial activism in developing common law principles, including the rules of judicial review applicable to many public bodies and organisations.[28] This has broadened the reach of the courts in terms of assurance that standards of proportionality, reasonableness and fairness are applied. A further dimension to this is the addition of the Human Rights Act 1998. The Act came into force in October 2000 and makes rights under the European Convention on Human Rights available in domestic law of the United Kingdom. The rights culture fostered by the Human Rights Act 1998 potentially has implications for environmental protection. A number of specific articles may be helpful in this regard, which include Article 8 on the right to respect for private life and Article 6 on the process of a fair trial. As with public law in general, the environment lacks the status as a foundation on which to build judicial protection. This is probably a deliberate omission on the part of Parliament since it leaves the courts untroubled by the need to adjudicate on the balance between the market economy and protecting the environment. Public law also potentially offers interest groups access to the courts to complain about illegality. This may allow pressure groups opportunities to litigate matters that are for the protection of the environment. Friends of the Earth, Greenpeace and the World Development Movement have taken the opportunity to use judicial review in attempt to challenge policy and protect the environment.[29] It is equally possible to see judicial review as a means of objecting to measures that may be intended to protect the environment and some may

[26] See: Wilkinson [1994] 57 MLR 799.
[27] *Eastern Counties Leather plc* v *Eastern Counties Leather Group Ltd* [2003] Env LR 13.
[28] See: *Ridge* v *Baldwin* [1964] AC 40.
[29] See *R v HM Inspectorate of Pollution, ex parte Greenpeace Ltd (No. 2)* [1994] 4 All ER 329; *R v Secretary of State for Foreign and Commonwealth Affairs, ex parte World Development Ltd* [1995] 1 WLR 386.

regard it as an interference with their individual liberty.[30] The success or failure of judicial review is often difficult to predict as decisions may fall to the smallest margins of agreement between upholding the decision of a public body and reviewing it. Judicial review deserves a detailed examination in the context of environmental protection, especially with regard to the significance of human rights.[31]

The market economy and the globalisation era: twenty-first century

The twenty-first century has begun as an era dominated by the market economy and globalisation, setting new challenges for our environment. This includes the development of a global economy in energy; the increase in the use of air transport and in car use; and in the consumption of fossil fuels. The impacts of globalisation are complex and not simply based on consideration of international markets. There is an attempt to resolve apparently competing aims, namely the maintenance of high growth in the world's economies against the protection of the environment. The way forward is found in attempts to reconcile market forces and environmental protection through the principle of sustainable development,[32] a term commonly used to cover the need to address the needs of future generations. There is a new urgency, largely driven by concerns over climate change, in facing the dilemma of how best to achieve both goals. The international dimension to environmental law also draws on aspects of rights supporting the social context of sustainable development. In 2001 the Aarhus Convention established the idea of environmental citizenship. This gives the citizen rights of participation and access to information and is supported by the concept of environmental justice. This important concept is likely to play a significant role in environmental matters in the future.

The planning system has a crucial role in achieving the goal both of economic growth and of environmental protection. It is interesting that this century has signalled the end of planning the environment partly on the basis of social objectives that formed an intrinsic part of the 1947 Town and Country Planning Act. Instead the emphasis now is on how planning will facilitate the market and at best protect the environment. The Planning and Compulsory Purchase Act 2004, which is one of the most controversial planning Acts passed because it introduced a more market-led solution to planning than in the past, illustrates this change in emphasis. The 2004 Act also marked a shift from the state as the main developer towards acceptance that the private sector is the major stakeholder in the planning system. This is consistent with the development of private sector partnerships in terms of financing major projects.[33] Today, the burden of financing major projects often falls on the private sector rather than the public purse.

[30] Examples are a challenge against the Mayor of London on congestion charges on the grounds that it offends against individual rights; see: *R (on the application of Westminster City Council) v Mayor of London* [2003] LGR 611.
[31] See Chapter 6.
[32] This term is discussed in full in the analysis in Chapter 1 and also examined in Chapter 16 in the conclusions; see pages 11–12, 358–60.
[33] See: Public Accounts Committee, *Achieving Value for Money in the Delivery of Public Services* HC 742. See: *Treasury Minutes on the Ninth and Eleventh Reports from the Committee of Public Accounts 2006–7* Cm 7076. (April, 2007) London, Stationery Office.

The 2004 Act is intended to provide a more positive approach to planning than in the past where prohibition was an underlying culture in the planning application process. Another important feature of the 2004 Act is a statutory requirement in section 39 for sustainability built into the rationale of development plans. The environment is thus protected with the concept that in making plans there must be an objective of 'contributing to the achievement of sustainable development'. This is widely drawn but would appear not to apply to those parts of the planning process related to individual planning applications (Part 4 dealing with development control is excluded from section 39). The question of policy-making addressed by section 39 leaves uncertainty as to the exact remit of the duty imposed by section 39. In fact, there is some leeway for local discretion. There is, however, increasing pressure for the sustainability doctrine to be applied more generally, especially in the context of the EC Strategic Environmental Assessment Directive 2004 2001/42/EC.[34] The 2004 Act has also some streamlining features in its aims to speed up the planning process and allow some participation while facilitating flexible decision-making by planning authorities.

The twenty-first century has seen a major shift in environmental protection. It is no longer considered adequate to address environmental matters simply on the basis of treating each sector of the environment individually and in isolation. The remarkable breakthrough in the present century is the realisation that protecting and enhancing the environment requires numerous techniques and strategies, as illustrated by the Kyoto Protocol. Some strategies are proactive and preventative, some have deterrent value, and other techniques are retrospective offering penalties and damages to meet clean-up costs. (See Chapters 7 and 14 for further discussion). The adoption of the concept of sustainable development sets the overarching framework for policy-making. In terms of putting the principle of sustainable development into practice and its implementation, there are many techniques including setting future targets and specific objectives. Many targets and objectives have come about as a result of the EU's influence. The Clean Air Act 1993 was an example of this approach that had desirable results through prohibiting smoke and setting emissions standards (see above).

There is also a remarkable consolidation of agencies and institutions in recent years. The creation of the Environment Agency by the merger of the National Rivers Authority and Her Majesty's Inspectorate of Pollution is one example. The National Rivers Authority was set up in 1989 for England and Wales to regulate water quality and water pollution. Her Majesty's Inspectorate of Pollution was set up in 1987 to create a single agency that would regulate discharges to air, water and land. The Environment Agency holds all the main pollution control functions including integrated pollution control, waste management and the regulation of water pollution.

Recently the environment appears to have become a major issue in the politics of the United Kingdom. This is illustrated by using congestion charging in London as an attempt to reduce traffic congestion. Taxation on the CO_2 emissions of cars is another example. This is a fairly new phenomenon and its future impact on the overall direction and creation of environmental policies is hard to predict. The driving forces for this change are complicated by issues beyond those strictly related to the environment. For example, there is considerable political interest in moving away from energy reliance on oil. The reason is not only environmental but substantially lies in the cost of oil and the realisation that developed

[34] The Assessment of Plans and Programmes Regulations 2004, SI 2004/1633.

economies must compete with the new economies of the world, including India and China, for limited oil resources. Energy security has risen on the political agenda and is inevitably intertwined with environmental issues.

In 2006 the United Kingdom government set up the Stern Review,[35] looking into the scientific background and economic consequences of climate change. It is worthwhile briefly considering the background to this review. The Kyoto Protocol had created the necessity for the introduction of measures to reduce greenhouse gas emissions and in order to help meet the targets required by the protocol, emissions trading schemes had begun between some developed economies. In 2000 the United Kingdom government made a commitment to reduce CO_2 emissions from 20 per cent of their 1990 levels by the year 2030. This target was increased, following the publication of a White Paper[36] requiring a 60 per cent reduction by 2050. In fact new legislation, the Climate Change Act 2008, has created a Climate Change Committee to oversee progress towards these targets. There had also been a number of IPCC Reports under the auspices of the UN that had detailed the scientific evidence for anthropogenic influences on global warming and the likely impacts of climate change.[37]

The Stern Review concluded that there was an undoubted need for intervention to tackle climate change. His calculations were based on assuming a rise in temperatures of between 1.4 °C and 5.8 °C by 2100 in total. Stern predicted substantial economic impacts and rises in costs linked to the consequences of this warming. In fact, determining the exact costs is difficult, but the Stern Review estimated that the global economy might decline by as much as 20 per cent based on the likely impacts of warming over this temperature range. This was calculated, in part, on predictions of higher transportation costs; higher insurance costs arising out of the increase in storm damage and a higher incidence of economic disruption because of weather factors. The Stern Review recommended the following:

- global policies are required to address global warming;
- there should be a reduction in the use of energy-intensive goods and services;
- there should be a corresponding increase in energy efficiency;
- there should be a reduction in non-energy emissions through deforestation strategies;
- low-carbon technologies should be adopted;
- there should be measures to ensure that the carbon cost is spread uniformly across the economy.

The Stern Review has been contested by other economic writers and commentators in terms of the predictions and also the calculations of net cost to the economy. However, there is consensus over the various mechanisms that may be used to address global warming. The United Kingdom has been active in putting in place a variety of 'green taxes' as new techniques in controlling the emission of greenhouse gases and also in environmental contexts

---

[35] N. Stern, *The Economics of Climate Change* London: HM Treasury, 2006.

[36] DTI: *Our Energy Future-Creating a Low Carbon Economy* Cm 5761 London, 2003.

[37] The most recent of these is the *Fourth Assessment Report of the Intergovernmental Panel on Climate Change* (2007) Cambridge: Cambridge University Press.

(Table 2.1). The use of economic instruments is an important step forward in the development and future of environmental law in the twenty-first century. It should be borne in mind that an environmental tax is one based on 'something that has a proven, specific negative impact on the environment'.[38] Yet other environmental taxes are being introduced, including for road pricing and congestion charging. The latter has been implemented in London and is designed to encourage the use of public transport and diminish traffic congestion. The future of 'green taxes' is likely to be assured,[39] given the need to provide incentives to protect the environment, and sets an important marker for environmental law.

Environmental law for the twenty-first century may be described as *the new environmental law*. Compared to the historical legacy of the previous centuries, the new environmental law has a number of distinctive characteristics. Some of the key issues that surround environmental law include the following:

- Environmental law is no longer state-focused. It is increasingly informed by European Union law and international law. This reflects the general need for environmental law to address issues globally and to recognise the limitations of any state to adequately address environmental issues on its own.

- The new environmental law is about preventing harm as much as reacting to the harm once it has occurred. In marked contrast to the historical legacy, setting discharge or emissions targets is useful as a way of inhibiting bad environmental practices, based on a scientific analysis of what is harmful.

- Scientific analysis and its integration into the setting of standards is a fundamental part of the current environmental law as well as providing the future direction for environmental policy-making. The scientific evidence of global warming, while still contested by a few, is generally accepted today by a large part of the scientific community. Without the science it would be impossible to address climate change satisfactorily.

- Setting satisfactory environmental standards requires not only an examination of the production process but also an assessment of how best to approach environmental protection in the design of a process. Reuse and recycling strategies are being adopted in engineering processes and the use of 'clean technologies' fostered.

- A wide variety of compliance and regulatory strategies may be used to create enforceable values and standards in environmental law. These range from civil and criminal liability to administrative penalties, clean-up costs and environmental taxes. The use of publicity and the media also has an important role.

Environmental law is increasingly shaped by ethical issues and related concerns. These will undoubtedly have an important role to play for the future. The sources, concepts and principles of environmental law are examined in the next chapter.

---

[38] See: Eurostat, *Environmental Guide – A Statistical Guide*, 2001.
[39] See: R. Eddington, *Transport's Role in Sustaining UK's Productivity and Competitiveness* London: HM Treasury, 2006.

Further reading

Environmental history

E. Ashby and M. Anderson, *The Politics of Clean Air* Oxford: OUP, 1981.

W.H. Booth and J.B.C. Renshaw, *Smoke Prevention and Fuel Economy* London: Earthscan, 1911.

T.J. Chandler, *Climate of London* London: Hutchinson, 1965.

B.W. Clapp, *An Environmental History of Britain* London: Longman, 1994.

A. Markham, *A Brief History of Pollution* London: Earthscan, 1994.

C.A. Moser, *Social Conditions in England and Wales* Oxford: Clarendon Press, 1958.

C.S. Orwin and E.H. Whetham, *History of British Agriculture 1846–1914* 2nd edition, Harlow, Essex: Longmans, 1971.

C. Ponting, *A Green History of the World* London: Sinclair-Stevenson, 1991.

N. Shaw and J.S. Owen, *The Smoke Problem of Great Cities* London: Constable, 1925.

D. Vogel, *National Styles of Regulation* Ithaca: Cornell University Press, 1986.

A. Wohl, *Endangered Lives: Public Health in Victorian Britain* London: Methuen, 1984.

The new environmental law of the twenty-first century

S. Bell and Donald McGillivray, *Environmental Law* 7th edition, Oxford: Oxford University Press, 2008.

A. Boyle and M.R. Anderson (eds), *Human Rights Approaches to Environmental Protection* Oxford: Oxford University Press, 1996.

G. Harris, *Seeking Sustainability* Cambridge: Cambridge University Press, 2007.

J. Holder and Maria Lee, *Environmental Protection, Law and Policy* 2nd edition, Cambridge: Cambridge University Press, 2007.

R. Lazarus, *The Making of Environmental Law* Chicago: University of Chicago Press, 2004.

A. Leicester, *The UK Tax System and the Environment* London: Institute for Fiscal Studies, 2006.

R. Revez, P. Sands, and R.B. Stewart, *Environmental Law, the Economy and Sustainable Development* Cambridge: Cambridge University Press, 2000.

B. Richardson and S. Wood (eds), *Environmental Law and Sustainability* Oxford: Hart Publishing, 2006.

Visit **http://www.mylawchamber.co.uk/mceldowney**
to access key issue checklists and practice exam
questions to test yourself on this chapter.

3 Sources, institutions and organisations in environmental law

Introduction

Identifying the sources of environmental law and explaining how environmental law is defined and interpreted provides a useful structure for the study of the subject. Environmental law is faced by complicated and daunting challenges, not only because of the technical nature of the subject but also because of the diversity of its sources. Deciding what is pertinent and finding the relevant law is sufficiently difficult to warrant a chapter in its own right.

At the outset it is necessary to define environmental law within the United Kingdom. The focus of this book is primarily on issues that are relevant to environmental law for England and Wales. In fact, since 2006, under newly granted devolved powers, Wales has been able to develop its own distinctive environmental law. This must, however, be within the framework of environmental law influenced by the European Union and also England. Environmental law in Scotland and Northern Ireland may also differ in certain key aspects from that in England and Wales, again, because of devolved arrangements. It is important that we take account of the influences of devolution on environmental law in the United Kingdom.

Identifying the legal sources for environmental law provides an important insight into the boundaries and regulatory context for the subject. In fact a wide range of agencies, institutions and government departments have a significant role to play in the administration and implementation of environmental law. The main values, principles and concepts that underlie environmental law also need to be considered and their role in tackling environmental problems identified. The diversity of techniques available within environmental law crosses the boundaries of traditional legal disciplines and touches on economics, political science and also science itself.

It is hoped that this chapter will provide a useful road map and analysis of how to find the law, together with an understanding of the role and function of legal rules. It is clear that while the courts provide a contribution to the development of environmental law, the European Union and our domestic legislature have provided significant and detailed legislation. There is no codified system of environmental law but there are codifying legislative acts that have provided some coherence to an otherwise diffuse subject.

We have already discussed how environmental law crosses many traditional subjects in the curriculum, ranging from private law to public law and including criminal and civil liability. There is also a remarkable emergence of legal principles and ideas from other jurisdictions as a result of the convergence of European Community law. This embraces civil and common law principles and the result is a largely hybrid subject that addresses many different cultural and national approaches to law and law-making. The result has the positive effect of allowing convergence between legal principles that apply to the environment drawn from different legal cultures. The negative side, however, is that this may cause some complexity, which makes technical skill necessary when attempting to understand environmental law and interpret its operation.

Environmental law is much more than the sum of the different influences that have shaped its development. It is true that environmental law has inherited from the past and from recent times a distinctive identity but this inheritance is matched by an expectation of continued transition. One important element in the future of environmental law may be the creation of environmental rights. This has a resonance with the current debate on human rights and the protection of rights. The focal point for the discussion is to what extent reliance should be placed on rights to protect the environment rather than practical solutions to prevent and remedy environmental pollution. It is wrong, however, to assume that this is the only context in which to consider environmental rights. Environmental law brings additional considerations to the value of rights. Searching for the ethics and philosophical underpinnings of environmental law is not new. It can be traced back to the issues surrounding the law of property and its protection embedded in the seventeenth-century discourse. This century also saw debate on the notion of nature and the rights of humans that formed part of theological, ideological and philosophical ideas that were thought to benefit human life and the environment. The idea that environmental law is mainly derived from technical and legalistic rules or economic concepts is mistaken. The broader moral and social issues that underpin society lie at the very heart of environmental law. They set where boundaries to protect the environment are drawn and how such boundaries are made effective. Within this broader analysis there is much to be gained by questioning how environmental law is to benefit society.

Sources, scope and remit of environmental law

There are a number of sources for environmental law (Table 3.1), but our starting point is to consider the role of the national legal system.[1] The United Kingdom was formed out of the union between England, Scotland and Northern Ireland and was often described as a unitary state. The term 'unitary' was used to distinguish the United Kingdom from a federal system of government such as in Germany, the United States and Australia. The description of a unitary or single state is misleading as there are several important differences in the different parts of the United Kingdom. Strictly speaking there are separate legal systems in Scotland[2]

Table 3.1 Sources of law

- National legal systems
- European Union law
- International law
- Comparative law

[1] Table 3.1 sets out where the main parts of environmental law may be found.
[2] See Barry K. Winetrobe, 'Scottish devolution: developing practice in multi-layer governance' in J. Jowell and D. Oliver (eds), *The Changing Constitution* sixth edition, Oxford: Oxford University Press, 2007, pp. 207–26.

and Northern Ireland. While Northern Ireland shares much in common with the English common law system, it has developed in it own way with a distinctly different regional organisation of local government and differences in planning and land use. In the case of Scotland, the legal system has drawn many influences from the continent. In private law and property, particularly, Scotland is different from any other part of the United Kingdom. Wales has followed more closely the law that is applicable in England, but this is unlikely to remain the case in the future. Since 1998 there has been substantial devolution to Wales, Scotland and Northern Ireland. In addition, under the Regional Development Agencies Act 1998 there has been devolution to the English regions. This is of limited importance as there are very few devolved arrangements in the English regions. Finally, London now has a directly elected Mayor and London Assembly with 25 members under the Greater London Authority Act 1999.

Devolution is a substantial change in the constitutional arrangements of the United Kingdom, and raises interesting questions for environmental law. At the level of EC law or international law, environmental law applies to the United Kingdom as a whole. The United Kingdom is a member state of the European Union and central government retains legal responsibility for ensuring overall compliance with EC law. This has remained the case after devolution, with only a few minor adjustments for each region. For example for historical reasons, there have been delays in implementing many EC Directives within Northern Ireland and the responsibility for this delay legally rests with the United Kingdom government. Devolution does, however, create new devolved administrations that have responsibility for environmental protection. Each devolved arrangement must be examined, because there are differences in powers and responsibilities given to each devolved administration. More generally the powers granted to the devolved administrations may be overridden by the United Kingdom Parliament as that Parliament has retained its sovereignty. Thus devolved powers to Wales, Scotland and Northern Ireland may be amended or repealed by United Kingdom legislation. In that respect the system of devolution does not confer overall sovereignty on the devolved administrations.

Scotland

The Scotland Act 1998 provides for a Scottish Parliament (129 members) and a Scottish Executive. In Scotland there are likely to emerge substantial differences in environmental law from England because sections 28–30 of the Scotland Act 1998 provide the Scottish Parliament with legislative powers that include the environment. This gives rise to differences in the approach to environmental law as well as in substantive matters. There are also likely to be contentious areas where responsibility is only partially devolved – for example rail and transport and where there is a devolved function but substantial European Union input, e.g. agriculture and fisheries. It is not possible to give full attention to the differences in Scotland, which requires a separate analysis related to that jurisdiction. The transposition of EU environmental law into Scotland is one of the most significant factors that has transformed Scotland's approach to environmental issues.[3] The points that follow are intended to

---

[3] Andrea Ross, Hazel Nash and Colin T. Reid, 'The implementation of EU environmental law in Scotland' (2009) *Edinburgh Law Review* 224.

highlight only the main differences from England and Wales. Scotland has separate regulatory agencies that deserve mention. The Scottish Environment Protection Agency (SEPA) was established to oversee pollution control.[4] This was set up under pre-devolution legislation, the Environment Act 1995, and the agency generally corresponds to the English Environmental Agency (see below). The unified nature of SEPA, however, through having control over all industrial regulation that exists under the Integrated Prevention of Pollution Control system (IPPC) gives it the advantage over its English equivalent. Criminal prosecutions involving environmental matters are determined outside SEPA by the independent Crown Office and Prosecutor Fiscal Service. This is very different from the powers in England and Wales given to the Environment Agency (see below). SEPA does not have any of the non-pollution related water management functions, as these fall under the jurisdiction of the unitary system of local government in Scotland.[5] Under the devolved arrangements the Scottish Parliament has powers over water pollution and its control. The public sector body Scottish Water runs the water supply and the treatment of sewage and trade effluent. Scottish Water operates like a private company but it has public functions and this is in marked contrast to that in England and Wales. It, in fact, has the status of a public and non-departmental authority since Scotland does not have privatised water companies unlike England and Wales. There is a Drinking Water Quality Regulator which monitors and enforces drinking water quality.[6] In 2005 the Water Environment (Controlled Activities) (Scotland) Regulations 2005[7] brought most of the EC Water Framework Directive into Scotland, resulting in greater divergence between Scotland and England than in the past.

Scottish Natural Heritage oversees conservation and enhancement of habitats, species and landscapes.[8] In 2000, after devolution, the Scottish Parliament was given powers under the National Parks (Scotland) Act 2000 to propose and designate national parks. This is a welcome addition to the powers of the Scottish Parliament as hitherto Scotland had no National Parks. There are now two designated areas in Scotland, Loch Lomond and the Trossachs (as one National Park) and the Cairngorms. Scottish National Parks are expected to follow the English model of areas of natural and cultural heritage protection of the environment. The 2000 Act also provides powers to promote sustainable use of natural resources and social and economic development of the communities.

Planning law in Scotland falls under separate legislation, the Town and Country Planning (Scotland) Act 1997, from England and Wales. As responsibility for town and country planning is a devolved matter under the Scotland Act 1998, the Scottish Parliament has considerable discretion for the planning laws in Scotland. This gives considerable potential for Scotland to develop differently from the rest of the United Kingdom[9] in terms of setting general policy priorities and environmental implementation strategies.

[4] See: the Environment Act 1995, the Environmental Protection Act 1990 and the Control of Pollution Act 1974.
[5] See: the Local Government etc. (Scotland) Act 1994.
[6] See: the Water (Scotland) Act 1990 and the Water Industry (Scotland) Act 2002.
[7] SSI 2005/348; also see: EC Water Framework Directive 2000/60/EC.
[8] See: the Natural Heritage (Scotland) Act 1991 and the Nature Conservation (Scotland) Act 2004.
[9] The Planning and Compulsory Purchase Act 2004 does not extend to Scotland.

Northern Ireland

Northern Ireland has developed very differently from other parts of the United Kingdom.[10] The Northern Ireland Act 1998 created a partnership form of devolution through an elected Assembly (108 members) and Executive. Section 4(1) provides the Northern Ireland Assembly with powers that include environmental matters. The administrative arrangements in Northern Ireland reflect the fact that for a long time there was no devolved administration, but responsibilities were carried out by the Secretary of State for Northern Ireland under direct rule powers from Westminster. Northern Ireland has a Department of the Environment and under its control there is an Executive Agency known as the Environment and Heritage Service with similar powers to the English equivalent, the Environment Agency, and the Scottish equivalent SEPA (above). Northern Ireland has a departmental responsibility for water and sewerage services combined with regulatory functions. Northern Ireland is likely to come under pressure to reform its current arrangements to take account of national environmental policies such as an independent water regulator and privatised water services. This a transitional period for Northern Ireland whose record on environmental protection is often criticised when compared to that of England and Wales. There are very few prosecutions for infringements; indeed, to date, prosecution has been given a low priority by the main Northern Ireland department responsible. There has also been a remarkable time lag in the implementation of European Community law, which is currently being addressed. The need for an independent enforcement agency in Northern Ireland is seen as pressing. The Department of Enterprise Trade and Investment has responsibility for economic development as well as energy, health and safety at work and mineral developments. There is also an important tourist function under the Department's control that relates to a broad environmental remit. The Department for Regional Development has strategic planning, transportation strategy, public transport and water policy as well as water and sewerage services within its remit.

The return to a devolved administration in May 2007 may well influence the future direction of environmental law and policy-making within Northern Ireland. The Department of Environment's Business Plan 2007–8 provides an overview of how the future strategy on environment is likely to develop. Planning legislation in Northern Ireland is also substantially different from that in England and Wales. The Planning (Northern Ireland) Order 1991[11] was an attempt to bring the Northern Ireland law into alignment with the Town and Country Planning Act 1990 and, more recently, in 2004 a new planning order has greatly assisted the presumption in favour of development plans.[12] The system of local government in Northern Ireland is also noteworthy. The Local Government Act (NI) 1972 established the current structure with a wide variation between designated areas both in terms of their population base and in terms of the number of staff serving each area. The main cities Belfast, Derry, Armagh, Lisburn and Newry have specific responsibilities. There are also borough and district

---

[10] See. C. McCrudden, 'Northern Ireland and the British Constitution since the Belfast Agreement' in J. Jowell and D. Oliver (eds), *The Changing Constitution* sixth edition, Oxford: Oxford University Press, 2007, pp. 227–70.

[11] SI 1991/1220 (NI11).

[12] SI 2003/430 (NI8).

councils across Northern Ireland. The current structure of local government is being reviewed and the reform programme proposed envisages the following:

- local councils are to be reduced from 26 to 7;
- the new councils will have a statutory duty to engage in a community-based planning process and are to be given a lead role (relevant agencies are to be obliged to work under their remit);
- the new councils will have a wider range of powers, including responsibilities for local roads, planning and rural development, bus services, fire and rescue and future European programmes with some housing-related functions.

Wales

In terms of environmental law England and Wales are generally classified together. This simplification, however, is not likely to continue. The introduction of devolution to Wales provides for a Welsh Assembly under the Government of Wales Act 1998. This legislation was amended by the Government of Wales Act 2006. This Act provides an enhanced legislative power to the Welsh Assembly to ask for legislative powers covering areas within the competence of the Assembly. Schedule 2 to the original Government of Wales Act 1998 included the following areas: agriculture, forestry, fisheries and food; ancient monuments and historic buildings; economic development; the environment; health and health services; highways; town and country planning; water and flood defences; transport; and also local government. The potential in terms of environmental matters is clear.

The Government of Wales Act 2006 has enhanced the Assembly's legislative powers in several ways. It has conferred wide powers to make subordinate legislation on the Assembly itself. There are, also, powers to make an Order in Council whereby the UK Parliament may grant enhanced legislative powers to the Assembly. This will enable the Welsh Assembly to pass legislation, known as Assembly Measures, on its own behalf (see sections 93–102 of the Government of Wales Act 2006). It provides an important mechanism for the Assembly to make laws within the area of devolved authority listed under Schedule 5 to the Act, which broadly mirror the powers listed above under Schedule 2. Thus a number of areas relevant to the environment fall within the legislative potential of the Welsh Assembly, including the environment, agriculture, forestry, fisheries, rural development, tourism, town and country planning, water and flood defences and social welfare. The 2006 Act provides that Welsh Assembly Orders in Council must be approved by the Assembly and also by both Houses of Parliament in the United Kingdom. The idea is that Orders will be proposed by Welsh ministers and then drafted following discussions between Welsh ministers and the relevant UK government department. Orders are subject to pre-legislative scrutiny by the UK Parliament and also the Welsh Assembly. There is the common requirement that such legislation is compatible with both the European Community as well as Human Rights legislation.

There is also another form of legislation. Primary legislation may be passed by the Welsh Assembly within the listed devolved areas outlined above (sections 103–106 of the Government of Wales Act 2006). Such legislative powers, however, are of a fundamental kind and would require a referendum before the Welsh Assembly is granted this form of legislation. At the moment there is the intention to keep the powers given to the Welsh Assembly distinct from the powers given to the Scottish Parliament. This intention may be changed in the next few years as Welsh devolution begins to gather its own momentum.

England

England is the seat of the United Kingdom Parliament in London and the major central government departments (set out below). For many years there has been movement towards decentralisation, with some government activities being based outside London. This has been achieved by using decentralised agencies and regional offices. Local government also makes an important contribution to policy-making and delivery of public services. One example is the use of congestion charges in London to deter traffic congestion in the capital. The implementation of smoke controls is also locally based. The Regional Development Agencies Act 1998 created regional development agencies as economic regions for the generation of 'sustainable development and social and physical re-generation' in their region. London has its own development agency with similar powers and functions to regional development agencies. Regional Assemblies scrutinise the work of the regional development agencies and, in 2002, it was decided that the regional assemblies should be directly elected where there is sufficient support for this in the region. There are currently eight regional assemblies outside London.

London has been given individual attention in terms of its governance. The Greater London Authority Act 1999 established the Greater London Authority (GLA), which consists of a directly elected Mayor and a London Assembly (25 members). The main functions of the Greater London Authority include economic development and wealth creation, which incorporates social development and the improvement of the environment in Greater London. The London Boroughs continue to perform their local government functions and where necessary are expected to coordinate with the Greater London Authority. The Mayor has a policy-setting remit that includes transport, land-use planning, biodiversity, air quality and culture. The Mayor must consult with the Greater London Assembly and is accountable to the Assembly. There are four functional bodies currently established and accountable to the Greater London Authority. This includes Transport for London, The London Development Agency, the Metropolitan Police, and the London Fire and Emergency Planning Authority. One example of proactive environmental policy development in London is the Low Emission Zone established early in 2008. The Low Emission Zone has been designed to improve London's poor air quality through requiring all diesel-engined lorries over 12 tonnes to meet strict emission standards or face daily charges for entry to Greater London. In July 2008 this was extended to all vehicles over 3.5 tonnes including buses and coaches.[13]

The brief outline above shows how important the environment has become in recent years. There is also a growing recognition of how necessary it is to have the environment integrated into the work of the various decision-makers.[14] This is an ongoing debate of how best to identify and solve environmental problems, which has begun to enter the public arena. Environmental policy and law has a higher public profile than in the past as a consequence of global warming and climate change. Increases in energy and transport costs have also heightened public awareness. It seems unavoidable that the environment will form a part of many different policy debates.

---

[13] Information on the Low Emission Zone is available at *www.london.gov.uk*.
[14] See: *A Mayor and Assembly for London* Cmd. 3897/1998.

Devolution and environmental law

It is clear that devolved government will have a significant effect on the future shape and form of environmental law within the United Kingdom. There is likely to be a variety of dimensions to this influence. For example, how energy needs will be addressed in each of the devolved administrations has important repercussions for achieving climate change commitments. The universal concept of sustainability is likely to be interpreted and acted upon differently at each level of government. This may provide a rich diversity of options and ideas that support sustainable development. It is probable that environmental law in each of the regions will take its own distinctive character under the general framework of central government and European Union oversight. This may encourage the recognition of diversity in the United Kingdom in a different way from the past. It may also serve to highlight the impact of global trends on local communities. Devolution will undoubtedly add to the complexity of environmental law, but it will also underline its uniqueness. It is likely that in future years the distinctiveness of regional variations on environmental law and policy will become more discernible. If regional variations continue it may help encourage a proliferation of responses to environmental problems.

Central government

The main sources of United Kingdom environmental law are primarily found through the major central government departments and their related agencies. The range and variety of environmental matters dealt with by central government is such that there are inevitable overlaps in departmental responsibilities. The Department of the Environment, Food and Rural Affairs performs a key environmental role but it has to share its responsibilities with other central government departments, local government and different agencies. The main departments and organisations that are relevant to the environment are set out below.

There are several important departments that provide policy on the environment and oversee the implementation and application of the law. Central government enjoys considerable autonomy in environmental matters, which consists of measures for pollution control as well as planning and related issues. The setting-up of the Department of the Environment in 1970 gave rise to the consolidation of environmental policies. In the important field of town and country planning, however, the Department's powers were overarching. The day-to-day urban and regional planning decisions are made by local authorities. The local level of planning decisions is an important mechanism to ensure that local communities are major stakeholders in the planning system. There have been major changes to the 1970 arrangements. In June 2001 the Department of the Environment became the Department of the Environment, Food and Rural Affairs (Defra). This is a large department with responsibility that includes food safety, fisheries and agricultural policy as well as rural affairs. Defra is also responsible for key areas such as access to environmental information, climate change, contaminated land and forestry. The role of Defra is examined in further detail below. After 2001, town and country planning policy and law, including environmental assessment, was transferred to the Office of Deputy Prime Minister.[15] Subsequently, in April 2007, the work of the Office

---

[15] For a period from June 2001, the Department of Local Government, Transport and the Regions was given planning responsibilities before the shift of those functions to the Deputy Prime Minister's Office.

of Deputy Prime Minister was transferred to the Department for Communities and Local Government. This department has ministerial responsibility for town and country planning and environmental assessment. There are additional areas of responsibility, including devolution, local government and the regions, housing, regeneration and urban policy. There is a new agency, the Homes and Community Agency, which will contribute to the delivery of new housing and regeneration.

Today the environment has a potential impact on the activities and work of almost every aspect of government. In terms of responsibilities that specifically cover the environment, a number of other government departments are worthy of consideration. The aim for the Department of Transport is to develop a transport system that 'balances the needs of the economy, the environment and society'.[16] The Department's role has an EU dimension through the implementation of relevant EU law in areas covering its responsibilities. Transport has a significant impact in terms of major infrastructure projects such as road building, railways, airports and ports. The Department for Business Enterprise and Regulatory Reform (BERR) has responsibilities for energy and this includes advancing nuclear power, one of the key elements of the government's recent energy White Paper.[17] Nuclear power has the advantage of not creating CO_2 emissions and consequently may be viewed as environmentally beneficial compared to coal and other fossil fuels. It has the disadvantage of costs and strong environmental concerns about waste disposal and safety.

One of the smallest departments in central government, but also the most powerful, is HM Treasury. This department is responsible for government spending as well as taxation policy. The environment is one of the key policy areas for HM Treasury, especially in terms of developing 'green taxes' and economic instruments applicable to the environment. Environmental taxes are wide-ranging and include the Climate Change Levy. This is a tax on energy use and relates to industrial and public sector users under section 30 of and Schedule 6 to the Finance Act 2000. The aim is to encourage less use of certain types of carbon fuels. Renewable energy is exempted. The Climate Change levy is different from a carbon tax levied on the supply of fuel.

Debt relief is another aspect of the Treasury's work and can include adopting sustainable development strategies for developing countries through the Foreign Office. This provides a mechanism for ensuring that large projects in developing countries adopt best practice when it comes to protecting the environment. The Treasury is also active in pursuing sustainable development[18] strategies across other government departments and agencies. This applies to the central government's own use of resources, their management and regulation.

The Treasury is also a key department when it comes to large-scale projects such as roads, airports and power stations. Even when there is private sector involvement the Treasury has an important influence. It oversees the details and regulation of the Private Finance Initiative (PFI). PFI is a way of encouraging private sector investment in public projects such as infrastructure projects, transport systems and large municipal buildings such as schools and hospitals.

---

[16] See the Department of Transport at *www.dft.gov.uk*.

[17] BERR: Meeting the Energy Challenge; a White Paper on Nuclear Power, London, (2007/8).

[18] The Treasury has the aim 'to raise the rate of sustainable growth, achieve rising prosperity and a better quality of life, with economic and employment opportunities for all'.

There are other government departments that have important influences because their role includes incidental environmental matters. Examples include the Foreign Office in the context of overseas development and diplomatic relations. The Home Office has responsibility for neighbourhood nuisances and licensing matters. The Cabinet Office acts as a forum for policy coordination, achieved through the use of committees and sub-committees that crucially enable policy-making to cross departmental boundaries. The existence of committees lies in the discretion of the Prime Minister. It is not uncommon for the structure and even the existence of committees to alter with time, reflecting the priorities of the government of the day. Currently, the Ministerial Committee on Economic Development has a Sub-Committee on Environment and Energy (ED(EE)). Its terms of reference are 'to consider international and domestic policy on environmental and energy issues'. There was a Cabinet Committee on Climate Change and the Environment, but in August 2007 this was subsumed into the main sub-committee ED(EE).[19] There are many opportunities for environmental policy-making to form part of the Prime Minister's strategy unit. One recent example is the Stern Report, originally commissioned by HM Treasury but discussed throughout all central government departments. This report also received wide media attention.

Department for Environment, Food and Rural Affairs (Defra)

Defra is the main United Kingdom department with environmental responsibilities and policy-making functions. It also covers the areas of food policy and countryside issues that find substantial links with environmental matters. Recently it has identified its goals as follows:

- to tackle climate change internationally and through domestic action to reduce greenhouse gas emissions; and

- to secure a healthy, resilient, productive and diverse natural environment.

These overall goals are divided into a number of strategic objectives, including tackling climate change; supporting a 'healthy' natural environment; achieving sustainable patterns of resource use; mitigating environmental risk and the impacts of climate change to protect society and the economy; reducing the environmental impact of farming; championing sustainable development policies across government; and protecting rural communities. The government's Comprehensive Spending Review 2007 established a new set of cross-departmental priorities called Public Service Agreements (PSAs). Defra was given responsibility for two of these cross-governmental PSAs, which set the government's environmental priorities for 2008 and 2011. This permits the government to encourage ministries and departments to engage with good environmental practices such as investing in energy-efficient buildings; the use of renewable energy and also best practice in offices e.g. the use of recycled paper. The first PSA that falls to Defra is the Climate Change PSA, which includes elements such as CO_2 emissions and the global and UK carbon market. The second is the Natural Environment PSA that encompasses elements such as water quality, biodiversity, air quality, marine productivity and pollution, and land management.[20]

---

[19] The Ministerial Committee on Sustainable Development was abolished in the Summer of 2007.

[20] For further information and links see *www.defra.gov.uk/corporate/busplan/spending-review/psa2007.htm*.

Defra, then, is central to the government's environmental strategy, but the separation of transport, and town and country planning from its main functions poses problems and may inhibit its effectiveness. It could be argued, however, that this gives Defra more time to engage in environmental protection and that it is an integrative function with relevant agencies and government departments.

Department for Communities and Local Government

Defra's main role changed substantially when its responsibilities for the planning system were transferred to the Office of Deputy Prime Minister (ODPM). In May 2006 the Department for Communities and Local Government was created as a successor to ODPM. The new department has an expanded and powerful role in the delivery of sustainable communities, including areas relevant to the environment, which are:

1. building more and better homes, and reducing homelessness;
2. improving local public services;
3. regenerating areas to create jobs;
4. working to produce a sustainable environment.

The Department's role in housing is a key element in the development of sustainability strategies to protect the environment. The role ranges from encouraging the building of low-cost homes to homes that are better insulated. The government has set a target that all new homes should be zero carbon, in other words carbon neutral, by 2016. There is also a planned expansion in the number of new homes built each year together with improvements in the process of buying and selling homes through the introduction of home information packs (HIPS). These include an energy performance certificate. A highly rated home that has effective insulation and low energy use is likely to sell more quickly and at higher price than less efficient housing.

A prominent part of the work of the Department of Communities and Local Government is its responsibility for planning policy and building regulations. Again the environment is uppermost in the policy strategies of the Department in this regard. The government has set a target for a 20 per cent reduction in carbon dioxide emissions by 2010 followed by a 60 per cent reduction by 2050. The planning system will be prominent in delivering these targets and is thereby intrinsically linked to the protection of the environment. The Department is also expected to work with local government in carrying out sustainable policies.

Parliament and the scrutiny of government

Parliament's role in holding government to account includes the scrutiny of environmental matters. Traditionally the role of Parliament is to uphold the convention of ministerial responsibility. This convention provides a link between accountability and scrutiny and holds that ministers should be accountable for failures in policy or in the department for which they have responsibility. In recent years it is rare for ministers to resign for policy failures. However, the mechanism of accountability allows Parliament authority to question ministers and to inquire into the facts. Information and accountability provide the means for exercising scrutiny over government. In order to facilitate this role, there are departmental select committees that monitor and scrutinise each department of government. Consequently there is a House of Commons Select Committee on the Environment, Food and Rural Affairs. In the House of Lords there is a Select Committee on the European Union and also on the Constitution. The various departments already outlined are each scrutinised by a select committee.

In addition to this there is a House of Commons Environmental Audit Committee formed as part of a government initiative to ensure that environmental appraisal and environmental issues are satisfactorily addressed in the operations of central government departments. This includes questions about the budget allocation to support environmental policies and also the operation of sustainable development strategies across all government departments. The committee acts as an auditor of 'environmental matters' across government departments. High up on the agenda is climate change and how to address this fast developing area.

There is also a link between the executive and the parliamentary scrutiny of government. Obtaining evidence and assessing scientific data, select committees provide a pivotal link aided in their task by experts and specialists. Indeed, select committee reports often provide a simply stated but incisive analysis of the relevant science that underpins the development of environmental policy.

The question is, however, whether such scrutiny is adequate. The answer to date is that the agenda for the discussion of environmental matters is commonly at the direction of the government of the day. This leaves little discretion for fact-finding and scrutiny outside the government's own remit. In fact, there are various Cabinet sub-committees that provide government with an overview of their environmental performance, and the Sustainability Commission (see below) also has a pivotal role. In addition there are influences from public opinion and from the media, which are critical in the future development of environmental strategies. In the ebb and flow of political life, however, this may in the end prove too precarious a system.

Agencies

The Environment Agency

The Environment Agency (EA) is an independent corporate body established under section 1(1) of the Environment Act 1995. The Environment Agency for England and Wales employs around 12,000 staff and has a budget of £9,000 million.[21] Almost 60 per cent of the funding comes from government; the remaining sums come from charges under various schemes. There is an Environment Protection Advisory Committee (EPAC) and with an individual EPAC for each of the Agency's regions. The regional offices work closely with other regulatory bodies in the discharge of their functions. The EA has a number of primary responsibilities, but does not have an exclusive responsibility for the environment. The work of the Agency covers the following:

- Flood protection: In 2007/8 the Agency protected around 30,000 people with flood defences and barriers.

- Cutting sulphur dioxide and working with industry to reduce the amounts emitted. Since 1990, a 75 per cent reduction has been achieved.

[21] In Scotland there is the Scottish Environment Protection Agency (SEPA).

- Using resources skilfully and efficiently. The Environment Agency employs strategies for the recycling and reuse of materials.

- Monitoring high-risk businesses and seeking to provide best practice in terms of standards and environmental protection.

- Taking direct action, including criminal prosecution of those who breach their environmental obligations. The Agency secures many millions of pounds in fines in the courts against offenders.

- Wildlife protection; use of waterways for anglers and others through monitoring lakes and rivers, as to their water quality and use including their navigation.

- Making use of the environment for the benefit of the community.

- Influencing government, local authorities and industry in giving the environment a high priority.

There are a number of aspects about the EA that are useful to consider in order to highlight its role. The title of Environment Agency gives the impression that it is responsible for all the regulation and regulatory matters that apply to the environment. It is clear that the EA falls short of this expectation. We have seen that a large part of the protection and regulation of the environment is allocated outside the EA's remit.[22] Its main aim is to act as a pollution control authority that includes aspects of flood defence, land drainage and assorted tasks such as issuing fishing licences and the control of disposal of hazardous waste. The establishment of the EA was a remarkable achievement even so and there can be no doubt that it holds a broad diversity of environmental aims and objectives. Its task is to set standards and enliven the public debate about the environment. The Environment Act 1995 provides a wide discretion in how to achieve a better environment. The Corporate Strategy published in 2000 covers the period up to 2011. This combines two roles: one as an efficient monitoring and reporting body, the other as a modern regulator with powers to take criminal prosecutions. The EA receives funding from a number of sources.

The Sustainable Development Commission

The commission was founded in October 2000 and later, in 2006, expanded to act as an independent watchdog with reporting functions. The main remit for the commission is to consider principles of sustainable development. This provides a surprisingly wide remit covering academic, scientific and policy-making issues. The work of the commission is divided into 10 policy areas, covering climate change, consumption and business, economics, education, energy, health, housing, regional and local government, and stakeholder engagement. The commission is unique in having to report to the Prime Minister, the First Ministers of Scotland and Wales and the First and Deputy First Minister of Northern Ireland. The main activities of the commission are as follows:

- production of reports on the environment;

- provision of advice and expert opinion, bridging the gap between science, economics and law;

- responding to government policy initiatives;

- undertaking reports and appraisal of the government's progress in sustainable development.

[22] The Drinking Water Inspectorate is not included and planning is covered by local authority planning decisions that are subject to central government policy-making.

The Sustainable Development Commission also helps to act as a coordinator for different aspects of government policy on the environment.

Royal Commission on Environnemental Pollution (RCEP)

The Royal Commission was established in 1970[23] and has since continued as a standing Royal Commission. Its role is to take an overview as well as to provide substantial scientific and policy advice on pollution issues. The advantages of the Royal Commission are that it provides a wide-ranging evaluation and analysis drawing on a multi-disciplined team. RCEP stands outside party political considerations and acts as a forum for debate and analysis that help to map out future environmental strategy. It may hold public meetings and make site visits whenever appropriate in its considerations. The normal method of reporting is through general reports that canvass major issues of the day. In 2002 the Royal Commission began to publish Special Reports that contain technical and more narrowly defined analysis of selected issues. The status of the Royal Commission is important. It commands considerable esteem and is recognised to provide independent analysis of major environmental issues. One of the commission's most important influences has been the early recognition, found in its 12th Report, of the *Best Practicable Environmental Option*. Another major contribution to environmental protection came in its 21st Report on *Setting Environmental Standards*. This report brought together wide-ranging views on the value of scientific and social criteria in risk assessment and their significance in standard-setting. The Royal Commission has also published an influential 22nd Report on *Energy – The Changing Climate*.[24]

The value of a Royal Commission is that it has time and appropriate resources to provide forward-looking analysis. This, however, may fall short of the expectation that it takes decisions or that its recommendations are acted on to improve the environment. Nevertheless, it is its advisory role that is pivotal. The government of the day can adopt its recommendations and through published White Papers take forward its policy ideas. The Royal Commission has sought to provide a link between expertise and the public and it has championed scientific approaches to establishing facts. It has embraced issues as diverse as aircraft noise, crop spraying and the urban environment, and continues to move forward with issues of substantial environmental concern. It is currently working on its 28th Report that will undoubtedly contribute to the national debate on our response to climate change, *Adapting the UK to Climate Change*.

Ofwat

The Water Services Regulation Authority (Ofwat) is the main economic regulator of the water and sewerage industry in England and Wales. The Water Act 2003 created the present arrangement and, from 1 April 2006, Ofwat was given its present remit. There had been previously the Director General of Water Services. A number of roles are performed by Ofwat relevant to the protection of the consumer and the maintenance of high standards. These are:

- setting limits on the charges set by the various water companies;
- ensuring that the water companies carry out their responsibilities set out in the Water Industry Act 1991 and section 39 of the Water Act 2003;

---

[23] See Table 3.2 for a list of publications.
[24] 22nd Report *Energy – The Changing Climate* Cmd 4794.

Table 3.2 Reports from the Royal Commission on environmental pollution

1st Report: Cmnd 4585 (1971)

2nd Report: Three Issues in Industrial Pollution, Cmnd 4894 (1972)

3rd Report: Pollution in Some British Estuaries and Coastal Waters, Cmnd 5054 (1972)

4th Report: Pollution Control: Progress and Problems, Cmnd 5780 (1974)

5th Report: Air Pollution Control: An Integrated Approach, Cmnd 6371 (1976)

6th Report: Nuclear Power and the Environment, Cmnd 6618 (1976)

7th Report: Agriculture and Pollution, Cmnd 7644 (1979)

8th Report: Oil Pollution and the Sea, Cmnd 8358 (1981)

9th Report: Lead in the Environment, Cmnd 8852 (1983)

10th Report: Tackling Pollution – Experience and Prospects, Cmnd 9149 (1984)

11th Report: Managing Waste: The Duty of Care, Cmnd 9675 (1985)

12th Report: Best Practicable Environmental Option, Cmnd 310 (1988)

13th Report: The Release of Genetically Engineered Organisms to the Environment July 1989, Cm 720

14th Report: Genhaz – a System for the Critical Appraisal of Proposals to Release GMO's into the Environment, June 1991, Cm 1557

15th Report: Emissions from Heavy Duty Diesel Vehicles, September 1991, Cm 1631

16th Report: Freshwater Quality, June 1992, Cm 1966

17th Report: Incineration and Waste, May 1993, Cm 2181

18th Report Transport and the Environment, October 1994, Cm 2674

19th Report Sustainable Use of Soil, February 1996, Cm 3165

20th Report Transport and the Environment – Developments Since 1994, Cm 3752

21st Report Setting Environmental Standards, Cm 4053 1998

22nd Report Energy – The Changing Climate, Cm 4794

23rd Report Environmental Planning, Cm 5459 2002

A Special Report: The Environmental Effects of Civil Aircraft November 2002

24th Report Chemicals in Products – Safeguarding the Environment and Human Health, June 2003, Cm 5827

A Special Report Biomass as a Renewable Energy Source, May 2004

25th Report Turning the Tide – Addressing the Impact of Fisheries on the Marine Environment, December 2005, Cm 6392

Special Report Crop Spraying and the Health of Residents and Bystanders, September 2005

26th Report The Urban Environment, March 2007, Cm 7009

27th Report Novel Materials in the Environment, 2008, Cm 7468

- protecting standards of service;
- encouraging competition;
- encouraging the companies to be more efficient;
- meeting the principles of sustainable development.

In discharging its functions Ofwat works partly as a complaints organisation and ensures that water supply is not interrupted. Ofwat has to work with the Environment Agency and the Drinking Water Inspectorate to meet environmental standards and to ensure the quality of the drinking water. It also has the important role of monitoring company investments in repairing and renewing their infrastructure. Recent years have seen Ofwat determined to meet the challenge of leaking pipes and to ensure that water is conserved appropriately. Equally important is the problem of flooding. In 2004 Ofwat provided, within its pricing review for the water industry, an investment of nearly £1 billion to tackle the challenge of flooding arising from overloaded sewers. Ofwat's responsibilities are significant in terms of coordinating the regulation of water companies in developing flood defences.

Ofgem

Ofgem is the main energy regulator. Its powers grew from arrangements put in place after privatisation of gas and electricity.[25] Ofgem's main powers arise from the Utilities Act 2000, the Competition Act 1998 and the Enterprise Act 2002. The Energy Act 2004 provides a duty on Ofgem to contribute and promote sustainable development in the shaping of gas and electricity industries. This includes consideration of the EU Emissions Trading Scheme and managing a low carbon economy. Ofgem's role is to manage the transition to a low carbon economy. It is also involved in overseeing the Renewables Obligation (RO) for renewable electricity in the UK, which is designed to provide incentives for the generation of electricity through renewable technologies. There is a certification process whereby accredited generators receive a certificate for each megawatt hour of eligible renewable electricity generation. Ofgem is also involved in the competition initiatives undertaken by the European Commission that form part of a single European energy market.

Natural England

Natural England is a new body[26] formed from the old English Nature and a revamped Countryside Agency on 1 October 2006. English Nature had the responsibility for the promotion of the conservation of wildlife, geology and wild places between 1990 and 2006. There is a long history of nature conservation in England which goes as far back as 1948 when the National Conservancy Council was established. Natural England has a wide remit covering the conservation and enhancement of biodiversity, landscapes and wildlife in rural, coastal and marine areas. It has four strategic outcomes, namely:

1. A healthy natural environment – this includes England's natural environment and its conservation and enhancement.

2. Enjoyments of the natural environment – this includes establishing appropriate arrangements for more people to enjoy, understand and improve the natural environment.

3. Sustainable use of the natural environment – this includes the sensible use and management of the natural environment.

4. A secure environmental future – this takes account of decision-making and policy-advising.

There is a Chief Executive and six Executive Directors with overall strategic responsibility for the activities of English Nature.

---

[25] See: the Gas Act 1986 and the Electricity Act 1989.
[26] See: the Natural Environment and Rural Communities Act 2006.

Nuclear Directorate

The Nuclear Directorate acts on behalf of Health and Safety Executive to ensure that general safety is provided at nuclear sites. There are extensive safety regulations, including the Nuclear Installations Act 1965, that ensure nuclear sites are licensed and their safety monitored. The Health and Safety at Work etc. Act 1974 provides a comprehensive code for employers to ensure that their operations on site are safe and that safety extends beyond employees to the general public. The UK Safeguards Office (UKSO) has extensive compliance regulations to ensure that the UK's nuclear operations are acting under international safeguards and obligations. There has been a general tidying-up of responsibilities and the Health and Safety Executive received an amalgamation of different roles from the then Department of Trade and Industry (now reformed into the Department for Business Enterprise and Regulatory Reform DBERR). Two hundred and fifty staff are employed by the Nuclear Directorate, and its work has many links with international organisations.

Health and Safety Executive (HSE)

The Health and Safety Executive (HSE) has an increasingly significant role in environmental matters. There are a number of areas where the HSE is particularly important and these serve to illustrate the wide range and scale of health and safety legislation in the United Kingdom. The European Union Regulations on the Registration, Evaluation, Authorisation and Restriction of Chemicals (REACH) came into force on 1 June 2007 and consolidates and replaces a number of EU directives and regulations dealing with industrial chemicals. The HSE is the competent authority within the UK responsible for REACH. This role includes a wide variety of regulatory functions including enforcement and compliance through authorisation and monitoring arrangements. This also covers whistleblowers who may inform the HSE of their concerns.

The HSE is also responsible for the Control of Major Accident Hazards Regulations 1999 (COMAH) and the implementation of the relevant Directive 96/82/EC amended by Directive 2003/105/EC. This also applies to the chemical industry. The HSE provides advice to planning authorities in respect of land use and access of the public to private land, including developments that are planned around major hazard sites.

The HSE has responsibility for onshore and offshore pipelines involved in the transportation of hazardous and non-hazardous substances throughout the United Kingdom. There are detailed rules applicable to pipelines under the Pipeline Safety Regulations 1996 (PSR) but the environmental issues surrounding pipelines are within the competence of the Environment Agency in England and Wales and the Scottish Environment Protection Agency (SEPA) in Scotland. Particularly important is supervision of the United Kingdom gas pipeline.

The control and regulation of any risks associated with the contained use of genetically modified organisms (GMOs), i.e. GMOs not released to the environment, is within the competence of the HSE who operate and enforce the main legislation in the United Kingdom (the Genetically Modified Organisms (Contained Use) Regulations 2000). The HSE acts as an inspector, watchdog and adviser on the containment facilities and the use of GMOs.

Finally, the HSE makes an active input into the risk management strategies of employers to ensure the safety of the place of work. The importance of risk management and carrying forward appropriate policies has given the HSE a major role in this field.

Local government

There is a wide range of environmental responsibilities delegated to local authorities. These include primary responsibility for town and country planning, waste management, air quality management, statutory nuisance and noise control. There is an historical responsibility for contaminated land.[27] The organisation and structures of local government is complex. It is also multi-functional in terms of the responsibilities it holds and in the delivery of its services. Following substantial organisational changes in 1996, local government in England is composed of 46 new unitary local authorities. There is, however, a two-tier structure of county and district local authority applicable in most of the non-metropolitan counties. Devolution for London and directly elected mayors for 11 local electorates also exist. In Scotland, local government was reorganised in 1994 under the Local Government etc (Scotland) Act 1994. The Act established 32 all-purpose unitary authorities.

The responsibilities of local government vary with the authority and are outlined in Table 3.3.

Table 3.3 Areas of local government responsibility

Responsibility	English metropolitan authority	English non-metropolitan authority	London
Planning	Borough and District	County with local planning at District	Greater London Authority (GLA)
Refuse collection	Borough and District		London Borough Council and GLA
Refuse disposal	Joint Authority*, Borough and District		London Borough Council and GLA
Environmental health	Borough and District		London Borough Council and GLA

*Joint Authorities are empowered to undertake multi-tasks as part of their role.

Local government, then, has an important role in the protection of the environment, which has recently been extended. The Sustainable Communities Act 2007 is intended to enhance protection of the environment through the adoption of sustainability policies. Significantly, this includes sustainable local communities, and local authorities are encouraged to make proposals to contribute to sustainability. The Secretary of State is enabled to short-list such proposals and assist local authorities in carrying out their plans. Action plans under these arrangements must be published and approved. The Secretary of State has a consultation requirement as well as the opportunity to make regulations to enable proposals to be taken forward.

National law

Environmental law can be examined in terms of the legal sources that define and explain the law. This is somewhat complicated by the fact that the legal system must be considered not only for England and Wales but also for each of the devolved administrations (see above). Even so, there are some generally applicable laws that contain the basic sources of environmental law. There are different categories of laws, which are worthwhile considering in brief.

---

[27] Each sector is analysed in Part II of the book.

Primary legislation

The term 'Act of Parliament' is frequently used to describe the sources of primary legislation. There are other terms in common usage such as 'statutes' or simply 'legislation'. The key feature of an Act of Parliament is that the Act is made by the United Kingdom Parliament which claims sovereignty. The question of sovereignty is not straightforward, as the United Kingdom Parliament has to give way on matters of European Union law to the Court of Justice. Public Acts of Parliament differ from Private Acts. The former are made by the government of the day, while the latter may be the result of a private member of Parliament introducing a Bill that reflects an interest or cause. The environment is an area that attracts the attention of private members of parliament and if they are successful in the ballot to bring forward legislation, it may ultimately result in environmental legislation being passed. A recent example of a Private Act in the environmental sphere is the Household Waste Recycling Act 2003.

The *Explanatory Notes* that accompany the legislation help with the interpretation of an Act of Parliament. Statutory interpretation, however, is often complex and technical. Since the decision in *Pepper* v *Hart*,[28] the courts may study Parliamentary Debates and other relevant material in order to understand the background to the legislation that is being interpreted. It is important to determine when the Act comes into force as not all sections or parts of the legislation come into force at the same time. There is a section in the Act that contains the short title, commencement and extent of the Act. This is important as the Act may only extend to England and Wales, which leaves Scotland and Northern Ireland requiring their own separate legislation.

The United Kingdom does not have a codified system of law. There are many examples, however, where Parliament has provided Acts of consolidation. For example, the Town and Country Planning Act 1947, although subsequently amended, is a major consolidation of planning law in the United Kingdom.

Delegated legislation

Primary legislation often provides for more detailed and specialist rules to be made through delegated or subordinate legislation. This is also known as secondary legislation. Delegated legislation is made through a process that does not require the full assent, which is three readings of Bills provided by both Houses of Parliament. The operation of delegated legislation is often under ministerial control and this means that delegated legislation may be made more quickly and efficiently than full-scale primary legislation.

In fact the forms of delegated legislation are varied. The term 'delegated legislation' covers different types of laws that allow ministers, the relevant Secretary of State, to legislate under the authority of the primary Act of Parliament. There are various names used to describe delegated legislation such as directives, rules, orders, regulations, or statutory instruments. Why is delegated legislation used? The complex and highly technical nature of environmental law makes it impossible for all the relevant powers to be set out in primary legislation. Environmental law is continually changing and the need for powers to meet the challenges of protecting and enhancing the environment is ever present.

---

[28] *Pepper* v *Hart* [1993] AC 593.

There are many aspects of delegated legislation that are a common cause of complaint. One point of criticism is that delegated legislation is not given the same parliamentary scrutiny as an Act of Parliament. This may mean that political oversight and accountability is not as robust. In addition, since delegated legislation is often immensely technical and detailed, the absence of full parliamentary oversight avoids detailed scrutiny. This may give the government of the day too much unfettered power. It is impossible to give a comprehensive outline of all the areas covered by delegated legislation in the field of environmental law. However, the following are indicative of the purpose for which environmental regulations are passed:

- the means of implementing EU directives and integrating UK environmental law with the treaty obligations;
- the setting of standards and the monitoring of Integrated Pollution Control categories or providing suitable exemptions to planning legislation;
- the means of setting procedural requirements and establishing protocols.

The use of delegated legislation has increased over the past two decades. Its role and remit is set to expand in response to the increasingly technical style and content of environmental law. There is a counter-movement, however, that favours the use of less technical regulation and incremental deregulation of many areas. The Deregulation and Contracting Out Act 1994 confers powers on ministers to amend or repeal delegated or primary legislation. The powers are known as Regulatory Reform Orders and their scope was expanded under the Regulatory Reform Act 2001 to remove or reduce burdens that affect any person carrying on any activity. More recent legislation, the Regulatory Reform Act 2006 has extended the role of regulatory orders still further.

Circulars, codes or memoranda

The use of circulars, codes or memoranda is also a useful way to provide those working in environmental law with guidance and assistance in the interpretation and application of the law. In many instances codes are not enforceable, and when they are enforceable this is clearly set out in primary legislation. The use of discretionary powers is a common feature of this area of law, which gives the decision-maker a wide range of options in how to make decisions. Codes, circulars and memoranda all provide a useful function in helping to make the law and practice of environmental law accessible to the public at large. Policy issues may also be addressed in this way, allowing the government of the day to influence and guide policy-making among decision-makers. The wide number of regulatory agencies that have an environmental role makes the use of informal guidance and rule-making the preferred option to establish the practical working of an agency. In fact setting standards of best practice involves agreeing a Code of Conduct. There are many examples of this kind. One of the most remarkable is the Environment Agency's Enforcement and Prosecution Policy which provides policy objective as a guide to discretion in prosecutions. The future of environmental law is likely to be influenced by the many ways guidance and codes of conduct are made effective.

The courts

The role of the common law in developing, on a case-by-case basis, the interpretation of existing common law principles is well illustrated by the discussion in Chapter 2. While judge-made law in the area of tort is influential, environmental law is primarily found in statutes and in the different forms of delegated or secondary legislation. This gives the courts the task of statutory interpretation. This role is not unique to the United Kingdom courts since statutory arrangements are very often part of the implementation of EU directives. The Court of Justice has, therefore, a key role as guide and interpreter of the main principles and concepts of EU law. In the future it is likely that the Court of Justice will not only influence the interpretation of EU law, but will also ensure that EU law is given full priority in the interpretation and implementation of United Kingdom law. National courts are bound by the Court of Justice when it comes to ensuring the implementation of EU law.

Environmental law cases can arise from disputes over legislative interpretation or from disputes concerning how regulators are expected to perform their statutory responsibilities. In addition to civil law cases the criminal law can be applied to the environment. The use of the courts to prosecute breaches of the criminal law brings enforcement before the criminal courts as a way of adjudicating disputes and upholding the law. There is also the possibility that the courts may be invited to consider the human rights aspects of an environmental dispute. This is a difficult area of law as human rights and the environment have an uneasy relationship. The expectation that once the Human Rights Act 1998 came into force in 2000 it would give rise to many more environmental rights cases has not been realised.

Environmental lawyers and their role

Interest in environmental law has increased over the past twenty-five years. The leading firms of solicitors have specialised teams of lawyers devoted to the environment together with energy and renewable energy sources. Privatisation of the major utilities has led to a substantial increase in the need for specialist skills in drafting contracts. The driving force of European Union law in the environment field has also resulted in more attention being devoted to the environment. This is reflected not only in the activities of law firms but also in societies such as the United Kingdom Environmental Law Association (UKELA), which has a large membership including academic as well as practitioner lawyers.

The environmental lawyer is faced by a number of challenges that arise from the characteristic features of environmental law and from the need to assess environmental rules. The most obvious problem is the complexity of the technical rules and the corresponding communication between primary and delegated legislation. Amendments are frequently made and there are often assortments of changes, reforms and consolidations in general procedural rules. Finding the relevant law on any particular environmental area is often more difficult than it might at first appear because of the different levels of legislation and procedures.

Primary legislation is often implemented in stages rather than at a single time and finding the time of implementation is painstaking and time-consuming. Environmental law often includes complex concepts, and definitions are often not only hard to interpret but are open to different understanding. There is a wide margin of discretion in interpreting key concepts such as sustainable development or the best practical means. Environmental law also contains very widely drafted discretionary powers and embedded in the law are many EU directives and regulations. The changing nature of environmental problems gives rise to the need for flexibility, which may encourage the drafting of discretionary powers so that they may be altered. This is particularly the case when it comes to the adjustment of standards based on scientific evaluations of risk. Indeed it may be necessary for scientists to provide expert opinion over an environmental dispute; one example of this is found in *Cambridge Water* where scientists identified the source of the groundwater pollution. More complicated still, the underlying science may not be certain but open to debate, e.g. the health impacts of mobile-phone masts. Advising clients may prove difficult and uncertain.

European Union law

There are 27 member states of the European Union, each with its own legal system but working together within the European Union to provide common policies. The European Union is a significant source of environmental law and it provides a policy-making function and takes forward initiatives on sustainable development. The content and details of European Union law are the subject matter of Chapter 5. In the United Kingdom context membership of the European Union came about under the European Communities Act 1972. Section 2(1) of the Act provides an obligation on the United Kingdom courts to give effect to the European Union law.[29] This provides the basis for legislation within the United Kingdom Parliament to comply with European Union law. It sets a major imperative on the United Kingdom to adopt EU law as part of domestic law. There are many examples where regulations have been made to incorporate EU law in domestic law such as the Pollution Prevention and Control Act 1999.[30]

The interpretation of EU law is aided by the Court of Justice. The EU Commission is an important source of policy-making and along with member states has promoted the protection of the environment. The EU commonly adopts the precautionary principle working within the framework of sustainable development. It ensures overall integration of environmental law into the law of member states and in force from 1st December 2009. The EU Reform Treaty signed in Lisbon on 19 October 2007 has to be ratified by the member states. Article 1 of the Reform Treaty defines sustainable development as part of the EU's internal market which

> shall work for the sustainable development of Europe based on economic growth and price stability, a highly competitive social market economy, aiming at full employment and social progress, and a high level of protection and improvement of the quality of the environment. It shall promote scientific and technological advance.

The Reform Treaty also integrates environmental protection into the Treaty establishing the European Community (TEC).[31] Many of the underlying principles of EU environmental law are based on social and economic concepts that do not easily translate into enforceable legal rules. There has been a recent tendency to draw together different directives into general framework directives providing comprehensive and often complex consolidations of the law.

---

[29] The term 'European Union law' is appropriate, following the signing of the Reform Treaty on the European Union in 2007.

[30] See Sch.1, para. 20. Also see other examples such as the Town and Country Planning (Assessment of Environmental Effects) (England and Wales) Regulations 1999 SI 1999/293.

[31] Article 6 of TEC will be replaced by 'Environmental protection requirements must be integrated into the definition and implementation of Community policies and activities, in particular with a view to promoting sustainable development'.

One example is the Water Framework Directive, which provides an overarching set of principles with universal application to water quality. There are inevitable difficulties in interpretation of technical and complex law. Indeed, interpretations may vary between different courts within the national legal systems of the 27 member states. The Court of Justice has an important role in providing guidance and assistance in extracting different layers of meaning. The dominant influence within the EU is the civil law tradition and as a result the UK common law interpretation of basic fundamental principles may not always be upheld by the Court of Justice.

While EU legislation is recognised in UK law, not all legislation is directly effective. EU regulations are directly effective but some directives are binding as to the results that can be achieved. In many instances this leaves member states with discretion over the interpretation and application of EU principles and concepts. When member states fail to achieve an adequate level of implementation the matter may become an issue before the Court of Justice. The failure to implement specific substantive or procedural provisions from a directive may also be actionable at the suit of the private citizen and damages may be awarded by the Court of Justice.

An example of the work of the EU in the policy field is the recent Commission Working Document, *Impact Assessment*.[32] The policy has come about as a result of discussion on climate change at Lisbon and illustrates the proactive role the EU plays in tackling current problems and in adjusting existing directives. The Working Document set the following targets:

- an EU commitment to achieving at least a 20 per cent reduction in greenhouse gas emissions by 2020 compared to 1990 levels and an objective for a 30 per cent reduction by 2020 subject to the conclusion of a comprehensive international climate change agreement;

- a mandatory EU target of 20 per cent renewable energy use by 2020 including a 10 per cent biofuels target.

This proposal is accompanied by a review on the role for renewable energy and amendments to the EU Emissions Trading Directive, modifying the EU emissions trading system. There are a number of related proposals to save energy through reviews of transport, buildings, services and smaller industrial installations and also agriculture and waste.

International law

Since environmental hazards and impacts transcend national boundaries, the protection of the environment must also cross national boundaries. The relationship between states forms an intrinsic part of trade relations and has global significance. The impact of continued globalisation and economic growth, and the cross-national nature of environmental problems is likely to make the role of international law pivotal in the future development of environmental policy and law. There is a sharp contrast between international law and EU law. International law is not directly enforceable in domestic law and many of the decisions taken

---

[32] Brussels 23 January 2008 Proposals of the EU Parliament and of the Council amending Directive 2003/87/EV to improve and extend EU greenhouse gas emission allowance trading system. SEC(2008) 85/3.

about the environment require political consensus before any effective action may be taken. There are many examples where the aspirational policy-making in international environmental law has created enormous discussion and worthwhile action. The Climate Change Convention and the Kyoto Protocol and latterly agreements reached at Bali in 2007 are indicative of major shifts in the way policy-makers confront environmental issues.

One of the most influential policies in environmental law came from the 1987 Brundtland Report of the World Commission on Environment and Development, *Our Common Future*, that defined sustainable development as the

> development that meets the needs of the present without compromising the ability of future generations to meet their own needs.

There are a number of reasons why international environmental law is significant and it is useful to indicate some of the relevant rationale behind the subject:

- Transboundary problems require a special kind of protection through international law.
- Standards are created through international agreements.
- International law can generate principles such as sustainable development and adapt others such as the precautionary principle.
- International procedures and practices allow for negotiation and arbitration between nations to deal with global and regional problems.
- Economic instruments are important tools in environmental protection and international law provides the correct formula for their implementation.
- Organisations and institutions that are international in character are important beyond the national systems of law that may be ineffective in dealing with cross-boundary problems.
- EU law has contributed greatly to the development of international law.

International environmental law has developed through several periods of history.

Period 1: the nineteenth century until the Second World War (1945). This period saw the creation of international organisations and agreements. The development of the industrialised society, the market economy and the growth in capital brought the need to protect the environment. The control of noxious fumes, noise and pollution began as part of public health, in tandem with ameliorating environmental impacts on human diseases. The first inspectorate, the Alkali Inspectorate, was established in the UK, and other nations also responded to urbanisation and industrialisation. Legal instruments developed to protect flora and fauna at an international level.

Period 2: after the Second World War until 1972. The creation of the United Nations and the UN Conference on the Human Environment 1972 in Stockholm are milestones in this period. A variety of problems that had environmental impacts started to be addressed internationally, including pollution and the conservation of the natural habitat, nuclear testing, wetlands, the marine environment, freshwater and prevention of dumping at sea.

Period 3: from 1972 until 1992 and the UN Conference on the Environment and Development. The UN coordinated action and the development of responses to issues such as production, consumption and international trade.

Period 4: between 1992 and the present century. This period has seen the attempt to integrate into political and economic policies the rules of international law that address environmental matters. There has been a marked growth in the reliance on science and evidence-based analysis of environmental impacts. This involves the use of hazard and risk assessment together with the use of predictive models of effects. There has been an attempt to create a stronger link between governance, national and international systems leading to the development of adjudications involving environmental issues.

The significance of international environmental law is explored in more detail in Chapter 4.

Comparative law

Comparative law is a means of learning from the experiences of other countries when tackling similar problems. There is increasingly appreciation of the value of comparative analysis particularly for global environmental problems. For example, combined heat and power (CHP) systems and their regulation in Scandinavian countries are being examined by other countries in the context of energy efficiency, renewable energy and reducing carbon emissions. Comparative environmental law is likely to become more significant in the future of environmental law.

Pressure groups and organisations

The significance of pressure groups in the development of environmental policy should not be overlooked. At the national and international level Friends of the Earth, Greenpeace and the World Development Movement and others have been active and effective campaigners and lobbyists for better protection of the environment. They are often successful in challenging government action (See: *R v Secretary of State for Foreign and Commonweath Affairs, ex parte World Development Movement* [1995] 1 All ER 611). Greenpeace has been particularly active in monitoring radioactive waste. Mr Justice Otton in *R v Inspectorate of Pollution ex parte Greenpeace* [1994] 4 All ER 321 at p. 349 described how the organisation had nearly 5 million supporters worldwide with 400,000 supporters in the United Kingdom and about 2,500 of them living in the Cumbria region where the British Nuclear Fuel's plant was situated.

Specific organisations that protect rights such as the Ramblers' Association also deserve mention. It was founded in 1935, following the setting-up of a National Council of Ramblers' Federation in 1931 and the creation of a number of other distinct federations in London. Its role is to preserve the national footpath network and support the creation of national parks. Such organisations perform an educative function as well as providing for the interests of members. There are many other national groups such as the Campaign for Rural England and the Royal Society for the Protection of Birds. Local groups taking action about a particular issue may campaign alongside these national pressure groups.

The National Trust, a charity which owns many buildings and areas of natural beauty also lobbies for the protection of the environment. The Trust has taken on a greater role in environmental controversy than hitherto by opposing genetically modified crops. The National Trust through ownership of a number of historic buildings and parkland also provides an important contribution to the protection of the environment. Founded in 16 July 1894, it was registered six months later under the Companies Act 1895 as 'The National Trust for Places of Historic Interest or Natural Beauty'. The Trust has become one of the largest private landowners in Britain and currently owns about 1 per cent of the land. It cares for over 200 historic houses. Independent of government, the Trust through endowments and gifts, seeks to conserve and preserve the historic aspects of its many buildings and land that it owns. In 1993–4 its income was £139 million, nearly 30 per cent coming from membership fees. In recent years it has had to respond to the increase in public awareness about the environment.[33]

There are a number of significant 'think-tanks' or policy-making bodies that have relevance to environmental law and policy. The Institute of Fiscal Studies offers an influential analysis of government fiscal policy. Its annual Green Budget Report provides a basis for evaluating taxation in the context of public spending. It also tackles issues connected with the environment in the context of policy-making. The Institute of Public Policy Research (IPPR)[34] is a centre-left policy group that also includes analysis of the environment. The Adam Smith Institute founded in 1977 addresses new policy ideas relevant to the state and regulation.[35]

Conclusions

The complex nature of environmental law is partly explained by the diverse influences that have brought about its transition from a purely domestic set of rules, procedures and principles to one where there are layers of obligation beyond the UK. Some of these stem from the European Union while others come from international law. There has also been a borrowing of ideas from other jurisdictions. The absence of any large-scale codification of environmental legislation is likely to remain the case. This adds to the ever-increasing complexity of the subject. The legacy of the past is also a factor. Legal change in terms of shaping and moulding environmental law has not been uniform or consistent. Adapting the law to meet new challenges and accommodating scientific discovery and data leaves environmental law in an almost continual state of flux. The wider political agenda is also a major factor, which has both underpinned and on occasion undermined the development of environmental law.

The administration of the environment is equally complex and devolution has brought changes that have far-reaching consequences. One of the main factors that drove forward devolution was the need to locate government decisions closer to the communities affected. This inevitably holds a particular resonance for the environment. Protecting and enhancing the environment in a sustainable way is a local as well as national and global responsibility, but citizens close to their own environment are likely to take a keen interest. There may be an inevitable tension between the economic developmental needs of the country and the need to take account of local residents' and citizens' rights. Setting the balance is quite simply one of the biggest challenges facing governments and environmental law today.

The United Kingdom has not consolidated environmental law into a coherent form. Instead many initiatives and policies are driven by the particular department that has

---

[33] See: Robin Fedden and Rosemary Joekes, *The National Trust Guide*, The National Trust, London: 1973.
[34] See for information *www.ippr.org.uk*.
[35] See *www.adamsmith.org.uk*.

responsibilities linked to the environmental problem. This approach to environmental matters can be criticised since environmental policy-making is diffuse and ill-coordinated. It crosses the boundaries of local and central government, which may lead to inconsistent approaches in each locality. A plethora of agencies and organisations are engaged in environmental regulation, which must raise issues about ensuring the effectiveness of regulation. There is no overall coordinating body that links all the strands of environmental law and policy into a single entity. There are some advantages, however, to the British system namely that environmental issues arise in the context of the jurisdiction of the responsible specialist body. This may not allow good coordination but it provides that environmental issues are fully integrated into decision-making supported by particular expertise. It is possible that the environment will be given a higher priority by government and when this happens any deficiency in the British approach will probably be addressed.

Finally, the articulation of the main guiding concepts and principles of environmental law is also complex and often problematic. There are always tensions in trying to implement and explain vague concepts such as the 'polluter pays' principle or sustainable development. Creating realisable targets and achievable goals is one way forward. Enforcing and regulating such goals and objectives takes time and effort and requires a continual reassessment of effectiveness. In examining the layers of law that make up environmental law there are two influences that have a distinctive contribution. One is international environmental law and the other is European environmental law which form the basis of the following two chapters.

Further reading

On law and interpretation of cases and statutes see: **C. Manchester and D. Salter**, *Exploring the Law* 3rd edition, London: Thomson, Sweet and Maxwell, 2006.

On constitutional arrangements and the role of administrative law see: **C. Turpin and A. Tomkins**, *British Government and the Constitution* 6th edition, Cambridge: Cambridge University Press, 2007.

On science and the direction of scientific research see: **Lord Sainsbury of Turville**, *The Race to the Top: A Review of Government's Science and Innovation Policies* London: HM Treasury, 2007.

On local government see: **T. Byrne**, *Local Government in Britain* London: Penguin, 2000.

On developing ideas about environmental law see: **J. Holder and M. Lee**, *Environmental Protection, Law and Policy* 2nd edition, Cambridge: Cambridge University Press, 2007.

Pressure groups and organisations

Amnesty International at *http://wwww.amnesty.org/*.

Anglers Conservation Association, 23 Caslegate, Grantham, Lincs NG31 6SW.

The Council for the Protection of Rural England, Warwick House, 25 Buckingham Palace Road, London SW1 0PP.

The Environmental Law Foundation, Lincoln's Inn House, 42 Kingsway, London WC2B 6EX.

Friends of the Earth, 26–28 Underwood Street, London N1 7JQ.

Greenpeace, Canonbury Villas, London N12PN.

National Society for Clean Air, 136 North Street, Brighton BN1 1RG.

Royal Society for Nature Conservation, The Green, Witham Park, Waterside South, Lincoln LN5 7JR.

Useful sources of information

Civil Service Year Book – available as an annual publication from HMSO (1995–).

ENDS Reports – Monthly publication from Environmental Data Services Ltd, Finsbury Business Centre, 40 Bowling Green Lane, London EC1R ONE.

The British Ecological Society, 26 Bloades Court, Deodar Road, London SW15 2NU.

The Geological Society, Burlington House, Piccadilly, London W1V OJU. Guidance to the Environment Agency on its objectives, including the contribution it is to make towards the achievement of sustainable development (DoE, 1995).

The Consumer Association, 2 Marylebone Road, London NW1 4DF.

Business and the Environment Programme: **The Environment Council**, 21 Elizabeth Street, London SW1W 9RP, and **Business in the Environment**, 8 Stratton Street, London W1X 5FD.

Websites

Central government

http://www.ukonline.gov.uk provides links to all the main central and some local government activities. There is a guide to government departments that allows easy access. In particular Defra may be found at *www.defra.gov.uk*.

Parliament

http://www.parliament.uk provides links to the UK Parliament including House of Commons and House of Lords. There are useful research papers prepared by the Library on the website. There are also links to select committees, and the evidence from government and agencies is regularly provided in *Hansard*.

Legislation

Primary legislation (Acts of Parliament) see: *http://www.legislation.hmso.gov.uk/acts.htm*.

Statutory instruments are available at: *http://www.legislation.hmso.gov.uk/stat.htm*.

The Environment Agency

Access to the work of the agency may be found at: *http://www.environment-agency.gov.uk*.

Regional assemblies

Scottish Parliament see: *http://www.scottish.parliament.uk*

Scotland legislation: *http://www.scotland-legislation.hmso.gov.uk*.

National Assembly of Wales: *http://www.wales.gov.uk*.

Northern Ireland Assembly: *http://www.ni-assembly.gov.uk*.

Northern Ireland legislation: *http://www.northernireland-legislation.hmso.gov.uk*.

The courts

The Courts Service website, see: *http://www.courtservice.gov.uk*.

The various judicial judgments are available from: *http://www.courtservice.gov.uk/judgments/judge_home.htm*.

The Court of Justice of the European Communities: *http://europa.eu.int/cj/en/index.htm*.

The European Court of Human Rights: *http://www.echr.coe.int/*.

The International Court of Justice: *http://www.icj-cjj.org*.

Law firms on the web

See: *http://www.lawontheweb.co.uk/lawyers-find.htm*.

European environmental law

There is a large amount of law available from the following:

See: *http://www.eel.nl*.

The different DGs in the European Commission include:

DG Environment: *http://europa.eu.int/comm/environment/*.

DG Fisheries: *http://europa.eu.int/comm/dg14.html*.

DG Agriculture: *http://europa.eu.int/comm/agriculture/index_en.htm*.

Visit **http://www.mylawchamber.co.uk/mceldowney** to access key issue checklists and practice exam questions to test yourself on this chapter.

4 International environmental law

Introduction

The study of international environmental law is an important part of our attempts to control environmental problems. The acknowledgement that environmental problems are not contained within national or territorial boundaries but have regional and global dimensions has brought a growing recognition of the significance of international environmental law. The environment is shared and the need to protect the environment is paramount in the relationship between states. We will focus on international environmental law in this chapter, specifically addressing a number of questions. What is international environmental law? What is the role of international environmental law and how does international law contribute to environmental protection?

International environmental law has a number of distinctive features, as follows:

- International law is not directly enforceable in the national legal system of the United Kingdom. Treaties are required to be given effect by implementation of national legislation before they are enforced.

- International law does not have the benefit of a single or coherent body responsible for its enforcement or monitoring.

- International law is often used to settle disputes between states. When economic issues of trade or markets are the centre for the dispute then environmental matters may not be a prominent consideration. This may make international environmental law ineffective, and a sustainable balance between rich and poor states difficult to achieve.

- International environmental law may provide a means to set standards and encourage improvements in environmental protection. If environmental standards are adjudicated correctly it may help to encourage poorer countries to adopt best practice.

- International environmental law may also encourage policy-makers to engage with environmental considerations and sustainable development strategies.

- International environmental law and EU law are mutually influential in the development of policy and strategy. Although international law and EU law are distinct and different from each other, they may join forces in bringing about environmental protection. The EU has acknowledged the need to address transboundary and global problems and through the European Court of Justice it may enforce its environmental legislation. This provides an opportunity for many policy decisions in international environmental law to be implemented in 27 member states, which can act as a spearhead for action by other countries.

● International environmental law struggles to be set as a priority because of the pre-eminence given to regulating international trade. Protecting the environment may take second place to other international concerns.

Why study international environmental law?

There are many reasons for studying international environmental law and considering environmental protection on the world stage. The most obvious comes from the fact that environmental problems do not recognise national boundaries, which quite simply means that national laws or domestic standards cannot fully manage the demands of environmental protection. The study of international law provides an important reflection on setting environmental standards that are broader based than national concerns. Principles of environmental law are likely to emerge from international law that have a wider perspective than those from a single country. International law may also act to facilitate discussion and help provide a set of common procedures and principles for the resolution of environmental disputes. International law offers a greater variety of regulatory ideas and influences than a national legal system. There can be no doubt that international law is the most appropriate way to tackle international environmental problems such as ozone depletion, global warming and climate change. Ultimately, this may be particularly relevant for the future development of environmental law. Finally, one of the earliest foci for international law was on trade and commerce and this may provide an effective mechanism for building environmental protection into its remit of activities. It is difficult to achieve effective regulation and compliance against a backdrop of strong national lobbying. It is possible that international law may create a bargain with stakeholders by combining the regulation of trade and the adoption of environmental principles.

International environmental law also faces a number of complex challenges. Among these, reconciling accepted principles of environmental protection while recognising the aspirations of emerging economies to develop and grow is one of the most difficult. Competitive tendencies between different national economies are also often at odds with environmental stewardship. The vested interests of national states to regulate and control their own resources may also affect their willingness to conform to international law or to accept the need for global interests to be prioritised over national ones.

How international law applies in the United Kingdom

In the United Kingdom legal system, international law is relevant for the creation and the continuous review of environmental policy. It may also find its way into the law itself. This can be achieved by adjusting rights and duties to take account of international environmental principles. It is possible that contributing to the development of international environmental law may provide the United Kingdom with a platform to have a significant influence on the strategies underpinning international environmental law as well as on its operation. Probably the best example of international law's influence on environmental policy within the UK is found in the application of sustainable development. The 1992 Rio Summit (The UN Conference on Environment and Development) brought forward Agenda 21 as part of the mechanisms for implementing the concept at a local level. The United Kingdom government rapidly introduced sustainable development[1] as a cornerstone for its approach to the environment. This proved influential since the concept of sustainable development subsequently found favour within the European Union and has been influential worldwide.

Sustainable development is part of an approach in international law known as 'soft law'. This is not directly enforceable but contains general ideas and principles. The concept of sustainable development has become a fundamental building block for environmental law. Ultimately its adoption may prove to be a turning point in the development of environmental law, since it engages diverse stakeholders – industry, business and government. There are many other examples of international agreements, including the 1998 Aarhus Convention on environmental justice, that are pragmatic in character and allow individual countries flexibility in their interpretation of the agreement. In contrast to 'soft law' there is 'hard law'. This is defined to mean treaties, conventions or agreements and is generally to be found as binding in the general way that international law is binding on a state. This is normally in respect of relations between states rather than enforceable within the state itself.

The United Kingdom has also considered international law as a way of building influence throughout the world. Aside from domestic politics where scepticism of the role of international law is often expressed, there are many instances where the United Kingdom has engaged and influenced the direction of international law. The Cartegna Protocol to the Convention on Biological Diversity is one where scepticism and opposition gave way to acceptance and negotiation. The convention applies to the transportation of living organisms, and the UK has agreed the substance of its provisions. Inevitably, however, there are sceptics about the power of international environmental law to meet the challenge of vested interest, wariness of change and unease about external rules being applied to internal and domestic markets.

There are two ways in which international environmental law can take effect: direct application and indirect application. These are worthy of a brief discussion here.

Direct application

The general rule is that under United Kingdom law international agreements only become part of national law once they are given effect by the United Kingdom Parliament. The rule is in part a reflection of the centuries-old idea that the United Kingdom Parliament is uniquely sovereign and of a reluctance to have laws imposed on the United Kingdom outside parliamentary scrutiny. It also reflects the tradition of an imperial power and the assertion of sovereignty over many colonial countries.[2] There is, however, another influence at work. The growth in global markets and the domination of transnational corporations has encouraged and shaped the modern market economy with free movement of capital and resources. In

---

[1] *Sustainable Development: The UK Strategy* Cm 2462,1994.
[2] See: Lord Denning in *Blackburn* v *Attorney General* [1971] 1 WLR 1037, p. 1040 discussing the role of the Statute of Westminster 1931. Also see: *Manuel* v *Attorney General* [1983] 1 Ch 77.

parallel with this is a rapid expansion of and advance in science and technology, not least in mass communication across national boundaries. Together these have brought the need to embrace international agreements and agencies rather than rely on national systems of law. Consequently necessity demands that national systems of law should adapt to and adopt international law. In the United Kingdom the negotiation of treaties, and the making of national law is in the hands of the government of the day. Thus, a treaty is not self-executing: it requires legislation to become part of domestic law – only then does it have direct application. This process of incorporation is maintained by the courts as an essential prerequisite of the law. The United Kingdom Parliament's role remains sovereign. This is so, notwithstanding the granting of independence to many countries in the last century; also the UK Parliament's sovereignty is unchanged with the introduction of devolution to Wales, Scotland and Northern Ireland, introduced since 1998.

Once an international treaty is signed it may create obligations that are binding on countries in terms of international relations and also in terms of international law. Not all such obligations, although binding on governments, may give rise to directly enforceable rights actionable at the behest of the citizen. Thus, it is the case that international agreements cannot be used as a basis for actions against the state on behalf of a pressure group or because of individual action. This is only possible once adopted by national law.

Indirect application

Once an international treaty is agreed it may confer rights and liabilities on individual states, and when given effect in national law it can be used as a source of interpretation in national courts. The presumption that Parliament does not intend to directly violate international law is the most obvious example of this. Thus the impact of international law may extend far beyond the simple translation of international law into the Act of Parliament through indirect application.

Important issues arise when environmental rights are construed from international law. In the United Kingdom, the Human Rights Act 1998 raised expectations about rights protecting the environment. The 1998 Act came into force in 2000 and brings the European Convention on Human Rights (ECHR) into domestic law. It allows the United Kingdom courts the opportunity to interpret legislation as well as common law doctrines in terms of protecting rights.[3] Human rights and their indirect effect on the environment may well become significant for the future development of environmental protection. Pressure groups and interest groups may find that the courts take the opportunity to develop environmental rights as part of the jurisprudence. The role of rights is examined in more detail in Chapter 6.

It is clear that beyond the simple legislative effect in domestic law, international treaties may provide an overarching influence on governments. This may ultimately press governments to engage with and collaborate over environmental rights. Eventually, as international environmental law develops to its full potential, it is likely that there will be a greater willingness to see treaty arrangements as providing a road map for domestic courts to follow.

---

[3] See: *McKenna* v *British Aluminium Ltd* [2002] Env LR 30 and also *Marcic* v *Thames Water Utilities Ltd* [2004] Env LR 25.

European Union law and international law

European Union law stands out as an example of treaty obligations uniquely binding on member states as part of the law of the European Union. This arises because of the nature of the United Kingdom's legal relationship with the European Union and the pivotal role of the European Court of Justice in developing the jurisprudence of the European Union. It is sufficient to explain that the European Union is actively engaged in treaty-making under international law. The EU Commission carries on the task of negotiation on behalf of the member states, and once concluded then the Council has legal authority to sign the treaty. This is an example of where unanimity is required and is subject to delicate horse-trading between the interests of the EU and those of the member states. The recently ratified EU Reform Treaty (Treaty of Lisbon) creates a new Article 3 of the Treaty of the European Union that the Union 'shall establish an internal market' and 'will work for the sustainable development of Europe based on balanced economic growth and price stability, a highly competitive social market economy, aiming at full employment and social progress, and a high level of protection and improvement of the quality of the environment' as part of the promotion of the 'economic, social and territorial cohesion and solidarity among member states'. This is an important guiding principle that makes the environment integral to the building of the sustainable development of the EU.

It is also the case that because the EU has legal competence it may engage in disputes that are subject to arbitration by the international court or tribunal. There is considerable room for disagreement over environmental matters, particularly in the context of trade disputes. Reconciling the interests of the EU and individual member states is difficult. A majority of member states may favour one course of action but the minority may block the EU from agreeing a treaty or providing a reconciliation through international arbitration. There are often irreconcilable differences in the attitudes of member states. In the case of a number of international environmental treaties, such as the 1997 Kyoto Climate Change Protocol, there is an overlap of responses between the United Kingdom and the EU since they are both parties to the agreement. The extent of international cooperation in environmental matters is also illustrated by the important role of the Intergovernmental Panel on Climate Change (IPCC)[4] in providing evidence-based assessment of global warming and its impacts for policy-makers. The IPCC takes account of EU and UK representations through the G8 summit. The IPCC provides information that contributes to negotiations and ultimately agreements under the UN Framework Convention on Climate Change. This convention provides the framework for an international strategy on climate change. Agreements reached at Bali in December 2007 at the start of the process to renegotiate the Kyoto Protocol have led the United Kingdom to take new national initiatives. A new Climate Change Bill has been proposed with emission targets set for 2012 and beyond, which is after the Kyoto Protocol has expired. The EU has not been able to meet its existing Kyoto commitments but has undertaken intensive action through the EU's action plan by buying foreign emissions credits in order to meet targets. Over 175 countries originally signed the Kyoto Protocol. Australia under a new government has recently ratified the protocol, in 2008, but the USA has not.

---

[4] See: Working Group III contribution to the IPPC fourth assessment report: mitigation of climate change, ENDS Report 388, May 2007, p. 11.

The EU is a unique example where the rules about trade and commerce are integrated with rules for environmental protection within a framework for sustainable development. There is a growing opportunity to devise techniques that test the needs of trade against those of environmental protection in order to strike a suitable balance between potentially competing objectives. The European Union did not at first prioritise the environment, and this gave ample opportunity for competition and market developments to take shape. The insertion of the environment into the EC Treaty has given room for negotiation on the environment as part of the future of the EU. The European Court of Justice has also had an important role in combining EU and international law and policy for environmental protection. Clearly the EU example is worth considering in more detail in its own right and the significant role of EU environmental law will be explored in detail in Chapter 5.

A short history of international environmental law

It is difficult to date the precise origins of international environmental law. The nineteenth century saw international agreements for wildlife protection including both flora and fauna. In the eighteenth century, Comte de Buffon[5] and others worked on listing and mapping the flora and fauna of the world. Their general interest was to consider evolution and the effects of humans on the environment. De Buffon became highly influential through his appointment as Director of the *Jardin du Roi* and the Royal Museum in France. Von Humboldt[6] and others traced the impact of deforestation on water levels. His study of the atmosphere provided a link between humans' activities and the environment. He made particularly important observations on species decline, which provided some evidence to support regulation of hunting and fishing to preserve species. This gave rise to early initiatives on conservation through bilateral fishing treaties.

International environmental law also addressed the legal problems associated with mineral extraction linked to industrialisation, and the impact on the environment. International environmental law grew alongside the era of scientific discovery, and the period of nineteenth-century industrialisation became significant in the history of trading nations and in the acquisition of colonies by the great powers.

◼ Treaties and other responses

A growing recognition that the environment existed outside national boundaries gave rise to bilateral and regional treaty agreements. The Whaling Convention of 1931 is but one example. The protection of birds and other conservation issues were initially lightly regulated though various societies and voluntary groups – for example, the Ornithological Congress. The first committee for the protection of birds was formed in 1844. In 1902 the Convention to Protect Birds Useful to Agriculture was agreed and this was followed by the 1979 Berne

---

[5] George-Louis Leclere, Comte de Buffon (1707–88), French naturalist published his 44 volume *Histoire Naturelle* from 1749 to 1767.

[6] Alexander von Humboldt (1769–1859) German naturalist and traveller. Worked at Freiburg and published *Flora Subterranea Fribergensis* in 1793. Worked with a leading French scientist, Christian Ehremerg, in Paris and studied the atmosphere.

Convention and, in 1992, the Biodiversity Convention. These illustrate how treaty agreements act almost like building blocks, with further agreements building on initial arrangements.

Wildlife constituted the first major treaty in 1900 on the Conservation of the Wildlife in African Colonies, followed in 1933 by the Convention on the Preservation of Fauna and Flora. Oddly, state boundaries were also the cause of the protection of the environment by international law. An early example of this is the 1909 Water Boundaries Treaty between the USA and Canada, which established a monitoring committee to ensure performance of the various treaty obligations. A further draft treaty was prepared in 1920 specifically on pollution control but, although drafted, it was not adopted.

Diseases also led to treaty agreements. The Poisonous Substances and Epizootic Diseases Treaty was adopted in 1876 in Europe by Italy and Austria-Hungary in 1876. Nature and its protection formed another organising category in 1909 when an International Congress for the Protection of Nature held its first meeting in Paris. A nature-protection body was proposed at the Congress and four years later this resulted in the formation of the Consultative Committee for the International Protection of Nature. The First World War interrupted these environmental endeavours but they are indicative of the approach taken, the recognition of environmental problems and the need for cross-boundary environmental protection even then.

Trade disputes also contributed to the development of international environmental law. The Pacific Fur Seal Agreement was a settlement between Britain and the USA on how to control the fur trade and avoid over-exploitation of the resource. The arbitration, however, was only of limited assistance and success. International law rejected the rights of states to step outside their own national boundaries to police or regulate environmental conservation. This severe limitation on the law is a reflection of the way that the early treaty obligations were expressed and also of the way disputes could be used to an individual state's benefit. On the other hand, the important potential for dispute settlement through international law had been revealed.

The Trail Smelter case (*USA* v *Canada*)[7] in 1941 is a famous example of the use of international law in the resolution of environmental disputes between nations. The dispute between the USA and Canada arose from the emission of sulphur by a smelter in Canada, which caused damage in the in the American state of Washington. The principle of international law that applied was that a neighbouring state had no right 'to use or permit the use of its territory in such a manner as to cause injury by fumes in or to the territory of another or the properties thereon'. This prohibition was qualified by the idea of serious harm and the 'establishing of the facts through clear and convincing evidence'. As an authoritative decision, the case provides a pivotal use of international law. It established international environmental law by declaring that the sovereign use of land did not include the right to cause injury to the adjoining neighbouring state.

◼ The United Nations and Stockholm (1972)

The UN and its agencies have helped to develop an institutional and regulatory approach to environmental problems using international law. Although the UN Charter does not mention the environment, it has provided conservationist and related activities through international agencies such as the Food and Agriculture Organisation (FAO) and the United Nations

---

[7] Trail Smelter Case *US* v *Canada* (1941) 3 RIAA 1907.

Educational, Scientific and Cultural Organisation (UNESCO). The chief responsibility for this, in fact, has fallen on the General Agreement on Tariffs and Trade (GATT). The GATT addresses not only issues of free trade but also, and crucially, the issue of conserving exhaustible natural resources. This theme of conservation was taken up by the UN Conference on the Conservation and Utilisation of Resources (UNCCUR) in 1949. The United States had a formidable and important early role in these developments of the GATT. The remit of the UNCCUR was limited, but it nevertheless had important if modest results:

- Global issues were addressed.
- Economic and scientific measurements were made and economic concepts were used to assess minerals, fuels and energy, water, forests and land, wildlife and fish.
- Conservation was given a high rating and attention.
- New technology was assessed.
- Education strategies were adopted.
- Developed and developing countries received consideration according to their economic situation.
- Integrated development of river basins was applied as a policy.

One of the outcomes from the UNCCUR was the gradual development of a system of international law aimed at the protection of the environment. Conservation conferences soon followed, the most notable was Conservation on the Law of the Sea in 1954. A conference on the atmosphere was held a year later, which attempted to address the issue of nuclear testing. The 1955 Test Ban Treaties were ultimately signed in 1963.

The International Maritime Organisation (IMO) first met in 1954 with conservation of the high seas and environmental matters becoming important agenda items. In 1971 the Ramsar Convention (The Convention on Wetlands of International Importance, especially as Waterfowl Habitat)[8] was an important milestone in international environmental protection. It was the first environment treaty to require protection and management of a particular type of ecosystem i.e. wetlands, based on named sites worldwide.

In 1948 the International Court of Justice adopted the principle that every state had an obligation not to knowingly allow its territory to be used for acts contrary to the rights of other states. In 1972 the UN general Assembly convened the Stockholm conference that included considerable scientific discussion on the use and conservation of the human environment. The issues canvassed included the impact of human activity on the biosphere, including pollution of the air, water and deforestation. Six main areas were discussed and became the basis for action:

1. planning and management of human settlements for environmental quality;
2. environmental aspects of natural resource management;
3. control of pollutants and nuisances as part of an overall strategy to address environmental issues;
4. education and information as key to an understanding of strategic development relevant to environmental matters;

---

[8] See the Ramsar Convention on Wetlands at *www.ramsar.org/*.

5. development to be accompanied by understanding the environment;

6. international organisational implications to include action protocols.

These elements formed part of a global environmental assessment programme that is still overseen by Earthwatch,[9] which was established as a result of the conference.

Stockholm to Rio 1972–92

The decades following 1972 were a period of considerable activity in international environmental law. Actions were taken to implement outcomes from Stockholm; there was a proliferation of treaties and agreements and new techniques for setting standards developed. Scientific expertise expanded and deepened, which led to many innovations in assessments and technology.

The UN Environmental Programme (UNEP) promoted environmental agreements such as Principle 21 and oversaw the development of over 30 different treaties and agreements. World Heritage sites were created and the United Nations Convention on the Law of the Sea was created. Significantly the GATT Group on Environmental Measures and International Trade was established, embedding environment matters at the heart of the international market. Other international institutions such as the World Bank also adopted environmental elements into their thinking and activities. International developments over this period included the following:

● environmental impact assessment;

● endangered species;

● biodiversity;

● transboundary harm;

● international law and cooperation over the Environment Resolutions 2997–3004;

● the World Conservation Strategy 1991 Caring for the Earth;

● the Brundtland Report 1987, probably the most significant of all;

● Environmental Perspective to the Year 2000 and Beyond.

The sources of international environmental law

Understanding international environmental law requires an explanation of the differences between 'hard' and 'soft' environmental law. The distinction is a familiar one to international lawyers. 'Hard law' refers to those international rules or principles that are binding on states in their relations with other states. The other category 'soft law' are rules that are not binding in themselves. These set norms and influence the way the government of a country may make decisions. The distinction between hard and soft international law is worth considering in greater depth.

---

[9] See the United Nations System-Wide Earthwatch at *http://earthwatch.unep.ch/index.php*.

Hard international law consists of treaties; customary international environmental law (see below); generally accepted principles of international law; judicial decisions and the writing of the international jurists. This list is accepted under Article 38(1) of the Statute of the International Court of Justice (ICJ). The most authoritative source of international environmental law emerges from treaties. States are said to be bound through consent and this consent is obtained through ratification. Treaties may also be called conventions, accords or agreements. The word 'protocol' is also given legal force in the same way as a treaty but it is a term used to apply to a sub-agreement to a treaty. There are some famous examples of environmental treaties such as the Whaling Convention, the Convention on World Heritage Sites, and the 1992 Climate Change Convention. This convention is often simply referred to as the Kyoto Protocol, which is a sub-agreement of the convention. It is difficult to make a definitive list of treaties that apply to the environment; estimates of the number vary but it is probably about 500. The form of treaties on the environment conforms to international legal rules and fall under the auspices of the UNEP or, as many countries in the developing world prefer, the UN General Assembly. Interpretation also conforms to international legal rules and Articles 31 and 32 of the Vienna Convention 1969 are relevant here. There is a tendency to adopt the help of the international courts when interpreting treaties, which provides an important step forward in laying down common standards for countries to follow. Environmental treaties can suffer from the problems of overlap and confusion – such issues can only be resolved thorough a skilful interpretation. In addition, there are also instances where a treaty may interfere with some environmental protections. One possible way forward is to call international conferences to detail a response to and resolve the problems of any conflict between treaties.

Customary international law

Customary rules also have a part to play in international environmental law. These rules arise through implicit rather than explicit agreements and are limited in scope, but they have an influence on creating binding obligations between states. The great advantage of custom as a source of international environmental law is that it creates flexibility. Custom often offers vague or imprecise arrangements and this may facilitate policy developments and agreements. There are now examples of international customary environmental law including the use of the 'polluter pays' principle, the development of the precautionary principle and also establishing best practice in the use of scientific advance. The evolution of such principles provides the future of environmental law with a vibrancy, as the principles provide a sound basis for bargain between the parties. There is a great deal to be gained by adopting best practice through the precautionary principle as a means of protecting the environment. Risk assessment and judgements about risk inevitably form a key component of protecting the environment.

Judicial decisions and the role of international environmental lawyers

The use of binding precedent familiar to the common law is not applicable to judicial decisions in international environmental law. International courts include the International Court of Justice (ICJ) and a number of regional courts such as the European Court of Justice in the European Union and national courts. The decisions of the ICJ are not binding as general precedent, but are binding between the parties. The ICJ is a UN body consisting of 15 judges elected by the General Assembly and the Security Council. There are a number of significant shortcomings in the remit of the ICJ:

- Only a small number, about three, of cases are heard each year.

- Less than one-third of the UN membership has accepted the authority of the ICJ.

- There is delay before cases are heard by the ICJ.

- The ICJ has difficulty in laying down general principles, in marked contrast to the EU Court of Justice, which has managed to build up an important jurisprudence in the area of environmental law.

The absence of much case law leaves the way for international lawyers to write opinions on international environmental law and their opinions can have considerable influence on the development of the law. The ICJ may be asked to give advisory opinions by the various United Nations agencies.[10] There is considerable scope for developing the ICJ and extending its influence. In 1993 an Environmental Chamber of the ICJ was established but to date there has not been a single environmental case. There are, however, examples where in trade disputes the ICJ has given consideration to the environment. In the Nuclear Test II case *New Zealand* v *France* [1995] ICJ Rep 288, the ICJ decided that states had responsibilities not to cause environmental damage beyond its national or jurisdictional boundaries. Thus, there is a general obligation to act with self-restraint and respect the environment of other states. In fact, there is only one specific case that has been referred to the ICJ on the basis of an environmental issue and that is in the Danube Dam case. It is worthwhile considering two cases that illustrate both the effectiveness and ineffectiveness of the ICJ.

1. The Danube Dam case *Hungary* v *Slovakia* (1998) J7 ILM 162 The question addressed by the ICJ was on the impact of the commonly agreed project, to build a dam to allow economic development between Hungary and the then, Czechoslovakia (1977). Was the impact sufficient to harm Hungary? Hungary was a co-signatory of a treaty to aid economic development and argued that the dam was not in the interests of economic development. The ICJ acted as an agreed arbiter and held that the Czech action in planning the dam was disproportionate. The Danube waterway should be protected and the environmental consequences of the dam considered.

2. The Fisheries Jurisdiction case *Spain* v *Canada* (1998) ICJ 432 Canada used force to stop a Spanish trawler, outside the Canadian exclusive 200-mile zone used to denote economic development. Canada amended its law to allow the power to stop and board fishing vessels. This was of dubious legality, but Canada refused to let the ICJ hear the case and consequently the ICJ did not have jurisdiction.

The international community has created a number of international courts and tribunals in addition to the ICJ. The European Court of Human Rights is notable because it permits individual petition as well as state disputes. This provides access to the ECHRs on the basis of arguing environmental rights. The adjudication of disputes between states may fall under the jurisdiction of the Appellate Body of the World Trade Organisation (see below) and also the International Tribunal for the Law of the Sea. It should be emphasised that in using such

---

[10] One example is the *Legality of the Threat or Use of Nuclear Weapons* 35 ILM 809, 1343 in 1996.

courts the main issue is not between individuals but rather the resolution of disputes between states. There are substantial issues in this context about how the environment should be protected when the main focus of these disputes is trade. The specialist nature of environmental matters today also raises questions over whether this is the best approach to tackle problems encompassing trade and environment. The Law of the Sea Tribunal is highly regarded for its expertise and competence in that field and there is a clear question as to why the environment should not be similarly protected. The Sellafield dispute between Ireland and the UK is one example where an environment tribunal would prove invaluable. A nuclear waste reprocessing facility had been built by the UK on the Irish Sea with waste water from the plant discharged into the sea. Ireland complained of radioactive contamination of the sea environment and their shores. In this dispute, which is still ongoing, Ireland:

1. took a case under the UN Law of the Sea Convention, as no proper environmental assessment was undertaken of the nuclear plant;

2. took action under the treaty OSPAR to make information about the environment surrounding the plant more widely known;

3. took action under the EC and Euratom Treaties Case 459/03 *Commission* v *Ireland*. The Grand Chamber decided that Ireland by taking such a case had done so without recognising the fact that the EU was a part to the convention.

All the above have limited effect because of the issues raised by competence and compliance.

Soft law as a source of international law

The term 'soft law' refers to non-binding principles of international law that are non-enforceable even between the parties. The use of soft law provides a pliable set of guidance that helps in discussions about the protection of the environment and in shaping policy. There are a number of useful examples that illustrate the flexibility and range of soft law. The first is the use of declarations, which set out policy and its significance. The most influential of these have already been mentioned, namely the 1972 Stockholm Declaration on Sustainable Development and in 1992 Rio Declaration on Environment and Development. Today declarations play a fundamental role in the development of environmental protection, as they allow a scoping exercise for policy-makers determining the content, direction and future of environmental law. There are many other examples that underline the significance of declarations. The Five Declarations of the North Sea Conference substantially influenced the EU's policy on the dumping of industrial waste and sewage at sea.

Soft law may also appear in the form of principles that set out aspirational ideals which over time may become attainable. Principles are not binding on states but have considerable influence over setting future agenda. Article 3 of the 1992 Framework Convention on Climate Change gave rise to a set of guidelines that set out principles for future generations on climate. These have become a foundation stone for identifying and setting targets to limit greenhouse gas emissions. Principles also provide recommendations for best practice found in some treaties or in previously enunciated principles.

International law also sets different forms of standards to protect the environment. These have become increasingly important. Standards can take the form of a binding and enforceable set of rules, such as standards for drinking water. They fall into a number of different broad categories, including product standards, emission standards and process standards. Invariably standards are based on the best available techniques and also come about through good practice in licensing arrangements, information systems and the like.

The international community is engaged in agreeing standards, and scientific input from organisations such as the World Health Organization are often highly influential. In the European Union the use of standards is seen as a way of changing and adjusting patterns of behaviour. Standards may also take the form of non-binding regulations that set norms to judge quality and achievements against and drive improvements.

Environmental law benefits greatly from the use of a variety of approaches with both proactive and reactive techniques needed. International law based around agreements and trade arrangements are often more important than the term soft law may imply. The technical complexity and details of international law often requires simplification into easily adopted and facilitative codes of practice and guides to interpretation. While these may suffer from the weaknesses of being non-binding they are likely to be more readily adopted into the working practices and culture of an organisation, and in this way construct a pathway for where enforceable rules may apply in the future. Undeniably, soft international environmental law may be so vague that it is unusable and so aspirational that it becomes virtually unenforceable. Soft law, however, can act as a mapping exercise that sets the range and remit of international environmental law for the future where treaty agreements may embed the aspirations into a binding form. Inevitably, even binding arrangements may never be enforced because of the paucity of legal cases and in some cases the relative weakness of the ICJ in addressing even major environmental issues.

International trade and the environment

The operation of agreements in international law to regulate and facilitate world trade has given rise to a number of organisations and procedures for trade adjudication. The agreements are between states and the main sanction to ensure compliance is the control of imports through restrictions or bans. Since 1933 and the London Convention that controlled and regulated imports, exports and the traffic in certain species, there have been many attempts to further limit trade on environmental grounds. These attempts usually take the form of a permit system which is designed to protect the interest of the different parties and allow for trade and the market to develop. There are also transit agreements and licences. Trade agreements represent an important opportunity for environmental matters to be raised but in the barter between states the environment may be used as another way to gain an advantage. Thus advanced economies can use environmental protection as a mechanism to set standards for or limit imports from rival markets and emerging economies. There are two methods that national governments can adopt to limit free trade between nations based on environment. The first is through quality controls that are included in product standards, which regulate the particular commodity to be exported. The second procedure is to impose restrictions on the production method for a commodity such as process and production controls and standards. There are two bodies engaged in the regulation of trade. The first is the World Trade Organization (WTO), and particularly its Committee on Trade and the Environment, which can provide trade and environmental measures in the context of sustainable development. The European Union also provides standards for the production, distribution and export of goods and service as part of EU law. Principles such as sustainable development and the precautionary principle are also commonly used.

The WTO has considerable potential to influence trade arrangements and give priority to environmental protection. It has 144 individual member states and the EU is also a member. WTO plays an important role along with the World Bank and the International Monetary Fund (IMF) in providing an international framework for development and trade. WTO uses an assortment of legal instruments and devices to achieve its aims, which include the optimal use of the world's resources to comply with objectives of sustainable development. The WTO also provides a framework for the implementation of different levels of trade agreement. It implements WTO agreements and multilateral trade agreements and finally provides a forum for negotiation and cooperation with the World Bank and the IMF. The WTO's role is complex and highly difficult since there are strong economic arguments between states that frustrate the protection of the environment. One step forward has been the role played by the Appellate Body of the WTO, where matters of dispute over sustainable development and global free trade may be settled. This is a highly controversial area and striking a balance that protects the environment is not easy. Essentially the arrangements within the WTO tend to give trade a higher priority than the environment; many critics compare this to the arrangements within the EU where trade and environment are formed into a unity through the jurisdiction of the ECJ. The ECJ is tailored to prioritising the environment through principles that it assimilates into the everyday law of the EU. There are some limited examples where the Appellate Body of the WTO has followed the example of the EU ECJ. This has given some expectation that in the future, sustainable development principles will be used to control trade practices that are against the interests of the environment. There is also some progress in protecting the environment through other bodies.

The 1987 Montreal Protocol provides that trade measures may be used to protect the global commons. Trade sanctions can be applied to implement environmental protection. Such use of sanctions has given rise to the potential for conflict between the general rules of international environmental law and free trade agreements. Such conflicts are not easy to reconcile or settle. The 2000 Bio-Safety Protocol on genetically modified organisms (GMO) provides either that conditions can be set or that a complete ban can be imposed on individuals to prevent/control imports. The decision is based on a risk assessment. However, even if the scientific evidence is not conclusive but there is potential for adverse effects on human health caused by a GMO, action may be taken. This gives rise to some difficulties of consistency and also conflict resolution particularly in the context of WTO and associated General Agreement on Tariffs and Trade (GATT) arrangements to encourage trade between states.

In December 1993 the Uruguay round of GATT was adopted by agreement forming the Final Act. This comprises a series of agreements and procedures that includes dispute settlements. The following year GATT and the WTO attempted to take the protection of the environment forward by embedding the objective of sustainable development to protect and preserve the environment in 'a manner consistent with the respective needs and concerns at different levels of economic development' in their arrangements. Even so GATT is primarily involved in setting arrangements for the trade of certain goods under the auspices of the WTO. Some international treaties might, in marked contrast, attempt to limit trade in some way to protect the environment. For example, the Montreal Protocol of 1987 provides that states should prohibit the import of certain controlled substances, such as refrigerators, which might be in conflict with the rules for the market under GATT.

It is useful to consider some disputes between states over international trade that have involved GATT and have an environmental dimension. These are illustrated by the following two cases.

1. The Tuna–Dolphin Dispute (1992) 30 ILM 1598 Import restrictions on tuna were imposed by the USA because of concerns about the impact of tuna fishing on dolphin populations in Mexico and other tuna fishing grounds. Mexico took a case to GATT over the import restrictions. The Mexican case was upheld because the GATT panel accepted that GATT's provisions on equal and fair treatment had been violated. The question addressed was whether the US action amounted to a quantitative restriction. Article XX holds various exceptions that could apply, if the restriction:

● was necessary to protect human, animal, and plant life or health;

● relates to the conservation of exhaustible natural resources, if such measures are made effective in conjunction with restrictions on domestic production or consumption.

It was held that the US action was unlawful since the above exceptions only applied to activities within the national jurisdiction of the country and not to action in international waters. Thus the primary objective of GATT was to reduce restrictions on trade and such barriers.

Following the Mexico dispute, the EC took action against the USA in a similar dispute (Tuna–Dolphin II (1994) 33 ILM 839). The GATT panel again found against the USA, but modified its view that there were circumstances where it might be possible to influence environmental protection beyond a national jurisdiction. It is interesting to note that in 1992 the USA and Mexico agreed that the use of dolphin-unfriendly nets should be phased out, eight other countries, who accounted for nearly 99 per cent of the tuna catch in the disputed area, agreed to this international accord.

2. Shrimp/Turtle Case (1999) 38 ILM 121 The case brought forward the issue of the US imposing an obligation on any state exporting into the USA to show that its shrimp harvesting methods were not putting at risk the sea turtle population and to set standards for conservation and protection. Were such restrictions compatible with the GATT provision of 'exhaustible natural resources'? It had already been agreed that the term was sufficiently flexible to apply to the endangered species in the world and were not confined to the use of finite resources such as minerals etc.

The GATT panel held that the US measures were substantially acceptable but that they were too arbitrary and that there was unjustified discrimination between two countries with much the same conditions, in this case the USA and Malaysia. It is important to consider what constituted unjustified discrimination? This is settled by considering what is in the interests of the nation state but in the context of a shared natural inheritance between states. The latter is an attempt to address the environment.

Environmental information

Principle 2 of the 1972 Stockholm Declaration set the foundation for the availability of environmental information by calling for free flow of information on scientific data and experience. Mitigating this is, of course, the reality of the confidentiality of information with a commercial purpose. The Stockholm conference also provided the basis for education initiatives (such as the Gore film) on global warming. Major accidents of the recent past have eloquently illustrated the need for ready availability of environmental information. In the late 1980s an explosion and fire at the Chernobyl nuclear power plant in the Ukraine released large amounts of radioactive materials that contaminated vast swathes of Europe. Major chemical accidents that have resulted in the release of highly toxic and long-lived chemicals include the release of a gaseous cyanide compound from a subsidiary of an American chemical company at Bhopal, India (1984) which caused the deaths of 2,500 people and countless other people being disabled. In Basle, Switzerland (1986) another major chemical accident resulted in the Rhine being heavily polluted. The value of sharing the experience and the availability of environmental information is clear from all these cases.

Following the Stockholm Declaration a number of treaties addressed the issue of availability of environmental information. These include the 1986 IAEA Notification Convention; 1989 Basel Convention; and 1992 Industrial Accidents Convention. The Rio Declaration sets out a detailed agenda in this regard. There is also the UNEP Legal Experts Group that contributes to the exchange of environmental information. The 1997 Kyoto Protocol establishes an important exchange of information, linked to the establishment of the International Panel on Climate Change. In Europe a Directive on Environmental Information was adopted in 1991 and the 1998 Aarhus Convention has established a Europe-wide regime for environmental information. This convention set out to clarify and define aspects of EU rules on the availability of environmental information across Europe.

Exchange of environmental information in operation

The framework for ensuring that environmental information is available and successfully exchanged at international level consists of the following stages.

1. **Information exchange** There is a general obligation on one state to inform another – for example, Principle 9 of the Rio Declaration. Examples that fall under this obligation include scientific cooperation and also coordination of national and international policies. The Tuna fisheries case (see above) is illustrative of this. The 1992 Climate Change Convention also draws on scientific cooperation and policy coordination as fundamental in international responses to climate change.

2. **Reporting and providing information** There is an obligation to provide reports and information on a regular or periodic basis and for this information to be used by another state to gather data on the environment. Organisations and institutions from earliest times of international law have, in fact, been under such an obligation. Examples of reporting requirements are found under the Climate Change Convention and Kyoto Protocol, and also in the event of emergencies such as Nuclear Installations etc. Also there are obligations on states to inform another of any transboundary harm.

3. **Auditing and accounting** Eco-auditing is an important and highly significant technique. Environmental accounting is intended to establish the environmental cost of activities as an aid to achieving environmentally neutral impacts. It provides companies with a mechanism for establishing their environmental footprint and setting their costs in the context of minimising impacts. The Intergovernmental Working Group of Experts on International Standards of Accounting and Reporting (ISAR) is involved in establishing best practice in this

area. It is, however, always difficult to impose this type of procedure on commercial organisations and at present adoption of environmental accounting is voluntary.

The EU's eco-management and audit scheme (EMAS) sets more demanding requirements than the international standards. It has the potential to set standards and allows, in some cases requires, audits to be carried out. Again, this scheme is voluntary.

Future directions

Resources, financing, technology and intellectual property

Sands argues that defining financial mechanisms to support environmental protection is likely to be the most effective means of addressing global environmental matters.[11] In 1990 amendments to the 1987 Montreal Protocol introduced a financial mechanism to address the global problem of atmospheric ozone depletion. It has been exceptionally successful. The use of financial mechanisms in this way is likely to lie at the heart of the future of international environmental law. Property rights and environmental protection needs to be reconsidered and analysed in an international context as global economies come to terms with recession.

There are some real achievements as follows: The 1992 Climate Change and Biodiversity Conventions and amendments in 1994 on drought and desertification, climate change in 1997 and biosafety in 2000 as well as persistent organic pollutants in 2001. There are also associated achievements to do with the role of multilateral development banks. There are examples such as the WTO Agreement on Trade and Related Aspects of Intellectual Property Rights (TRIPS), the European Patent Convention 1973, and the International Treaty on Plant Genetic Resources for Food and Agriculture 2004 are all important.

Financial resources

Financial resource issues undoubtedly have significant implications for the capabilities of nations to address environmental protection. A number of key questions in the area of financial resources must be addressed. First, to what extent are loans and agreements granted bilaterally by states subject to compliance in international law? Second, what are the institutions and bodies that are empowered to establish suitable mechanisms for the oversight of financial instruments? Chapter 33 of Agenda 21, entitled Financial Resources and Mechanisms, sets the scene for the use of financial resources. This has been estimated to cost over US $600 billion annually. Providing debt relief; the employment of adequate resources to tackle foreign investment; and private funding with an environmental focus is an important element in the future of international environmental protection.

There are a number of examples where these elements come together.

The Organisation of Economic Cooperation and Development (OECD) There has been a political commitment by OECD members to meet a UN target of 0.7 per cent of GNP for overseas development assistance. A proportion is set to be targeted specifically on the assistance for environmental matters. The OECD also provides a model contract and compliance over environmental issues. It is as yet unclear to what extent this is going to be successful.

---

[11] P. Sands, *Principles of International Law* second edition, Cambridge: Cambridge University Press, 2003.

Multilateral development banks The World Bank's terms of conditions for contracts, employment of consultants and compliance systems is a further example of an international organisation drawing together financial and environmental foci. The International Development Association (IDA) and the International Finance Corporation (IFC) have also moved forward in this way.

Agenda 21 (see above) sets limits on regional and sub-regional banks in the way they deal with environmental matters, by providing that contract should consider their environmental implications. Most banks have now developed a departmental structure for examining and responding to environmental issues as part of their role.

Environmental funds Environmental funds also fall within the Multilateral Funds Protocol. There are many examples of these in operation that encompass elements related to the environment; these include the UNEP Environmental Fund, the World Heritage Fund, the Wetlands Fund and the Montreal Protocol Multilateral Fund.

The Global Environment Facility (GEF) This Facility was established in 1990 as part of a three-year experiment to advance the use of grants for investment that incorporated global environment matters. It continues today and provides grants that support projects covering biodiversity, climate change, international waters, land degradation, the ozone layer and also organic pollutants. The GEF is an independent organisation that assists developing countries as part of an overall project to benefit the environment by adopting sustainable development strategies.

Conclusions

International environmental law is at the apex of global responses to environmental protection. At present it provides impressive coverage of many of the major areas where environmental protection is most acutely needed. The examples are numerous: perhaps the most momentous for our future is found in attempts to draw together an international response to global warming and climate change. In managing scientific advances with potentially substantial economic and environmental consequences, for example in the area of biotechnology, then international law on world trade is central. Even given impressive successes such as control of ozone depletion, there are a large number of shortcomings in international environmental law.

- The context, complexity and technical nature of international environmental law gives rise to ambiguity and uncertainty.
- International environmental law operates too often with a fundamental lack of clear objectives or priorities.
- There is an untidy relationship between the theory and practice of international environmental law that can give rise to scepticism and opposition.
- Enforcement of agreements is limited owing to limitations in the role of the ICJ and in building a consensus among trading nations over environmental rules that have an impact on the balance of trade.
- There are also considerable political constraints on making international environmental law effective.

International environmental law also suffers from the shortcomings of a system that is focused primarily on relations between states rather than the role of individuals or organisations. One of the most challenging problems facing the environment is the growth of new economies such as China and India. Their desire for market share, economic growth and success confronts the environment with contradictory claims, one based on growth and resource exploitation and the other based on conservation and protection. It is likely that global pressure for environmental protection may well be resisted and delayed as the new economies grow and develop. There undoubtedly remain a number of unresolved questions for international environmental law including:

1. How to implement environmental law policies;

2. How to make environmental law fit the context of social and economic needs;

3. What are the most effective techniques for environmental law and what role should law perform?

4. What is the future role for science in identifying and addressing environmental problems?

There is considerable scope for international environmental law to adopt a rights-based approach to provide constitutional and fundamental protection of environmental rights. There are two strands to the rights-based approach. The first is based on substantive rights that are enforceable. Rights to sustainable development, for example, might provide litigation strategies but this may not be sufficient to provide adequate protection or become robust enough to ensure that good environmental policy-making is prioritised. The second strand consists of procedural rights that include individual rights to environmental information and participation in the decision-making systems. There is considerable scope for such procedures to operate at different levels – international, the European Union and national through domestic courts and decision-makers. The 1998 UN Aarhus Convention on Access to Information, Public Participation in Decision-making and Access to Justice in Environmental Matters is an example in this direction. We have yet to see if this direction for environmental rights will bear fruit. At the same time there is increasing economic pressure as oil prices escalate and in an economic recession it may be necessary for international environmental law to provide a stronger input into the market economy of the world.

Further reading

There is a wide range of international environmental law texts. The following is a selection of the main works.

P. Birnie and A. Boyle, *International Law and the Environment* 2nd edn, Oxford: Oxford University Press, 2002.

A. Bodansky, 'The United Nations Framework Convention on Climate Change: a commentary' (1993) 18 *Yale Journal of International Law* 451–558.

E.D. Brown, 'The conventional law of the environment' (1973) 13 *Natural Resources Journal* 203.

J. Coleman, 'Environmental barriers to trade and EC law' (1993) 2(11) EELR 295.

J. **DiMento**, *The Global Environment and International Law* University of Texas Press, 2003.

R. **French**, 'The changing nature of environmental protection: recent developments regarding trade and the environment in the European Union and the World Trade Organization' (2000) XLVII *Netherlands International Law Review* 1.

A.P.J. Mol (ed.), *Globalisation and Environmental Reform: The Ecological Modernisation of the Global Economy* MIT Press, 2003.

V.P. Handa and G.W. Pring, *International Environmental Law and Policy for the 21st Century* Transnational Publishers, 2003.

J. **and S. McEldowney**, *Environmental Law and Regulation* Blackstone Law Series Oxford: Oxford University Press, 2001.

J. **and S. McEldowney**, *Contemporary Issues in Environmental Law* London: Edward Elgar, 2007.

M. **Redclift and G. Woodgate** (eds), *The International Handbook of Environmental Sociology* Edward Elgar, 1997.

B. **Richardson and S. Wood** (eds), *Environmental Law for Sustainability* London: Hart Publishing, 2006.

P. **Sands** (ed.), *Greening International Law* London: 1993.

P. **Sands**, *Principles of International Law* 2nd edition Cambridge: Cambridge University Press, 2003.

Reports

OECD, *Report of the OECD Workshop on Environmental Hazard/Risk Assessment.* Environment Monograph No. 105. (OECD, 1995).

OECD, *OECD Guidelines for the Testing of Chemicals, Plus the 9th Addendum.* (OECD, 1998).

The Stern Report HM Treasury, 2006.

UK Sustainable Development: The United Kingdom Strategy (HMSO, 1994).

UNDP, *Human Development Report 1992* (Oxford University Press, 1992).

United Nations Economic Commission for Europe (UNECE), *Policies for Integrated Water Management* E/ECE/1084 (1985).

United Nations, *Agenda 21: The United Nation's Programme of Action from Rio* (United Nations, 1992).

WHO *Guidelines for Drinking-water Quality.* Vol. 2 pp. 290–2. (World Health Organisation, 1984).

World Bank, World Development Report 2003: *Sustainable Development in a Dynamic World* Washington, 2003.

Visit **http://www.mylawchamber.co.uk/mceldowney** to access key issue checklists and practice exam questions to test yourself on this chapter.

5 European environmental law

Introduction

The European Union has a dominant influence on the development of the United Kingdom's environmental law.[1] The significance of the EU is not only in terms of policy-making but also in creation of a whole range of flexible and often innovative approaches to environmental law. The EU Commission has estimated that 80 per cent of national environmental legislation stems from the European Union's environment policy.[2] The EU Reform Treaty (the Treaty of Lisbon)[3] which was agreed in 2008 and ratified by all member states in 2009, reinforces the significance of the environment in the European agenda and the continued influence of EU policy-making on environmental law. A new Article 3 of the Treaty of European Union emphasises the protection of the environment as a key part of sustainable development set in the context of balanced economic growth and price stability intended to ensure full employment and social progress. We will consider the potential impact of the Treaty of Lisbon in this chapter. The Treaty of Lisbon provides an important insight into the likely future for environmental policy-making within the EU. EU environmental law has been proactive and inventive. It brings a commitment to environmental protection that is not always found in individual member states and there is an exciting possibility that the influence of the EU may stretch beyond its borders to sway international environmental policy. Studying EU environmental law is, then, a key element in understanding our current successes and failures in environmental protection and provides an indication of the future direction for environmental law.

The expansion of EU law into the environment area has helped catalyse the development and adoption of a range of legal, economic and social instruments into environmental law. This achievement is all the more remarkable when it is remembered that in 1957 the Treaty of Rome made no direct reference to the environment or how it fitted into the development of a market economy and free market for all the member states. Today the EU is composed

---

[1] Andrea Ross and Hazel Nash, 'European Union environmental law – who legislates for whom in a devolved Great Britain' (2009) *Public Law* 564.

[2] COM(2007) 225 *Mid-term review of the Sixth Community Environmental Action Programme* EU Commission, Brussels.

[3] The Lisbon Treaty has been brought into law by all member states at the beginning of December 2009.

of 27 member states and this expansion has placed environmental issues at the top of the EU's agenda. Concern about global warming and its impact on the environment and economies has led the EU into considering how international relations should encompass environmental concerns. In the future, EU policy-making is set to address how to engage trade and trade relations within the context of a sustainable environmental policy. The European Union is today one of the most important trading and political blocs in the world and, as a consequence, it is one of the most important international actors in the world economy. The EU is not only growing in membership and territorial coverage but also expanding through a complex network of regional agreements that are not solely restricted to trade, but include detailed rules on investment, environment, competition, telecommunications, services and labour. This new legal network is more comprehensive than that of the WTO and in many respects has already achieved what the major oil exporting OECD countries failed to achieve with its negotiations on the Multilateral Agreement on Investments. It is estimated that the addition of the new member states will add up to one per cent extra growth for each member state during the first 10 years of membership. The result will provide weaker economies with considerable economic potential. The addition of the new member states will add 75 million consumers and provide greater opportunities for manufacturers and exporters in an increasingly global market. The total population of the European Union now stands at more than 450 million. Over the next 15 years the European Union is likely to expand further with up to five new members, including Turkey. The implications of this expansion on the world role of the EU, member state economies and social development should not be underestimated.

This chapter will provide the basis for understanding EU environmental law. It includes an overview of the main components of EU environmental law and will illustrate how the environment is seen as integral to economic development within the EU. The specific nature of the EU, its institutions and how environmental policy is developed in the EU will also be examined.

EU law, policy and the environment

There are two fundamental questions about environmental protection within the EU. First, how has EU law addressed environmental problems and second, how adequate is the law in safeguarding the environment? The EU has sought to lay general standards on environmental matters that are directly enforceable by the member states, and this has substantially advanced the protection of the environment and human health. The European Court of Justice has also been instrumental in advancing environmental protection through the interpretation and implementation of EU environmental law and the various aims and objectives set by the EU to engage with member states. There are, however, many instances where the EU directives are not directly enforceable. This leaves member states, including the United Kingdom, considerable flexibility in the interpretation and implementation of environmental law. The EU has also been influential in guiding and encouraging member states towards favouring the environment in policy-making. There are many instances, for example, where the United Kingdom has followed EU policy direction through incorporation into the national legal system, which has included changes in United Kingdom statute law. It is accepted that the EU, as a treaty-making body, can enter into international agreements relating to the environment. This holds the possibility of the EU not only influencing the behaviour of individual member states but also contributing to international environmental policy development.

The EU is a good example of how an international organisation is capable of building environmental strategy incrementally. We have already remarked that the Treaty of Rome, which established the European Community in 1957, had no specific provision for the environment. Moreover, subsequent amending treaties were slow to accept the significance of the environment. The emphasis on harmonisation and market integration was the main focus of the treaties for some time. The 1972 Stockholm Conference asserted the relevance of international institutions for the environment, and its sustainable development strategy received acceptance in the European Community. This is an excellent example of international environmental law setting standards and developing strategies of significance for the environment that are adopted at regional and national level (see Chapter 4 for a discussion of such influences). The absence of express treaty provision for the protection of the environment, however, left a legal lacuna but one that was readily filled through policy-making – the creation of Environmental Action Programmes. The first Action Programme began in 1972 and it, together with subsequent action programmes, provided the basis for the development of environmental legislation. There had already been a 1970 directive on car pollution and air, and this was followed, under the action programmes, in 1984 by a directive on industrial plant pollution (84/360/EEC). In a 1985 ruling the European Court of Justice accepted that the environment was an essential element in the interpretation of the free movement of goods, even though there was no legally enforceable regime for its protection at that time.[4]

The Single European Act 1987 gave rise to the single market and by amending the original Treaty of Rome specific law-making powers were finally granted in the general field of environmental protection. There was a chapter in the 1987 Act that outlined environmental objectives for policy-making. The treaty, however, was vague in respect of the environment and lacked legal clarity. The creation of the European Union came under the Treaty on European Union 1992, but the opportunity to settle with clarity the legal role of the EU in environmental policy-making was missed in this treaty. In 1997 the Treaty of Amsterdam took the important step of clarifying the use of a co-decision procedure for environmental matters. This was highly significant since it put the environment on a par with trade and other areas of European Competence and moved the environment centre stage in the promotion of sustainable development strategies. Article 3(1) of the EC Treaty admits the need for 'a policy in the sphere of the environment' and this environmental policy is generally set out in Articles 174–176. It allows binding measures on member states or private persons to be taken in environmental matters. The articles, however, are not sufficiently specific to give the environment precedence and there is no legal priority given to the environment over other market considerations. It is clear that the environment has to compete with the free movement of goods and other assorted parts of the market. Articles 174–6 do provide for Community policy to pursue objectives that are intended to preserve, protect and improve the quality of the environment; protect human health; provide for a prudent use of natural resources; and promote measures at international levels for regional and worldwide measures to tackle environmental problems. There are accompanying principles found in Article 174(2) that

---

[4] See Case 240/83 *Procureur de la République v Association de défence des brûleurs d'huiles usagées* (ADBHU) [1985] ECR 531.

provide a general acceptance of the 'polluter pays' principle (see Chapter 7). This principle acts as a general guidance to legislative decision-making functions. There are many policy areas driven by the EU in addition to the 'polluter pays' principle, such as environmental rights, and the precautionary principles but these have not found express articulation in the main treaties.

It is clear that in future there will be greater priority given to protection of the environment within the EU. This will require a delicate balance to be struck between environmental protection, the costs of materials and production, employment, and the various goods and services of the market. There are specific restrictions on limiting free movement of goods between member states, but under Article 30 it is possible for member states to derogate if necessary for the protection of health and the life of humans, animals or plants. What precisely may fit into this category is unclear. There is some case law of the European Court of Justice that allows the argument of environmental protection to be used as part of a generous interpretation of national import and export controls, provided it is proportionate and justified.[5] The EU is expected to protect and improve the quality of the environment in a way that is compatible with 'the raising of the standard of living and quality of life, and economic and social cohesion and solidarity among Member States' (Article 2 of the EC Treaty). It remains to be seen whether or not this is achievable, but the environment is likely to remain one of the most contested areas of policy-making.

The Treaty of Lisbon

The EU has currently entered a period of significant change, including the adoption of the Treaty of Lisbon[6] (the Treaty on the functioning of the European Union, TFEU) signed in 2007 ratified by each of the 27 member states by the end of 2009. There were doubts about the ratification of the treaty, following its rejection by Ireland in a referendum. It is important to recognise the potential of the Lisbon Treaty for the environment. The treaty confirms the existing status quo, namely that the environment is an area of shared competence between the EU and the various member states.[7] There are, however, a number of welcome clarifications and additions to existing arrangements. In terms of the EU's general objectives, Article 3 of the TEU covers sustainable development and its application to the aims of promoting 'solidarity' between generations. This is likely to have far-reaching consequences since it goes beyond the definition of sustainable development solely in economic matters.[8]

More significantly the treaty recognises the strategic significance of climate change and places mitigation and adaptation as a fundamental part of EU policy. Measures to tackle climate change at international level are also promoted under Article 191(1). An important innovation is the addition of an Article on energy that encompasses energy efficiency and

---

[5] Case 302/86 *Commission v Denmark* [1988] ECR. 460 (the Danish Bottles case). Case 120/78 *Rewe-Zentral AG v Bundesmonopolverwaltung für Branntwein* [1979] ECR 649 (known as the Cassis de Dijon case).

[6] See Treaty of Lisbon Cm 7294 December 2007 and the European Union (Amendment) Act 2008 which sets out the necessary amendments of the European Communities Act 1972, which is the legal basis for the United Kingdom's membership of the EU.

[7] Article 4(2)(e) of TFEU.

[8] The Treaty of Lisbon also integrates fisheries into Article 3(1) on agriculture within the treaty. The protection of marine diversity is likely to be controversial.

the development of new forms of energy. This is a welcome addition since it identifies the importance of modifying our energy usage to ameliorate climate change and for the future of the environment. There is a related solidarity arrangement on civil protection that recognise the need for joint protection and cooperation in the event of human-made or natural disasters. This extends to a cooperation arrangement in the event of a terrorist attack.

The Lisbon Treaty also adopts procedural changes to decision-making that apply to a variety of nationally sensitive issues such as land use, water resources and town and country planning. The changes omit areas such as waste management and the choice of energy; in these cases individual member states are able to adopt best practice. Under the past arrangements nationally sensitive areas are subject to unanimity after consultation with the EU Parliament (Article 175(2) TEC), even though in general the Council adopts most environmental legislation by qualified majority voting (QMV). The new arrangements for nationally sensitive areas under the Treaty of Lisbon permit the Council, acting unanimously, to switch all or some of the relevant measures to fall under ordinary legislation rather than qualified majority voting. This would expand the role of the EU Parliament. It should be remembered, however, that adoption of this procedure is subject to the Council's unanimous decision. There is also a link in this decision-making to national parliaments. The European Union (Amendment) Act 2008 requires that a UK Minister must obtain parliamentary approval in favour of agreeing to the EU Council's decision to apply ordinary legislative procedures in the case of nationally sensitive legislation.

There is considerable speculation about the effects and the future of the Lisbon Treaty and it is worthwhile here to briefly assess its possible significance for the environment. The House of Lords European Union Committee[9] concluded that the introduction of a 'specific reference to climate change is of strategic rather than legal significance'. The committee points out, however, that the EU has taken an important step in being the first to adopt into a treaty a politically sensitive area and recognise its long-term significance. It should also be recognised that energy issues are likely to confront the future of environmental law much more than in the past. As an area of 'shared competence' the internal market in energy is likely to be fundamental to the adoption of new energy-efficiency measures and the use of different forms of renewable energy. There, of course, remains the right of member states to choose the energy sources, but once an environmental priority is adopted the choices of member states are likely to become more restricted. Energy conservation and renewable energy use will probably form one of the most challenging and controversial areas of environmental law in the future.

EU Action Programmes and policy-making

The EU has a number of mechanisms for the creation and implementation of environmental policy and law. The absence of express legal authority for measures to protect the environment left a gap that was readily filled by initiatives known as Action Programmes. Lasting up to five years normally, the action programmes helped keep the environment to the fore of the Community. It also embedded environmental matters into the policy-making process.

[9] House of Lords European Union Committee 10th Report: The Treaty of Lisbon; an impact assessment HL Paper 62-I (13th March 2008) paras 10.11–10.13.

Initially, many regarded action programmes as a mechanism for building consensus but in 1993 it was accepted that the action programmes were legally binding. The First Environmental Action Programme was in 1973 when the UK joined the European Community. Its aim was to advance the idea of the 'polluter pays' principle, while encouraging the principle that urgent pollution problems should be remedied. Although the policy was a reactive one, contained within it were the ideas of prevention and anticipatory controls. This was an important beginning for the view that environmental harm was preventable. The following three programmes were intended to strengthen the protection of health and the management of natural resources. The strength of the programmes was the philosophy that prioritising the environment as part of economic and social policy did not have to conflict with trade and market power. Proactive environmental policy could be sensitively handled and embedded in economic growth. This gave rise to strategies such as eco-labelling and the operation of better access to information. The need to integrate environmental policy-making with trade was a legal necessity for a common market based on fair competition but it was also a useful strategy to build the environment outwards as part of a general growth in the European Community. Thus the Fourth Action Programme in 1987 was linked to the economy and jobs. The Fifth Action Programme in 1992 was path-breaking and far-reaching. *Towards Sustainability* (1992) introduced the concept of sustainable development, and argued for a combination of preventative and precautionary strategies as part of a fundamental responsibility for both public and private bodies. The areas addressed in this action programme included climate change, air quality and noise as well as biodiversity and the management of resources. Significantly for environmental protection, policy was not to be shaped by individual sectors, i.e. land, air and water, but rather across the sectors. Thus transport, agriculture, energy and tourism were to be examined across sectors, providing integration in policy-making and recognising the inevitable cross-sectoral environmental effects of different economic activities. Thus environmental integration, as it became known, developed as part of the Amsterdam Treaty (Article 6) but also as part of the shared responsibility that applied across the public and private sectors based in an action programme. There are many examples of this approach in various directives, for example the WEE Directive 2002/96/EC on Waste Electronic and Electrical Equipment. The Fifth Action Programme also saw sustainable development as an economic concept begin to be translated into practical measures that included civil liability. The breakthrough in conceptual thinking that came about with the Fifth Action Programme arose from a combination of social, political and economic circumstances. Acceptance that regulating the environment involves a variety of stakeholders including NGOs and regulatory agencies was coupled with agreement that the environment is best tackled by utilising a diverse range of economic, financial and legal instruments. Today, there is a growing realisation that legal instruments won't work unless tied to fiscal and other financial incentives.

The Sixth Action Programme began in 2002 is set to run until 2012. It builds on past policy success in the area of sustainable development, which it develops further along with the following four key priorities:

- climate change;
- nature and biodiversity;
- health and the quality of life; and
- natural resources and waste.

Each priority is seen as settling environmental policy for the immediate future. The programme includes a number of important strategic initiatives that tackle soil protection, marine environment, air pollution, waste recycling, the urban environment and pesticides. Sustainable use and the management of natural resources is also generally applied across the action programme. The EU Commission, in its mid-term review of the environment is clear that scientific knowledge is at the centre of environmental policy-making. The challenges of global warming, chemicals and pesticides in the environment and air pollution, to name but a few environmental pressures, have brought a general acceptance of the need for scientific understanding to support environmental policy-making. There is, however, obedience to the linkages that have been made previously. Thus environmental policies should not detract from and if possible should contribute to competitiveness, economic growth and enhancing jobs so that social well-being is fostered. Examples of where sustainable development may drive forward sustainable economic growth commensurate with the protection of the environment is the operation of wind energy and the development of environmental technologies.[10] The action programme has also supported the use of innovative practices such as carbon taxes, the operation of trading permits and the use of emissions trading scheme as part of the response to controlling greenhouse gas emissions. Taken together, the Sixth Action Programme is an ambitious one and may not ultimately be able to deliver all that is promised. There are a number of reasons for this, not least the absence of political will in the many areas where unanimity was required by the member states, set to change under the Treaty of Lisbon. The programme has set some demanding targets, which include:

- reduction of emissions of greenhouse gases by at least 20 per cent now increased to 30 per cent by 2020;
- the operation of 20 per cent target for renewable energy production and 10 per cent of consumption for biofuels;
- increase energy efficiency and reduce EU energy consumption by 20 per cent compared to projections for 2020.

It remains to be seen whether such ambitious targets are attainable. We have already fallen behind our schedule for reducing greenhouse gas emissions and the biofuel target has been controversial largely because of unforeseen consequences for food production and food prices. Moreover, some biofuel crops may actually not reduce carbon emissions because of the energy costs in their harvest, transport and conversion to liquid fuels.

The EU plans to enhance cooperation at an international level to assist with meeting targets. One strategy currently being adopted is to work with the WTO on liberalising the trade in environmental goods and services, thus supporting environmental protection through commercial opportunity. Other strategies expose the efficiency and impact of regulation to scrutiny and encourage making better regulation as part of environmental policy. Good regulatory practice has become a significant part of policy-making. Policy-makers working with major stakeholders are seen as a key element in the success of policy integration. A significant weakness in EU policy development was the absence of integration between the different policy fields such as agriculture and transport with the environment. This is addressed in the Sixth Action Programme but remains a major challenge for the future.

---

[10] This is estimated by the EU Commission as worth over €227 billion.

Despite the profound optimism in the aspirations of the commission, there are substantial impediments to progress. Integrating environmental policy across sectors is difficult as is the adequate enforcement of EU environmental law. The Sixth Action Programme is in its mid-term but it is unclear if it will meet its ambitious objectives. There are inherent pitfalls in using scientific data to set tangible and realisable targets, which must be carefully managed. Scientific data is couched in terms of uncertainty and probabilities that need interpretation through socially acceptable risk rather than in terms of the science alone. There is, also, a danger that standards become technology-driven, with advances in analytical equipment resulting in the adoption of lower targets simply because our ability to detect a pollutant has improved. Despite these problems there are clear examples, such as the EU Directive on Drinking Water 80/778/EEC or the Directive on Bathing Waters 76/160/EEC, that illustrate how standards once set at a suitable level may become the basis for real improvements.

The progress made since the introduction of the First Action Programme may not necessarily indicate how we will view its ultimate success. Member states are unlikely to find it easy to accept the enforcement of environmental regulation especially when it comes to politically sensitive questions of taxation. It is clear that the EU is crucial for environmental policy-making. This is because the EU has as its main focus the creation of a single internal market for all 27 member states and it is also at the centre of negotiations on international trade and economic policies with market rivals such as USA.[11] Economic and environmental policies are inextricably linked with industry, agriculture, tourism and other economic sectors, a key backdrop for environmental strategy-making. The emphasis on economic growth over the past decades has often been at the expense of the environment. In times of recession or smaller economic growth, hard choices on environmental policy may be more politically acceptable than in the past and may raise opportunities for the environment to be given priority. The EU has also the potential to take a lead in laying down environmental policies in sensitive or difficult areas. Genetically modified organisms (GMOs) are a good example of where the EU has embarked on policy-making that is intended to address the future need for growth and diversity in the competitive field of agriculture, while protecting the environment.

Institutional and other mechanisms for EU environmental law

Environmental protection has formed an important concern of the European Union. It must be remembered that, while there is general competence to legislate on environmental matters, there is also responsibility to ensure that the legislation is enacted in conformity with EU policy. At the same time, however, there is a shared competence to work with member states. Article 174 EC makes clear that member states are expected to adopt environmental provisions where the Community has not legislated or taken action. There is, in fact, wide scope for member states to take tougher measures than under EU legislation where appropriate (Article 176 EC), with the general proviso that they should not conflict with the obligations set out in the various treaties. The idea of subsidiarity acts as a balance to any encroachment by the EU into areas of the member states' competence. This idea of subsidiarity is important under Article 5 of

---

[11] See Damien Geradin, *Trade and the Environment: A Comparative Study of EC and US Law* Cambridge: Cambridge University Press, 2007.

the EC Treaty. It acts as a brake on general EU encroachment on member states' activities but subsidiarity may also act as a check that environmental legislation is only justified if the objectives of the legislation cannot be properly achieved by the member states alone.

Even allowing for subsidiarity it is clear that membership of the EU has a profound influence[12] on how national decision-making takes place. As Paul Craig, a leading EU lawyer, has noted, the first 30 years of the Community decision-making 'was dominated by the Council and Commission'.[13] This has been substantially changed in recent years with the growing significance of the EU Parliament and the operation of co-decision-making powers between the Parliament and the Council. This means that the commission must ensure that the Council and the Parliament receive legislative proposals. It should be noted that the main institutions of the EU, the Commission, the Council of Ministers, the Parliament and the European Court of Justice are integral to the creation of EU environmental law. It is worthwhile briefly considering each institution in the context of the environment.

The commission is a key element in environmental policy-making. Its main responsibilities include implementing and enforcing EU law but it also has an investigative and evaluative role. It is a major stakeholder in environmental matters and has driven forward the environmental agenda so that it is given a high priority in EU policy-making. The commission is the author of six different Environmental Action Programmes and it is fair comment that without the commission's considerable efforts, the environment would not have received the attention it has or the attention it needs. The commission has a staff of nearly 25,000 with an organisational structure that contains the College of Commissions, the Directorate-Generals and the Cabinets. The College of Commissioners has 27 members, one drawn from each of the member states. Each commissioner has a specialist portfolio that is allocated by the President of the Commission. There is a commissioner for the environment, one for agriculture and one for energy. The commissioners are appointed for a term of five years, which runs concurrently with that of the president. Although drawn from the member states, the commission is required to act independently and to operate for the benefit of the EU. Article 211 EC provides that the commission must uphold the treaties, as their guardian, and participate in shaping the measures taken by the Council and the European Parliament. Each commissioner acts through a Directorate-General, similar in function and activity to a government department. There is a small cabinet, of about six, members to oversee the work of a Directorate-General. In the case of the Directorate-General for the Environment there is an obvious need for links and close coordination of activity with the directorates for energy, agriculture and transport. The strength of the directorate system is that it allows specialist activities to grow within house, but this may create a weakness in the commission's ability to take proactive decisions across departmental boundaries. In recent years, there have been attempts to address this problem and ensure that environmental policy is better coordinated and integrated throughout the EU institutions. In summary, the commission is the guardian of the treaties, oversees and initiates policies, particularly in the environmental sphere through the six action programmes and carries out decision-making. The role of the commission does not conform to any strict separation of powers doctrine. It may set its own

---

[12] It is estimated that over 100 different environmental provisions were passed before 1987 relating to trade, covering the wide areas of water and air quality, waste management and chemicals. This has been increased to over 200 different elements of environmental legislation.

[13] Paul Craig, 'Britain in the European Union' in J. Jowell and D. Oliver (eds), *The Changing Constitution* Sixth Edition, Oxford: Oxford University Press, 2007, p. 86.

agenda, ensure policy-making through networking and strategic planning; exercise executive functions of proactive policy formulation and implementation, and supervise the operation of the European Union. It also has legislative powers, largely concerned with delegated legislation and rules agreed by the Council.

The Council of Ministers is composed of representatives of the national governments of the member states, with representatives at different levels of government coordinating policy. Environmental ministers meet when there is the need to address a particular issue relevant to their remit. The same is true for the other sectors, e.g. transport and agriculture, whose decisions might affect environment. On one view the Council represents the interests of member states, and voting in the Council may operate along the lines of these interests. On another view their role is to coordinate the economic and social policy of the European Union. The European Parliament has been strengthened and a joint role with the Council created to form the main legislative function of the European Union. Consequently, voting arrangements within the Council are a critical part of decision-making. Broadly, there are two ways of voting, either unanimously or through a qualified majority voting system (QMV) that gives weighted votes to the various member states. QMV is intended to make decision-making more efficient. Since the expansion of the EU to 27 members the future of QMV is seen as critical, and is incorporated in the Lisbon Treaty as the only effective way to ensure that EU decision-making remains possible. It is envisaged under the Lisbon Treaty that, from 2014, the qualified majority will be calculated on the basis of a double majority. This will be secured when a decision is taken by 55 per cent of the member states representing at least 65 per cent of the Union's population. It is hoped that this will achieve political consensus and maintain legitimacy. The authority of the Council is at its best when it can achieve consensus. It is weakened when there is inertia or the self-interests of member states prevail.

The European Council comprises the heads of government of the member states and meets on a regular basis. It received formal recognition under the Single European Act 1986. The main role of the European Council is to set out and develop general policy guidance. It also brings together the governments of the member states and the President of the Commission. By setting broad policies the Council acts as the guide for the future.

The European Parliament, recognised by the Single European Act 1986, has been directly elected every five years since 1979. Each member state is entitled to a number of seats, with the balance adjusted to provide appropriate representation for the smaller states.[14] Voting is based on member state electoral practice; currently the United Kingdom elects members of the European Parliament (MEPs) through a closed-list system of proportional representation. In theory, MEPs are expected to vote on an individual basis but there is considerable evidence that they operate on the basis of groupings within the European Parliament. This provides an important opportunity for pressure group activity and lobbying over particular issues or causes. Environmental issues have come to the fore through the various committees of the European Parliament, most notably Environment, Public Health and Consumer Protection. A major issue for the European Parliament is how citizens may participate in the EU's institutions and how this participation may be rewarded. Not least in these concerns is the environment. Maria Lee, a leading European Union environmental lawyer, writing about the 'EU's democratic deficit' argues that the citizen's right of access to information on the

---

[14] The smaller states are over-represented as Germany has one MEP for about 820,000 citizens, whereas smaller countries have one for smaller numbers of citizens – Luxembourg has one for every 65,000 citizens.

environment is key and that this includes openness in decision-making through the much vaunted Aarhus Convention (see Chapter 6). She concluded:[15]

> And yet the mechanisms available are both weak in themselves and strikingly inadequate for any attempt at democratisation. 'Participation', certainly as currently conceptualised by the Commission, is far from significantly robust an instrument to bear the weight of democratising the Union; quite heroic institutional arrangements would be required.

There is also the difficulty of reaching sufficient consensus amongst member states to ensure that environmental matters debated by the parliament are not lost in the lobbying and infighting between different self-interests. The technical reality is that the European Parliament has few legal powers when compared to national parliaments, but this does not leave it without authority. Its powers of dismissal and appointment (Article 214 EC) are not insignificant and can be used to good advantage. This was clearly demonstrated by the dismissal of the commission in 1999 following a motion of censure and concerns about probity in the commission. The parliament also has powers (Article 193 EC) of investigation and inquiry so that it is able to pursue important issues. The power to bring the various EU institutions before the European Court of Justice held by the parliament may become a means to pursue investigations of legality. The European Parliament also has budgetary powers that can be used to supervise policy-making and its implementation.

The European Court of Justice (ECJ), which sits in Luxembourg, is important in legal arrangements for EU environmental law. The main role for the ECJ is to judicially interpret the treaties and ensure that member states implement the law correctly. The ECJ also provides judicial review of the implementing regulations, directive treaties, in particular of the interconnections between the treaties. We have already noted how the ECJ has helped to inform EU policy on the environment (see above) and also that, when interpreting the various strands that go to the free movement of goods, it has given effect to the protection of the environment. Underlying this role there is the question of adjudicating the legality of environmental law and establishing the fundamental principles for the development of environmental law. The Advocate-General plays an important part in the procedures of the ECJ by advising on EC law, including environmental law, and providing of well-articulated and authoritative analysis. Interpreting the use of the precautionary principle is one example of how the Advocate-General has assisted in the understanding and development of EU environmental law. The judges of the ECJ are drawn from the member states, one judge for each member state. Their tenure is for renewable terms of six years. The independence of judges has considerable protection and their important role within the EU ensures them a high profile. Normally decisions are made by a chamber of three or five judges, although there is the possibility of the Grand Chamber of 13 judges making a decision in an important case. The eight Advocate-Generals help to secure high quality decision-making through their advisory role; their opinions are normally published in advance of the decision of the chamber. The Advocate-General's opinion provides a good guide to the detailed considerations that may have influenced the judges' decisions. In fact, the judicial opinion itself is given in fairly short and unanimous findings. Bringing a case before the ECJ is not difficult: Article 234 permits any court or tribunal in a member state to refer to the ECJ a matter of law. This is especially helpful when there are doubts and uncertainties about the law.

---

[15] Maria Lee, *EU Environmental Law* Hart: Oxford, p. 148.

There is, also, the opportunity to use the ECJ as part of infringement proceedings. The commission can alert the ECJ to a possible infringement of EU law, and further may ask the ECJ for an opinion on the matter. Pressure groups and lobbying organisations are well versed in making the ECJ aware of potential infringements of EU environmental legislation, which has given the ECJ an opportunity to develop and deepen environmental law. As far as national courts are concerned, the ECJ stands as a shadow ensuring that EU law is correctly interpreted. This gives the national courts considerable support for the interpretation and analysis of environmental law in a way that would not have been considered possible if the main reliance for interpretation was national law. There is in effect a continuous dialogue between national courts and the ECJ. Even when national courts feel reluctant to draw in the ECJ directly, they are aware that it may ultimately become involved. The courts are conscious that the ECJ has taken a reasonably firm line against affording any latitude to administrations when interpreting EU environmental legislation. One recent example is the decision by the ECJ that the commission was wrong to exempt decaBDE, a fire retardant, in electrical and electronic equipment. The ban against decaBDE came under Directive 2002/95 EC restricting the use of certain hazardous substances for electrical and electronic equipment. The issue of the exemption arose in the *European Parliament and Denmark* v *Commission* C-14/06 and C-295/06 ECJ 1 April 2008. The commission's decision to grant decaBDE an exemption was considered by the ECJ. The list of substances banned under the directive included decaBDE, but was contained in an annex subject to the requirement that for a substance to be included, there had to be a stringent risk assessment undertaken as 'a matter of priority'. The commission undertook a review of the risk posed by decaBDE based on two studies of long standing and concluded that there was no need to ban decaBDE. The commission, therefore, recommended that that substance should be exempted from the ban. Both the EU Parliament and Denmark took the commission to the ECJ to determine the legality of the commission's decision. The ECJ found against the commission. As Richard Macrory has recently noted,[16] the decision in the case is an example of the tendency of the ECJ to strictly interpret the directive as requiring the granting of exemptions only in defined and special circumstances. A number of issues were pertinent to the decision of the ECJ. First, the availability of alternative fire retardants to decaBDE should be considered. Second, it might be possible to find reports of studies after 2006 when the directive was made and not have to rely on work undertaken four years earlier in 2002. This evaluation of the legality of the commission's decision illustrates another way by which the ECJ can influence the protection of the environment. Requiring stringent observance of risk assessments is an important element in establishing appropriate action to give voice to the precautionary principle. The ECJ is likely to remain instrumental in the interpretation and implementation of environmental law within the EU.

The EU Environment Agency, based in Copenhagen, has also been important for environmental protection since its inception in October 1993. Strictly, the European Environment Agency is not a formal institution of the EU: a reflection of low priority given to the environment in the early treaties. The Environment Agency, as an agency of the European Union, collects environmental information and data from member states and provides an independent assessment of the information (as part of the European environment information and observation network Eionet). It produces three yearly reports that provide highly influential analysis of the state of the environment within the EU. The European Environmental Agency

---

[16] ENDS Report 400, May 2008, pp. 58–9.

has a number of mandates. It provides member states with accurate and reliable information, which forms a basis for decisions to improve the environment and takes account of sustainable economic policies. The Agency also has a coordination role in the setting of priorities especially among the various European Union institutions, and supports infrastructure-building within the European Union in collaboration with the Economic and Social Committee and the Committee of the Regions. The Agency, however, does not have strong enforcement powers or regulatory supervision over environmental legislation. In the future it might be useful to expand the Agency's role to provide the commission with a means to oversee best practice and benchmarking for the environment as a whole.

An important new agency was established in June 2008 for the management of environmental and human health risks from manufactured chemicals (see Law in context, below). The European Chemicals Agency (ECHA) is responsible for the supervision of the EU Regulation for the Registration, Evaluation, and Authorisation of Chemicals (REACH). The ECHA essentially oversees the administration of chemical regulation, and more fundamentally is responsible for the technical and scientific aspects of REACH. In marked contrast to the European Environment Agency it also has responsibility for harmonising enforcement of chemical regulation across member states. REACH saw a controversial shift in the onus of carrying out and baring the cost of chemical risk assessment from member states to the manufacturers. Data from companies on individual chemicals is considered by the Risk Assessment Committee of the ECHA, which provides opinions on chemical risk, risk reduction measures, labelling and classification etc. There is also a Committee for Socio-economic Analysis under the ECHA, which considers the social and economic consequences of applications for authorisation and restrictions on individual chemicals effectively entrenching a sustainable development element in the working of the ECHA. This Committee is also charged with examining the feasibility of safer replacement chemicals for particular applications. The Agency works through these committees as well as a member state committee, which resolves disputes over draft decisions and identifies chemicals of very high concern, a Board of Appeal and an Enforcement Forum.

LAW IN CONTEXT

Chemical regulation

Chemicals pervade every aspect of our daily lives. Both humans and the environment are exposed on purpose and by accident to a diverse range of chemicals. There is a yearly production of approximately 400 million tonnes of 100,000 different chemicals worldwide, and of this total volume the EU produces 30,000 chemicals in quantities from 1 to more than 10 tonnes. Roughly 200 new chemicals are manufactured every year. These chemicals have a range of potential impacts, from those that have acute effects e.g. are highly toxic, or those that have chronic affects e.g. carcinogens or hormone-mimics capable of disrupting reproductive capacity, to those that are considered to have little associated risk with their use. The assessment of the risks posed by manufactured and marketed chemicals and the adoption of appropriate risk reduction measures, from a total ban to labelling for correct use, is clearly essential. Assessing chemical risk prior to marketing is a useful example of the precautionary principle in operation. Regulation of chemicals also provides an example of the difficulty of applying the concept of sustainable development. The chemical industry is of notable economic success and of considerable significance within the EU. Some three million jobs are supported by the industry in approximately 36,000 small- and medium-sized industries as well as large conglomerates. The total value of the chemical industry to the EU is €425 billion annually. Regulation to protect human health and the environment must be achieved sensitively so that the economic success and the competitiveness of the EU chemical industry are not affected.

EU environmental law and its impact on the United Kingdom

Since joining the European Community in 1972, the common law tradition of the United Kingdom has ensured that its notions of sovereignty have been sufficiently flexible to adjust. The United Kingdom has followed the dualist theory of international law. This means that treaty obligations are accepted into domestic law only after the United Kingdom Parliament has passed specific legislation. In 1972, the United Kingdom not only signed the various European treaties but also passed the European Communities Act 1972 to ensure that the United Kingdom would follow EU law. Over the years, there has been controversy over how best to implement EU law at the level of the member states. In the case of the United Kingdom, section 2(1) of the European Communities Act 1972 ensures that the United Kingdom courts have to give effect to EU law and that EU law forms the domestic law of the United Kingdom. Precisely what this means, however, requires careful interpretation. It has already been noted that the environment did not form a major pillar of the EC Treaty (see above). This left some doubt as to how environmental law gave rise to obligations at the level of the member state. In fact the vagueness of the EC Treaty made the environment part of Community policy-making fall far short of enforceable legal obligations. That said there are various ways in which the protection of the environment can be considered to form enforceable obligations.

EC directives form the bulk of environmental law. Directives are binding on member states, but there is some discretion at the level of member states. Normally the United Kingdom will pass primary legislation – an Act of Parliament to effect the introduction of a directive. It is also possible to adopt secondary legislation in the form of statutory instruments. There is an important doctrine that applies to directives, namely the principle of direct effect. While directives are normally implemented through domestic legislation, such as an Act of Parliament or statutory instrument, there are some situations where this may not occur or where legislation imperfectly translates the directive into domestic law. The doctrine of 'direct effect' is a means of allowing individuals to rely on any rights or obligations in the directive even if not fully in national law or imperfectly translated into national law. The doctrine may be used to enforce environmental obligations. The ECJ has been instrumental in promoting the doctrine to allow EU citizens rights as against member states. Thus, the direct effect doctrine is primarily a means of achieving member states' compliance. It does not interfere with the rights of private parties or individuals against each other.

The circumstances where the ECJ will invoke the direct effect doctrine vary but depend on the nature of the directive, the extent to which member states have attempted to comply and whether there are rights conferred on individuals against member states. There must be sufficient clarity in the wording of the directive for the ECJ to be able to interpret rights in this way.

There are examples in environmental law where the direct effect doctrine can be found and applied. There must be clarity, however, for example, in setting levels of pollutants and their discharge or where there are specified substances that are prohibited. The largely discretionary framework directives or programmes, which give the member states some latitude in implementation, are essentially excluded from the effect of the direct effect doctrine. The UK courts have been active in interpreting the doctrine of direct effect in environmental law after guidance given by the ECJ. In *Van Gend en Loos* v *Nederlandse Belasting administratie*[17] the ECJ set out principles for interpreting the general scheme of a directive, the wording and how rights are created. While in *Foster* v *British Gas plc*[18] the nature of the organisation that the indirect effect doctrine applies to was examined. The designation of a state or public body depends on its legal form, whether it provides a public service under the control of the state and whether it exercises special powers above ordinary individuals. The idea of state service brings organisations such as central and local government and related agencies including the UK Environment Agency within the influence of the doctrine. Indeed it is possible that private bodies, if they are exercising state functions, may be included within the doctrine's application. If so, the utility companies, Company Act companies formed after privatisation, fall within its scope.

There is also an 'indirect effect' doctrine. This provides for member states to give effect to EU law through the interpretation of the domestic law of the member state. Constitutional issues may arise, however, if the national courts in the United Kingdom operated the indirect effect doctrine to circumvent the sovereignty of parliament on a regular basis. As a consequence there is some reticence in developing the indirect effect doctrine.

Finally, some mention should be made of the nature of state liability. Broadly defined, this arises from the ECJ's decision in *Francovich and Bonifaci* v *Italy*.[19] The principle adopted by the ECJ is one of general application: namely that for certain types of breaches of EU law, the courts may impose damages. The exact nature of the breach must come within the discretion of the courts where it is regarded as sufficiently serious to warrant damages as a remedy. This may depend on the nature and extent of the responsibilities imposed by the law on the state. A failure to implement a directive may be sufficiently serious.[20] The action may be taken by an individual, and the principle is widely regarded as giving the ECJ a means of ensuring that domestic legal effect should be given to directives. The liability of member states arises out of three conditions articulated in the case. These are: the breach must be sufficiently serious; there must be a causal link between the breach of the obligation and the obligation on the member state; and that there must be some damage sustained by an injured party. The

---

[17] Case 26/62 [1963] ECR 1.
[18] Case C-188/89 [1990] 3 All ER 897.
[19] Cases C-6 and 9/90 [1991] ECR I-5357. P. Craig, 'Once more unto the breach: the Community, the State and damages liability' (1997) 113 LQR 67 and C. Harlow, '*Francovich* and the problem of the disobedient State' (1996) 2 ELJ 199.
[20] See: *Bowden* v *South West Water Services Ltd* [1999] Env LR 438.

application of the doctrine largely rests on the national courts of the member state. This is also subject to the vigilance of the ECJ[21] to ensure that national courts apply the law correctly. The scope for state liability is broad but the principle has not, to date, become a basis for broadening the scope of environmental liability.

Judicial interpretation of a directive

One of the most difficult issues faced by the United Kingdom national legal system is how to give effect to EU law. Very often interpreting an EU directive involves readjusting the traditional way of interpreting or analysing legal principles. In *R (on the application of Edwards)* v *Environment Agency*[22] the question of whether Rugby Cement, who wished to change its main fuel for the purposes of making cement, came within the requirements of the Environmental Impact Assessment (EIA), Directive 85/337/EEC was considered. Setting the criteria as to when an assessment is required is an important part of the responsibility of national authorities. In a previous case, *Berkeley* v *Secretary of State for the Environment*[23] the House of Lords quashed a planning permission that did not conform to the requirements of the EIA. The reasoning of the House of Lords was based on the treaty obligations that require effect to be given to European law. In *Berkely* there was a complete absence of an EIA which gave rise to the decision. The absence of an EIA as the basis for the decision to quash the planning permission was explained by Lord Justice Carnwath in *Brown* v *Secretary of State for Transport, Local Government and the Regions*[24] when he followed the *Berkeley* principle. The *Berekely* decision was a much tougher stance on the requirements of the directive than there had been in the past.

In the case of Rugby Cement the various alterations including the change of fuel did not require planning permission. If it had, then the EIA arrangements would have applied and an environmental statement under the EIA would have been required. The proposed change of fuel, however, potentially fell within the requirement to have an EIA. The Environment Agency for England and Wales claimed that it did and the question for the House of Lords was whether an EIA was required. The answer turned on what interpretation of 'project' would mean if it came within the scope of EIA arrangements. What is a project? Lord Hoffman envisaged that the definition depended on whether there was 'something new and not merely a change in the way existing works are operated'. This view was endorsed by the majority, Lords Hope and Walker. It was strongly contended by the minority comprising Lords Brown and Mance that the change of fuel required an EIA. Lord Hoffmann examined the totality of the European regulatory arrangements that included pollution control (IPPC), waste incineration and air quality. His analysis was that the 'change' of fuel had to be assessed on information supplied for the pollution prevention and control regime (IPPC). The same information also satisfied EIA requirements and therefore the information supplied by Rugby Cement was adequate to the requirements of an EIA. One of the findings of fact made by the High Court was that a change of fuel did not have an adverse effect on the environment. One interesting part of the case was that the Environment Agency had predicted that the change

---

[21] See: Case C-224/01 *Köbler* v *Austria* [2003] ECR I-10239.
[22] [2009] 1 All ER 57 and ENDS Report 400, pp. 56–9.
[23] [2001] 2 AC 603.
[24] [2004] Env LR 509.

of fuel would adversely effect the environment; in reality when air quality was monitored by Rugby Cement and the local authority, emission standards were not exceeded.

National courts have a large margin of discretion over the EIA since the ECJ has allowed a broad interpretation to be applied to EIA arrangements.[25] The Rugby Cement decision of the House of Lords raises two important issues. First, does a change of fuel represent a project that requires an EIA? Second, does the regulatory regime under the IPPC Directive meet the requirements of the EIA Directive? There are also some differences in the information required under IPPC regulation and EIA. There are also issues about how a directive is best interpreted in the context of how courts in the member state are accustomed to interpret the law. Given the general importance of the issues raised and the general approach taken by the ECJ on environmental matters, it is only a matter of time before these issues are considered by the ECJ. Until this happens it will be a matter for national courts to navigate around their approach to the EIA Directive.

Implementing a directive

Member states face considerable challenges when faced with implementing directives. The implementation of the Environmental Liability Directive[26] illustrates some of the problems. This directive is intended to establish mechanisms for the prevention and remedy of significant environmental damage and to operate the 'polluter pays' principle.[27] The directive was adopted on 30 April 2004. Its principal effect is to place on certain operators who cause a risk of significant damage to land, water or biodiversity a duty to avert such damage. Where damage does occur their obligation is to reinstate the environment. There are responsibilities to notify 'the competent' authority of the imminent threat of damage or of actual damage and there are accompanying responsibilities to set out plans to avert or repair the damage. The content of the directive proved controversial and there was a protracted eleven-year discussion before the final directive was adopted in 2004. Member states were given until 20 April 2007 to transpose the directive into their national legal system. The main driver for the implementation process is through building on the pre-existing 'polluter pays' principle. The directive that was finally agreed, however, resulted in a shift from the private law to a public law scheme for compensation. The simple principle underlying the directive is that public authorities are required to ensure that the polluter takes responsibility for damage to the environment and provides the necessary compensation to remediate the damage and restore the environment. The directive appears not to affect the damage suffered by private persons in terms of economic loss or physical injury. It significantly reinforces a burgeoning administrative law responsibility on regulatory bodies.

In order to bring forward the directive within the UK there have been a number of consultation documents,[28] which are intended to be followed by legislation in the form of regulations. Designating the competent authorities under the directive is critical to its

---

[25] *Commission v Italy* Case C-486/04 [2006] ECR I-11025.

[26] Directive 2004/35/EC European Parliament and Council 21 April 2004.

[27] Sixth Report: House of Commons, Environment, Food and Rural Affairs Committee: Implementation of the Environmental Liability Directive 2006–7 HC 694 contains a useful analysis and overview.

[28] This means Defra undertook arrangements for England, Wales and Northern Ireland, working with the Northern Ireland department of the Environment and the Welsh Assembly Government. There are separate arrangements for Scotland.

success. These are public authorities with responsibility for the environment such as the Environment Agency. Under the directive the 'operator' is designated as the person who operates or controls the occupational activity which poses a threat of damage or causes actual damage. There is a very wide definition of occupational activity, which extends from economic activity through to business and industry or other undertaking, and is irrespective of the private or public nature of the body. Article 2 of the directive sets out the definition of environmental damage which is also wide-ranging and includes:

- damage to protected species and natural habitats;
- water damage including the affect on the ecological, chemical and or quantitative status of water;
- land damage, including contamination of land that creates a significant risk of human health being adversely affected;
- damage which causes a measurable adverse change in a natural resource or service directly or indirectly.

There are some exclusions from liability, such as diffuse pollution and damage, that falls within the remit of international conventions, such as oil pollution and nuclear radiation. There are also defences such as when the actions of third parties are responsible or where damage occurs despite the fact that the operator complied with existing conditions contained in a permit.

There are also obligations set out in the directive that must be complied with when it comes to taking immediate action to prevent any threat of damage. There are rules about notifying the competent authority if the preventative measures fail and also in the event of significant environmental damage. Further rules relate to taking immediate action to control, contain, remove or manage any potential causes of damage and to make proposals for taking the necessary remedial measures. There are similar duties about taking preventative and remedial action on the competent authority responsible under the directive. How costs are to be distributed in the discharge of such duties remains to be seen as, in theory, the costs should fall on the operator. The main thrust of the directive is to address serious environmental incidents and this may limit its scope. As already noted the directive seeks to be both preventative and remedial.

The directive was transposed into UK law under the Environment Damage (Prevention and Remediation) Regulations 2009 but this was not without controversy.[29] The consultation on the directive was undertaken by the Department for the Environment, Food and Rural Affairs, Defra, with the final stage, which included draft regulations, completed in February 2008. The UK Environmental Law Association claimed that the consultation process failed to live up to expectations on providing access to justice. Up until now, the common law nature of the United Kingdom legal system gives a large part of the development of environmental liability to the case law developed by judges. This leaves a considerable space for pragmatic and ad hoc developments. The use of the reasonableness test and the application of foreseeability as part of liability make proving environmental liability similar to that in ordinary private law. There are many public authorities that have environmental powers that may be

---

[29] See Gerd Winter, Jan H. Jans, Richard Macrory and Ludwig Kramer, 'Weighing up the EC Environmental Liability Directive' (2008) *Journal of Environmental Law* 20: 2, pp. 163–91.

used to require remediation. Water pollution is a good example of where the Environment Agency may require remedial works. Contaminated land is another example of where remediation of the land may be required. The hotchpotch nature of current arrangements suggests that transposition of the Environmental Liability Directive offered a valuable opportunity to harmonise and consolidate the arrangements into a coherent whole which was not taken. As Gerd Winter, Richard MacRory and Ludwig Kramer, all influential environmental lawyers, however, explained:

> In respect of the Environmental Directive, it is clear that to date the Government has adopted a minimalist approach, and does not intend to use the opportunities provided to strengthen and harmonise national legislation concerning liability for environmental damage.[30]

The UK's approach is consistent with the evaluation that while the directive is directly effective and can be relied upon in national courts, there is a very wide margin of interpretation and national governments may choose to adopt an incremental style of implementation. This is a high-risk strategy as it is possible for there to be state liability arising from the failure to implement the directive and the obligations that flow from the directive may become the basis for individual liability. There is also the further possibility of a member state being taken to the ECJ by the commission for not fully implementing the directive.

The Environmental Liability Directive provides a valuable case study of how EU law and policy operate. Subject to intense political and interest group pressures, the directive is intended to bring coherence to the system of prevention, remediation and management of environmental damage. The directive also encourages greater availability of environmental information. The Environmental Liability Directive has moved forward the agenda on environmental liability; however, the technical outcome is to create within the sphere of public law a range of remediation measures that traditionally were found within the private law field. There is also a remarkable discretion accorded to member states that may require the ECJ to supervise the application of the directive. Critics of the United Kingdom minimalist approach to transposing the directive include many green groups and the Environment Agency.[31] There was a desire to see GMOs included within the regulations and that the onus for assessing and proposing remedial measures should be on the operator and not the regulator. There are concerns that there is inadequate protection afforded to water bodies, and some confusion and lack of clarity over the relationship between different regulatory bodies relevant to marine areas. This is also the case for the Control of Major Accident Hazard sites and damage caused by sites regulated by local authorities. A more general concern was that UK regulations are focused on a narrow definition of regulated sites, mainly commercial, rather than the broader definition preferred for occupational activity used in the directive. This has been addressed in the Regulations.

Conclusions

EU law has developed the field of environmental law and policy in many directions, sometimes in advance of the expectation of member states and often in ways that increases regulation

---

[30] Gerd Winter, *op. cit.*, fn 26.
[31] ENDS Report 401, June 2008, pp. 48–9.

and technical rules. The fact that the EU has adopted, and may adopt for the future, many legally binding environmental instruments makes an analysis of the EU experience a worthy case study in its own right.

EU environmental law is often identified with adding regulatory burdens to different sectors of business and industry and with the increasing costs of regulating the environment. The ambit of EU environmental law embraces all the sectoral areas of land, air and water. In setting standards and being proactive the EU stands out at the apex of enforceable rules that govern human activity in each of the 27 member states. In setting environmental standards there is an emphasis on sustainable development and the operation of the collective action by member states. Significantly, in the arena of tackling climate change the EU has contributed to international agreements and has led the way in terms of strategic implementation of a global policy for sustainable development. Ludwig Kramer summarises the distinctive quality of the EU as:

> the only regional organization that has the declared policy to pursue both the objectives of economic growth and environmental protection, because it accepts that, in the long term, it cannot reach one objective without the other.[32]

The significance of EU environmental law coincides with a period of rising oil prices and many urgent voices that argue for prioritisation of the environment in response to climate change, as well as concerns about food stocks and the positioning of China and India in the world's economies. The challenges that face EU environmental law include the appropriate monitoring and protection of the environment with the application of the precautionary principle and appropriate risk management strategies. There is greater transparency and accountability over EU policy-making and the generation of a political agenda with member states that resists short term decision-making in favour of long-term strategies. Durable strategies are also sought in politically sensitive areas such as GMOs and transport policy. The latter is likely to require much more coherence between policies for aircraft, road transport and shipping. The attention to the technical details in environmental law has often masked the political realities, which has tended to obscure open public debate and analysis. The need for public engagement is essential for the future.[33] Providing better public information and a more active engagement with business and industry should be regarded as indispensable to the future success of EU environmental law. There is also a need for technical and bureaucratic decision-making to be simplified so that EU environmental law can be properly assessed.

Evaluating EU environmental law

The pivotal role of EU environmental law makes an assessment of its effectiveness especially important. Evaluating EU environmental law, however, is a difficult task. At the heart of EU environmental policy-making is the EU Sustainable Development Strategy. Delivering

---

[32] Ludwig Kramer, 'Regional economic integration organizations: the European Union as an example' chapter 37 in D. Bodansky, Jutta Brunée, Ellen Hey, *The Oxford International Environmental Law* Oxford: Oxford University Press, 2006, p. 854.

[33] See: Maria Lee, *EU Environmental Law Challenges, Change and Decision-Making* Oxford: Oxford University Press, 2005.

the strategy requires a cross-cutting approach covering a number of areas and themes. These include:

- climate change and clean energy;
- sustainable transport;
- sustainable consumption and production;
- public health and policies that include demography and immigration;
- managing natural resources.

The EU Commission has undertaken a review of its own performance around these themes[34] that has sought to identify and assess progress. The conclusions of the study are that sustainable development policy continues to provide an agenda for change and that the framework for its future development is linked to regional i.e. EU, national and local policy-making. There is also a desire to set priorities in the development of different themes. The overarching problem of climate change has taken the highest priority and this is likely to continue. The commission is aware of a wide variation in the adoption of policy by different member states and this is linked to a growing acceptance that 'no one size fits all'. There are notable areas where real progress is clear – recycling waste is one example of real achievement but less success is evident in setting and meeting energy-efficiency targets. Clearly, the outcomes from EU developments will take time to reach fruition and evolve. Generally, it was noted that conservation and natural resource management is relatively weak and that there is considerable divergence in resource management between member states. The review found that the time lag between environmental policy formulation and implementation is unacceptable and should be addressed. It was recommended that support for cohesion in implementation through the use of structural funds should be improved. It was also noted that complexity and over-technical information often impeded progress. The review concluded also that EU environmental law needs a better defined hierarchy of objectives – especially in the transport area and also with an increase in the operation of cross-cutting policies (see above). There is also a need for greater internal cohesion within the EU, and a better synergy between different policies and implementation needs to be found. Fuller and more detailed assessment of objectives and targets is essential. Finally there is a need to keep the EU's Sustainable Development Strategy under review, with 2013 set as an appropriate date for the next one.

EU environmental policy is not only found in its Sustainable Development Strategy but also in the various Environment Action Programmes. Currently the operation of the 6th Environmental Action Programme (2002–12) is subject to review. Many of the points outlined above are reiterated in the assessment undertaken by the commission of its own progress.[35] The energy and climate change strategy, intended to place the EU on the pathway to an ultimate 30 per cent reduction in greenhouse gases, is one of a number of important steps towards a unilateral reduction of at least 20 per cent by 2020. A further element is the recent introduction of a Climate Action and Renewable Energy Implementation Strategy from January 2008. The EU has also shown interest in developing and expanding the use of

---

[34] See ECORYS, *Final Report: Progress on EU Sustainable Development Strategy* Brussels: 29 February 2008.

[35] *Communication from the Commission to the Council and the European Parliament: 2007 Environment Policy Review* COM (2008) 409 final.

new financial instruments to encourage eco-innovative small- and medium-sized enterprises to develop energy and natural resources efficiently. There is also recognition that better regulatory strategies can be used to encourage good environmental policy-making. The need for cross-cutting environmental strategies is also a key element in integrating the environment into the fields of agriculture, industrial policy, and trade and industry. Engagement with citizens over environmental matters is also seen as complementary to giving the environment the pivotal status it deserves. In conclusion, EU environmental law is at the apex of implementing policies for sustainability and adapting to climate change. Cross-cutting environmental policies are of fundamental importance and likely to engage the main stakeholders at a time when they are sensitive to rising oil prices and concerned about the implications of climate change.

EU environmental law has developed incrementally. It is obvious that the commission has developed environmental policy through the economics of the EU and has helped create a sustainable development focus for the EU. This focus has the potential to guide the main policy areas such as agriculture, transport and energy. The work of the ECJ in creating a legal basis for many EU environmental initiatives is also significant. The combination of the ECJ and the commission has given the EU an important legal framework. There, however, remain significant issues about the method of decision-making and citizen participation as well as accountability. Pre-eminent in the EU is the use of scientific advice and data, and the technical importance of legal rules. The development of sophisticated economic tools and risk assessment strategies may alienate member states and citizens. Often the EU is criticised for its 'over-regulation' and lack of proper enforcement strategies.[36] The increasing use of fines and penalties, which has the potential for expansion under the EC Directive on Environmental Liability, suggests that the EU is entering a new phase in its development of environmental law and policy. The expansion of EU membership and the potential of the Treaty of Lisbon to prioritise environmental law suggest new horizons for environmental law within the EU.

Further reading

An introduction to EU law is necessary as a guide to the main institutions and decision-making systems.

C. Archer, *The European Union* London: Routledge, 2008.

D. Bodansky, Jutta Brunée and Ellen Hey, *The Oxford International Environmental Law* Oxford: Oxford University Press, 2006.

P. Craig and G. de Burca (eds), *The Evolution of EC Law* Oxford: Oxford University Press, 1999.

L. Kramer, *EC Environmental Law* 5th edition, London: Sweet and Maxwell, 2003.

[36] See: M. Hedemann-Robinson (ed.), *Enforcement of European Union Environmental Law Legal Issues and Challenges* Abingdon: Routledge-Cavendish, 2007.

Policy-making in the EU is well covered in the following:

W. Grant, D. Matthews and P. Newell, *The Effectiveness of European Union Environmental Policy* London: Macmillan, 2000.

J. McCormick, *Environmental Policy in the European Union* London: Palgrave, 2001.

Han Somsen (ed.), *The Yearbook of European Environmental Law* Oxford: Oxford University Press, 2000–.

Select bibliography

A. Bodansky, 'The United Nations Framework Convention on Climate Change: a commentary' (1993) 18 *Yale Journal of International Law* 451–558.

J. Coleman, 'Environmental barriers to trade and EC Law' (1993) 2(11) EELR 295.

Peter G.G. Davies, *European Union Environmental Law* London: Ashgate, 2004.

R. French, 'The changing nature of environmental protection: recent developments regarding trade and the environment in the European Union and the World Trade Organization' (2000) XLVII *Netherlands International Law Review* 1.

L. Gormley, 'Free movement of goods and the environment' in J. Holder (ed.), *The Impact of EC Environment Law in the UK* (1997) 289.

W. Grant, D. Matthews and P. Newell, *The Effectiveness of European Union Environmental Policy*, London: Macmillan, 2000.

L. Kramer, *Casebook on EC Environmental Law* Oxford: Hart Publishing, 2002.

L. Kramer, *EC Environmental Law* London, 5th edition, London: Sweet and Maxwell, 2003.

M. Lee, *EU Environmental Law* Oxford: Hart Publishing, 2005.

J. and S. McEldowney, *Environmental Law and Regulation* Oxford: OUP, 2000.

J. Scott, *EC Environmental Law* London: Sweet and Maxwell, 1998.

Han Somsen (ed.), *Yearbook of European Environmental Law* Oxford: Oxford University Press, 2000–.

S. Tromans, 'EC waste law – a complete mess?' (2001) 13(2) JEL 133.

H. Wilkinson, 'Subsidiarity and EC environmental policy: taking people's concerns seriously' (1994) 6(1) JEL 85.

Useful periodicals

European Environmental Law Review (monthly)

The Yearbook of Environmental Law (yearly)

Review of EC and International Environmental Law (tri-annually)

Visit **http://www.mylawchamber.co.uk/mceldowney** to access key issue checklists and practice exam questions to test yourself on this chapter.

6 Human rights and the environment

Introduction

The concept of environmental rights as part of human rights has gathered momentum[1] in recent years. Rights are increasingly seen as the focus of how citizens interact with government and how government should respond to citizens' desire for empowerment. The values and norms of a rights-based culture appear to fit the challenges of protecting the environment and the threat that environmental degradation poses to humankind. Individual rights are accorded to the citizen such as the right to life or the right to a fair trial, and it is arguable that environmental rights are just as important since the environment is fundamental to the survival of the species. Merrills has noted that there is an argument in favour of the addition of 'a broad right to the environment, to the list of traditional human rights'.[2] The transcription of environmental rights into some form of guaranteed rights has already been achieved in the 1981 African Charter on Human and People's Rights and also in the 1988 San Salvador Protocol. A healthy environment is axiomatic to the moral, legal and economic considerations that are to be found in many principles of environmental law such as the precautionary principle and sustainable development, though it is not always articulated as such. There is a seductive quality about rights being subsumed into mainstream environmental law. There is also a strong belief that environmental rights will fill the gap in the current legal arrangements and enhance the protection of the environment. The arguments in favour of a rights-based approach to the environment have gained strength through the perspective of constitutional rights.

In contrast to the rights-based approach, the United Kingdom, for many years, proceeded on an opposing idea of freedom, namely that unless there was a law forbidding or preventing a certain course of conduct then there was freedom to do as you please. Freedom, thus defined, left little room for the articulation of positive and enforceable rights. The introduction of the Human Rights Act 1998 has changed this approach and opens the possibility for human rights to include environmental rights. There is a delicate balance to be made, however, in the progression of environmental rights and the acceptance of ideas about freedom. That balance is explained by Baroness Hale in the House of Lords:

---

[1] A. Boyle and M. Anderson (eds), *Human Rights Approaches to Environmental Protection* Oxford: Clarendon Press, 1996. Also see: *Dobson v Thames Water Utilities Ltd* [2009] 3 All ER 319.

[2] John G. Merrills, 'Environmental rights' in D. Bodansky, J. Brunnée and E. Hey, *The Oxford Handbook of International Environmental Law* Oxford: Oxford University Press, 2006, p. 664.

the purpose of such human rights instruments is to place some limits upon what a democratically elected Parliament may do: to protect the rights and freedoms of individuals and minorities against the will of those who are taken to represent the majority. Democracy is the will of the people, but the people may not will to invade those rights and freedoms which are fundamental to democracy itself. To qualify as such a fundamental right, a freedom must be something more than the freedom to do as we please, whether alone or in company with others.[3]

The question arises as to whether the environment qualifies as such a fundamental right that it requires express protection? There is also the related concern that should environmental rights become the main focus, it is inevitable that there will be a preference for litigation-based solutions to environmental problems. This may have its problems in securing judicial law-making which may be at odds with the idea of democratic governance and government authority.[4]

In the United Kingdom, the courts have shown some reluctance and at times timidity in developing environmental rights. It is clear that in the absence of express environmental rights, various violations of human rights such as the right to life, health or family may provide protection of the environment through a human rights route. This requires identifying the various human rights instruments that may give rise to environmental rights, and engages with a broader analysis that places environmental rights as a means of securing justice. The impacts and aftermath of serious pollution incidents are clear from events at Bhopal in India and Chernobyl in Europe and provide a case for group rights to engage with environmental justice (see Law in context, below).

LAW IN CONTEXT

Bhopal, India

In 1969 a chemical plant, owned jointly by Union Carbide India and by Indian authorities, was built in a densely populated area of the city of Bhopal. The plant manufactured the pesticide carbaryl. In the late 1970s additional facilities were built on the site to produce methyl isocyanate (MIC), a highly toxic intermediate in the manufacture of the pesticide. Liquid MIC was stored in several holding tanks on the site. Water entered one of these tanks causing a chemical reaction that ultimately resulted in the release of 40 tonnes of gaseous methyl isocyanate during the early morning of 3 December 1984. The gas cloud enveloped the inhabitants of the surrounding area and between 3,000 and 4,000 people died immediately. Estimates vary as to the final death toll but it may have reached 20,000 people. Large numbers of animals also died and even vegetation was affected. Today the impacts of the Bhopal chemical disaster linger. Over 100,000 people still suffer the chronic effects of methyl isocyanate poisoning, some of which are serious e.g. blindness. The groundwater in the area is contaminated by a variety of pollutants arising from the pesticide manufacturing plant and there is still debate about how to remediate the contaminated land. Litigation in the Indian courts followed the events of 1984, ultimately ending in an out-of-court settlement in 1989 with Union Carbide

---

[3] R (on the application of the Countryside Alliance) v A-G [2008] 2 All ER 95, p. 135 at d.

[4] See: Phillipe Sands, 'Why no redress when EU breaks its own laws?' ENDS Report 402, July 2008, pp. 34–7.

agreeing to pay $470 million for damages caused by the Bhopal disaster. There had been allegations of poor safety procedures and equipment maintenance at the plant. Over 500,000 people have received compensation arising from this settlement, which was administered by the Bhopal Gas Tragedy Relief and Rehabilitation Department. Union Carbide also sold its stake in the pesticide plant and established a charitable trust for victims of the disaster. This trust supported the building of a hospital specifically for victims of the accident and continues to support the running of the hospital. The accident was of such magnitude that in 1993 the International Medical Commission on Bhopal was established and to this day the effects of the disaster continue to be felt.

LAW IN CONTEXT

Chernobyl, Ukraine

In April 1986 workers at the Chernobyl nuclear power plant in the Ukraine undertook an experiment that was to lead to a runaway nuclear reaction and a series of explosions in the reactor. This resulted in a plume of radioactive material to be released in the atmosphere from the nuclear plant. The radioactive cloud was carried over large swathes of Europe and even to the eastern seaboard of North America. Worst affected were those countries closest to the reactor, in particular Balarus, which received 60 per cent of the radioactive fallout, the Ukraine and parts of Russia. Here in the order of 350,000 people had to be evacuated and resettled. Today, most of the severely affected areas are safe, except for the Chernobyl Exclusion Zone itself and a few other limited areas. One of the major problems after the accident was the contamination of reservoirs and rivers in the area, and the quality of drinking water was of concern for months after the accident. Plants in the immediate disaster area died as did some animals although stunted growth and a decline in reproductive health was commoner. The international scale of the disaster was remarkable, with populations exposed to radioactive fallout in countries ranging from Greece to Sweden and the United Kingdom. Agriculture was affected, with crops unusable and farm animals contaminated through the ingestion of polluted grass. In the UK severe restrictions on the sale of sheep from highly polluted pastures lasted for decades. The human health impacts are still being played out. The International Atomic Energy Agency and the World Health Organization established the Chernobyl Forum, which published a Report in 2005. It was estimated that the number of direct deaths from the accident included 47 accident workers, mostly from radiation sickness, and 9 children from thyroid cancer. Predictions of 4,000 extra cancer cases in the 600,000 most exposed individuals, with a further 5,000 in the 6 million living near the power plant were made in the report. Much lower increases in cancer cases can be expected across the rest of Europe. Most of the radioactive material remains within the nuclear reactor, which was contained within a concrete sarcophagus in the immediate aftermath of the accident. The sarcophagus must remain safe while the site is decommissioned, both technologically demanding but essential. The economic, human health and environmental costs will continue for many decades.

Justice, however, has a wider frame of reference that embraces the relationship between humans and the world in terms of fairness embodying ethical and moral issues about society and the fair distribution of wealth. Given the nature of rights that embody notions of fair procedures, transparent and accountable decision-making, environmental justice may prove difficult to achieve and impossible to manage. A major component of social justice is transparency in information and many advocates of a rights approach to the environment see environmental information as a key component. This chapter addresses environmental rights in terms of rights available under international law, followed by an analysis of the European Convention on Human Rights. The Human Rights Act 1998 offers the prospect of a human rights protection being extended to the environment within the UK. The major UK human rights cases are considered in the chapter as is the possibility of providing environmental justice through the UN Aarhus Convention on *Access to Information, Public Participation in Decision-making and Access to Justice in Environmental Matters.*

Environmental rights and international law

The starting point in international law is to consider how human rights and the environment can be linked. The United Nations recognised the connection between human rights and the environment in 1968 but this was no more than the obvious recognition of scientific and technological progress and the rights of individuals.[5] In 1972 Principle 1 of the Stockholm Declaration made the link between human rights, the freedom and equality of life and an environment 'of a quality that permits a life of dignity and well-being'. The Declaration goes on to articulate that man 'bears a solemn responsibility to protect and improve the environment for present and future generations'. Philippe Sands makes a number of substantial points about the nature of the pre-existing legal order before the Stockholm Declaration.[6] The first is the idea of 'permanent sovereignty' over natural resources that reside in the state. This is a principle of very long standing and in its modern form received acceptance despite the obvious conflict that might exist between the rights of the citizen to a safe and wholesome environment and the desire to exploit the environment to its full potential. Various resolutions adopted by the UN General Assembly after 1952 related to foreign private companies and their exploitation of the environment through the use of natural resources. Oil extraction and mining are two examples where exploiting natural resources were considered essential for the economic growth of underdeveloped poor countries. The need for balance between the sovereign rights of the state and international companies were met by market economies and the autonomy of the state. The United Nations has accepted that nation states enjoy full autonomy over natural resources. The 1971 Ramsar Convention acknowledged this national sovereignty alongside the recognition of wetlands as part of the establishment of international protection for these important habitats. Indeed Principle 21 of the 1972 Stockholm Conference recognises permanent sovereignty over natural resources and responsibilities, meaning stewardship of natural resources. The 1972 Stockholm Declaration included recognition that the environment should be 'of a quality

---

[5] The Proclamation of Tehran UN Doc. A/CONF.32/41; see para. 18 quoted in P. Sands, *Principles of International Environmental Law* second edition, Cambridge: Cambridge University Press, 2005, p. 294.
[6] *Ibid.*

that permits a life of dignity and well-being'. This set an important principle upon which to build. A novel attempt to reconcile individual rights with rights to public participation was made in the 1982 World Charter for Nature. Seven years later in 1990, the Declaration of the Hague on the Environment contained the idea of the environment linked to 'human dignity'. There have also been statements of a number of broad and generalised environmental aspirations. The UN General assembly declared 'all individuals are entitled to live in an environment that is adequate for their health and well-being' in 1988. Another way of viewing human rights is to see the environment and its protection as being dependent on the avoidance of pollution that affects humans. Thus the environment and human rights is involved in frameworks that are designed against toxic chemicals.

The 1992 Rio Declaration advanced the idea of sustainable development linked to the entitlement 'to a healthy and productive life in harmony with nature'. The relationship between environmental rights and sustainable development is one that raises fundamental questions about how rights and sustainable development may be reconciled. These are difficult to answer as the priority given to economic development in industrialised countries as part of sustainable development is unlikely to be kept in check by environmental rights that are often individualised and localised. Rights empower citizens and empowerment may constrain the policy-making agenda. Even more difficult is to know the precise moment when the rights of the majority as defined by national government policy should be set aside for the rights of a minority or ethnic group. There are numerous examples where such tensions are seen in ethnic rights of indigenous minorities.[7] The difficulties of reconciling sustainable development with rights have translated into a patchy framework of environmental rights such as the 1981 African Charter recognising 'a right to a general satisfactory environment favourable to their development'. The 1988 San Salvador Protocol includes the right to a healthy environment and to the state having an obligation to promote, protect, preserve and improve the environment. There are many other conventions that recognise the environment as linked to indigenous people. The 1989 Convention on Indigenous and Tribal People in Independent Countries associates state obligations to the protection of the people and their environment.

The literature on human rights and the environment has been added to substantially by the UN Commission on Human Rights affirming the relationship between the preservation of the environment and the promotion of human rights. There is a Sub-Commission on Prevention of Discrimination and Protection of Minorities that receives reports on the Human Rights and the Environment – notably the famous Ksentini Report.[8] This charts the protection of the environment and the need for states to protect human rights. The Council of Europe has also followed a similar approach and encouraged protection of the environment with advancing human rights.

Despite the obvious achievements of mapping the environment through human rights values, there is a surplus of aspirations over actual achievements. This is mainly because international law has been slow and cumbersome in delivering real economic and social rights, and rights that include the environment must inevitably engage with economic and

---

[7] See for example in New Zealand and Australia and also in Canada. There is a good analysis of the perspective of environmental rights to be found in T. Hayward, *Constitutional Environmental Rights* Oxford: Oxford University Press, 2005, pp. 185–215.

[8] E/CN.4/Sub.2/1994/9: this includes a Draft Declaration on Principles of Human Rights and the Environment.

social rights. This has the potential of conflict with market economies and causes trade imbalances between countries with good human rights protection and those that do not. A violation of economic and social rights should give rise to enforceable and substantial liabilities. Defining environmental rights requires setting standards and observing controls that ultimately become binding agreements in international law. There is a risk of imposing unacceptably high and unachievable standards on poorer countries that might inhibit their development and growth. Setting, implementing and enforcing standards for drinking and bathing water, for example, can be expensive and costs may bear down disproportionately on consumers that are poor. It is likely that future developments in human rights will have to take account of the shifting economics of environmental rights. There is a growing number of environmental organisations and groups that are developing rights-based legal actions determined to create justice through a more rights-focused approach.[9] Examples include Greenpeace, Friends of the Earth, the World Development Movement, each with their own agenda and policy focus.[10] Their impact on environmental rights is yet to be seen. In Europe the emergence of environmental rights is one of the issues to come from the European Convention on Human Rights (ECHR).

Environmental rights and the Human Rights Act 1998

The European Convention on Human Rights (ECHR), drafted after the Second World War and signed in 1950, contains a code of rights that was intended to address the problems that arise from totalitarian government. The ECHR also provides for the European Court of Human Rights (based at Strasbourg) to adjudicate on rights. The ECHR together with the European Court of Human Rights provides access to human rights for many citizens. When the ECHR was drafted, it was heavily influenced by the English common law. Rights protected under the ECHR were individually based and freedom was defined in negative terms, ensuring that the individual was protected from any 'unjustified' interference. Individual liberties were defined in a traditional way and left little scope for social, economic and environmental rights.

There is no explicit mention of environmental rights in the ECHR. There are a number of articles that may be relevant in environmental cases but the European Court of Human Rights has shown reluctance to interpret the ECHR so that the environment falls directly under one of the articles of the convention.[11] There has, however, been some limited extension to convention rights over the years. Reliance on case law has given the European Court of Human Rights a proactive role in developing rights. This has the advantage of allowing the law to develop to fit the circumstances of the time. It has the disadvantage common to judicial decision-making of requiring careful interpretation, which may not always lead to clarity. The reliance on case law also falls far short of a radical rethink of the scope, extent and

---

[9] This is especially the case in Latin America and South Asia. It is also an inevitable result of the experiences in India and China of environmentally damaging projects.

[10] *R v HM Inspectorate of Pollution, ex parte Greenpeace Ltd (No. 2)* [1994] 4 All ER 329.

[11] *X and Y v Federal Republic of Germany* Application No. 7407/76; Decision of 13 May 1976 on the Admissibility of the Application 5 DR 161 (1976). An application made by environmental protestors about the use of land for military purposes with implications for the environment *was* rejected by the court. There was no explicit recognition of environmental rights to be found in any of the rights and freedoms in the ECHR.

breadth of rights appropriate for a time very different from the post-war era. If the ECHR were to be drafted today it would undoubtedly be necessary to give the environment some direct mention. This would reflect the growing awareness of the importance of environmental rights and also acceptance of international law in this area. Similarly, any priority given to the environment would require reconciliation with social, economic and political rights. This is controversial and would probably need negotiation, especially as environmental rights may give rise to economic consequences and costs that government and industry may be anxious to resist. Finally, the operation of convention rights centred on the individual may not always be consistent with the democratic wishes of the majority. Applying environmental rights to individuals may not in itself be bad but it is likely to be controversial and difficult to reconcile with democratic government. It is a major question whether incremental increases in judicial power through human rights litigation is a desirable means of protection.[12]

Complaints made under the ECHR provide the European Court of Human Rights with the opportunity to investigate and ensure that the convention is observed. Inadmissibility of a complaint can rest on procedural as well as substantial grounds. There are strict time limits and there can be complaints that do not fall within the remit of the convention. There are complaints that are ill-founded or there is an adequate remedy in domestic law and this has not been explored. There is a strict rule of standing, namely that an individual or group must satisfy the European Court of Human Rights that they are a 'victim'. This is defined to mean that the complainant is affected directly or indirectly by the act or omission that is complained about. This is strictly applied and leaves a hurdle to be overcome, much greater than that which applies in the United Kingdom courts.

Given the procedural and substantial obstacles, it is hardly surprising that there are relatively small successes in using the European Court of Human Rights to advance environmental rights. Pressure groups and 'green activists' have found that the ECHR is limited in scope and application to the environment. There are some examples where the European Court of Human Rights has been able to interpret environmental rights under the ECHR, which has given rise to an expectation that environmental rights may at last come to dominate environmental law. There are a number of articles under the ECHR that can be adapted to apply to the environment. Article 8, the right to respect for private and family life, provides the basis for arguments of privacy related to various forms of air pollution such as noxious smells and fumes from industrial processes and also in terms of dust and noise pollution. There are many cases where arguments are made around the application of Article 8, as the individual seeks protection from the results of living beside large airports or industrial premises. In *Guerra* v *Italy*[13] Article 8 was breached on the basis that the state (the Italian government) had failed to provide adequate protection to local inhabitants living beside a chemical plant. The decision by the full Grand Chamber is a significant application of Article 8 to provide environmental protection. There is, however, a marked reluctance to extend the scope of Article 8 beyond a narrow construction. In *Hatton* v *UK*[14] on appeal to the Grand Chamber the court held that there was no breach of Article 8 by the state authorities in respect of night-time flights that residents living hear Heathrow complained interfered with their

[12] J. Waldron, *Law and Disagreement* Oxford: Oxford University Press, 2003; also see: R. North, 'A Response to Jeremy Waldron's Law and Disagreement' (2003) 12 *Political Studies Review*, Vol. 1, no. 2, pp. 167–78.

[13] Application 14967/89 (1998) 26 EHRR 357.

[14] *Hatton* v *United Kingdom* Application 36022/97 (2003) 37 EHRR 28 15 BHRC 259.

private lives. Hitherto there had been some support for intervention in respect of human rights protecting the citizen, but it was clear that the protection afforded by rights left a large margin of discretion with the state authorities as to how to regulate night-time flights. In that way the courts showed reluctance to go beyond a legal interpretation into the broader canvass of assessing the most effective way of protecting individual environmental rights.

The approach in *Hatton* is indicative of how the European Court of Human Rights perceives its role. Rather than being interventionist, it acts in a passive way to oversee the role of the state.[15] There is nevertheless a positive duty on state authorities to refrain from interfering with the right to private and family life This places arguments about the environment to the fore; while not guaranteeing an outcome in favour of environmental rights it establishes an arguable case. Many of the issues associated with the environment fail because there is always a balance to be struck between state intervention that is permissible and the individual's rights. The *Hatton* case outlined above shows how difficult it may be for the judges to agree when the balance has been correctly decided. The judges do not substitute their views for those of the decision-maker.[16] It is also necessary for there to be a high standard of evidence to support the view that the effect of the state's interference is unreasonable or that it causes deterioration in the quality of the individual's life, balanced against the interests of the community.

Article 2 is the right to life, which is clearly linked to the protection of the environment, although this is not articulated in the article as such. Put into the concepts that lie behind the article, there is a question of whether the right to, for example, clean water to drink, or the quality of the air or the standard of housing, will fall under the terms of the article. Despite the obvious connection between life and a healthy environment, there are few cases where the article has been used. We have already seen the decision of *Guerra* v *Italy*, where the evolution of environmental rights was considered and it was suggested that Article 2 might be useful for the protection of the physical environment. While the case law is disappointing, there is an acknowledged right to information about the environment that runs alongside the application of rights to a healthy environment. Judges are often critical if the citizen is deprived of the necessary information on which to base a measured view. Article 6, the right to a fair trial has wide-ranging significance in terms of setting both procedural and substantive rules that apply to decision-makers. The scope of Article 6 extends to regulators, planning authorities and also confronts the issue of how public consultation is best achieved. Among other things, this brings into human rights the issues associated with the grant or renewal of permits or licences. The scope of Article 6 extends to criminal and civil adjudications, including penalties or fines levied by regulators.

Article 1 of Protocol 1 is the right to peaceful enjoyment of possessions, which provides a very broadly drafted right that may allow the courts to inquire into the levels of dust, pollution more generally or noise. Inevitably it is necessary to set an appropriate balance when deciding whether or not there is an acceptable level of interference into the enjoyment of property or possessions. The scope of Article 10, the right to freedom of expression, also extends into the area of environmental information and the method of deliberation used by environmental decision-makers. The overall ambit of Article 10 is to provide a judicial oversight that balances different interests in establishing the boundaries of freedom of

[15] *Powell and Rayner* v *United Kingdom* Application 9310/81 (1990) 12 EHRR 355.
[16] See: *Buckley* v *United Kingdom* Application 20348/92 (1996) 23 EHRR 101.

expression. Defining the public interest is very much part of the balancing exercise undertaken by the courts.

Finally, Article 13 is a general right to an effective remedy. This is an overarching responsibility that falls on the grievance mechanisms that are 'reasonable' and suitable to provide an effective remedy in the national courts. The adequacy of the remedy is the key – not simply the availability of the remedy.

The Human Rights Act 1998

In the United Kingdom the possibility for environmental claims to raise human rights issues comes as a consequence of the Human Rights Act 1998. This Act provides the UK courts with the opportunity to give the European Convention of Human Rights a limited form of domestic effect. A singular feature of the Human Rights Act 1998 is its potential to affect the common law and many of the assumptions, as well as the substance, of statute law. Rights-driven, judge-made law infiltrating into the political process of decision-making could alter the balance between the judicial, executive and legislative functions and limit the freedom of elected politicians to create policy. The potential for conflict between the principle of pre-eminence given by Parliament to democratic decision-makers and the role of the judiciary is at the centre of the *Alconbury* case. In the High Court, for the first time, the courts granted a declaration of incompatibility under the Human Rights Act 1998. The declaration was reversed on appeal to the House of Lords. Lord Hoffmann in the House of Lords in *Alconbury* explained:

> There is no conflict between human rights and the democratic principle. Respect for human rights requires that certain basic rights of individuals should not be capable in any circumstances of being overridden by the majority, even if they think that the public interest so requires. Other rights should be capable of being overridden only in very restricted circumstances. These are rights which belong to individuals simply by virtue of their humanity, independently of any utilitarian calculation. The protection of these basic rights from majority decision requires that independent and impartial tribunals should have the power to decide whether legislation infringes them and either (as in the United States) to declare such legislation invalid or (as in the United Kingdom) to declare that it is incompatible with the governing human rights instrument. But outside these basic rights there are many decisions which have to be made every day . . . in which the only fair method of decision is by some person or body accountable to the electorate.[17]

There is no doubt that the development of a rights-based culture as part of the United Kingdom's domestic law took a new direction and vigour with the coming into force of the Human Rights Act 1998 on 2 October 2000. The Act does not empower the judiciary to strike down legislation or ignore its contents, but there is a duty on courts and tribunals to avoid incompatibility between UK domestic legislation and the ECHR. The duty applies to existing and future legislation as well as secondary and primary legislation. The courts must uphold convention rights unless the legislation is so incompatible that this is impossible. This gives the courts considerable scope in judicial interpretation and in developing the case law. It is possible that the courts may apply a different emphasis and approach depending on the

---

[17] *R (on the application of Alconbury Developments Ltd)* v *Secretary of State for the Environment, Transport and the Regions* [2001] 2 All ER 929 at p. 980, para. 70.

nature of the legislation. Convention rights require weighing up different rights and interests[18] and the judicial interpretation of their duties of interpretation under section 3 of the 1998 Act is emerging as the case law develops.[19]

The boundaries of judicial discretion are also influenced by the specialist nature of legislation and some scepticism[20] that judges are suitably qualified to make choices involving competing social and economic claims. The environment presents particular challenges and really requires specialist expertise given the complexity of legislation and the technical nature of environmental regulation, which includes economic and legal instruments to enforce environmental law. The high expense of human rights litigation[21] and the fact that the costs of meeting environmental liabilities are often difficult to quantify makes the task of the judiciary particularly difficult, especially if there is substantial scientific uncertainty.

As well as interpreting the nature of convention rights, judges are faced with striking difficult balances when interpreting UK legislation. The weighing-up of political, social and economic issues is a responsibility of the legislator and settling the right balance between competing claims is considered a matter for political consideration and policy-making. Environmental issues often involve government deciding resource allocations that involve complex questions and the balancing of short-term and long-term considerations. This is especially true in areas such as town and country planning, waste disposal and pollution control. There is a strong tradition in the United Kingdom of ministerial accountability to Parliament for policy-making and of acknowledging parliamentary sovereignty to enable legislation to settle economic and social priorities. Judges' interpretation of statute under the Human Rights Act is clearly a sensitive and delicate matter in the context of the United Kingdom's constitutional arrangements. These arrangements place ultimate authority in the sovereignty of Parliament (with the exception of the European Union where the European Court of Justice has the final say).

Section 4 of the Human Rights Act 1998 allows the courts to make a declaration of incompatibility but this excludes the striking-down of legislation. In this way the Act provides a solution to the conundrum of competing legislative and judicial powers by recognising Parliament's sovereignty as paramount. The higher courts may only make a declaration of incompatibility when it is impossible to interpret legislation in a way that is compatible with convention rights. Such a declaration is not binding on the parties. The legislation remains valid and effective. The government may bring amending legislation by way of a remedial order[22] or the government may refuse to remedy the incompatibility. This may be a ground for a complaint to the European Court of Human Rights at Strasbourg, and it leaves the government of the day the option of arguing that the legislation is, in fact, compatible with the ECHR.

In *Alconbury*, the first case of its kind, the House of Lords considered how rights set out under Article 6 of the ECHR might affect how planning decisions are made. The system of

---

[18] J. Jowell, 'Judicial deference: servility, civility or institutional capacity?' [2003] *Public Law* 592.

[19] See *Re S (Minors) (Care Order: Implementation of Care Plan)* [2002] 2 AC 291.

[20] See Lord Bingham in *R v Secretary of State for the Environment Transport and the Regions, ex parte Spath Holme Ltd* [2001] 2 AC 349 at p. 395.

[21] *R (on the application of Burkett) v Hammersmith and Fulham* [2004] All ER (D) 186 (Oct); see the comments of Lord Justice Brooke.

[22] See the Mental Health Remedial Order 2001 SI 2001/3712 *R (on the application of H) v MHRT (North and East London Region)* [2001] 3 WLR 512.

planning in the UK is important for the protection of the environment. This is achieved through the following:

- a system of development plans that allows environmental protection to be considered in policy-making. Central government issues policy guidance related to this that provides a road map of convention and practice throughout the country;

- development control which requires that acts of development must conform to planning permission from the relevant local authority. This provides an opportunity to survey matters of pollution control and engage various environmental agencies;

- the planning system, which provides the power to control activities by imposing various conditions for a grant of planning permission.

Significantly, an applicant for planning permission has a right of appeal to the Secretary of State against any refusal or any condition of planning permission. The Secretary of State is part of the planning process and hears appeals on the main issues of planning applications. When considering such appeals the Secretary of State may bring broader government policy to bear. Effectively this gives the Secretary of State the ultimate decision over planning policy and its implementation. There are no express rights for third parties and no right of appeal against a grant of planning permission. The Secretary of State's decision may be appealed to the High Court on the same basis as judicial review. Such an appeal is confined to legal issues: the courts do not intervene on the grounds of fact or policy.

In the *Alconbury* Case the High Court first examined the application of Article 6 of the ECHR under the Human Rights Act to the Secretary of State's powers. Article 6 requires that 'everyone is entitled to a fair and public hearing within a reasonable time by an independent and impartial tribunal'. Specifically at issue were the Secretary of State's powers to 'call in' an application for consideration either on his or her own initiative or on that of the planning inspectorate. The number of call-ins is, in fact, very small compared to the number of planning applications.[23] The High Court concluded that the Secretary of State's powers were inconsistent with Article 6. It was reasoned that the Secretary of State acted as both a policy-maker and a decision-maker. Judicial review was an inadequate protection because the courts had limited powers of intervention and there was not a full appeal on the merits of the case.

On appeal, the House of Lords considered the full implications of human rights for the planning system. It was held:

- that disputes involving planning matters such as compulsory purchase orders and the determination of planning conditions did involve rights protected by the convention;

- that the House of Lords reviewed many cases determined under the convention where ministers take decisions and are answerable to Parliament. Article 6, however, does not require the court to have full jurisdiction over every aspect of the powers of those making decisions on planning matters. Lord Hoffman reasoned that the jurisdiction of the courts was one that related to a full jurisdiction to deal with the merits of the case in circumstances where the nature of the decision required it;

---

[23] Richard Macrory estimates that there are about 130 call-ins out of some 500,000 applications and only 100 recovered cases out of 13,000 appeals.

- that it was not appropriate nor required that the court should have every aspect of planning law fall under the review: it was sufficient that there should be a review of the legality of the decision and of the relevant procedures followed;

- that the extent to which judicial review had been expanded over recent years was sufficient to provide the necessary protection for the individual.

The decision of the House of Lords to uphold the powers of the Secretary of State in exercising a political discretion as compatible with human rights under the Act marks a significant development in how rights may be attached to our existing system of planning and environmental protection. The Lords have recognised the development of a rights-based culture, but the area of policy and its implementation appears to fall under parliamentary accountability.

A number of important outcomes follow from the case. First, the development of a new system of planning appeals – be it a tribunal or a court – is possible, but not at the insistence of the courts. Second, rights impact on the way decisions are reached, the factual basis of the decision, and the legal principles that apply. Rights and ethics are to be found not simply through a formalistic application of rules but also through the development of policy. The *Alconbury* case underlines the role that a rights-based analysis is likely to play in the future development of environmental law in the UK.

Although the Human Rights Act 1998 has considerable potential to influence the development of environmental law this remains largely unrealised. After *Alconbury* it might be concluded that the courts are likely to adopt a relatively restrictive interpretation. At least in the initial reaction to the decision this would appear to be the case. A similarly restrictive approach has been taken in *R (on the application of Vetterlein) v Hampshire County Council.*[24] In a judicial review to the administrative court, a challenge under Article 8 (protecting the right to home and family life) was rejected. The facts concerned local taxpayers whose claim was that a proposed incinerator was a threat to the enjoyment of their home. The decision reinforces the need to show a strong connection between the harm complained of and the protection offered by Article 8. This is also consistent with the approach of the European Court of Human Rights in *Hatton* outlined above.

One of the most significant cases in recent years is the landmark decision of the House of Lords on flooding caused by sewerage in *Marcic v Thames Water Utilities Ltd.*[25] The case is illustrative of the approach the House of Lords may take to a rights-based analysis involving the environment. In *Marcic* overturning the Court of Appeal,[26] a decision that had concluded rights had been infringed, the House of Lords adopted a restrictive approach to expanding human rights into environmental rights. Thames Water's appeal to the Court of Appeal was decided on 7 February 2002. The Court of Appeal[27] took considerable account of the law of nuisance and extensively reviewed the case law which up until then had concluded that the failure of a sewage authority to lay new sewers did not constitute grounds for an action in nuisance. While accepting, in common with the High Court that Mr Marcic had no claim in damages for breach of statutory duty, the Court of Appeal considered how Thames Water was in the same position as any other landowner on whose property the hazard accumulates.

---

[24] [2001] All ER (D) 146 (Jun).
[25] *Marcic v Thames Water Utilities Ltd* [2004] 1 All ER 135.
[26] *Marcic v Thames Water Utilities Ltd* [2002] 2 All ER 55.
[27] *Marcic v Thames Water Utilities Ltd* [2002] 2 All ER 55.

Thus by adopting or continuing with a nuisance the sewage authorities had a common law duty to prevent overloaded sewers continuing. In reaching this conclusion the Court of Appeal had to consider a number of leading authorities decided in the nineteenth century. The result was that it was accepted that the courts had denied that such a common law duty might come about because Parliament had created a distinct statutory duty on the sewage authorities and this had restricted remedies to that of an enforcement notice and not actions in nuisance.[28] Instead of following that line of cases, the Court of Appeal adopted a different approach that relied on a series of cases that held that a landowner might be under a common law duty to take positive steps to remove a nuisance that was not created by the landowner.[29] Lord Phillips[30] in the Court of Appeal concluded[31] that the earlier cases had depended on distinctions between misfeasance and non-misfeasance while the more recent line of authority in *Leakey* represented a 'significant extension' to the law in laying down a general principle that owners of sewers have a duty to remedy a potential nuisance. Thus by passively allowing an inadequate sewer system to be used they might be said to have continued the nuisance.

Having decided in favour of a common law claim in nuisance, on the Human Rights Act 1998, the Court of Appeal upheld the finding made by the High Court in respect of the claim in human rights. The Court of Appeal gave particular attention to the question of whether the regulatory regime set up under the Water Act 1991 satisfied the requirements of convention rights by providing a balance between private and public interests. The Court of Appeal found that the regulatory scheme was inadequate and failed to protect Mr Marcic's convention rights. While it accepted that the rights interfered with were not unqualified and might fall within the defence under Article 8(2) as being justified where necessary on the basis of the economic well-being of the country or for the protection of the rights and freedoms of others,[32] it found that this justification was not met. The Court of Appeal agreed with the High Court that because Thames Water had failed to establish that their scheme of priorities for upgrading sewage work had struck a fair balance between the competing interests of Mr Marcic and that of the other customers, Mr Marcic's convention rights were violated. The Court of Appeal upheld the High Court analysis of how rights might be interpreted in terms of the Human Rights Act 1998.

It may be concluded that the Court of Appeal had adopted a similar approach to rights to the High Court, but did so notwithstanding their finding that Mr Marcic also had common law rights available in an action for nuisance. The potential scope for human-rights-led environmental litigation seemed to be widening as a result of the decision. At the very least, and as a result of the approach taken by the Court of Appeal, this had pointed to the inadequacy of the priorities scheme for upgrading sewers. Thames Water took action to revise the scheme in the light of criticisms made by the Court of Appeal. The Director of Ofwat also noted the concerns expressed by the Court of Appeal in a discussion paper.[33] There

---

[28] *Glossop* v *Heaton and Isleworth Local Board* (1879) 12 Ch D 102; [1874–80] All ER Rep 836; A-G v *Guardians of the Poor of Union of Dorking* (1881) 20 Ch D 595 [1881–5] All ER Rep 320.

[29] *Sedleigh-Denfield* v *O'Callaghan (Trustees for St Joseph's Society for Foreign Missions)* [1940] 3 All ER 349; *Pride of Derby and Derbyshire Angling Association Ltd* v *British Celanese Ltd* [1953] 1 All ER 179.

[30] [2002] 2 All ER 55 at p. 83 [103].

[31] See: *Goldman* v *Hargreave* [1966] 2 All ER 989; *Leakey* v *National Trust for Places of Historic Interest or Natural Beauty* [1980] 1 All ER 17.

[32] The Court of Appeal relied on *Powell* v *United Kingdom* (1990) 12 EHRR 355.

[33] Ofwat, *Flooding from Sewers – A Way Forward* March, 2002.

is also considerable potential for rethinking the exact scope of the law of nuisance, given the Court of Appeal's findings about a positive duty to abate a nuisance on a landowner. Finally it would appear from both the High Court and the Court of Appeal that more thought might be given to setting up a robust compensation scheme for flood victims. Having lost in the Court of Appeal, Thames Water appealed to the House of Lords.[34]

The House of Lords decided the appeal on 4 December 2003,[35] overturning the decision of the Court of Appeal. Lord Hoffmann and Phillips each delivered speeches. The approach taken in the House of Lords was markedly different from that of the Court of Appeal. At the outset the House of Lords considered in some detail the comprehensive nature of the Water Industry Act 1991. It was noted how the powers of making an enforcement order lay exclusively with the director, leaving the ordinary citizen with judicial review of the director's powers but with no redress in an action for damages. The statutory scheme also underlines the need for considerable expertise and specialist knowledge needed to draw up priorities and the question of what is unfair or not 'is a matter inherently more suited for decision by a regulator than by a court'.[36] This leaves the courts looking on and only adjudicating disputes when the necessity requires. There is also a common thread to this approach found in other decisions of the House of Lords with a similar line of reasoning. The courts appear to weave a delicate line, balancing Parliament's intent to allow the regulator to regulate the industry with its role to adjudicate rules for that purpose.

On the question of whether Mr Marcic had a common law action in nuisance, the House of Lords rejected the approach taken in the Court of Appeal, instead following the reasoning in the High Court. Lord Hoffmann distinguished those cases such as *Leakey* and *Goldman* relied on by the Court of Appeal to assert Mr Marcic's common law right in nuisance, as cases involving disputes between neighbouring owners of land in their capacity as landowners, from the claims that arise in disputes against a statutory sewage undertaker. In disputes between neighbours he claimed that it is 'fair and efficient to impose reciprocal duties upon each landowner to take whatever steps are reasonable to prevent his land becoming a source of injury to his neighbour'.[37] The question arises as to what measures should be taken by a statutory sewage undertaker. The answer depends on what in the courts' view is reasonable, considering the nature of a statutory undertaker. Lord Hoffmann's implicit assumption, when applying such a test, is that the court should decide the boundaries of a proportionate response when reaching its decision. Lord Hoffmann's analysis is that this is a difficult task that may fall outside the types of decisions courts are equipped to make.

> the court in such cases is performing its usual function of deciding what is reasonable as between the two different parties to the action. But the exercise becomes very difficult when one is dealing with the capital expenditure of a statutory undertaking providing public utilities on a large scale . . . This in turn raises questions of public interest. Capital expenditure on new sewers has to be financed; interest must be paid on borrowings and privatised undertakers must earn a reasonable return. The expenditure can be met only by charges paid by consumers . . . These are decisions which courts are not equipped to make in ordinary litigation.[38]

---

[34] *Marcic v Thames Water Utilities Ltd* [2004] 1 All ER 135.
[35] *Ibid.*
[36] Lord Nicholls, p. 148 [38].
[37] Lord Hoffmann, p. 153 at [62] c–d.
[38] *Ibid.*, Lord Hoffmann, p. 153 [63]–[64].

Lord Nicholls also agreed that the Court of Appeal had been wrong in applying the same standard of conduct between neighbours to the conduct required of a statutory undertaker. He held that the cause of action in nuisance was inconsistent with the statutory scheme set out in the 1991 Act. He concluded:

> The existence of a parallel common law right whereby individual householders who suffer sewer flooding may themselves bring court proceedings when no enforcement order has been made, would set at nought the statutory scheme. It would effectively supplant the regulatory role the Director was intended to discharge when questions of sewer flooding arise.[39]

The existence of the statutory scheme appears to block the possibility of the courts recognising any action in nuisance. This approach appears consistent with the view expressed by the courts in cases on negligence.[40] On that line of authority, because the common law might provide a parallel right in negligence covering the same areas of activity as the statutory arrangements, the duty of care could not be applied if its existence interfered with the ability of the statutory body to carry out its responsibilities. The House of Lords adopts this approach because of constitutional and administrative reasons. In terms of constitutional arrangements it accepts that because Parliament has allocated responsibility to the regulatory authorities then such an allocation must be respected by the courts. In administrative terms, the Director's substantial duties under Part I of the Water Industry Act 1991 are sufficient to ensure that balancing the interests of customers, shareholders, consumers and the prices charged by the sewerage companies fall within their remit. This approach preserves the autonomy of the regulator, and subject to the rare occasion for an intervention by way of judicial review, avoids the courts becoming greatly involved in the detail of regulation or having to assess its effectiveness.

On convention rights, the House of Lords departed from the interpretation offered by the High Court and the Court of Appeal. The former had concluded that the Human Rights Act with its protection of privacy and the peaceful enjoyment of possessions had been infringed in circumstances where the statutory arrangements were inadequate and where there might at best be a limited action in the common law of nuisance to remedy a positive act which had resulted in damage. The Court of Appeal had upheld the human rights point agreed by the High Court, while also holding that a remedy in nuisance might be available, not only for a positive act, but also for a failure to act and this applied in Mr Marcic's circumstances. As we have seen the House of Lords held that the remedies provided by the statutory scheme were adequate and consequently provided an adequate safeguard for Mr Marcic's rights. Also influential in reaching this conclusion was the decision of the Grand Chamber of the European Court of Human Rights in *Hatton* v *UK*[41] (see above) decided after Mr Marcic's High Court decision.

Marcic is a significant decision because it touches on common law and statutory rights as part of the consideration of environmental human rights. The House of Lords' approach illustrates a trend, in line with the judgement of the Grand Chamber of the European Court of Human Rights on night-time flights[42] in *Hatton* v *United Kingdom* reversing a previous

---

[39] Lord Nicholls, p. 147 [35].

[40] *X (Minors)* v *Bedfordshire County Council* [1995] 2 AC 633 and *Phelps* v *Hillingdon London Borough Council* [2001] 2 AC 619.

[41] *Hatton* v *United Kingdom* Application 36022/97 (2003) 37 EHRR 611.

[42] *Hatton* v *UK* [2003] All ER (D) 122 (Jul); (2004) JEL 127.

decision of the European Court of Human Rights. This judgment drew a wide margin of appreciation that allows national authorities considerable latitude and denies any special status to environmental human rights when determining environmental claims. In *Marcic* the House of Lords has shown little inclination to develop a rival interpretation of convention rights to the Strasbourg court. Interpreting the convention requires the courts to adjudicate between competing interests and striking a fair balance between the parties. In line with Lord Hoffmann's approach in *Marcic* the House of Lords has recognised the deeply complex issue of balancing interests in areas involving special expertise and competing social and economic issues. The *Marcic* case is an example in point when the House of Lords defers to the expertise of the regulator and admits the limits of its own competences. As Lord Bingham noted[43] the allocation of public resources 'is a matter for ministers and not courts'. Similarly in another leading House of Lords' decision on the call-in powers of the Secretary of State in planning appeals, Lord Hoffmann commented on how convention rights should be interpreted.

> All democratic societies recognise that while there are certain basic rights which attach to the ownership of property, they are heavily qualified by considerations of public interest.[44]

In setting general standards for review involving convention rights, the UK courts have developed considerable discretion,[45] not only, in terms of applying the proportionality test, in balancing the interest of the parties, but also in how much deference to give to convention rights.[46] The proportionality test allows the courts to consider the balance of convenience measured in outcome and effects of whether or not to review a decision of a public body.[47]

Judicial review and environmental law

Pressure groups are an important part of the political life of Britain. Professor Grant[48] has defined a pressure group as one that 'seeks to influence public policy'. Falling within the definition are a wide range of social groups, individuals and societies ranging from the formal to the informal. A pressure group, to be recognised officially, would usually have to meet the criteria of having a defined membership, stated objectives in terms of public policy, and paid staff. Pressure groups, sustained by self-interest in promoting their cause, sometimes have marked effects and can even create their own social movement.

An interesting question is whether pressure groups contribute to democracy or are anti-democratic because they represent the view of a minority. It is worth noting that in the seventeenth and eighteenth centuries private Acts of Parliament for granting specific redress were popular with the wealthy, who used them to petition Parliament for a cause. Pressure

---

[43] *R v Secretary of State for the Environment, Transport and the Regions, ex parte Spath Holm Ltd* [2001] 2 AC 349.

[44] Lord Hoffmann in *R (on the application of Alconbury) v Secretary of State for the Environment, Transport and the Regions* [2001] 2 All ER 929 at p. 980 [71].

[45] *R (on the application of Daly) v Secretary of State for the Home Department* [2001] 2 AC 532.

[46] *R on the application of Mahmood v Secretary of State for the Home Department* [2001] 1 WLR 840.

[47] *R (on the application of Daly) v Secretary of State for the Home Department* [2001] 2 All ER 532 [2001] 3 All ER 433, *R v Home Secretary of State for the Home Department ex parte Turget* [2001] 1 All ER 719.

[48] Wyn Grant, *Pressure Groups, Politics and Democracy in Britain*, 1989, p. 3; C. Harlow and R. Rawlings, *Pressure Through Law*, 1992.

group activities can be traced back to the period after the 1832 Reform Act, which broadened the franchise. Parliament became increasingly responsive to public opinion, and the contest for the popular vote spilled over into lobbying for causes or reform movements. Pressure groups lobbied for law reform on a wide range of social, economic and political issues. Popular causes included women's property rights, Catholic emancipation and the abolition of slavery. Lobbying the establishment for a vested interest or group was also popularly undertaken. Today, pressure groups undoubtedly provide an outlet for public opinion and allow grievances to be made public. They enrich the political life of the nation because they act outside party politics, allowing a plurality of interests to be represented.

A range of pressure groups are familiar today and are often identified with well-known campaigners who are prominent among their membership. Greenpeace, Friends of the Earth, and the Campaign for Nuclear Disarmament (CND) are examples of well-known environmental pressure groups; the World Development Movement is another environmental action group. Various bodies represent 'sectional' interests, such as the Royal Society, and British Medical Association. They may not appear as pressure groups but their role and tactics share some similarities, such as lobbying for their members' interests. It is estimated that business alone has over 1,800 associations representing their interests. In addition, the Confederation of British Industry (CBI) and the various trade unions represent their members' interests and engage in active lobbying and persuasion. In the recent foot-and-mouth crisis, farmers' unions representing the agricultural sector had an enormous influence on development of government policy on vaccination of the national herd. The effectiveness of pressure groups providing an outlet for public opinion has a profound influence on the democratic process. Elected politicians and government receive a mandate at the point in time when an election is held, but pressure groups have a continuous existence, well beyond the life cycle of the normal government limited to a five-year term in office. In that sense, pressure groups engage in a form of unbroken 'participatory democracy'. Ironically, they may prove a more effective opposition than the main opposition party. Their special knowledge and expertise may also help inform decision-makers. For example, the Royal Society for the Protection of Birds contributes to government policy through monitoring and reporting on bird populations. Many pressure groups have moved away from confrontation towards contributing to the process of policy-formulation, and find their views well received by policy-makers and government. Pressure groups may thus broaden the canvas of decision-making. This permits minority parties or views to be better represented.

There are, however, dangers when pressure groups assume the mantle of representing public opinion as a whole. Instead of strengthening the democratic system, pressure groups may weaken the democratic process. Samuel Brittan[49] has argued that entrenched 'industrial, economic and political interest groups' will limit what may be achieved by any economic management, new or old, attempted by government. Further dangers are that pressure groups will hide vested interest, and lobbying from financial interests may invade the political system. This may lead to financial corruption of the political system and to business practices inevitably becoming inconsistent with the parliamentary system. The 'cash for questions'

---

[49] S. Brittan, 'The economic contradictions of democracy' 5 *British Journal of Political Science* 129–59; W. Grant, 'Insider and outsider pressure groups' (January 1990) *Social Studies Review* p. 10–15; M. Smith, *Pressure Power and Policy* London: Harvester, Wheatsheaf, 1993.

affair in the 1992–7 Parliament revealed that some MPs received cash of up to £1,000 per question to ask parliamentary questions on behalf of paid lobbyists. MPs had failed to declare the payments or their financial links with lobbyists in the Parliamentary Register of Interests.

The contribution of pressure groups is an eclectic one. They may, through their activities, improve the quality of governmental policy and decisions. Inside groups, however, may achieve unwarranted influence and unduly tip the balance against a more open style of government. Within political parties, pressure groups may operate largely undetected and provide a counterbalance to the public debate outside. In the final analysis, pressure groups can be seen as an inevitable result of the close bargaining of party politics. Not everyone may join in and the temptation is to split off and join a single-issue group representing only one's pet interests. While the dangers of pressure group activity should be recognised, such groups perform the valuable task of ensuring that the distance between government and the governed does not become too great.

Pressure groups and standing

What is the role of the courts when asked by a pressure group to consider the legality of a government decision? Once the court is made aware of the perceived illegality it is very hard to resist intervening and considering the case in the usual way. The ability to mount a legal challenge may, therefore, become pivotal in changing the policy itself. There is a fear that politically motivated litigation will involve the courts in political struggles, and judges may regard such a use of judicial review as an unacceptable abuse of the proper role of the courts. Distinguishing acceptable from unacceptable motives for seeking litigation, however, may not be easy, and flexible rules of standing may permit the courts a much-needed discretion. As a result the courts have developed rules of standing that protect administrators against vexatious litigants and permit government business to be conducted without outside inter-ference. Setting limits on who may litigate helps prevent government from adopting an over-cautious and over-legalistic approach to problem-solving. It is equally true, however, that the value of interest group litigation is to bring to the attention of the courts matters that require consideration in the public interest. Not allowing standing to pressure groups would act as a disincentive for interest groups and organisations to obey the law; it may force matters to be resolved outside the law and the normal parliamentary process.

The law relating to standing, *locus standi*, is important in both private law actions and in the application for judicial review. The rules of standing set out (see below) the entitle-ment of the aggrieved citizen to seek redress in the courts for the particular remedy sought. They have a 'gatekeeping' function and provide the means to exclude vexatious litigants or unworthy cases. Standing may appear to be a procedural requirement, but procedural rules in this instance are linked to substantive issues. The arguments in favour of liberal rules of standing are compelling. Access to the courts as a means of complaint should be open to the citizen. Wide rules of standing permit the courts a large discretion in remedying the abuse of public power. This fits Dicey's view that the rule of law requires disputes as to whether acts of the government are legal ought to be decided by judges independent of the executive. This implies, as a necessary corollary of enforcing the law, that illegal conduct should be prevented or stopped. Flouting of the law may occur where the procedures for redress are inadequate. If illegality is not checked then the law has diminished in status.

There are some notable examples[50] where an individual or pressure group has taken legal action. In *Gillick*[51] the rights of an under-age schoolgirl to receive information on contraception were considered. The case was brought as part of a crusade against contraceptive advice being available to schoolgirls without the consent of their parents. The case was taken by Mrs Gillick and was broadly supported by religious groups and organisations. The Pro-Life Alliance, an anti-abortion group, has pursued legal cases directly in a legal case.[52] An intervention by the Pro-Life Alliance setting out moral issues was accepted as part of the court's consideration of the legality of a decision. These two examples highlight the unmistakable tactics of pressure groups to make use of the courts, in this case as part of an effort to protect the unborn and to advance that cause through legal rights. The courts have increasingly shown willingness to allow interested parties or groups to represent their views in cases where the interpretation of law or international agreement might require explanation or expertise. The flexibility in allowing such a development appears from the introduction of new civil procedure rules. As Harlow has noted:

> To sum up, we are seeing a shift away from the traditional bipolar and adversarial law suit familiar to common lawyers, to something more fluid, less formal and possibly less individualistic in character. By making access easier, judges are subtly changing the rules of the game. A novel public interest action is in the making, with the help of which campaigning groups are gaining entry to the legal process. No serious credentials in the form of 'democratic stake' are required of them.[53]

The 'rules of the game' include the possibility that public interest challenges, when they raise public law issues and the claimant has no private interest in the outcome of the case,[54] may be heard by the courts. Though the number of applications for judicial review[55] has increased to over 5,398 for the year 2008, per year, however, this does not reflect a marked increase in pressure group activity. In fact, judicial review cases neatly fall into four categories: those taken by homeless people, those arising out of immigration disputes, those involving the police in relation to criminal matters and matters relating to central government or cases involving local authorities.[56] One reason for pressure groups' small role in litigation is that, despite the liberalisation of the rules of standing, there is general reluctance on the part of the judiciary to encourage a widespread use of judicial review to settle disputes. There is marked sensitivity to maintaining strict discipline in applying the rules of procedure. The rules of standing are therefore important as a procedural route of access to the administrative court.

The Human Rights Act 1998 introduces a new dimension to the role of the courts. Rights issues may now be more openly addressed through legal action taken by pressure groups. There is a contrast between the 'sufficient interest' test in judicial review, outlined above, and

---

[50] See: Carol Harlow, 'Public law and popular justice' (2001) 65 *Modern Law Review* 1. Also see: D. Feldman, 'Public interest litigation and constitutional theory' (1992) *Modern Law Review* 44.

[51] *Gillick v West Norfolk and Wisbech Area Health Authority* [1986] AC 112.

[52] *Re A (Children) (Conjoined Twins: Surgical Separation)* [2001] 2 WLR 480.

[53] Harlow, *op. cit.*, pp. 7–8.

[54] *R v Lord Chancellor, ex parte Child Poverty Action Group* [1999] 1 WLR 347.

[55] Practice Statement [2002] 1 All ER 633.

[56] L. Bridges, G. Meszaros and M. Sunkin, *Judicial Review in Perspective*, 1995.

the restricted 'victim' test for standing adopted by section 6 of the Human Rights Act 1998 as part of the jurisprudence of the Strasbourg Court of Human Rights.[57]

Standing and environmental cases

The application for judicial review under Order 53 and section 31 of the Supreme Court Act 1981, (for convenience referred to as Order 53), requires consideration of the applicant's standing. The procedure under Order 53 is a two-stage process. At the first stage there is a leave requirement. Obtaining leave requires that an arguable case is made out; if this is not found leave may be refused. In practice this sets a low threshold but it may be seen as a procedural sieve or as a hurdle to be surmounted before the full hearing of the issues is considered at the second stage. There is no such leave requirement in ordinary civil actions, and the leave requirement is criticised by some as wrong in principle because it creates a special procedure for the administrative court rather than a single system of procedure.[58] The requirement of leave may, however, be justified as an important way to exclude vexatious litigants or busybodies from taking judicial review. The leave requirement, also, acts as a means to filter out hopeless or unmeritorious cases. Originally the Law Commission envisaged that the standing rule should be part of the consideration of whether to grant any of the remedies sought. As matters presently stand, however, the question of standing is raised as to the grant of leave to apply for judicial review under section 31(3) of the Supreme Court Act 1981. There remains, however, the possibility that standing may be considered also at the second stage when there is a substantive hearing of the case.

The current law of standing is explained by the House of Lords in *R v Inland Revenue Commissioners, ex parte National Federation of Self-Employed and Small Businesses*[59] (hereinafter the Fleet Street Casuals case). An application for judicial review was made by an association of taxpayers who objected to the Inland Revenue waiving the arrears of income tax for 6,000 workers in the printing industry in Fleet Street. The association objected to preferential treatment, which it viewed as condoning illegality in newspaper practices in hiring casual labour for the printing industry in Fleet Street. This case raised important issues over the interpretation of the existing law of standing but the decision unfortunately leaves uncertainty as to the precise legal principles that apply. The case favoured a flexible and liberal approach to standing but failed to set out clear principles, preferring to leave a large measure of judicial discretion and policy-making. It may be concluded that the Court of Appeal had adopted a similar approach to rights as the High Court.

The law of standing before the introduction of Order 53 varied according to the particular remedy sought. After the Fleet Street Casuals case there is still some doubt as to whether there is a single test for standing in the new procedures under Order 53. It may, thus, still remain relevant to consider the nature of the particular remedy that is sought. It is broadly accepted that in the Fleet Street Casuals case the general preference in judicial opinion was in favour of a uniform test for standing, freed from any undue procedural or technical differences based on the remedy sought. Lords Diplock, Scarman and Wilberforce agreed that standing had to

---

[57] N. Garnham, 'A Sufficient Victim?: Standing and the Human Rights Act 1998' [1999] JR 39. See: *R (on the application of Pelling) v Bow County Court* [2001] UKHRR 165.
[58] R. Rawlings, 'Courts and interests' in *A Special Relationship? American Influences on Public Law in the UK*, I. Loveland (ed.), 1995.
[59] [1982] AC 617.

be considered not in isolation but as part of the legal and factual context of the application. Lord Fraser dissented on this point but it was commonly agreed that the applicants had failed to show any breach of the duty of the Inland Revenue and that the Revenue had wide discretionary managerial powers which allowed them to make special agreements of this kind. The nature of the Revenue's discretion was such as to make it difficult to argue that policy matters did not fall within their discretion. Consequently, according to Lord Scarman, the association had failed to show sufficient interest to justify any further proceedings.

On the general matter of standing, Lords Diplock, Scarman and Roskill agreed that the law on standing was the same for all remedies. The consensus of opinion in favour of liberal rules of standing raises the question about the nature of the rules that should apply to determine standing. The judges refer to standing being determined as a question of 'mixed law and fact'. Statutory interpretation and the general context of the application are relevant to determine the nature of the applicant's interest in the case. Legal principles, rather than general discretion, are expected to be applied to determine standing, though Lord Diplock admitted that he regarded the judges as having an unfettered discretion to decide what sufficient interest may mean in a particular case. Searching for legal principles from the Fleet Street Casuals case, it emerges that every person who has a good case has standing. This might be interpreted to mean that standing no longer forms a distinct category, as every good case will fulfil the standing requirement on its merits. Standing only becomes a relevant issue for those cases where there is doubt about the merits of the discretion of a public body. This view, however, does not find universal acceptance and the matter remains uncertain.

The Fleet Street Casuals case, by joining the issue of the applicant's status and interest to the merits of the case, appears to move in favour of presuming that citizens have the right of legal redress. This does not, however, always guarantee that citizens' action is approved of by the courts. Consistent principles in this area of the law are difficult to formulate. Factors that contribute to the uncertainty include the use of the discretion of the courts. In addition, in some cases the Crown waives any consideration of standing if it considers an issue requires adjudication by the courts.

Pressure groups and judicial review

It is worthwhile to consider the issue of standing in relation to pressure groups. In *Covent Garden Community Association Ltd v Greater London Council*,[60] the Covent Garden Community Association was a company formed to protect the rights and interests of Covent Garden residents. Woolf J accepted that this gave the Association sufficient interest and therefore standing to challenge planning permission, but *certiorari* was refused on the merits of the case. A similar approach was evident in *R v Hammersmith and Fulham Borough Council, ex parte People Before Profit*,[61] where a company limited by guarantee sought leave to object to the local authority's grant of planning permission after a planning report, following a public inquiry, had favoured objectors. Standing was established because any person (individual or company)[62] was entitled to object in a planning matter, provided they were bona fides

---

[60] [1981] JPL 183.

[61] (1981) 80 LGR 322.

[62] In *Wheeler v Leicester City Council* [1985] AC 1054 Lord Roskill accepted that the appeal was in reality to do with the club, and this was accepted.

and had reasonable grounds. The application was refused, however, because the case was not a reasonable one.

A more fundamental objection to citizens challenging decisions appears from *R v Secretary of State for the Environment, ex parte Rose Theatre Trust Co.*[63] Schiemann J considered the standing of a trust formed from local residents, renowned archaeological experts and leading actors who applied for judicial review to preserve a site in London that was claimed to be the remains of the Rose Theatre and of great historical interest. The case raised the fundamental question of the role of a pressure group and the law of standing. Leave was granted to apply for judicial review but the question of standing became a central issue at the full hearing of the application. Schiemann J considered whether standing was established. He observed that even after leave was granted, the court which hears the application ought to consider whether the applicant has sufficient interest. Whether an applicant has sufficient interest is not purely a matter for the court's discretion. Not every member of the public can complain of every breach of statutory duty. The fact that[64] 'some thousands of people join together and assert that they have an interest does not create an interest if the individuals did not have an interest.' Having a particular power within its memorandum to pursue a particular objective does not create for a company an interest in the case. It remains to be seen whether this restrictive view of public interest litigation will be followed by the courts in future.

The *Rose Theatre* case adopts an approach that emphasises the importance of establishing a sufficient interest even if the effect is to allow the legality of the Secretary of State's powers to remain unchallenged. In deciding that the applicants failed to meet the standing requirement the question of who might have sufficient standing was also considered, and it was concluded that 'no individual has the standing to move for judicial review'. This reasoning appears unduly protective of the powers of the Secretary of State, but the interpretation may arise from the particular statutory arrangements under section 1 of the Ancient Monuments and Archaeological Areas Act 1979, which did not envisage any appeal or review. It may also be, however, that the courts are reluctant to become an instrument of pressure group activity and to develop public interest litigation, for two reasons: first, administrative pressures on the courts to cope with the increased volume of judicial review, and second, a concern that policy formulation is best left to parliamentary supervision rather than judicial review.

Greenpeace has been particularly active in monitoring radioactive waste. Mr Justice Otton in *R v Inspectorate of Pollution, ex parte Greenpeace Ltd*[65] described how the organisation had nearly 5 million supporters worldwide, with 400,000 supporters in the United Kingdom, about 2,500 of whom lived in the Cumbria region where the British Nuclear Fuels plant was situated. On that basis, sufficient standing was established to allow a legal challenge to be considered by the courts.

The Law Commission, in their report on administrative law,[66] acknowledged that interest groups may have good grounds for having standing in the public interest to make an application for judicial review. This might apply in cases where the pressure group feels that the public are adversely affected by an administrative decision of a government agency or government itself. Clearly there is some flexibility in permitting pressure groups a role

[63] [1990] 1 QB 504.
[64] *Ibid.*, per Mr Justice Schiemann, p. 516.
[65] [1994] 1 WLR 570.
[66] Law Commission, *Administrative Law: Judicial Review and Statutory Appeals* Report No. 226 (1994).

in bringing public interest matters before the courts. Concern arises out of the *Rose Theatre* case, however, if interpreted to mean that in the absence of an express statutory right the ordinary citizen is debarred from challenging decisions, even where it appears that there may be a public interest served by such a challenge. This may leave a gap in the arrangements for public challenge and may restrict standing to a few.

The broad liberalisation of the rules of standing since the Fleet Street Casusals case raises the question of whether the rules of standing are required today. The Woolf Reforms on civil procedure provide a case management system sufficient to act in a gatekeeper function. Standing may therefore be seen as less of a substantive hurdle to be overcome, but more as an unnecessary procedural requirement. In terms of developing systems for the simplification of the procedures for judicial review, rules of standing may be substituted by the exercise of a straightforward judicial discretion on the merits of each case.

Pressure or lobby groups often play a controversial role and in recent years their activities have become more significant in the area of legal challenge. One of the most noteworthy judicial review cases brought by a pressure group is the Pergau Dam case (see Case study, below).

CASE STUDY

Protecting the environment through judicial review

At both the national and international levels, pressure groups such as Friends of the Earth, Greenpeace, and the World Development Movement have been active campaigners and lobbyists for better protection of the environment and changes in government policy. In *R v Secretary of State for Foreign and Commonwealth Affairs, ex parte World Development Movement*,[67] the World Development Movement successfully challenged payments from the overseas aid budget to build a dam in Malaysia. The World Development Movement was described as 'a non-partisan group, over 20 years old and limited by guarantee' that has 7,000 full voting members throughout the United Kingdom with a total supporter base of some 13,000. There are about 200 local groups, and campaign activities include letter-writing and petitioning MPs. The Pergau Dam case marks an unusual and significant use of public assess to official documents and greater transparency in government decision-making. The pressure group relied on information obtained through a National Audit Office report and information gleaned from debates within, and evidence taken by, the Public Accounts Committee and the Foreign Affairs Committee.[68] The National Audit Office and the Public Accounts Committee assumed the legality of the aid but criticised aspects of its value for money. The National Audit Office regarded the allocation of money as falling under policy matters within the remit of ministers. This excluded the merits of the policy from its consideration. It appeared, however, that the Accounting Officer had serious reservations about the project. As Lord Justice Rose noted, the Accounting Officer's view was that the Pergau project was 'an abuse of

➡

---

[67] [1995] 1 All ER 611.

[68] Pergau Hydro-Electric Project HC 155 (1994/5) See F. White, I. Harden and K. Donnelly, 'Audit, accounting officers and accountability: the Pergau Dam affair' [1994] *Public Law* 526.

the aid programme in the terms that this is an uneconomic project' and that 'it was not a sound development project.'[69] Despite such reservations, written ministerial instructions were given to proceed with the financial aid. The Pergau project was funded, purportedly under section 1 of the Overseas Development and Cooperation Act 1980. Considering whether the aid for the Pergau dam fell within the ambit of the 1980 Act, Lord Justice Rose concluded:

> [a]ccordingly, where, as here, the contemplated development is, on the evidence, so economically unsound that there is no economic argument in favour of the case, it is not, in my judgment, possible to draw any material distinction between questions of propriety and regularity on the one hand and questions of economy and efficiency of public expenditure on the other.[70]

The Secretary of State under section 1(1) of the 1980 Act had extensive powers as follows:

> The Secretary of State shall have power, for the purpose of promoting the development or maintaining the economy of a country or territory outside the United Kingdom, or the welfare of its people, to furnish any person or body with assistance, whether financial, technical or of any other nature.

The case hinged on the interpretation of this section. Was the grant in question 'for the purpose of promoting the development' of Malaysia? This depended on whether the aid flowed into a development that might be described, according to the Foreign Office test for funding development, as one that was 'sound, financially viable and [would] bring economic benefits'. As doubts had been expressed during the consultation process within the government departments, the divisional court held that the provision of aid was *ultra vires* the 1980 Act. As a result of this decision, the Comptroller and Auditor-General qualified his opinion of the aid on the basis of irregularity. Despite this finding and the decision of the divisional court, the government found the necessary additional aid required to finance the dam from a repayable charge on the Contingency Fund. Eventually the money was found from the Reserve Fund.

The World Development Movement was able to show how the dam project had limited use in terms of promoting development but had enormous potential for encouraging arms sales and other markets for UK companies. The project also failed on the criteria of its potential damage to the environment and limited benefits for the community. Evidence used in the case provided a broad cost–benefit analysis of the project, beyond the narrow view of the government in favour of economic trade. The case signifies that issues of the legality of public expenditure may involve questions of value for money. There is a stark warning here. As Lord Justice Rose noted, the government had taken no legal advice in the first instance on the legality of the aid; and as Daintith and Page observe:

> The question of the relationship between the legislation and the Department's power to incur expenditure subject only to the authority of the Appropriation Act does not appear to have been raised or discussed.[71]

---

[69] [1995] 1 All ER 611 at 617A–B.
[70] [1995] 1 All ER 611 at 626J–627B.
[71] T. Daintith and A. Page, *The Executive in the Constitution*, 1999, p. 35.

There are a number of reform proposals, such as the possibility of setting up a Director of Civil Proceedings[72] as an alternative to individual public interest litigation. The Lord Chancellor has argued that a Community Legal Service may provide sufficient cover to canvass issues of judicial review and human rights. Lobbyists and pressure groups, however, display unabated enthusiasm for litigation. Indeed, today, there appear to be a plethora of groups willing to campaign for individual rights as well as common causes. As Harlow has noted:

> [a] new Public Interest Advisory Panel, designed to 'represent consumers', advises the Legal Service Commission and several leading public advocacy groups including the Public Law project, the Legal Action Group and JUSTICE have been involved. Some – Liberty, the Public Law Project and the Joint Council for the Welfare of Immigrants – have also signed contracts to provide back-up and training services to the Community Legal Service in their area of expertise and to maintain telephone help lines and web sites.[73]

There is an inherent problem in shifting democratic participation from the parliamentary political process to courts. This problem is exemplified in the Pergau Dam case (see Case study, above), where government policy, however misconceived, eventually prevailed over the technical legal arguments accepted by the courts. The World Development Movement is an effective pressure group with international standing, and that can hardly be questioned, but as a representative group of the public at large it appears to be a small minority. However worthy its cause, pressure group activity has the potential for abuses of the legal process. Until the day the United Kingdom creates a constitutional court and a written constitution delineating the boundaries of legal and political power, the ultimate parliamentary authority and sovereignty vested in the government of the day prevails. Meanwhile, confusion and lack of clarity remain over how legal and political authority may best be defined and where the boundaries between them should be drawn.

Environmental democracy, rights and justice

A human rights perspective on the environment has the effect of prioritising the need for environmental information and transparency. Citizen participation also accompanies the analysis that better decision-making is the result of more open discussion and consultation. As Richardson and Razzaque attest, public participation has 'become an indelible feature of many regulatory systems world-wide over the past few decades'.[74] Principle 10 of the Rio Convention alludes to the principle of information availability and participation of citizens. It continues thus:

> At the national level, each individual shall have appropriate access to information concerning the environment that is held by public authorities, including information on hazardous materials and activities in their communities, and the opportunity to participate in decision-making process. States shall facilitate and encourage public awareness and participation by making information widely available. Effective access to judicial and administrative proceedings including redress and remedy, shall be provided.

[72] Sir Harry Woolf, 'A possible programme for reform' [1992] *Public Law* 221.
[73] Harlow, *op. cit.*, p. 9.
[74] B.J. Richardson and J. Razzaque, 'Public paricipation in environmental decision-making' in B.J. Richardson and S. Wood, *Environmental Law for Sustainability* Oxford: Hart Publishing, 2006, p. 164.

The question arises as to the extent the above aspirations are fully met by the United Kingdom. The answer may be found in the Aarhus Convention and its implementation. The Aarhus Convention[75] is a UN convention that was signed in 1998 and came into force in October 2001. It builds on the Rio Declaration and provides a link between citizenship, the protection of the environment and participation in environmental issues. The key elements are built around the essential idea that, in order to protect the environment adequately, there is recognition of the environment as a basic human right, linked to the right to life. As already mentioned, the Aarhus Convention links environmental justice, environmental information and the right of participation. These three pillars, as they have become known, require elucidation. The convention provides a broad definition of environmental information to include information on policy and government decisions and actions. There is a timetable of one month for the release of information and its proper dissemination. On participation there is an expectation that public authorities should consult with citizens and that the consultation process should be a substantial one. Comments and analysis are expected to be fed back to policy-makers with an opportunity for the policy-making to take account of the information. Finally, there is the idea that justice requires appropriate judicial remedies.

Today, there is a plethora of public registers available to every citizen that make finding and disseminating information about the environment much easier than in the past. This has partly addressed the information pillar of the Aarhus Convention, and is a welcome development. It provides the citizen with access to the working of government in a much greater way than in the past. It must be remembered that much of the technical information that is available requires careful analysis and this may be beyond the reach of the average citizen. Lobby groups and pressure groups are likely to find the information very useful. Regulators such as the Environment Agency in England and Wales perform a useful function of communicating the information and data and making it available on their own website. Building up a general analysis of the state of the environment is a difficult and time-consuming activity. Understanding how best to protect the environment is, however, inextricably and undoubtedly linked to making best use of the available information on the environment.

Environmental information

The EU response to implementing the Aarhus Convention has been through a number of directives. The main Directive 2003/4/EC provides access to environmental information held by public authorities and relevant bodies under their control. The implementation of this directive in United Kingdom law is discussed below. There are some exemptions from access such as commercial information or where there are matters of national security or legal proceedings. There is a requirement of a prompt response or within two months. There is also a system of appeals. Additional to these arrangements are requirements that apply to the various institutions of the EU. The European Commission and Council are formally included in a *Code of Conduct on Public Access to Commission and Council Documents*. This has been followed up by the inclusion of Article 255 of the EC Treaty of a right to documents held by the European Parliament and Commission. Eventually this gave rise to Regulation 1049/2001

---

[75] *The United Nations Convention on Access to Information, Public Participation in Decision-making and Access to Justice in Environmental Matters*, June 1998, signed at Aarhus Denmark and known as the Aarhus Convention.

on Public Access to European Parliament, Council and Commission Documents covering all the main European institutions. A further broadening to a general right to information for EU citizens has occurred and this includes corporate entities under Article 2(1). Environmental information is at the heart of the role of the European Environment Agency. This has given rise to transparency regulations such as Regulation 1641/2003. Access to environmental information in general is greatly fascilitated by the Agency, and its excellent website,[76] provides a much-needed resource on policy, implementation and statistical data on each of the member states and their progress on environmental protection.

The United Kingdom has taken steps to implement the requirements of Directive 2003/4/EC. The main source of the implementation may be found in the Environmental Information Regulations 1992.[77] This is in marked contrast to its historical approach to information. Excessive secrecy has been the hallmark of the United Kingdom's past approach to the environment. Partly motivated by commercial and business interests, there has always been a general presumption in favour of secrecy that covers most of the workings of the civil service and government. The legislation that applied to environmental pollution often mirrored this approach.[78] There is a marked change today in both culture and legal attitude within the UK. A number of statutory arrangements provide access to environmental information on a scale that hitherto has not occurred. The Control of Pollution Act 1974 provides access to information on discharges to water and under the Environmental Protection Act 1990 there is access to information on waste management operations. The Local Government (Access to Information) Act 1985 was another step in the direction of transparency through providing better information on planning matters. Some general legal frameworks also provide access to environmental information from local authorities. In this regard, the Freedom of Information Act 2000, supported by the Environmental Information Regulations 2004[79], is relevant. The local authorities hold public registers of information specifically for the purpose of allowing citizen access. A formal request is required in many instances but there is also a general access right to information.

In fact, the Freedom of Information Act 2000 has only limited impact on access to environmental information. The Environmental Information Regulations 2004 help the public establish, subject to various exemptions, the existence of environmental information and whether access may be given. The request must normally be in writing along with a description of the information. The application is subject to a list of exemptions, which are technically difficult because there are qualified exemptions as well as absolute exemptions; section 39 states that environmental information is qualified. The main consideration is whether the public interest in maintaining an exemption is justified. This justification in the public interest does not apply to an absolute exemption. Underpinning the Freedom of Information regime are a number of key procedures, various Codes of Practice and an Information Commissioner. The Information Commissioner has the power to instruct public authorities to disclose information. Environmental information may, then, become available under the 2000 Act, but the application of the Environmental Information Regulations 2004 is in fact required in most cases.

---

[76] Also see the European Environment Information and Observation Network (EIONET). See the Environment Agency at *www.eea.eu.int*.

[77] SI 1992/3240.

[78] See: The Rivers (Prevention of Pollution) Act 1961 and the Health and Safety at Work etc. Act 1974.

[79] SI 2004/3391.

Directive 2003/4/EC is implemented through the application of the Environmental Information Regulations 2004. This places all public authorities under a duty to provide 'environmental information' to the public. The definition of environmental information can be found under Regulation 1 and is sufficiently broad to cover the bulk of the information relevant to the environment. The definition of 'public authorities' is also broad and includes the various key regulators and government departments. Local authorities, the Environment Agency and bodies with an environmental duty are included in the definition, as are the various privatised utilities.

The procedures for obtaining environmental information require that information be made available within 20 working days of receipt of the request. This may be extended to 40 days if the request is complex. There are rules about refusing to give the requested information. It is possible for a refusal that neither denies nor accepts that the information is available in circumstances where knowledge of the very existence of the information may be prejudicial. There are circumstances where refusal is because the request is vague, or unreasonable. Equally there are matters of protecting personal data or internal communication or where the material information is incomplete. There is a range of exempt information where information may be refused disclosure. The existence of exempt information may affect the disclosure if it adversely affects one of the exempted categories of information. There is an appeal system if the applicant is refused the information sought.

Exempt information includes information that would adversely affect matters such as international relations, defence, national security or public safety. Also included is information which may affect the course of justice or where disclosure might affect a fair trial. Exempt information may also include intellectual property rights, confidentiality of proceedings or, where this is required by law, commercial confidentiality. In addition, it includes information that has been voluntarily supplied to the public authority or information that would adversely affect the environment.

Public registers

There is a long-standing culture in the United Kingdom of using public registers as a means of providing public information. The different categories of public register are based on statutory provisions that cover a wide range of interests and specialist areas from contaminated land to water resources. Access to the various registers is provided through Defra's website *www.defra.gov.uk/environment*. This provides a comprehensive and detailed list of the various types of information, their location and how to access them. The coverage includes[80] the main areas of the environment where information is required. The Environment Agency itself holds a number of public registers that are accessible online (Table 6.1). Other environmental registers are organised around information on contaminated land, genetically modified organisms, industrial processes, planning, trade effluent, waste management, water resources abstraction licences and water discharge consents.

There are some common rules and procedures that apply to all public registers. These include the hours and stipulated conditions for the availability of the information and the

---

[80] Air, eco-design, energy, environmental impact assessment, energy labelling, environmental management systems, environmental reporting, genetically modified organisms, pesticides, planning radiological surveillance, sustainable development, waste, water and wildlife.

Table 6.1 Public registers available from the Environment Agency

Waste related registers	Pollution related registers
Hazardous waste	Water quality and pollution control
Waste carriers	Integrated pollution prevention and control (IPPC)
Waste brokers	Integrated pollution control (IPC)
Waste management licensing	Radioactive substances information

facility for photocopies to be made. There are also details of the information held, the operation of exemptions such as disclosure of information that might affect national security or commercial confidentiality, and the rights of appeal that may be exercised for the failure to disclose certain information.

The complexity and number of registers leaves a lot to be desired. There is a strong case for simplification of the system of public registers and their interconnection. There is a wide discretion provided to the relevant authority not to disclose information especially if the request is too vague, unreasonable or the information is not held or is incomplete.[81] The question of whether the information is complete and therefore capable of being disclosed can be subject to judicial review.

The question arises as to the adequacy of access to environmental information in the United Kingdom today. As noted above, there has undoubtedly been considerable progress in developing a more transparent approach to environmental information and to subjecting the information to public scrutiny. There is, however, considerable discretion and ambiguity in the scope of obligations. In the main, the role of the Information Commissioner is critical to the operation of the system. The technical nature of the information available on the environment requires careful explanation and analysis, and it may not be easily interpreted by many people. The use of the internet has greatly fascilitated the dissemination of information and its availability to the wider public. Greater transparency and access to environmental information undoubtedly helps pressure groups and politicians as well as the media and journalists examine and prioritise environmental problems. Access to environmental information can be seen as a key element in the provision of environmental rights, since it provides a route to obtain important and otherwise largely unobtainable data on environmental quality.

Conclusions

UK courts and other national courts may provide the best way to go forward in developing and protecting environmental rights. A compliance and enforcement strategy, however, is needed if environmental rights are to progress. Consider the environmental problems posed by war and armed conflict. Controlling such impacts would involve the application of general rules of environmental protection as part of the international law of war and would probably also include limits on the use of different types of weapons. Such rules would

---

[81] See: *Maile v Wigan Metropolitan Borough Council* [2001] Env LR 11.

be exceptionally difficult to agree internationally and enforce. This is perhaps an extreme example of how environmental issues are integral to human rights, particularly rights associated with the home or person. There are many occasions when the activity of commercial organisations has considerable environmental consequences and may interfere with individual human rights. In fact community rights may be easier to apply than the rights of states in these contexts. It is certainly useful to consider the potential for extending environmental rights further than at present.

Judicial review procedures have proved useful in the environmental field by allowing pressure groups to bring actions against public authorities. There is a requirement of standing (*locus standi*) in judicial review procedures. Generally this has been interpreted liberally[82] and allowed environmental groups to challenge decisions where environmental issues arise. Greenpeace was successful in being granted standing in a challenge to the THORP reprocessing plant at Sellafield[83] on the basis of their expertise and standing as an environmental group. Members of a local preservation society were also allowed standing to appear at an inquiry and were entitled to challenge the legality of the order[84] in a planning matter. One of the most significant examples is the Pergau Dam case[85] involving the World Development Movement, a pressure group, in a challenge to the legality of aid granted by the Secretary of State for Foreign Affairs to fund the construction of the controversial Pergau Dam in Malaysia. The World Development Movement relied on assessments of possible environmental impacts and their own expertise to question the economics of the project. Through reports compiled by the National Audit Office, the financial watchdog, it was possible to question the legality of the funding and it was revealed that the Accounting Officer for the department had concerns about the project. This gave rise to a successful challenge in the courts based on the public interest to allow the World Development Movement to take its case. There is no guarantee of success[86] in such cases as the courts are limited in their role. The functions of policy-makers and decision-makers are usually left outside the discretion of the courts.

Judicial review has offered limited scope to develop environmental rights, but it has gained access to the courts for pressure groups[87] and other interested parties.[88] Even liberal standing rules set by the courts are not always applied,[89] as when Schiemann J, as he then was, considered the standing of a local group of residents who formed a pressure group to preserve the site of the Rose Theatre, said to be of great historical interest. The pressure group included archaeological experts and leading actors who had formed a small company to protest against the development. Standing was refused because the pressure group was perceived as attempting to develop a form of public interest litigation which was denied by the court.

Even before the Human Rights Act 1998 came into force, the European Convention of Human Rights had a limited influence in helping to develop the potential scope of judicial

---

[82] *Inland Revenue Commissioners* v *National Federation of Self-Employed and Small Businesses Ltd* [1982] AC 617.

[83] *R* v *HM Inspectorate of Pollution, ex parte Greenpeace Ltd (No. 2)* [1994] 4 All ER 329.

[84] *Turner* v *Secretary of State for the Environment* (1973) 28 P & CR 123.

[85] *R* v *Secretary of State for Foreign and Commonwealth Affairs, ex parte World Development Ltd* [1995] 1 WLR 386.

[86] *R* v *Swale Borough Council ex parte RSPB* [1991] 1 PLR 6.

[87] See C. Harlow, 'Public law and popular justice' (2002) 65(1) *Modern Law Review* 1 and D. Feldman, 'Public interest litigation and constitutional theory' (1992) *Modern Law Review* 44.

[88] *R* v *Hammersmith and Fulham Borough Council, ex parte People Before Profit* (1981) 80 LGR 322.

[89] *R* v *Secretary of State for the Environment, ex parte Rose Theatre Trust Co* [1990] 1 QB 504.

review[90] and extend the intensity of review when rights were involved.[91] Despite developing a more sensitive approach to fundamental rights, however, generally the courts acted in deference to the decisions of the executive. The basis for such self-restraint was an unwillingness to encroach on executive powers, and the absence of rights in domestic law. The Human Rights Act 1998 provided a basis for judicial discretion to adopt rights at the centre of the jurisprudence of the courts.[92] In that context, the question is how far will the Human Rights Act advance environmental litigation?

Environmental litigation gives rise to the possibility of the protection of the individual from agents or substances that may cause a danger to health or impair the quality of life. English tort law, for example has been slow to develop damages in respect of mental distress or loss of amenity.[93] Only by adding convention rights to the common law claims in negligence or nuisance might it be possible to develop the law in this broad direction. There is room to think that this might occur. In the case of *Dennis* v *Ministry of Defence*[94] the Divisional Court considered the impact of the Human Rights Act on the law of nuisance in a case brought against the Ministry of Defence in respect of noise caused by the operation of military aircraft near Wilmot Hall, a large estate near an RAF station. The claim in nuisance depended on expert evidence on the impact of the levels of noise on the estate. This included its potential commercial impact as well as the annoyance caused to the residents of the estate. In considering a traditional nuisance case, the courts weigh up the balance of interests between the parties to consider whether any interference with the enjoyment of property has been infringed. In addition to the nuisance claim, in *Dennis* v *Ministry of Defence* it was argued that Article 8 of the Convention was breached as the aircraft noise caused interference with respect for private and family life. Convention rights seemed to tip the scales in weighing the public interest in favour of providing a claim for compensation while allowing the aircraft to continue to fly. This approach to rights fell short of providing grounds for the court to grant an injunction but it satisfied the discretion of the court to award damages. As a result the Divisional Court awarded damages of £950,000. This marked a flexible approach to rights and the potential to develop rights more generally in the area of environmental litigation where the quality of life is impaired by a nuisance.

The *Marcic* decision of the House of Lords was decided after the decision of the Divisional Court in *Dennis*. It is clear that the *Marcic* approach is different from the approach taken in *Dennis* and this has far-reaching consequences. It shows a marked reluctance to allow rights to develop beyond the existing case law of the ECHR or to allow a rights-based approach to extend the common law of nuisance or negligence. *Marcic* is also consistent with other decisions of the House of Lords[95] where, in considering the general development of judicial review, the House has shown a traditional self-restraint in terms of deferring to the executive on the basis of a separation of powers between Parliament and the courts.[96] Lord Hoffmann,

---

[90] *Bugdaycay* v *Secretary of State for the Home Department* [1987] AC 514, the role of rights in deportation matters.

[91] *R* v *Ministry of Defence, ex parte Smith* [1996] QB 517, the role of rights when considering sexuality when dismissed from the armed forces.

[92] See *R* v *Secretary of State for the Home Department, ex parte Simms* [2000] 2 AC 115.

[93] *Hunter* v *London Canary Wharf Ltd* [1997] 2 All ER 426.

[94] *Dennis* v *Ministry of Defence* [2003] 2 EGLR 121.

[95] See *R (on the application of Alconbury Development Ltd)* v *Secretary of State for the Environment, Transport and the Regions* [2001] 2 AC 295.

[96] See *R* v *Secretary of State for the Home Department, ex parte Daly* [2001] 3 All ER 433.

in a lecture to the Common Law Bar Association,[97] a month after the passage of the Human Rights Act 1998 and before the Act came into force, predicted that the potential impact of the Act 'has been greatly exaggerated'. In interpreting legislation and convention rights under the Human Rights Act 1998, the courts have a wide discretion but equally this margin of appreciation gives government considerable latitude. Convention rights that are most likely to be raised in environmental claims come within a broad band of discretion when reviewing the compatibility of state action by the authorities with convention rights.

In interpreting common law rights in the past the UK courts have given 'special weight' to interpreting a citizen's rights in terms of access to the courts, which in the words of Lord Justice Laws, 'could not be abrogated except by express statutory words'.[98] Prior to the enactment of the Human Rights Act 1998, the courts had been ready to adapt various areas of the law on defamation,[99] confidentiality,[100] free speech and personal privacy[101] and this might have developed in a way that gave environmental rights some recognition, as part of a broader canvass of 'citizens' rights'. At least one leading writer[102] believed that 'the impact of the Act on both statute-based and common law of tort is bound to be immense'. In contrast, in the environmental field, the House of Lords in *Marcic* has shown marked reluctance to develop convention rights within the law of tort covering actions for negligence and nuisance, even in circumstances when the statutory arrangements as in *Marcic* were inadequate in terms of compensation provision. Since *Marcic* follows the Grand Chamber's decision in *Hatton*, there is no 'special approach' or 'special status' to be given to environmental human rights.[103] The *Marcic* decision stands out as one that illustrates a marked 'conservatism' in the approach taken by the courts when dealing with the environment, in marked contrast to the approach taken in other areas of the law such as freedom of speech and expression. This illustrates a reluctance to develop rights beyond the boundaries set by the European Court of Human Rights.

Environmental law is by its nature bound up with complex public and private policy considerations. This often involves technical economic and fiscal instruments deserving of specialist treatment before qualified adjudicators. Environmental regulation[104] involving environmental liability is also difficult and requires special expertise. If the courts had adopted a more broadly based rights-approach to environmental claims, what would be the probable consequences? It is unlikely to lead to widespread litigiousness, although after the original decision of the European Court of Human Rights in *Hatton* there was widespread media concern that 'thousands of claims' would arise:[105] unfounded, as the case was reversed by the Grand Chamber. However much an increase in litigation is feared, the practicalities need to be noted. Generally environmental litigation is narrowly confined to pressure groups

---

[97] Lord Hoffmann 'Human rights and the House of Lords' (1999) 62 *Modern Law Review* 159 at p. 161.

[98] *R v Lord Chancellor, ex parte Witham* [1998] QB 575 at p. 585.

[99] *AG v Observer Ltd and Times Newspapers* [1990] 1 AC 109 and *Reynolds v Times Newspapers Ltd* [1999] 3 WLR 1010.

[100] See: A. Lester, in J. Jowell and D. Oliver (eds), *The Changing Constitution* Oxford: Oxford University Press, 2004, p. 83.

[101] *Ibid.*

[102] C. Gearty, 'Tort law and the Human Rights Act' in Tom Campbell, K.D. Ewing and Adam Tomkins, *Sceptical Essays on Human Rights* Oxford: Oxford University Press, 2001, p. 245.

[103] See: P. Cane 'Are environmental harms special?' (2001) 13 JEL 3.

[104] Mark Stallworthy, 'Environmental liability and the impact of statutory authority' (2004) 15 JEL 2003.

[105] David Hart and Marina Wheeler, 'Analysis' *Journal of Environmental Law* Vol. 16 no. 1 (2004) p. 132.

and individuals who are adversely affected by pollution or other environmental harm through no fault of their own. Lawyers specialising in this area of the law are often dependent on public funds and are often inhibited by costs and the technical complexity of the cases. Environmental justice requires that there should be adequate legal redress and that civil litigation ought to facilitate members of the public to challenge acts of public authorities involving environmental claims. There is the general question of the inadequate compensation available to those that suffer the effects of night flights or the escape of sewerage onto their property. Environmental litigation might seem to offer some solution in the absence of adequate statutory compensatory arrangements. This appears to be problematic, however, not least because of *Marcic* but also because of the high costs of litigation, a point of concern raised by Lord Justice Brooke recently in the Court of Appeal.[106]

The future of environmental human rights litigation in the UK may have suffered a setback because of the House of Lords in *Marcic*. Human rights issues, however, are continually being taken and argued in suitable cases. This is clear from cases that are decided in the lower courts up to the Court of Appeal. There are signs that the lower courts are prepared to consider rights when dealing with environmental matters even though the outcome may be disappointing to the claimant. In *Andrews v Reading Borough Council*,[107] a case concerning a road traffic regulation order, Article 8 issues were raised when the claimant argued that noise levels from traffic flows infringed his convention rights. The case was not struck out because of the *Marcic* decision. The availability of a discretion to provide grants for double insulation of a home only applied where there had been a physical alteration to the highway. This was inapplicable to the claimant's case, leaving him with no claim. This might be an arguable point in terms of interference with the claimant's convention rights.

There is considerable pragmatism in how environmental human rights are likely to be viewed by the courts. In considering third party rights to respect for privacy and peaceful enjoyment at major planning decisions, the Court of Appeal in *Lough v First Secretary of State*[108] showed reluctance to use convention right to change the way planning decisions are reached. The degree of seriousness in the effect on the individual must be substantial before the courts will hold that there has been any breach of convention rights.[109] The decision-maker is supposed to take account of human rights as an intrinsic part of decision-making, leaving the courts a limited role to intervene.[110]

In the future it might be possible for the House of Lords to decide in a suitable case to depart from the Grand Chamber decision in *Hatton* and thereby offer a rival interpretation to the narrow interpretation of environmental human rights. It remains to be seen, in the absence of a specialist Environmental Court (see Chapter 7), whether or not in the future the UK courts will be willing to take a lead in the development of environmental human rights. The signs are not optimistic. There is a sensitivity on the part of the judiciary not to review policy matters – especially when environmental issues are sensitive and often carry significant cost effects.

---

[106] *R (on the application of Burkett) v London Borough of Hammersmith and Fulham London Borough Council* [2004] All ER (D) 186 (Oct).

[107] [2004] All ER (D) 319 (Apr).

[108] [2004] 1 WLR 2557.

[109] See *R (on the application of Paul Rackham Ltd) v Swaffham Magistrates' Court and the Environment Agency* [2004] LLR 759 on the uncertainty of the definition of waste giving rise to arguments about incompatibility with the convention.

[110] See: *R (on the application of Fisher) v English Nature* [2004] 4 All ER 861.

Further reading

R. Barnes, *Property Rights and Natural Resources* Oxford: Hart Publishing, 2007.

A. Boyle and M. Anderson (eds), *Human Rights Approaches to Environmental Protection* Oxford: Clarendon Press, 1996.

E. Brandl and H. Bungert, 'Constitutional entrenchment of environmental protection: a comparative analysis of experiences abroad (1992) 16(1) *Harvard Environmental Law Review* 1–100.

R.D. Bullard, *The Quest for Environmental Justice: Human Rights and the Politics of Pollution* California: UCLA Press, 2005.

S. Coyle and K. Morrow, *The Philosophical Foundations of Environmental Law: Property, Rights and Nature* Oxford: Hart Publishing, 2004.

T. Hayward, *Constitutional Environmental Rights* Oxford: Oxford University Press, 2005.

M. Hunt, *Using Human Rights Law in English Courts* Oxford: Hart Publishing, 1998.

B. Richardson and S. Wood, *Environmental Law for Sustainability* Oxford: Hart Publishing, 2006.

Select bibliography

A. Dobson, *Justice and the Environment* Oxford: Oxford University Press 1998.

J. Hancock, *Environmental Human Rights: Power, Ethics and Law* Aldershot: Ashgate, 2003.

W. Howarth, 'Environmental human rights and parliamentary democracy (2002) 14 *Journal of Environmental Law* pp. 353–89.

J.G. Merrills, 'Environmental protection and human rights: conceptual aspects' in A.E. Boyle and M. Anderson (eds) *Human Rights Approaches to Environmental Protection* Oxford: Clarendon Press, 1996.

T. Pogge, *World Poverty and Human Rights: Cosmopolitan Responsibilities and Reforms* Cambridge Malden: Polity Press/Blackwell, 2002.

D. Shelton, 'Environmental rights' in P. Alston, *People's Rights* Oxford: Oxford University Press, 2001.

M. Stallworthy, 'Whether environmental human rights?' (2005) 7 *Environmental Law Review* 12–33.

J. Waldron (ed.), *Theories of Rights* Oxford: Oxford University Press, 1984.

Visit **http://www.mylawchamber.co.uk/mceldowney**
to access key issue checklists and practice exam
questions to test yourself on this chapter.

7 Regulation, standards and the environment

Introduction

Our discussion in previous chapters has clearly illustrated the distinctive nature of environmental law. We have seen, during its historical transition, the development of environmental law as a composite of different experiences ranging from the law of nuisance to criminal law and administrative law. Even though these all remain important elements of environmental law, there is a marked difference today from the past. Our recent efforts to protect the environment have created a diversity of standards and regulatory strategies. Some of these are simply reactive forms of law where liability or consequences come about because someone is at fault or through a mistake. In other instances, however, the law is proactive in protecting the environment. It applies the precautionary principle through setting environmental standards and attempting to change behaviour. Today, standards have a central role in environmental law. It is essential to our understanding of environmental law to examine the different forms of standard-setting and how distinct formulations of the law have captured economic instruments as well as traditional command–control systems of regulation to implement and enforce standards. Setting environmental standards rests on assessing risks and managing a delicate balance between protection and economic development. Risk-based regulation is also seen as an important way forward in tackling global warming and climate change. Science is a major contributor to a risk-based analysis of environmental problems and provides a knowledge base, albeit incomplete, on which to judge environmental change and our impacts on environmental health. It forms a critical part of regulation and legal forms of environmental supervision.[1]

The use of legal regulation to improve the environment has traditionally followed the command and control system of regulation. There are many different forms of regulation available and while command and control has a role to play, there is a growing literature expressing dissatisfaction with this system and looking for more effective modes of regulation.[2] There have been two major reviews of regulation and penalties that are set to have a major impact on the future development of regulatory controls in the UK. The Hampton

---

[1] J. Corkin, 'Science, legitimacy and the law: regulating risk regulation judiciously in the European Community' (2008) EL Rev. 359.

[2] R. Baldwin and J. Black, 'Really responsive regulation' (2008) 71(1) MLR 59–94. C.T. Reid, 'Regulation in a changing world: review and revision of environmental permits' (2008) CLJ 126.

Review, undertaken by Sir Philip Hampton,[3] has questioned the effectiveness of regulation especially when considering its complexity and the duplication of regulatory systems. The review by Professor Richard Macrory, *Regulatory Justice: Sanctioning in a post-Hampton World* (the Macrory Review),[4] considered the role of regulatory penalties and their appropriate use in environmental regulation. Macrory advocated a more flexible approach and that a greater range of penalties should be available for particular types of regulatory crimes. The Regulatory Enforcement and Sanctions Act 2008 provides a new structure for regulatory activities including a Local Better Regulation Office, set up to coordinate and provide consistency between central and local government, regulators and the system of regulation. The details of the 2008 Act are explained below.

This chapter is intended to draw together the main techniques available for environmental regulation and to explain how different regulatory principles can advance environmental protection. Since science plays an important role in environmental regulation and is key in environmental risk assessment, the role of science in the regulatory system is also considered.

Science and the environment

Advances in science and technology have been fundamental to the development of modern societies and remain a key element in underpinning our prosperity. It is a double-edged sword, however, with the use of scientific developments on occasion having unforeseen and adverse consequences. Extensive urbanisation, the need for effective transport systems and intensive agriculture all bring their own and substantial impacts on the environment. Our energy use also has impacts, not least of which is climate change. Understanding the effects of our activities on environmental and human health is difficult and demanding, and it is only through science that we can hope to begin to unravel and control our impacts. Scientific assessment provides a method to help us establish the boundaries for acceptable levels of technological, environmental and health risk that form the framework for public safety. Science, however, can only describe the levels of risks: it is for society to determine their acceptability.

The development of standard-setting as a technique in environmental law comes from a number of distinct influences. First, there is the experience of the nineteenth century, especially in respect of the Alkali Inspectorate and the development of health and safety arrangements in industrial and domestic premises (see Chapters 1 and 2). The history of health and safety law has had a pronounced impact on how risk and safety are calibrated. In fact, the significance of health and safety legislation has increased in recent years, especially since the introduction of corporate criminal liability and the development of increased EU regulation in this area. Second, the enhanced role for science has come about because of the need to avoid civil and criminal liability to prevent hazardous substances from injuring the public. This stems from stronger litigation strategies arising from a more rights-centred idea of citizenship to meet rising expectations about a healthy and safe environment. Science is used as a protection against legal action. The use of standards affords protection on the

---

[3] Sir Philip Hampton, *Reducing Administrative Burdens: Effective Inspection and Enforcement* London: HM Treasury, 16 March 2005; also see: Better Regulation Task Force Less Is More, March 2005.

[4] Professor Richard Macrory, *Regulatory Justice: Making Sanctions More Effective* November 2006, London.

basis of defining and elaborating a standard of safety that addresses the precautionary principle and is embedded in a risk assessment. Thirdly, there is also a strong political agenda for the use of scientific data linked to risk assessment as an important role in policy-making, which has partly been driven by public concern. Politicians use science to act as a convenient barrier between political accountability and the attribution of any fault. There have been a significant number of health and environmental scares in the recent past that have created a marked increase in public demands for scientific proof that a substance, product or process is safe (see Law in context, below). Defining the acceptable levels of safety is as much to do with public perception as it is with science, but credible evidence can assure public confidence and provides a basis for standard-setting. Finally, science is advancing at a rate and in ways (e.g. genetically modified organisms and nanoparticles) that present substantial regulatory challenges often at the limits of scientific knowledge and understanding.

LAW IN CONTEXT

The BSE crisis

Bovine spongiform encephalopathy (BSE) was unknown until first identified in a few cattle showing characteristic symptoms of the disease, such as drunken gait. Probably present in the national herd as early as the mid-1970s this identification of a new prion disease, which affected the brain, was not made until 1986. The disease has a long incubation period and it is estimated that as many as 50,000 animals were probably infected at this stage. BSE probably arose because of changes in farming practice, the recycling of animal protein in ruminant feed, during the 1970s. In 1988 the government, because of the increasing incidence of BSE, set up an expert working group into the disease under the chairmanship of Sir Richard Southwood. The terms of reference for the group were wide and included consideration of the implications of BSE. The working group reported in 1989. One of the recommendations in the report was for diseased animals to be slaughtered and their carcasses destroyed. The government moved on this recommendation and public awareness of the disease became acute and concern about its possible human implications began to be raised. The Southwood Report, however, concluded that 'it was most unlikely that BSE would have any implications for human health'. The government of the day keen to protect the farming industry and reassure the public used the Southwood Report to substantiate claims that English beef was safe to eat. In reality the working group had insufficient scientific information on BSE to substantiate this claim. In 1990 the first non-ruminant, a pet cat, died from the disease. It was not until 1996, under a new government, that BSE was recognised to infect humans in the form of variant Creutzfeldt–Jakob disease (*v*CJD) an incurable and fatal disease. The transmission to humans and other animals was through eating infected beef and beef products. By the end of the BSE epidemic, approximately 170,000 cattle died or were destroyed and as a result of precautionary measures many more were slaughtered. Virtually the whole national herd was destroyed. Restrictions on English beef sales and cattle husbandry by the farming industry lasted many years. To date 167 people have died and a further 3 have been diagnosed with *v*CJD. The long incubation period for and considerable uncertainty about the disease means we do not know how many of us are infected or indeed if infected whether we will develop the disease. Original scenarios suggested that the numbers infected could number in millions; this may prove to be a substantial overestimate but remains a possibility.

Public confidence in government response to such a crisis and in scientific advice on matters where there was considerable uncertainty was dealt a considerable blow by the BSE crisis. The 2000 BSE Inquiry into the affair chaired by Lord Phillips, then Master of the Rolls, made the point that the government's ultimate admission that vCJD probably arose through the transmission of BSE to humans left 'the public feeling betrayed'. The Inquiry Report highlighted the need for openness and transparency by government and scientists. The inquiry also considered a proper provision of information on risk and when precise scientific evaluation is impossible because of uncertainty.

Scientific evidence and regulation

The role of science and scientific assessment in environmental law and regulation has steadily and substantially increased in recent years. In court cases it is becoming increasingly more commonplace for scientific analysis and data to be used when determining criminal and civil liability. Science also makes an important contribution to setting environmental standards, which requires careful consideration and definition of risks. Building standards on the basis of acceptable levels of safety and economic considerations means that standard-setting brings science into a social context. It cannot be assumed that science offers certainty: it does not and risks are normally phrased in terms of probabilities and likelihoods. Scientific data is often limited; there may be considerable scientific uncertainty associated with data; consequences may be unsure and, on occasion, events or effects may be unforeseeable. Scientific evidence and analysis, however, provide a tool, a methodology to help us gauge risk and attempt to use an objective base for setting standards. Science can also support us in deciding how we might manage or mitigate the consequences of an event appropriately. There is a further important role for science in environmental regulation and law: monitoring standards and the environment. For example, drinking water is monitored regularly across a broad range of chemical and microbiological standards. The Environment Agency monitors river quality and traces pollution incidents to their source whenever possible.

Perhaps the best illustration of these roles is found in the contribution that scientific assessment is making in the climate change debate. The reports of the Intergovernmental Panel on Climate Change (IPCC), which inform international negotiations on climate change under the auspices of the United Nations, illustrate this combination of uses for scientific evidence, analysis and monitoring. The IPCC reports have provided scientific explanations for the causes of climate change, predictions of its impacts, together with an assessment of the likelihood of these impacts occurring, e.g. sea level rise, and provided suggestions and analysis of mitigating measures. There was considerable scientific uncertainty about climate change in the IPCC's early reports and considerable scientific debate over the causes of climate change. The growing amount of scientific evidence, including the results of monitoring programmes, e.g. of atmospheric carbon dioxide concentrations, glacier melt and the diminution of the Artic ice cap, has now resolved these uncertainties. The IPCC's most recent report allows little room for doubt about human-produced greenhouse gas emissions being primarily responsible for the undoubted social, economic and environmental consequences of climate change.[5]

Science and standard-setting

The use of science in setting environmental standards provides part of the objective basis for this process. It should not be overlooked that economic analysis and social considerations are also key elements in setting environmental standards. A good example of the interaction between these different components is found in the Bathing Water Directive (Directive 2006/7/EC repealing Directive 76/160/EEC) (see Law in context, below).

LAW IN CONTEXT

Bathing Water Directive

The Bathing Water Directive sets quality standards for sea water and fresh water used for swimming. The microbial standards of the initial directive (Directive 76/160/EEC) were fairly demanding and when the directive was introduced there was a considerable debate in the United Kingdom about the costs and benefits of achieving them. The economic costs were considerable, since to meet the standards substantial sewage treatment is needed before discharge from sewage outflows near designated bathing waters. This meant quite extensive new investment in sewage plant infrastructure by sewage undertakers. It was strongly argued at the time that the costs were disproportionate when set against the number of people who would develop illness, or indeed the seriousness of the likely illnesses, as a result of swimming in water that did not meet the standards. The risk was argued to be low, the social benefit marginal but the economic burden on water companies considerable. In reality it is difficult to establish the number of illnesses arising from swimming in infected sea water. Most people only have short holidays at the seaside, leave and subsequently develop the illness when they return home, anywhere across the country. The illness is rarely linked back to swimming in the sea, so there is considerable uncertainty about numbers infected. The economics are also more complicated than simply considering the costs to water companies. There is the issue of any costs to the NHS in the treatment of resulting illnesses, e.g. antibiotic treatment of ear infections, and the costs of missed days at work through illness, e.g. diarrhoeal illness.

The government at the time did not fully implement the Directive. In 1985, the date set in the Directive for implementation, only 27 resorts had been designated as bathing waters. This left the vast majority of swimming areas, including Blackpool, out of the remit of the Directive. The European Commission took action against the UK for a failure to conform to quality standards in the Directive and the European Court found that the United Kingdom had failed to appropriately implement the Directive (*Commission v United Kingdom* (Case C-56/90)). The UK complied with the ruling and more bathing waters

[5] IPCC (2007) *Climate Change 2007: Synthesis Report. Contribution of Working Groups I, II and III to the Fourth Assessment Report of the Intergovernmental Panel on Climate Change* [Core Writing Team, Pachauri, R.K. and Reisinger, A. (eds)]. IPCC, Geneva, Switzerland, 104 pp.

were duly designated and the standards implemented. Britain has something like 475 beaches and a £2 billion investment programme was put in place to meet the directive in 1990. In 2006 our compliance rate with the standards in the directive in England was 99.5 per cent and in Wales 98.8 per cent. Since then a new Bathing Water Directive (Directive 2006/7/EC) repealing the original Directive has been put in place with still tighter microbiological standards. The Department of Environment has estimated that this new Directive will cost between £1.6 and £4.2 billion to implement. Needless to say, the debate about cost and benefits began all over again. It is worth noting, however, that the Bathing Water Directive that has resulted from a raft of directives has contributed to the general improvement in sea-water and freshwater quality (see Chapters 12 and 13).

Science is used to establish a number of distinct components that together make the assessment of risk possible. These are most commonly, though not exclusively, applied to chemicals and pollutants in our environment. There are generally four components to risk assessment – hazard identification, hazard characterisation, exposure assessment and risk characterisation. Hazard identification and characterisation go together in a process called hazard assessment. Hazard identification is intended to establish the inherent ability of a substance to cause harm. Clearly some chemicals, because of their particular characteristics, are more harmful than others. Hazard assessment determines the nature and extent of the harm. In other words, hazard assessment describes the toxicity of a compound and the levels of exposure, i.e. the dose, at which the substance is harmful. The remaining two elements of risk assessment look beyond the chemical itself to the environment. Exposure assessment attempts to predict the likely routes of environmental and human exposure to the substances and the probable levels of exposure. It includes consideration of factors such as sources, chemistry and extent of use, i.e. market size. It includes, wherever possible, environmental monitoring data. Drawing on these three elements, risk characterisation goes on to estimate the probability that humans or the environment will be harmed and how severe the harm is likely to be under particular exposure conditions. Risk assessment is not an exact science and the outcomes are stated in terms of the probability of harm. Indeed as our knowledge increases and scientific uncertainty is reduced, or as monitoring programmes throw up unexpected problems, then risk assessments need revisiting and perhaps standards either tightened or relaxed.

It is worthwhile briefly considering the methods used to predict risk and help set regulatory standards, and to examine limitations in the techniques. There are a number of different reasons why humans and the environment may be exposed to chemicals. The first is through the intended use of a product (e.g. biocides), the second as part of a controlled release of waste to the environment (e.g. sewage outflows), through incidental environmental exposure (e.g. car exhaust fumes), or accidental environmental contamination (e.g. oil pollution from a shipping accident). In any of these cases impacts are described in terms of the potential harm through risk assessment. Key here is the potential effects on human health through exposure to the pollutant and the effect on aquatic and terrestrial environments. Important in assessment of human and environmental impacts is toxicity testing, which provides data that contributes to hazard assessment. Quantifying the risk to aquatic and terrestrial ecosystems involves examining the toxicity of a chemical to selected species.

This forms part of a relatively new science called ecotoxicology. It is possible to make attempts to assess a more general impact of chemicals on an ecosystem as a whole. This is challenging since we understand surprisingly little about the working relationships and interactions between organisms, and between them and the physical environment in many natural systems. Ecotoxicology, in fact, developed as a discipline because of the need to predict the environmental fate, i.e. whether a chemical remains in solution or adheres to surfaces etc., and adverse affects of substances in the environment. The question arises as to what we mean by an adverse effect. This was defined by the Royal Commission on Environmental Pollution[6] as

> the effect of exposure to a substance on an organism is defined as adverse when it represents a change in morphology, physiology, growth, development, or life-span which results in impairment of functional capacity or impairment of capacity to compensate for additional stress, or increase in susceptibility to harmful effects of other environmental influences.

Adverse effects are clearly defined very broadly and range from acute toxicity effects to chronic impairment of some biological function. Designing techniques to establish such a range of impacts is extremely difficult.

Toxicity testing

Let us briefly consider the scientific techniques that are currently available to assess impacts on humans and other organisms. It is also worthwhile to consider factors that influence the outcomes of chemical or pollutant exposure. We will not look at the techniques in any detail[7] but it is useful to examine the limitations of the techniques that provide us with the scientific foundation stones for much environmental standard-setting. Toxicity testing can essentially be used to establish the impact of chemicals and pollutants on humans and other organisms. Ecotoxicology[8] goes a step further and describes the fate and impacts of pollutants and chemicals in ecosystems, i.e. the community of diverse species and the physical environment in which they live. It assesses the impacts of chemicals on populations and communities. Toxicity testing and ecotoxicology are used in a number of ways relevant to environmental regulation and provide fundamental information for the application of the precautionary principle. They contribute to establishing the toxicity of compounds to selected plants and animals, individually and in communities. In this way they provide an important element of risk assessment and the regulation of a range of products including biocides and industrial chemicals etc. Toxicological studies and ecotoxicology can also provide information on the quality of the air, soil and water in ecosystems and contribute to the development of quality indicators and the definition of quality standards. In addition, by determining the concentrations of substances above which harm is likely to occur, they can provide a basis for regulatory agencies such as the Environment Agency to set discharge consents for various industries discharging liquid or gaseous waste to the environment.

---

[6] Royal Commission on Environmental Pollution Twenty-First Report. Setting Environmental Standards. Page 14.

[7] The 21st Royal Commission Report. *Setting Environmental Standards*. October 1998, London: HMSO; provides a useful overview of the procedures and definition of terms.

[8] Walker, C.H., Hopkin, S.P., Sibly, R.M. and Peakall, D.B. (2005) *Principles of Ecotoxicology* (3rd edn) CRC Press.

Table 7.1 Examples of the adverse effects of chemicals determined as part of toxicity testing

Effect of chemical	Description
Skin irritation or corrosion	
Immunological sensitisation	Allergic reactions
Carcinogenicity	Ability to cause cancers
Mutagenicity or genotoxicity	Ability to cause permanent genetic changes that can be passed to the next generation
Teratogenicity	Foetal abnormalities
Neurotoxicity	Damage to the nervous system
Reprotoxicity	Adverse effects on reproductive capacity
Phototoxicity	Skin reactions induced by exposure to light

Toxicological testing involves a number of different methods, from laboratory-based controlled exposure to chemicals, to epidemiological studies to the more recent use of cell lines and computer models. All have limitations and advantages. It provides a technique to determine the impact of a chemical and provides a basis for obtaining a dose–response relationship between the concentration of a chemical or pollutant and its effect. It is normal in toxicity testing on humans to use surrogate animals. In toxicological testing of other organisms and as part of ecotoxicology, laboratory-based tests are carried out on specified animals such as the water flea *Daphnia magna*, earthworms and fish, and plants, e.g. algae, either as single species or multi-species tests and are then extrapolated to other species. Different organisms, of course, respond differently to chemicals, but the philosophy behind toxicity testing is that there are common reactions to toxins across species. How one species behaves predicts how others are likely to behave. The types of adverse effects that can be assessed are quite diverse (Table 7.1).

It is normal for regulators to require standardised tests to be performed in order to determine toxicity of products and pollutants. Within the EU a new regulation,[9] which deals with chemicals and their safe use, came into force on 1 June 2007. The regulation sets out the requirements for the Registration, Evaluation, Authorisation and Restriction of Chemical substances (abbreviated to REACH) and supplies guidance on all these different elements, including evaluation, i.e. testing procedures and risk assessment.[10] The toxicity tests that are required vary with the size of market for the chemical, i.e. the amount produced, and are classified on the basis of a number of criteria (see Table 7.2). REACH is one of the most important pieces of EU environmental legislation implemented in recent years and will undoubtedly play a valuable role in the proactive protection of environmental and human health. The Environment Agency provides a variety of guidance on testing water and soils[11] and the Organisation of Economic Cooperation and Development (OECD) also provides guidelines on testing regimes.[12] The OECD has an important role in coordinating international efforts to develop improved testing methods.

[9] 1907/2006/EC.

[10] REACH Guidance on Information Requirements and Chemical Safety Asssessment available at *http://reach.jrc. it/docs/guidance_document/information_requirements_en.htm*.

[11] Environment Agency *Index of Methods for the Examination of Waters and Associated Materials 1976–2008*.

[12] Organisation of Economic Cooperation and Development, Environment Directorate *OECD Guidelines for Testing of Chemicals* available at *www.oecd.org*.

Table 7.2 Classification of toxicity tests

Test classification	Description
Length of exposure to substance	Acute studies – up to a few days
	Chronic studies – the lifetime of a test species, i.e. months to years
Method of contact with the substance	Ingested, oral, skin, eyes, inhaled
End point of test	Death, tumour development, reproductive or developmental effects, allergic reactions, neurological or behavioural effects

There are two major types of toxicity testing: acute which can be over hours or days, and chronic which may last weeks, months or over the lifetime of the organism (discussed more fully below). The organisms selected for acute toxicity testing are different for terrestrial and aquatic environments and are specified by regulators as part of standardised testing regimes. Acute toxicity testing related to aquatic systems is further developed and less problematic than for terrestrial systems. Organisms such as worms, and some other invertebrates, can be used as marker organisms for terrestrial systems as can some insects, e.g. bees. Key vertebrates include birds. Acute impacts are just that: rapid, obvious, non-reversible and often fatal. The majority of such tests last no more than 14 days. The outcome of acute toxicity tests are described in terms of lethal concentrations (LC). They are commonly expressed as LC_{50} or LC_{70} of a substance, which indicate the percentage of organisms, 50 per cent or 70 per cent respectively, killed at a given concentration of the chemical under defined conditions. The exposure time to this effect is also included in the expression, thus $48\ h\text{-}LC_{50}$ simply means that 50 per cent of the test organism died during 48 hours of exposure to the chemical in specified conditions, e.g. chemical concentration etc. There are other ways of expressing the results of acute toxicity tests, for example in terms of the median effective concentrations (EC). For example, EC_{50} is the concentration of a substance that results in 50 per cent of the maximum response, e.g. death, again under stipulated conditions.

It is not uncommonly the case that the concentration of a chemical has to reach a threshold level before there is a toxicity effect; below this dose there is no observed effect. This 'no observed effect concentration' (NOEC) is the maximum concentration at which the substance has no detectable impact on the test organisms. This is really the ideal concentration in the environment. The concentration of NOEC is, of course, not only influenced by the target species but also by test conditions, e.g. the sensitivity of methods used. In other words, NOEC varies and in order to cope with this variability and uncertainties safety factors are applied in risk assessments (see below). It is also possible to describe the impact of chemical concentration in another way: the lowest observed effect concentration (LOEC). Sometimes it is impossible to find a concentration at which there is no response, i.e. NOEC, and in this case LOEC is used. LOEC is the lowest exposure concentration to have an observed effect on the test organisms. In reality LOEC is determined by the lowest detection limits of the methods used, so it may not actually be the lowest concentration at which there is an effect. It is above the threshold and does not supply information on the actual threshold concentration of a chemical that will have an impact. Data from acute toxicity tests provide the hazard characterisation and are subsequently linked to exposure assessment, i.e. likely levels of exposure in the environment, before determining the probability of harm and completing the risk assessment (see below). In EU legislation this relationship between predicted, or

153

occasionally known, exposure levels and the concentration at which there are adverse effects is called risk characterisation.

The attractions of using acute toxicity testing for environmental regulation are clear. It provides a quantifiable estimate of safety that can be used in the development of environmental standards. The tests are laboratory-based, relatively simple and rapid. The procedures are easily standardised and their conditions and requirements can be tightly controlled by regulators. Since these tests have been used for some time, there are useful data sets on commonly used tests organisms and diverse chemicals that allow easy comparisons between results. The European Chemicals Agency, for example, maintains a database of chemical testing results that is accessible through the web.[13] Much acute toxicity testing undertaken is used to provide part of the basis for environmental regulation of individual chemicals marketed in the UK and EU. This chemical data, however, is a valuable resource for other types of standard-setting.

It is important to understand that acute toxicity testing is not a panacea. It has obvious limitations. Chosen species may not be representative of particular ecosystems, and for the test to be really meaningful they should be the organisms most likely to be exposed (e.g. perhaps sediment organisms) and most sensitive to the toxicity of the chemical. None of these criteria are easy to meet and are probably rarely achieved through the standard test methods. The vast majority of organisms in most ecosystems have never been tested, which raises the question of how robust the current regulatory requirements for testing are. Moreover, environmental conditions can alter the impact of chemicals as can the stage in the life cycle of an organism, e.g. juvenile or reproductive stages. In the final analysis acute toxicity tests are considerably handicapped by the fact that they extrapolate laboratory-based tests to real-world ecosystems, and the responses of single species to other organisms and mixed assemblages of species, i.e. communities. There is a good deal of work at present to develop acute toxicity testing strategies that address some of these problems, but they are some way from use in tests set by regulators.

Tests on animals are in themselves controversial and expensive both in monetary and resource terms. The number of animals likely to be used in chemical testing under the EU REACH regulation for industrial chemicals has been estimated by animal rights groups to be of the order of twelve million animals. This may be an overestimate, but nonetheless the numbers used to test existing and new chemicals are likely to be in the millions. Using animals to test the acute or chronic toxicity of chemical to the environment and humans may sit uneasily with ethical concerns in our society today. There has been a good deal of pressure to develop alternative methods to using animals in tests,[14] and there is considerable international cooperation in developing alternatives. Such methods are difficult to develop and validate. Policy-makers will have to strike a balance between ensuring robust risk assessment that allows regulation to apply appropriately precautionary standards, while reducing the use of animals in toxicological testing.

So far we have considered the role of acute toxicity testing in environmental regulation. Testing the chronic impacts of chemicals and pollutants is even more demanding. Chronic toxicity tests last longer and over more of the lifespan of organisms used in the test. They fit

---

[13] See the European Chemicals Agency website for details.

[14] Select Committee on Animals in Scientific Procedures, *Animals in Scientific Porcedures*, Session 2001–2, Report HL 150-I of 24 July 2002.

within the definition provided by the Royal Commission on Environmental Pollution (see above), and relate to more subtle affects on plants and animals than those of acute toxicity testing. Thus, chronic effects include reductions in reproductive success, or lowered growth and development rates, and even behavioural changes. Chronic toxicity testing is particularly important when substances are likely to have a very large market since this will increase the frequency of environmental exposure and may even mean continual exposure. Testing chronic effects, then, has to take account of prolonged exposure periods and the chemical's persistence in the environment as well as its distribution in that environment. A further complication is the likelihood of biomagnification, which must be taken into account. This is the term used when a chemical's concentration in the body of organisms increases with each level in a food web, i.e. plant to herbivore to predator. A classic example of biomagnification is shown by the impact of DDT, with predators at the top of food chains substantially affected by the biocide. Thus, in the UK, the reproductive success of birds of prey, e.g. hawks, was severely affected by DDT, resulting in their population size decreasing markedly to the point of placing the birds on the 'at risk list' for extinction.

The reality of pollutants and chemicals in most ecosystems is probably chronic, long-term exposure. Chronic toxicity tests are, therefore, likely to be more revealing and useful in terms of characterising risks than acute toxicity tests. The impact of chronic exposure, as with acute toxicity, is affected by many factors, from the species and stage in the life cycle to the characteristics of the chemical and to environmental factors. Periodic doses of a chemical may be cumulative and it is possible that a threshold dose, at which an organism is affected, may ultimately be reached. Chronic toxicity testing is challenging, and together with the problems associated with acute toxicity testing they pose other difficulties. Chronic effects may be masked by perfectly normal changes in communities, populations or organisms that occur with time. From a regulatory perspective chronic toxicity tests require a significant time investment, and may substantially delay needed regulatory action. Standard-setting in an acceptable time-frame meets the concerns of industry who may, for example, have invested significantly in a new product. There are a number of tests that shorten chronic toxicity assessment, including early life stage (likely to be the most vulnerable stage) tests for aquatic organisms and screening tests for mutagenicity and teratogenicity (see Table 7.1). The acute to chronic ratio can also be used to extrapolate estimates of chronic toxicity between organisms and chemicals. The ratio is calculated by dividing acute LC_{50} by some measure of chronic toxicity, e.g. the mean of the no-effects and the low-effects concentrations (the maximum acceptable toxic concentration). This is a rather rudimentary estimate of chronic toxicity. None of these measures offers a robust and reliable method for determining long-term subtle effects.

There is a further technique that may provide clues to the effects of chemicals on organisms. These toxikinetic studies revolve around assessing how an organism takes up a chemical, e.g. in its food or through exposed surfaces, whether it is metabolised by the organism, and whether it is excreted or accumulates in particular organs. Toxikinetic data can be used as a tool to predict the likely physiological impact of chemicals and may contribute to toxicity testing in this way. These tests are again time-consuming and expensive in resources and do not offer readily usable information for regulators.

More often than not organisms, humans and ecosystems are exposed to more than one polluting compound at the same time. This essentially further complicates the extrapolation of toxicity testing to the real world. Exposure is most often to mixtures of chemicals that may interact and have effects that are:

1. additive – the effect of the mixture of pollutants is the sum of their individual effects;

2. synergistic – the effects are significantly increased owing to interactions between the compounds;

3. antagonistic – the compounds again interact, but the overall effect is to reduce toxicity.

Put into this variability the fact that environmental conditions can change chemical interactions and the complexity is evident. The Environment Agency has been examining the use of toxicity tests on complete effluents together with the toxicity of receiving waters in part to address this problem. The latter is important since a stretch of river, for example, may receive discharges from several different sources, e.g. road run-off, sewage treatment works, food processing company, a chemical manufacturer etc. The so-called Direct Toxicity Assessment Programme is proving a success and is being expanded as one way forward to aid the setting of discharge consents.[15]

Toxicity testing on single species or even assemblages of species provides a poor database to extrapolate to effects on ecosystems, which reflect complex diverse interactions between many different types of organisms, and between them and the physical and chemical environment. A pollutant might quite often have a type of domino effect, as the impact on one organism influences the fate of another organism not directly affected by the pollutant. We know surprisingly little about pristine ecosystems, which presents us with substantial problems in trying to describe ecological 'harm'.

Our knowledge base on chemical and pollutant toxicity is not particularly impressive and establishing chronic effects is especially difficult. Any testing method is limited to particular end points, in time and to target organisms. It is further limited by the sensitivity of the testing methods and the limit of detection of impacts. Subtle effects are the most difficult to establish, but are nonetheless significant. Extrapolation to other, perhaps very different, species increases uncertainty substantially, well illustrated by the fact that species-specific responses to chemicals have been frequently reported. There may also be unforeseeability in effects. For example, we have only relatively recently become aware of the problem of endocrine-disrupting chemicals, or hormone mimics, first detected because of the feminisation of freshwater fish near a sewage outfall in a UK river. A worrying range of chemicals now appear capable of acting as hormone mimics, affecting reproduction and development. Endocrine-disrupting chemicals induce responses at exceptionally low concentrations and we are still attempting to design appropriate regimes to test for their effect. Long-term effects are particularly difficult to establish, given that tests must inevitably be limited in time. How, for example, can a NOEC value derived from a test that has lasted 90 days on one species be relied on to accurately reflect the NOEC for possible lifetime exposure of a human? Moreover toxicity testing considers only direct effects on organisms, not the indirect effects that might arise, say, from the substance having an effect on the physical environment. Indeed, the impact of multiple chemicals in diverse mixtures is exceptionally difficult to try to predict. Toxicity testing, then, is not perfect and there is considerable research to improve the techniques. The inclusion of rather arbitrary safety factors in the calculations of risk is intended to account for these types of uncertainties and build in considerable safety margins in the calculation of risk.

---

[15] Environment Agency (2000) State of the Environment. See *http:www.environment-agency.gov.uk* for a brief description of developments in this area. See also Environment Agency (2001) *Ecotoxicity Test Methods for Effluent and Receiving Water Assessment – Comprehensive Guidance.*

Even so, toxicity tests provide us with at least a handle on establishing safe levels of exposure to chemicals and pollutants.

Exposure assessment and contaminants in the environment

The sources of chemicals in our environment are many and varied and exposure can arise at any stage in their life, including extraction, production and processing, transport, storage, product formulation, use and disposal. This makes exposure assessment no less problematic than toxicity testing. Exposure assessment involves obtaining some quantitative measure of organisms' exposure to chemicals from the surrounding environment. A variety of factors effect the fate of a chemical in the environment, among other things the concentration and characteristics of the chemical itself, e.g. whether it is soluble, whether it degrades or is long-lived, and the physical and chemical characteristics of the environment because they influence the reactions of the chemical. These factors have an influence on two key elements: first, how quickly the chemical is transported through the different parts of an ecosystem (e.g. water, sediment) or whether it is immobilised in one part of an ecosystem; second, and related to the first, whether the chemical is 'bioavailable', that is can be taken up by organisms. It is unlikely, for example, that a solid will be bioavailable. It is ironic that if a chemical is degraded it may actually become more harmful. Degradation may not be complete and the products may be more toxic than the original pollutant. This was the case with DDT. The mobility, fate and bioavailability of chemicals essentially describe the likely exposure of organisms in an ecosystem and the pathways, i.e. the pathways between the target organism and the source of the chemical or pollutant, of exposure. Ecosystems are highly variable in physical and chemical terms and often change substantially over very small distances. This makes the assessment and prediction of chemical fate in the environment difficult. Exposure assessment normally uses both measured values of the chemical in the environment, which is the ideal, and predictive models that, based on the factors outlined above, predict the concentrations in all the different parts on an ecosystem. Exposure values for humans in risk assessment take account of exposure through consumer products, occupational exposure and environmental exposure.

New approaches to exposure assessments are being developed. At present, human and environmental assessment are carried out separately. It is suggested that this should be integrated so that the total exposure of humans and the environment are considered in one assessment. This would require an integrated assessment of exposure levels in all the different components of our environment.

Risk characterisation

Characterising the risk of adverse effects, how severe they are likely to be and how long they will last is termed risk characterisation. This is the final part of the risk assessment jigsaw. In order to attempt to establish safe levels of chemical exposure the predicted no-effect concentration (PNEC) is derived from data produced in toxicity testing, most often from acute toxicity testing. PNEC is simply defined as the maximum level of pollutant that would have no effect on a target organism. Calculation PNEC is actually quite simple: it is the lowest LC_{50}

or EC_{50} normally divided by 1,000 (under EC procedures), an arbitrary safety (application) factor used to account for scientific uncertainty (see below). The application factor can be 10, 50, 100 or 1,000 depending on the length of the test and the species used in the test. The smaller application factors are normally applied when longer term tests have been undertaken for organisms at more than one level in the food chain, e.g. plant, herbivore, omnivore and predator. Whatever the PNEC value, it is important that it is higher than the predicted environmental concentration (PEC). Estimates of PEC arise from exposure assessments. Put simply, there must be at least a 1,000-fold difference between PEC and the lowest LC_{50} to assume that a chemical has no significant environmental hazard. The application factors are an attempt to account for all the uncertainties that are embedded in the risk assessment and are intended to provide a sufficient safety margin in risk assessments.

Assessing impacts on human health

A surprisingly large amount of environmental regulation is focused on protecting human health; in fact historically this was the major emphasis (see Chapter 2). It is worthwhile then to briefly consider in more detail hazard assessment for humans. Two methods are used: toxicity tests and epidemiological studies.[16] We have already discussed toxicity testing in some detail above and there are a variety of toxicity tests used in human assessments, from mammalian cells to studies on laboratory mammals. Testing focuses on chronic effects that may result from prolonged exposure. There are laboratory-based tests that assess mutagenic effect of a chemical on cells, i.e. if it causes genetic mutation. Toxicity testing on mammals has all the problems we have already discussed, e.g. extrapolation to another species, in this case to humans. As with other toxicity testing there are differences in susceptibility with age: children and the elderly are particularly susceptible to the impact of pollutants. There are still further variations in susceptibility, for example pregnant woman and those with pre-existing health conditions may be vulnerable. The mapping of the human genome has suggested that it is possible for certain groups of people to be particularly susceptible to environmental toxins because of their genetic make-up.[17] Such susceptibility may not be mimicked by animal models. Risk assessments must somehow take account of these variations in susceptibility.

Real data is always more helpful in risk assessment and data that relates directly to human responses is no exception. Epidemiological studies, then, should be particularly useful. Again the aim of the studies is to determine dose and effect relationships but in this case using data from the general population, groups within the population or occupational groups. As with toxicity tests the type of study must be carefully stipulated: extrapolation from one group to another may not be valid. Epidemiological studies again have substantial limitations, for example the test groups will usually be exposed to a range of different chemicals and this is difficult to control. They will have different levels of nutrition and different levels of disease. All these factors make establishing responses to chemical exposure difficult. Estimating the extent of chemical exposure in epidemiological studies may also be challenging. For example,

---

[16] Royal Commission on Environmental Pollution Twenty-First Report. Setting Environmental Standards. See pp. 15–21 for a more detailed description of these tests.

[17] S. McEldowney and L. Warren (1998), 'The new biology: a challenge to law' *Int. J Biosciences & the Law* **4**, pp. 315–25.

exposure to volatile organic compounds from car exhausts will vary between a town centre and a suburban street, between measurements taken at child height and adult height. The lifestyle of individuals will also affect exposure and so it goes on. In fact the best data on exposure is available for occupational groups. For all these reasons, linking exposure to effects is challenging. Epidemiological studies are only possible after the human population has been exposed to the compound, which has certain self-evident disadvantages. They are, of course, highly relevant and useful in terms of reviewing possible impacts or monitoring responses when concerns have been raised from other data. In the United States the Centers for Disease Control and Prevention routinely monitor the exposure of humans to chemicals; while in the United Kingdom the Food Standards Agency funds monitoring programmes for dietary exposure to chemicals in food.

In general, epidemiological studies have not contributed substantially to providing quantitative data for risk assessments and therefore to setting standards and environmental regulation; that is not to say it may not in the future as methods improve. There have been occasions when the epidemiological data has been relatively clear and has contributed to standard-setting. A nice example of this has been summarised by The Royal Commission of Environmental Pollution in the development of an air quality standard for benzene.[18] The setting of the benzene air quality standard relied on animal laboratory tests and occupational exposure epidemiological studies.

Science, socio-economic assessment and environmental monitoring

We have considered risk assessment in terms of the scientific methods that can contribute to quantifying risks. Undoubtedly science is fundamental to environmental standard-setting and regulation. It would, however, be totally inappropriate for it to be the only element deciding regulatory requirements. Moreover, it is clear from our limited discussion that there is considerable scientific uncertainty surrounding the data generated during risk assessments. Ultimately it is a social question as to the acceptability of risk and uncertainty balanced against the economic cost of control and mitigation. The question goes to the heart of regulation that embraces the precautionary principle while not undermining social and economic development that is sustainable development.

A range of socio-economic considerations cannot be separated from the scientific outcome of risk assessment. Some examples include:

1. The estimated costs of implementing standards based on risk assessment. This has been a clear problem in the implementation of the Bathing Water Directive (see Law in context, p. 149).
2. The technical feasibility of achieving the standards. Techniques may not be available to achieve levels of pollutants in effluents or chemicals in drinking water etc. set by risk assessment.

---

[18] Royal Commission on Environmental Pollution Twenty-First Report. Setting Environmental Standards. See p. 21.

3. The public perception of risk. The public may be prepared to accept different levels of risk for different activities.

4. The tolerability of the risks. Establishing whether a level of risk can be tolerated may vary with the context of the risk. These levels of 'acceptable risk' are in increasing usage and are being applied to delineate levels of risk considered tolerable for a variety of industrial processes. This is often put in terms of the probability of any individual dying in any one year, e.g. 1 in every 100,000. For a new nuclear power plant, for example, 1 in 100,000 is put as the 'maximum tolerable risk' for members of the public.[19] Setting the limits to tolerability is a social, political and regulatory process.

Development of these types of probabilities also allows the risks associated with different processes and substances to be compared. Factors other than the risk in terms of an individual dying in any one year may also contribute to decisions on the tolerability of a risk. There are costs if insufficient precautionary action is taken. These include costs of remedying any damage arising if controls are not sufficiently stringent. Adverse effects may not be reversible or may only be reversible on a long timescale. This is particularly the case in terms of 'harm' to ecosystems.

Social and economic public values are not very successfully taken into account in risk assessments and environmental regulation at present. This is generally recognised and there have been a number of proposals of mechanisms to successfully link socio-economic assessments to risk assessments.[20] Certainly transparency and openness with regard to risks associated with a chemical or process etc. is essential and this should be put in readily understandable terms without over-simplifying the issues. The EU publishes the results of risk assessments on the European Chemical Agency website and publishes decisions on the regulation of chemicals. These are highly technical and may not provide many people with insights into the risks. There are also mechanisms that regulators use to help establish a proper balance between cost and precaution, including instruments such as best available techniques not entailing excessive costs principle (BATNEEC) (see Chapter 12). The European Chemical Agency as part of the authorisation process under the EU REACH Regulation is required to undertake and publish not only the risk assessment on a chemical related to its use but also a socio-economic assessment. Both these are considered in deciding on the regulation of a chemical.

Using numerical standards should be tempered by a willingness to review the underlying science and to monitor the environment. Our scientific knowledge is incomplete and limited in many areas particularly relevant to risk assessment. New scientific methods are continually being developed. There should be willingness on the part of regulators to adopt new methods once appropriately verified and to revisit assessments in the light of new science and evidence. An example we have already mentioned are the risks posed by endocrine disrupters to human and animal health, reproduction and development. This has only come to light in recent years with a variety of chemicals implicated, including some pesticides, phthalate plasticisers (that can enter the human food chain from food packaging), anti-fouling paints

---

[19] Royal Commission on Environmental Pollution Twenty-First Report. Setting Environmental Standards, p. 53.
[20] See Royal Commission on Environmental Pollution (2003) *Chemicals in Products. Safeguarding the Environment and Human Health* Twenty-fourth Report Cm 5827.

Table 7.3 Types of environmental monitoring

Type of monitoring	Purpose
Compliance	Ensuring statutory limits on emissions, effluents etc. are met
Quality	Determining chemical and biological quality, e.g. river quality, drinking water quality, air quality
Investigative	Part of an investigation into specific effects or concerns, e.g. the Endocrine Disruption in the Marine Environment programme
Research	Improve understanding of the environment and our impacts
Epidemiology	Determine chemical and pollutant effects on human health

and dioxins. This chronic effect of some chemicals was largely unforeseen and scientific evidence on the effects of hormone mimics on animals in aquatic ecosystems, e.g. fish and alligators, grew over a number of years before the issue began to be addressed by regulators. It is still a troublesome and difficult area; there is no validated method as yet to determine if a chemical substance disrupts endocrine systems.

Some of the uncertainties in unexpected and unforeseen impacts or other factors that confound risk assessments can be resolved by environmental monitoring. Environmental monitoring takes several forms and is used for a number of distinct purposes (Table 7.3). Monitoring relies on regular environmental sampling at designated locations, which depend on the type of monitoring being undertaken. Inevitably there are difficulties with monitoring, not least in obtaining samples that are representative of the environment and, of course, monitoring is also after exposure of humans and ecosystems to the substance. The harm may already have occurred. There is growing pressure to incorporate monitoring programmes into the management and regulation of pollutants and chemicals, but the success of doing so is patchy. Thus the regime for regulating pesticides includes monitoring pesticide residues in food and drinking water and any evidence of potentially adverse effects, but monitoring data on the environmental impact of pesticides is not included in risk assessments. Monitoring schemes are also often limited to, say, one group of chemicals, e.g. pesticides or to one part of an ecosystem e.g. the sediment in a river, so that the coverage of monitoring is rather fragmented.

There are a number of ongoing environmental monitoring programmes within the UK. These are best developed for aquatic environments and the air. Freshwater quality is monitored in England and Wales under the Environment Act (1995) by the Environment Agency (see Chapter 12). As part of our obligations under a number of international agreements – e.g. the OSPAR Convention (see Chapter 4) – and EU Directives, the concentrations of chemicals in marine environments is monitored in the UK National Marine Monitoring Programme. The EU Air Framework Directive (96/62/EC) and daughter directives require the monitoring of particular substances in air, and the UK Air Quality Strategy 2003–2008 sets standards for particular pollutants. There is a national network of air-monitoring stations overseen by the Department of Food and Rural affairs. Local Authorities also contribute to air monitoring (see Chapter 14). The poor relative in terms of environmental monitoring is the terrestrial environment. There is only one programme that monitors chemicals in one component of the terrestrial environment nationally: this is the National Predatory Bird Monitoring Scheme set up by the Joint Nature Conservation Committee. Although there are some other environmental monitoring programmes, from a regulatory perspective these are the key ones.

Over recent years, setting environmental standards and environmental regulation has increasingly employed risk assessment. This trend is likely to continue. It is also likely that the process of risk assessment will be continually refined with improvement in scientific techniques, proper inclusion of socio-economic assessment and public values, and better use of data from monitoring schemes in deriving acceptable levels of risk.

Environmental impact assessment and environmental audit

Environmental impact assessment is used to evaluate the potential environmental and ecological harm of large infrastructure development. Environmental assessment has been an intrinsic part of the planning system since 1998, when Directive 85/337/EC *The Assessment of the Effect of Certain Public and Private Projects on the Environment* was implemented. It has had a substantial impact on the day-to-day practicalities of large-scale planning. The directive has subsequently been amended through Directive 97/11/EC, which came into force on 14 March 1999. This has been added to by the Directive on Strategic Environment Asessment (SEA) Directive 2001/42/EC that came into effect in 2004.

The regulatory details of environmental assessment are found in the Town and Country Planning (Environmental Impact Assessment) England and Wales Regulations 1999 SI No. 293 which contain the basis for planning and projects. Environmental impact assessments are required on major projects, including highways, land drainage, harbour works, electricity and pipeline works. They have three elements:

1. An environment statement is provided by the developer setting out the terms of the planning application and the potential impact on the environment.

2. Environmental information provided by the developer is used to evaluate the planning proposal. The information includes queries raised about the impact of the project, responses given by the developer on the queries, any third-party consultation and correspondence with any of the statutory authorities.

3. The developer must also publicise the planning proposal. Four copies of the environment statement must be provided to the local planning authority.

The environmental impact assessment, then, provides essential information on the scope of the development and its potential impact on the environment.[21] Planners must weigh the outcome of the environmental impact assessment against the other elements that go to a determination of planning permission. Recently the ECJ has ruled that EIA may be required at the reserved matters stage of a planning application and also at the outline planning stage. This gives rise to the possibility of planning at different stages including the initial screening stage.

The United Kingdom has developed an 'audit culture' over the last several decades. Audit is a strategy that has been adopted by successive governments to achieve effective public expenditure and identify wasteful practices.[22] This is the type of audit that most of us are familiar with, but audit has also been utilised in the context of the environment. Internal

---

[21] See: Victor Moore, *A Practical Approach to Planning Law* seventh edition (Blackstone Press, 2000) pp. 231–85.
[22] M. Power, *The Audit Society: Rituals of Verification* (Oxford: Oxford University Press, 1997).

management and control systems that meet international standards (e.g. ISO 14000) and British standards (e.g. BS 7750) contribute to companies managing resources, their production processes and the life cycle of their products to minimise environmental impacts and increase their efficiency. Risk assessment plays its part in this process. Policy-makers must also evaluate the costs and benefits of specific environmental policies and it is essential that objective criteria are used to make a reasoned analysis.

The Environmental Audit Committee of the House of Commons (EAC) was established in 1997. EAC monitors the environmental performance of government departments and programmes and their progress in developing strategies for sustainable development. There are considerable advantages in adopting an environmental audit process. First targets and indicators can be set and regularly monitored to determine performance. The targets can be short, medium and long term. Second it is possible as part of environmental audit to use 'value for money'-type evaluations. This provides useful data and a mechanism to compare the performance of the public and private sectors. Finally the audit process allows reviews of performance, and improvements for the future based on these reviews.

Central government departments are subject to audit of their public expenditure by the National Audit Office under the Comptroller and Auditor-General. It may be possible to adapt this model to environmental audit, which would provide a valuable means of external scrutiny. There are, however, some disadvantages associated with public sector auditing. This type of audit sometimes favours a static or non-interventionist approach or encourages risk aversion in audited departments. Despite these potential problems, audit is a useful device for improving the environmental performance of government. The tools for developing an environmental audit assessment of government are, in fact, already in place. These include considering environment matters as part of the Comprehensive Spending Review, the adoption of environmental appraisal in government policies, and the use of environmental targets and reporting by government departments. Additional strategies include setting environmental taxes and government policy on public procurement.[23] It remains to be seen whether such strategies will be adopted over the long term.[24]

Preventative and remedial techniques

We have discussed how science and the assessment of risk are used by regulators as a mechanism to help identify, quantify and manage risks. In fact a number of legal techniques can be used for regulating the environment, either preventing or remediating environmental harm. It is these techniques that we turn to now, starting with those of the common law.

Common law techniques

Environmental law began life as a classic example of the methods that underlie the common law approach to problems. It was not defined as a distinct area of law but rather was embedded in a number of different legal disciplines. Property and planning lawyers

[23] ENDS Report 276, pp. 29–30.
[24] Kathryn Hollingsworth, 'Environmental monitoring of government – the case of an environmental auditor' (2000) 20 *Legal Studies* 241.

could point to the development of the environment as a feature of land use or built environment planning. The Housing, Town and Country Planning etc. Act 1876 set in train the development of the system of town and country planning[25] in Britain. Public health and housing lawyers saw the environment as an important focus of their work. Legislation such as the Public Health Act 1875 formed the foundation of the modern law on public health. The Alkali Acts of 1863 and 1868,[26] intended to control emissions from a part of the heavy chemical industry in nineteenth-century Britain, created the first inspectorate. Preventing and controlling river pollution began with the Rivers Prevention of Pollution Act 1876. Together, these Acts heralded the beginning of a pollution control strategy and laid the foundations of the 'inspectorate' approach to solving environmental problems. Tort lawyers, expert in negligence and nuisance liability, could see environmental law as a development of the case law approach to pollution control. Cases such as *Rylands* v *Fletcher*[27] highlighted the private law approach in applying remedies to ensure environmental protection. How to reconcile the rights of the private landowner with the need for environmental protection was an important question in the development of the law of nuisance.[28] Similarly, the law on trespass was applied to meet environmental problems.

Building up environmental law in this ad hoc way also found resonance in the statutory response to environmental problems. The Public Health Acts of the nineteenth century required statutory procedures for their enforcement. The development of statutory nuisance was also a response to the protection of the environment in the areas of public health and in the powers granted to local authorities to enforce environmental law. The development of public nuisance followed a similar pattern of applying existing legal remedies available under the common law to the new, or newly recognised problems of noise, smell, and air pollution.

Remedies, such as damages and injunctions, provide only limited redress to the private citizen seeking legal resolution for environmental problems. Over the past decade in public law there has been a growth in the application of judicial review in the area of the environment. Application for judicial review allows a variety of public law remedies to be used to protect the environment. Remedies under judicial review[29] are available against public bodies, including regulators and environmental enforcement agencies such as the Environment Agency.

In common with the study of many legal problems, environmental law is commonly defined in the way the subject has developed. This approach, however, is unsatisfactory for several reasons. First, the environment and its protection are not capable of exact legal definition. Many environmental problems are intimately related to economic and social issues,[30] and environmental policies involve a broader definition of law than one that is narrowly focused on legal remedies and their application. Second, in recent years environmental law has

---

[25] See: the Housing, Town Planning etc. Act 1909 and the Town and Country Planning Act 1947. There are proposed changes to be found in the government's Green Paper, *Planning: Delivering a Fundamental Change* London: HMSO 12 December 2001.

[26] See: the Alkali, etc. Works Regulation Act 1906.

[27] See: *Rylands* v *Fletcher* (1868) LR 3 HL 330.

[28] See: *St Helen's Smelting Co.* v *Tipping* (1856) 11 HL Cas. 642.

[29] See: *R v Secretary of State for Foreign and Commonwealth Affairs, ex parte World Development Movement Ltd* [1995] 1 WLR 386. See generally J.F. McEldowney, *Public Law* 2nd edn, 1998.

[30] See: A. Gouldon and J. Murphy, *Regulatory Realities. The Implementation and Impact of Industrial Environmental Regulation*, 1998.

developed quite successfully its own specialist responses to environmental problems. A wide variety of mechanisms and techniques, both proactive and reactive, unique to environmental law have been built up. Third, understanding environmental law itself requires economic, scientific and policy evaluations. Not only is this an interdisciplinary task, but it also requires a focus on the question of environmental standards. This is an area where environmental law has most developed its own identity. It is also the area where further growth is likely.

Environmental law and regulatory instruments

There has been a marked shift in environmental law from reactive provision of remedies for environmental pollution to the more proactive provision of standards to meet environmental problems. Various preventative measures have been adopted in environmental law, which are designed to reduce or eliminate the risk of environmental damage. The main textbooks and literature on environmental law reflect very well how environmental law has developed in the ad hoc way described above. Gaps were filled through legislative and judicial creativity, and solutions to environmental problems were developed case by case. Environmental law has now come of age. Preventative measures and the regulation of processes and activities attempt to prevent or mitigate harm. It is time for a fresh consideration of the role and function of environmental law, with a clear focus on regulating the environment through standards. While acknowledging the complexity and diversity of the subject, it is possible to distil three main principles that have come to guide environmental law: sustainable development, the 'polluter pays' principle and the precautionary principle (see Chapter 1):

1. The principle of sustainable development[31] sets the agenda by attempting to ensure that environmental problems are addressed and controlled. This involves trying to reconcile the conflicting demands of economic development and social, environmental and resource protection so as to ensure that the benefits of any development outweigh its costs, including costs to the environment.

2. The principle of 'polluter pays'[32] is currently in vogue. It asserts that the polluter should pay for any costs that arise from harm to the environment, or ill health or injury to individuals caused by the pollution. The law has developed a number of strategies to implement this principle.

3. The 'precautionary principle'[33] means that the absence of scientific proof for a risk of environmental harm is not a sufficient reason for failing to take preventative action. In recent years it has largely been interpreted in terms of risk assessment (see above).

[31] Sustainable development was first defined in terms of social, economic and environmental criteria by The World Commission on Environmental Development (the Brundtland Commission) in *Our Common Future* (the Brundtland Report, United Nations, 1987).

[32] This principle originated from the UN Conference on the Human Environment held in Stockholm (1972). The principle is embedded in Article 130r(2) of the Treaty Establishing the European Community 1957 (as amended).

[33] First found as 'Vorsorgemassnahmen' in the Bremen Declaration of the First International Conference on the Protection of the North Sea. The principle now has a broader definition and is also embedded in Article 130r(2) of the Treaty Establishing the European Community 1957.

All three principles are open to differing interpretations. Assessing risk, balancing costs, and predicting harm are inevitably open to widely different assumptions and assessment methodologies. Even so, it is possible to devise strategies for implementing the three principles through setting standards for the environment.

Setting and developing environmental standards

There are different categories of environmental standards. The following list is not exhaustive, and the categories are not exclusive.

● Emission standards set the levels of discharges into different media. For example, under the Environmental Protection Act 1990, it is possible to set limits on the total amount of any particular substance which may be released into the environment. Limits may be established by the Secretary of State. The range and extent of emission standards are immense, involving controls on discharge of organic and inorganic substances and particulates to each medium, i.e. air, water and soil, and controls for the disposal of solid waste. Emission standards can relate to emissions from sources as diverse as the food industry, the chemical industry, the energy-producing industries, and transport.

● Quality standards set the maximum allowable levels of pollution in the environment with specific targets set for the levels. Examples are noise levels for aeroplanes, air quality standards for sulphur dioxide levels, and water quality standards for different purposes, such as drinking or bathing.

● Process standards apply to fixed installations such as factories or chimneys. These standards stipulate the means of production, leaving no discretion to the polluter. Such standards are useful as a means of regulating a hazardous activity and preventing accidents. As process standards may be targeted at specific types of manufacturers, this may require information on, and analysis of, dangerous stages in the manufacturing process.

● Product standards are familiar in relation to pharmaceuticals and food packaging and labelling. Scientific information is often contained in the information supplied in the labelling. Instructions for safe usage and warnings about hazards may also comprise the standard required for the product. Pesticides and chemicals in everyday use also conform to these requirements set by the product standard. The information on labels is based on data from risk assessments and is part of the risk management process.

The range of standards goes beyond these and their diversity can be further highlighted by additional examples. Environmental management standards such as ISO 9000 provide certification ensuring that companies have an effective environmental management structure and environmental programmes. There is also an international standard related to the green claims made by manufacturers for their products: ISO 14021.[34]

All standards are under continual development as scientific knowledge and data improve or the risks of harm are more fully resolved. Changes to standards and the introduction of new standards may also be related to social and economic criteria. The development of new

---

[34] See ENDS Report 280, May 1998, ISO 14021.

standards can require industry itself to provide additional information on the impacts of products[35] and will often involve policy discussion in development of the standard.[36]

The European and international standards

Standards are exceptionally important in the proactive protection and management of the environment. There have been a number of contributions to and influences on the growth in standard-setting. Perhaps the most important influence on British environmental law is the development of the environmental policy of the European Community (see Chapter 5). In its own right, European environmental law has created an emerging specialist literature on Community aspects of regulating the environment. An important step was taken by the creation of the European Environment Agency.[37] This Agency sets regulatory standards for the environment and its role is likely to become more important over the next decade. The recent establishment of the European Chemicals Agency is also important. The new Agency is responsible for chemical risk assessment, the management of that risk and product labelling. One of the major sources of law for environmental standards is the many recent directives and laws of the EU (see Chapter 5). These often contain standards, which require interpretation within British law, as the means of regulating the environment. A number of illustrative examples serve to make this point:[38]

- setting standards for water: in addition to the Directive on Bathing Water (76/160/EEC) and Directive on Drinking Water (80/778/EEC), a number of directives similarly set standards for Dangerous Substances in Water (76/464/EEC), Groundwater (80/68/EEC), Shell-Fish Water (78/659), Freshwater Fish (78/659/EEC), and Nitrates (91/676/EEC);

- setting standards for air: there are Air Quality Standards Regulations 1989 (SI 1989 No. 317) and, for noise, the Noise in the Workplace Directive 86/188/EEC;

- setting standards for waste: a plethora of different directives range from the Framework Directive on Waste 75/442 (amended by Directive 91/156/EEC) to the Urban Waste Water Treatment Directive 91/271/EEC;

- setting standards for genetically modified organisms: there are Directives 90/219/EEC and 90/220/EEC now amended by Directive 94/15/EC;

- setting implementation standards for environmental law: Directive 85/337 on Environmental Impact Assessment provides one of the key ways to assess the impact of the array of standards in the environment.

Setting environmental standards also falls under the influence of the international community (see Chapter 4). The Convention on Wetlands of International Importance Especially as Waterfowl Habitat (1971), known as the Ramsar Convention, and the Vienna Convention for the Protection of the Ozone Layer (March, 1985) provide general guidance as to acceptable standards in the environment. A further example is the Kyoto Protocol intended to curb

---

[35] See: ENDS Report 285, October 1998, 'ISO 14021 pushed as basis for implementing green code', pp. 23–6.
[36] For example see DETR (1998) UK Climate Change Programme Consultation Paper.
[37] Established in 1990 (1212/90 EEC 7 May 1990).
[38] A list of relevant directives is to be found in Stuart Bell and Donald McGillivray, *Ball and Bell on Environmental Law*, 2000, pp. 84–5.

fossil fuel emissions in an attempt to limit changes to the climate and a rise in the sea level. This protocol is currently being renegotiated under the auspices of the United Nations.

Managing environmental change

Over recent years there has been a shift to reliance on economic instruments in environmental law. These instruments require new techniques for their implementation and enforcement. Invariably, this leads to the creation of new institutions with the precise purpose of regulating the environment using the techniques of legally enforceable standards. In Britain the Environment Agency provides a formal enforcement code that encapsulates the policy for environmental regulation. The four principles contained in the code are consistency, transparency, targeting, and proportionality in the approach to enforcement. Enforcement strategies must conform to this code of practice.

Enforcement of standards also takes the form of self-regulation through voluntary agreements such as the Regulation on Eco-labelling (Regulations 880/92/EC and 1836/93/EC which were replaced in 2000 with Regulation 980/2000/EC). There is also an advance of eco-labelling through an energy labelling scheme, for example washing machines under Directive 95/12/EC.

Environmental standards can also be implemented by using some innovative taxation devices.[39] These are intended to secure compliance through influencing consumer choices. The cause of 'green taxes' has been advanced as a further commitment to a proactive and preventative approach to the environment.[40] Linked to this is the strategy to increase the costs of energy sources that are *not* environmentally friendly in order to subsidise sources that are. The fossil fuel levy used in the calculation of electricity prices is intended to provide an initial period of subsidy for more expensive electricity produced by wind, solar, or non-fossil fuel systems. Electricity distributors are required to buy a certain percentage of non-fossil fuel. The government has set a target to produce 10 per cent of all electricity in this way by the year 2010.[41]

Democracy and science

Science contributes to democracy and governance in a number of ways. The first we have already alluded to in its contribution to decision-making and policy-making through risk assessment. The tension between science and social, economic and political considerations is particularly apparent when deciding the balance between development and precaution in the arena of sustainable development (see above). This, however, is not the only way that scientific data is highly sensitive. It is often at the heart of court disputes over environmental matters.

The case of *Cambridge Water Co v Eastern Counties Leather plc* [1994] 2 AC 264 is an example of this tension between scientific knowledge and legal principle in courts. A borehole used by Cambridge Water as a source of drinking water was severely contaminated by the solvent perchlorethylene. The contamination came from land that belonged to Eastern Counties

---

[39] See: T. O'Riordan (ed.), *Ecotaxation*, 1997.
[40] See: The White Paper on Transport Policy (1998).
[41] See: DETR (1998) UK Climate Change Programme Consultation Paper.

Leather, a long-established tannery. Cambridge Water sued Eastern Counties Leather for more than £1 million. The House of Lords found in favour of Eastern Counties Leather because it could not been reasonably foreseen that the tanning process might result in the borehole becoming contaminated. In the nineteenth century the possible impact of solvent contamination was unknown. Scientific understanding of the impact of solvents has increased considerably in recent years and the levels of detection for the contamination have improved substantially. Since the *Cambridge Water* case was decided, scientific research has shown that solvent vapours may pose a threat to health.[42] The House of Lords' decision, therefore, did not include consideration of the dangers of vapour pollution; the key issue in the case was the question of water contamination. This is a nice illustration of how scientific knowledge continually changes, raising new issues that may not have been foreseen.

A further important contribution to democracy made by science is found outside the formal proceedings of a court. Scientific evidence can be offered as evidence at an inquiry, e.g. the BSE inquiry (see Law in context, p. 147). The basis of an inquiry, of course, may subsequently provide grounds for future action against a company or public body. Thus science makes important contributions to our democratic processes in a number of important ways.

Improving regulation: civil and administrative penalties

The use of enforcement powers and adequate sanctions is a crucial part of environmental regulation. There is an historic resistance to using criminal penalties for breaches of environmental regulations. Moreover, there is growing evidence that recourse to the courts is impractical when dealing with environmental matters. Regulators actually have quite a wide discretion when determining how to meet environmental requirements. In *Wandsworth London Borough Council* v *Rashid* [2009] EWHC it was held that it could be an abuse of process if enforcement policy of a regulator involving civil and criminal sanctions was not published and made clear and then it may be an abuse of process for prosecutions to take place. While the courts may be reluctant to interfere, there is a need for some flexibility in the way prosecution policy is developed and analysed. The intention to broaden the use of civil sanctions to various agencies such as Natural England and the Countryside Council for Wales is in line with the Regulatory Enforcement and Sanctions Act 2008. Nevertheless there has been increasing concern over the burden of regulation and technical complexity in the way regulation has developed. The Hampton Review[43] under Sir Philip Hampton identified high costs; over-complexity in the systems of regulation; duplication and inefficiency in the delivery of targets and outcomes as particular regulatory problems. The review found many instances where regulation was unnecessary and simply added to the regulatory burdens on business. Common to most forms of regulation is some form of risk assessment. Hampton concluded that risk assessment could be better coordinated, which would reduce the regulatory burden and minimise costs. Many of the conclusions reached in the Hampton Review argue for simplification and streamlining of regulation and a reduction in the scope of regulation. Hampton considered that the aims of regulation should be business-led and achieve better performance. Thus, reducing the regulatory burden through deregulation strategies is strongly supported in the Hampton

---

[42] ENDS Report 293, June 1999, p. 5.
[43] Sir Philip Hampton, *Reducing Administrative Burdens.*

Review. Since the Hampton Review, there have been tentative steps towards the creation of rolling programmes to reduce regulatory burdens and, where necessary, remove regulation. The deregulation agenda has been supported by new legislation, the Regulatory Reform Act 2006, which is intended to improve on the strategies to reduce the burdens of regulation on business and has renewed pressure to reduce regulatory structures.

There have been a number of direct influences on the system of environmental regulation. First was the 2003 *Modernising Environmental Justice Report*[44] that considered the twin questions of the role of civil justice in environmental matters and the idea of an Environmental Tribunal. The Report advocated a streamlining of the civil justice system and simplifying access to justice for environment cases. The argument that a specialist tribunal or court might provide a more efficient mechanism to deal with environmental disputes, including permits and licensing matters, was made in the Report. This was considered more appropriate for resolving environmental disputes than recourse to the ordinary courts. The government has consistently rejected the idea of an independent environmental court or tribunal.

The Hampton Review was followed by the Macrory Review, *Regulating Justice: Sanctions in a post-Hampton World*. This undertook a review of the system of penalties relevant to the application of regulatory sanctions. The Hampton Review's advocacy of risk assessment was seen as a means of taking stock of the multitude of penalties and enforcement practices. Macrory did not reject the idea of criminal sanctions in the area of environmental law but advocated a greater flexibility in sanctions and a deeper analysis of the range, variety and cost benefit of penalties. Thus, the range and scope of penalties and their effects should be better coordinated and assessed.

The direction of Hampton, in favour of deregulation and better risk assessment, and Macrory, in favour of greater flexibility and the appropriate use of more efficient sanctions with a greater range of penalties, requires serious consideration to be given to the way regulation works. A major innovation is the recent Regulatory Enforcement and Sanctions Act 2008. This legislation is intended to implement the risk-based approach to enforcing regulations recommended by the Hampton Review. It remains to be seen how effective the use of sanctions and regulation will become in future years.

The Regulatory Enforcement and Sanctions Act 2008

The Regulatory Enforcement and Sanctions Act 2008 came about after the government took account of the Hampton and Macrory Reports outlined above. The Macrory Report recommended that a set of key principles should form the basis of regulation. The principles encapsulate much of the thinking that was at the heart of the report and are set out in a Ministry of Justice Guidance on Creating New Regulatory Penalties and Offences as follows:[45]

- aim to change the behaviour of the offender;
- aim to eliminate any financial gain or benefit from non-compliance;

---

[44] R. Macrory and Michael Woods, *Modernising Environmental Justice – Regulation and the Role of an Environmental Tribunal* Centre for Law and the Environment, Faculty of Laws, University College, London, 2003.

[45] The list may be found in: *Ministry of Justice: Guidance on Creating New Regulatory Penalties and Offences* London: 2008.

- be responsive and consider what is appropriate for the particular offender and the regulatory issue;
- be proportionate to the nature of the offence and the harm caused;
- aim to restore the harm caused by the regulatory non-compliance, where appropriate, and
- aim to deter future non-compliance.

The new legislation is intended to deliver a more risk-based approach to regulation. This applies specifically in the environmental area to the work of the Environment Agency and also to the Health and Safety Executive. The aim is to simplify and streamline arrangements for regulation. This includes establishing a Local Better Regulation Office (LBRO) as part of the statutory framework of the Act. The function of LBRO is one of coordination and achieving consistency among local and central government. This includes issuing guidance to local authorities and ensuring that the guidance is complied with. It also brings into analysis the role of revising and reviewing national priorities and finding a sensible local authority strategy. There is also the role of achieving best practice and adopting, whenever relevant, innovation in the way local authorities provide regulatory services. There is also a major role in advising ministers and promoting consistency of enforcement by local authorities.

Part 3 of the Regulatory Enforcement and Sanctions Act 2008 provides a variable range of different penalties and sanctions. The aim is to tailor the penalty much more closely to the needs identified by the regulator. This provides a much more flexible and dynamic approach to regulation and this may depart from the current usage of criminal sanctions. It may be concluded that criminal sanctions for environmental matters have been used more frequently in recent years and the scale of the penalties available has increased. One example of a regulatory body employing criminal sanctions is shown in action taken by Ofwat, the regulator for water services. Ofwat has levied fines that amount to 10 per cent of a company's turnover. This is likely to be more severe than the fines that might have been levied by the courts. One estimate is that Severn Trent Water has been fined £34.7 million for deliberate misreporting and £1.1 million for providing sub-standard services.[46] The tenth report from the Environment Agency, which reviews the past 10 years, noted how serious pollution cases had declined but there was an increase in the number of prosecutions.

> The number of serious pollution incidents in 2007 was the lowest on record, while fines of just under £3 million were levied on businesses and individuals. Despite a record low number of serious permit breaches, the number of companies fined in Agency prosecutions rose to 284.[47]

The use of the criminal law by regulators is set to continue as the need for a sanctions-based approach to regulation is linked to a greater use of risk assessment.

Conclusions

Regulation in general and environmental regulation in particular is undergoing a fundamental reappraisal. There is a tension between using expert knowledge and specialist skills that provides scientific data in any regulatory structure and at the same time aspiring to democratic

---

[46] ENDS Report 402, July 2008, p. 61.
[47] ENDS Report, 24 July 2008.

governance. The media attention given to science often creates a counter-culture against the scientific lobby, with often unpredictable results. Science has also been under the spotlight in terms of expert witnesses and the use of scientific information and data in court cases. This creates tension between legal and non-legal approaches to the acceptance of science.

Consider how regulating the environment has progressed over the past few centuries. Science is linked to sustainable development and the concept of sustainable development[48] is aimed at enhancing the environment, protecting future generations against harm and securing a rise in the living standards of society as a whole. This rests on measuring change and preventing harm. Economic indicators rely on factual evidence rather than conjecture or subjective opinion. Scientific data sets the parameters for informed discussion and analysis. Risk assessment and the evaluation of harm is based on objective indices. The precautionary principle[49] supported by both European law and in international treaties requires an analysis of risks. As the Royal Commission concludes, risk assessment is central to the future strategy in developing environmental policy:[50]

> Risk assessments prepared in support of decisions on environmental policies or standards should start with information about the nature of the hazard which the policy or standard seeks to address and the extent and quality of the evidence available for assessing the risks it poses. This part of the analysis should indicate whether the hazard is of the relatively well-understood type; if it is unfamiliar, an attempt should be made to identify the most nearly analogous hazards and the aspects which are not understood.

Great care must, however, be taken when science is used in different settings and subject to different levels of certainty. In order to effectively set standards and determine risk scientific information is the obvious and necessary starting point. In the application of that science to standard-setting, however, it is essential to have a high degree of confidence in the experimental techniques used to acquire the information and in the rigour of the analysis. A firm perception and appreciation of the uncertainties in the science and methods used is also needed. The range of interpretations based on the available evidence should be clear. The scientific method and interpretations that underlie any standard setting should be transparent and available not only to regulators but also to the public.[51] Standard-setting must be an open-ended process. Science and scientific understanding that contributes to individual standards and the processes of standard-setting generally must be open to review. Increasingly the courts demand a more open and accountable formulation of standards, an inevitable consequence of the availability of judicial review.[52] The absence of a specialised regulatory environmental court remains a continuing weakness in the United Kingdom system of control. Streamlining risk management, standard-setting, and enforcement mechanisms fits the growing deregulation agenda to minimise the regulatory burden on businesses while increasing regulatory efficiency.

---

[48] The Amsterdam Treaty introduced this concept as part of Community law. The concept may also be found in a variety of Community legislation such as Regulation 306/95/EC. See L. Kramer, *EC Environmental Law* Sweet and Maxwell, 2000, p. 7.

[49] This is contained under Article 2(exB) of the Treaty of the European Union and Article 2 of the European Communities Treaty as part of the environmental objectives of the European Union; see EC Treaty Article 174.

[50] Royal Commission para. 4.50, p. 61.

[51] ENDS Report 289, p. 3.

[52] See Chapter 6 for an analysis of the role of the courts. See: *R v HM Inspector of Pollution, ex parte Greenpeace Ltd (No. 2)* [1994] 4 All ER 329.

Further reading

J. Alder and D. Wilkinson, *Environmental Law and Ethics* London: Macmillan, 1999.

C. Hilson, *Regulating Pollution: A UK and EC Perspective* Oxford: Hart Publishing, 2000.

R. Macrory, 'Regulating in a risky environment' [2001] *Current Legal Problems* 619.

R. Macrory, *Modernising Justice: Regulation and the Role of an Environmental Tribunal* March 2003 Centre for Law and the Environment. Faculty of Laws, University College, London (available through Defra)

R. Macrory, *The Environmental Justice Report* Environmental Law Foundation 2004 (available through Defra).

C. Scott, 'Accountablity in the regulatory state' (2000) 27 *Journal of Law and Society* 38–60.

F. White and K. Hollingsworth, *Audit, Accountability and Government* Oxford: University Press, 1999.

G. Winter, 'Perspectives for environmental law – entering the fourth phase' *Journal of Environmental Law* vol. 1 no. 1 p. 42.

C. Wood, *Environmental Impact Assessment* Harlow, Essex: Longman, 1996.

Reports and references

OECD, *Report of the OECD Workshop on Environmental Hazard/Risk Assessment*. Environment Monograph no. 105 (OECD, 1995).

OECD, *OECD Guidelines for the Testing of Chemicals, Plus the 9th Addendum* (OECD, 1998).

Ofwat, *Paying for Quality: The Political Perspective* (Ofwat, 1993).

Ofwat, *Paying For Water: A Time for Decisions* (Ofwat, 1991).

Ofwat, *Future Charges for Water and Sewerage Services: The Outcome of the Periodic Review* (Ofwat, 1994).

Visit **http://www.mylawchamber.co.uk/mceldowney** to access key issue checklists and practice exam questions to test yourself on this chapter.

 mylawchamber

8 Environmental law: issues for the twenty-first century

Introduction

Environmental law is at an interesting stage in its development. We have seen in previous chapters how a number of key issues cross boundaries between politics, law, economics and political science. These issues include sustainable development, particularly in the light of global warming and climate change, the regulation of agencies and the influence of EU and international law on the UK environmental law. It should not be forgotten, also, that all these aspects can be seen from the perspective of environmental rights.

Increasing concerns about oil prices and a downturn in the global economy have helped to propel the environment to the top of the political agenda. There is a growing concern that natural resources require direct and explicit legal protection. The growth of the economies in the developed world also underlines the need for environmental rights. Poorer countries lack the delivery and governance systems to effectively regulate the environment, making it essential that developed countries take on global responsibilities.

The EU provides a useful case study of the delivery of different techniques and strategies through legal structures. Setting environmental priorities and cross-cutting environmental protection through different sectors, for example, agriculture, energy and transport, is also a key prerequisite for the future development of environmental law. In this chapter we will draw together the arguments set out in the book so far about how improvements in the techniques and systems to protect the environment might be achieved. The chapter provides a summary of some of the main conclusions reached in the previous chapters. It is intended to help you develop different perspectives on environmental issues, engaging not only with law but also with the other subject disciplines that contribute to environmental law. This is particularly helpful when undertaking research into the social, economic and political background of legal rules. Moreover, seeking to integrate legal doctrine with different aspects of empirical understanding of environmental law is also important. The precise value of law and legal rules may also be questioned in a post-Hampton era where regulation is expected to deter non-compliance rather than simply penalise it. The road map of the different approaches to environmental law canvassed in previous chapters is set out below. It is hoped that the considerations set out in this chapter will encourage advanced study and research in environmental law and regulation. The idea is that by setting out some of the issues in anticipation of examining different sectors such as land, air and water, the reader will have a detailed understanding of the direction and trends in environmental law.

Researching and evaluating techniques and systems for the protection of the environment

Sources and institutions

In Chapter 1 the convergence of private and public law into a form that allows environmental law[1] to address environmental problems was examined. The product of nineteenth-century responses to environmental pollution, this approach enabled environmental law to adopt criminal or civil sanctions when appropriate. There is much to be gained through an historical analysis of how environmental law developed,[2] tracing the role of planning law and various inspectorates from the nineteenth century until the present day. An institutional approach that focuses on key institutions, such as the Environment Agency and the Royal Commission on Environmental Pollution, involved in environmental law and regulation is also valuable. The European Environment Agency is also a useful resource for environmental information as are the various pressure groups and organisations identified in Chapter 2. It is also possible to use a case-study approach to analysing environmental law that allows interrogation of the main lessons from experience. A theoretical analysis of environmental law allows us to engage with the main elements of philosophical and sociological thought about society.[3]

Recently the *UKCLE Law Subject Survey – Environmental Law*[4] reviewed the teaching and assessment of environmental law in England and Wales through analysis of a questionnaire. Group research work[5] and dissertation research revealed the growing use of websites and organisational investigation in studying environmental law.[6] A further approach is to follow the example of Brian Simpson in his *Leading Cases in the Common Law*.[7] There are two good examples drawn from Simpson's book where the usefulness of a case study analysis is apparent. His first example is the famous case of *Tipping* v *St Helen's Smelting Company*[8] in 1865 which examines the problem of social cost analysis in the private law of nuisance. The issue arose when Tipping sued St Helen's Smelting Company on the basis of private nuisance arising from pollution from copper smelting at the time of the industrial revolution in England. The claim of pollution was contested by the St Helen's Smelting Company on the basis of not having any better way to conduct the smelting business. There was the social cost of not having factories that had to be weighed up against the problems of pollution.

---

[1] See T.R.S. Allan, *Constitutional Justice: A Liberal Theory of the Rule of Law* Oxford: Oxford University Press, 2001.

[2] John McNeill, *Something New Under the Sun* London: Penguin Books, 2000.

[3] D. Wirth, 'Teaching and research in international environmental law' (1999) *Harvard Environmental Law Review* 423.

[4] S. Bell, D. McGillivray, A. Ross Robertson, S. Turner, *UKCLE Law Subject Survey – Environmental Law* UKCLE, University of Warwick, 2002.

[5] R. Hammer, 'Integrating interdisciplinary perspectives into traditional environmental law courses: the challenges of interdisciplinary teaching in environmental law' (1999) 23(3) *Journal of Geography in Higher Education*, 367.

[6] The main sources used included Open.gov UK, UK university sites at Cardiff, Keele and Kent as well as access to the main Parliament website and the devolved governments. Also listed are ENDS, Monsanto, Greenpeace, Friends of the Earth, FIELD, CIEL, IUCN, UKELA. Government departments included Defra.

[7] A.W. Brian Simpson, *Leading Cases in the Common Law* Oxford: Clarendon Press, 1995; see in particular chapters 7 and 8.

[8] (1865) LR 1 Ch App 66.

Although Tipping won damages and this was upheld on appeal, Simpson's case study showed that the smelting continued. It was only after an injunction was obtained to prevent a nuisance that the value of locating the smelting plant in close proximity to residents was questioned. After this the smelting plant moved away from the region. Subsequently, in 1874, the government intervened with legislation that provided a more adequate set of remedies than the common law provided. This is a good early example of the inadequacy of a remedy-based approach to the environment centred on the common law, and where state intervention eventually addressed the problem.[9] The case resulted with the setting up of a Royal Commission in 1878 to address the problems of industrial pollution. This example also illustrates how theoretical and interdisciplinary approaches may be used to address social and environmental problems.[10] This gives rise to the discussion of what is an efficient way to counter pollution and whether government intervention is amenable to an economic cost–benefit analysis.[11] The law of nuisance in particular is a fertile area for research and analysis in the development of environmental law.[12]

Simpson's second example[13] is *Rylands* v *Fletcher* in 1868. This case established a well-known rule that an escape of a dangerous thing in the course of a non-natural use of the land left the occupier liable for damage as a result of the escape. The main principle of liability under the rule was that liability came about irrespective of whether or not the occupier was at fault. Liability was limited to only the foreseeable consequences of the escape. The facts in *Rylands* v *Fletcher*[14] involved the damage caused by a reservoir bursting and flooding an adjacent colliery. There was no loss of life but some damage and the principles discussed in the case became important in the development of the law. This coincided with legislation, passed in 1853 and 1864, to require liability on waterworks with general application to the waterworks industry. The example of *Rylands* v *Fletcher* is illustrative of how environmental issues confront the common law and through interventions from the courts and parliament various solutions are found and explored. Private law offers useful insights into how environmental law developed through the law of pollution control, specifically nuisance and cases in negligence.

There is also much to be gained from adopting philosophical or theoretical approaches to environmental law. Environmental law can be interrogated though the medium of public law – how state power and governance addresses environmental protection. This involves issues about environmental regulation (see below). Equally important is how humans and the environment are in dialogue. Coyle and Morrow in their work[15] trace how the political philosophy of the seventeenth century has advanced ideas of public health and how private property rights had to be adjusted to take account of the competing demands between public and collective social duties and individualised property rights. The analysis offered by the authors challenges the assumption that the sum total of environmental law is the

---

[9] 37 and 38 Vict.c.43.

[10] A.W. Brian Simpson *op. cit.*, chapter 7.

[11] R.H. Coase, 'The problem of social cost' (1960) 3 JLS and also R.H. Coase (1996) 25 JLS 53–101.

[12] See: J.F. Brenner, 'Nuisance law and the industrial revolution' (1974) 3 JLS 403; J.P.S. McLaren, 'Nuisance law and the industrial revolution. Some lessons from social history' (1983) 3 OJLS 155.

[13] *Ibid.*, chapter 8.

[14] (1866) LR 1 Exch. 265.

[15] S. Coyle and K. Morrow, *The Philosophical Foundations of Environmental Law: Property Rights and Nature* Oxford: Hart Publishing 2004.

accumulation of statutory interventions by the state. An alternative analysis consists of a more holistic approach to environmental law:

> Environmental law, viewed as a series of arguments concerning responsibility and justice, might be thought of as the product of a sustained reflection upon the relationship between property, rights and nature; a body of philosophical speculation which has its roots in the deliberations of the natural rights of theorists of the seventeenth century.[16]

The approach taken is to avoid reliance on doctrinal interpretation of black letter rules devoid of much of the moral and philosophical foundations that underpin property, rights and nature. Thus it is argued that the most effective way to understand sustainable development is to see the underpinnings:

> The concepts of sustainable development, of inter-generational justice, and of human rights are best understood as attempts to offer an account of property rights according to underpinning conceptions of justice and responsibility . . .[17]

The value of such studies advances our knowledge and understanding of the environment and the role of law.[18] The advances in science have also shown how law, regulation and science may form the basis of a useful analysis.[19] Examining how environmental regulation can be sufficiently flexible and responsive to changes in scientific knowledge and technology is a key issue. Genetically modified organisms (GMOs) and nanotechnology are the obvious examples where research and understanding of legal rules may be helpful. A comparative analysis of how other jurisdictions achieve appropriate responses to scientific developments may also prove informative. Furthermore, examining how science can be successful incorporated as one element in policy-making and how scientific outcomes can be made more open and transparent to the public would be exceptionally valuable research.

Cultural studies are also relevant to understanding law and the environment. The wider social sciences have gained currency in the literature on culture and the environment.[20] General theories involving the social sciences have received slow acceptance among policy-makers on environmental law. Indeed, the growth of interest in environmental issues has spawned anew social science discourse that addresses the environment. There is a distinct discipline of environmental sociology that relates to regional and epistemological contributions. The emergence of environmental sociology[21] follows the acceptance of the subject as a distinct section within the American Sociological Association in 1976. This type of environmental study included the examination of energy and resource allocation with the perspective of how environmental decisions may affect society. Attitudes to the environment and the social impact assessment of the environment were in vogue and informed much of the sociological analysis of the period.[22] As the twenty-first century approached, environmental sociology moved towards an understanding of cause and effect, the impact of humans

---

[16] *Ibid.*, p. 215.

[17] *Ibid.*, p. 215.

[18] C. Manchester and D. Salter, *Exploring the Law* 3rd edn, London: Sweet and Maxwell, 2006.

[19] Joseph Corkin, 'Science, legitimacy and the law: regulating risk regulation judiciously in the European Community' (2008) *European Law Review* 359.

[20] K. Milton, *Environmentalism and Cultural Theory* London: Routledge, 1996.

[21] John A. Hannigan, *Environmental Sociology* London: Routledge, 1995.

[22] Michael Redclift and Graham Woodgate (eds), *The International Handbook of Environmental Sociology* London: Edward Elgar, 1997.

on nature and the different structural elements of society. The narrative of how society and the environment interact is linked to different concepts of human development and the interrogation of what sustainable development may mean in the context of society as a whole.

There is also a political aspect[23] to environmental law that addresses the role of the state and society.[24] Robin Attfield's study[25] on the *Ethics of the Global Environment* considers the fairness of environmental decisions seen in the context of global warming. The questions posed go to the heart of society and how biodiversity and global environment issues are to be addressed. One focus of the analysis is 'world citizenship' and how it informs societal responsibilities and how these are to be applied. This goes to a sharing of responsibilities and the acceptance of an ethical underpinning for the development of environmental law. There is a strong implication of a common stewardship and shared responsibility.[26]

Environmental stewardship and 'world citizenship' stretches beyond global warming. Conservation and the protection of biodiversity also fit into an ethical framework with societal responsibilities. The 2005 UN Millennium Ecosystem Assessment[27] that spanned the previous 50 years found substantial loss of biodiversity. While the Organisation of Economic Cooperation and Development[28] environmental outlook to 2030 paints a similarly bleak picture, warning of the need for urgent action to conserve natural habitats and biodiversity. The cost of this loss of biodiversity has been addressed in an interim EU Report,[29] which strongly argued for the substantial economic cost of biodiversity and ecosystem loss. The report is intended to provide an analysis of the costs of loss set against the cost of taking no action in the manner of the Stern report on the economics of climate change. It has been advocated by several groups that business profits from conservation, and that markets can be formed to avoid biodiversity loss, e.g. deforestation. The costs are economic with the loss of substantial resource, social with loss of earnings for example from the fish industry, and environmental with degradation of ecosystems and impacts on climate change from effects such as deforestation. Habitat and biodiversity conservation does not rest on the action of individual countries but, particularly in the context of globalisation, involves government and business engagement with environmental stewardship. How this is to be achieved offers an interesting and important area of further study.

In the UKCLE survey, one of the key challenges identified by the respondents to the survey is the difficulty of engaging in interdisciplinary research. Environmental law as a subject discipline undoubtedly requires this approach but despite this there are very few links between disciplines or active collaborations. Cooperation across disciplines would provide environmental law with enormous potential for the future and opens the way to exciting analysis at the boundaries of our knowledge. It is clear that the pathway to the successful completion of a dissertation or research project is a willingness to engage in the interdisciplinary aspects of environmental law.

[23] Jared Diamond, *Guns, Germs and Steel* London: Norton Company, 1997.

[24] Nicolas de Sadeleer, *Environmental Principles* Oxford: Oxford University Press, 2002.

[25] Robin Attfield, *The Ethics of the Global Environment* Edinburgh: Edinburgh University Press, 1999. Also see: I.G. Simmons, *Humanity and Environment* Longman, 1997.

[26] Also see: Philippe Sands QC, *Lawless World* London: Penguin Books, 2005, especially chapter 5.

[27] Available at *www.millenniumassessment.org/en/index.aspx*.

[28] Available at *www.oecd.org/dataoecd/29/33/40200582.pdf*.

[29] European Communities (2008) *The Economics of Ecosystems and Biodiversity Interim Report.*

One of the disciplines that is perhaps most difficult to engage with is science. Nonetheless the interaction between science and environmental law and regulation is worthy of study, since it throws up significant issues for the protection of the environment. These go from the best ways to deal with uncertainty to using sound science in regulation and policy development.[30] Other difficulties surround interactions between science and environmental law. How, for example, do we ensure that environmental law is sufficiently responsive to deal with and respond to scientific advances and knowledge? It may be the case that environmental regulation runs in front of scientific capability. The Water Framework Directive (2000/60/EC) requires member states to determine why surface water and groundwater fails to, or may fail to, meet 'good ecological status'. This raises a conundrum, since there really is no scientific definition or description of 'good ecological status' for water bodies, which reflects our paucity of knowledge about many systems. How should we proceed in such a situation? Engaging with science may be difficult but the issues generated are fundamental to environmental law.

International environmental law

The role of international environmental law has changed considerably as part of the shifting role of law and the state. International human rights has become one of the main aspects of that change and, consequently, international environmental law has had to elaborate and respond to world economic and social conditions that have global consequences. The focus of international law has also been adjusted to take account of the need to respect natural habitats and species as well as to prevent the degradation of the natural environment. Stakeholders engaged in developing companies to exploit natural resources are often the same stakeholders that should be engaged in resource protection. They are, in the end, dependent on the resources they exploit. Designing international environmental law norms is difficult because of the need to reconcile competing economic claims. Contracting states need to create a new legal order while at the same time preserving and enhancing the existing one.

Developing strategies that address environmental problems involves new techniques and modes of delivery in environmental law. The role of traditional legal values and the need for adaptation is recognised by Kiss and Shelton in their analysis of the future 'retooling of environmental law'. First they note how the values of law are often directed at the maintenance of the status quo:

> The objective of law is traditionally the safeguarding of present rights and interests: the respect for human rights, property, contracts, family relations, maintaining public order and security and peace. Environmental protection also tends to maintain and protect existing situations, such as the quality of water and air, the survival of certain wild species and the integrity of ecosystems.[31]

There is also the idea of preserving the environment for future generations, which is considered as part of the responsibility of citizenship. This gives rise to the concepts of prevention and precaution often based on a risk analysis that may not be rooted in scientific uncertainty.

[30] J. Jones (2007) 'Regulatory design for scientific uncertainty: acknowledging the diversity of approaches in environmental regulation and public administration' *Journal of Environmental Law* 19: 347–65.

[31] Alexandre Kiss and Dinah Shelton, *Guide to International Environmental Law* Leiden/Boston: Martinus Nijhoff Publishers, 2007, p. 272.

One could speak of a fundamental change in law: the irruption of the time perspective in legal orders traditionally aimed at the continuation and respect of present situations. The emergence of the concept of sustainable development also illustrates the temporal element: although development in itself is not a legal concept, the requirement that it should be sustainable, that is to say that it should continue, which involves the protection of the environment contributes to reinforcing role of the time dimension and in particular international law.[32]

International environmental law has created a new dimension to the traditional notion of law and its role in society. This is further extended by the idea that international legal principles should be adapted to apply beyond the single notion of trans-frontier harm and damage to the environment. The recognition that individuals living along state boundaries should be protected and have access to adequate remedies ensures that planned activities that are likely to have environmental repercussions might be better regulated.

Allied to the shifting role for international environmental law is the 2001 Aarhus Convention and its idea of environmental citizenship. This has considerable scope to enhance the development of environmental law. Citizenship is likely to further extend the idea of individualised rights in international law and may develop international environmental law beyond its current remit. The theory of international law and its practical application is undoubtedly fertile ground for analysis and elaboration.

European environmental law

In Chapter 5 we have seen how influential the European Union has been in shaping environmental law in the member states. The development of EU environmental policy-making is based around the implementation of an EU Sustainable Development Strategy. This embraces cross-cutting developments that identify and assess the environment in terms of legal rules, economic and political policy-making. The characteristic of EU law is setting priorities and developing through incremental means the acceptance of strategies that fit across the fields of agriculture, industrial policy, trade and industry. The work of the European Court of Justice is critical to this development and its successful implementation at the level of member states. The success or failure of EU environmental law will depend on getting the balance right between the avoidance of over-rigid rules and regulation and the opportunities to reduce pollution and manage natural resources satisfactorily. Success also requires good quality scientific data and advice, partly through risk assessment, to effectively contribute to decision-making and policy-making. It is the breadth and scale of EU regulatory activity that allows for a diverse and multi-layered approach. The role of the ECJ has been influential in the development of EU law. Policy-making of an incremental kind has ensured that the EU through its various Environmental Action Programmes is at the heart of the future of environmental law.

Human rights and the environment

Environmental human rights have brought a new expectation for citizens. Pressure groups are empowered through test cases and judicial review to bring actions against public

[32] *Ibid.*, p. 272.

authorities. In the United Kingdom liberalised laws of standing, *locus standi*, to sue help empower pressure groups to challenge the legality of decisions that could adversely affect the environment.[33] This creates a link with the media as a strategy for airing environmental issues and bringing public notice to environmental problems. We have seen in Chapter 6 that transparency in understanding environmental issues comes from an expanded role for environmental information. Environmental human rights engage with ordinary citizens and provide opportunities for public participation in environmental issues. They also allow individual cases that claim to be taken and the law to be enforced. A recent example highlights the line taken between accepting common law forms of remedies and integrating them into a human rights jurisprudence. The case in question, *Dobson v Thames Water Utilities*[34] was decided after the *Marcic* case extensively discussed in Chapter 6. Claimants who lived in close proximity to a sewage treatment works owned by Thames Water complained of smells and mosquitoes from the treatment works. Their claim was based on nuisance and negligence but also the Human Rights Act 1998. The claim was that Thames Water were in breach of their statutory and related duties because they failed to 'effectively deal' with the contents of the waste treatment plant. Thames Water argued that there was no common law right infringed and in any event the matters raised by the claimants fell within the powers of the statutory regulator Ofwat. The court held that in the absence of any negligence there was no liability in any nuisance claim. There was, however, the possibility that if the claimants' human rights were breached. This would allow damages to be granted, under the Human Rights Act 1998, in the award of compensation for inconvenience, mental distress and physical suffering. The decision gives considerable support for the view that human rights may help provide a healthy environment and, through the empowerment of minority groups or individual litigants, provide access to information as well as a basis on which to build environmental justice.

The theme of environmental justice is fundamental to the development of the next generation of environmental rights. The potential provided by the Aarhus Convention is intended to increase public participation[35] and substantially adopt the Aarhus Convention into the full context of environmental law. The full potential of allowing public participation in the environmental decision-making process has not yet been fully realised.

The value of environmental rights may also encourage a robust approach to the adaptation of the precautionary principle in environmental law. A rights-based approach may challenge decisions, such as the location of mobile phone masts or the positioning of electricity cables or power stations.[36] Balancing the environmental rights is not always clear-cut, and whether this balance changes with country is an interesting question (see 'Law in Context' box overleaf).

---

[33] S.M.C. Gibbons, 'Group litigation, class actions and Lord Woolf's three objectives – a critical analysis' (2008) *Civil Justice Quarterly* 208.

[34] *Dobson v Thames Water Utilities* [2008] 2 All ER 362.

[35] C. Nadal, 'Pursuing substantive environmental justice: the Aarhus Convention as a "pillar" of empowerment' (2008) Env LR 28.

[36] N.Y. Turgut, 'Mobile phone base stations and precautionary principle in the light of a civil court's judgement' (2008) *Journal of Business Law* 269.

LAW IN CONTEXT

Genetically modified organisms

The debate surrounding genetically modified organisms is a clear example where the boundaries of rights are blurred. The EU is two years into a six-year moratorium on the cultivation and import of GM crops. Some crops have already been given authorisation for import into the EU, some have been authorised for cultivation. There is a general consensus that there will be increasing pressure to allow cultivation within the EU in the context of rising food prices and biofuels.[37] The organic farming lobby is particularly concerned about the prospect; pollen does not respect boundaries between fields so that organic crops may be contaminated by GM pollen. At present there are no 'co-existence measures' in place in the UK. Such measures are intended to avoid cross-contamination of crops and provide compensation if contamination occurs. What of the environmental rights of organic farmers? On the other hand, GM research holds much promise for the development of drought-resistant crops, for example. Drought is likely to be an increasing problem in parts of Africa as a result of climate change. If the EU moratorium on GM crops delays the research and development of drought-resistant crops, are we infringing the environmental rights of individuals in parts of Africa? An analysis of the environmental costs and benefits of GM is difficult and may vary with circumstances. Engaging with rights takes public health and scientific research into the legal regulatory framework.

Regulation and standards in environmental law

Regulating the environment is regarded by many writers as the key function of environmental law. There is a rich and growing literature on regulation that has been neatly integrated into environmental problems. As Jane Holder notes in her study of environmental impact assessment:

> Analysis of the environmental assessment process in this book has revealed a functional fit between environmental governance and environmental assessment because of the way in which the assessment process is capable of dealing with the varying scale of environmental problems and engaging a range of public and private individuals and groups in decision-making thus encouraging environmental awareness. The importance of environmental assessment is a neat focal point for theories of environmental governance and the regulation of decision making.[38]

The significance of environmental governance is increasing. There is a growing collection of different environmental techniques and processes, divided among different regulators that provide a wide range of legal and economic options. The operation of a hybrid system of regulation that addresses both public and private sectors and uses public and private techniques of analysis provides another element of the jigsaw. This hybrid system also engages

---

[37] ENDS Report 398, March 2008, pp. 38–42.
[38] J. Holder, *Environmental Assessment: The Regulation of Decision Making* Oxford: Oxford University Press, 2004, p. 286.

with risk assessment and a new force in regulation namely *Really Responsive Regulation*.[39] Regulating the environment, then, adopts different regulatory tools and strategies together with different and variable enforcement tools and outcomes. This means that assessing the regulatory system is not static or fixed in time but requires a process of continuous monitoring. As set out in Chapter 7 in the post-Hampton world, regulating the environment has to fit into the current culture on regulation. The focus of good regulation is intended not to penalise and deter on its own but to change and educate the behaviour of the offender. It is also intended to act in a responsive and proactive way in ensuring that regulation is suitable and addresses the possibility of non-compliance.

Conclusions

Regulating the environment, the theme of Chapter 7, sets the parameters of modern environmental law. The hybrid nature of many of the bodies engaged in decision-making, which may affect the environment, also underlines the multidimensional nature of how the environment is best protected. Sustainable development sets the challenge of protecting the environment and of securing the market economy. How to reconcile economic growth and sustainable environmental policies is *the* challenge of the twenty-first century. Benjamin Richardson offers an interesting and provocative analysis. He questions the ethical considerations that underline the basic assumptions applied to protecting the environment. He argues that financial institutions, despite their current state, are fundamental to the future approaches that environmental law should take. His reasoning is that the general structure of financial markets fails to provide the correct institutional base on which to build good environmental decision-making.

> The domain of environmental law is not intuitively associated with banks, pension funds, and other financiers, the economy's unseen polluters.[40]

This creates the need for developing some form of socially responsible investment law (SRI). It provides a method as well as a working hypothesis of how to engage with financial business. As a method it provides a legal means of negotiating social and environmental issues into the true cost of goods and commodities. This can be done compulsorily or through price negotiation. Pricing the environment in this way brings to the fore the means of transforming the tensions between competing business interests into one of setting priorities that favour the environment. It also may be a means of bringing investment, business and the environment into some form of balanced economy. There is considerable scope for this approach as the market is also willing to negotiate 'good bargains'. Thus, the energy-efficient model might be chosen because it saves money, is more efficient than any competitive alternative that uses more resources and is less wasteful. It is likely to bring environmentally friendly products on to the market but raises the question of whether the financial markets will accept that protecting the environment is a requirement of good business practice. This is the hypothesis part of the analysis. Socially responsible investment law may be a

---

[39] R. Baldwin and J. Black, 'Really responsive regulation' (2008) 71(1) MLR 59–94.

[40] Benjamin Richardson, *Socially Responsible Investment Law: Regulating the Unseen Polluters* Oxford: Oxford University Press, 2008, p. 4.

means of encouraging investors to engage with environmental issues. Profit-making and social responsibility need to be intertwined, built on the ethics of environmental protection. Richardson also considers the various mechanisms that may underpin social responsible investment law. Essentially, economic instruments such as taxes on pollution, emission trading and other aspects of environmental law that provide incentives for environmental protection are essential. The crucial point is that the environment is not led by company-specific policies but through the financial instruments that underpin them and that this is a key element in setting a pathway towards sustainable development.

Is it possible for socially responsible investment laws to work? The opportunity is greatest in the current economic downturn as it is now that economic restructuring is likely to occur. As Richardson argues:

> Among the menu of reforms, the reformulation of fiduciary duties is crucial. They define the core goals and processes of decision-making within financial institutions. Through fiduciary duties we can redefine the traditional concept of 'benefit' to investors and thereby steer financiers toward sustainable development.[41]

It is this link that makes the idea of protecting the environment through socially responsible investment laws so intriguing. The twenty-first century may be the appropriate time to consider this interesting perspective, so that we can meet the challenges of sustainable development and global warming.

There are many questions surrounding the protection of the environment that will warrant careful consideration for the future. A few you might want to consider include:

- What is the future for environmental law in the face of economic constraints?
- How effective is environmental law likely to be in tackling climate change?
- To what extent does sound science inform the debate about the safety of new products and technologies, e.g. GMOs and nanomaterials?

Further reading

General

J. Alder and D. Wilkinson, *Environmental Law and Ethics* London: Macmillan Press, 1999.

K. Alexander, *et al.*, *Global Governance of Financial Systems* Oxford: Oxford University Press, 2006.

Dieter Helm, *Environmental Policy: Objectives, Instruments and Implementation* Oxford: Oxford University Press, 2000.

R. Lazarus, *The Making of Environmental Law* Chicago: University of Chicago, 2004.

B. Lomborg, *The Skeptical Environmentalist* Cambridge: Cambridge University Press, 2001.

[41] *Ibid.*, pp. 569–70.

Benjamin Richardson and Stephan Wood (eds), *Environmental Law for Sustainability* Oxford: Hart Publishing, 2006.

Benjamin Richardson, *Socially Responsible Investment Law: Regulating the Unseen Polluters* Oxford: Oxford University Press, 2008.

M. Woolf, *Why Globalisation Works* Yale University, 2004.

D. Zillman *et al.* (eds), *Human Rights in Natural resource Development* Oxford: Oxford University Press, 2002.

Case studies

I.J. Bateman, 'Environmental impact assessment, cost–benefit analysis and the valuation of environmental impacts' in J. Petts (ed.), *Handbook of Environmental Impact Assessment: vol. 1 Process, Methods and Potential* Oxford: Blackwell, 1999.

A. Boyle and D. Freestone (eds), *International Law and Sustainable Development* Oxford: Oxford University Press, 1999.

P. Harremoës *et al.* (eds), *The Precautionary Principle in the 20th Century: Late Lessons from Early Warnings* London: Earthscan, 2001.

J. Holder, *Environmental Assessment: The Regulation of Decision Making* Oxford: Oxford University Press, 2004.

Royal Commission on Environmental Pollution is an important source of information and analysis.

International environmental law

Daniel Bodansky, Jutta Brunnée and Ellen Hey, *The Oxford Handbook of International Environmental Law* Oxford: Oxford University Press, 2007.

Jane Holder and Maria Lee, *Environmental Protection, Law and Policy* 2nd edition Cambridge: Cambridge University Press, 2007.

Alexandre Kiss and Dinah Shelton, *Guide to International Environmental Law* Leiden/Boston: Martinus Nijhoff Publishers, 2007.

P. Sands, *Principles of International Environmental Law* 2nd edition Cambridge: Cambridge University Press, 2003.

European environmental law

C. Archer, *The European Union* London: Routledge, 2008.

D. Bodansky, Jutta Brunée and Ellen Hey, *The Oxford International Environmental Law* Oxford: Oxford University Press, 2006.

P. Craig and G. de Burca (eds), *The Evolution of EC Law* Oxford: Oxford University Press, 1999.

P.G.G. Davies, *European Union Environmental Law* London: Ashgate, 2004.

L. Kramer, *Casebook on EC Environmental Law* Oxford: Hart Publishing, 2002.

L. Kramer, *EC Environmental Law* London: 5th edition Sweet and Maxwell, 2003.

M. Lee, *EU Environmental Law* Oxford: Hart Publishing, 2005.

J. Scott, *EC Environmental Law* London: Sweet and Maxwell, 1998.

Han Somsen (ed.), *Yearbook of European Environmental Law* Oxford: Oxford University Press, 2000–.

Human rights and environmental law

A. Boyle and M. Anderson (eds), *Human Rights Approaches to Environmental Protection* Oxford: Clarendon Press, 1998.

S. Coyle and K. Morrow, *The Philosophical Foundations of Environmental Law: Property Rights and Nature* Oxford: Hart Publishing, 2004.

Tim Hayward, *Constitutional Environmental Rights* Oxford: Oxford University Press, 2005.

Science and environmental law

U. Beck *Risk and Society* London: Sage, 1992.

Han Somsen (ed.), *The Regulatory Challenge* London: Edward Elgar, 2007.

J. Steele, *Risks and Legal Theory* Oxford: Hart Publishing, 2004.

Regulation and standards in environmental law

I. Ayres and J. Braithwaite, *Responsive Regulation* Oxford: OUP, 1992.

R. Baldwin and J. Black, 'Really responsive regulation' (2008) 71 *Modern Law Review* 59–64.

J. Black, 'The emergence of risk based regulation and the new public risk management in the UK' (2005) *Public Law* 512.

M. Cave and R. Baldwin, *Understanding Regulation* Oxford: Oxford University Press, 1999.

N. Gunningham and P. Grabosky, *Smart Regulation: Designing Environmental Policy* Oxford: Clarendon Press, 1998.

C. Hilson, *Regulating Pollution: A UK and EC Perspective* Oxford: Hart Publishing, 2000.

T. Jewell and J. Steele (eds), *Law in Environmental Decision Making* Oxford: Clarendon Press, 1998.

M. MacNeil, N. Sargent and P. Swan (eds), *Law, Regulation and Governance* Oxford: Oxford University Press, 2003.

J. McEldowney and S. McEldowney, *Environmental Law and Regulation* Oxford: Oxford University Press, 2001.

21st Report of the Royal Commission on Pollution: *Setting Environmental Standards* Cm 4053.

Visit **http://www.mylawchamber.co.uk/mceldowney**
to access key issue checklists and practice exam
questions to test yourself on this chapter.

Part II

Sectoral coverage of environmental law

Introduction to Part II

Substantive environmental law is found in the main sectoral areas, which are land, water and air. In part this is a legacy of the past but it serves to emphasise the specialist and technical nature of environmental law. One approach to studying environmental law is through an institutional focus. This is a common method used in many textbooks and it has great value. It illustrates the contribution of local and central government to environmental law in the United Kingdom and provides the opportunity for useful discussion of why this is the case.

The role of local government in environmental law is an attempt to engage with local communities and citizens in a way that reflects cultural diversity. Local government has specific legal responsibilities over contaminated land, waste collection and disposal, the prevention of fly-tipping and litter controls as well as disposal of abandoned vehicles. They also have important roles in the operation of a system of statutory nuisances and in planning law. The various district councils and also London borough councils as well as unitary authorities are under a duty to inspect their area for any statutory nuisance and to take action as part of an inspection process or on the initiative of an individual citizen with a specific grievance. There are broad and general categories of statutory nuisance organised around the central concept of anything complained of that is 'prejudicial to health or nuisance'. A variety of powers are extended to allow the nuisance to be abated or, where there are specific powers such as noise pollution, that regulate sounds and allow local authorities to investigate and take preventative steps. There are considerable powers over neighbours, including restricting the size of hedges.

Aside from statutory nuisance powers there are various statutory arrangements for specific problems, such as contaminated land or the control of waste. In fact, the most substantial area of local authority powers is over the planning process and system. Since 1947 town and country planning has developed to provide a complex, technical and proactive as well as reactive means of achieving planning development in the context of a social, political and economic framework. Planning is based around development plans that incorporate the main features of environmental protection. The planning system is policy-driven but under strict and enforceable legal controls. These are subject to the supervisory powers of the courts but also more directly: for an applicant in the planning process there is an appeal to the Secretary of State for a refusal or relating to the conditions of a planning permission. The development control process consists of planning permission obtained from the relevant local planning authority. The submission of plans, their agreement and eventual ratification allows participatory involvement of planners, local planning officials, lawyers, and ultimate political control through the creation of planning policy guidance. There is also a link in the planning process to what might be loosely described as the principle of sustainable development. This is an important shift in the way planning operates once a direct element of planning law incorporates sustainable development principles. As Chapter 9 explains, the potential for bringing environmental protection into the planning system is at its highest, given the rise in energy costs and the impact of global warming on the economy.

An important element of environmental concerns relate to contaminated land, waste disposal in landfill, and land use. Local authorities have the power to impose planning conditions and enter into agreements relating to environmental protection as part of the planning system and the granting of permission. There are many environmental issues raised in the planning process and the developer engages with the planning authorities in a negotiation of how best to implement plans while incorporating environmental protection. Increasingly this process is a 'barter' between the developer and the planning authority. The agreed bargain may form a demonstrable part of planning gain.

One of the difficulties of the planning system, particularly where there is conflict over policy, is to ensure that sufficient priority is given to environmental matters. The opportunity for local authorities to combine the interests of developers and the environment is high, but too often the environment has been the weaker part of the bargaining that inevitably accompanies planning decisions. It is not surprising that the environment is at the centre of considerable conflict between interest groups, and planning law often provides the context for disputes. It is also clear that there is an inevitable tension between local and central government. In part this may come from party-political differences but there are also different expectations linked to central government policy-making. It is not uncommon for local interests to be unrecognised in central government policies. There are also competing economic needs between rich and poor regions. Competing for scarce resources inevitably brings environmental issues to the fore – especially when jobs and economic growth are at stake. This is likely to become particularly evident in the future when natural resources continue to dwindle and energy costs become increasingly expensive. In fact, energy is often overlooked as an important basis for many environmental disputes. Regional geography amply illustrates how the North–South divide is recognisable in terms of different natural resources. Agriculture is also a basis for differentiation between regions. Large urban areas generate more taxes than sparsely populated areas but have substantial environmental implications. In some ways the problems of urban conurbations and industrial sites are self-evident. Industry brings with it the risks associated with accidental or permitted release of diverse pollutants to the environment. Concentrations of people bring problems of waste and sewage disposal. Historic pollution from industry brings problems such as contaminated land. The environment of pavements and roads, of houses and factories built on flood plains bring increased difficulties for flood control, particularly in the extreme weather events that appear more common. Urban environments are demanding to manage and plan appropriately but reliance on intensive agricultural production is no less difficult and also has an important environmental dimension. Management of agricultural land influences how areas flood; it affects the conservation of biodiversity, and the health of soil. Farming also has significant polluting effects. Intensive animal husbandry generates large volumes of waste and this, together with the application of biocides and fertilisers to crops, make substantial contributions to diffuse pollution of water bodies. The friction between overarching planning policy and local plans are felt just as keenly in agriculture as in urban developments. The solutions that provide environmental protection are often local not central.

We have so far briefly focused the institutional approach to studying environmental law through the central and local government divide. There are, of course, other institutions that contribute to environmental law, including agencies, regulators and courts (Chapter 3). The operation of the Environment Agency is a good example of where an institutional approach to studying environmental law is helpful. In this regard environmental assessment is a key mechanism for the determination of the potential environmental impact on development projects. As a procedural hurdle the system of environmental assessment is both a deliberative and preventative technique that integrates into the decision-making system of environmental law.

The institutional approach, however, is not the only way to study environmental law and if an institutional-based approach is not adopted entirely then it is possible to see environmental problems and challenges in a wider context. Principles and policies are focused on environmental problems that are defined not simply by the legal rules, but by the nature of the problem itself. In recent years, as outlined in Part I of the book, there has been a major shift in the direction that environmental law has taken law. This has been through its development of techniques and practices that go beyond the traditional private and public law solutions to environmental problems. This means that modern environmental law cannot be perceived as merely the application of nuisance, negligence or judicial review actions to environmental problems. The sectoral areas allow an analysis of how local and central government come together with a hybrid of different varieties and types of control. It also provides the opportunity for specific case studies of the challenges and issues that confront our land, water and air.

Land and the environment

In terms of organising the sectoral areas in this section of the book, our account begins with land and the environment in its three dimensions. In Chapter 9, the role of planning and how this may impact on the environment is assessed. Since the Second World War the United Kingdom planning system has had to satisfy competing demands. The need to build new cities and towns expanded the urban environment into many green spaces particularly in the main industrial areas of the North and Midlands. High population density resulted in many industrial areas becoming urban slums, with poorly managed architectural design in the 1960s leading to major housing problems. The main impact of land-use planning on land and the built environment is explained in this chapter and how planning controls may assist in environmental protection is considered. There is also specific consideration of the operation of environmental impact assessment and how this process may help environmental protection. The second element of land and the environment is the management of waste. In Chapter 10, the control of waste is discussed as one of the most important ways to address the protection of the environment. There is a range of devices and techniques applicable to waste control that cover the life cycle of materials from initial production to final disposal. The application of different strategies, including steps to minimise waste through techniques such as recycling and recovery, is considered. The effectiveness of waste minimisation strategies is assessed, as is the use of various economic instruments, including taxation in waste control and the regulation of waste through the EU and international law.

The third element of land and the environment relates to strategies to manage land and protect the natural environment. In Chapter 11, the protection of our countryside and the protection of plants, animals and the natural habitat are discussed. This is a subject that is easily overlooked in terms of how the law addresses environmental issues. Environmental law has a proactive role in protecting wildlife and habitats. A substantial number of UK species and habitats are endangered and at risk. The extent of the problem is well illustrated by the fact that Natural England has action plans for the 'recovery' of 93 species – e.g. the native oyster and the pennyroyal – and 15 habitats – e.g. fens and lowland calcareous grassland – in England alone. Competing interests and conflicts over priorities create enormous pressures on the system of protection at every level of development. Gradually over the years there has been greater integration between nature conservation and environmental decision-making. Species and habitat protection is also a good example of laws at domestic, European Union and international levels providing different regimes. The loss of species and habitat is the consequence of a variety of factors most commonly human-made, including the global impacts of climate change and even pollution and more local impacts such as agricultural practices. The conservation of nature, then, links environmental law to the difficult global dimension of the environment as well as to the practicalities of local protection.

Water and the environment

There are two chapters that address the quality of the water environment. In Chapter 12 the operation of domestic, EU and international law for the regulation of water quality, one of the most significant developments in environmental law for many years, is considered. In addition to addressing issues that surround water quality there is also an explanation of how water is regulated and how setting quality standards is an essential element in the future of environmental law. The marine environment is given specific analysis in Chapter 13 outlining in particular how international and EU law protects the marine environment. Estimates vary but a large proportion of marine pollution is the result of discharges from land – either from agricultural run-off or because of discharges from industrial processes. There is a growing concern that marine pollution and the effects of global warming on our seas will have long-terms effects on future generations.

Air

The legal controls over atmospheric emissions and air quality are the subject of this section. There are two chapters. In Chapter 14, air and pollution is considered. The issues of climate change and ozone depletion have given this area a singular importance. Despite the significant nature of these problems, there are also important attempts to address health and environmental effects that come about because of poor air quality. In common with the other sectors, land and water, the consideration of air quality also incorporates domestic, EU and international law. The approaches to address air quality have varied from attempts to set air quality standards to preventing pollution through techniques such as integrated pollution control and preventative measures aimed at protecting the environment through controls over smoke and fumes. You will remember that the early history of environmental law was significantly shaped through techniques and regulations to control emissions (Chapter 2). Chapter 15 considers noise and its control. Significant advances have been made in addressing noise pollution and setting up a local system of control. This is an area where local controls in the United Kingdom gives considerable powers to local authorities, involving statutory nuisance, the application of standards to noise and the general protection of the environment. The problem of noise pollution has increased largely because of the scale and nature of modern industrial processes, transport and domestic appliances. Environmental rights are important when citizens complain about noise and seek redress in the courts.

Conclusions

The final Chapter 16, addresses the overarching themes of environmental law and conclusions that arise from its study. There are several conclusions that will be discussed and are briefly summarised here.

- Environmental law has developed its own identity through a series of complex, often interrelated techniques that provide reactive, proactive and preventative means to protect the environment.

- There is an overlapping use of different regulatory systems that apply to the environment generally but also specifically to different sectors. Assessing whether competing values and norms are working is a difficult task.

- Environmental law operates at different levels of legal control: domestic, EU and international. This provides a great variety of ideas and influences – perhaps leading to unnecessary complexity.

- Today environmental law has developed significant complex and interwoven techniques for the protection of the environment. Assessing the effectiveness of how environmental law is working is difficult and challenging.

- The need to assess environmental law in terms of whether the law is adequately addressing risks and harm is paramount to the future.

- Competing interests are prevalent in setting a balance for sustainable development. Assessing market needs and environmental necessities are controversial and it is important to establish how environmental law addresses the changing needs of society.

- Protection and conservation strategies often have limited success especially in the context of significant impacts on the environment, such as climate change and rapid economic development.

- Economic growth without adequate environmental protection is likely to prove prohibitively expensive if the costs of environmental pollution are accurately assessed. In the post-Stern era the economic cost analysis of environmental pollution may ultimately provide an incentive to protect the environment that is more effective than reliance on legal regulation alone.

- Environmental law lacks a comprehensive and easily understood formulation of its aims and objectives. This may lead to a multiplicity of competing ideas that make decision-making difficult and policy-making almost impossible to agree upon.

- Science is one of the foundations for environmental law, providing evidence and evaluation. Public participation and understanding of environmental law faces a significant challenge because of the demands of communicating scientific ideas and values. Concepts such as scientific uncertainty and risk must be carefully explained and if science cannot provide a definitive answer because of lack of knowledge this must be made clear. Addressing our understanding of science is a major hurdle that must be overcome if the public is to be informed and involved in the protection of the environment.

- The development of environmental law and policy relies on 'good' science which is sufficiently robust and reliable to be used in the assessment of environmental risks, and as information sources that forms part of the basis for policy-making.

- Studying environmental law is an interesting way to provide an analysis of how law addresses different problems in society. Environmental law crosses the traditional discipline-focused boundaries, and requires an evaluation of economic, scientific and theoretical subjects. The use of legal rules to protect the environment as part of a global responsibility to safeguard our world for future generations should not be underestimated.

- Environmental protection may be achieved through incentives as well as punitive measures. The function of environmental law is multidimensional. As well as its primary aim, protecting the environment, it must also offer solutions to disputes over the environment. Reconciling competing interests is one of the greatest challenges facing the environment today.

- Traditionally legal systems and laws may be judged on how effective the rules and laws are in resolving disputes and in providing adequate remedies for conflicts and problems. Environmental law has the potential to move legal discourse to the dimension of setting priorities for policy-makers, and building the protection of the environment into the fabric of society through taxation and financial instruments.

- Environmental law is developing a rights-based dimension that, at both procedural and substantive levels, may enhance scope for environmental protection. The future shape of public and private rights may ultimately have to be adjusted to take account of fundamental environmental rights.

- There is much scope for the development of environmental law in the twenty-first century. It is likely to succeed, provided public confidence and political awareness recognises and agrees that protecting the environment is a priority. The assortment of legal and economic tools and techniques open to environmental law may change the nature and shape of how legal rules are generally perceived and applied.

9 Land, planning and the environment

Introduction

Town and country planning is an important means of regulating land use and shaping the urban environment. The scale and diversity of planning activity is vast. In England alone, for example, in 2007–8 the planning authorities received 649,000 planning applications and made decisions on 596,000 applications. Over 82 per cent of applications decided were granted – an average that appears consistent with those of previous years. There is clearly a robust and active planning system at work as the following statistics for the year 2007 to 2008 indicate:[1]

- 71 per cent of planning decisions on major applications were made within 13 weeks;
- there were 5,565 enforcement notices and 5,039 planning contravention notices issued at district council level.

There are many different dimensions to a planning system – from social and political to the nature and scope of economic development and to the environmental impact. The placing of a major development – a factory, a major road or even a town may have enormous significance for the employment, economic wealth and well-being of the citizens living nearby. Undoubtedly planning[2] has a major impact on the economy and this may impact on ordinary people in quite significant ways – the high cost of home ownership is partly attributable to a scarcity in housing, and realising appropriately the government's planned increase in new housing is highly dependent on an efficient planning system. It is also dependent on the staff and quality of the planning officers who are essential for the implementation of planning policy – currently there is a serious shortage of planning officers. Planning may equally have serious consequences for the environment. The interaction between the planning system and the state of the environment is the particular focus of this chapter.

The planning system offers expertise and specialist knowledge that contributes to a diverse range of building developments, engaging with both the design and building of these

---

[1] Communities and Local Government, Development Control Statistics for England, 2007–8. August, 2008.
[2] 11th Report House of Commons Select Committee, Communities and Local Government Committee: Planning Matters–Labour Shortages and Skills Gaps, HC 517-I 24 July 2008.

projects.[3] It also permits local communities to be involved in developing their own distinctive identities and preserve or enhance their cultural and historical heritage. Democratic input is another important hallmark of the planning system in the United Kingdom. The planning system provides an opportunity to balance competing interests and adjudicate on the needs of ordinary citizens as well as the demands of business and the market economy. It is both reactive and anticipatory in the forms of the controls it provides. Specific developments from large airports or power stations to large-scale industrial developments or retail outlets have to be accommodated, while more modest developments such as individual housing must also be accommodated by the planning system. These differences in scale and the difficulties of balancing the competing needs for social and economic development in the context of environmental protection often make planning a controversial activity.

In the past, planning also faced many stresses and strains as the agricultural community in Britain increasingly moved to cities and industrial work from the end of the nineteenth century. At that time the planning system was relatively unsophisticated and these developments were given priority. The modern system of planning dates back to the period just after the Second World War. The need for rebuilding towns and cities and the continued growth in the industrial population required new towns to replace the old, destroyed during the war. The focus of much of the planning arrangement was not to provide a solution to environmental problems but to develop, through a wide range of strategies, controls over the built environment. The influences of modern architecture and urban planning were linked to the provision of social and economic strategies for living. Environmental issues fell very broadly within the spectrum of these strategies but were not given the prominence that perhaps they should have received. This chapter addresses how planning law and the environment interact. It begins with an outline of the planning system, followed by an examination of the current process and procedures. Finally, there is a discussion of the application of environmental impact assessment (EIA) and how as part of the planning system EIA may offer environmental protection greater priority than hitherto. The chapter provides some conclusions on how planning law may have the potential to protect the environment, provided politicians and lawyers recognise the priority of that protection. In recent legislation there has been a strong focus on linking energy conservation in buildings with environmental protection. A further link between energy and planning can be found in the target for renewable energy to provide 10 per cent of the UK's electricity generation by 2010. The need for energy-efficiency and non-fossil fuel generation of energy reflect our international obligations to reduce carbon emissions in an effort to limit global warming and also the changing cost of oil with its deleterious impact on the economy. This will involve the planning system in the consideration of both small- and large-scale projects such as wind turbines, electricity-generating tidal barrages and even nuclear sites (see Law in context, below). The recent White Paper, Planning for a Sustainable Future,[4] provides a more detailed analysis of the requirement for speed, responsiveness and efficiency in land-use planning especially when it comes to major structural plans.[5] There is also the beginning of a sea change in how we view cities

---

[3] There are several recent consultations on planning as an indication of the high priority given to planning and the environment. The first is a Defra consultation paper on a new planning policy for development and coastal change. The second is a Defra paper on Planning Policy Statement 25 relating to Development and Flood Risk.

[4] *Planning for a Sustainable Future* Cm 7120, 21 May 2007.

[5] See HM Treasury, Kate Barker and Rod Eddington.

and towns as part of the sustainability agenda that will substantially affect planning. The Royal Commission on Environmental Pollution reported on the urban environment[6] and included consideration of improving the environmental performance of the built environment and the 'green' urban environment generally through planning policy. In similar vein, the government has announced that between 10 and 15 'eco-towns' are planned for the future. These are based on the premise that the built environment can be sustainable and designed with the lowest possible environmental impact through water efficiency measures and ensuring a carbon footprint of zero.[7] The change in the way we view our towns and cities will have substantial impact on planning into the future.

LAW IN CONTEXT

Climate change and planning

Planning will form a central plank in our response to climate change. The UK government has recently set a target to cut greenhouse gas emissions to 80 per cent of their 1990 levels by 2050. Such a target will require substantial changes in our energy infrastructure as well as in our built environment. Renewable energy options, such as water, wind, solar, geothermal and biomass produced energy, are likely to become increasingly important in our attempts to reach greenhouse gas emission targets. As part of the strategy to reach this reduction the proposal is for 15 per cent of our energy needs to be from renewable sources by 2020. This is a substantial increase in our present renewable capacity, which stands at 1.4 per cent of energy consumption. The National Audit Office, in a recent report,[8] has pointed out that this will require the removal of barriers to renewable technologies, including planning constraints. Renewable technologies are not without environmental controversy. Wind farms, for example, are often opposed on the basis of their visual impact on the landscape, and they are noisy. There is a programme for the development of offshore wind farms but this has also proved controversial, raising issues such as risks to shipping. Nevertheless, British offshore wind capacity currently stands at 864 megawatts with a further five winds farms being built or completed in the near future, bringing the total to 10,281 megawatts. The Sustainable Development Commission supports the plan for a £15 billion tidal barrage to be built across the River Severn that could supply up to 5 per cent of the UK's electricity. The commission views that lost wetlands would be compensated for elsewhere so that the benefits outweighed the disadvantages. The National Trust, the RSPB and the WWF disagree, claiming that up to 35,000 ha of protected wetland would be destroyed. Balancing such difficult issues falls within the ambit of the planning system. Whatever happens, renewables cannot meet all of our energy needs. There is the evolving policy to build new nuclear plants to fill the gap.[9] Nuclear

➡

---

[6] Royal Commission on Environmental Pollution 26th Report *The Urban Environment* March 2007 Cm 7009.

[7] See for information, Dept. for Communities and Local Government, *Eco-Towns Living a Greener Future: Progress Report*, July 2008.

[8] The National Audit Office *Renewable energy: Options for Scrutiny*. July 2008.

[9] Department for Business, Enterprise and Regulatory Reform, *Meeting the Energy Challenge: A White Paper on Nuclear Power, January 2008* CM 7296.

power stations are even more controversial, with concerns over their safety, security and the environmental impact of any accident and of their decommissioning and nuclear waste disposal. The last nuclear power plant given planning permission in the UK was Sizewell B. Sir Frank Layfield delivered the planning inquiry report for this installation in 1987; the inquiry began in 1982. Energy-efficiency measures in buildings and new plans for eco-towns all fall within the remit of planning. Our management of climate change will require proactive solutions throughout the planning system. This will require a radical break from the past and a determination on the part of government to make tough planning decisions as part of the policy-making system.

CASE STUDY

Planning as a tool to help protect the environment

One interesting characteristic of the planning system today is the requirement to promote environmentally friendly and sustainable options. This is a proactive function and is a departure from the traditional role of planning to prevent building and enhance the natural environment through greenfield sites. Wind farms, for example, are best situated in exposed windy areas of countryside, not unusually in areas of unspoilt countryside, National Parks and even sites of scientific interest. Over the past five years there has been a significant increase in applications to build wind farms and the government is under pressure to build and resource at least 28 gigawatts (GW) of electricity through wind. This forms part of the drive to reduce our reliance on fossil fuels and lower the production of greenhouse gases during energy production. Currently, in 2010, 3939 megawatts of wind power generating capacity have been built. An average of 2,000 planning applications has been made each year since 2006, with over one-third of applications gaining approval. There have been inevitable time delays as each application is considered, and there remains a considerable pressure to build at least another 6.7 GW by 2020. It would appear that there are sufficient planning consents given to meet that target, indicating that the planning system is coping with the extra demand on its activities and has also developed and applied its own specialist knowledge of this area.[10] The future of planning law will increasingly find a role for developing proactive policies to protect the environment in the broadest sense.

Planning strategies and the environment

The key mechanisms used to develop town and country planning need to be explained at the outset. The main framework is set by the development plan. This designates the overall strategy for a specific area and acts as a guide to what can take place. The planning authorities are expected to make specific decisions, taking into account the overall framework set by the

[10] ENDS Report 415, August 2009, p. 4.

development plan. The definition of what constitutes development is broadly defined in the relevant planning legislation. This includes change of use as well as all physical development. The planning authorities are usually the local authority in the area – this gives planning a local characteristic and provides a community a link to planning and developments in their neighbourhoods. There are specific areas where planning permission is rarely given – conservation areas where there are listed buildings or historical sites of national interest. There are a range of fairly minor changes to buildings which do not require formal planning permission but where building controls are used instead. House extensions and conservatories are within this category, but building control does not apply to listed buildings which require specific permission for any alterations. Change of use of all buildings, however, requires planning permission. In the light of the Hampton Review (explained in Chapter 7), which seeks to reduce regulation, the government plans to change the planning arrangements, allowing more extensive minor developments to be exempt from planning permission. The process of making an application for planning permission is essentially a study in a consultation process. Those likely to be affected by the planning permission are notified and may make representations about the proposed plan. The specific details of the plans are made open to the public and a public consultation takes place. The plans are accessible to the general public and can be inspected by them. There is a period of days for objections to be made.

Central government has input into the planning process by putting forward overall objectives and strategies. Material considerations may be set out in these strategies for consideration by and guidance of the planning authorities. While the decision to grant or refuse permission falls within the remit of the planning authorities, there is a broad discretion for the basis of the decision. This includes careful consideration of the development plan, the policy guidance provided by central government and the merits of each case. Planning permission may be subject to conditions and in certain cases, such as large-scale developments, there is express provision for planning conditions or even contributions to the development costs for infrastructure in the area or for environmental requirements to be addressed.[11] The latter may form a useful basis for planning to be linked to environmental considerations. For example, comprehensive building regulations apply to new housing intended to up-rate the energy efficiency of new housing and insisting on higher housing standards.

The planning system in the United Kingdom has not favoured third-party appeals against the grant of planning permission or of any conditions set by the planners when agreeing a planning application. If an applicant fails to obtain planning permission, however, there is a right of appeal to the Secretary of State under section 78(i) of the Town and Country Planning Act 1990 against that refusal or against any planning conditions set in the planning permission. There can also be an appeal by the applicant under section 78(ii) of the 1990 Act if the authority fails to decide within the statutory period of appeal ('non-determination') or such other period as agreed by the parties. The process of appeal involves a rehearing of the issues raised by the planning application, including general policy issues defined by the general social, economic and political framework of the planning process.

The appeal process provides the Secretary of State with proactive powers and a position at the apex of the planning system. This effectively is a way of ensuring a degree of local planning authority compliance with the general policy set by the government of the day. There is also an incidental but significant effect – namely that the planning process is subject

---

[11] See: Planning-gain Supplement (Preparations) Act 2007.

in the final analysis to the overarching political agenda set by the government. This is the ultimate form of citizen participation – allowing politicians to set the direction and purpose of planning. The role of the Secretary of State may appear to interfere with the concept of fairness – a political decision being incompatible with an opportunity to have an unbiased hearing. This issue was discussed by the House of Lords in *Alconbury*. It was held that the provisions for the Secretary of State to consider appeals on planning issues was theoretically compatible with the Human Rights Act 1998, but subject to the supervision of the courts through judicial review. There is also a right of appeal against a decision by the Secretary of State to the High Court through judicial review. This gives the courts both a substantive and a procedural role of overseeing the planning process. There is an important restriction on this oversight, since the merits of the policy are not within the scope of judicial review.

It is often asked how planning is enforced in the United Kingdom. The answer is that planning permission is a means of ensuring the legality of the project. Failure to have permission, while not in itself a criminal offence, is subject to enforcement notices. Such notices are subject to criminal and civil penalties. Failure to comply with permission or certain conditions set out in the permission may allow the planning authorities to directly intervene and require compliance. Demolition of part or all of the contested development may well be required.

In the description given above, it is clear how few environmental matters are raised directly in the planning process. The need to provide environmental priorities within the scope of the planning law is apparent – but this takes time and effort. Energy-efficiency homes are now recognised as an important part of protecting the environment and this has been the subject of recent attention in planning policy. If sensibly used, planning has a great potential to develop and enhance the environment. As development plans are essential to the planning process it is arguably that there should be environmental plans that set sustainable goals for each new development – including traffic, incidental costs to the environment and issues such as vulnerability to flooding. This may seem to be too idealistic a vision but, even on the grounds of cost today, cutting energy bills and protecting against flood damage must rank as a higher priority than before.

Central government guidance is also an important means of ensuring that government objectives and targets are set and met. Here, as with development plans, there are important opportunities for inputs from various public bodies, including the Environment Agency and the Utility Regulators. Many of the principles set out in government objectives are examples of anticipatory planning controls and this makes them very relevant to environmental protection. Equally it is possible for environmental matters to be seen as an ongoing and continuous problem. The planning system has enormous potential in providing environmental protection on a continuous basis. The wealth of possibilities for the use of the planning process to protect the environment is yet to be fully realised. This is partly because of inertia on the part of government and partly because of the fear that environmental considerations will lead to additional costs. There are concerns that developers will be inhibited from investing in developments if environmental standards are set too high. The approach of bringing environmental matters to the heart of planning can be seen as overly prescriptive and too interventionist for many commentators.

The planning system can also be viewed as deliberative or conflict-resolution-focused. Planning is primarily expected to negotiate between participants at community level. Thus local government, with its experience of its own community, is given enormous scope for deliberation on planning issues. Developers and local authorities are increasingly working in partnership. In fact planning gain allows a local authority to extract financial rewards from developers that provide for the development of the community – a new swimming pool or an upgrade for a park or a community centre. Incentivising planning in this way links planning into the market economy and allows many developers to feel that planning and the market are intertwined. This has not always worked out. Developers complain of inconsistency between local authorities and delays, regulatory burdens that are too great, and too much technical interference in the operation of building controls. Citizens complain that their voices are not heard, that developers are given too much influence and that the overall effects lead to poorly planned infrastructure, and traffic congestion. There is also little scope for environmental protection to be seriously given a high priority. As much of the planning process is to do with the urban environment, many critics argue that this leaves agriculture hardly regulated and it is here that the environment may need greatest protection. The current system of planning law is an historical legacy that leaves the environment as an afterthought and, as will be seen, this is particularly true of large-scale planning projects. The environment requires active attention as part of a continuous process of control. Managing the environment needs to be built into the planning system, where the implications of developments are more actively assessed. Even as far back as 1976 the Royal Commission on Environmental Pollution warned about the need to give greater priority to the role of the planning system in environmental protection. In recognition of the growing significance of the environment to planning, the government has launched a strategy for sustainable development *Securing the Future*[12] that sets environmental issues in the context of using natural resources effectively.

There is recognition that protecting the physical and natural environment needs new objectives to be set – *Planning Policy Statement 1: Delivering Sustainable Development.*[13] The intention is to encourage 'healthy and sustainable communities', with the express aim under the Planning and Compulsory Purchase Act 2004 to have sustainable development at the heart of planning and to make planning an important tool for future generations. One way to achieve this aim is to use the Planning Policy Statements to identify policies in the following key areas:

- the protection of biodiversity and geological conservation;
- sustainable development in rural areas;
- waste management;
- renewable energy and;
- assessment of flood risk.

The implementation of these aspirations will take some time. Moreover, it still leaves planning decision-making loosely defined in terms of prioritising decisions that make sustainable development a reality.

Planning has a significant impact on energy resources since it decides on the construction of power stations and other energy-generating structures (see Case study, p. 198); on noise in terms of the location of major roads and airports; on air in terms of pollution from factories, industry and major roads; and on waste in terms of waste disposal site licenses and on the

[12] *Securing the Future – delivering UK Sustainable Development Strategy* March 2005, Cmnd 6467.
[13] *PPS1 Delivering Sustainable Development*, OPDM, February 2005.

regulation of waste sites. In order to ensure that the environment is protected and sustainability in planning law achieved, the law must take a proactive approach. One approach is to make use of enforceable planning conditions that take account of climate change and global warming. If there is a conflict between the environment and the developer, it should be resolved in favour of protecting limited resources and the environment. The extent to which planning permission may become a useful environmental tool has yet to be fully assessed, but can it be correct that planning permission for a development will override the designation of a site of scientific interest? This is the reality of how careful thought needs to be given to changing the system of planning control and of how planning takes account of available science (see Law in context, below).

LAW IN CONTEXT

Planning and the use of scientifically based advice

Sites of Special Scientific Interest (SSSIs) are designated on the basis of scientific surveys of wildlife or geology. They are the responsibility of Natural England, to identify and protect under the Wildlife and Countryside Act 1981 (as amended by the Countryside and Rights of Way Act 2000). Many of the designated sites are not only SSSIs but also Ramsar sites, Special Protection Areas etc. There are more than 4,000 SSSIs, which include wetlands, chalk rivers, upland moors, beaches and many other habitats. They may equally be in the middle of industrial estates and reflect the presence of a unique habitat for a single endangered plant. Local planning authorities are informed of the designation and location of SSSIs in their area, which brings into the ambit of planning authorities scientific advice on important geology and wildlife within the locality. Natural England provides an annual update on the condition of SSSIs and indicates the reason for their adverse condition. In the year to October 2008 planning permission accounted for damage to a total of 47 sites.

There are other examples of scientific advice being made available to planning authorities: an important one is through the activities of the Environment Agency. The Environment Agency is a statutory consultee in the drawing up of Local Development Documents (in Wales these are Local Development Plans). This includes Strategic Environmental Assessment. Consequently the Environment Agency provides advice on land contamination, development and flood risk, setting up catchment flood management plans and strategies as well as waterway plans. This is an important role in terms of providing good advice and scientific analysis. It also provides a pathway to environmental information and analysis.

Planning law and practice

The planning system has undergone many changes since its earlier inception. Intervention in terms of planning law began with very light interference from the state and a general protection afforded to private property rights. The paramount respect given to private property and land ownership is indicative of why the law was reluctant to interfere. The courts supported private party disputes to be resolved on the basis of the law of nuisance or negligence. The triumph of land law was that it also contained many devices to ensure that land was freely alienable which future generations would enjoy through restrictive covenants ensuring that the land was protected. Heritage and building reflected a view of the land as being appropriately managed as a visual display of nature. The great gardeners of the nineteenth century[14] showed a mastery of form and substance and supported in many instances the use of reusable agriculture to promote health, wealth and prosperity. There were many mills used to generate electricity as well as provide for flour-making. The urban environment was not so fortunate. There are instances of planned environmental triumphs such as large-scale public parks and civic centres. However, the early planning legislation – the Housing, Town Planning etc. Act 1909 – left abundant discretion outside any planning control or regulation and fell to the initiative of the private developer. The planning system was left to develop on its own until the aftermath of the Second World War. The Town and Country Planning Act 1947 provided a single consolidation and set the basis of modern planning law that has remained in place today. It is surprising that the fundamentals of planning law should be so settled although recent changes have made substantial differences to the procedures, practices and thinking behind much planning law. There are two major works of consolidation:

1. the Town and Country Planning Act 1990 and the Planning and Compensation Act 1991;

2. the Planning and Compulsory Purchase Act 2004.

There is also an increasing preference for making use of various subordinate powers found in the General Development Procedure. This is in keeping with the view that the planning system has been too restrictive and what is required is a more relaxed scheme of control allowing many more permitted developments than previously. This highlights one of the main tensions within the planning system – namely to develop and enhance investment to secure employment and economic opportunities for citizens, as opposed to securing a wide definition of public interest that looks to future generations and ensures that sustainable development and land-use planning are interconnected. Into this mix may be added tensions between local and central government over the allocation of powers and decision-making.

The tensions acknowledged above are not confined to current events or interests. The 1960s witnessed the rise in new architecture designed to confront the housing shortage, attacking the causes of poverty, crime and urban squalor and at the same time introducing social housing with shared values and experiences. By the late 1970s many of the new buildings attracted critics that pointed to the new squalor of the 'high rise' building and the high crime attracted to common walkways and passageways that became unsafe for the public. Despite the rejection of many of the values of the 1970s, the 1980s remained a period that linked amenity and social values into the urban environment. The ultimate rejection of social value planning came in the late 1980s with a Conservative government that pursued the right to buy for all public housing tenants and the operation of a private market solution to social problems. In the 1990s and commonly today, this pursues the value of deregulation and the need for developers to be given a priority in the planning system. This may be seen to be a return to the traditional view that private property rights should triumph over social and economic values; public participation in the planning process should be minimal

---

[14] Capability Brown and J. Hawkes.

and that the role of government should act not as a provider of services, including public housing, but as a facilitator of the planning system. These shifts in government thinking are also a noteworthy feature of how the planning system is politically sensitive and adjusts to the prevailing ideology of the planning system.

The British planning system is remarkably open to the political controls that give politicians an ultimate say in its policy and direction. Through the use of circulars and policy guidance, it is possible to set the conditions of planning policy. The government could introduce presumptions in favour of development, taking account of such factors as the needs for small businesses and the requirements of housing. In recent years the unprecedented housing boom in prices was seen as demanding a large-scale housing plan to provide lower prices and 'affordable' homes. Such presumptions[15] about planning were subject to the caveat that such developments 'would not cause demonstrable harm to interests of acknowledged importance'. Any conditions that might be attached should be made only where they could be justified.

The active role of politicians many may see is the hallmark of a system that may react to the changing needs or ideological shifts in society. Others may be concerned that political control is too often at the whim of the government of the day and this may divert from the specialist expertise of the professional planner. The stronger intervention of central government may be seen to be at the expense of local government. Centralisation has been a highlight of the way government has moved since the 1980s. Ironically, privatisation and the use of the market has given rise to an increase in market power but equally a centralising influence of central government. In recent years including the past two, there is a marked willingness on the part of central government to continue this trend of centralisation and control.

The role of the courts in the planning system has always been peripheral. There is no environmental court and no planning court – notable absences from the legal system that has specialised in establishing specialist courts and tribunals to address specific areas of conflict. The overarching role of the courts is to take a hard look at the legal principles when required but not to directly intervene in the merits of policy. The Human Rights Act 1998 has brought some planning issues to the fore in terms of testing the planning system but also in ensuring that rights are enforceable. The legalism of planning decisions is partly as a result of litigiousness among the developers and a proactive legal profession that is linked to the commercial and business world.

Environmental law and planning law make curious allies in terms of environmental protection. Planning law is likely to offer limited help to environmentalists, given its primary focus and role.

Planning in the twenty-first century

Planning law inherited from the Town and Country Planning Act 1947 has been greatly modified by the Planning and Compulsory Purchase Act 2004. The 2004 Act reflects a modern approach to planning – more focused on citizen or consumer interests and based on higher expectations than in the past of a speedy and simplified system of decision-making. Some see this as making planning more positively focused on the basis of presumptions that planning approval will be given, as against a negative approach that sets too many constraints on development and assumes that planning permission will not be granted. The introduction

---

[15] Circular 22/80 and Circular 14/85.

of so-called regional spatial strategies has been designed and intended to coordinate and assist in laying down a framework for development that coordinates development control and hopefully will incorporate future-looking strategies such as transport, and environmental quality assessments. However, it is not clear that all the ambition of the strategies are realisable and in fact only some of the spatial strategy will be found in the development plan, which remain the key planning document. A positive view of such spatial strategies is that there is an inclusion of key environmental issues within them. A negative view is that unless such spatial strategies are given support, this may be of little significance. The regional spatial strategies replace the county-level structure plans.

How is the planning system to be viewed today? The idea of a national-based planned urban strategy around central government policy-making seems to have given way to a hybrid of different and often competing interests. The objectives in the 2004 Act appear to favour private sector market-led planning solutions that fit within a more streamlined and pragmatic system. Section 39 of the 2004 Act for example requires all plan-making bodies to have the responsibility of exercising their functions in accordance with the principle of sustainable development. This does not apply to Part 4 on development control and it begs the question as to how, if at all, this is to be consistent with environmentally friendly decision-making. There must be specific and clear guidance if sustainability is to work and, if this is to be a feature of central government controls, it must be carried out systematically. The most likely impact of the inclusion of section 39 is simply to reinforce the need for economic development to take place, rather than a prescription of how the environment may need protecting.

Consistent with this approach is the idea allowed under the 2004 Act to give local planning authorities the power to make local development orders to advance decision-making that may relax planning controls when appropriate. This does not interfere with the primacy of the development plan, but it allows local planning authorities individual choices commensurate with their needs. The system of local planning authorities mirrors the organisation of local government. This varies with the location and region. There are unitary authorities, also district authorities, metropolitan districts and single-tier London Boroughs. The 2004 Act at the regional level of planning replaces the county level and we have seen how county-level authorities have regional spatial strategies. The new system of devolution devolves the powers from the Secretary of State to the local assembly.

In Scotland planning legislation falls under the Town and Country Planning (Scotland) Act 1997, similar in terms of the Town and Country Planning Act 1990. Similarly Northern Ireland has its own planning system under the Planning (Northern Ireland) Order 1991 amended substantially in 2003 (SI 2003/430 N.I. 8).

The nature of the development plan is important as it sets the main aims, policies and priorities believed to be worthy goals by the local planning authority. Development plans are drawn up after due consultation, including a variety of inputs that come from specialist planners, pressure groups or individuals. It is fair to say that the tone and culture of the development plan is intended not to be restrictive but permissive. There is much to be said for this approach, as it does not fix rigidly or in a binding way the planning system[16] based around legally enforceable obligations. The position prior to 2004 was that there was a two-tier system of structure plans and local plans.

---

[16] This allows negotiation and bargaining. In *Bovis Homes Ltd* v *New Forest District Council* [2002] EWHC 483 (Admin) the application of Article 6 to the development plan was not generally accepted as necessary.

The 2004 Act makes the regional spatial strategies (RSS) the upper tier of development planning and thus replaces structural plans. There are arrangements in place under Part 1 of the 2004 Act that permit the RSS to take account of the Secretary of State's policies and to encourage the take-up of central government policies. This falls short of an overall national system of planning but allows the Secretary of State considerable latitude in the fashioning of planning strategy. Put simply the aim is to drive forward economic development, secure a speedy transition in the way in which that development operates and secure a positive management of resources at the locality. Thus in a number of instances it is possible to use the RSS system to create some form of loose and generally defined national strategy. This is also a means of locating a device that allows the national policy guidance, often issued as planning policy, into a more comprehensive whole.

The local aspect of planning may now be addressed. Local development plan documents are adopted by local planning authorities and together with waste and minerals development plans (to be discussed in Chapter 10) form the core basis of planning. However, the law requires each to be distinguishable and the inclusion of each in the development plan is not a foregone conclusion. There are a number of key documents that comprise the local planning portfolio:

- non-statutory material including designs, local draft plans and priorities;
- supplementary planning documents forming guidance, targets for affordable housing and the operation of local policies.

The preparation of development plans has to take account of the various documents and includes the submission of the draft plan to the Secretary of State for approval. Again this is another centralising influence and representations may be made to the Secretary of State by interested parties. There are under the 2004 Act powers to call in and modify or alter development plans. Interestingly there is no specific and direct mention of environmental matters and this underlines the problem of not giving the environment sufficient specific attention.

Nationally significant infrastructure planning

One of the principal features of the 1947 planning system has been the key element of public participation. This is a recognisable quality of the democratic process. Public participation is aimed at engaging with the public and providing access to decisions that may affect ordinary people. It also encourages the role of pressure groups and lobbying to secure aims and objectives that may not always be in keeping with government policy. Ultimately the planning system has to reflect the views of the majority and the political role of policy-making engages with the ideals of elected and accountable government. Equally, public participation may act as a fetter on quick decision-making and inhibit large-scale planning projects. The history of public participation and large-scale planning has been an unhappy one. In London, delays and procrastination has continually deferred decisions on the third London airport. In the United Kingdom, public opinion has acted as a deterrent in planning nuclear power stations. Examples abound of indecision and delay that have resulted from the planning process. There have been delays in building new airports or expanding existing ones; power stations and electricity schemes and large-scale urban planning, including roads and railways. Generally the decisions are taken within the ordinary planning process, but increasingly there are special statutory arrangements created for distinct areas. Sir Rod Eddington and Kate Barker published their reports *The Eddington Transport Study* and the *Review of Land Use Planning* in December, 2006.[17] The government's response is found in the White Paper, *Planning for a Sustainable Future*[18] and after due consultation it was proposed that a new Planning Bill should be passed setting out how large economic projects might be assisted. The results are to be found in the Planning Act 2008 that received the Royal Assent in November 2008. The Act extends to England and Wales but only partly to Scotland, in that it covers oil or gas pipes. It creates a new system of development consent for nationally significant infrastructure projects applicable to energy, transport, water, waste water and waste projects. The approach of the Act is to place nationally significant infrastructure projects within the following framework.

- National Policy Statements will set the framework for the policy of defining and categorising nationally significant infrastructure schemes.

- The Secretary of State will have wide powers to set the policy and categorise the projects for inclusion in the scheme.

- The creation of a new independent body called the Infrastructure Planning Commission will have powers to decide on the projects that are suitable for inclusion within the relevant national policy statement.

- The Infrastructure Planning Commission will be able to recommend projects for the scheme and inform the policy-makers of the issues to be considered.

- Development consent will be granted subject to various conditions but will include rights for developers to compulsorily acquire land for the projects where there is a public interest.

- There will be compensation powers applicable to any compulsory purchase scheme and there are requirements for public consultation in respect of any proposed project.

The new arrangements are intended to consolidate some existing special statutory schemes available for laying pipelines and electricity cables into a form that will assist in the economic prosperity of the nation.

The Planning Act 2008 provides a fundamental alternative to the existing planning arrangements for 'nationally significant infrastructure projects'. The past history of delays over airports and power generation as well as major transport schemes has become a major stimulus for change. The new arrangements need to be considered in the light of a number of criticisms:

- a missed opportunity in terms of failing to address climate change and give priority to sustainable energy sources;

- reduces public participation in terms of streamlining processes that may make objections more difficult to deter large-scale projects;

- may not encourage transparency and openness in the way decisions are made.

---

[17] London: HMSO, December 2006.
[18] Cm 7120.

Environmental impact assessment (EIA)

Environmental impact assessment (EIA) offers an 'environmental assessment' that enables decision-makers to take account of the environmental impact of their decisions. Its origins date back to the USA in the 1960s.[19] In the planning process environmental matters may form a material consideration in making planning decisions. The collection of information and analysis about the environment makes good sense in terms of providing a material consideration in the decision of whether or not to grant planning permission. Assessments were often used by developers to persuade planners of the value of the planning project, and the evaluation of the environment became a way to overcome any local objections. The rise in the use of environmental assessment accompanied large-scale public inquiries. It was in part also recognition that planning was a professional and specialist subject that brought expertise and technical skills to the planning process. The rise in the use of environmental assessment is very much a product of government pressure and the role of the EU.

In addition to the system of EIA there is also the operation of a strategic environmental assessment (SEA). This is the use of systematic analysis of environmental information, employing the best available techniques. Taken together the operation of environmental assessment gave rise to better transparency and an increase in the opportunities open to the citizen to participate in the planning process. The engagement with interested groups and the expertise of specialists in the field of science, technology and biology is also a consideration in favour of the system of environmental assessment. In theory, environmental assessment should be a minimum standard for all planning decisions. The opportunities for consultation and deliberation also support the view that deliberations on environmental information provide the means to improve decision-making.

In EU law the first steps were taken in the 1985 EIA Directive 85/337/EEC. The aims were limited to providing some form of monitoring system and very much based on the ideas at the heart of the project. The need for EIA is clear right across the planning system, although where it is most useful is at the earliest stages of the planning system. EIA combines techniques for assessment with appropriate procedures for analysis. It may identify specific areas where it is appropriate to adopt environmental measures. This allows the decision-maker in terms of the planning decision to make a more informed decision with sufficient information to assess a project in terms of its environmental impact. The operation of EIA is very much focused on the decision-maker and provides an assessment based on procedural principles. The 1985 Directive was based on the provision of environmental information on private and public projects as part of a requirement of the decision-making process. This provided considerable flexibility and in many instances EIA was adopted by developers as part of their planning strategy beyond what was strictly required. After 1985 there were some amendments to the directive. In 1999, Directive 97/11/EC came into force. This broadened the scope of the 1985 directive and brought within the EIA regime projects that were thought to

---

[19] See: The US National Environmental Policy Act (NEPA) 1969, A. Kiss and D. Shelton, *Manual of European Environmental Law* (Cambridge, 1993) p. 58). In the United States the 1969 Act incorporated a requirement for assessing the environmental impact of major Federal actions significantly affecting the quality of the human environment.

Table 9.1 Annex I and Annex II projects

Schedule 1 Projects Annex I

- Major projects such as power stations; chemical installations, motorways and major roads.
- Projects that fall within the scope of a major project but where there is some doubt because the scale of the project may be relatively small in terms of likely effect on the environment.
- There is no clear guidance from the ECJ, but each case must be carefully considered.

Schedule 2 Projects Annex II

- Projects are to be judged on their facts.
- EIA is applicable only where there is 'a significant environmental effect', which by nature of the project is 'likely to have significant effects on the environment by virtue of its nature, size or location'.
- Thresholds are often set to determine the size and scope of the EIA.

have a significant effect on the environment (Annex II projects) (see Table 9.1). In those cases the assessment became a mandatory part of the decision-making. A distinction was made between Annex I where the operation of EIA is compulsory and Annex II projects where EIA is only required if there are significant effects. The details of the procedures needed to carry out EIA were more clearly spelt out and the direct and indirect effects of projects were to be assessed in terms of the variety of factors, such as the flora and fauna of the habitat of the site where the project was to be undertaken.

The 2001 Directive 2001/42/EC on Strategic Environment Assessment (SEA) is also relevant and came into force in 2004. This relates to ensuring that environmental impact assessments are part of the process before planning consent or approval is granted. There is no guarantee that at the end of the process the environment will be better protected. As an important tool, EIA provides an imaginative means to secure information and assessment of the environment. The EU's involvement is to provide a step-by-step approach across all member states for the consideration of the environment. It is also intended to provide a framework for development and ensuring that across all levels of member states' development, there is a concurrence of ideas.

In the United Kingdom the main mechanism for the adoption of EIAs is through the planning process. This is achieved through section 15 of the Planning and Compensation Act 1991 which inserted an amending section 71A into the Town and Country Planning Act 1990. Various regulations apply, including the Town and Country Planning (Environmental Impact Assessment) (England and Wales) Regulations 1999 which provides wide powers for the adoption of EIA in the UK. This links the EIA process with planning and the application process required for most large projects. In cases where planning permission is not required there are separate regulations that cover such cases.

In 2000 the 1999 Regulations were amended to bring EIA to cover applications for the determination of new mineral workings. In 2006 legislation was introduced as a result of proceedings in the European Court of Justice in *R (on the application of Barker)* v *London Borough of Bromley*,[20] and amendments were made to the EIA arrangements through the Town and Country Planning (Environmental Impact Assessment) (Amendment) (England) Regulations 2008 SI 2008/2093. The effect of the 2009 regulations is to make EIA mandatory for not only the

---

[20] C-290/03 and C-508/03 *Commission* v *UK* judgment of 4 May 2006.

interim outline planning stage, but also the full planning hearing. The 2008 regulations relate to England only and also covers the planning stage when approved matters are being considered.

There are a number of key question and issues that have to be addressed. In terms of establishing EIA there are a number of steps that must be taken.

What is a project that is subject to EIA consent? The preliminary question of whether or not EIA is required can be the most difficult. There are certain projects where there is a requirement for an EIA since they will effect the environment. These are broadly outlined in Annex I of the directive (see above). Annex 1 projects are mandatory and include major projects such as large chemical installations, thermal power stations, motorways and major projects that may impact on the environment. The list was supplemented under Directive 97/11/EC to include pig and poultry farms and major groundwater abstraction schemes. The inclusion of large projects may also be considered by the ECJ in determining the types of projects or modifications required.

Annex II projects are in less sensitive areas or where the environmental effects are less controversial, with a more minor impact on the environment. Figure 9.1 sets out a helpful guide on EIA provided by the Environment Agency.

It is always difficult to know precisely whether or not a project might have an environmental effect. This can be judged by its size and scope and the location and sensitivity of the operation of the project, e.g. if it is near or in a greenfield site or Site of Special Scientific Interest. The potential for pollution discharges or emissions are also relevant.

What is an environmental statement? This is regarded by many planners as the key component part of the EIA.[21] The statement allows proper consideration of the environmental effects of a development. There may be more or less information according to the nature of the development but there is a minimum under the regulations (reg 2(1) and Part 2 Schedule 4) These are:

● the main description of the development including details of the site, its design, specifications and size;

● the data necessary to assess, identify and consider the main effects of the development and its likely impact on the environment;

● the identification of any adverse effects and strategies to tackle any adverse effects in the development and reduce the environmental impact of undesirable effects;

● a general outline specifying the main alternatives that the applicant has considered and explanations for choices made and options taken.

There is also a reasonable expectation built into the EIA process. This is the inclusion of information that might be reasonably required to assess the environmental effects of developments and how the applicant may tackle such developments. There is also an expectation that a balance should be struck between the development going ahead and the alternatives. Most EIA statements are detailed on technical specifications, including the operation of any processes. The inclusion of data on energy efficiency and conservation measures is also to be expected. There is an inherent trade-off between the benefits sought and the environmental impact. The latter has to be fully considered in terms of alternatives and include

---

[21] See: *Berkeley v Secretary of State for the Environment, Transport and the Regions* [2001] Env LR 16.

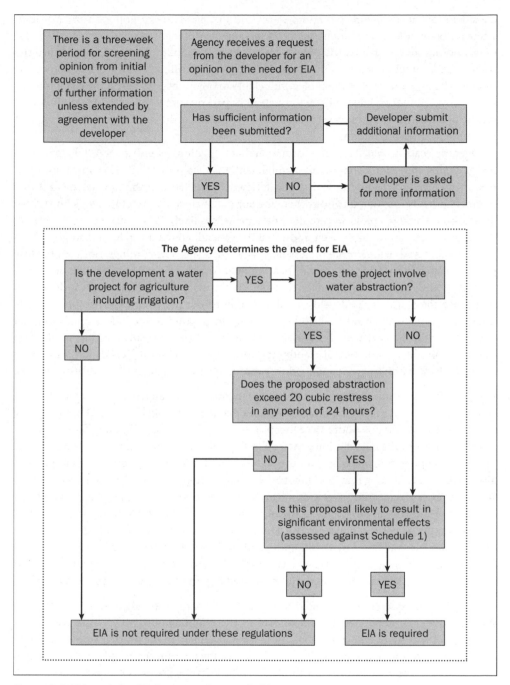

Figure 9.1 EIA and the Environment Agency Guide

Source: Defra.gov.uk

consideration of the use of natural resources and the avoidance of pollution or emissions. There is also an acknowledgement that processes and developments may be at the cutting edge of technology and, therefore, there should be an attempt to indicate any potential difficulties or events that might impact on the environment. One difficult area is the estimation of any indirect effects, which makes the project vulnerable to objectors especially if the claim is made that the overall indirect effect will be through an impact on climate change. In addition to the technical data and specifications there is a requirement that the information is summarised in simple non-technical terms.

Over the years the inclusion of information that was voluntary under the 1999 regulations has gradually moved to a mandatory requirement; the details of exactly how much information is open to judicial interpretation and review.[22] The essence of the EIA statement is that planners must be put in a position where the key parameters of a development's impact can be assessed. There is a presumption that the statement is likely to be reasonable provided all the issues noted above have been addressed. In general, courts are reluctant to go behind the statement and require more than is necessary. There are shortcomings, not least because judicial inspection is likely to offer only a limited form of review. The most obvious shortcoming is that only the alternatives that the developers opt to consider are included. In that sense the statement is developer-led and only robust planning expertise can properly interrogate any assumptions that do not stand up to scrutiny. There is an implication that developers may be too narrowly focused or financially driven to really consider all the best options from an environmental standpoint. Moreover, general environmental scrutiny of indirect effects has to be given some priority through the engagement of appropriate experts.

How are EIA applications determined? EIA statements are considered as part of the planning process. There are, however, a number of features that are worth highlighting. Developers may use the 1999 regulations under the Directive 97/11 EC to request planning authorities for their responses to the information provided in the statement. This is a mechanism generally known as scoping opinions and gives the planning authorities the opportunity to respond. It also means that planning may become reactive rather than proactive. There is no general consultation process on scoping statements. This misses an opportunity to allow the engagement of public opinion at an early stage in the planning process. Although not required, however, it is commonly accepted as good practice. Public consultation is generally viewed as a desirable objective and is sought by many planning authorities. The United Kingdom has refrained from requiring a mandatory scoping consultation. Perhaps the scoping statement is regarded as less critical as the matters it raises are considered as part of the planning system overall.

The planning system in the United Kingdom has favoured general consultation. The first stage is when the developer decides to consult the planning authorities. This also allows engagement with an interested party on the scope and content of the project. Various statutory bodies can have an input such as Natural England or the Environment Agency. Ensuring that consultation takes place is a responsibility placed on developers. This provides information and analysis that is relevant to the planning system as a whole but is also important for the specific planning application. At this stage interested parties, including pressure groups or expert organisations, may be consulted. The public consultation part of the process is very important as it provides a means of identifying environmental issues and enables projects

---

[22] *R (on the application of Blewett) v Derbyshire County Council* [2004] Env LR 29.

to become compatible with good environmental practice from the outset. The consultation is also a way of ensuring efficiency in decision-making and this is also to be encouraged in terms of setting a dialogue between developer and development planning.

Generally environmental statements are regarded as a good development in the planning system. Critics may worry whether it gives the developer a more proactive role than previously. This may favour developers who have access to consultants and expertise. Many concerns are expressed at the uneven quality of some environmental statements and the advantage that this may give the developer in second-guessing planning authorities. Do planning authorities have access to sufficiently high quality advice? Are the environment statements a fair description of the development and how useful are such statements in terms of their depth and quality? Setting standards for good quality or setting benchmarks for environmental statements would seem desirable but difficult to achieve in practice. If EIA is to be effective then environmental statements have to be regarded as a pivotal part of the process.

The determination of EIA applications as part of the planning system is important to consider. The standard planning application procedure is followed, but in the case of an EIA there is an additional 16 weeks allocated to determine the application to provide time to assess and analyse the EIA. The key point is that the planning decision has to take account of the EIA. This must be considered carefully and with due deliberation including public consultation. Sufficient copies have to be made available and the public must be given access including only reasonable charges for any photocopies. The views of the various statutory consultees must also be considered and made available to the public. In cases where the EIA is regarded as inadequate this must be queried by the planning authorities and followed up as part of the planning decision-making system. In that regard decisions must be taken reasonably and be fully reasoned in their explanation. The EIA is often a key part of whether planning permission should be given. Since Directive 97/11/EC, regulation 21 has required that reasons should be fully articulated. This includes the basic content of the decision and any conditions that are attached. It should also mention reasons,[23] which is effectively an explicit duty on the planning authorities. Inadequate reasons may have serious implications for the legality of the planning decision.

We have already seen that the use of an EIA is always good practice but often the development proposal will not require this to happen. The courts are reluctant to step in and ask that an EIA should be imposed on a developer. However, as the practice becomes commonplace, especially in controversial planning applications, the use of EIA is a good strategy on the part of the developer. This falls a long way below the expectation that perhaps EIA should be used in every planning decision. The cost and additional burdens make this an impractical idea.

The future of EIA

EIA is at the heart of future strategies to integrate environmental protection into the planning system. The significance of EIA is accepted as a global phenomenon that is located inside many international agreements, and intrinsic to the work of many agencies and organisations throughout the world. The World Bank and the United Nations make use of EIA in their contracts and agreements. Since 1989, the World Bank has incorporated EIA into its formal requirements[24] that engage with transboundary risks and assessments. Cross-border effects

---

[23] *R v Cornwall County Council, ex parte Hardy* [2001] Env LR 25.
[24] World Bank, *Operational Policy 4.01 (1999) Environmental Assessment* as revised.

are measured and assessed. The assessment is drawn around the support of experts appointed to carry out the assessment. There are strict guidelines and also the division of projects into two different categories according to risk. The first category is projects that are likely to have a significant adverse environmental impact. These are projects that are unusual or are likely to have by their nature a significance for the environment. Such projects are deserving of more robust assessment and the assessment has to be detailed and comprehensive. The second category of project is one that is given less scrutiny and the consequences on the environment are regarded as likely to be minimal.

The operation of EIA in general addresses some of the critics of large dam projects or projects where international donors are likely to receive adverse comments. In many instances meeting EIA targets require addressing the role of NGOs and local agencies. Community-based projects are likely to be given support. However, the challenges are many in the light of pressure from within developing countries to be led by market choices that will provide a pathway to economic growth and prosperity. This sets a stark challenge for developers and funding agencies. EIA strategies by their nature have to be largely consensual and are centred on specialist and expert opinion. Large multinational corporations and developers will often employ a range of specialists to bring projects within the boundaries of what is likely to be successful in order to achieve approval under EIA. This has a clear advantage of empowering experts early on and the EIA route engages in the debate over the standards to be followed and the objectives to be achieved. International law has thus favoured EIA as a structural and procedural device that allows engagement in the dialogue of development. This can form the basis of treaty agreements or understandings.

On the debit side there are many instances where EIA set high expectations that are simply not being met in the realities of practical experience. EIA also suffers from the fact that it does not empower individuals or even groups. In the international context this raises the question about how national groups with an environmental agenda may engage with the process and participate in the decision-making.

Conclusions

Town and country planning law has developed with a primary focus on permitted development and land use. This has meant that planning law has not engaged directly with environmental priorities. In sharp contrast, housing policy has in recent years focused on energy-efficient homes and takes account of the reality of scarce and expensive energy. Sustainable development strategies have, in general, failed to be fully implemented into the planning system, except for steps taken to bring energy and efficiency savings into many aspects of housing and planning. If sustainable development and planning decisions were more closely interwoven, this would achieve a workable link between planning and the environment. It would allow environmental protection through planning strategy with reactive and continuous mechanisms to safeguard the environment. Over 60 years have elapsed since the 1947 Town and Country Planning Act, which secured green-belt protection around major towns and cities and helped shape our environment. There is a clear case for a significant step to be taken now in terms of embedding proactive environmental protection in planning law.

In marked contrast to the expectation that the environment should be safeguarded by the planning process, developers and business interests have been very successful in developing

market-led priorities for the planning system. This is reflected in the Barker Review of land-use planning that argued for a more targeted approach to planning decisions, and the need for speed, efficiency and effectiveness in decision-making. In this context sustainable development is used as a means of securing primacy for market forces rather than for environmental protection.

The planning system is illustrative of the various tensions at work in decision-making. As the review by Kate Barker has shown, the demands on the planning system are to promote the UK's competitiveness and this is geared to the creation of a vibrant infrastructure that enhances a thriving economy and creates an improved environment. The potential for incompatibility is high and there are a number of fundamental questions for the planning system:

- how to encourage citizen participation at a local level;
- how to make an enhanced environment compatible with infrastructure growth and a thriving economy;
- how to deliver high standards of employment and at the same time protect and enhance the physical and natural environment.

The use of brown-field sites is often claimed to provide the solution to at least the last two questions. Yet this is barely adequate to meet demands on housing and new retail developments.

Further reading

J. Adler, 'Environmental impact assessment: the inadequacies of English Law' (1993) 5 JEL 203.

E.P. Bosselman and A.D. Tarlock, 'The influence of ecologcal science on American law' (1994) 69 Chicago-Kent L Rev. 847.

B. Cullingworth and V. Nadin, *Town and Country Planning in Britain* 13th edition, London: Routledge, 2002.

J. Holder, *Environmental Assessment* Oxford: Oxford University Press, 2004.

J. Holder and D. McGillivray (eds), *Taking Stock of Environmental Assessment* London: Routledge-Cavendish, 2007.

P. McAuslan, *Ideologies of Planning Law* Oxford: Pergamon Press, 1980.

M. Stallworthy, *Sustainability, Land Use and the Environment* London: Cavendish, 2002.

C. Wood, *Environmental Impact Assessment: A Comparative Review* 2nd edition Harlow, Essex: Pearson, 2002.

Visit **http://www.mylawchamber.co.uk/mceldowney** to access key issue checklists and practice exam questions to test yourself on this chapter.

10 Land: waste management and controls

Introduction

The legal control of waste offers a fascinating case study of different regulatory forms and mechanisms that can be used to address one of the major by-products of industrialisation and our way of life: the need for waste disposal. The disposal of waste is an economically important industry in its own right and stretches across continents. Developing different strategies of waste management and control has been one of the most daunting challenges facing the United Kingdom, with an average of nearly 500 million tonnes of waste produced annually. The definition of waste is broad and includes a variety of different types of waste from domestic waste to agricultural and industrial waste. Today, there is a greater amount of recycling and reuse than ever before, but regulating all the different forms of waste has proved an almost impossible challenge. The legal controls mainly operate on municipal, industrial and commercial waste.

Historically, the United Kingdom has favoured landfill as the main disposal method. Up to 80 per cent of waste used to be discarded in this way. Recycling and reuse strategies achieved relatively limited success with only 12 per cent of waste falling under this umbrella. In recent years, however, primarily driven by the European Union there have been significant changes in this balance. There have been strong centralising tendencies within the United Kingdom, but nevertheless local government powers and responsibilities for waste management have been retained. The introduction of devolution to the regions[1] in 1998 has encouraged regional decentralisation[2] of waste management, although this change is actually quite hard to evaluate in terms of increasing local autonomy. At the same time there have been many new structures and management arrangements that have been intended to transform the role of local authorities. These include public contracts, private finance initiatives as well as other devices that have changed the complexion of local government. A corporate identity has become an increasingly important part of local government. Thus, both public and private participants are present in the delivery of waste management goods and services.

The EU has also facilitated change in the management of waste, becoming particularly active in setting targets and overarching strategies for waste disposal in recognition of the size of the problem. From the 1970s onwards the increased wealth of Western European

[1] Scotland, Wales, Northern Ireland and London.
[2] The system of waste management is examined for England only.

216

countries has resulted in a dramatic rise in the amount of waste produced. In 2003 the municipal waste market in Europe came to 248 million metric tonnes. The UK alone in 2005 produced over 550 kg per person per year of municipal waste, but only ranked eighth in the European league of municipal waste production. Inevitably, reusable resources and recycling have become a central part of EU strategy to manage waste. Such strategies not only have their intended effect of improving the environment, but also save costs and contribute to sustainable development through resource recovery and reuse. The EU has undoubtedly had a significant impact in the way waste is managed today. Landfilling has diminished, matched by a concomitant rise in waste treatment activities such as incineration and recycling. Incineration, especially when used for energy recovery has increased in importance, but is usually linked to waste sorting activities and the recycling of a variety of material. There has been a marked shift away from the use of landfill to reuse and recycling systems, the preferred options, in order to meet EU targets and as a consequence there is a new regulatory regime for waste disposal, which involves the active engagement of local authorities. Apart from the overarching influence of the EU there is a more pragmatic reason for the UK's need to reduce the use of landfill for waste disposal. Landfill sites are commonly positioned on low lying and low value land and the reality is that such sites are becoming increasingly difficult to find. Moreover the breakdown of organic material in landfill contributes to greenhouse emissions through the production of carbon dioxide and methane, a potent greenhouse gas. Part of our drive to meet greenhouse emission targets (see Chapter 14) also includes reducing our reliance on landfill disposal of waste. Landfill that is not properly managed and sealed can also contribute substantially to the contamination of soils, surface and groundwater through run-off of pollutants. Reducing the use of landfill reduces this risk.

Despite the centralising tendencies of recent years, waste management strategies have actually placed local authorities at the apex of control. The outcome has been to revitalise the role of local authorities as pivotal actors in the development of policy, the enforcement of good practice and in the management of resources. As recycling and reuse becomes commonplace as best practice, there are questions over how to improve poor practice. The debate about incentives and disincentives on waste producers, including households, has been quite contentious at times. We have all become used to source-sorting our waste into different types for collection and recycling, but should we be fined if we dispose of too much non-reusable or recyclable waste?

Historically waste disposal, particularly of industrial waste, often resulted in land and water courses near disposal sites becoming polluted. Land contamination also arose from industrial practices failing to contain chemicals properly and from gaseous waste-products causing contamination through, often local, deposition of pollutants. Many common practices at the time of the industrial revolution have contributed substantially to the bank of contaminated land across Europe and the UK. We are not immune, however, from contributing to the problem and today accidental release of pollutants can cause severe land contamination, e.g. the Bhopal accident in India, as can bad containment or waste management practices on the part of industry. Even small-scale operations, such as a petrol station or a local scrapyard can contribute to contaminated land problems. Contaminated land contains pollutants that can cause harm to human and environmental health and requires remediation before it can be used. We do not know exactly how much land is contaminated in England: estimates suggest about 325,000 sites covering approximately 300,000 hectares. In fact, contaminated sites are usually fairly small in area but often contain multiple and varied contaminants making remediation difficult. Given this and the number of contaminated sites, remediation is likely to be a costly activity. Local authorities again have a substantial role in managing contaminated sites, with significant responsibilities for inspection, identifying sites and remediation shared with the Environment Agency. This chapter will examine our strategies for and the regulation of waste management and how we manage contaminated land.

The European Union: a common legal framework

Waste management with the EU has a common framework. The legal definition of waste is contained in Article 1(a) of the Framework Directive on Waste (75/442/EC). This defines waste in broad terms as 'any substance or object in the categories set out in Annex 1 (of the directive) which the holder discards or intends or is required to discard'. Annex 1 to the directive contains over 16 categories of waste, covering a very wide range of products and substances.[3]

National legislation has followed the same path. Defining the type of waste has large economic and environmental implications as it will determine the mode of treatment e.g. recycling, incineration etc. Moreover, the classification of waste determines the regulatory authority responsible for overseeing the management of waste. This includes control of a number of tasks such as collection, sorting, treatment, recovery, reuse, transport and storage. A great variety of actors are concerned with these activities, some of which are specific and require a technical expertise. This is normally provided by private companies or third parties, as are many of the activities that make up the waste disposal chain. As a result of this variety, provision of waste management services is far from being harmonised in either the methods or organisation across the EU. The answers to the challenges raised by waste management are very much national.

It is important to remember that historically waste management was a response to the common practice of disposing of rubbish in streets and public sites, and the public health problems this caused. Authorities where entrusted with the responsibility of developing a public policy in order to solve the problem. The problems were local so the issue of control was primarily viewed as local; thus waste services became organised at the level of local authorities. Their role consisted mainly of the collection and the disposal of waste. Eventually environmental concerns about the impact of solid waste became a major issue for public opinion in many EU countries, influencing the political discourse. Together concerns about public health and environmental harm became a driving force for action at local level and within the EU.

---

[3] The significance of the 16 categories is their general remit. They include: (i) production or consumption not specified in the other categories below; (ii) off-specification products; (iii) products whose date has expired; (iv) materials spilled, lost or having undergone mishap, including any material, equipment contaminated as a result; (v) residues from cleaning operations, packaging materials and containers; (vi) unusable parts such as rejected batteries or the like; (vii) substances that no longer perform satisfactorily; (viii) residues of industrial processes; (ix) residues from pollution abatement processes; (x) machine finishes, residues such as from sawmills; (xi) residues from extraction processes; (xii) adulterated materials or substances; (xiii) any materials banned by law; (xiv) products for which the holder has no further use such as agriculture; (xv) products for which there is remedial action with respect to land; (xvi) any materials, substances or products not contained in one of the above categories.

During the 1970s the EC, in principle, could not legislate on environmental matters under the treaty. In reality, by using the harmonisation provision of the treaty (Art. 94 EC Treaty) and through an economic approach to the question of waste, the Council was able to intervene in issues related to waste. The 1975 Waste Framework Directive 75/442/EEC was built, first, on arguments by the Council that national provisions on waste disposal might distort competition. Then, second, on the basis of the 'flexibility clause' (Art. 235 EC Treaty), the Council claimed the importance of the protection of the environment for the EC. The first framework directive[4] provides a definition of 'waste' and developed a common approach for member states, giving priority to preventing waste production, the 'polluter pays' principle, and appropriate waste treatment. It creates obligations for the member states and waste authorities regarding the management of waste services. This includes elements such as the establishment of waste plans and the use of permits.

The obligations set out in the waste framework directive, now consolidated in Directive 2006/1/EC, were substantially added to over the years by a raft of further directives on different type of wastes or activities linked to waste (see Table 10.1). Some quantitative standards were fixed, such as a prohibition on the marketing of batteries containing more than 0.05 per cent mercury (Directive 91/157/EEC on batteries and accumulators) or the obligation to ensure by 31 December 2008 the recovery or incineration, using incinerators capable of energy generation, of a minimum of 60 per cent of package waste weight (Packaging Directive 94/62/EC).

Managing waste under the requirements of these directives represents a considerable challenge for small local authorities. Inevitably, therefore, national legislative frameworks

Table 10.1 EU waste directives

Directive	Specific field
75/439	Waste oils
75/442	General Framework (now replaced by 2006/12)
78/176	Titanium dioxide
86/278	Sewage sludge
91/156	General Framework
91/157	Disposal of batteries and accumulators
91/689	Hazardous waste
94/62	Packaging and packaging waste
96/59	Waste PCBs
96/61	Integrated pollution control (replaced by 2008/1)
99/31	Landfill
2000/53	Management of end-of-life vehicles
2000/76	Incineration (amended previous directives)
2002/96	Waste electrical and electronic equipment
2004/12	Amends Dir. 94/62 Packaging and packaging waste
2006/12	Consolidates and replaces Dir. 75/442 Waste Framework
2008/1	Integrated pollution control (replaces Dir. 96/61)

[4] The directive was preceded by only one other regarding waste: Council Directive 75/439/EEC of 16 June 1975 on the disposal of waste oils.

slowly started to be reformed to allow a more efficient organisation of waste management and to comply with obligations set out in the directives.

There remains a wide range of waste management options open to waste authorities, including:

- **Landfill** – this is at the bottom of the waste hierarchy and is regarded as the least desirable option, because it has the potential to generate up to 40 per cent of a countries methane emissions (see above).

- **Recycling and composting** – are regarded as effective disposal options. They have the advantage of producing usable products from waste and have the potential to reduce the material costs of and conserve resources.

- **Reuse** – is considered an excellent environmental practice and is generally encouraged as part of a sustainable development strategy.

- **Energy from waste** – either as heat or electricity is primarily, though not exclusively, linked to incineration. Lower than recycling and reuse in the waste hierarchy, incineration linked to energy generation is nonetheless a feasible option.

Under the Waste Framework Directive (2006/12/EC) then, there are a number of specific directives and regulations aimed at pursuing the overarching control and policy mechanisms set by the framework in specific areas of waste management. For example, under the European Landfill Directive (99/31/EC) the United Kingdom has adopted clear targets for the reduction of waste sent to landfill, including an assessment of the role and future of local authority participation in waste management:

- an analysis of the future directions in terms of the public/private sector divide;

- an identification of how the environmental dimension has taken a dominant role in the waste management sector and how local authorities are best suited to deliver on environmental targets;

- an analysis of the corporate strategy that is part of waste management.

Other waste directives not only encourage reuse and recycling, but similarly place the emphasis on waste reduction. The new Integrated Pollution Prevention and Control Directive (2008/1/EC replacing 96/61/EC) includes the requirement to prevent, recycle or dispose of waste in the least polluting way. It is interesting to note that in 2007 the waste sector was responsible for 28 per cent of the most serious incidents resulting in land pollution. Household waste, vehicle parts and asbestos were the most common waste materials involved. The Packaging Directive is also intended to drive forward reduction in packaging use, and thence, packaging waste. The reduction and prevention of waste is likely to be a continuing theme for the future in the EU as a major part of environmental protection.

United Kingdom

A key element of waste management involves the collection and appropriate disposal of municipal waste. This includes household waste and any waste collected by the various waste collection authorities, such as waste from municipal parks and gardens, beach-cleansing waste and commercial or industrial waste arising from clearing 'fly tipping' waste (waste that has been illegally disposed of and abandoned). The definition of municipal waste can be found under the Waste and Emissions Trading (WET) Act 2003. The guidance available to local authorities under the Local Authority Trading Scheme (LATS), however, is simply 'all waste under the control of local authorities'. Defra (the central government department responsible) is of the view that the LATS definition should be of universal application. This would broaden local authority responsibility and increase the volume of waste that comes within local authority control. There are conflicting views as to the desirability of widening the definition of waste and any likely expansion of local authority responsibilities.

Local government operates as part of an integrated approach to waste management and related services. In terms of both policy development and legislation it operates alongside the Environment Agency. Under the Environment Act 1995, the Environment Agency licenses and supervises waste management activities. The responsibility for the actual collection and disposal of waste, however, is delegated to local authorities. The Waste Collection Authorities are composed of District Councils in England and Wales. Their role is to arrange for the collection of waste and its delivery to designated sites that have been approved by the Waste Disposal Authorities. Waste collection authorities are also charged with the responsibility of drawing up proactive recycling plans. The waste disposal authorities are mostly County Councils in England and District Councils in Wales. Their responsibilities include monitoring and operating places for the disposal of waste.

UK waste management policy follows the direction set by the European Union. In May 2007, the government announced a detailed Waste Strategy for England 2007 (Defra). This is an important strategy document that provides a comprehensive analysis of waste and its management. One of the distinctive features of the United Kingdom's arrangements has been the relatively extensive use of landfill as the preferred option for disposal over many years. The EU Landfill Directive requires that the amount of biodegradable waste (BMW) disposed of in landfill is reduced to 5.2 million tonnes in England by 2020. The Waste Strategy for England incorporated this target and the Landfill Allowances Trading Scheme (LATS) was introduced in 2005 to help achieve this aim (see below). In 2007–8 78 per cent (10.6 million tonnes) of waste sent to landfill was BMW, a drop from 2004–5 when 13.9 million tonnes of BMW were landfilled. In fact, there has been a slow decline in the total amount of waste that goes to landfill. In 2000–1 80 million tonnes of waste was landfilled; by 2006 this figure was 19 per cent less, at 65 million tonnes. In 2006 commercial and industrial waste accounted for 21 million tonnes of the total waste sent to landfill. The significance of household waste for waste reduction is clear from these figures. The Waste Strategy sets targets for reuse, recycling and composting of household waste, with an overall target to reduce household waste that is not treated in these ways (residual waste). In 2007–8 approximately 35 per cent of household waste was recycled or composted. We, householders, are still profligate in waste production: residual waste in 2007–8 accounts for 324 kg per person, amounting to 16.6 million tonnes.

Legal, financial and general framework of local waste services

The UK has a highly complex and technical system for waste payments and financing. Local authorities are financed by local taxes leviable at the local level and part of the expenditure of local authorities is on waste management. Central government responsibilities are paid

Table 10.2 The responsibilities of institutions in waste management

Organisation	Activities and jurisdiction	Sources of powers for the role
Central government	Sets general waste policy and has monitoring and reporting role	EU Directive and policy-maker
Environment Agency	Licenses waste sites	General regulator: Environmental Protection Act 1990
District councils England and Wales and London boroughs	Waste Collection Authorities: responsibility for collecting waste and recycling	The Environmental Protection Act 1990, sections 45, 46–47 and 49
County councils in England	Waste Disposal Authorities: monitors and operates sites for waste disposal	The Environmental Protection Act 1990, section 51 and the Waste and Emissions Trading Act 1003
District councils in Wales	Waste Disposal Authorities: monitors and operates sites for waste disposal	The Environmental Protection Act 1990, section 51

out of central taxes. There are, however, also environmental taxes based around the 'polluter pays' principle that relate to waste. Perhaps the most important of these is the Landfill Tax. This is a tax levied on local authorities or organisations for the volume of waste sent to landfill. Degradation of organic matter in landfill produces over 40 per cent of all UK emissions of methane, an important greenhouse gas. In part, Landfill Tax was intended to reduce the amount of biodegradable waste going to landfill, thus reducing greenhouse gas emissions. Since the inception of the tax in 1999, there has been an annual increase in the tax, known as a landfill accelerator. There is, also, a Landfill Tax Credit Scheme to further encourage eco-friendly disposal of waste. Landfill owners are responsible for paying the tax, which they commonly pass on to the waste producer. At present the standard rate of tax is £48 per tonne, providing net receipts of £0.95 billion. The owners of landfill can receive up to 6 per cent relief by way of tax credits annually as part of the Landfill Tax Credit Scheme. There is also a tax on the extraction of primary aggregates, the aggregates levy, which is set at £2.50 per tonne (net receipts £0.33 billion). In addition to these taxes, licences for waste sites and disposal are collected as part of a self-financing system over waste. There range of institutions with a role in waste management and their jurisdiction is shown in Table 10.2.

Waste management and controls

In 2005/6 over 28.7 million tonnes of municipal waste was collected by various local authorities in England. Municipal waste is defined under the Landfill Allowances and Trading Scheme (England) Regulations 2004 as waste that comes under the control of a waste disposal authority or waste collection authority. There is a steady increase of around 0.5 per cent in total waste annually. This trend is, however, subject to fluctuations in the light of individual company strategies to reduce waste overall.

The main enabling legislation applicable to waste is the Environmental Protection Act 1990 sections 45–49 and subsequent changes including the Household Waste Recycling Act 2003. The main regulatory provisions under the 1990 Act together with the Waste Management Licensing Regulations 1994 sets out the definitions of what is waste and sets the main licensing institutional and regulatory framework.

The Control of Pollution Act 1989 provides for a system of registration for carriers of waste. There are significant changes to the licensing regime, intended to modernise and bring the law in England and Wales into line with European Community law. These are as follows:

- Waste and Emissions Trading Act 2003 provides a waste quota system, setting the amount that may be deposited in landfill sites;
- Household Waste Recycling Act 2003 provides for the phased introduction of separate waste collection before 2010;
- Clean Neighbourhoods and Environment Act 2005 provides a regulatory structure for waste that includes fixed penalty notices for certain waste offences.

Various implementation strategies for the adoption of the Waste Framework Directive (75/442/EC) as amended in 1991 by Directive 91/156 and Directive 91/689 on hazardous waste have been adopted. The Household Waste Recycling Act 2003 places a legal duty on local authorities to provide kerbside collection for recycling, composting and energy recovery by 2010. This has created an incentive for all local authorities to meet their targets based on performance indicators.

In order to meet the demanding requirements of the European Landfill Directive, the United Kingdom has embarked on a strategy to reduce landfill (See: Defra, 2007 Report on Waste Management Strategy) by setting targets:

1. 2010, to reduce landfill to 75 per cent of that produced in 1995;

2. 2013, to reduce landfill to 50 per cent of that produced in 1995;

3. 2020, to reduce landfill to 35 per cent of that produced in 1995.

In order to achieve these targets the government introduced a Landfill Allowance Trading Scheme (LATS) in April 2005. This means that among the 121 waste disposal authorities, there are tradable allowances to permit authorities who expect to landfill more than they should to trade with those authorities that are landfilling less. This mechanism should result in the targets being achieved nationwide. The use of a trading arrangement for landfill is a means of encouraging local authorities to reduce the use of landfill. There is also a Waste Strategy Board and a focus group to work with stakeholders.

LAW IN CONTEXT

Hazardous waste consultation on a waste strategy: trends and directions

Defra engaged in a waste strategy consultation concluded in October 2009. The aim is to provide a basis for the publication of a waste strategy for hazardous waste management in England. This is in the light of the revised Waste Framework Directive 2008/98/EC. Part of the revision is to take account of shifting priorities identified in the revised waste hierarchy: prevention, preparing for reuse, recycling and other recovery methods such as energy and, finally, disposal. The aim is to facilitate the provision of an improved infrastructure for the management of hazardous waste. There is an ongoing debate over how best to address future trends with a specific need to make provision for waste producers and waste managers to adopt appropriate treatments for certain kinds of hazardous waste streams. The need for clarity and certainty is apparent if waste is to be treated appropriately. Tackling waste is also linked to the need to address issues surrounding climate change and to recover material or energy from hazardous waste. The approach taken is instructive of how best to encourage waste managers and producers to adopt strategies that will address future needs.[5]

Special waste

Special waste is defined under the 1980 regulations (see: the Control of Pollution (Special Waste) Regulations 1980 SI No. 1709) as any controlled waste which contains one or more listed substances, the presence of which makes the waste dangerous to life. There is a specific list of chemicals (Schedule 1 to the regulations) which are dangerous to life or have a low 'flash point' or are a medicinal product available only on prescription. It is estimated that special waste covers about 2 per cent of United Kingdom controlled waste. The largest proportion is from industry but also included are ordinary household products such as battery acids, pesticides and household cleaners.

The statutory controls for special waste are more stringent than for other controlled wastes. Defra have noted the following controls on special waste (see: A Waste Strategy for England and Wales Consultation Draft (DoE, 1995) p. 93):

- closer supervision of movements (pre-notification to the WRA);
- recording of location of deposits within a landfill;
- fewer waste management licensing exemptions than for other waste;
- higher licensing charges than for other controlled waste;
- mandatory environmental impact assessment for the development of facilities (SI 1988/ 1199) (see Chapter 9).

It is likely that the 1991 Directive on Hazardous Waste (EEC Directive 91/156) will be extended to include many more types of wastes within its powers. The potential for harm arising out of special waste requires its segregation from other wastes. This is an expensive operation that requires the waste stream at point of collection to have effective separation of the various types of waste.

Radioactive waste

Radioactive waste arises from a number of different sources, including nuclear power stations, reprocessing of spent fuel rods, hospitals and research laboratories (see: 6th report of the Royal Commission on Environmental Pollution, Nuclear Power and the Environment Cmnd 6618, September 1976, HMSO). Radioactive waste can be gaseous, liquid or solid and must be stored or disposed of safely. A number of hazards arise from radioactive waste, depending on characteristics of the radioactive material present. For example, waste produced

---

[5] Defra, Consultation on a Strategy for Hazardous Waste Management in England July, 2009.

during the reprocessing of fuel rods is highly radioactive, toxic and physically hot. It contains radioactive elements that are exceptionally long-lived, i.e. have long half-lives (see Law in context, below). High-level radioactive waste is defined as containing >37000 TBq tritium, 37 TBq of beta- and gamma-emitters, 3.7 TBq of strontium-90 and caesium-137 or 0.037 TBq of alpha-emitters with half-lives over 50 years. In contrast, low-level waste normally contains short-lived radioactive elements (30 years or less) in low concentrations: in fact, the bulk of this waste is often organic, e.g. packaging etc. Techniques for the safe disposal of solid and liquid radioactive wastes are currently being developed by many countries, including the UK.

The safe disposal of radioactive waste requires that the health of the general population and industrial workers are not put at risk through exposure to radiation. The International Commission on Radiological Protection (ICRP, 1991) estimates that a radiation dose of 0.05 Sv-1 may induce cancer. Exposure levels are kept well below this dose.

LAW IN CONTEXT

Radioactive material in the environment

The impact of any accidental or deliberate discharge of radioactive material to the environment is difficult to predict. The mobility and fate of radioactive elements in the environment is affected by the chemistry of the radioactive material and environmental conditions and varies with the particular element. Different radioactive elements are also accumulated to different extents by different organisms, e.g. scallops (Pecten maximus) accumulate manganese and oysters (Ostrea) accumulate zinc. Thus the environmental impact of released radioactive elements must be considered on the basis of individual elements. Moreover, radioactive elements change (decay) to other elements when they emit radioactivity and these may themselves be radioactive. Each radioactive element has a characteristic decay sequence, with a number of different daughter radioactive elements formed in series until a stable element (i.e. not radioactive) is formed. Each radioactive element in this series is chemically distinct: they are, after all, different elements with different radioactivity and different half-life. Predicting the impact of a sole radioactive element is therefore insufficient: even if there is only one contaminating radioactive element to begin with, the mobility and ultimate fate of all the daughter radioactive elements in the decay series should be considered.

The basis for controlling exposure to radioactive waste is through the system of dose limitation recognised by the Radiological Protection Board and recommended by the International Commission on Radiological Protection in 1977 (see: Radioactive Waste Management 1982 Cmnd 8607). The Radioactive Substances Act 1993 provides a comprehensive system of controlling the handling of radioactive substances and materials. The 1993 Act is a consolidation of an earlier statute, the Radioactive Substances Act 1960, which was heavily amended by the Environmental Protection Act 1990 (also see: the Control of Pollution (Radioactive Waste) Regulations 1989 (SI 1989 No. 1158). The 1993 Act regulates all aspects of the use and storage of radioactive material and the disposal and the accumulation of radioactive waste. There is a system of registration of premises supervised by the Environment

Agency under the Environment Act 1995. Central controls under the 1993 Act are exercised by the Secretary of State and various licences fall under the Nuclear Installations Act 1965. There are various inspectors with enforcement powers and a rigourous system of record-keeping and inspection. Transport of radioactive materials is regulated by the Radioactive Material (Road Transport) Act 1991. Current policy on radioactive waste management is under review.

Contaminated land

Contaminated land is an important and often neglected area of land use management.[6] It is pivotal to good soil quality, which has important links to agriculture and building when land use may have important implications for human health. As far back as 1996, the Royal Commission on Environmental Pollution in their 19th Report made the link between good soil quality and the sustainable use of the land. Establishing what levels of pollutants present on contaminated land are likely to be injurious to health is problematic and the focus of some debate. The nuclear industry has been continually plagued by costs associated with clean-up, and the safe disposal of nuclear waste remains an ongoing challenge. Amelioration of chemical pollutants is an important factor in making contaminated land reusable and suitable for building purposes. Public perception of land contamination is more accentuated than in the past, although there has always been a tension in making use of old Victorian industrial sites. Setting standards for contaminated land based on risk assessments is also difficult and requires realistic establishment of safety margins. There is also some difficulty in situating the 'polluter pays' principle within the boundaries of liability and cost-sharing for contaminated land remediation. Who was the polluter may be impossible to establish as the pollution may not have been scientifically detectable or may not have been considered problematic by policy-makers when the pollution first occurred. The common use of lead and asbestos, once considered relatively safe are now known to represent threats to human and animal health and well-being in different ways. Similarly, the risks associated with mercury only came to light in the relatively recent past.

Sites where existing industrial buildings have been demolished, i.e. 'brown-field sites', are prime building sites in the centres of many town and cities. Who pays for the clean-up costs when previous owners and activities have been lost to present-day knowledge? There is a strong unfairness if historic pollution is used to place liability on previous owners or occupiers ignorant of the pollution and abiding by the regulations of the time. The Environmental Liability Directive in 2004 (Directive 2004/35/EC) makes clear this limitation, and liability for environmental damage caused by substances that are released into the environment before 20 June 2007 is excluded from liability under the directive. This, however, leaves open potential liability under different headings such as negligence, nuisance and statutory nuisance. The end of the industrial revolution of the nineteenth century and, over the past century, the demise of large industrial plants, has offered new possibilities to improve the standard of contaminated land. It has also, however, exposed many tensions in the contaminated land regime.

---

[6] See: S. Tromans and R. Turrell-Clarke, *Contaminated Land* 2nd edn, London: Sweet and Maxwell, 2008. Also see note 7.

■ Challenges in the regulation of contaminated land

There are many powers to control and regulate contaminated land. Contaminated land has proved problematical and not susceptible to easy solution[7]. The estimate is that 27,000 hectares of land fall within the category of contaminated land, which is land contaminated with noxious substances. Contaminated land has historically arisen from a variety of activities, including mining and smelting, town gasworks, steelworks and foundries, and railway goods yards. These types of operations are the origin of a large proportion of the contaminated land in the UK. In the present day, contamination of land may arise from a variety of commercial and industrial sources either as a result of accidents or through the activity itself, e.g. landfills and scrapyards. Contaminated sites commonly have a large number of potentially harmful substances present which may be solids, in solution, liquids or gaseous. Substances such as heavy metals (e.g. cadmium, lead and copper); inorganic compounds (e.g. asbestos and sulphate); organic compounds (e.g. PCBs, dioxins, chlorinated hydrocarbons, polyaromatic hydrocarbons, phenolic compounds); and gases (e.g. methane), are relatively common contaminants. A number of hazards can arise from contaminated land, including:

- prevention and inhibition of plant growth and toxic effects on invertebrates and vertebrates;
- contamination of surface water and groundwater;
- uptake of contaminants by food crops and entry into the human food chain;
- human ingestion, inhalation or skin contact with the contaminants;
- chemical degradation of building materials;
- fire and explosion.

The extent of the ecological impact depends on the ecotoxicity and toxicity characteristics of the substances, their physical and chemical characteristics, their concentration, and site environmental conditions (see Chapter 7). Heavily contaminated sites are often associated with severe disruption to ecosystems. Plant species diversity and abundance is often low, i.e. the species are restricted to those tolerant of the contaminating substances. Other components of the ecosystem, e.g. micro-organisms and invertebrates, are also adversely affected, showing low abundance often linked to low activity. The impact of the contaminating substances on the microbial community may have a deleterious effect on the cycling of nutrients, enhancing further the degeneration of the ecosystem.

The first attempt to legislate on contaminated land was in section 143 of the Environmental Protection Act 1990. This section requires that a register of contaminated land should be maintained by each district council or London borough. This was regarded as a first step to enable the land to be cleaned up. However, this left a number of questions unanswered. Who is responsible for paying the costs of any clean-up? Once land is identified as contaminated land what are the implications for future land use? The answers have been provided by a number of key initiatives. The Contaminated Land (England) Regulations 2006[8] builds on to the statutory framework that came about in 1990 and also had been amended to take account of defining and identifying contaminated land and the works needed to improve

---

[7] D. Lawrence, and R. Lee, 'Permitting uncertainty : owners, occupiers and responsibility for remediation' (2003) 66 *Modern Law Review* 261.

[8] SI 2006/1380. There are also corresponding regulations that are applicable to the devolved regions.

the land. It also applies to special sites and to the detailed arrangements needed to remedy contaminated land, including the process and procedures for notice and the publication of information on the contaminated land in public registers. The latter is an important step forward in public awareness and in disseminating environmental information. In addition to the 2006 Regulations there is an important Circular 2/2006 Part 2A of the Environmental Protection Act 1990: Contaminated Land, available from Defra. This includes guidance on risk assessment, the allocation of environmental liability and the most appropriate way to assess environmental harm.

◼ Statutory definition and powers over contaminated land

Contaminated land is defined as land which appears to the relevant local authority to be causing or to have a significant possibility of causing significant harm.[9] Harm is defined as: 'harm to the health of living organisms or other interference with the ecological systems of which they form part and in the case of humans, includes harm to his property'. This is broadly defined, leaving the Secretary of State with a wide discretion to issue statutory guidance and advice. Broadly the guidance under Circular 2/2006 has a number of aspects that include a link between contamination and a fundamental concept of pollutant 'linkage'. The formation of such a link is a key component of the system of control. The link must be significant and must cross the boundaries of the land to a target such as human or property and the pathway must be clearly established. The presence of a linkage is necessary as is the requirement that such a link must be 'significant' and also harmful. There is a clear requirement that local authorities will have to inspect their areas to identify contaminated land and to decide whether any such land should be designated a special site with the Environment Agency, the enforcing authority. There is a catalogue of targets or types of receptors. These include human beings; nature conservation sites, buildings, other property including crops, animals and general stock. The excluded categories such as wild animals, motor vehicles and areas that are not protected under the nature conservation laws are deemed outside the contaminated land regime under Part 2A.

The degree of the harm must be significant and this is a matter of judgment made by the local authority in each case. There is an implication that the degree of harm must be associated with damage to property or persons that results in impairment of functions. The other part of significant harm is harm that must be regarded as a possibility. Thus harm that has occurred is covered as well as harm that might flow from the consequences of the contamination. The risk assessment that must be undertaken provides a basis for establishing any link. This can be based on a statistical assessment or come from setting standards to assess the likely impact of contamination on humans or crops, for example.

A further aspect of the contaminated land regime refers to situations where the contaminated land may cause pollution of controlled waters. This is an important part of the statutory regime. Contaminated land may result 'in entry into controlled waters of any poisonous, noxious, or polluting matter or any solid waste matter', under Part 2A. The

---

[9] Section 57 of the Environment Act 1995 had inserted 28 new sections after section 78 of the Environmental Protection Act 1990. There is a statutory definition of contaminated land and there are regulatory procedures for the control of contaminated land which follows the scheme for statutory nuisances contained in the Environmental Protection Act 1990.

breadth of this part of the contamination gave rise to the possibility of small amounts of contamination falling under the contaminated land regime. Section 86 of the Water Act 2003 qualifies the above with the addition of the word 'significant' to qualify within the legislation. There are also considerations about the scope of the Water Framework Directive (see Chapter 12) and its application in this area if the law.

Identifying and dealing with contaminated land

A critical part of the contaminated land regime is an attempt to distinguish between degrees of contamination. Local authorities have the primary duty to inspect for contaminated land and also special sites. There are wide powers of investigation to track down contamination. Indeed there are duties on local authorities to consult with Natural England and the Environment Agency in respect of controlled waters and the potential for harm on a conservation site. In other cases landowners are encouraged to undertake voluntary investigations to establish facts and work out any link with pollutants and the potential for harm. Local authorities are given similar rights of entry and inspection powers under section 108 of the Environment Act 1995. The protection given to special sites is important. The designation of special sites ensures that they receive adequate protection through the Environment Agency. Special sites also bring landowners and occupiers responsibilities for ensuring that the costs of remediation are met.

Contaminated land, once identified, brings duties on the local authority to ensure that all owners and occupiers or anyone associated with the land should be liable to pay for the costs of clean-up. Notification is first required and this also extends to notifying the Environment Agency. This follows with a period of consultation and discussion over the remedial action to be taken. A minimum period of three months applies for the consultation, although in certain examples where there is imminent danger there are specific powers. The three-month period is basically a voluntary scheme allowing agreements to be reached. This is intended to give some scope for expertise and specialist advice to be taken and also decide the best method to bring about remediation. At the end of the period of consultation there is a remediation declaration and this sets out action to be taken or, where appropriate, no action is needed.

There are different remediation standards and this may apply to the site depending on its future purpose. One set of standards is to provide land to a state that it could be possible to make use of the land for any purpose – a multifunctional approach. Another set of standards is to bring the land to a standard where it is fit for a specified suitable purpose. Setting the standards and clarifying their application is a difficult and complex task that may not always work in practice. Too low a standard may be applied in situations where landowners are reluctant to do more than the minimum. There are questions as to whether the standards are adequate.

The main tool for the securing of assessment and the clean-up of a site is the issuing of a remediation notice.[10] Failure to comply with the remediation notice is an offence. There are appeal procedures against a remediation notice. Remedial works may be carried out in certain cases and the enforcement authorities will be able to recover costs from the polluter, including the power of sale of the land in appropriate circumstances. There is a register of remediation notices maintained by the enforcement authorities.

[10] See: ENDS Report 243, April 1995, p. 27.

The arrangements under the 1995 Act implement the 'polluter pays' principle and occupiers of land are responsible for certain aspects of its conditions if the original polluters cannot be found. In general terms the new provisions do not appear to create new liabilities but serve to clarify existing arrangements. The Environment Agency makes regular reports on contaminated land and may give guidance to local authorities on specific sites.

The contaminated land provisions of the 1995 Act attempted to settle liability of polluters and landowners, waste producers and carriers. It should not be overlooked that the normal process of development and redevelopment of land continues to afford one of the best means of cleaning up contaminated land. Contamination is a material consideration for planning authorities in the grant of planning permission. Registers of contaminated land under section 143 of the Environmental Protection Act 1990 will remain a valuable guide for the planning authorities. Will there be a different standard for contaminated land applied by the planning authorities compared to the standard applied by the enforcement authorities under the 1995 Act? This may prove to be one of the major controversial issues left unresolved by the 1995 Act. It may also be difficult to establish who the most appropriate person is to ensure that liability is fairly and reasonably apportioned. There are two elements to the apportionment of liability. First, the question of whether or not a person has caused the contamination. Here liability is regarded as one of strict liability and this means that the absence of knowledge or intention is no defence in law. The storage of materials or the presence of an unknown risk may seem to attract an unfair penalty if it is later shown that the result is contamination. In many cases there may be rebuttal evidence from the defence that if good practice is followed and standards applied, no cause ought to be established.

The second question is the definition of 'knowingly permitted' which is a key part of the contamination land regime. In general law 'knowingly' brings the need to show real knowledge of the presence of the substance. This would exclude cases where there was no knowledge or the extent of the knowledge was limited by the available scientific data. Indeed the nature of land transfer makes it improbable that such knowledge would be transferred to new owners. The test of knowledge is a high threshold. Cases involving awareness of scientific tests do not impute real knowledge unless the contrary could be proved.[11] The law of property and that of company law takes the view that newly established companies or entities are new bodies from their previous incarnation – either as nationalised companies or where there has been a liquidation or winding-up. The question of whether National Grid, a successor company to a series of gas companies including British Gas and Transco, could be said to be liable for contaminated land in a housing estate on the site of a former gas works required the House of Lords to consider this matter. The House of Lords in *R (on the application of National Grid plc, formerly Transco plc) v Environment Agency*[12] held that it was impossible to construe the contaminated land regime was applicable to National Grid as a polluter because National Grid could not be said to cause or knowingly permit pollution. The new company could not be expected to remediate the harm caused by previous companies. This is undoubtedly a narrow interpretation of the law but one that suggests that only very clear words could bring National Grid into the statutory contaminated land regime.

There is a broader question of the public interest and how it is best protected. This is an open question; contaminated land can pose serious risks that may cause lasting damage for

[11] *Circular Facilities (London) Ltd v Sevenoaks District Council* [2005] All ER (D) 126 (May).
[12] [2007] 3 All ER 877.

individuals and the community at large. The contaminated land scheme has a detailed way of allocating liability through the identification of the different classes of category of persons that 'knowingly' permitted pollution or different types of pollution. This may help settle different groups and categories of engagement. The result is to provide a mechanism for the remediation of contaminated land. Under these arrangements effect may be given to any private arrangement or agreements for liability. This encourages a private settlement of such cases and allows parties to attempt to mitigate the effects of the statutory arrangements. It is justified in terms of ameliorating costs and on the economic principles of allowing markets to determine the best solutions to sharing liabilities.[13] This leaves unanswered, however, whether the public interest is best served through these arrangements. It might be desirable for a state system of contaminated land compensation based on a taxation principle on land users. This might provide a fair balance between costs and the public interest in the goal of achieving appropriate remediation.

Remediation notices once served give rise to a right of appeal. There is a 21-day period for appeal and there are various grounds of appeal listed in the 2006 Regulations. In appropriate circumstances the Secretary of State may hold a public inquiry, which may involve a hearing of the issues. The inquiry may involve planners, assisted by experts in the specialist field. When the remediation notice has been served and no appeal lodged then it must be complied with or an additional notice may be served. Once the land has been classified as contaminated there are no formal powers to have it declassified.

In addition to the remediation notices that can be issued under the Environment Act 1995 there are planning powers under section 215 of the Town and Country Planning Act 1990 which allow planning authorities to require owners or occupiers of land to remedy the condition of their land so as not to affect adversely the amenity of other neighbouring land. At first glance this may appear to be a valuable power. Its effectiveness, however, is diminished by a number of factors. An appeal against a notice under section 215 is possible on the basis that even if the condition of the land does adversely affect the amenity of the neighbouring land, provided it is attributable to the ordinary course of events and it is not in breach of planning control, then the notice must be quashed. Even if there is non-compliance with the notice, the penalty is set at a level 3 summary offence. Given the limitations of the section and the low penalty, it is unlikely to provide a realistic means of enforcing the notice.

The contaminated land regime has a number of additional features relevant to the regulation of the land. The first is the public register containing information about contamination and remediation notices and related matters in terms of procedure, appeals and special sites. This is an important advance in terms of providing environmental information and openness. There are detailed Schedule 3 Regulations that apply to the Register. The second feature is that contaminated land and its listing may impact on the property market. Built into the system is voluntary bargains and agreements to ensure that the market continues to support land values but also anticipates costs and remediation action. This is sensible as contaminated land may come with burdens that may make it uneconomic. As a consequence planning controls and contaminated land are co-joined as a means of achieving suitable use.

---

[13] The insurance industry may seek to limit liabilities especially in the light of their recent experience over asbestos claims and pleural plaque compensation; see: *Rothwell* v *Chemical and Insulating Co. Ltd* [2005] [2005] All ER (D) 219, (Feb).

New technologies and scientific knowledge is likely to improve the chances for contaminated land to be successfully remediated in the future (see Law in context, below). At present, however, remediation still tends to rely on physical methods such as removing the contaminated top layers of soil from a site and disposal elsewhere. This is a messy and costly process that raises other environmental and health risks. It may, in fact, sometimes be safer to leave the contamination *in situ* since it is possible that contaminants are bound up in the soil and are present in forms that are effectively unavailable for uptake by organisms. In reality we know relatively little about the impact and risks that are associated with contaminated land. Indeed the risks are site-specific since the environment and mix of contaminating substances will vary with site.

It is difficult to assess how effective the contaminated land regime is. There are to date relatively little land designated as contaminated land.[14] The recent economic downturn in the property market may also be a factor in the way land is being developed. Perhaps the system is only gradually having an impact on the majority of contaminated sites. It is considered that around 100,000 sites in England and Wales[15] are affected in part, with an estimated 20,000 sites potentially affected with unacceptable levels of contamination. The legislation is complex and technical. Cases take time to progress and local authorities may be stretched to provide enough resources. Strategically there may be concerns that a robust approach will give rise to fluctuations in the housing market. Since 2008 the housing market has been depressed and the economics of regulatory intervention might be regarded as counter-productive at this stage in development planning. Contaminated land sets challenges for the future of land use. Its importance to the environment and its protection is increasingly being recognised, however.

LAW IN CONTEXT

Remedial treatment and contaminated land

Remedial treatment may take several forms and involves the removal or treatment of the contaminated land and eventual restoration and reclamation of the land. There are a limited number of techniques available for treating contaminated land, including:

- removal of the contaminating substances from the site for subsequent disposal elsewhere under appropriate containment conditions;

- on-site retention and isolation of the material, e.g. by encapsulation systems or the use of appropriate barriers etc;

- dilution of the contaminating substances with clean material;

- the elimination or immobilisation of contaminants through biological, chemical and/or physical treatments.

Among the newest technologies being applied to contaminated land treatment are bioremediation techniques. These utilise the ability of micro-organisms to break down a range of organic contaminants. This often, though not always, involves enhancing degradation by the *in-situ* microbial community through the manipulation of site conditions, e.g. through the application of nitrogen and phosphate fertilisers. Oil from the

---

[14] One estimate is that there are 538 determinations between 2000 and 2007, with only 29 special sites.
[15] Environment Agency, *The State of Contaminated Land*, London: Environment Agency, 2000.

grounded Exxon Valdez oil tanker which contaminated large areas of beaches and rocky shores in the vicinity of Prince William Sound, Alaska (March 1989) was in part treated through bioremediation.

One of the problems inherent in using novel technologies such as bioremediation to eliminate or immobilise contaminants is the great variability in soil and sediment composition. This can affect the rate and efficiency of bioremediation. In addition, there is often a mixed cocktail of contaminants present on a site which may vary in their distribution and concentration across a site. Remediation technologies, therefore, require site-specific investigations and are usually selected and specifically designed for the particular site, even a particular area of a site.

Following remediation of the contaminated land, further treatment involves land reclamation or habitat restoration. Land reclamation is a process by which the land is returned to productive use. The final use of the land may be very different from the original use, e.g. a woodland may have been disrupted owing to mineral extraction and subsequently reclaimed for agricultural production. Land restoration involves the return of the original ecosystem, i.e. the ecosystem prior to disturbance, to the land. In practical terms this is unlikely to be an entirely achievable goal. There is a grey area between reclamation and restoration owing to the limitations of fully restoring a habitat. Both reclamation and restoration imply the development of a fully functioning and self-sustaining ecosystem. Land reclaimed for productive use will require a degree of subsequent management depending on the end-use. Land subsequently used for building either housing or other industrial properties will have different end points in remediation and reclamation. There are soil and groundwater quality standards set as guidance on the assessment and redevelopment of contaminated land, e.g. ICRCL 59/83: guidance on the assessment and redevelopment of contaminated land; ICRCL 70/90: notes on the restoration and aftercare of metalliferous mining sites for pastures and grazing. These often offer guidance on acceptable levels of contamination by named substances linked to final end-use.

Conclusions

Trends and future directions in the provision for local waste services

There are a number of competing themes in the provision of local waste service that have emerged in recent years. Coinciding with the strategy of privatising public services, local authorities have retained the main statutory duties related to waste. This has ensured their continued role in the regulation of waste. Reforms in public administration to the delivery of public services, and specifically a preference for private sector and market-led solutions, has had a substantial affect on waste management. This has engaged a new public management ethos that has prioritised market and competition in order to gain efficiency in public services. Business-style management is particularly apt as a description of the way local authorities embrace their role. This has arisen out of mixed motives, partly economic and partly political. The result is often pragmatic and charts a way forward that engages with aspects of market-led solutions while continuing to maintain a public service ethos. Other countervailing trends are also detectable, however. These mainly stem from economic factors but also from the EU and community-based local politics. There are acknowledged contradictions in the way policy and management strategies are developing. Local citizens and communities are articulate and strong-minded about aspects of waste disposal and collection. Public opinion can shape policies and may tend to result in higher objectives for environmental protection. It may be the case that the outcome to this type of pressure will be higher targets in the management of household waste. The industrialisation and the technicality of dealing with waste will probably result in continued and growing delegation of the service to privatisation. In this context it is probable that the economic value of the activity will also grow.[16] Whatever influences dominate the future of waste management, it is important that standards in the disposal and separation of different types of waste support reuse and recycling.

The common framework in the EU applies in the United Kingdom. The EU influence is dominant and has led to significant changes in the attitudes and standards set for waste management. In the UK there is a trend in favour of using economic instruments as a means of achieving more effective pollution control and thereby higher environmental standards. The use of taxation for particular types of wastes that are placed in landfill sites offers the possibility of encouraging best practice and reducing the amount of waste that is landfilled (see above). The taxation scheme also allows waste disposal authorities to trade in landfill allowances, linked with recycling strategies. The use of economic instruments provides an incentive to encourage good practice and the achievement of high standards. The expectation is that this will lead to the further development of a waste strategy towards higher targets.

Waste disposal policy is influenced by issues that arise from town and country planning considerations. The historic use of landfill sites in England and Wales gave rise to complex planning issues. The link between land use and landfill sites as part of the planning system remains, despite the complex system of waste management regulation and licensing outlined above. Thus the deposit of waste on land is part of a deemed development and requires planning permission. Land used for waste management purposes is treated similarly. The storage of waste and the incidental collection of waste can constitute a material change of use that also requires planning permission.

There is, therefore, a significant input from local planning authorities into waste planning. This is achieved through the use of compulsory purchase schemes or through Regional Spatial Strategies. The Planning and Compulsory Purchase Act 2004 and Regional Spatial Strategies are used to replace planning guidance. There has also been a phased introduction of a Minerals and Waste Development Framework, which provides a coordination of pre-existing policies and may be developed as part of the development plans for local areas.

The details of development control and its application to waste are to be found in section 55(3)(b) of the Town and Country Planning Act 1990. There are important overlays between the implementation of the Framework Directive on Waste and the Integrated Pollution Prevention and Control (IPPC) Directive 96/61/EC. Waste management facilities can be covered by both directives. There are also related issues associated with the control of groundwater that is contaminated by waste, and civil liabilities that may emerge through the unlawful disposal of waste. In the latter case this may be through common law cause of action or through the statutory arrangements under section 73(6) of the Environmental Protection Act 1990. The style and content of enforcement strategies is also important.

Waste policy is continually evolving as we come to terms with a complex but important area of environmental protection. Strategies to reduce waste must be foremost not only to limit disposal needs but also to protect limited resources (see Table 10.3).

---

[16] Between 1993 and 2000 the turnover of the waste sector increased 48 per cent passing from 334 thousand millions of euros to 495 thousand millions.

Table 10.3 Developments in waste reduction strategies

Key new targets and actions

- Establishing a **Waste Strategy Board** to provide leadership within and across Government with **responsibility for taking forward the delivery of this strategy and developing new policy actions** as necessary; and a **Waste Stakeholder Group** to provide external advice, challenge and assistance with delivery.
- Publishing periodic reports on progress with delivery of the strategy.
- Reducing greenhouse gas emissions from waste management by at least 9.3 million tonnes carbon dioxide equivalent per year by 2020 compared to 2006/07.
- Setting a **new target to reduce the amount of household waste not re-used, recycled or composted** from over 22.2 million tonnes in 2000 and 18.6 million tonnes in 2005 to 15.8 million tonnes in 2010 with an aspiration to reduce it to 14.3 million tonnes in 2015 and 12.2 million tonnes in 2020 – a reduction of 45% between 2000 and 2020.
- Setting **higher national targets for re-use, recycling and composting of household waste** – at least 40% by 2010, 45% by 2015 and 50% by 2020.
- Setting national targets for the **recovery of municipal waste** – 53% by 2010, 67% by 2015 and 75% by 2020.
- Expecting the reduction of **commercial and industrial waste going to landfill** by at least 20% by 2010 compared to 2004.
- Considering in conjunction with the construction industry, a target to halve the amount of **construction, demolition and excavation wastes going to landfill by 2012** as a result of waste reduction, re-use and recycling.
- Further developing the **evidence base** to underpin the evaluation and development of future policies and **review of the strategy.**

Source: www.defra.gov.uk.

Regulating contaminated land

The effective regulation of contaminated land is increasingly perceived as an important part of protecting the environment. Much of our contaminated land finds its routes in past practices and is as diverse in character as it is difficult to remediate and restore. We are only relatively recently addressing the problem of contaminated land through the development of appropriate strategies, but we still have some distance to go. How the current arrangements will work will take some time to unfold. It is an area, however, where much depends on scientific assessment and development so that progress in policy is closely linked to science. The scientific understanding of the hazards and risks associated with polluted land and advances in remediation technologies will feed directly into future strategies to both identify and remedy contaminated land problems.

Further reading

R. Baldwin and J. Black, 'Really responsive regulation' (2008) 71 *Modern Law Review* 59.

Germa, Bel, Xavier, Fageda, 'Why do local governments privatise public services? A survey of empirical studies' (2007) 33(4) *Local Government Studies* 517–34.

T. Besley and S. Coate, 'Centralized versus decentralized provision of local public goods: a political economy analysis' *National Bureau of Economic Research Working Paper* (1999) No. 784.

G.A. Boyne, 'The determinants of variations on local service contracting – garbage in, garbage out? (1998) 34(1) *Urban Affairs Review* 150–63.

Nicholas Buclet *et al.*, *Municipal Waste Management in European Policy: Between Harmonisation and Subsidiarity*, London: London University Press, 2002.

Defra, *Waste Strategy for England, 2007* Defra: London, 2007 (*www.defra.gov.uk*).

R.B. Denhardt and J.V. Denhardt, 'The new public management: serving rather than steering' (2000) *Public Administration Review* 60(6) 549–59.

G.P. Hawkins and H.S. Shaw, *The Practical Guide to Waste Management Law* London: Thomas Telford, 2004.

A. Heftz and M. Warner, 'Privatization and its reverse: explaining the dynamics of the government contracting process' (2004) 14(2) *Journal of Public Administration Research and Theory* 171–90.

R.E. Hester and R.M. Harrison, (eds) Assessment and reclamation of contaminated Land *Issues in Environmental Science and Technology Vol. 16*. Royal Society of Chemistry.

D. Lawrence and R. Lee, 'Permitting uncertainty: owners, occupiers and responsibility for remediation' (2003) 66 *Modern Law Review* 261.

R. MacRory, *Regulatory Justice: Making Sanctions Effective* London: Better Regulation Executive, 2006.

J. Pitchtel, Waste management practices: municipal, hazardous and industrial, CRC Press, London: Taylor and Francis, 2005.

C. Reid, 'Regulation in a changing world: review and revision of environmental permits' (2008) *Cambridge Law Journal* 126.

Royal Commission on Environmental Pollution, *Setting Environmental Standards* 21st Report CM 4053, 1998.

R. Sackville, 'Mega-litigation: towards a new approach' (2008) *Civil Justice Quarterly* 244.

S. Tromans and R. Turrell-Clarke, *Contaminated Land* 2nd edition, London: Sweet and Maxwell, 2008.

M. Walls, M. Maculey and S. Anderson, 'Private markets, contracts and government provision. What explains the organization of local waste and recycling markets?' (2005) 40(5) *Urban Affairs Review* 590–613.

Case law

Commission v *Italy* C-194/05, C-195/05, C-263/05.

R (on the application of Anti-Waste Ltd) v *Environment Agency* [2008] 1 WLR 923.

R (on the application of Edwards and another) v *Environment Agency and Others* [2009] 1 All ER 57.

Visit **http://www.mylawchamber.co.uk/mceldowney** to access key issue checklists and practice exam questions to test yourself on this chapter.

11 Land, countryside and the environment

Introduction

The countryside of the United Kingdom has been moulded and shaped by our activities over many centuries. Nevertheless a diverse and interesting natural heritage remains, reflected in both the ecology and geology of our environment. Together these make up our natural environment. The demands of a dense and urbanised population and an agricultural sector that relies on modern methods to be economic, however, places considerable pressures on our countryside. Protecting the countryside relies on land-use planning for towns and cities as well as managing the amenity use of the natural environment and agriculture. The protection of the plants, animals and natural habitats that go to make up the natural environment are an important part of environmental law. The preservation of wildlife and the protection of the natural habitats are essential[1] if we are to continue to benefit from our interactions with the natural environment and for its survival. Our considerable vulnerability to perturbations in our natural environment and the importance of its protection is well illustrated by the fate of the honey bee and other pollinating insects. We rely on them for the fertilisation of many plants, including many agriculturally important crops. A decline in the populations of these insects augers ill for food production in the UK and indeed across the world, and in a domino effect their loss would play out into loss of other species, from other insects to birds and beyond. The human food chain is sensitive and precarious – from bees and insects involved in pollination of food crops and vegetation to the management of animal resources and farming. Even though the United Kingdom is heavily populated, agriculture and forestry in fact make up 90 per cent of land use. Inevitably, the law applicable to the land and the countryside covers a diverse range of issues, including – the Common Agricultural Policy (CAP) of the European Union; agricultural land use (including the application of pesticides and fertilisers); the operation of National Parks, Green Belts, Areas of Outstanding Natural Beauty and areas of Special Scientific Interest. The areas designated are set out in a map on Defra's website and the roles of each designation are carefully observed. The EU has set a goal to preserve and manage natural resources as part of its annual policy strategy agenda for 2010.[2]

---

[1] See: B.A. Holderness and M. Turner (ed.), *Land, Labour and Agriculture, 1700–1920: Essays for Gordon Mingay* London: Hambledon Press, 1991.

[2] COM (2009) 73 final EU Commission, *Annual Policy Strategy for 2010*.

The past century has seen competing demands placed on the rural environment. The need for a healthy rural economy has to be balanced against the preservation and conservation of nature. The agricultural use of pesticides and fertilisers must be set against the need to protect the health and safety of both humans and wildlife. In fact, agriculture is less important than it once was for the UK economy. The UK only derives 1 per cent of its GDP from agriculture, a major shift from its historical past of self-sufficiency, and is no longer in the top 10 per cent of countries that count as the biggest agricultural producers. These include the United States of America and France. Given the size of the UK this is not surprising. It does, however, point to the vulnerability of our economy to any rise in agricultural production costs, as costs are passed on in terms of higher prices, for example caused by increased oil prices, and indeed to the vulnerability of our food supply if world food production declines as a result of global change. Recreational pastimes such as sport and countryside pursuits, e.g. rambling, are not without impacts on the natural environment and have to be reconciled against the interests of other groups in society. Linked to all these issues are significant and very real concerns about the impact of climate change and pollution on plants, animals and other organisms in often fragile natural habitats. The impact of humans on the environment in the building of cities and towns has to be appreciated in terms of the preservation of natural habitats. The principle of sustainable development is essential for future generations and the rights of generations to come (see Chapters 1–3). Various international attempts to pursue nature conservation are apparent and include the 1982 UN World Charter for Nature and the various activities related to the World Wildlife Fund. This is in the context of saving animals such as the tiger or panda. Protecting biodiversity has also been acknowledged internationally and linked to agriculture and economic development. In 1992 the Convention on Biological Diversity acknowledged the intrinsic value of biodiversity and sustainable use of nature. This was an international agreement that recognised the importance of protecting natural habitat.

There are current predictions that the United Kingdom is set to lose many naturally occurring plants and animals. It is difficult to be precise over the possible extent of losses. Predications are based in part on climate change reflected in unusual winter and spring rainfall and temperature patterns, and partly on habitat loss due to land-use change. This underlines how natural systems are influenced by a complex array of factors and are inextricably linked to a variety of human-made environmental pressures. The protection of our natural inheritance then involves far more than a distinct set of protective controls aimed at species and habitats but arguably rests more generally on the success of environmental law as a whole. One of the most effective measures of our capacity for sustainable development then is, perhaps, our stewardship of the countryside.

Historical and contemporary developments in nature conservation

The end of the nineteenth century saw the desirability of preserving game and other animal species established, although the response to preservation and nature conservation was rather pragmatic. The National Trust and national groups such as the Campaign for Rural England, the Ramblers' Association and the Royal Society for the Protection of Birds all played a role in purchasing land, protecting nature and creating public awareness of wildlife. Ironically it was the two World Wars and the need to compulsorily acquire land for defence purposes that revealed the potential for wildlife preservation. The end of the Second World War saw the publication of two influential reports in 1947. The Huxley Report in England and Wales[3] and the equivalent Ritchie Report in Scotland[4] both recommended some form of designation to protect areas of nature conservation and the setting-up of some agency or body to oversee nature conservation. These recommendations also coincided with the creation of the regime for Town and Country Planning (see Chapter 9). The result was the creation of the National Nature Reserve and the designation of Sites of Special Scientific Interest (SSSI). The creation of the conservation body, the Nature Conservancy Council (now replaced by Natural England, The Countryside Council for Wales and the Scottish Natural Heritage) was also undoubtedly a major step forward.[5] The rationale for these initiatives was largely science based – and emphasised the role of education and the need for further research. Amenity and recreational use of land were to be considered but were regarded as ultimately subservient to the landscape and its preservation.

The position of agriculture in the equation of nature conservation and protection was somewhat incongruous. The Agriculture Act 1947 was basically enabling legislation intended to accompany the Town and Country Planning Act 1947. The former regulated agriculture and set up systems of payment and controls; the latter helped to create green belts around major cities and towns, thus preventing scarce agricultural land from being used for factories or housing. Ironically the fundamental concept of development control did not apply to agricultural land, which was remarkably unregulated. Perhaps it was believed that nature was likely to face greater challenges from industrialisation and urbanisation than from the industrialisation of agriculture. The limitations on the use of development control (a planning term that is intended to set limits on building as part of planning permission) for agricultural land has given rise to a number of problems. The maintenance of traditional hedgerows, stone walls and the operation of new forms of agriculture – for example the recent use of large plastic sheeting to provide hothouses for all-year-round crops appears to be outside the parameters of development control and the planning system. The scope of section 55(2) of the Town and Country Planning Act 1990 provides that a change of use to agriculture or forestry is not development. Under the related section 336 of this Act the term 'agriculture' is widely defined to permit diverse activities related to livestock production, fish farming, horticulture and intensive farming. There are also exemptions for agricultural use from the terms of the Town and Country Planning (Permitted Development) Order 1995 (S1 1995/418). This relates to fence construction, walls up to two metres in height and temporary use for up to 28 days. Under the same Order there is a wide range of development, including roads, buildings and drainage works, that fall within more generous rules than would normally be the case. There are specific allowances made for the storage of farm waste and for the accom-modation of animals. General guidance is available from the Planning Policy Statement 7, *Sustainable Development in Rural Areas*, which provides general government policies on agri-cultural land use. It may be concluded from the above that generally the United Kingdom has tight planning controls over towns and cities and where building may take place. This

---

[3] Cmd 7122.
[4] Cmd 7184.
[5] See: William M. Adams, *Future Nature: A Vision for Conservation* London: Earthscan, 2003.

is in sharp contrast to the relatively unregulated arrangements that apply to agricultural planning. Planning protects agriculture by limiting building on agricultural land but there are very lax controls over what agricultural landowners can do in carrying out their agricultural activities. This may seem strange but it is a reflection of the way the law in 1947 perceived the special status of agricultural land.

There are only a few instances when the controls are specifically aimed at limiting farming and related activities. There are limitations placed on development within national parks and the Suffolk Broads and the Norfolk Broads, which are singled out for special protection. This also may apply to areas of Outstanding Natural Beauty and to areas specified by Defra under the Wildlife and Countryside Act 1981 section 41(3). There is a notification system whereby there are 28 days prior notice required before the development may take place. This gives the local planning authority time to set controls and limitations on the visual effects and the likely impact on the surrounding landscape. There is also the idea that such notice may help preserve ancient monuments and where there are listed buildings. Incidental amendments have been made since 1999, including ground-based mobile-phone masts and their location especially when they are sited near school buildings. There are restrictive conditions that may be imposed by local planning authorities, such as design and the operation of local custom on buildings. There are defined and unusual circumstances where Article 4 of the General Planning Development Order may allow specific interventions such as draining marshes or ploughing up agricultural land. The moratorium against building on green belt land established since 1947 is normally enforced up to the present day, but there are special circumstances when it may be relaxed.[6]

The operation of Annex II of the EC Environmental Impact Assessment Directive (85/337/EEC) is also relevant to nature conservation. In theory the directive was expected to integrate agriculture and environmental sustainable development. In practice, because so little of the planning controls applied to the environment and farming, it left a lot to be desired. The Environmental Impact Assessment (Uncultivated Land and Semi-Natural Areas) (England) Regulations 2001 SI 2001/3966 are an attempt to fill the gap. Projects with an environmental impact fall under the consent procedure. An Environmental Statement must be submitted to the Secretary of State setting out the nature and impact of the proposed project. There are detailed guidelines that cover matters such as conservation and the protection that designated conservation areas should be given. Thus development and agricultural use of uncultivated land requires consent through the application of EIA. A failure to obey and apply the guidelines may lead to criminal prosecutions.

Nature conservation

Agencies and their roles

The Environment Protection Act 1990 helped to create a number of agencies with responsibilities related to nature conservation. In England there was English Nature, which became an integrated countryside and management agency with a new name, Natural England, in 2006. The integration of different aspects of countryside planning came after careful consideration.

---

[6] See: Planning Policy Guidance Note 2, *Green Belts* (1995).

Lord Haskins carried out a review of the Government's Rural White Paper and Rural Strategy in November 2003, which led to consideration of new structures and ideas for rural England.[7] There followed considerable debate and pre-legislative scrutiny of the draft Natural Environment and Rural Communities Bill. The result is enabling legislation for the regulation of nature conservation contained in the Natural Environment and Rural Communities Act 2006. This was an Act of consolidation over the previous legislation. It also helped refocus existing ideas and allow for the allocation of funding where appropriate to assist with the various roles of each of the bodies.

The role of Natural England[8] is complemented by an independent advisory Commission for Rural Communities that advise the government on policy. This provides a link to ensure central government has coordinating functions over policy. Consequently, the role of the commission under the Natural Environment and Rural Communities Act 2006 is to provide independent advice to government and to ensure that government policies reflect the needs of communities. In addition to Natural England there is the Countryside Council for Wales and, for Scotland, there is Scottish Natural Heritage.

The current structure at first glance seems over-complicated and perhaps lacking in the benefits of a UK-wide body. The Nature Conservancy Council (now replaced by Natural England) had a major input into policy-making and protecting the environment. The new structure, however, is more in keeping with the desire to integrate landscape, access and recreation with environmental land management. The term 'land management' relates to how best practice in managing land to ensure natural habitats are maintained is implemented. In fact the full integration of resource management to include nature conservation, the protection of biodiversity, landscape access and recreation is a step forward in balancing competing needs and successfully meeting the challenges of the countryside (see 'Law in Context' below). An indication of what Natural England does is reflected in the large number of statutory duties that have been given to Natural England with the agreement of the Secretary of State. A glance at the list below indicates just how significant the integration of land management into general policy has become:

- pest and weed control;
- control of pesticides and plant protection products;
- Farm Woodland Scheme and Farm Woodland Premium Scheme;
- wildlife Licensing;
- agri-environment;
- heather and grass burning;
- Energy Crops Scheme;
- minerals and waste planning;
- overgrazing and unsuitable rural supplementary feeding;
- England Rural Development Programme enforcement.

---

[7] Lord Haskins, *Rural Delivery Review* November, 2003; see: *www.defra.gov.uk/rural*.
[8] See: Julie Lunt and Kyle Lischak, 'Natural England – a new dawn? Rights and responsibilities towards the natural environment and how these may change – the "Dilly Lane" case' UKELA (2008) ELM 246.

LAW IN CONTEXT

Soil erosion and land management

Soil erosion is a recognised problem of upland areas in England and Wales and of some agricultural land. There are a number of types of erosion, primarily water erosion (e.g. as a result of intense rainfall) and wind erosion. Some British uplands have high erosion rates not only because of having soils that are prone to erosion, heavy rainfall and steep slopes but also because of a number of human-made impacts. Thus moorland management techniques including heather burning can increase erosion. Overgrazing, recreational uses and tree planting also have important impacts that require careful control. Some arable agricultural land is also vulnerable to erosion and degradation of the soil. The extent of erosion varies not only with the soil type, but also with the crop and can be exacerbated by removal of hedges. An area of approximately 26,000 km² may be vulnerable to erosion in England and Wales. Careful management of erosion-prone land is important in the protection of natural environments and agricultural systems.

Effective stewardship and protection of the natural environment requires Natural England to work in close partnership with other organisations. There is an established framework for future relations between the Natural England Confederation (Natural England, the Countryside Council for Wales and the Scottish Natural Heritage), the Environment Agency and the Forestry Commission. In addition, Natural England is expected to cooperate with English Heritage and local authorities in protection of our natural heritage. There is considerable opportunity for regional and local input into rural-land management through prior consultation, as well as the planning of open spaces in cities and towns. Moreover, there is a need to integrate actions taken by Natural England and regional and local authorities for the recovery and conservation of seas and coasts. The extent of the challenge facing the various agencies is set out in Countryside Surveys. The first Countryside Survey was carried out in 1978 with the express aim of providing a detailed study of natural resources in the UK. Since 1978 there have been regular surveys.[9] The latest in 2007 collated data from a number of surveys taken across Great Britain and in Northern Ireland. The surveys cover a variety of habitats, vegetation types, freshwater bodies and soils.[10] Their findings indicate that protecting the countryside needs constant vigilance and that the stewardship of the countryside is likely to require considerable resources.

Setting priorities for the natural environment is often difficult. One mechanism that is being used is through the adoption of Public Service Agreements (PSA) as part of the government's Comprehensive Spending Review (CSR). The Natural Environment Public Service Agreement was established as part of the 2007 spending review. This covers the period from April 2008 to March 2011. The Natural Environment PSA applies across water sustainability, land and soils, biodiversity and sustainable development. Natural England has published a *Strategic Direction for 2008–13* and *A Manifesto for the Natural Environment*. Taken together

---

[9] In 1984, 1990, 1998, 2000 and 2007.

[10] Available at *www.countrysidesurvey.org.uk*.

the documents provide the important overall strategy for the development of the natural environment. The *Manifesto* includes:

- support for the basics of life including clean air, clean water and productive soils;
- support for economic activity including raw materials for sustainable energy production;
- reducing carbon emissions and moderating temperature extremes as a means of protecting against flood damage and the spread of diseases;
- ensuring cultural identity and also contributing to the health and well-being of the nation as a whole.

It may be concluded that in terms of strategic direction, Natural England is there to conserve and enhance the natural environment. This gives a large discretion to the organisation as to how best to carry out its tasks.

The impact of devolution means that the Countryside Council for Wales supports the Welsh Assembly by carrying out its role in managing the natural environment in Wales, which contributes £9 billion to Welsh economic output. The role of the Council is proactive and engages with all sectors to ensure sustainable policies underlie rural development. The Council's role includes the following:

- protecting the distinctive landscape character of Wales and its biodiversity;
- managing land and sea to support more wildlife;
- overseeing the economic aspects of the natural environment, including history and culture;
- ensuring greater access to the countryside coast for the public.

The Countryside Council has a Corporate Plan 2008–12 and implementation strategy in order to perform its role and deliver its functions.

In Scotland, Scottish Natural Heritage provides a proactive agency for the following:

- caring for nature, including biodiversity in part through a species action framework;
- responding to climate change through increasing renewable energy use and delivering a sustainable development programme;
- enhancing access to the outdoors including green spaces;
- supporting the Scottish economy and delivering sustainable projects in areas such as tourism.
- delivering health and well-being based on the natural heritage adding to the quality of life.

Scottish Natural Heritage also has a Corporate Plan 2008–11, which sets out its strategic objectives and how to achieve them in an economic, sustainable and cost-effective way. Many different programmes and work activities are applied throughout the natural environment by Scottish Natural Heritage (SNH). These include the Natural Care Programme that provides individual management agreements and management schemes to help landowners and managers with SSSIs on their land; the Ancient Wood Pasture classification and management initiative; and the Species Action Programme. SNH also has various agri-environmental schemes.

Sites of Special Scientific Interest (SSSIs)

SSSIs are part of a national scheme to ensure that the diversity of habitats across the country is retained. Such sites are protected because of their scientific interest. Designation may be given to sites where the flora or fauna, or other biological characteristics or geology of a site, requires protection. SSSIs are a means of recognising the importance of the major habitats and wildlife areas. Currently there are more than 4,100 SSSIs in England, covering over a million hectares of land and representing about 7.6 per cent of the total land area. In Wales there are 1,019, in Scotland 1,456. The size of SSSIs varies but one of the largest is 62,000 hectares in Wales covering a coastal and marine environment. The inclusion of the coastal and marine environment makes sense as the land boundaries include territorial waters. Invariably the sites are subdivided into different units to reflect ownership and occupancy responsibilities. The sites are not all in the countryside as over 39,000 hectares of SSSI land are in or near urban areas. For example, there are 36 SSSIs in Greater London. Indeed, sites can be in the heart of apparently unprepossessing industrial areas. The government has estimated that £395 million in public money was spent managing SSSIs between April 2000 and March 2008. A small portion, £77 million, of this has come from the European Union, the remainder from central government.

In the case of England, Natural England is the main regulatory body for SSSIs. Section 28 of the Wildlife and Countryside Act 1981 amended by Schedule 9 to the Countryside and Rights of Way Act 2000 and the Natural Environment and Rural Communities Act 2006 provides the main means of enforcement and protection. In Scotland the Natural Heritage (Scotland) Act 1991 is relevant. The legislation is aimed at protecting the habitat and ensuring that the main features of the SSSIs are not damaged, disturbed or destroyed. There are investigatory powers and, in the case of criminal offences, powers given to the police to prosecute. The work of Natural England is both regulatory and advisory. The main aim is to ensure that the various owners and land managers are proactive in their responsibilities to protect SSSIs, and receive good guidance and advice. Enforcement strategies are also designed to meet this purpose. Letters may be sent to landowners and, under criminal sanctions, investigations undertaken (see above). There is also the opportunity to take civil action in the form of an injunction or damages as part of protecting SSSIs.

The Countryside and Rights of Way Act 2000, only applicable to England and Wales, has created the need for management strategies and targets. Scotland and Northern Ireland have still to decide what direction to take regarding public rights of way in the context of their own special circumstances. This has generated a greater working partnership on principles of management and evaluation of SSSIs between Natural England and owners of SSSIs than was the case in the past. The aims and objectives and quality of the management of SSSIs are at the centre of the strategy. There is a Public Service Agreement (PSA) target that at least 95 per cent of all land within SSSIs should be categorised as in a favourable condition by 2010. This sets a very high standard and expectation. The target is a response to the UK's international responsibilities under the 1992 Rio Convention on Biological Diversity. The use of a PSA is intended to strengthen standard-setting and build SSSIs into the parent central government department overall Departmental Strategic Objectives. The reason is that a PSA aids scrutiny and evaluation. As part of monitoring and tracking there is a Departmental SSSI PSA Programme Board. This has an added benefit of being departmental-led and subject to several reviews by the National Audit Office. There is a whole series of regulatory devices open to use by Natural England when attempting to manage and develop SSSIs. Five are identified in an NAO report:[11]

1. regulatory powers under the legislation to prevent damage;

2. financial incentives to require positive management of sites and their maintenance;

3. advice in the form of practical help in setting up the management of resources for the SSI;

4. policy and advocacy to include initiatives to encourage good management;

5. practical action to encourage active intervention and influence in the way in which the environment is used.

The main aim behind the Countryside and Rights of Way Act 2000 is to bring forward improvements to SSSIs despite reluctance on the part of landowners. Landowners often feel that government intervention may interfere with their property rights and freedom to enjoy the land, though many are generally sympathetic to the need for environmental regulation. The Act applies to England and Wales and there is legislation for Scotland. Designation of an SSSI is an important procedural matter and involves English Nature in making a notification that in their opinion the land is worthy of protection. The notice of notification is provided to every owner or occupier. This is a fundamental responsibility of English Nature and requires a careful analysis of the site and a list drawn up of any potential operations that may damage the site. There is a positive duty that is directed to landowners. The absence of adequate stewardship had been a failing in the past, partly due to the legislation being weak. A recent National Audit Office Report in 2008 concluded that since 2002, the reported condition of SSSIs has improved from 52 per cent by area in target condition to 83 per cent in March 2008.[12]

The Countryside and Rights of Way Act 2000 made provision for management of the sites, and all SSSIs were expected to have developed management statements by April 2006. There are also useful powers under Natural Environment and Rural Communities Act 2006 that provide reasonable steps to serve a notification, which makes notification easier than in the past when there was the stricter requirement of having to ascertain the landownership.

Section 28(1) of the Wildlife and Countryside Act 1981 provides for notification of a site, meaning that there is a procedure to be followed for notification to be made and this may ultimately lead to designation of the site. The section predates the Human Rights Act 1998 and was drafted at a time when approaches to discretion and decision-making were very different to the present orthodoxy. Section 28(1) was the subject of considerable judicial interpretation both before and after the Human Rights Act 1998 took effect. *R v Nature Conservancy Council (NCC), ex parte London Brick*[13] is one of the leading cases in this area and preceded the passage of the Human Rights Act by two years. The issue arose out of a challenge to the notification of old clay pits on a Peterborough brickworks by the NCC, the responsible agency at that time. The analysis offered in the case suggested that notification should operate on a two-stage basis. In cases where there is the appropriate scientific evaluation and the scientific criteria are met, then there is a duty to impose notification on

---

[11] National Audit Office, *Natural England's Role in Improving Sites of Special Scientific Interest* (19 November 2008) HC 1051 Session 2007–08.

[12] *Ibid.*

[13] [1996] Env LR 1.

the site. This is for a provisional period of three months and during this time representations or objections can be made. It is after this discretionary stage, when representations or objections are made, that the regulator may confirm notification. There is an additional requirement, namely that if the confirmation is not made within nine months of the date on which the notification was served then the notification must lapse.[14]

Another perspective on the notification of SSSIs is found in R *(on the application of Fisher)* v *English Nature*,[15] decided after the Human Rights Act 1998. Here the emphasis was on the prior criteria for listing. The analysis drew a distinction between making a judgement and exercising a discretion. It was accepted that once the regulatory body believes that the site meets the criteria for listing then there is a duty to list. The only caveat to this is that during the course of confirmation there must be an open-minded and full consultation process between the notification and confirmation. There is clearly considerable overlap between the approaches in *Fisher* and *London Brick*. It follows that in circumstances where the regulator believes that unless confirmation of the notification is made, for example where the site is likely to be destroyed, it is reasonable to act and make confirmation follow out of the duty that arises from notification. In *Fisher*, however, the main emphasis is to ensure that the process of notification and confirmation should share the common rules of natural justice and fairness. The regulatory agency is not able to consider notification even if the criteria are satisfied simply because of the political or ideological tactics of a pressure group or organisation. This leaves open the possibility that confirmation of a site might be refused on the basis of scientific evidence or expert opinion during the discretionary stage after notification. Once the science is in place in favour or against designation of a site, there is little that can be done to challenge the decision, provided the points made in *Fisher* are followed namely that proper consultation and natural justice applies in a fair, proportionate and reasonable manner. The question arises as to how any conflict in the scientific expert opinion can be resolved. It is perfectly acceptable for the regulatory agency to make a decision that is based on its own expertise, provided it follows the correct procedures.[16] There is a strong implication that the notification and confirmation of SSSIs is likely to reflect expert opinion based on the best available science at that time. Information and scientific understanding is always changing and this will be reflected in the way the regulatory agency considers SSSIs. There are powers to denotify an SSSI. This had been undertaken in the past, provided various bodies including the Environment Agency and interested parties are informed. There is a nine-month period between denotification and confirmation of denotification that allows the parties to make representations.

It is also clear from *Fisher* and the discussion in R *(on the application of Aggregate Industries UK Ltd)* v *English Nature*[17] that the Human Rights Act 1998 has to be taken account of to ensure that the processes and procedures used to notify and confirm a SSSI are compliant. The role of the agencies and the use of expert evidence must also comply with the fairness provisions of Article 6 of the European Convention on Human Rights (ECHR). The ECHR, it will be remembered, underpins the Human Rights Act 1998 which brought the majority of its provisions into United Kingdom domestic law (Chapter 6). In essence this means that all

---

[14] See section 28(5) of the Wildlife and Countryside Act 1981, as amended by the Countryside and Rights of Way Act 2000.

[15] [2004] All ER 861.

[16] See: R *(on the application of Western Power Distribution Investments Ltd)* v *Countryside Council for Wales* [2007] Env LR 25.

[17] [2003] Env LR 3.

the procedures must be fair. The significance of the *Aggregate Industries Ltd* case is that the regulatory structure must be compliant with Article 6, of the European Convention on Human Rights. A concern was that making decisions based on in-house expertise might be inconsistent with Article 6, as the independent evaluation of the evidence might be lacking. In fact the checks and balances within the existing decision-making system were human-rights compliant. This is formally a matter for legal advice, and policy-makers have to take account of the possibility of a judicial review to the courts if there is a failure to act fairly.

Once a designation is made and notification correctly undertaken, there are a number of obligations on landowners and occupiers. SSSIs are a protective device and therefore the landowner must comply with certain responsibilities and duties. These include:

- A written notice must be provided by the landowner before carrying out any operations that may damage an SSSI.
- Provided written consent is obtained and it is four months after the written notice was given, then the operations may go ahead, subject to planning permission. This arrangement has been changed and modified by the Countryside and Rights of Way Act 2000 (set out below).
- Criminal offences apply if there is a breach of the obligations.
- Under the arrangements found in section 29 of Wildlife and Countryside Act 1981 amended by the Countryside and Rights of Way Act 2000, there are powers to require immediate protection of a site and ultimately powers of compulsory purchase, after initial attempts to get a landowner's consent to undertake or refrain from any activities harmful to the SSSI.
- Since the Countryside and Rights of Way Act 2000, there is the power to withhold consent over any activity that may damage a SSSI. Consequently this gives considerable leverage in achieving compliance. In such cases there is an appeal to the Secretary of State or Welsh Assembly or, in Scotland, to the Scottish Land Court where appropriate. Deciding whether there is any potentially damaging operation rests on the general duty to further conservation and enhance SSSIs.

The management of SSSIs has apparently entered a new phase. Instead of relying mainly on self-regulation or voluntary agreements with landowners to manage a site appropriately, the Countryside and Rights of Way Act 2000 provides for reasonable management agreements with landowners. If this proves impossible, then there are powers to issue management notices requiring reasonable measures to conform to a management plan.

Management notices can be appealed. The grounds of appeal are widely drawn to include responsibilities that should be met by other landowners and not the occupier or landowner who is the subject of the notice. The appeal is to the Secretary of State. The use of management notices is in response to the decision to subject SSSIs to a public service agreement target (PSA) that aims to ensure that 95 per cent of all SSSIs should be in a favourable condition by 2010. The historical approach, based on self-regulation and consent through voluntary agreements failed to deliver good management standards for many sites. The arrangements under the Countryside and Rights of Way Act 2000 are, in part, aimed at strengthening the control over public funds by shifting the burden from the public finances to the finances of the landowner or occupier. There are signs that public access to the countryside has improved and there is greater awareness about such rights in the popular press. The real likelihood is that voluntary arrangements might be easier to agree in the shadow of a more interventionist approach. There is little evidence of the regulators wishing to use the powers available to enforce standards for SSSIs. The recent NAO Report[18] on meeting the PSA target and making better use of resources made a number of observations. In summary these were:

- Improving the conditions of SSSIs require that Natural England should build good relationships with landowners and this includes working with the financial incentives on offer to improve environmental stewardship.

- Financial incentives that are tied into contractual management agreements need to be carefully monitored with good record keeping.

- There needs to be realistic plans in place if the target set for 2010 is to be met.

- The assessment process needs to be strengthened and a comprehensive means of checking introduced.

- Good practice and case management needs to be regularised. Natural England has not yet exercised its powers fully to regulate the appropriate management of land resources. The need to improve record-keeping is a high priority.

- The true cost of SSSIs requires careful calculation and this has yet to be fully worked out. It is likely that owing to the nature of funding, costs will fluctuate from year to year.

The effective regulation of SSSIs is also contingent upon planning permission controls as well as the exemption of land operations carried out in an emergency. There is Planning Policy Statement 9 (2005) that outlines the role of *Biodiversity and Geological Conservation*. The fact that planning permission, however, may override the SSSI system is undoubtedly a major weakness. There is further problem that many statutory undertakers with specific powers may be able to undertake work that is detrimental to the SSSI regime. Thus planning permission, if properly given, may act as a defence to any liabilities from environmental damage injurious to the protection given to the SSSI. Overturning or revoking planning permission is expensive, as the denial of planning permission once granted is subject to compensation. Even compulsory purchase may prove economically difficult.

In *R (on the application of Peter Charles Boggis Easton Bavents Conservation) v Natural England*[19] Mr Justice Blair considered a challenge against English Nature on its designation of a coastal site as an SSSI as *ultra vires* and that English Nature was required to consider the effects of SSSI designation on the adjoining lagoon, which was part of the Easton Bavents Special Protection Area known for rare birds. The claim was that Natural England had not taken into account the need to undertake an environmental impact assessment on the designation of the SSSI required under the European Habitats Directive (Directive 92/43/EEC). The case is important for showing how environmental assessment is an important evaluative tool in assessing how to proceed. Mr Justice Blair concluded:

- that section 28(1) affords scope for judgments; it affords no scope for discretion. This follows *Fisher* and the role of English Nature in assessing whether to notify that an SSSI should exist. This approach gave Natural England the necessary legal powers, which had been correctly applied in this case;

---

[18] National Audit Office, *Natural England's Role in Improving Sites of Special Scientific Interest* (19 November 2008) HC 1051 Session 2007–08.
[19] [2008] EWHC 2954.

- the requirement to have an environmental impact assessment came from the Habitats Directive (92/43/EEC). English Nature had failed to comply with this requirement. The risk of designating the SSSI had to be objectively considered in terms of the legal requirements to protect the adjoining land which fell under the Habitats Directive.

The decision in *Easton Bavents Conservation* reinforces the analysis that SSSIs require careful consideration within the overall responsibilities of the regulatory agency. The importance of an integrated approach is reinforced in the discussion of habitat conservation requirements discussed below.

It is also possible to provide special sites where additional protection might be given. This may be based on particular topographical features such as woodlands or hedgerows. There is also the possibility of providing special schemes or incentives to promote tree conservation or the protection of specific species. The operation of international and EU controls are also relevant in this context. There has been a concerted attempt to build the basis of protection through international agreement. The 1972 World Heritage Convention is a good example of building a consensus to provide and protect natural heritage as of 'outstanding universal value'. States are obliged to keep their natural heritage under review and to monitor and list areas that are worthy of protection. Assistance is available from the World Heritage Fund under UNESCO in terms of finance and also publicity. This has in the past favoured buildings and cultural sites – the United Kingdom has 25 sites currently listed. In 2004 there was a Council of Europe European Landscape Convention; this had a more general application, intended to give similar protection of the landscape to that provided more narrowly by the World Heritage Convention. The EU has also favoured the integration of agricultural and environmental objectives into its policy-making. The Habitats Directive 92/43/EC encourages member states to make land-use policy integral to the conservation of the landscape. The protection of habitats' biodiversity is included as part of conservation.

Habitat conservation

Nature conservation strategies include a number of protective designations that apply to different habitats. There are National Nature Reserves (NNRs) and Sites of Special Scientific Interest (SSSIs), already discussed above. Each has their own distinctive role in habitat conservation and species protection. Historically there was one body responsible for Nature Conservation, the Nature Conservancy Council. Under the Environmental Protection Act 1990 there are now three bodies responsible, namely English Nature (now Natural England), the Countryside Council for Wales and Scottish Natural Heritage. This is a rather complicated arrangement but illustrates the importance of having regional and devolved responsibilities in the distinct areas of devolved administrations in the United Kingdom (see above).

NNRs are managed primarily for the study of or research into flora, fauna and geological or physio-graphical features. There are 352 NNRs in Great Britain that cover 226,000 hectares. Just how significant an area this represents is best illustrated by comparison with the size of a county. Buckinghamshire has a geographical area of 156,494 hectares. An NNR is established through the creation of a nature reserve agreement. This can be achieved by ownership and agreement through private property rights. In this case the operation of a site may be through a specified governing body such as the Wildlife Trust. Private ownership of NNRs is, in fact, a cost-sharing device that is intended to increase the scale and scope of NNRs without incurring public costs, leaving costs on landowners. In Northern Ireland there are 47 nature reserves as an alternative to NNRs. In tidal and coastal waters, the equivalents of NNRs are Marine Nature Reserves (MNRs).

International treaties also make important contributions to habitat protection. The UK has 70 Ramsar sites designated under the 1971 Convention on Wetlands of International Importance. So-called Ramsar sites are designated under an international agreement implemented into UK law. The scope of habitat conservation has also been increased by the impact of two significant EC directives. There is Directive 79/409/EEC, the Wild Birds Directive (see Case Study below), and Directive 92/43/EEC on the Conservation of Natural Habitats and of Wild Fauna and Flora. The United Kingdom has currently 77 Special Protection Areas classified under the Wild Birds Directive.

CASE STUDY

Hart District Council v Secretary of State for the Communities and Local Government

In *Hart District Council v Secretary of State for the Communities and Local Government*[20] the role of Natural England was reviewed by the courts. The case arose over the views of Natural England with regard to the designation of a special protection area for rare bird species under the European Wild Birds Directive 79/409/EEC. The designated area covered the Thames Basin Heaths. This comprised 13 heathland sites in Berkshire, Hampshire and Surrey. The bird species under protection included the nightjar, woodlark and Dartford warbler. The process of setting up a special protection area includes an assessment of the impact of any development proposals. Regulation 48 of the Conservation (Natural Habitats etc.) Regulations 1994 provide that when assessing a development proposal the competent authority, in this case Hart District Council, must carry out an 'appropriate' assessment of the proposal. This includes consulting with the relevant nature conservation body, in this case Natural England. The decision to adopt the Habitats Regulations came from an application for the development of 170 residential homes at a site 1.5 kilometres from the Thames Basin Heath. Hart District Council was the competent body to consider the application and also under the Habitats Regulations the competent body to ascertain, after an appropriate assessment, whether the proposed development would adversely affect the special protection area.

Natural England considered that any development within a five-kilometre radius of the special protection area would be likely to disturb the heath and the habitat of the birds. This was based on the analysis that recreational traffic on the heath would increase. Natural England objected to the development and argued that the development required an appropriate assessment. Hart Council rejected the planning application and the applicant appealed. This resulted in a public inquiry. The opportunity was taken to consider how to reconcile a special protection area being close to a residential area.

---

[20] [2008] All ER (D) 21 (May).

Considerable debate and consultation took place, with the outcome that a strategy was agreed between Natural England and the applicants. Under section 106 of the Town and Country Planning Act 1947 a planning agreement was reached. The agreement provided the basis for the applicants entering into a strategic plan and this was agreed by the Secretary of State.

Hart District Council as the local planning authority decided to appeal the decision of the Secretary of State. In the High Court, the District Council claimed that it was wrong to consider the planning application together with the designation of the special protection area. The District Council was not inclined to accept the accommodation reached between the developer and Natural England. However, the High Court upheld the decision of the Secretary of State and the advice given by Natural England.

The result of the case is as follows:

- Natural England has the opportunity to inform and develop nature conservation strategies as part of the planning process.

- Significantly the case highlights the role of science, specialist expertise and analysis.

- The opportunity to undertake detailed and analytical assessment of natural habitats provides an environmentally sustainable future for habitat protection.

- The future of integrating adequate species protection into residential and community housing may pave the way for a proactive engagement with environmental issues for the future.

Trees and woodlands

Among the most striking features of our landscape is woodland, trees and hedgerows. This is an area where the law has been much more active in affording stronger protection than was the case in the nineteenth century. There are duties on many agencies to ensure that woodlands are protected. These extend to the Forestry Commission which must ensure when granting tree-felling licences that appropriate conditions apply. While there are negative restrictions stating what cannot be done under the Hedgerows Regulations 1997, there are also positive requirements about tree management under the Environmental Impact Assessment (Forestry) (England and Wales) Regulations 1999. Section 55(2)(e) of the Town and Country Planning Act 1990 excludes from the definition of permitted development any change of use of land from forestry or woodland. This provides important protection as permitted development would give landowners too wide a discretion over the land which is not in keeping with the protection required. There are wide powers to make tree preservation part of planning conditions. Local planning authorities have a general duty to make provision for trees when planning permission is granted. Sections 197–214 of the Town and Country Planning Act 1990 applies a regime of tree preservation that permits local authorities powers to require adequate protection of trees when planning permission is granted.

One of the innovative mechanisms used to protect trees comes under the operation of the Tree Preservation Order system (TPOs) under the main sections (sections 197–200 of the Town and Country Planning Act 1990). This is a system intended to protect individual or large groups of trees. The test for local planning authorities to apply TPOs is whether 'it appears

. . . expedient in the interests of the amenity'.[21] This is likely to mean that the amenity and its well-being is linked to what is expedient and necessary. This, in fact, may apply to an individual tree, though it is interesting to note that the term 'amenity' is distinctive from simple nature conservation purposes. As a general principle the use of a TPO is not likely to apply to an area where there is a good systematic conservation plan in operation. In areas where there is a good conservation plan, there is an acceptance that appropriate measures are in place to address the conservation and management of trees.

There is a wide range of offences connected to contravention of a TPO. This includes cutting, uprooting or 'wilfully' destroying a tree or damaging a tree in such a manner that is likely to destroy it. The criminal law provides a penalty at summary conviction of £20,000. This rises to an unlimited fine if the prosecution is on indictment. The question of whether the level of conviction is appropriate is linked to the fact that the most likely offenders are large property developers who stand to gain considerable sums. The system of fines may not be adequate to developers who are prepared to pay fines and recoup the costs from their profits. Related to the TPO system are offences connected with various conditions as part of the TPO regulation and which are enforceable as part of the regulatory regime.

There are a number of cases in the courts that have sought to define the mental elements of the offences and the idea of 'deliberate'.[22] The courts have taken a fairly strict interpretation of the responsibilities for inquiries to be made to ensure that there are no TPOs on a particular development site. The use of the term 'deliberate' in the definition of the offences associated with the breach of a TPO may also be interpreted to mean a negligent act.

The system of making TPOs falls to the District Planning Authority or the National Park Authority in a national park. There are reserve powers delegated to the Secretary of State to make a TPO under the little-used section 220 of the Town and Country Planning Act 1990. The procedures used for making a TPO are that the Local Planning Authority draws up a draft order that is made public and open to consultation. Twenty-eight days are allowed for objections. The draft is circulated to all those who may have an interest, such as owners, occupiers, or those with felling rights over the land. Once the 28-day period is concluded then the draft TPO is confirmed after due deliberation of any objections. While there is no appeal against a TPO, it is possible to challenge the validity of a TPO in the High Court under section 288. The process of confirmation of a TPO and the period of deliberation may take some time. As a result there are powers for interim TPOs to be made under section 201, pending the outcome of the TPO arrangements for making a permanent order. Interim TPOs have immediate effect. The use of an interim TPO provides an immediate response to the challenges of preventing a valuable asset from being demolished.

The TPO is detailed in its application and is accompanied by a map and a designation of the tree or trees to be preserved. This is seen by many as time-consuming and cumbersome. It is clear that local authorities require resources and time to invest in the process, which may act to self-regulate the system. There is some evidence to suggest that TPOs are not being made by local authorities because of the time, trouble and expense.

---

[21] There is a detailed guide; see: *Tree Preservation Orders: A Guide to the Law and Good Practice* DETR, 2000 – see the new edition published in 2009 for an analysis of recent changes and procedures. The Department of the Environment Transport and the Regions (DETR) is the central government department responsible.

[22] See *Maidstone Borough Council* v *Mortimer* [1980] 3 All ER 552; also see: *Barnet London Borough Council* v *Eastern Electricity Board* [1973] 1 WLR 430.

There are inevitably some defences to the various offences created under the TPO regime. The most commonly used include that it is still possible to prune fruit trees and, in certain circumstances where planning permission has been given, then, it is possible to cut down, uproot or lop a tree. There are also various permissions arising from work on dead or dying trees or trees that are dangerous or where it is necessary for the abatement of a civil nuisance. The most obvious application of the latter is in the case of roots that under-mine a neighbour's foundations or sewers. While it is not a nuisance to deprive a neighbour of the right to a view or the right to light to his land, it is possible for a high hedge to be unjustified and to fall under local authority regulations.[23] Local authorities may make use of their own independent legal powers. There are specific regulations concerning conifers and their use in urban surroundings. The most common form of exception to the TPO arrangements is through an application for consent made to the Local Planning Authority. This provides on a case-by-case basis some limited form of exception. It is possible to appeal to the Planning Inspectorate (previously the Secretary of State, before 2008) in cases where consent is refused. Another strategy is to offer replacement trees. This may be part of the conditions attached to the TPO or it may be a condition attached to the granting of planning permission under section 206 of the 1990 Act. In cases where a tree is dead or dying a replacement may be planted in the same place as soon as possible. There are special and detailed provisions for woodlands and their maintenance. There are also exceptions to the TPO regime for the Forestry Commission and its management of land and forestry planning under the Forestry Acts.

A breach of the TPO is itself a criminal offence. The local planning authority, however, may decide to make an enforcement notice using its own legal powers. Section 207 of the 1990 Act provides that such a notice must be served within four years of the failure to abide by the conditions or where there is a breach of the TPO. There is a right of appeal against an enforcement notice to the Secretary of State.

In conservation areas there is a general rule that all trees are subject to a statutory restriction that prohibits the cutting down, lopping, topping, uprooting, wilful damage or wilful destruction of any tree under section 211. There are more limitations than would normally be applied to an individual TPO. It is possible for any prohibited act to go ahead six weeks after there is notification to the local planning authority of the decision to undertake the works. This is designed to give time for forward planning and to give con-sideration for the operation of a TPO. The penalties and regime for enforcement are the same as for TPOs in general. There is no compensation scheme for the imposition of a TPO but in circumstances where consent is refused there is some compensation under section 203. The compensation goes beyond the value of felled trees and after a Court of Appeal case it is assessed on the basis of the value of the land.[24] The value of the land is centred around an assessment of its market rate. This might limit the use of TPOs, given the high price of land values and their fluctuation over time. One way to achieve the same objectives might be to certify refusal on fairly narrow grounds, such as the interest of good forestry or that the trees were a necessary part of the outstanding amenity value of an area. Another way was to follow the practice of refusal through an amended regulation (SI 1988/963), and follow the Forestry Commission practice in respect of woodland. This would provide

---

[23] Anti-social Behaviour Act 2003.
[24] *Bell v Canterbury City Council* [1989] 1 JEL 90.

compensation from the commission under the Forestry Act 1967 relating only to the value of the timber. Amendments to the TPO regulations in 1999 have effectively given statutory effect to the role of the Forestry Commission in enforcement and regulatory matters that had previously been done through agreement with local authorities rather than the Forestry Commissions' own powers.

The Town and Country Planning (Determination of Appeals by Appointed Persons) (Prescribed Classes) (Amendments) (England) Regulations 2008 SI 2008/595 came into force on 6 April 2008 together with the Town and Country Planning (Trees) (Amendment) (England) Regulations 2008 on 1 October 2008 SI 2008/2260. The main changes in the law relating to TPOs are as follows:

- simplification of the application process and procedures, including a standardisation of application form;
- a fast-track procedure for cases where the Local Planning Authority refuse consent and impose conditions;
- to make use of the Planning Inspectorate to process appeals and
- empower planning inspectors rather than the Secretary of State to make decisions.

The reforms are welcome additions to the law on TPOs that will assist in streamlining the application process and simplify procedures. There is also a greater use of electronic data than hitherto. The use of the Planning Inspectorate is also an important step forward in achieving more speedy resolution of cases and also for implementing a fast-track procedure.

Forests and their protection

There are specific rules applicable to forests and their protection. This includes regulation of forestation and deforestation. Forestation is where planting makes possible for the forest to be regenerated. Deforestation is where the forest has lost many trees, e.g. through acid rain, diseases or other causes.

There are many voluntary schemes and a variety of licensing and private property protections applicable to forests. A Woodland Grant Scheme has existed since 1990. This is designed to move forestation away from simply supplying a resource for the timber industry, which had been common practice in the 1980s, to a more varied forestation scheme including the restoration of many native species.[25] This would include broadleaved trees such as the horse chestnut, beech or oak. The scheme provides incentives in the form of grants and funding, including a premium for the planting of broadleaved trees. The Farm Woodland Premium Scheme SI 1992/905 also encourages the planting of new woodlands on farms and the movement of farmland into woodland production. This is supported by the EC Rural Development Regulations 1257/1999.

There are regulations applicable to felling trees within forests. Section 9(2) of the Forestry Act 1967 provides for a system of licensing, covering the felling of trees of a certain size and dimension.[26] The absence of a licence and any attempt to fell a tree makes anyone liable for a fine. Section 1(3)(a) inserted into section 4 of the Wildlife and Countryside (Amendment) Act 1985 provides that the Forestry Commission must attempt to strike a balance between

---

[25] *Our Forests – the Way Ahead: Enterprise, Environment, Access* Cm 2644, 1994.
[26] Trees over 8 cm in diameter or 15 cm in coppices when measured 1.3 m from the ground.

the management of forests and the conservation of landscape and nature. There are various widely drawn exceptions when a licence to fell a tree is not required, such as for fruit trees, trees in gardens, orchards and churchyards or public spaces. There is no licence required when the felling is part of a development authorised by the planning authorities. Similarly when the aim is to abate a nuisance or to prevent danger then no licence is required. Disputes may be settled by the local authority. The operation of a felling licence and the existence of a TPO are matters to be resolved by the Forestry Commission. This is an attempt to give some consistency to decision-making.

There are many initiatives on forest and woodlands. A joint venture between Natural England, then the Countryside Agency, the Forestry Commission and local authorities is run under the initiative known as *Forests for the Community*. There is a new National Forest in the Midlands and also 12 Community Forests in operation in England with more to be planned. The designation of National Forest status provides protection and allows careful management of the forest and its habitat.

Despite their obvious importance for wildlife, hedgerows have not been given as much protection as trees under the TPO regime. In England and Wales they only received some protection under section 97 of the Environment Act 1995. The Act provides that the Secretary of State may make regulations prohibiting the destruction of certain hedgerows. The Hedgerows Regulations 1997 SI 1997/1160 apply generally to a wide range of types of hedgerows, but specifically to hedgerows that are 20 metres or more long and are adjacent to land. The owner is required to notify the local planning authority that it is intended to remove or make major alterations to an existing hedgerow. There are 42 days for the Local Planning Authority to decide whether or not to serve a retention notice. There are two categories of hedgerow – important and unimportant. The former is defined by age – not less than 30 years old – and also special qualifying criteria set out in great detail in the regulations. The current hedgerow regulations attempt to set objective criteria on which to decide whether or not to afford protection. A different approach might be to emphasise the value of the hedgerow in terms of local and cultural significance. This would undoubtedly bring many more hedgerows under protection but it would intensify the need for appropriate resources to regulate this important part of the environment. There was a review of the hedgerow regulations in 1998, which accepted that any implementation of the United Kingdom's Biodiversity Action Plan needed greater protection for hedgerows. It is clear that the future of hedgerow protection should be linked to the preservation of natural habitat – an indispensable part of any environmental regulation if nature conservation is to be optimised. This is unlikely to occur for some time to come. Hedgerow protection provides wildlife and birds a natural habitat. Their removal takes away an important environmental protection.

Landscape and management

The system of town and country planning outlined in Chapter 9 is mainly concerned with the built environment and the threat of urbanisation on the countryside. The countryside itself requires additional and specific protection. There are many human activities ranging from farming to recreational pursuits that may have impacts on the countryside. In a sense the tendency for people to move out of towns and cities, increased in the 1990s, has served to increase pressures on the countryside and rural life.

The landscape of great poets, artists and musicians is often idealistic, but it does find a common chord in public opinion and awareness. This is supported by a survey undertaken by the Countryside Agency in 2003 where the respondents appeared to want to keep the countryside as it is now, unchanged. Nevertheless how we manage the landscape is burdened by different, often conflicting and sometimes strongly held views. The fact that the national identity and culture can be influenced by the landscape is all the more reason to maintain a lively debate about its future. Three recent examples of incursions into the countryside highlight the dilemma. The first is the use of mobile-phone masts – the twenty-first century successor to the controversial National Grid power lines of the 1950s and 1960s. There are public concerns about cancers and effects on human health. These concerns remain difficult to prove in terms of scientific evidence. Mobile-phone masts have alerted many conservationists to the delicate balance between serving the needs of a large economy while securing the natural habitats and preserving natural landscapes. The second example is the introduction of large wind-powered energy farms. Usually situated in areas of great beauty and unspoilt wilderness primarily because these are the areas of reliable wind, their aim is to harness the wind and convert its use to electricity. Wind farms again attract conflict and debate over their position, potential noise and their visual impact. The environmental case in their favour is that wind turbines provide energy that does not release greenhouse gases to the atmosphere. They also provide an important contribution to the 15 per cent renewable target set by the European Commission as the UK's contribution to the EU's 2020 target.[27] In 2007–8 the UK only managed to reach 1.8 per cent of energy generation by renewable sources. It is calculated that to make the 15 per cent target, some 32 per cent of electricity, 14 per cent of heat and 10 per cent of transport fuels will have to be sourced from renewables.[28]

Wind farms are also an important part of the climate change agenda contained in the UK's Climate Change Act that is set to reduce CO_2 emissions. The capacity for wind farms to fill the gap in energy needs, however, is limited. According to two recently commissioned independent reports,[29] for the government 'only 10.7% of offshore wind can be built in the UK by 2020'. This is far below the target of 14 GW anticipated to be needed. This is primarily because of limited industrial capacity to manufacture the new technology and the need to give incentives to the industry to meet current expectations. Incentives to build offshore wind farms would also provide much-needed jobs at a time of economic downturn. The British Wind Energy Association has carried out a study demonstrating how this might be achieved.[30]

The third example of dilemma facing landscape protection is also highly controversial. The Common Agricultural Policy (CAP) resulted in new rules for agricultural production with many farms being paid to 'set aside land' and leave it fallow. The main aim of the scheme was to reduce over-production of food and also ensure that land was being treated as a scarce resource that needs to be protected. In 2007 there were approximately 300 thousand hectares of set-aside land, in fact a decrease of 14 per cent since 1996. Payments for set-aside were

[27] ENDS Report 397, February 2008, p. 48.
[28] ENDS Report 402, July 2008, p. 38.
[29] ENDS Report 403, August 2008, pp. 13–14.
[30] ENDS Report 406, November 2008, p. 18.

abolished under CAP in 2008. In recognition of some of the environmental benefits of set-aside Defra initiated a voluntary scheme, the Campaign for the Farmed Environment, in 2009. Should farmers be paid or given incentives to take their stewardship of the land responsibly and, for example, manage set-aside land, to encourage natural habitat recovery? This question was originally posed in 1991 when the then Countryside Commission for England introduced the Countryside Stewardship Scheme. The scheme is intended to provide a wide-ranging means of achieving countryside conservation. Currently it is run by Defra and the areas selected are to be restored and enhanced as part of nature conservation and landscape management strategies. There is a ten-year agreement, with over 10,000 agreements in place in England and is likely to provide public access to the countryside. There are similar arrangements in Wales (Tir Gofal), which extends to whole farms. Many farmers and landowners object to such government intervention as over-burdensome and unnecessary. Others see it as an important recognition of the long-term farming and land-owning responsibilities.

A recent innovation, from 2005, is for the introduction of the Environmental Stewardship Scheme (see below). This has a two-tier payment scheme setting entry-level participation that is relatively limited and graduating to the full scheme over time. The European Union has added to it's repertoire of agricultural innovations the operation of Chapter VI of the EC Rural Development Regulation (1257/1999)[31] from 1 January 2000. The regulations allow for financial support to maintain the countryside as part of a land management strategy. The conditions of the EU scheme are met by the Countryside Stewardship Scheme. One advantage of the scheme is that it is also supportive of farmers remaining on the land in cases where farming is uneconomic. This may apply when the price of some crops is too low or where milk prices make dairy farming uneconomic. Under section 98 of the Environment Act 1995 there are also schemes that permit Defra and the Welsh Assembly to make grants for the purposes of conservation and enhancement of the countryside. In short the aim is that conservation of the countryside is promoted and that the countryside is accessible to the public as part of the stewardship of land by farmers.

Strategic management of the landscape

It is difficult to design a comprehensive strategy for integrated management of different aspects of landscape. We have already seen how the use of town and country planning legislation helps designate agricultural land and provide an overall protection for the natural landscape. Strategic management of the landscape is largely addressed through development control. This is an inheritance that goes back to the 1947 planning system and has remained largely unaltered. The main concerns behind the 1947 use of development control were that the need for housing and rebuilding towns and cities after the Second World War was likely to put considerable pressure on land resources. Green belts were designated around the major centres of population as a means of protecting large areas of the countryside from large-scale urban development. A surprising outcome of planning after the 1947 Town and Country Planning Act was to allow agricultural developments to remain largely unrestricted and this is reflected in the rural landscape today.

---

[31] This replaced EC Rural Development Regulation 1257/99.

The agri-environment

The impact of agriculture, meaning farming in general,[32] on our natural heritage cannot be underestimated, particularly if you consider that approximately 75 per cent of the total land area of the UK is used for agriculture. Some of the greatest changes to our landscape have been a direct result of evolving farming practices. The end of the Second World War saw a drive for the UK to be self-sufficient in food, which brought substantial changes in farming practice. Land that had not been agriculturally productive was managed for farming use: it was drained or coppices (hedges and boundaries, including small woods) were removed, etc. The increased mechanisation needed for intensive arable farming resulted in the loss of vast swathes of hedgerows, producing extensive fields that were easily managed using large agricultural machinery. In some parts of the country the visual change to the landscape was immense and the loss of habitat considerable. Such large field systems are vulnerable to soil erosion, an increasing problem in some parts of the country. Intensive crop production also requires large applications of fertilisers to optimise crop yield, which has resulted in the eutrofication (excess nutrients in rivers etc. resulting in major ecological changes) (see 'Law in Context' box on p. 260) and degradation of many of our waterways. Large field systems are also particularly vulnerable to pests, largely controlled by the application of biocides. These chemicals can affect non-target organisms, with potentially alarming environmental and health consequences. Crops need water, and farmers abstract large volumes of water from rivers and groundwater to irrigate fields. All this has resulted in substantial habitat loss and considerable pressure on our natural environment. Intensive animal husbandry can be no less damaging, with large amounts of animal waste raising water pollution risks as well as potentially releasing ammonia to the atmosphere, and the use of biocides e.g. sheep dip. There is also a concern that the use of chemicals will enter the food chain and cause injury to human health. Intensive animal farming is also a substantial contributor to greenhouse gas emission because the metabolism of ruminants results in the release of methane, a greenhouse gas, to the air. Animal-feed supplements such as copper and zinc can contaminate soils and water. It is clear that any protection of the natural environment, from habitats to soil and water and the atmosphere, must include consideration of agriculture.

We have already discussed the role of landowners in protecting designated sites in our environment. As landowners, farmers, estate managers and market gardeners must also protect designated SSSIs and Natura 2000 sites, including Special Areas of Conservation and Special Protection Areas, either on their own land or on adjacent land. Natura 2000 sites come from the EC Habitats Directive (92/43/EEC) and form a European network of protected sites. The sites incorporate the highest-value natural habitats and those that contain rare, endangered or vulnerable plant or animal species. Landowners and managers have to seek permission to cultivate soils, and apply fertilisers or biocides in order to protect designated SSSIs. More generally there is a cross-compliance obligation on farmers and direct payments to farmers, under the CAP Single Payment Scheme that subsidises farming, to meet set standards for agriculture. Since 2007, this has also included compliance with Rural Development schemes, which are designed to help deliver the government's Strategy for Sustainable Farming and Food.[33] Rural Development schemes include Environmental Stewardship

[32] This includes arable and non-arable and dairy farming.
[33] See for information *www.defra.gov.uk/farm/policy/sustain/strategy.htm*.

(see below), Environmentally Sensitive Areas Scheme, Countryside Stewardship Scheme (see above), Woodland Grant Scheme and England Woodland Grant Scheme, among others. Cross-compliance requires that farmers meet:

1. Standards for good agricultural and environmental condition. These include standards to maintain habitat and landscape features, and protect soils.

2. Statutory Management Requirements. These are set by the EU and were phased in between 2005 and 2008. The requirements affect a variety of areas linked to agriculture, including the environment, human, plant and animal health, and animal welfare.

Failure to meet cross-compliance requirements can mean that agricultural payments are withheld.

The Environmental Stewardship scheme is a recent innovation under the auspices of Natural England. The objective of this scheme is the protection of soil and water. Farmers can enter the Environmental Stewardship Scheme at a number of levels:

1. entry-level stewardship;

2. organic entry-level stewardship; and

3. higher-level stewardship.

The latter, for example, has a number of options relating to land and fertiliser use, and the management of grazing. Land management techniques that protect and enhance the environment can attract specific payments. These include contributions such as planting hedgerows and ditch restoration.

Historic heritage sites, whether above or below the soil surface, should be protected from agricultural practices, including ploughing, uprooting trees and even from pigs disturbing the ground. The protection of Scheduled Monuments with an important historical legacy, e.g. prehistoric stone circles, is a legal requirement.

Much of the agricultural industry relies on good soil quality to maintain crop yields and fertile grazing land: the only exception to this is aquaculture where water quality is fundamental. The protection of soil is, of course, a fundamental part of water quality since soil erosion and run-off can have significant impact on the ecology and chemistry of water systems. The importance of the soil resource is under substantial reassessment today. Defra issued a consultation on the draft Soil Strategy for England in March 2008, which is an extension on its First Soil Action Plan (2004–2006). Part of this Strategy, adopted in 2009, is directed at sustainable soil management in agriculture and forestry, which will require good soil management in these sectors. Among other things the strategy emphasises soil management to protect peat soils, as many potting products used in gardening and the sale of indoor and outdoor plants use peat. Peat bogs are substantial carbon stores as well as being an important habitat. The improvement of soil quality by encouraging recycling of organic waste materials to land is also included and is linked to the development of quality standards to reduce health, contaminant and nutrient pollution risks from organic waste applications such as farm slurry. All of this is likely to impact on farming practices. The strategy has been designed to be compatible with the proposed EU Soil Framework Directive.

Farming is responsible for both point source pollution (i.e. coming from a single point) and for diffuse pollution (i.e. arising from a much larger area such as fertilised fields). Pollution control is not the topic of this chapter but it is worthy of mention in the context of our countryside, since the impact of agricultural pollution on natural habitats and the environment can be considerable (see 'Law in Context' below).

LAW IN CONTEXT

Diffuse pollution from farms

We will consider two examples of pollutants arising from farming activities.

1. The use of nitrogen and phosphorus fertilisers is a common reason for the eutrofica-tion of rivers, lakes and even coastal water. Eutrofication occurs when the water is nutrient-enriched by fertiliser being washed out of farmland by rain. This results in algal blooms and rapid growth of other plants, disrupting the ecological balance of the system. One consequence is the loss of biodiversity from a system. Water quality standards may not be met as a consequence of eutrophication, depending on the vulnerability of the river or other water body; moreover it may be impossible to meet Water Framework Objectives (see Chapter 12). There are a variety of sensitive areas where particularly careful management of and controls on fertiliser use is needed, including Groundwater Source Protection Zones and Nitrate Vulnerable Zones (NVZ). NVZs are part schemes that protect Nitrate Sensitive Areas and are designated by the EA. They are areas of land that drain into waters that are or could become polluted by nitrate. In fact about 70 per cent of land in the UK drains to water identified as meeting the EC Nitrates Directive's definition of nitrate polluted. This is a significant problem for the UK because of very intensive farming methods. Farmers are expected to manage fertiliser addition through such techniques as reducing fertiliser use, land-spreading animal waste and applying fertiliser when there is least likelihood of run-off occurring.

2. Biocide treatment of crops is a controversial area. The European Parliament approved the new EU pesticide legislation, a Directive on the Sustainable Use of Pesticides, in 2006. This is intended to ensure safer use of pesticides through strengthening controls and banning some pesticides considered an unacceptable risk to human health or the environment because of their toxicity. The use of biocides in agriculture is prob-lematic in a variety of ways. Biocides can have acute environmental impacts but more often they have chronic effects on flora and fauna. These effects may be cumu-lative and persistent, affecting biodiversity and the health of water and land habitats. For example, the decline in a variety of bird species, e.g. Corn Bunting, Yellowhammer and Grey Partridge, has been partly linked to pesticide use. The directive requires farm-ers, and others, to change current practices. For example, aerial crop spraying will be banned; they will have to establish 'buffer zones' around water bodies, and 'safe-guard zones' around surface or groundwater used for drinking.

There can be no doubt that the agricultural industry has a substantial role to play in the protection and stewardship of our countryside.

Genetically modified organisms (GMOs)

Genetically Modified Organisms (GMOs) are controversial. GMOs are organisms that have been altered in a way that does not occur naturally but through a process of genetic modification. This is at the cutting edge of scientific discovery, and the use of genetic modification has widespread medical and scientific applications that are often controversial because of concerns about human health and also the effects on the natural environment. The main concern in this part of the chapter is on the modification of plants that has a direct implication for the production of food and agriculture. This is, of course, primarily in terms of crop plants a range of which, including corn, cotton, soybean, oil-seed rape, have been modified for a variety of traits, e.g. herbicide tolerance, insect resistance, virus resistance, colour alteration and oil alteration. There is some scepticism about our ability to provide appropriate risk assessments for GMOs and control any unforeseen outcomes from large-scale planting of GMO crops in agri-environments. In reality, large-scale use of GMO crops is common across most of the world, although not yet in Europe. The EC Council Directive 2001/18/EC notes how the potential impact of the release of GMOs into the environment is such that the effects may be irreversible. Knowing the extent of any unwanted impact of GMOs is so difficult to quantify that there are many groups opposed to GMOs. Scepticism about science and public distrust of scientific evaluation is commonplace – especially in the aftermath of the BSE crisis in agriculture in the UK. In 1989 the Royal Commission on Environmental Pollution undertook a study of GMOs,[34] which considered the risks and evaluated the science. An influence on this study was the history of the involvement of Health and Safety Executives (HSE) with contained use of GMOs in biotechnology. In the 1980s the HSE made recommendations about risk assessment and monitoring based on voluntary self-regulation. There was an early attempt to put the voluntary arrangements into a statutory form under SI 1989/1810, which represents one of the earliest attempts to set a framework for the use of GMOs. The Royal Commission built on this early history with an important finding that there should be new and comprehensive legislation to set controls on GMOs and their release into the environment. The Royal Commission Report was very influential and contained some details on a statutory scheme that monitors, authorises and screens as well as controls releases. Built into the Report was the idea of risk assessment – difficult to make when scientific advances mean that there is a continual reshaping of the characteristics of GMOs. The Royal Commission also suggested strategies for regulation that include licensing, registration of GMOs companies, access to public information as well as a duty of care. The paramount aim was to protect health and the environment.

The bulk of the recommendations are to be found in Part VI of the Environmental Protection Act 1990. The aims of the legislation are 'to prevent or minimise any damage to the environment which may arise from the escape or release from human control of GMOs'. There is an Advisory Committee on Releases to the Environment (ACRE) to advise on human health aspects of release. Section 109 of the 1990 Act has an interesting series of general duties to identify the risk to environmental damage that their releases may have and cease activities where, despite all due care, the risks cannot be eliminated. The Secretary of State has wide-ranging powers to regulate GMOs that include prohibition notices, and the result of any breach may cause the offender to come within the criminal law. There is also a list of activities

---

[34] 13th Report of the Royal Commission on Pollution, GMOS.

under section 111 where consent must be obtained from the Secretary of State. There are public notices and registers of information as well as any prohibitions.[35]

The EU has been very active in this area. Since the 1990s there has been EC legislation that also aims to protect health and environment from risks associated with GMOs. At the same time there is common ground that finding the correct market for biotechnology is an important part of the future for entrepreneurial science and for the EU a recognisable economic commodity. Directive 92/219/EEC, commonly called the Contained Use Directive, required a system of classification in order to set boundaries on the use and control of GMOs. This approach sought to distinguish small-scale use, such as in laboratories for non-commercial purposes, from larger-scale operations. Directive 98/81/EC added to this system and refined it in the light of new scientific knowledge.

The next step was Directive 90/220/EEC on the Deliberate Release of GMOs into the environment.[36] Balancing protection of the environment and human health and also ensuring market developments is a delicate and difficult operation. In 1997 the EU decided to amend the directive after consultation and analysis. This has taken some time. The key issues include:

- adequate scientific analysis and effective risk assessment;
- managing longer-term effects and ensuring member states were adopting a consistent approach;
- evaluating and assessing the post-market strategies for GMOs, especially products produced through the use of GMOs;
- public consultation and the operation of adequate controls over experiments involving GMOs; and
- adequate transparency in the procedures used to make decisions about GMOs.

In 1998 a number of European countries within the EU effectively started a moratorium on the environmental release of GMOs because of concerns over risks, substantially influenced by public opinion. In recent years, however, there have been a number of key changes that open up the possibility of GMOs being more widely used and the moratorium being relaxed. These include the following:

- Rises in food prices and pressures on food production has increased the likelihood of wider use of GMOs.
- The demand for biofuels and industrial starch has given a further impetus to GMOs.
- US manufacturers are no longer separating out non-GMO produced products such as maize and soya beans – this inevitably places pressure on EU countries to accept the new crops.
- EU arrangements for the authorisation of GMOs have seen an increase in authorisations.

The EU Directive 2001/18/EC replaced the earlier Directive of 90/220/EC from October 2002. This provides a detailed and comprehensive set of standards and processes for GMOs. The UK implemented the Directive in the Genetically Modified Organisms (Deliberate Release) Regulations 2002 SI 2002/2443. The result is a detailed and comprehensive code on GMOs. The principles and procedures are as follows:

---

[35] Legislation also includes: Genetically Modified Organisms (Contained Use) Regulations 2000, SI 2000/2831 replacing the earlier 1992 regulations; see: Genetically Modified Organisms (Contained Use) Regulations 1992 SI 1992/3217.

[36] In the United Kingdom see: Contained Use Regulations 1992, SI 1992/3217 and also the Deliberate Release Regulations 1992, SI 1992/3280.

- the adoption of the precautionary principle for GMOs;
- the operation of preventative and risk-assessed action to prevent any damage to the environment through GMOs release. There are comprehensive steps that must be taken to ensure that clean-up of any damage is undertaken;
- there is a detailed guide setting out the procedures for the regulation of GMOs, including the scale of release and the circumstances whereby releases should be evaluated;
- contained use of GMOs and their release has to take place after a detailed risk assessment based on scientific evaluation. It is unclear to what extent ethical issues may be considered.

In England and Wales the main regulatory regime is enforced by Defra in collaboration with the GM Inspectorate at the Central Science Laboratory and by the Food Standards Agency, the Local Authority Trading Standards Officers and the Port Health Authorities. Specific statutory powers are given under Part VI of the Environmental Protection Act 1990 that cover inspection, enforcement and release as well as marketing of GMOs. In the case of food, regulation is through the Food Standards Agency and local authorities. The current arrangements for GMOs fall under an authorisation process and also risk assessment.

Conclusions

Nature conservation and human development requires a fine balance between conflicting and often contradictory pressures. Economic growth led by market forces has encroached on many of our natural habitats. It is remarkable that so much natural habitat has been preserved. In part this is due to the structure of planning laws since 1947. One approach to conservation is through National Parks, established to preserve and enhance the natural beauty, ecology, cultural heritage and amenity value of areas designated under the National Parks and Access to the Countryside Act 1949. The Act has been substantially amended, most recently under the Natural Environment and Rural Communities Act 2006 and the National Parks (Scotland) Act 2000. There are now 15 National Parks, 10 in England, 2 in Scotland and 3 in Wales. National Park Authorities, which are independent statutory organisations, are charged with protecting the natural and cultural heritage of National Parks. They produce a five-yearly National Park Management Plan after consultation with local communities, landowners and organisations such as the National Trust and the Forestry Commission, for the strategic management of the National Park. It is equally the case that SSSIs and habitat protection strike a new balance for the future of the environment. The challenges for the future include GMOs, an increase in the need to protect individual animals and plants and the pressures on conservation.

Further reading

General

W.M. Adams, *Future Nature Conservation* revised edition, London: Earthscan 2003.

R. Caddell, 'Biodiversity loss and the prospects for international cooperation: EU law and the conservation of migratory species of wild animals' (2008) *The Yearbook of European Environmental Law* 218–64.

G. Harvey, *The Killing of the Countryside* London: Jonathan Cape, 1997.

P. Marren, *Nature Conservation: A Review of the Conservation of Wildlife in Britain 1950–2001* London: Harper Collins, 2002.

S.W. Martins, *Farmers, Landlords and Landscapes: Rural Britain 1720–1870* Cheshire, England: Windgather Press, 2004.

J.C. Nagle and J.B. Ruhl, *The Law of Biodiversity and Ecosystems Management* 2nd edition, New York: New York Foundation Press, 2006.

M. Overton, *Agricultural Revolution in England: The Transformation of the Agrarian Economy 1500–1850* 5th edition, Cambridge: Cambridge University Press, 2006.

O. Rackham, *The History of the Countryside* London: Orion, 2000.

C. Reid, *Nature Conservation Law* 2nd edition, Edinburgh: W. Green, 2002.

T. Smout, *Nature Contested* Edinburgh: Edinburgh University Press, 2000.

T. Williamson, *The Transformation of Rural England: Farming and the Landscape 1700–1870* Exeter: University of Exeter Press, 2003.

Genetically modified organisms (GMOs)

This is a highly specialist area but worth careful study.

Thomas Bernauer, *Genes, Trade, and Regulation: The Seeds of Conflict in Food Biotechnology* Princeton: Princeton University, 2003.

Julia Black, 'Regulation as facilitation: negotiating the genetic revolution' (1998) 61 *Modern Law Review* 621.

Environmental Audit Committee, Second report 2003–4, *GM Foods: Evaluating the Farm Scale Trials* HC 90-I.

J. Holder, 'New age: rediscovering nature law' (2000) 53 *Current Legal Problems* 151.

Websites

Defra: *www.defra.gov.uk*

Agencies

Countryside Council for Wales: *www.ccw.gov.uk*

European Commission Nature and Diversity homepage: *www.ec.europa.eu/environment/nature/index_en.htm*.

Joint Nature Conservation Committee: *www.jncc.gov.uk*

Natural England: *www.naturalengland.org.uk*

Northern Ireland Environment Agency: *www.ehsni.gov.uk*

Scottish Natural Heritage: *www.snh.org.uk*

Visit **http://www.mylawchamber.co.uk/mceldowney** to access key issue checklists and practice exam questions to test yourself on this chapter.

12 Water and pollution controls

Introduction

Ensuring water quality and protecting water resources through pollution controls are central to any effective system of environmental protection. Water is big business. Ofwat, the water industry regulator, expects that water companies will invest up to £27 billion over the next five years. The Environment Agency for England and Wales alone has spent over £124 million during 2007–8 in its work ensuring water quality. At all levels,[1] national, EU and international, the setting of standards and the protection and assurance of water quality is of fundamental importance. Water is a topical subject. Climate change affects the amount of rainfall that provides rivers and groundwater, and the usable water resource. Predictions of rainfall and water usage into the future are challenging. The average rainfall may not be a true reflection of the problem. Downpours may cause disruption, floods and problems in maintaining the quality of fresh waters. Periods of drought may lead to water shortages for agriculture and domestic use and will affect the health of aquatic ecosystems. Predicting weather patterns and rainfall is a notoriously difficult and uncertain science, but essential nevertheless in order to plan for the future. In recent years flood plains in many parts of Europe, including the United Kingdom, have been unable to cope with sudden and unexpected periods of high rainfall. As a consequence some highly populated low-lying areas have been flooded. This may be partly due to the impact of global warming but other factors have an influence. The need for more homes has led to building in areas prone to flooding. High housing density and increased areas that are made of impervious material, e.g. roads, drives etc., means that rainwater cannot seep into soils but runs off into rivers. Changes in agricultural practices have also tended to increase the amount of rain run-off to rivers. In many developing as well as developed countries abstracting water is often the most contentious element of the state's involvement with private citizens.

Water also defines sovereignty, and the need for healthy and drinkable water is likely to be at the centre of many conflicts in the world. Water is also a source of energy and large hydroelectric schemes may convert developing countries into developed economies. In many continents the building of dams is high on the agenda and this creates tensions between funding agencies, governments and environmental interests. In China the Three Rivers Dam

---

[1] Environment Agency, *Water for People and the Environment: Water Resources Strategy for England and Wales* Environment Agency, March 2009.

project highlights the problems of the state seeking to expand their market economy but having to address environmental concerns with difficult environmental forecasts and risk assessments as to the likely ecological damage.

Water is essential to life; protecting water quality and controlling pollution is a key concern. Its varied uses at home, in industry and agriculture make it vital to the sustainable development of humankind. Water is essential to domestic consumers; for a variety of commercial uses including waste disposal, commercial fishing, agriculture and food manufacture, various industrial processes; as a means of transport, and for many recreational activities. The responsibilities of the Environment Agency (EA) in the protection and regulation of water resources are diverse and considerable. The EA is active in monitoring water pollution in rivers and lakes and incidents are logged and followed up. Each river is given an assessment against water quality benchmarks such as the levels of oxygen and nitrates. There is a General Quality Assessment Scheme (GQA) in use and this has proved to be a useful means of monitoring water quality. Four elements are involved – chemical and biological content; nutrient content; and finally the aesthetic quality of the water. The incidents of pollutant discharges into rivers that cause contamination are carefully monitored. Criminal prosecutions are taken and fines are set on a scale of seriousness and effects on water quality. Prevention is intended to be *ex ante* but it relies mainly on *ex post* surveillance and deterrence. Do fines serve as an adequate deterrence?

There is, in fact, some ambiguity over what constitutes water quality. The European approach has been to set standards for specific activities such as drinking water or bathing water. In the final analysis this serves to act as a standard that may be imposed to deter pollutants entering the water system. Another approach is to set targets and levels of substances found in water. This is exemplified by the pesticides standards set in the Drinking Water Directive (98/83/EC). The Water Framework Directive (2000/60/EC) is one of the most significant and innovative approaches fostered by the European Union. It is comprehensive and provides a framework for the classification of water bodies; the setting of objectives and the monitoring of achievement as well as identifying what measures are required to maintain and achieve the objectives set. It is hoped that the directive will foster continual improvements in water quality. There is a specific section in the chapter for the discussion of the implications of the directive.

Water is an important resource and providing sustainable water supplies is one of the greatest challenges of the twenty-first century. Approaches to water pollution and water quality are more holistic than in the past. There is a more integrated approach to water quality, including price controls, water pollution controls and standards for waste. There is a need for even greater integration between the legal regimes that exercise controls over oceans and marine life with the regime that applies to freshwater sources.

Water pollution and quality

An overview

Water pollution control is the subject of much legislation. In England the privatisation of water gave rise to new legislation; a fresh approach to regulatory issues and as a consequence a greater public awareness of water costs. The perception has grown that the cost of water services is higher for consumers because of water companies investing in large capital projects and addressing the problem of water leakage. A number of relatively dry seasons in the 1990s as well as increasing demands for water drew attention to the potential for water shortages. Universal water metering is planned but has not been implemented. In England, *Future Water* provides an outline of government water strategy.[2]

The current law is complicated and found in six major pieces of legislation: the Water Resources Act 1991, the Water Industry Act 1991, the Statutory Water Companies Act 1991, the Land Drainage Act 1991 and the Water Consolidation (Consequential Provisions) Act 1991. The Environment Agency established under the Environment Act 1995[3] is the major environmental regulator and takes responsibility for water pollution enforcement. In the area of water resources one significant change is the Water Framework Directive 2000 (Directive 2000/60/EC). This is an ambitious part of an ongoing strategy to develop and improve water quality in member states. There is also the Water Act 2003 that amends the previous regulatory system over water set up at the time of water privatisation. This has resulted in Ofwat becoming, in 2006, a regulation authority as part of a panel of regulators. Ofwat's role as the water industry regulator is a key element in ensuring water standards.

The main challenges facing the regulation of water need to be considered. These are to ensure sustainable water resources that are well managed and are in keeping with securing a balance between natural habitats and humans' need for water resources. The primary focus of this chapter is to consider the arrangements for the management of water and the monitoring, prevention and detection of pollution of inland waters, rivers, canals and groundwater. The setting of standards for water quality and the regulation of drinking water are also discussed in this chapter. The legal regime that applies to water is greatly influenced by the European Union but is also in line with international law. Aspects of water that come within waste are considered in the chapters on land (Chapters 9, 10 and 11) and marine (Chapter 13).

It is important to note at the outset that there are some differences in the way water is considered in the devolved system of government operating in Scotland, Wales and Northern Ireland. In Scotland, unlike England, the water industry is not privatised. Scottish Water provide water supply and sewerage services. The Scottish Environment Protection Agency (SEPA) is the Scottish equivalent of the Environment Agency, but does not have responsibilities for flood control or fisheries. It does act in flood risk assessment. The Scotland Act 1998 that created the Scottish Parliament devolved responsibilities for legislating in the area of water to the Scottish Parliament. This is subject to the United Kingdom Parliament retaining legal authority over EU negotiations and treaty obligations. The EC Water Framework Directive 2000/60/EC was enacted in Scotland under the Water Environment and Water Services Act (Scotland) 2003, resulting in the Water Environment (Controlled Activities) (Scotland) Regulations 2005. In Wales the Government of Wales Act 1998 (amended by the Government of Wales Act 2006) provides the Welsh Assembly with powers to initiate proposals for additional fields of competences to be given to the Welsh Assembly. Responsibility for water pollution is a matter for the Assembly and this falls under the powers set out in the

---

[2] *Future Water: The Government's Water Strategy for England* (February 2008) Cm 7319.

[3] The Environment Agency took over the role of the National Rivers Authority, set up under the Water Resources Act 1991 and abolished by the 1995 Act, and also takes on responsibilities of Her Majesty's Inspectorate of Pollution (HMIP).

Water Resources Act 1991. Finally, in Northern Ireland, there is a devolved assembly under the Northern Ireland Act 1998 and the Water (Northern Ireland) Order 1999 (N.I. 6) applies under the responsibility of the Department of the Environment (Northern Ireland).

Challenges and issues: science and law

The different demands made on water require an integrated approach to water management. It is becoming increasingly accepted that the management of water resources must take account of the variety of uses and impacts of water. This includes water extraction for agriculture, domestic and industrial use; fisheries; hydro-power generation; navigation; leisure and recreation; and flood defences. The preservation of aquatic ecosystems requires the highest priority. The water quality found in rivers and groundwater affects the quality of water available for public or private water supply. Pollution of rivers through discharges affects the quality of water and substantially adds to the cost of making water wholesome for drinking or other purposes. The Environment Act 1995 contains powers for the creation of flood defence committees, and the dilemmas set by climate change provide a real challenge for the future of flood defences and the protection of towns and cities. The pollution of groundwater and surface waters is a serious problem which has a considerable impact on the use of water by humans and on aquatic ecosystems. Pollutants in aquatic environments include a variety of organic, inorganic and microbial agents discharged, leached, or precipitated from the atmosphere, either singly or as a cocktail, into freshwater systems. In addition physical agents such as heat can pollute water (see Law in context, below). One of the important shifts in tackling water is the marked improvements in water monitoring, particularly for drinking water, together with improved standards. There is also evidence of a difficult learning curve in the UK's approach to regulating pollution. Increasingly the Environment Agency has taken a more robust view of pollution controls and mounted successful prosecutions against polluters. The EU adoption of targets and setting standards is also an important way of addressing pollution problems.

LAW IN CONTEXT

Effects of pollutants in fresh water and groundwater

Pollution of freshwater and groundwater ecosystems is exceptionally diverse in character involving a wide range of agents, for example suspended solids, organic nutrients, pH, and a wide range of chemicals. In fact some 1,500 compounds have been listed as freshwater pollutants. These pollutants arise from a variety of sources, both point sources (e.g. from sewage outfalls) and diffuse (e.g. agricultural run-off) sources. Any one source of pollution may contain more than one type of pollutant. The specific impact of the pollutants on aquatic ecosystems is difficult to predict but some generalisations can be made. The effects of a toxic chemical on an organism or community depends primarily on the distribution and concentration of the chemical, the length of time that organisms are exposed to it, environmental transformations of the compound (e.g. chemical reactions and biodegradation) and if the pollutant is biologically available, i.e. its bioavailability.

Many of these factors are interrelated and are affected by the nature of the receiving water and by the types and lifestyles of the organisms present. For example, consider a pollutant which after discharge to a river becomes associated predominantly with the sediment. Organisms that live primarily in the water will be very little exposed to the pollutant, while sediment dwelling organisms may be exposed for long periods. The lifestyle of an organism may also vary during the organism's life cycle so the eggs or juvenile stages may be exposed to pollutants to different extents from adults.

The impact of individual pollutants on any individual organism may be either acute or chronic. Acute effects are rapid, obvious, often fatal and normally non-reversible. Lethal concentrations (LC) of chemicals to selected organisms are often expressed as LC50 or LC70, which indicates the percentage of organisms killed at a given concentration of chemical. Since exposure time is important this is normally linked to a specific exposure time, e.g. 48-hr LC50. An example of an acute pollution incident happened at Camelford in 1988 where aluminium sulphate was released to the Rivers Camel and Allen, resulting in acidic water with high aluminium concentrations. Between 43,000 to 61,000 salmon and brown trout alone were killed.

Chronic toxic effects occur after long-term exposure to low concentrations or doses of pollutants, e.g. pesticide run-off from agricultural land and pharmaceuticals from sewage. These effects are often sub-lethal although on occasion may ultimately cause death. Sub-lethal effects are reflected in a lowering of the growth or reproduction of an organism, i.e. physiological impact, or perhaps impairment of behavioural responses. As a consequence its impacts are not only on individual organisms but also on whole populations and communities. Chronic pollution may also be cumulative, with the effect increased by a series of doses. Add to this the fact that pollutants may exert individual influences, or they may interact, the problems of prediction are evident. Moreover, some aquatic ecosystems are substantially more vulnerable to the adverse effects of pollutants than others. For example, streams high in nutrients, organics and solutes, e.g. lower clay streams, tend to be reasonably stable when a number of low toxicity compounds are added. Fragile streams easily disrupted by effluent discharges are generally nutrient- and solute-deficient, e.g. acid sand streams in the New Forest.

Trying to establish the impact of pollutants has catalysed the development of a relatively new scientific discipline called ecotoxicology. Basic ecotoxicology techniques (often using LC values; see above) are currently employed to predict the impact of a given chemical on specified freshwater organisms in an attempt to quantify the toxicity of the chemical. These are largely inappropriate to the prediction of community and ecosystem level impacts, or even to predict the response of other organisms to a pollutant. Considerable scientific work is still needed in this respect. Monitoring to establish the extent and nature of any ecosystem damage is also essential. (See Chapter 7 for more details.)

River pollution, of course, is important for the quality of drinking water. Equally important is the contamination of groundwater which has considerable impact on achieving drinking water quality standards (see the *Cambridge Water* case below). This is especially the case in South East England where there is a heavy dependence on aquifers for public water supply. Contamination arises from both point source and diffuse pollution, and includes the same range of pollutants as surface water. Particular concerns in the UK relate to pollutants arising from old landfills; pesticides and nitrates from agricultural land; acid mine drainage; and industrial chemicals especially solvents.[4] Contamination of groundwater supplies vary with meteorological conditions, for example flooding may lead to high levels of contamination. There is an important link between groundwater and surface water. Groundwater recharges surface water from springs and seepages into rivers and maintains wetland ecosystems. Any decline in the quantity or quality of groundwater has a subsequent impact on surface water and the achievement of river water quality. Remediation of groundwater is often technically complex and expensive to achieve; ideally this precious water resource should be adequately protected from contamination.

Clearly, water resources are contaminated by pollutants that originate not only from effluent discharged directly into the water, but also as diffuse pollution from land and from the atmosphere. Protecting our water resources, therefore, involves control over both land use and atmospheric discharges. Only a truly integrated and holistic legal approach will achieve adequate protection of our water.

The main statutory and regulatory framework

The Water Resources Act 1991 provides for the management, regulation and operations of water resources. The major part of water resources, including water management, licensing and extraction, flood defences and drainage, water pollution control, fisheries management, flood defences and conservation, are within the remit of the Environment Agency under the Environment Act 1995.

The Water Industry Act 1991 provides for privatised water companies to carry out the functions of providing water and sewerage services. The Land Drainage Act 1991 applies to the land drainage aspects of water management carried out by internal drainage boards. Many of the powers in the 1991 Act have been consolidated from the now repealed Land Drainage Act 1976. The Water Consolidation (Consequential Provisions) Act 1991 incorporates a consolidation of the various past Water Acts and fills in the gaps in the incorporation of the law undertaken by legislation.

The legislation outlined above envisages several organisations with regulatory functions over water quality. There is also a limited role for local authorities (see below). The main organisations and their key functions in water regulation are as follows:

- The Environment Agency oversees discharge consents and supervises the system of integrated pollution control (IPC) under Part 1 of the Environmental Protection Act 1990 and under section 138(2) of the Water Industry Act 1991.

- The quality of drinking water is regulated by the Drinking Water Inspectorate, while pollution is the specific responsibility of the Environment Agency and Defra.

- Under the Water Resources Act 1991, originally the National Rivers Authority and now the Environment Agency under the Environment Act 1995, enforces the provisions for discharge consents under IPC. The discharge of prescribed substances falls under the application of the 'best available techniques not entailing excessive costs' principle (BATNEEC).

---

[4] See: W. Howarth and D. McGillivray, *Water Pollution and Water Quality Law* Crayford: Shaw and Sons, 2001.

- Waste disposal that falls under Part 2 of the Environment Protection Act 1990 imposes a duty of care to take all reasonable steps to ensure that the disposal is not harmful to others. Originally the NRA worked in close cooperation with HMIP, which was also subsumed into the Environment Agency. The monitoring of effluent discharges into watercourses and the general quality of rivers fall within its remit.

The setting of standards for discharges is an important responsibility. This is carried out through:

- monitoring facilities and equipment for sampling and the maintenance of quality assurance;
- maintaining the means to record discharges;
- maintaining permanent records of discharges and the conditions relating to discharge consents.

As noted above the Environment Agency is required to protect and enhance the environment taken as a whole and to contribute to sustainable development subject to legislation and taking into account any likely costs.

Water management, pollution and standard-setting

Considerable progress has been made in tackling point-source pollution from specific effluent discharges. The basis of the current regime is the use of consent for discharges of sewage that is into controlled waters, or any discharge of trade or sewage effluent that is carried out through a pipe from land or sea outside controlled waters, and any discharge where there is a prohibition in force.

Historical developments and the Environment Act 1995

Part 2 of the Control of Pollution Act 1974 concerns water quality and effluent discharges. After privatisation of the water industry the Water Act 1989 repealed much of the 1974 Act. Reorganisation of the legislation on the water industry took place in 1991 following the Law Commission Report No. 198 Report on the Consolidation of the Legislation Relating to Water (Cmnd 1483), and resulted in the Water Industry Act 1991 with the setting-up of the National Rivers Authority (NRA) for England and Wales (in Scotland the Rivers Purification Boards). Since then the Environment Act 1995 has set up the Environment Agency, which possess the powers of the NRA for England and Wales. In Scotland the Scottish Environmental Protection Agency (SEPA) has general duties as to pollution control and water. The Environment Agency for England and Wales has statutory duties under the 1995 Act to promote:

- the conservation and enhancement of the natural beauty and amenity of inland and coastal waters;
- the conservation of flora and fauna which are dependent on an aquatic environment;
- the use of waters and land for recreational purposes.

The SEPA has statutory duties for Scotland under the 1995 Act to promote:

● the cleanliness of rivers and other inland waters and groundwater in Scotland;

● the cleanliness of tidal waters in Scotland;

● conserve, as far as practicable, the water resources of Scotland and, in addition;

● the conservation and enhancement of the natural beauty and amenity of inland and coastal waters;

● the conservation of flora and fauna which are dependent on an aquatic environment.

Comprehensive powers are provided under the Water Resources Act 1991 for the proper management of water resources. There are general duties on the Environment Agency to conserve, redistribute, augment and secure the proper use of water resources in England and Wales. This includes powers under section 20 to make water resource management schemes with water undertakers, and under section 21 to provide the Secretary of State with draft schemes for the minimum flow of inland waters. Part II of the 1991 Act contains powers for the licensing of the abstraction of water (see: sections 24–37 of the Water Resources Act 1991). There are detailed regulatory controls over the issuing and modification and revocation of licences under Chapter II of Part II of the 1991 Act.

Section 93 of the Water Industry Act 1991 has a new Part IIIA and section 93(a) inserted by Schedule 22, article 102 of the Environment Act 1995. This imposes a duty on every water undertaker to promote the efficient use of water by its customers. Additional powers are contained in new sections 93 B–D inserted into the Water Industry Act 1991. These powers supplement the powers granted to the Office of Water Services (Ofwat) for the economic regulation of the water companies. Sections 93 B–D provides the Director of Ofwat with powers to determine and publish standards of performance related to the new duties to promote the efficient use of water. In this context it is useful to note that recently published government policy favour the use of water meters.

There are additional powers under Chapter III of Part II of the 1991 Act for dealing with drought. Section 73(1) provides the Secretary of State with powers to make an ordinary drought order where because of 'an exceptional shortage of rain' a serious deficiency of supplies of water in an area exists or is threatened. The meaning of the term 'exceptional shortage of rain' is not clear, and the period of time over which this is determined is not stipulated. For example, should average rainfall over a year be used, or is a shorter period, such as four months, appropriate even if rainfall was normal prior to this period? A drought order may provide prohibitions on the use of water and may specify modifications or restrictions to the licensing of the abstraction of water. There are powers to make an 'emergency drought order' where there is a serious deficiency of supply because of shortage of rain and the economic or social well-being of persons in the affected area is likely to be affected as a consequence. An emergency drought order may provide for the same restrictions as set out above for an ordinary drought order. In addition, an emergency drought order may authorise the use of standpipes and water tanks.

The request to make a drought order may be made by the EA or the water undertaker. It is an offence to breach a drought order under section 80 of the 1991 Act. Drought orders are made in the form of statutory instruments and there are procedural rules about public consultation, including the holding of a public inquiry under the Drought Order (Inquiries Procedures) Rules 1984 (see: SI 1984 No. 999 and see Schedule 8 to the 1991 Act). While there is provision for compensation payable (Schedule 9) where existing rights are affected and loss or damage caused, these provisions are primarily aimed at the entry or occupation of land or restricting the taking of water or its discharge. There is no provision for any reduction in water bills because of a failure of supplies during a period of drought. In fact a drought order may be an effective indemnity against any claim for a reduction of water charges. Section 79(3) specifically excludes from compensation payments the interruption of supply by preserving the rights of water or sewerage undertakers to recover their charges. The use of drought orders is likely to be controversial.

The Environment Agency has powers under Schedule 22 to the Environment Act 1995, which inserts into the Water Resources Act 1991 a new section 79A, allowing the grant of a drought permit to a water undertaker. A drought permit may specify the source of water and the period for which water extraction may be granted. This enables water undertakers to have access to a wider variety of water resources than would otherwise be possible. There is a similar system of enforcement for drought permits as that which applies for drought orders under section 80 of the Water Resources Act 1991.

Water pollution control: the statutory controls

The water pollution control system under Part II of the Water Resources Act 1991 applies to coastal waters and territorial waters extending 3 miles from shore. It also has application to inland fresh waters, including lakes, ponds, specified reservoirs, rivers and watercourses. Finally, the definition of controlled water under the 1991 Act extends to groundwater. The breadth of the definition of controlled water is sufficient to cover almost all water sources, including artificial constructions such as canals.

Pollution control rests on a distinction between 'point' source pollution and 'diffuse' pollution[5] (see Law in context, below).

LAW IN CONTEXT

Sources of water pollution

Water pollution arises from two kinds of source: 'point sources' and 'non-point' or diffuse sources. As the names indicate, point sources are clearly identifiable sources of discharges into water courses, e.g. a pipe deliberately constructed to conduct effluent into a watercourse. Non-point sources are diffuse and not so easily identifiable. Commonly the discharge is an incidental and unintended consequences of other activity, e.g. using nitrate fertiliser on crops. There, are however, areas of overlap. Accidents, for instance can cause both point source and diffuse pollution. Point source contamination arises from industry, agriculture and fisheries, and the urban environment, and may be intermittent or continuous. Intermittent pollution events, e.g. stormwater discharges exacerbated by heavy rainfall, can be as damaging to an ecosystem as continuous discharges. The amount

---

[5] Albert Mumma, *Environmental Law* McGraw-Hill Book Company, 1995, p. 25.

of pollutants originating from point sources often tends to decline rapidly with distance from their point of origin. Commonly diffuse pollution originates from sources such as agricultural run-off and may have severe ecological implications. In the case of toxic chemicals, e.g. biocides, diffuse sources of pollution tend to result in low environmental concentrations of the pollutants, their presence and impact often only becoming apparent after accumulation in organisms or long time periods.

Adopting the distinction, in the case of 'point sources', pollution is controlled principally through a regulatory authority giving in advance consent for effluent to be discharged into a water course, subject to specified conditions and controls. In the case of 'diffuse' pollution the pollution is primarily intended to be prevented through tight controls precluding discharges from taking place. Where discharges do take place there are legal controls in an attempt to minimise the effects of the discharges. However, both 'point sources' and 'diffuse' systems of control are subject to accidental or unintended events. In the case of 'point source' pollution an attempt is made to build into the system of pollution control strategic plans where, for example, there is unexpected flooding.

The lawful discharge of polluting effluent through the granting of consents must be confined to certain limits in order to prevent pollution becoming too burdensome for the water courses. Setting limits on lawful discharges is therefore an important part of the system of water pollution control. Under the Water Framework Directive (see below), water bodies are classified as to their ecological and chemical status (e.g. high, good or moderate) and with water type (e.g. river, lake, transitional and coastal). Environmental quality standards (EQS) are put in place for the water body depending on this classification. They are set for a range of characteristics and significantly in the context of discharge consents (see below) for 'priority substances'. Limits on discharges will be determined by the overall load of the receiving water body. There are a variety of Community Directives that contain reference to such substances, such as the Dangerous Substances in Water Directive 76/464/EEC which sets out a prescribed list of substances and chemicals that are banned or any discharge which must be reduced to safe levels (also see: the Trade Effluents (Prescribed Processes and Substances) Regulations 1989 SI 1156 as amended by SI 1990 No. 1629 and SI 1992 No. 339). The Surface Waters (Dangerous Substances) (Classification) Regulations 1989 SI No. 2286 provide a list of dangerous substances according to various EC Directives which include mercury (82/176/EEC and 84/156/EEC), cadmium (83/513/EEC), hexachlorocylo-hexane (84/491/EEC), carbon tetrachloride, PCP and DDT (86/280/EEC), and aldrin, dieldrin, isodrin, hexachlorobenzene, hexachlorobutadine and chloroform (88/347/EEC). There is provision for further directives to be made as 'daughter directives' to the main Dangerous Substances Directive. Also included in the United Kingdom is the Surface Waters (Classification) Regulations 1989 (SI 1989 No. 1148). Currently a Water Framework Daughter Directive on priority substances is being negotiated with the planned repeal of the Dangerous Substances Directive in 2013 (see Water Framework Directive below).

The Secretary of State is empowered under section 82 of the Water Resources Act 1991 to set water quality objectives. This involves the Environment Agency, exercising their water pollution powers to ensure that such objectives are met.

The Ground Water Directive 80/68/EEC provides two lists of dangerous substances, i.e. priority substances. List 1 includes organohalogens, mercury, cadmium, cyanides and substances with carcinogenic properties. Discharges containing any of the substances on list 1 are prohibited. There is to be a Water Framework Daughter Directive on groundwater and the Groundwater Directive will be repealed in 2013 (see below).

Account has been taken in the law in the United Kingdom of Directive 91/271/EEC on urban waste-water treatment. This directive stipulates minimum requirements for the treatment of urban waste water and sludge disposal. Its aim is to encourage reuse of water and the development of improved waste-water management. Originally in the UK sewage treatment was designed to avoid disease and odour and to protect potable water sources. Now approximately 30 per cent of all UK potable water supplies are connected with reuse of effluent after abstraction downstream from its discharge point and further treatment. The treatment and disposal of sludge is exceptionally important and accounts for as much as 40 per cent of the operating costs of a waste-water treatment plant. In the UK approximately 40 million tonnes (wet weight) of sludge is produced annually. There has been considerable debate about the best means of disposing of this waste. The sludge is treated, e.g. by anaerobic digestion and volume reduction processes, not only to minimise nuisance and adverse environmental impacts, but also to make for easy and cheap transport and disposal. The majority of sludge is disposed of to land. The largest portion of this is used in agriculture and horticulture, while the remainder goes to land reclamation or landfill. A small amount of sludge is incinerated.

There is also considerable importance attached to Directive 91/676/EEC on the protection of waters against pollution caused by nitrate from agricultural sources. This directive places restrictions on fertiliser use and sets maximum permissible nitrate levels in drinking water. Geographical areas are zoned according to their vulnerability to nitrate pollution (see 'Law in Context' box on p. 260).

At present there are also directives on Fishlife, but these will be repealed as part of the Water Framework Directive in 2013 (see below). Directive 78/659/EEC (as amended by Directive 2006/44/EC) is on the quality of fresh waters that require protection or improvement to support fish life. The directive divides water into salmonid and cyprinid according to fish species to be found in the water. In the United Kingdom the majority of water (88 per cent) is salmonid, the remainder cyprinid. The designation sets water quality standards that must be monitored. There is a directive on shellfish (Directive 79/923/EEC as amended by Directive 2006/113/EC) that is intended to ensure that member states will meet designated standards and monitor compliance.

Preventative measures

The Environment Act 1995 provides the Environment Agency with powers to serve a notice on potential polluters requiring them to carry out works to prevent pollution or to clean up water pollution. Schedule 22 to the Environment Act 1995 contains sections 161A–C inserted into the Water Resources Act 1991, which make it an offence not to comply with such a notice. There are procedures contained in these sections for serving notice and, in the event of non-compliance, taking action. If the person on whom the notice is served fails to comply with the notice then powers under section 161 of the 1991 Act may be used, which allow the Environment Agency powers to carry work out and recover costs.

Discharges

The requirement of a discharge 'consent' is authorised under the Water Resources Act 1991 through a consent document that may set the limits on effluent discharged into water courses or rivers. The 'consent' is analogous to a licence, which contains the authorisation for the discharge together with details of procedures and conditions. A consent provides the legality for discharges of effluent. Schedule 10 to the Water Resources Act 1991 prescribes procedures for the obtaining of consents for the discharge of effluent (see Department of the Environment Circular 17/84). There is a periodic review of consents undertaken by the Environment Agency. There are powers to revoke or modify a consent as a result of the review. However, each consent must specify a period or periods where there cannot be a modification or revocation. A modification or revocation must also contain a specified period, not less than four years, during which a subsequent notice may not be served (see: new sections 90A–B inserted into the Water Resources Act 1991 by Schedule 22 to the Environment Act 1995). In a situation where it is deemed necessary to issue a revocation or modification within the protected period, then compensation is payable to the discharger of effluent should there be a modification or revocation. These procedures are intended to give some security to the discharger. A limited amount of deregulation to these procedures has been introduced by amendments contained in Schedule 22 to the Environment Act 1995. This includes the removal of the provision for objectors to be able to call in a consent application and the suspension of modifications or amendments until appeals are heard. The only exception is in a matter where the Environment Agency considers there has to be immediate effect on public health grounds or to minimise pollution.

Consents may take two forms: numeric and non-numeric. Numeric consents specify quantitative limits for discharges usually expressed in terms of the concentration or load of the determinants. Limits may be expressed as a percentage of the whole or in absolute limits. The former is a standard that the discharge must not exceed at any time. For example, many different discharge consents relate to permitted effluent biological oxygen demand (BOD). BOD is a measure of the biodegradable material present in an effluent. This is significant because too high a BOD and water is likely to become deoxygenated and therefore unable to sustain many aquatic organisms e.g. fish. There can be instantaneous spot-sampling in order to discover if there is compliance with the standard. The latter is measured over a period of time and compliance is based on a standard that need not be complied with all the time. Non-numeric consents deal with discharges where it is not possible to set quantitative limits on discharges. The consent may require technical conditions, which are requirements that apply to the process of discharge to ensure that there is a satisfactory standard.

Direct discharge consents are issued by the Environment Agency, under Schedule 10 to the Water Resources Act 1991. There are four procedural steps that must be followed after receipt of an application:

1. In two successive weeks notice of the discharge must be published in a local newspaper in the vicinity of where the discharge is intended to take place.

2. A copy of the notice must also be published in the *London Gazette*.

3. The relevant local authority or water undertaker in whose area the discharge is proposed should be informed with a notice setting out the details of the intended discharges.

4. In cases where the discharges are into coastal waters or within or outside the relevant territorial waters then a notice should be served on the Secretary of State for the Environment, Food and Rural Affairs.

If it is considered that the discharge will not have an 'appreciable effect' on the water then the first three steps do not have to be taken and a discharge consent may be granted. Determining what is an appreciable effect falls under the guidance contained in DoE Circular 17/84. Broadly this covers matters relevant to the amenity of the area or of environmental significance, or where the discharge might result in a major change in the flow of the receiving waters or result in changes in water quality that may damage or effect future use of the water. It can, of course, be argued that there are inherent scientific difficulties in accurately predicting the environmental significance of a discharge (see Law in context, p. 268).

The procedures outlined above also include the receipt of written representations and call-in powers granted to the Secretary of State that may result in the holding of a local inquiry into the application. It is possible for the Environment Agency to consider the past history of the discharge operator and if necessary conditions may be attached to the discharge. Such conditions as the EA 'may think fit' include matters such as the place at which the discharge may be made, the nature, volume, origin, composition and rate of discharge, the steps that are taken to provide discharge treatment and the minimisation of the discharge. In addition, conditions may stipulate the facilities for taking samples and the keeping of records and the making of returns.

The regulation of discharges is carefully monitored. Periodic regular reviews are undertaken which may result in notice being served on the discharger, revoking consent or setting conditions. Some degree of certainty for the operators of discharges is provided. There is a restriction that conditions when imposed must settle a time period to be not less than two years, during which no revocation or variation in the discharge conditions may be made. If a modification or revocation is made within the two-year period then compensation is payable. The compensation is not payable as a consequence of circumstances that are not reasonably foreseen.

There are similar powers of revocation and modification granted to the Secretary of State. These powers are expressed in the form of allowing the Secretary of State to make a Direction to the Environment Agency. Such a direction may be made in three situations:

1. to enable the government to comply with any Community Directive;

2. to make provision for the protection of public health or of aquatic flora and fauna;

3. as a result of advice or representations received by the Secretary of State.

It is noteworthy that the two-year rule whereby no modification or revocation may be made does not apply in the case of the first two grounds.

Disposal of waste through sewers

Approximately 6.8×10^6 m^3 (1.5×10^9 gal) of industrial and other waste water are discharged directly to sewers daily in addition to the 8×10^6 m^3 (1.8×10^9 gal) from domestic sources. The majority of this waste water is treated by conventional treatment processes at approximately 5000 sewage treatment works. Sewage treatment is a three-stage process involving (1) preliminary treatment during which large objects and grit are removed, and storm flows are separated; (2) primary sedimentation during which suspended solids are removed, forming sludge; and (3) secondary or biological treatment during which dissolved organics are removed microbially. Occasionally tertiary treatment is undertaken, which results in a high-quality effluent. It is important that any industrial or trade effluent entering sewage works is carefully controlled (see below) so that the biological part of sewage treatment is not disrupted.

The disposal of waste through sewers forms a distinct part of the system of discharge controls. Historically the provision of water and the discharge of sewerage have been treated as forming a coherent whole. Private water and sewerage undertakers provide the public water supply and operate sewerage treatment works. This is a lucrative commercial enterprise. There are important environmental controls that are required to be operated by the sewerage undertakers under Chapter III of Part IV of the Water Industry Act 1991. The sewerage undertaker is under a statutory duty to provide a sewerage system under section 94 of the 1991 Act. This duty to allow for discharge and disposal of waste applies to both domestic and trade or industrial effluent. Schedule 22 to the Environment Act 1995 introduces into the Water Industry Act 1991 new section 101A, which places a duty on sewerage undertakers to provide a public sewer under certain conditions, with the costs being borne by the customer.

Account must also be taken of future trends and the future needs of the industry when making provision for the disposal of trade effluent. The crucial requirement for trade effluent is a trade effluent consent. It is a criminal offence to discharge trade waste without such a consent. The definition of trade effluent is under section 141(1) of the Water Industry Act 1991 and is widely drafted to include any liquid wholly or partly produced in the course of any trade or industry carried on in trade premises. Thus the definition is sufficiently broad to include liquid discharges from industry, shops, agriculture, research institutions and launderettes.[6] The main exception is from domestic premises. The sewerage operator receives an application for consent from the person wishing to make the discharge at least two months prior to the commencement of the discharge. The costs of undertaking the discharge are a central feature of the discussion between the undertaker and the discharger. The emphasis is placed on the discharger to minimise costs by using processes that make discharges less harmful. There is a statutory framework contained in sections 121(4)(a) and 142 of the 1991 Act.

There are a number of detailed procedural arrangements regarding applications for a trade effluent consent. The application must state the nature and composition of the effluent, the maximum quantity of effluent that is proposed to be discharged in any one day, and the maximum rate of discharge. There is wide provision for agreements to be reached between the discharger and the sewerage undertaker.

The regulatory system for trade effluent discharges rests on a number of enforcement procedures. A strict liability offence is committed by the occupier who discharges from the relevant trade premises without consent. The enforcement of this requirement may involve the commercial sewerage operator. It is assumed that consent conditions may operate to control effluent discharges. This involves a degree of self-regulation. It is expected that the sewerage operator will control discharges in the light of the most economical costs and available techniques. While it may appear that the undertaker has the crucial decision whether

---

[6] See: *Thames Water Authority* v *Blue and White Launderettes Ltd* [1980] 1 WLR 700.

to grant a consent or not, there is an appeal open to the discharger to the Director General of Water Services on the basis that any reasonable application for consent cannot be refused by the sewerage undertaker.

There is also some flexibility in the way the system operates. Consent conditions may be varied, revoked or added to by notice issued by the sewerage undertaker under section 124 of the Water Industry Act 1991. Similar provisions, as those discussed above, concerning discharge consent apply for a two-year period. There is a right of appeal to Ofwat against a variation.

Drinking water

The Water Supply (Water Quality) Regulations 2000 (SI 2000/3184) implement the revised Drinking Water Quality Directive 98/83/EC and provide for good-quality drinking water. There are a number of requirements, including the need for public information and continual monitoring of drinking water. It remains an offence under section 70 of the Water Industry Act 1991 to sell water that is unfit for human consumption. The Chief Inspector of the Drinking Water Inspectorate (DWI) has statutory powers of inspection under section 57 of the Water Act 2003. There have been a number of successful prosecutions, including for water that is discoloured or of 'unfit' quality. There is also in operation a system of risk assessment applicable to water supply companies and this is largely designed to prevent unhealthy water entering the water supply. There are various procedures in place to address any problems that may be identified and to report obligations to the Secretary of State. In the past year, the Drinking Water Inspectorate has had concerns over compliance with drinking water standards. There was an increase in the number of incidents where drinking water was contaminated to 144 incidents in 2008, compared to 129 incidents in 2007. While there is generally a high compliance rate with water standards, the rise in incidents from a low of 92 in 2005 is clearly a cause for concern.[7] Many of the incidents related to over-fluoridsation or the influx of pesticides into the water systems. The rise in incidents may be partly due to more testing and greater accuracy of the tests, but it also reflects agricultural land use.

Techniques in water regulation

Criminal offences and other remedies for water pollution

The use of the criminal law is a recurring theme in the legislation regulating the water and sewerage industries. The Water Resources Act 1991 contains enforcement through consent procedures where the criminal law applies for failure to obtain the relevant consent. Section 85(1) creates a number of offences to cause or knowingly permit any poisonous, noxious or polluting matter or solid waste to enter any controlled waters. If a defendant is charged with the 'cause' part of the offence, it is unnecessary to show that the defendant acted intentionally or negligently.[8]

---

[7] ENDS Report 414, p. 20.
[8] *Alphacell Ltd* v *Woodward* [1972] AC 824.

Section 90(1) makes it an offence to remove any part of the bed of inland waters so as to cause it to be carried away in suspension. Section 90(2) makes it an offence to cause or permit vegetation to be cut or uprooted so as to fall into inland waters, and fail to take reasonable steps to remove the vegetation. Many of these offences employ the term 'causing or knowingly permitting'. The interpretation of this term was considered in the House of Lords' case of *Alphacell Ltd* v *Woodward*.[9] Polluted water from the appellants' paper factory entered two settling tanks adjoining a river. There was an overflow system which became activated when the water reached a certain level. Owing to a blockage in the inlet to the pumps, the polluted water overflowed and entered the river. The defendants failed to prevent the overflow. The defendants were found guilty contrary to section 2(1)(a) of the Rivers (Prevention of Pollution) Act 1951. Although there was no evidence that the defendant knew that pollution was taking place or that they had been negligent, the House of Lords upheld the conviction on the grounds that, as Lord Salmon explained, although the defendants 'did not intend to cause the pollution they intended to do the acts which caused it'. There is no hard-and-fast rule that the courts will always adopt a strict interpretation of the statute thereby finding guilt without proof that the defendant either ought to have seen the pollution or was negligent.[10] The fact of pollution taking place appears sufficient to find criminal liability even if full intention is not proved on the part of the defendant. The interpretation of the statute will largely depend on the facts of each case. The degree of knowledge on the part of the defendant required by the court to uphold a prosecution will be assessed in all the circumstances of the case.[11] It is also possible to interpret quite widely various statutory defences. One example of judicial approaches to interpretation is the decision of the House of Lords in *National Rivers Authority* v *Yorkshire Water Services Ltd*.[12] The material facts of the case were that one night when no one was on duty at the sewerage works, an unknown person unlawfully discharged iso-octanol into the sewer. Yorkshire Water Services operated this sewer with a discharge consent for sewerage into the River Spen. The iso-octanol was an unauthorised discharge. The first issue raised by the case was whether an offence had been committed. On a strict interpretation of section 107(1)(a) of the Water Act 1989 Yorkshire Water was in breach of its consent to discharge effluent when a third party caused the discharge to be poisonous and exceed the prescribed limits of the consent. The result of the unlawful addition of iso-octonal was that the discharge by Yorkshire Water was contrary to section 107. The second issue was whether any statutory defence was available. This involved difficulty over interpretation. The magistrates convicted Yorkshire Water, who appealed. The Crown Court quashed the conviction, ruling that the water authority in law had not caused the chemical to enter the controlled water. An important point of law, however, was raised and this was accepted on a case stated by the Divisional Court, and the case was considered by the House of Lords. The House of Lords held that the water company had caused poisonous, noxious and polluting matter to enter controlled waters. This finding was decided even though Yorkshire Water was not responsible for the presence of the iso-octanol. There was strict liability in the interpretation of the offence and the magistrates had correctly interpreted the law on this point. The House of Lords, however, found that the company had a defence under section 108(7) and allowed the appeal

---

[9] [1972] AC 824.

[10] See: *Southern Water Authority* v *Pegrum* [1989] Crim LR 442.

[11] *Price* v *Cromack* [1975] 2 All ER 113 and *Wychavon District Council* v *National Rivers Authority* [1993] 2 All ER 440.

[12] [1994] 4 All ER 274, reversed [1995] 1 All ER 225.

against conviction. In the interpretation of the special defence contained in section 108(7), namely that the sewerage undertaker could not reasonably have been expected to prevent the discharge into the sewer or works, the House of Lords took a flexible approach. The case is a good illustration of the approach the courts may be likely to take in the future.

There are other examples of criminal offences in the area of water pollution. There are criminal offences specifically intended to protect fish from the effects of pollution (see Law in context, p. 268). Section 4(1) of the Salmon and Freshwater Fisheries Act 1975 makes it an offence to pollute water containing fish so as to cause the waters to be poisonous or injurious to fish, their food or spawning grounds. There are specific regulations concerning the use of lead weights (see: Control of Pollution (Anglers' Lead Weights)) Regulations 1986, SI 1986 No. 1992 and amendment regulations 1993 SI 1993 No. 49) and an assortment of regulations concerning the use of certain tri-organotin paints and chemicals (see: Control of Pollution (Anti-Fouling Paints and Treatments) Regulations 1987 SI 1987 No. 783). Organotin compounds have a number of applications, including use as biocides. Particularly important as a pollutant in aquatic environments is tributyl tin (TBT) used as anti-fouling material. Its use has now largely been curtailed, but only after it became evident in the 1980s that commercial oysters (*Crassostrae gigas*) were severely affected by this chemical leaching from ship hulls etc. It subsequently became evident that other aquatic organisms were adversely affected. There is also the potential to take a private prosecution in respect of a breach of the law relating to pollution.

Regulating pollution and the criminal law

The Environment Agency has adopted a proactive approach to the use of the criminal law, in keeping with its role in ensuring that the water industry complies with water quality standards. The table below gives an indication of the use of fines and costs against water companies (Table 12.1). The majority of cases are taken in the magistrates' court.

The trends are upwards with both fines and costs per offence gradually rising. There is greater frequency than in the past of courts being asked to look at serious pollution offences. Some water companies have better track records than others in terms of the number of successful prosecutions taken against them. Anglian Water has had some of the largest fines against it. There are some headline cases such as the prosecution against Thames Water in May 2008 after an old sewerage pipe burst in July 2006 killing thousands of fish and crayfish on a National Trust property.[13] Thames Water, however, is now notable for the decline in the fines made against the company.

The expectation is that criminal cases will serve as a means of bringing water companies into line with high standards and that public awareness of serious cases puts pressure on the industry to achieve high standards. What is the future of criminal sanctions and

Table 12.1 Pollution offences and fines against water companies

Year	2007	2008
Number of offences	53	61
Total fines and costs	£401,463	£591,465

[13] ENDS Report 400, pp. 60–1. The table is taken from ENDS Report 408, p. 61.

environmental law? The answer is to be found in the general discussion about regulation and the debate about the use of civil penalties following the recent MacRory Report (see Law in context, below).

LAW IN CONTEXT

The Better Regulation Agenda

The 'better regulation agenda' as it was optimistically called had begun under the Conservative government in 1985 based on the idea of reducing administrative burdens and decreasing the cost of regulation.[14] Deregulation policy was shaped by a series of White Papers in 1985, 1986 and 1988.[15] A Cabinet Committee on regulation was established and this led to an anti-red-tape virus that spread across Whitehall, culminating in the Deregulation and Contracting Out Act 1994 after another series of White Papers.[16] The 1994 Act has been further extended by the Regulatory Reform Act 2001 and then again by the Legislative and Regulatory Reform Act 2006. The movement in favour of deregulation was not confined to the UK, as a similar approach is evident in the European Union.[17] The invigoration of the 'light touch' agenda was reinforced by the Hampton Report[18] and the setting up of a Better Regulation Programme under the Better Regulation Executive, separated from the Cabinet Office in 2007. Hampton recommended the streamlining of many regulatory bodies and at the same time the coordination of regulatory policy with a regulatory impact assessment as part of each policy initiative. Adopting single strategies, reducing administrative burdens and driving regulation from the centre appear to offer an attractive style of regulation. Central government using traditional command and control techniques seeks to master the role of regulators while regulators look to decreasing controls and increasing autonomy among those regulated. The tensions are well explained by Black:

> Indeed, rather than negating the decentred analysis, the observation that the state is seeking to increase its centralised control is its natural corollary. Either through the establishment of 'meta-regulators' to regulate non-state regulators as in the case of the accounting, medical and legal professions, or through the internal regulation of other governmental regulators, central government is seeking to enhance its steering capacity.[19]

The Macrory Review[20] that followed the Hampton Report was asked to look at the role of sanctions and the functioning of criminal sanctions. This is a critical part of

---

[14] See: the DTI White Paper, *Lifting the Burden* Cmnd 9571 (1985).

[15] DTI White Paper, *Building Businesses Not Barriers* Cmnd 9794 (1986) and *Releasing Enterprise* Cm 512 (1988).

[16] DTI, *Deregulation: Cutting Red Tape*, (1994); *Thinking About Regulation: A Guide to Good Regulation* (1994); *Getting a Good Deal in Europe* (1994).

[17] R. Baldwin, 'Is better regulation smarter regulation?' (2005) *Public Law* 485.

[18] Philip Hampton, *Reducing Administrative Burdens: Effective Inspection and Enforcement* Final Report London: HM Treasury, 2005.

[19] J. Black, 'Tensions in the regulatory state' (2007) *Public Law* 58 at p. 66.

[20] R. Macrory, *Regulatory Justice: Sanctioning in a post-Hampton World: A Consultation Document* London: Cabinet Office, May 2006 and *Regulatory Justice: Making Sanctions Effective* London: Cabinet Office, November 2006.

the regulatory system. Regulators require a range of incentives and sanctions in order to be effective. The Macrory Review accepted that the existing use of criminal sanctions for regulatory offences was required. Macrory also recommended that a new punitive regulation system was necessary rather than reliance on simple moral persuasion or good behaviour. He recommended an extension of the range and variety of penalties available to regulators. He adopts the principle that ensuring that regulators' own sanctioning powers should be adopted rather than recourse to the formalised use of the criminal courts.

Macrory's recommendations were largely accepted by the government. New compliance codes and greater managerial controls are also favoured as a way of making the compliance arrangements more effective. The implementation of many of the Macrory Review's recommendations may be found in the Regulatory Enforcement and Sanctions Act 2008. This underlines the shift beyond the criminal courts for the application of sanctions to regulator-based systems of sanctions and enforcement. The Act underlines the five principles of regulation set out in Hampton, namely enforcement action should be transparent, accountable, proportionate, consistent and targeted.

The impact of the Hampton and Macrory Reports is important in setting the future direction for regulation in the United Kingdom. The Hampton Report reinforces and encourages a targeted approach to regulation that requires all regulators to perform risk assessments and to adopt an effective, efficient and proportionate response and not placing unnecessary burdens on business. The underlying philosophy is that financial information should only be sought when required. Intervention should be targeted and not invasive to the detriment of market conditions.

While Hampton and Macrory favour a continuation in the deregulation strategy, their analysis of the need for risk assessment and strategic use of tougher penalties is also consistent with the Environment Agency's approach to regulation. High-profile fines and convictions are used as a means of enhancing the profile of the regulator. Both reports raise issues about how in general regulators are to be held to account. The reliance on legal forms of accountability through penalties and sanctions makes the assessment of regulatory decisions to be based primarily on compliance with codes and legal rules. Risk-based accountability often enhances managerial accountability within the regulatory body.

Civil penalties may assist in more effective regulation and this is likely to be used in areas such as illegal waste disposal and under the EU ETS Directive (2003/87/EC) failures to meet emissions standards.[21] In the area of water pollution, however, there are many grounds for assuming that the importance of criminal prosecutions is set to continue. The Environment Agency has a published detailed prosecution code.[22] Generally the Agency adopts a 'name and shame' culture by highlighting the worst cases. There is, however, a generally admitted low level of fines and it is unusual for custodial sentences to be used (see Case Study below).

---

[21] See: EU Emissions Trading Scheme: *Guidance to Operators on the Application of Civil Penalties*, Environment Agency, January 2009.

[22] See: the Environment Agency Guidance for the Enforcement and Prosecution Policy *www.environment-agency. gov.uk*.

CASE STUDY

Criminal penalties and water pollution

The use of custodial sentences for environmental harm applies when it is a repeated or blatant offence and where in a public place the offence is such as to subject the public to hazardous substances. In *R v O'Brien and Enkel*[23] illegally storing 2,000 waste tyres at an unlicensed site gave rise to an eight-month prison sentence for O'Brien. On appeal the Court of Appeal quashed the sentence because it was regarded as excessive. Environmental pollution crimes have also not been included as part of the tariff approach to sentencing. This gives rise to the need to consider each case on its own facts rather than using the Sentencing Advisory Panel's Advice. There are two leading cases that establish the case-by-case approach: *R. v Yorkshire Water Services Ltd*[24] and *R v Anglian Water Services Ltd*,[25] that considered the relevance of individuals' circumstances in sentencing. This is despite the Advisory Panel's advice in 2000 to have guidelines to help achieve consistency. In *R v Anglian Water Services Ltd* Scott Barker LJ outlined the arguments for stricter culpability when a major industrial water company is involved. The idea of proportionality in the fine and penalty was also explicitly referred to as an important way of preventing future offences from occurring.

Common law pollution controls

Water pollution is also subject to liability under the common law. Liability for the pollution of groundwater may give rise to an action for negligence, nuisance or under *Rylands v Fletcher*[26] as follows:

- Negligence arises from a failure to exercise the care demanded in the circumstances. A plaintiff must show that he is owed a duty of care, that the duty has been breached and that any harm suffered is due to the breach of the duty that the plaintiff is owed. Damages may be awarded upon proof that the harm caused was foreseeable by the defendant.

- Nuisance is an interference with an occupier's use or enjoyment of land where there has been substantial injury to property or personal discomfort.

- The rule in *Rylands v Fletcher* is where a landowner is strictly liable for the consequences of escapes from his property and where the landowner is engaged in a 'non-natural' use of his land. The term 'non-natural' use has never been clearly defined.

Discussion of how the three grounds apply in cases involving water pollution may be found in the landmark decision of the House of Lords in *Cambridge Water Co Ltd v Eastern Counties Leather plc*.[27] This case is likely to have a significant influence in the future development of

---

[23] [2000] Env LR 156.
[24] [2002] Env LR 18.
[25] [2004] Env LR 10.
[26] (1868) LR 3 HL 330.
[27] [1994] 2 WLR 53.

this area of law for some considerable time. The House of Lords have placed restrictions on the availability of liability for past or historic pollution.

The facts of the case are that Eastern Counties Leather plc manufactured leather at their works at Sawston, Cambridgeshire since 1879. The processes used organochlorine chemicals. Up until the mid-1960s they used trichloroethene and thereafter perchlorethene. In the 1970s scientific evidence emerged that both chemicals were a possible threat to health. In the 1980s the European Community and the World Health Organization set drinking water standards that only permitted very low quantities of these compounds (see: 80/778/EEC and DoE Circular 20/82, also: Water Supply (Water Quality) Regulations 1989 No. 1147). The EC Drinking Water Directive set guide standard for wholesome water of no more than $1 \mu g \, l^{-1}$ organochlorines, in the specific case of tetrachlorethene, also called perchlorethene, a lower standard of $10 \mu g \, l^{-1}$ was set. The impact of these standards on the Cambridge Water Company was considerable. The water company had been extracting groundwater from the area of Sawston through bore holes, and by the mid-1980s perchlorethene concentrations in the groundwater were found to be $70-170 \mu g \, l^{-1}$. As a result of the new standards the water company found it impossible to continue using the extracted groundwater as a source of drinking water. As a consequence the water company moved its bore holes to an unpolluted zone and built a new plant at the cost of nearly £1 million. The Cambridge Water Company sought an injunction and damages from Eastern Leather who they alleged caused the pollution. Perclorethene was used by this company to degrease pelts and had been stored on site in drums. It was assumed that the drums had either leaked or that there had been accidental spillage, allowing organochlorine to leach into groundwater. The legal basis of the claim made in *Cambridge Water* was based on negligence, nuisance and the rule in *Rylands* v *Fletcher*.[28]

The case raises an important question concerning historic pollution. Should there be liability for acts done in the past on the basis of present-day knowledge and standards? The standards that apply to drinking water today and the scientific evidence about the harmful effects of the chemicals were not available at the time the pollution began. It can be seen that liability for historic pollution is an important principle with potentially great financial significance to commercial and industrial activities.

It is valuable to consider historic pollution in its scientific context. There is very often a delay in scientific understanding of the impact of chemicals on health and the environment. More often than not health issues become clear first. The effect of compounds in the environment often remain unclear for prolonged periods (see Law in context, p. 268). The assessment of 'safe' environmental concentrations of chemicals is still largely based on predictions from ecotoxicology studies on single selected species. These may subsequently prove to give an inaccurate prediction of the potential impacts in the environment. Thus even though the prescribed techniques may at present have been applied to determining safe environmental concentrations in the future they may subsequently prove invalid. Should industrial concerns be held responsible where they have followed current best practice and any future problems remain unknown?

The High Court dismissed the action against Eastern Leather on the grounds that Eastern Leather could not reasonably have foreseen that the chemicals used in their processes could cause harm. Cambridge Water appealed to the Court of Appeal, relying on the rule in

---

[28] *Rylands* v *Fletcher* (1868) LR 3 HL 330.

Rylands v *Fletcher*. There was no appeal made against the High Court's ruling on nuisance and negligence. However, the Court of Appeal upheld Cambridge Water's case against Eastern Leather. The Court of Appeal followed the case of *Ballard* v *Tomlinson*[29] where a brewery successfully sued for contamination of its groundwater taken from its own well. The groundwater had been contaminated by a neighbour's discharge of sewerage. The Court of Appeal accepted that Eastern Leather had interfered with a natural right (the water company's ownership of the boreholes and various riparian rights that accrue) and that liability was therefore strict. The water company had shown that the pollution was caused by Eastern Leather and this was sufficient grounds for damages.

On appeal to the House of Lords the nature of liability was considered in relation to the claims made in respect of both nuisance and the rule in *Rylands* v *Fletcher*. Lord Goff, who delivered the speech for the whole House, held that there was no rule of law imposing liability for unforeseeable damage simply because the right affected was a natural right. The House of Lords held that some degree of foresight of risk is required to be proven, even in circumstances where there might be strict liability and in cases where past activities are the subject of present-day litigation. Eastern Leather's appeal was granted on the reasoning that at the time they made use of the chemicals they could not have foreseen the harm caused by the chemicals. As a result Eastern Leather could not be liable in damages.[30] The decision is of major significance. It would seem that a defendant is liable for the reasonably foreseeable consequences of the unreasonable user. This also brings the torts of nuisance and negligence more closely together than in the past. It is clear that the House of Lords were reluctant to impose any form of strict liability on highly hazardous activities. Consequently, the House of Lords appears to have limited the effects of imposing strict liability through *Rylands* v *Fletcher*. This is particularly important in contaminated land cases.

The House of Lords' decision brought some relief to the concerns of commercial enterprises that arose from the Court of Appeal's decision because of the threat of the imposition of strict liability for historic pollution. There are a number of conclusions that may be drawn from the *Cambridge Water* case:

(a) Historic pollution or retrospective liability, that is liability for past acts, is now made more difficult to prove because foreseeability is a requirement of both *Rylands* v *Fletcher* and nuisance liability. Foreseeability of damage of the relevant type if there was an escape from the land of things likely to do mischief is a prerequisite of liability.

(b) The House of Lords has accepted that liability in nuisance and in *Rylands* v *Fletcher* is based on strict liability (where fault need not be proven). *Rylands* v *Fletcher* did not create liability any more strict than liability for nuisance. Strict liability renders the defendant liable where there was an escape occurring in the course of the non-natural use of the land, notwithstanding he had exercised all due care to prevent the escape from occurring.

(c) The definition of 'non-natural' used in *Rylands* v *Fletcher* is sufficient to cover the storage of substantial quantities of chemicals on industrial premises. In *Cambridge Water* the House of Lords held that Eastern Leather's use of the land through the storage of

---

[29] (1885) 29 Ch D 115.
[30] See: *The Wagon Mound (No. 2)* [1967] 1 AC 617 upheld by Lord Goff in the *Cambridge Water* case.

chemicals was almost a classic case of 'non-natural' use. No further definition of what 'non-natural' included was attempted but it was accepted that the creation of an industrial estate and employment was not a natural use of the land. Lord Goff explained: 'I myself, however, do not feel able to accept that the creation of employment as such even in a small industrial complex is sufficient of itself to establish a particular use as constituting a natural or ordinary use of the land.'[31]

The *Transco* decision and its importance

The impact of the *Cambridge Water* case was considered in the decision of the House of Lords in *Transco plc* v *Stockport Metropolitan Borough Council*.[32] The House of Lords broadly followed the approach set out in *Cambridge Water*. The facts of *Transco* are that water supplied to a Council-owned flats complex was subject to flooding through an undetected water leak. The leak had managed to flood an old railway embankment, resulting in a collapse of a gas main. Transco had to make good the gas pipe and claimed from the Council, Stockport Borough Council costs associated with the water leak. The House of Lords considered whether the supply of water to the flats was particularly risky and held it was not. Everything involved in the supply of the water conformed to existing practice. Although the water had accumulated, it was unforeseen that it would have escaped and that the escape would lead to a collapse in the soil supporting the gas pipe. There was no extraordinary use of land or a high or extraordinary degree of risk. *Transco* is in line with the approach in *Cambridge Water*. It is clear that the main elements of liability fall on the defendant's use of the land that must be extraordinary and give rise to some extraordinary degree of risk. This represents a more modern approach than the traditional non-natural use regime. It is a high threshold for claimants to reach in order for there to be liability. Thus whether the activity is likely to give rise to liability will depend on not only the natural use of the land but also whether the dangerousness of the operation on the land makes a high risk inevitable. The fact that standard-setting is commonplace makes the degree of risk, if there is an escape, dependent on whether or not the activity is dangerous. This applies to all sorts of activities involving chemicals, water, electricity, gas and so on.[33]

There are also a number of other current trends. The rule in *Rylands* v *Fletcher* applies to someone who must have an interest in land. There must be something that passes from the land belonging to the claimant. The escape must be such that it must be felt beyond the land of the defendant.

Damages for nuisance remain an important remedy for many pollution problems. In *Dobson* v *Thames Utilities Ltd*,[34] the Court of Appeal showed a willingness to consider the assessment of damages at common law for transitory nuisance such as smells or odours from a sewage works. This was also relevant in terms of offering human rights protection and ensuring that Article 8 rights are upheld.

[31] See: [1994] 1 All ER 53 at p. 79e.
[32] [2004] 2 AC 1.
[33] Also see *LMS International Ltd and ors* v *Styrene Packaging and Insulation Ltd* [2005] All ER (D) 171 (Sep).
[34] [2009] 3 All ER 319 and also case comment Justine Thornton, 'Sewage works nuisance and Human Rights Act damages' (2009) Env LR 328.

Public water supplies

Defining the role of the water companies

'Public water' is used to describe water that has some use that is provided through reservoirs, groundwater, rivers and the marine environment. Public water supplies come from a company licensed to supply water under the Water Act 1989. There are ten water and sewerage companies which provide the vast bulk of water supplies, approximately 20 billion litres per day. The 10 companies also provide sewerage services and are described in some statutes as 'water and sewerage undertakers'. The term 'public water supplies' is in contrast to 'private water supplies' which refers to water taken from private sources or supplied by unlicensed suppliers (discussed below). There are 28 such smaller private statutory water companies. Many were set up in the nineteenth century and have a long history of supplying water. All suppliers of water must be licensed and the licensing arrangements are undertaken by the Secretary of State for Environment and Ofwat under section 6 of the Water Industry Act 1991.

Setting standards for water quality

Public water supplies

Section 68 and Chapter III of Part III of the Water Industry Act 1991 provides that water suppliers or undertakers are under a duty to supply wholesome water and to ensure, as far as it is reasonably practicable, that the sources of the undertakers' supply do not deteriorate in quality. The Act makes it a criminal offence for a water undertaker to supply water that is unfit for human consumption. Part IV of the Water Supply (Water Quality) Regulations 1989 prescribe the steps to be taken by the water undertaker where there is a danger from contamination from copper, lead, or zinc present in the consumer's pipes.

Under section 70(2) there is a defence for the undertaker to show that there was no reasonable grounds for suspecting that the water would be used for human consumption, or that the company exercised 'all reasonable steps and exercised all due diligence for securing the water was fit for human consumption on leaving its pipes or was not used for human consumption'. The test of what is wholesome is prescribed under section 67 of the Water Industry Act 1991 and set out in the Water Supply (Water Quality) Regulations 1989 (SI No. 1147), which have been amended by the Water Supply (Water Quality) (Amendment) Regulations 1989 and 1991 and the Water Supply (Water Quality) Regulations 2000 (Amended 2007). These regulations take account of EC Drinking Water Directive (80/778/EEC as amended by 98/83/EC). Water supplied for domestic purposes of drinking, washing and cooking or for the purpose of food production will be regarded as wholesome provided it meets three criteria, commonly described as Regulation 3 of the Water Quality Regulations:

1. that the water meets the standards prescribed in the regulations for the particular properties, elements, organisms, or substances;

2. that the hardness or alkalinity of water which has been softened or desalinated is not below prescribed standards;

3. that the water does not contain any element, organism or substance whether alone or in combination at a concentration or value which would be detrimental to public health.

The monitoring of water is undertaken on the basis of a discrete water supply zone. This is defined as an area designated by the water company by reference to source and where not more than 100,000 people reside. It is possible that the designation of a zone may have an effect on the monitoring of water quality. In Scotland, for example, the number of small supply zones was high. Gradual improvements have been made to water quality by reducing the number of zones from 682 in 1992 to 663 in 1993 (see ENDS Report 240 January 1995, p. 10, Drinking Water Quality in Scotland 1993 (Scottish Office, 1995), but raising the number of people residing in a zone from 50,000 to 100,000.

The regulations contain 11 national standards that are interpreted over either three-monthly or twelve-monthly periods. There are specific parameters (66 in total) and descriptive standards for the testing of water quality. These are categorised into six groups:

1. Organoleptic (4 parameters) e.g. colour, odour;

2. Physicochemical (15 parameters) e.g. temperature, pH, conductivity;

3. Substances undesirable in excessive amounts (24 parameters) e.g. nitrates, oxidisability, zinc;

4. Toxic substances (13 parameters) e.g. arsenic, cadmium, pesticides;

5. Microbiological (6 parameters) e.g. faecal coliforms, sulphite-reducing clostridia;

6. Minimum concentration of softened water (4 parameters) e.g. total hardness, alkalinity.

Consumers' taps within the supply zone are used to monitor supply. The exact number of samples depends on the population served, the parameter and the water source. The Secretary of State has powers to authorise sampling from strategic points other than consumers' taps. There are guidelines for the method of taking samples as a result of a ruling from the Court of Appeal (see *Attorney General's Reference (No. 2 of 1994)* [1995] 2 All ER 1000).

It is clear from the above outline that there is a degree of self-regulation in the application of water quality standards. In the first instance the monitoring of water quality is undertaken by the water companies, subject to checks by local authorities and the Drinking Water Inspectorate. Local authorities receive regular amounts of information from water companies on the quality of drinking water in their area. The local authority may also take its own samples. If it is dissatisfied with the results of its findings it is under a duty to inform the water company. If it fails to receive adequate satisfaction then a report may be made to the Secretary of State for enforcement action. Monitoring consists of taking a minimum number of samples over a specified timescale. There is a Public Register of results of monitoring that must be made available on demand. Annual reports are made by local authorities in a prescribed manner and water companies must, in their annual reports, include a commentary on the supply of water.

There are considerable enforcement powers available under section 18 of the Water Industry Act 1991 where there is reasonable cause to believe that a public water supplier is in contravention of any enforceable statutory duty. This includes contravention of regulations or lapses in the system of monitoring supplies. Section 19 provides some exception from prosecution in cases where the breach is trivial and does not warrant prosecution or where there is an undertaking to stop current practices and introduce changes. Prosecution proceedings may be instituted in respect of section 70 of the 1991 Act for the offence of supplying water unfit for human consumption.

The procedures for enforcement are straightforward. A 'notice of intention to enforce' is first issued, giving the undertaker time to respond. This response may include a programme of work or the introduction of new measures to facilitate or to comply with the required standards for drinking water quality. The Secretary of State may take into consideration the parameters covered by the Drinking Water Directive and may make provisional or final orders to ensure compliance.

The Drinking Water Inspectorate is responsible for initiating enforcement action on behalf of the Secretary of State in the following circumstances:

- when water quality is breached and the breach is not trivial or where it is likely to recur;
- when there is a breach of one of the enforceable regulations (for example Regulation 3 of the Water Quality Regulations (see above)), such as sampling analysis or providing information on water treatment, has occurred;
- when existing undertakings or time-limited relaxations authorised by Regulation 4 expire before the necessary improvements have been made.

Normally no action will be taken in circumstances where the company takes remedial action and demonstrates that there is compliance with the regulations.

Private water supplies

The definition of 'private water supply' is any supply of water provided otherwise than by a statutorily appointed water undertaker (see section 93 of the Water Industry Act 1991). In recent years private water suppliers have become more numerous, especially, for example, in answering the increasing demand for bottled water. There is no legal prohibition against water suppliers or undertakers who wish to supply water in their private capacity. Private water suppliers have much the same requirements placed on them as public suppliers. There are similar requirements for wholesome water in regulations consolidated in the Private Water Supplies Regulations 1991 (SI 1991 No. 2790). The 1991 regulations set out a twofold classification system and require local authorities to monitor private suppliers on the basis of the classification. Category 1 water is used for domestic purposes; category 2 water is used for food production or in premises used as staff canteens; for educational, hospital and other residential use or in camp sites or other places providing short-term accommodation on a commercial basis. The regulations cover most matters relevant to the setting of water quality standards. The regulations provide that local authorities may serve a notice specifying the steps that are necessary to bring the water supply up to the standard of 'wholesome water' and a period of at least 28 days when objections may be made to the notice. The regulations:

- specify how local authorities are required to classify private suppliers in their areas;
- specify the parameters for which local authorities are required to monitor private supplies, including the frequency of monitoring and the taking of samples;
- allow local authorities, with certain exceptions, the right to enter into arrangements for the taking of samples and their analysis;
- prescribe the maximum charges local authorities are permitted to make for sampling and analysis.

The 1991 Act maintains the long-standing obligation on local authorities to keep informed about the wholesomeness and sufficiency of water supplies in their respective areas. Local authorities are given powers to secure the improvement of private water supplies or connection to a mains supply. This includes powers to serve a notice on the occupier of land where the source is situated and specify the improvement steps to be taken and the timescale for the improvements to be implemented. Such a notice must also be submitted to the relevant Secretary of State for confirmation. In certain circumstances there may be a public local inquiry or hearing at the discretion of the Secretary of State.

The Drinking Water Inspectorate also has a role in respect of private water supplies. It is responsible for the provision of scientific advice and for monitoring the arrangements made by local authorities. It also oversees the responsibility of local authorities to comply with the relevant regulations noted above. The increasing popularity of bottled water is a commercial development that is relatively lightly regulated. The Drinking Water in Containers Regulations 1994 SI No. 743 sets some standards for bottled water, broadly in line with the requirements of EC Directive 80/778/EEC. Local authorities have a duty to enforce these standards. The sale of bottled water also comes under the provisions of the Food Safety Act 1990 and the Act gives local authorities powers as food authorities.

There is little regulation over the contents of bottled water. The regulation of the use of various labels to describe bottled water is surprisingly lax. Mineral waters that are described as 'natural mineral waters' fall under the Natural Mineral Waters Regulations 1985 (SI No. 71), now the Natural Mineral Water, Spring Water and Bottled Water Regulations 1999 which implements EC Directive 80/777/EEC on the marketing and exploitation of mineral waters. Official recognition of a 'natural mineral water' requires the applicant to apply to the local authority in writing, giving details of the source of supply, the physical, chemical and microbiological properties of the water and evidence that the source and the supply is not polluted. Details are published in official journals and, if recognition is to be accepted in the EC, in the *Official Journal* of the EC.

The Water Framework Directive: the way ahead

The extensive involvement of the European Union in water quality throughout all the member states has expanded its legislative role and influence. Water policy was one of the first sub-sectors of EC environmental policy and it has now developed into a comprehensive area of Community activity.[35] Many of the changes, including the large-scale investment in improving standards and the introduction of new legislation have come about because of the Community's role in developing water policy. For example, the Drinking Water Directive 80/778/EEC as amended by 98/83/EC provides an important set of standards for drinking water quality.

The Water Framework Directive (WFD) envisages that there will be a number of directives phased in over the coming years until 2013. There are two key daughter directives in the form of the WFD Daughter Directive on groundwater and the WFD Daughter Directive on priority substances, which is currently being negotiated. At that time some key directives will be replaced (see Table 12.2). This includes the Dangerous Substances Directive 2006/11/EC, the Groundwater Directive 80/68/EEC and the Freshwater Fish Directive 2006/44/EC and

---

[35] See: N. Haigh, *Manual of Environment Policy: The EC and Britain*, Longman, 1994.

Table 12.2 The Water Framework Directive and other water directives

New directives and remaining directives	Directives to be repealed		Other relevant directives
	By 2007	By 2013	
WFD Daughter Directive on Groundwater	Surface Water for Abstraction of Drinking Water Directive (75/440/EEC)	Water for Shellfish Directive (79/923/EEC amended 2006/113/EC)	Integrated Pollution Prevention and Control (IPPC) Directive (96/61/EC)
WFD Daughter Directive on Priority Substances	Exchange of Information on Quality of Surface Freshwater Directive (77/795/EEC)	Water for Freshwater Fish Directive (78/659/EEC amended 2006/44/EC)	Major Accidents (Seveso) Directive (96/82/EC)
Bathing Water Directive (76/160/EEC, as replaced by 2006/7/EC)	Surface Water Sampling/ Analysis Directive (79/869/EEC)	Groundwater Directive (80/68/EEC)	Environmental Impact Assessment Directive (85/337/EEC)
Drinking Water Directive (80/778/EEC, as amended by 98/83/EC)		Dangerous Substances Directive (76/464/EC codified 2006/11/EC)	Sewage Sludge Directive (86/278/EEC amended 97/11/EC)
Urban Waste Water Treatment Directive (91/271/EEC)			Plant Protection Products Directive (91/414/EEC)
Nitrates Directive (91/676/EEC)			Habitats Directive (92/43/EEC)
			Birds Directive (79/409/EEC)

the Shellfish Water Directive 2006/113/EEC. The Water Framework Directive is intended to provide a more systematic approach to the protection of water, rationalising past directives. It has been built on the fundamental principle of sustainable development, safeguarding the valuable resource of water while maintaining benefits from its use for services. The directive sets demanding environmental quality standards for water and requires all inland and coastal water bodies to be classified as to their type and quality status – i.e. high, good and moderate, against set standards. It is proactive and requires good status to be achieved in all inland and coastal waters by 2015, with continual improvements thereafter. There is a balance between costs and benefits in improving the status of water bodies, but little leeway in terms of a deterioration of water quality. Water quality is described in terms of chemical environmental quality standards and environmental ecological quality standards. There has been considerable debate in setting ecological quality standards since this had not previously been attempted and there was no scientific consensus in choosing appropriate measures and defining them in terms of high, good and moderate status. The Water Framework Directive provides for a holistic approach to river basin management since achieving environmental quality standards in water bodies requires not only reduction in point source pollution but also lowering diffuse pollution. The management of water will thus stretch into land use, e.g. agriculture, housing, roads, industry.

Defra and the Environment Agency engaged in a major consultation process to bring the UK system into alignment with the needs of the Water Framework Directive. The government's water strategy is set out in *Future Water*[36] with a vision for 2030. There are a number of strands to the vision:

- water demand
- water supply
- water quality
- surface water drainage
- water charges and adequacy of regulatory structures.

The vision seeks to provide an overhaul of the main water environment directives.

Water and sewerage competition

The privatisation of the water and sewerage companies generated a great deal of discussion as to how to make market-led competition in the water industry compatible with protecting the environment. An interim report of an independent review chaired by Professor Martin Cave was published in December 2008. The conclusions from the review[37] address some of the concerns about how a free market in water services might be compatible with the environment. It was suggested that competition throughout the sector should help improve innovation and that the abstraction and licensing system should be reformed to bring to bear full costs on the industry. This should support the need for rationing and protecting water against scarcity. At present, there are many unsustainable abstractions, which might be possible to address through better competition. The final report is expected later in 2009, but the lessons to be drawn from the review are that water services require more innovation and greater competition. It remains to be seen whether environmental concerns are best addressed through more competition and greater efficiency.

Conclusions

The Environment Agency's recent *Water Resources Strategy for England and Wales* makes the important analysis that water resources are linked to a sustainable environment:

- to enable habitats and species to adapt better to climate change;
- to adjust the protection of the water environment to the flexibility required of a changing climate;
- to reduce pressure on the environment by the use of water for human use;
- to encourage options that are resilient to climate change;
- to protect water supplies and infrastructures;
- to reduce greenhouse gas emissions from the use of water;
- to improve understanding of risks and uncertainties of climate change.

[36] CM 7319 February, 2008.

[37] Professor Martin Cave, 'Interim review of competition and innovation in water markets' December 2008; see ENDS Report 407, pp. 50–1.

As water is a scarce resource used for a variety of purposes, it is essential that there is effective management, not only to conserve the resource but also to maintain and improve its quality. Water management and pollution controls are at the centre of the future development of environmental law. The law is heavily influenced by scientific and technical expertise. It is undoubtedly the case that scientists are faced by a number of challenges in contributing to the development of effective water law. It must be remembered that the protection of water does not come only from legislation directly targeted at water, but, significantly, also from other sources. Some of the most important developments for the protection of water bodies is found in the EU legislation on chemicals, particularly the Biocide Directive and REACH (see Chapter 7).

There is continued pressure from public opinion, and the work of pressure groups maintains water pollution at the centre of media attention. Privatisation of the water industry has affected public understanding and perceptions about the water industry. There are issues about rising costs and accountability over the industry. The abstraction of water, the use of licences and the level of protection expected today requires the water industry to be carefully managed. Achieving a sustainable environment places water at the centre of how effective environmental law really is.

Further reading

S. Elworthy, 'Finding the causes of events or preventing "state of affairs"? Designation of nitrate vulnerable zones' [1998] JEL 92.

N.F. Gray, *Drinking Water Quality: Problems and Solutions* London: John Wiley, 1994.

N. Gunningham and D. Sinclair, 'Policy instrument choices and diffuse source pollution' (2005) 17 JEL 51.

R.M. Harrison (ed.), *Pollution: Causes, Effects and Control* London: The Royal Society of Chemistry, 2001.

S.M. Haslam, *River Pollution: An Ecological Perspective* London: John Wiley & Sons, 1990.

J. Holder and M. Lee, *Environmental Protection, Law and Policy*, 2nd edition Cambridge: Cambridge University Press, 2007.

N.J. Horan, *Biological Wastewater Treatment Systems: Theory and Operation* London: John Wiley & Sons, 1990.

W. Howarth and D. McGillivray, *Water Pollution and Water Quality Laws*, London: Crayford: Shaw and Sons, 2001.

D. Kinnersley, *Coming Clean: The Politics of Water and the Environment* London: Harmondsworth, Penguin, 1994.

A. Kiss and D. Shelton, *Guide to International Environmental Law* Leiden and Boston: Martinus, Nijhoff, 2007.

C.F. Mason, *Biology of Freshwater Pollution* 3rd edition, Harlow, Essex: Longman Scientific & Technical, 1995.

G. Richardson, A. Ogus and P. Barrows, *Policing Pollution* Oxford University Press, 1983.

Royal Commission on Environmental Pollution 16th Report Freshwater Quality June, 1992 (Cm 1966).

Additional sources

The main environmental law journals all provide very good coverage of water management and pollution issues. There is a dedicated journal devoted to water: *Water Law* (Publishers: Wiley Chancery). Also see: ENDS.

Future Strategy, The Government's Water Strategy for England (February, 2008) Cm 7319.

Ofwat, Paying For Water: A Time for Decisions (Ofwat, 1991).

Ofwat, Paying for Quality: The Political Perspective (Ofwat, 1993).

Ofwat, Future Charges for Water and Sewerage Services: The Outcome of the Periodic Review (Ofwat, 1994).

UK Groundwater Forum, Groundwater in the UK: A Strategic Study, UK Groundwater Resources (June, 1995).

Visit **http://www.mylawchamber.co.uk/mceldowney** to access key issue checklists and practice exam questions to test yourself on this chapter.

Protection of the marine environment

Introduction

The coastal and marine environment sets a distinctive challenge for environmental law. The current law in the United Kingdom is scattered and diverse, with a number of agencies and organisations engaged in marine protection and conservation. Over the years there has been considerable discussion about legislation to promote the effective management and protection of the UK's marine resources and environment. There is a need to provide the United Kingdom with a unified approach to the protection of the marine environment. Recently these efforts have come to fruition in the Marine and Coastal Access Act 2009. The new Act sets a framework to promote effective management and protection of the UK's marine resources and environment. The outcome is to provide a fundamental break with past efforts to address pollution and conservation in favour of a proactive policy adopting a 'stewardship approach' to marine life and resources. The dedication of a specific chapter to the coastal and marine environment is recognition of the need to isolate the specific problems confronting the marine ecosystem and identify the relevant laws that apply. It is timely to consider the new Bill and its wider implications.

A wide variety of sources and different forms of law are relevant to the protection of the marine environment. Water resources include not only freshwater and groundwater but also coastal and marine habitats. It is estimated that at least seventy per cent of the earth's surface is covered by seas. Oceans and seas serve as a primary resource for life and have a significant influence on climate. In modern times, in common with the exploitation of many natural resources, the oceans are seen as a resource for food, for minerals and metals, for energy generation, for transport and for many forms of recreational use. Increasingly the oceans are used as dumping grounds for waste disposal and sewerage discharges. The self-renewing properties of the seas are seriously under threat from pollution. Pollution is mainly from rivers, estuaries and coastal run-off, although there is increasing recognition of the effects of shipping on the marine environment. There is some concern that oceans may be becoming acidic because of atmospheric CO_2 dissolving in the sea water. This process appears to be speeding up[1] as atmospheric CO_2 levels increase. Ocean acidification is likely to have a major

---

[1] J.T. Wootton *et al.*, *Proceedings of the National Academies of Science* (2008) vol. 105, p. 18. ENDS Report 407, p. 30 (December 2008).

effect on productivity of the sea through an impact on some types of phytoplankton, a primary source of food for many marine animals. It will also damage coral reefs, one of the most productive and diverse habitats on earth.

Pollution from ships and waste disposal at sea have a significant impact on the coast and marine life. The transportation of oil in bulk carriers and mishaps causing oil pollution have an impact on the self-regenerating qualities of the seas. Over-fishing and a failure to conserve fish stocks has also had an impact on the sea as a food resource.

Historically the marine environment was a rich source of food. Fish stocks taken from the sea in the waters of the North-East Atlantic supported large fishing communities for generations. It is estimated that Total Fish Catches (TFC) in the North Sea rose from an annual average of 1.7 million tonnes in the late 1940s to a peak of 3.2 million tonnes at the beginning of the 1970s. Catches have since declined and fish stocks are at substantial risk from over-fishing. Some fish types have already been over-harvested so that their populations will take many years to recover. Excessive catches and catches of juvenile fish have a major impact on the reproductive capacity of a fish population and the ability of the population to regenerate. Defra has been actively engaged in creating a sustainable fisheries strategy since 2007 that is consistent with the EU Common Fisheries Policy. In addition, there is increasing evidence that pollution of the marine environment is having an adverse effect on fish. This in part is being manifested as morphological abnormalities in the fish, resulting from chronic low-level exposure to pollutants; other impacts are not yet clear.

The impacts of pollutants originating from both land sources and shipping are complex. It is possible that the density and diversity of marine communities will be adversely affected and that energy flow-through and nutrient cycling within marine ecosystems may be disrupted. As with terrestrial ecosystems in marine ecosystems, it is possible for pollutants to be bio-magnified through a food chain with predators – e.g. birds, aquatic mammals, predator fish – at the top of the food chain accumulating most pollutant and being greatly affected. The impact of pollutants in marine ecosystems are difficult to predict and often difficult to monitor and study. It should be remembered that there can be major population shifts with season: for example phytoplankton community composition and density fluctuates with season, and some fish are migratory, adding to the difficulty in assessing and predicting pollutant impact.

In the past the dumping of waste at sea offered an apparently cheaper alternative, based on the economic argument that land-based disposal was too expensive. This was short-term decision-making. When measured over the longer term the pollution of the marine environment was likely to be much more costly. Oil pollution is caused both by the spillage of oil from vessels and from oil exploration. These pollution incidents often have major acute effects, including large bird and other animal kills. They may also result in chronic pollution, with shorelines and sediment remaining contaminated for many years (see below). The *Torrey Canyon* disaster in 1967 illustrated the inherent dangers of the transportation of oil in bulk carriers, when large quantities of oil caused hazards to fisheries, coastal resorts, marine wildlife and humans. Other disasters, such as *Amoco Cadiz* and the *Exxon Valdez* and in January 1993 the Shetland tanker accident, have shown the scale and potential severity of pollution from bulk oil carriers. It should also be remembered that ships commonly discharge oil pollutants during their normal passage and that deep-sea oil installations contribute to the hydrocarbon pollutant load of marine habitats.

Legal responses to the diverse challenges arising from the protection and conservation of marine ecosystems involve laws at the level of the member state as well as both community law and international law. As Kiss and Shelton explain:

> Deterioration of the marine environment demands legal responses with some universal aspects and others that are individualized, according to the different regional and local problems. In numerous cases regional or even global cooperation is required, even where the issue appears to be a local question like the cleanliness of several kilometres of coastland.[2]

There are a number of government departments in the United Kingdom with responsibilities that cover marine pollution. The Department of Transport is concerned with the control of oil and chemical pollution at sea and, since 1979, a Marine Pollution Control Unit (MPC) has been responsible for counter-pollution measures in the North Sea. The role of the MPC is likely to be subsumed into a new Marine and Fisheries Agency (discussed below). The Secretary of State for Transport is under a duty to make an annual report to Parliament under section 26 of the Prevention of Oil Pollution Act 1971. There is a moratorium on dumping at sea and this is carefully monitored by the UK Government department. Effectively, dumping of waste has ceased since 1972. In the case of pollution from offshore installations and the responsibility to deal with pollution there is an emergency crisis system under the Cabinet Office to work with various government departments, including the Department of Transport and Defra. In cases of oil pollution involving naval vessels there are responsibilities within the Ministry of Defence.

This chapter provides an outline of the main legal powers found in international law, European Union law and in the national law of the United Kingdom for the control of marine pollution and the management of the marine environment.

Sources of law

The main sources of law that apply to the marine environment are international law, EU law and the national law of the United Kingdom. The law covers matters as diverse as marine pollution and ownership of the seas. Marine pollution does not recognise national boundaries but legal frontiers are helpful in defining responsibility and enabling regulation of the marine environment. International law in this area primarily rests on the assumptions that there can be cooperation between states and that the protection of the marine environment may best be achieved through international regulation. This is a fast-developing and specialised area of law with particular emphasis on trans-frontier pollution.[3]

International law

There are a number of international organisations that are relevant to marine pollution and a number of international conferences that provide a forum for discussion of particular areas of marine pollution. There is an International Maritime Organisation (IMO), which is part of the United Nations, with membership of about 125 states. Its headquarters are in London and it acts as a facility to extend cooperation between governments on shipping matters. The United Nations Food and the Marine Environment Protection Division of the IMO draws

---

[2] A. Kiss and D. Shelton, *Manual of European Law*, Cambridge: Grotius Publications, 1993, p. 277.
[3] See: *Trail Smelter Arbitration* (1938) and (1941) 3 UNRIAA.

up conventions on shipping and marine pollution. There is a United Nations Convention on the Law of the Sea which has been ratified by over 60 states since it was agreed in 1982. The United Nations Environment Programme followed from the Stockholm Conference in 1972 where 113 states participated and a Declaration on Human Environment was agreed. The programme was established with its headquarters in Nairobi, Kenya. Protection of the marine environment forms part of the United Nations Environment Programme. There is an International Convention for the Prevention of Pollution from Ships (MARPOL) signed in 1973 and later amended by protocol in 1978. The convention, which came into force in October 1983, is intended to eliminate international pollution of the marine environment. There are a number of important regional conventions. In 1984 the North Sea States met together to prevent any pollution of the North Sea. There have been conferences held in 1987, 1990, and in 1995 with the result of a number of declarations elaborating agreed general principles. Over the past decade the conferences have focused on sustainable management of North Sea resources.

International law is important in designating ocean waters into zones. In 1982 the diffuse number of treaties and conventions was codified by a global convention signed by the majority of states of the world. The United Nations Convention on the Law of the Sea (UNCLOS) 1982, provides five distinct categories of marine space:

1. The sovereignty of a coastal state is defined to include internal waters consisting of ports, harbours and bays whose openings do not exceed 40 km.

2. A coastal state may exercise its territorial sea as a sovereign zone up to 20 km. Foreign shipping may have rights of passage but the sovereign state may legislate to protect its marine environment.

3. A coastal state is defined as consisting of the sea and seabed to the outer limit of the continental plateau, that is to the beginning of the deep-seabed.

4. An exclusive economic zone consists of the maritime area that extends between the territorial sea and a line situated 360 km from the coast. This designation has existed from the 1970s and gives the coastal state rights to exploit the resources of marine life in the zone. The coastal state is under a duty to ensure that there is environmental protection of the area.

5. Waters outside the designated zones, outlined above, are described as the high seas. These are open to exploitation by international shipping.

International law also consists of a number of other treaties and conventions that afford environmental protection to the various oceans of the world. As noted above, the United Nations Environment Programme initiated attempts to set out a programme for regional seas in 1974. The programme covers ten areas where regional plans are under development or are operative. The Barcelona Convention which came into force in 1978 applies to the Mediterranean. It is hoped that the principles of combating pollution will be extended to other seas through a series of framework conventions. These include the Persian Gulf, the Red Sea and the Gulf of Eden, parts of the Indian Ocean, the South Pacific, the Northeast Pacific, the Caribbean and parts of the South Atlantic. There are a number of additional cooperation agreements being planned; the Caspian was added in 2003. In addition there are a number of treaties which apply to the North Sea and the North-East Atlantic. There is a 1983 Treaty dealing with oil-based pollution. The 1972 Oslo Dumping Convention amended by subsequent protocols applies to the North Sea, the North-East Atlantic and the adjacent Arctic seas. In 1974 the Helsinki Convention for the protection of the Marine Environment of the

Baltic Area adopted a comprehensive approach to pollution control. There is a standing conference on Straddling Stocks and Highly Migratory Species that attempts to persuade states to conserve fish stocks. The United Kingdom has ratified the Agreement on the Conservation of Small Cetaceans (small marine mammals) of the Baltic and North Seas in July 1993 to protect dolphins and porpoises in the North Sea and to fund research into preventing them from being caught in fishing nets.

The European Union

The EU is also an important source of law for setting standards to protect marine habitats. Article 130r(3) requires that the EU should take account of available scientific and technical data when considering its environmental policy. European Community directives relating to the sea include Directive 76/464/EEC codified 2006/11/EC which applies to the pollution caused by certain dangerous substances discharged into the aquatic environment of the Community. There are a number of directives on the quality of shellfish, and Directive 76/160/EEC amended by 2006/7/EC on the quality of bathing waters, discussed in more detail below (see the Water Framework Directive in Table 12.2). There are directives prohibiting the discharge of specific chemicals into an aquatic environment. There is also a UK-wide transposition of the EU Council Directive 85/337/EEC amended 97/11/EC on Environmental Impact Assessment that applies to the marine world. The Marine Works (Environmental Impact Assessment) Regulations 2007 provides that environmental impact assessment applies to the various aspects of harbour and coastal protection, including offshore operations.

United Kingdom law

National laws are important in tackling marine pollution. For example, there are a variety of laws in the United Kingdom that prevent tankers from discharging oil or waste while at sea (see: the Merchant Shipping Act 1979 and the Merchant Shipping (Prevention of Oil Pollution) Regulations 1996 SI 1996/2154). Many national laws implement international agreements, or set out in United Kingdom law those obligations introduced by the European Community. Thus the Merchant Shipping (Salvage and Pollution) Act 1994 implements the International Convention on Salvage 1989, (Cm 1526) and various international conventions and protocols for oil pollution damage. Section 1(1) of the Territorial Seas Act 1987 sets UK territorial seas to be 12 nautical miles. Included within the definition of 'relevant territorial waters' under the 1987 Act are a number of straits used for international navigation. Under the Fisheries Act 1976 the United Kingdom set up an Exclusive Fishing Zone of 200 nautical miles. Since 1978 the Crown Court has jurisdiction over indictable offences committed on board or by means of a foreign ship in United Kingdom territorial waters. British ships are registered under the Merchant Shipping Act 1988.

Fisheries

Historical background

In 1983, after protracted negotiations, a legally enforceable Common Fisheries Policy (CFP) was agreed by the member states of the Community. Past attempts to arrive at a common policy had been unsuccessful and current attempts to find a workable fishing policy among all member states remain controversial. The competence of the Community to make laws for the conservation of the biological resources of the sea has been approved by the Court of Justice (see: Cases 3/76, 4/76 and 6/76 *Kramer* [1976] ECR 1279). The agreement in 1983 has four elements. First, all community fishermen are entitled to fish within the community's 200-nautical-mile limit of their own shores. The 200-nautical-mile limit came into operation in January 1977 and represented a considerable expansion in the territorial scope of Community law. Within this framework, member states are free to reserve fishing to their own fishermen and those fishermen with traditional fishing rights. Fishing the Atlantic and North Sea fish stocks are subject to additional controls. There are allowable catches that are divided into national quotas. The Total Allowable Catch (TAC) is fixed annually on the basis of Regulation 4194/88. Fishing from vessels flying the flag of a particular country may be stopped from fishing for a specific period.

Secondly, the Community operates a price system and market organisation for fish that come within the price system. There is also an external trade policy. Regulation 379/81 (amended by Regulation 3468/88) sets the guide prices, classification, market standards, packaging and labelling of fish products. Thirdly, there are international negotiations conducted by Community representatives on behalf of all the member states that concern access to waters and conservation of fish stocks. Finally, there are structural provisions for market development and modernisation of the industry that includes redeployment of resources. The Common Structural Policy falls under Regulation 101/76 (OJ 1976 L 20/19).

Community fishing policy, the subject of quotas and the use of exclusion of certain types of ships in conservation zones have all been highly controversial areas of Community policy and often the subject of litigation before the courts.[4]

A strategy to 2027

Concerns remain that diminishing fish stocks in the North Sea and Atlantic require a tougher policy if the replenishment of an important food source is not to be severely impaired. The Sea Fisheries Regulation Act 1966 has been amended by section 102 of the Environment Act 1995. The Environment Agency sea fisheries committees and ministers have been granted powers to regulate fisheries for environmental as distinct from fish management purposes. Membership of the sea fisheries committees may now include experts in environmental matters. The Sea Fish (Conservation) Act 1967 contains powers to restrict fishing for sea fish. The 1967 Act has been strengthened by section 103 of the Environment Act 1995. A new section 5A provides powers to make an order for the purposes of conserving the marine environment. This includes conserving the natural beauty or amenity of marine or coastal areas. In effect these are important conservation powers to restrict fishing or to prohibit the carriage of specified types of net for marine environmental purposes. It is likely that it will become increasingly necessary to make use of conservation powers of this kind.

Section 104 of the Environment Act 1995 also contains powers for the Environment Agency to operate a fixed penalty system for dealing with offences, under legislation protecting salmon and freshwater fish, under amendments made to section 37 of the Salmon and

---

[4] See: Case 63/83 *R v Kirk* [1984] ECR 2689, and the *Factortame* litigation (Case C-213/89 *R v Secretary of State for Transport, ex parte Factortame Ltd (No. 2)* [1991] 1 AC 603).

Freshwater Fisheries Act 1975. Section 37A sets out detailed procedures and fixed penalties. There are additional miscellaneous powers for setting standards for fish farm intakes and outfalls to be screened to protect wild fish stocks.

The Environment Act 1995 also attempts to provide the Environment Agency with unified grant-in-aid powers derived from Defra and also unifies the administration of the grant and approval of fish passes. There is a Fisheries 2027 – a long-term vision for sustainable fisheries. The aim is to provide a sustainable development strategy linked to protecting the environment, which will

- provide administration for the new European Fisheries Fund;
- engage with stakeholders;
- provide long-term plans that promote sustainability;
- engage in cost-sharing between the various stakeholders in promoting conservation and setting economic, social and environmental priorities;
- encourage long-term management plans for key fishing stocks;
- encourage and promote environmentally responsible decision-making.[5]

Pollution

The significance of marine pollution and its effects on the food chain should not be under-estimated (see Law in context, below).

LAW IN CONTEXT

Marine pollution

Marine pollution is due to a diverse number of causes (Clark, 1989; GESAMP, 1990). These pollutants may arise from both point and diffuse sources. They may be continuous or intermittent and may originate from humans' activities on land or on the sea. Indeed, pollution from land may be the most significant, particularly in coastal regions. Diffuse sources of marine pollutants include run-off of fertilisers and pesticides from agricultural land. Point sources include sewage outfalls, industrial effluents, mining wastes etc. and contribute a wide variety of different pollutants to marine habitats. Pollutants are also discharged to the marine environment through rivers carrying their pollutant load to the sea. Gaseous and particulate atmospheric emissions, primarily from land-based sources, may also contribute to the marine pollutant load through wet or dry deposition.

The significance of pollutants in marine ecosystems became apparent to the public in the late 1980s. In 1988 there was an epidemic of Phocine Distemper Virus in the

---

[5] Defra, *Fisheries 2027 – A Long-term Vision for Sustainable Fisheries* London: Defra, 2009.

common seal populations which spread from the Danish to the UK coast. Approximately 16,000 dead seals were washed up on beaches. The cause of this massive epidemic was thought to have been through the action of polychlorinated biphenyls (PCBs) and other pollutant chemicals impairing the seals' immune systems. Also in 1988, there was a large toxic algal bloom of *Chrysochromulina polylepsis* in the spring and early summer. The coast of Norway and Sweden were severely affected, with large numbers of marine invertebrates dying. Trout and salmon died at fish farms although most wild fish were able to avoid the contaminated area. The algal bloom was attributed to eutrophication of the coastal waters, primarily arising from fertiliser run-off from land.

The impact of these pollutants are dependent on a variety of factors, including the local physical conditions: for example, tides, currents, water depth, the nature of the sediment. These will influence the concentration and duration of exposure of an organism, population or community to a pollutant. The littoral zone is particularly prone to fluctuations in conditions such as temperature, wave action etc. This zone also tends to be relatively high in nutrients (many originating form land run-off) and have a highly diverse flora, fauna and microbial community which are dense and active. The deep sea in comparison is, in general, relatively stable, low-nutrient and has less biological activity. The biological characteristics of the ecosystem are also important in determining the impact of pollutants. At the individual or population level the sensitivity of the organism to the compound, and its tendency to bioaccumulate the compound, are important. The life cycle of the organism and its lifestyle will also affect an organism's exposure to pollutants. Some marine organisms are pelagic: that is, they either float (planktonic) or swim (nectonic) in the water. Other organisms are bottom-dwelling: that is, benthic. Some organisms have diurnal patterns of behaviour. Their way of life will affect their exposure to a chemical, e.g. whether it remains predominantly in the water phase or associates with the sediment. The characteristics of the particular pollutant is important: its longevity, its chemistry and distribution etc. in the marine environment affect the impact on organisms. Most often exposure is chronic and low-level rather than acute and toxic. Chronic effects on individual organisms and populations are particularly difficult to predict but may be highly significant.

Marine pollution controls, however, also need to be considered in the wider context of conservation in the United Kingdom. In section 11 of the Countryside Act 1968, there is a general duty on ministers and government departments to have regard to the conservation of the natural beauty and amenity of the countryside. This duty is balanced by various duties found in the National Parks and Access to the Countryside Act 1949; the Countryside Act 1968; and the Wildlife and Countryside Act 1981 (see Chapter 11). Broadly these Acts provide that due regard should be given to the needs of agriculture and forestry and to the economic and social interest of rural areas. The Environment Act 1995 provides the Environment Agency with the aims of protecting or enhancing the environment with the objective of achieving sustainable development. The future of marine conservation lies with achieving the exacting requirement of balancing the competing needs and uses of the sea with its proper management and conservation.

The Shellfish Waters Directive

The Shellfish Waters Directive 79/923/EEC amended 2006/113/EC is intended to protect shellfish populations and set water quality standards to ensure that the shellfish can spawn and reproduce. Various standards are used to ensure that samples are monitored and checks made to establish that standards are achieved. The aim is partly to ensure that there is no evidence of any harm from various organohalogenated compounds. The scale of the site inspections undertaken by the Environment Agency has grown. In the 1980s there were only 18 shellfish waters designated as falling under the directive. In 1999 this had risen to 119 shellfish waters and is supervised by Defra. Over the years the scheme has been extended from England and Wales to Northern Ireland with a total of 241 designations.[6]

Coastal management

Historical overview to 2009

Marine Nature Reserves (MNRs) occupy tidal and coastal waters. Land or water can be desig-nated from the high-tide mark to a line three miles from the baseline under the Territorial Sea Act 1987 and section 36 of the Wildlife and Countryside Act 1981 on a similar basis as National Nature Reserves (see Chapter 11). There is a procedure whereby designation may be made by the Secretary of State for Environment which allows representation from interested parties and if necessary a public inquiry. The English Nature manages MNRs and has been given by-law making powers. The scope of by-laws is set out in section 37 of the Wildlife and Countryside Act 1981. Restrictions may be made on the killing, taking and disturbance of animals as well as the deposit of litter. There are provisions included under section 37 for the restriction or prohibition of people and vessels to the MNR. This does not apply, however, where there is a right of access to tidal waters or the right of passage. In reality this limitation curtails the usefulness of these powers.

Coastal flood defences are the responsibility of Defra. The Environment Agency is directed in its work by local flood-defence committees composed of local landowners and local authority councillors. The control of coastal erosion falls to the district councils bordering the coast under the oversight of Defra. In effect the district councils are responsible for the coastal zone inwards of the sea. They receive some funding for coastal protection schemes from Defra but most costs are met directly by the councils. The impact of the predicted sea-level changes associated with global warming may substantially increase the costs of already expensive sea defences.

The Marine and Coastal Access Act 2009

The new Act provides a number of important initiatives[7] (there is an equivalent for Scotland and the Act applies to England and Wales). The setting-up of a new Marine Management

---

[6] See: the Surface Waters (Shellfish) (Classification) (Amendment) Regulations (Northern Ireland) 2009, SI 2009/61.

[7] See Explanatory Notes to the Marine and Coastal Access Act 2009; also see House of Commons Library Research Paper 09/56 (16 June 2009) Marine and Coastal Access Bill (HL).

Organisation is a significant step in coordinating the activities of many of the existing bodies. It promises a more holistic and joined-up management of the marine and coastal environment. The Act also introduces:

- a streamlining of the existing marine licensing system and an integrated approach to marine planning policy;

- the introduction of new marine conservation zones;

- the creation of a national route that allows access around the English coast through a new duty placed on Natural England to allow public access for walking and recreation activities;

- there are also reforms to the management and enforcement of fisheries, clearer licensing and a single process of consents.

The Act is controversial in terms of issues that have arisen about the adequacy of protection and enforcement provided for the marine environment. There is likely to be opposition to coastal access and the provisions that apply to landowners. There has been a lengthy consultation process undertaken by Defra, which started in 2007. The draft Bill was published in April 2008 and was subjected to pre-legislative scrutiny and a joint committee of both Houses. The Bill was introduced in the House of Lords in December 2008 and made steady passage through debates and committee stages. The Act mainly applies to England but there is a corresponding Marine (Scotland) Act for Scotland and framework powers under the Government of Wales Act 2006 for legislative competence to be granted to the Welsh Assembly. The main aspects of the new Act are worth discussion.

The Marine Management Organisation (MMO) is intended to act as a non-departmental public body that may draw up plans for a new system of marine planning. This includes matters such as environmental licensing, the management of marine fishing and undertaking conservation functions. The aim is to create a unified approach to enforce fisheries, licensing and nature conservation legislation. In planning terms the MMO will take responsibility for creating a series of new marine plans intended to apply the newly drawn up Marine Policy Statement. The MMO will also have licensing and enforcement powers[8] that span environmental, navigational, human health and other impacts of construction, deposits and removals in the marine areas. Important powers will be exercised over tidal and wave projects, jetties and moorings, coastal dredging, aggregate extraction and the laying of submarine cables.[9] The current powers exercised by the Marine and Fisheries Agency are to be transferred to the MMO. This will also result in the MMO becoming a key agency in terms of the Common Fisheries Policy and will provide the UK with compatibility under the EU rules that require a unitary body. In terms of marine conservation the MMO is likely to have a decisive role. Natural England and the Joint Nature Conservation Committee (JNCC) are the government's main statutory advisers for England. In the case of Wales the Countryside Council for Wales is the main statutory adviser. The intention is that the new MMO will work with Natural England and the JNCC and that the MMO will become the main regulator.

---

[8] Powers currently under the Food and Environment Protection Act 1985, the Coast Protection Act 1949 and Telecommunications Act 1984 Schedule 2 (Electronic Communications Code).

[9] The Marine Works (Environmental Impact Assessment) Regulations 2007 SI 2007/1518; the Marine Minerals Permissions under the Environmental Impact Assessment and Natural Habitats (Extraction of Minerals by Marine Dredging) (England and Northern Ireland) Regulations 2007 SI 2007/1067.

There are important enforcement powers in the Act. The MMO will, under Part 8, be able to appoint the existing Marine Enforcement Officers who will transfer to the MMO. There are much needed powers given to the MMO in order to address emergencies. Currently the Marine Fisheries Agency works with Defra to deal with emergencies and the aim is for the new MMO to take over this role. Given the nature of climate change, responding to emergencies is likely to become an increasingly important task. The MMO will also accommodate the scientific research undertaken by the Marine and Fisheries Agency.

One of the most important aspects of the Act is the creation of Marine Conservation Zones in UK waters. This will include a new designation of Marine Nature Reserves. There will be a number of different zones related to marine conservation. There is an illustrative map available from Defra setting out the proposed ideas and the use of different protections for the various zones.[10] The intention is to provide the following:

- a mechanism to protect nationally important species and habitats;
- marine planning to find space for competing activities such as sea fishing, windfarms and so on;
- inshore fishing will be managed to protect important marine habitats and biodiversity;
- MMO will provide an effective means to enforce the law.

The importance of the various proposals is that the new arrangements for the first time attempt to provide an integrated approach to the management and protection of the marine ecosystem. The government strategy is also to engage with public rights of way at the coast through an extension of access to the countryside that is currently available under the Countryside and Rights of Way Act 2000.

Pollution control

Discharge of effluent

The regulation of effluent discharge under the Water Resources Act 1991 has been examined in Chapter 12. There are other statutory provisions relevant to the marine environment. The Dangerous Substances in Harbour Areas Regulations 1987 SI No. 37 provides extensive regulations for the carriage, loading and unloading, and storage of dangerous substances within harbour areas. The regulations require periods of notice to be given to the harbour master where it is intended to berth any dangerous substance. There must be provision by the harbour authorities of an emergency plan and regulations over the entry, access, the method of carriage and handling of dangerous goods. The correct forms and procedures, including the labelling of the dangerous substances, are also included within the regulations. Vessels carrying dangerous substances must display flags and conform to the procedures set out in the regulations.

---

[10] See: Defra, *Protecting our Marine Environment Through the Marine Bill*, London: Defra, 2009.

A range of waste is discharged to the sea from land, including untreated or partially treated sewage which may pose a health risk (see below). It may also contribute to eutrophication (waters becoming nutrient-rich, with major impacts on fauna and flora) of coastal water. In some cases where exceptionally high biological oxygen demand (BOD) waste (waste that is readily degraded by micro-organisms respiring oxygen) is released then estuaries may become deoxygenated, again with major impacts on the flora and fauna. A range of other industrial waste may be discharged, the impact of which will depend on the particular compounds involved and a variety of other factors (see Law in context, p. 268). Attempts can be made to determine the toxicity of specific chemicals to selected marine organisms in ecotoxicity tests. The limitations of predicting other species' reactions, community and ecosystem level impacts from such studies have already been discussed (see Chapter 7). Power production in the UK also contributes to marine pollution. Thermal pollution can arise in coastal regions and estuaries from the discharge of cooling water from power stations.

Radioactive waste management

Nuclear power stations are permitted to discharge radioactive effluent to marine environments. These discharges are site-specific and depend on the receiving water. Currently, controls are set in terms of the total amount of radioactivity released and the maximum levels of specified radionuclides (radioactive elements) discharged (see Law in context, below). Reprocessing plants which reprocess the spent fuel rods from nuclear reactors are similarly controlled in levels of discharges. It is proposed that discharge authorisations will be set at the same low dose level for all new nuclear installations and wherever possible existing ones.[11] This proposal appears to be adopting the same strategy as that of uniform emission standards (UESs) followed in some European countries.

LAW IN CONTEXT

Radionuclides in the environment

The mobility, distribution and fate of discharged radionuclides (radioactive elements) in the marine environment vary with the chemistry of the radionuclide, and the physical and chemical characteristics of the receiving water. These factors influence the biological availability of individual radionuclides. The uptake and accumulation of radionuclides varies with organism and with particular radionuclide. Radionuclides change to other elements during radioactive decay; this means that any prediction of the impact of a radionuclide on marine habitats must include consideration of the potential fate and impact of all its decay daughters. A number of discharged radionuclides may have no stable counterparts and essentially do not occur naturally in the biosphere; assessing their likely environmental fate and biological interactions may be exceptionally difficult. This, of course, can also be said for many human-made chemicals which do not occur naturally.

---

[11] See: The Government's White Paper, Review of Radioactive Waste Management Policy (Cm 2919, HMSO, July 1995).

The regulation of radioactive waste under the Radioactive Substances Act 1993 has been amended by the Environment Act 1995. The Environment Agency and the Scottish Environment Protection Agency have responsibilities for its regulation. The authorisation procedure whereby Defra determines applications for the disposal of radioactive waste is directed by the Environment Agency.[12] The Health and Safety Executive (HSE) regulates the nuclear industry through its Nuclear Directorate (ND). This falls under the Health and Safety at Work etc. Act 1974 as amended by the Radioactive Substances Act 1993 and also the Nuclear Installations Act 1965.

Bathing Water Directive

EC Directive 76/160/EEC amended 2006/113/EC remains an innovative directive that requires the member states of the Community to provide a quality standard for bathing water.[13] There is much anecdotal evidence about illness developing after swimming and surfing etc. in coastal water. The illnesses range from gastroenteritis to ear infections, and include the more serious disorders that may include paralysis. It has proved epidemiologically very difficult to verify the link between swimming and such illness. This is partly because the reported illnesses are so varied and partly because the population using beaches is often transient. Many people spend holidays at the seaside and only develop symptoms when they return to their homes. The infectious agents causing the illness are likely to be varied with different incubation periods before symptoms become apparent, adding to the epidemiological complexity. It is thought that viruses may be particularly important in causing bathing-water-related illness and that the main contribution to the health risk from bathing water originates in the discharge of untreated or only partly treated sewerage effluent into coastal waters (see below).

LAW IN CONTEXT

Bacterial indicators of water quality

The water quality criteria for the Bathing Water Directive are based on water quality assessed through the presence of bacterial indicators of faecal pollution. A range of bacteria occur as normal flora in the human gastrointestinal tract and these are excreted in faeces. Estimating the numbers of these bacteria – e.g. *Escherichia coli*, faecal streptococci such as *Streptococcus faecalis*, and *Clostridium perfringens* – in water gives an indication of the amount of faecal pollution and therefore the risk of enteric pathogens being present in a water body. Isolating and enumerating pathogens themselves is more time-consuming and difficult than determining the presence of indicator organisms. However, one assumption must stand if indicator bacteria for faecal pollution are to be useful in determining the disease risk associated with water. The indicator organisms

---

[12] The Government's White Paper, *Review of Radioactive Waste Management Policy* (Cm 2919, HMSO, July 1995) contains details of how radioactive waste management policy should share the same principles as applied more generally to environmental policy.

[13] See: Case C-56/90 *Commission v United Kingdom* [1993] ECR I-4109. The UK was in breach in terms of beaches at Southport and Blackpool.

must survive longer in the water than pathogens. There is evidence that this is not always the case and it depends on species of indicator bacterium and species or type of pathogen, particularly in sea water – e.g. *E.coli* does not appear to survive as long in sea water as certain enteric viruses. This raises a question about the suitability of the monitoring technique accepted and used internationally.

CASE STUDY

Bathing Water Directive

There are a number of distinctive features about the EC Bathing Water Directive. First the directive was phased in over a period of time: two years to bring their laws into line with the directive and 10 years to bring the standards of bathing water into conformity with the directive. Secondly, the requirements of the directive can be waived where there are exceptional circumstances such as bad weather. For example, heavy rain can overwhelm a treatment works, resulting in poorly treated effluent being discharged into water. In recent years heavy rainfall has washed enteric micro-organisms arising from farm animals on agricultural land into sea water, resulting in a decline in water quality. In the past, the United Kingdom found it difficult to comply with the directive. In 1989 25 per cent of the designated bathing waters failed to reach even the minimum standards of the directive. Over the past 20 years our record has improved substantially. Past complaints that the United Kingdom failed to take adequate measures to ensure the quality of bathing waters at various resorts were upheld in *Commission* v *United Kingdom* (See: ENDS Report 222, p. 47, July 1993 Case C-56/90). The United Kingdom had argued that there was no requirement to authorise all bathing beaches under the directive. In designating beaches to qualify to come within the standards set by the directive, the United Kingdom adopted the criteria of counting the number of bathers in the water at any one time. As a result, only 27 beaches were designated in the United Kingdom and many well-used beaches were excluded. The court rejected this approach and also the argument that the ten-year period to comply with the directive could commence on the basis of the time of designation. The outcome was that another 389 beaches were required to be designated, and the standards of the directive applied and had to be in place within the ten-year period (1977–87).

The United Kingdom has about 599 beaches. Since 1990 it has sought to bring the majority within compliance of the directive. A £2.5 billion investment programme began in 1990 to meet the standards. It is clear that there have been a number of improvements. The compliance rate for England and Wales is, in 1994, 82.5 per cent, Scotland 69.5 per cent, N.Ireland 93.7 per cent (see ENDS Report 238, p. 24 November 1994). Since then there have been further improvements, not least in the design and installation of sewerage works in major towns and cities adjoining the beaches. The Environment Agency announced in May 2009 that it was taking further action on sewage effluent to ensure rivers and coastal waters are protected. The compliance rate at present is 98.3% for England, 100% for Wales, 93.5% for Scotland and 91.7% for N. Ireland.

The new Bathing Waters Directive 2006/7/EC came into force in 2008. The directive will require better publicity about the standards of beaches, and the prohibition of bathing areas where the pollution constitutes a threat to human health. In addition there is a new category of excellent quality for bathing waters. The new directive requires: (1) an improved standard for faecal streptococci which are thought to mimic the survival of enteric viruses better than other indicator bacteria; and (2) improved monitoring of water quality to enforce a zero limit for enteroviruses. Defra[14] has been engaged in a proactive analysis of how to monitor and bring into line current practices to meet the directive. This includes working with the Water Services Regulation Authority (Ofwat) through periodic reviews of sewage treatment works and pollution sources.

Deep-sea dumping

International law and United Kingdom legislation apply to the dumping of waste at sea.[15] Regulation of sea dumping has been much improved since Part II of the Food and Environment Protection Act 1985 replaced the Dumping at Sea Act 1974. The 1985 Act has been amended by the Environmental Protection Act 1990. Under sections 5 and 6 of the 1985 Act there is a system of licences for the depositing of substances from vessels, vehicles, aircraft or marine structures. A licence is required for the scuttling of vessels or for the loading of any vessel with substances that are intended to be deposited at sea. Licences are also required for incinerating substances on vessels or marine structures in United Kingdom waters. Licences may be granted by Defra. There are extensive regulations on the application procedure, the conditions that may be attached to licences and changes in licensing arrangements. There are conditions about keeping a public register detailing the licences issued and for carrying out periodic inspections. Section 10 of the 1985 Act permits the ministry to carry out operations for the protection of the marine ecosystem, human life or the legitimate uses of the sea.

The United Kingdom has been perceived in the past as having a poor record regarding sea dumping and discharges into the sea. At the 1990 North Sea Conference the United Kingdom agreed an extension of the lists of hazardous substances by 50 per cent of 1985 levels before 1995. A 70 per cent reduction was agreed for cadmium, lead, mercury and dioxins (ENDS Report 244, May 1995, p. 19). Public awareness of the sea dumping was heightened in the 1990s through the proposal by Shell to tow an oil installation the *Brent Star* into deep waters and sink it. This was opposed by Greenpeace who claimed that the deep-sea environment would be substantially affected by the toxic waste in the installation. There were large public protests, particularly in Holland and Germany, and a boycott of Shell products. Shell eventually gave way to public opinion and cancelled its plans to dispose of the structure in the sea. This led to considerable embarrassment, as the government had given approval to the scheme for sea dumping of the structure. Greenpeace subsequently admitted that they had overestimated the potential pollution risk arising from the rig. Sea

[14] See: HL Select Committee on the European Communities, Session 1994–5 7th Report, *Bathing Water Revisited* (HMSO, 1995).

[15] See: the Oslo Convention for the Prevention of Marine Pollution by Dumping from Ships and Aircraft 1972 Cmnd 4984, the London Convention for the Prevention of Marine Pollution by Dumping Wastes and Other Matters 1972, Cmnd 5169.

dumping may be a disposal option for this and other oil platforms.[16] There is some debate as to the potential environmental and health risks associated with the technically difficult decommissioning of the *Brent Star* on land compared to sea disposal. There are, for example, some toxic wastes that were present on the installation and disposing of these by incineration or landfill are not without associated risks. It is argued that the deep sea has a relatively low density of organisms present and should efficiently dilute and disperse any pollutants. It is almost impossible, however, to monitor either the fate of pollutants from deep-sea dumping of any type or to assess the impact of dumping on the marine ecosystem. The balance in safety for ecosystems and human health between sea dumping and land disposal is difficult to establish and verify. The economic cost and the cost to the environment through choosing the wrong option may well be large. Not only are the environmental consequences of sea dumping difficult to foresee, but also future economic costs of the dumping may be difficult to predict. For example, Beaufort's Dyke, a 1,500-foot trench in the seabed between Scotland and Ireland was the UK's main munitions disposal site for 50 years up to 1992. This dump even received some nuclear waste in 1981. Occassionally material from the dump is washed up on surrounding coasts with associated costs, of removing and disposing of the material.

The North Sea is a special area under the 1973/78 MARPOL Convention which would require ship owners to observe more stringent rules on discharges of waste. The MARPOL agreement has been amended many times, including in 1999, 2001 and 2008. The North Sea appears particularly vulnerable to pollution. This shallow shelf sea is surrounded by eight highly industrialised nations and as such receives a high pollutant load from land. In addition exploitation of oil and gas fields beneath the North Sea contribute to the contamination of this marine environment.

Some progress has been made on sea dumping. Disposal at sea of liquid industrial waste and of power station fly ash was brought to an end in December 1992. In 1998 the disposal of sewage sludge at sea was ended. At the end of 1992 the Ministry of Defence ended the dumping of redundant munitions at sea. There are proposals for the improvement of the disposal of garbage on war ships (see Third Report: This Common Inheritance Cm 2549 HMSO, 1994, p. 101). This falls under the jurisdiction of the Ministry of Defence.

Oil pollution

Oil is a complex mixture of many different types of aliphatic (straight chain) and aromatic (ring structure) hydrocarbons which vary with the oil field and method of processing. This has several implications, for example:

1. The toxicity of oil discharges will vary with the hydrocarbons present. It is possible that the hydrocarbons may interact in their impact.

2. The volatility of the compounds will be different, i.e. their tendency to evaporate from the aquatic environment and disperse in the atmosphere.

3. The solubility of the compounds will be different as will their tendency to form emulsions with water, i.e. become finely dispersed in the water. These characteristics will affect the rate of their biodegradation and the toxicity of the compounds.

---

[16] S. Mankabady, 'Decommissioning of offshore oil installations' 28 (1997) *Journal of Maritime Law and Commerce* 603.

4. The rate of degradation of the compounds will vary. Oil degradation is predominantly an aerobic process, i.e. occurs with the presence of oxygen, and varies with the size of, branching and presence of ring structures in the hydrocarbon, as well as with environmental conditions e.g. temperature. Ironically sites where oil pollution is common, e.g. in the vicinity of oil rigs, will have a large population of oil-degrading bacteria capable of rapidly degrading hydrocarbons. Sites where oil pollution is unusual, e.g. has only occurred because of an accident, may be not have a population of bacteria capable of removing the oil immediately, although such as population will evolve after a period of time.

All these factors will influence the biological and ecosystem impact of oil pollution. Some hydrocarbons will not be entirely removed from the marine environment by evaporation or degradation. The final residues of degradation may form tar balls which remain floating for up to a year but ultimately sink to the sediment. These are not particularly toxic since they are highly insoluble. Released oil sludges may carpet sediment – with severe impacts on the sediment community, often through physical effects. Prior to the removal of an oil slick by natural processes the adverse effect on marine organisms can be large. The physical properties of oil means that it tends to coat organisms, e.g. sea birds and mammals, and result in their death. The risk of coating lasts as long as a coherent oil slick remains. The length of time the oil slick persists depends on the types of hydrocarbons present in the oil and on physical conditions. For example, the oil from the *Braer* accident off the Shetlands was rapidly dispersed and evaporated because it was a light oil and the weather conditions were bad. Even though 87,000 tonnes of oil were accidentally released to the marine environment very little environmental damage occurred. It appears that intertidal communities are greatly at risk of severe damage – which can last for some years – if oil is washed ashore, partly because of this coating effect. This range of variables makes the impact of oils on marine environments difficult to predict. As with so many other pollutants the specific impact of individual incidents of oil pollution may not be known until long after contamination has occurred.

Techniques to control oil spills are fairly basic, including the use of booms to contain the oil so that it can be removed (e.g. by skimming) or treated. These physical techniques rely on calm weather or they are often inefficient at containing a slick. Treatments include the detergent dispersal of the oil. This is problematic since detergents have proved in the past, e.g. at the *Torrey Canyon* oil tanker accident off the UK coastline, to be more toxic to marine life than the hydrocarbons they are intended to treat. Less toxic dispersants are now available but they still may pose an environmental risk in themselves. Recently techniques to enhance the capacity of micro-organisms to degrade the oil have been used. The addition of nutrients (e.g. nitrogen and phosphates), often limiting in marine environments, to encourage faster degradation of the oil have been used: for example, the oiled beaches in Prince William Sound, Alaska were fertilised after an oil tanker accident.

Pollution may arise as a result of oil production in the North Sea. It is estimated that there are about 150 oil and gas production platforms producing about 100 million tonnes of oil and 40 billion cubic metres of gas each year. The industry employs around 50,000 people in Britain. Pollution may be caused as a by-product of extraction through oil-contaminated muds or through accidental spillage. There have been a number of oil spillages caused by poor tanker construction, insufficient training of the crew and inadequate maintenance of vessels and inadequate action on the part of coastal authorities.

The discharge of oil into a non-territorial water by a UK-registered ship or into UK waters by any ship are criminal offences under sections 1 and 2 of the Prevention of Oil Pollution Act 1971. There are ancillary provisions that apply to harbours under sections 10 and 11 of the 1971 Act. Accidental oil spills may be responded to by the use of comprehensive emergency powers contained in sections 12–15 of the 1971 Act. There are important enforcement provisions given to the Secretary of State (Defra) and delegated powers to make regulations under section 17 of the 1971 Act. These regulations have been strengthened by the Merchant Shipping (Prevention of Pollution) Regulations 1983 (SI No. 1680), the Merchant Shipping (Prevention of Oil Pollution) (Amendment) Regulations 1993 (SI No. 1106) and the Merchant Shipping (Prevention of Oil Pollution Regulations 1996). A variety of international agreements apply to prevent oil pollution and to prescribe action to be taken when such pollution occurs. In 1990 the International Convention on Oil Pollution Preparedness, Response and Cooperation was signed but remains unratified by 15 states. Nevertheless the convention aims to set out a standard of response to combat oil pollution that applies to both ships and offshore installations. There are various reporting procedures and measures to be adopted set out in the convention. Training exercises and detailed response strategies are contained under the convention.

Oil platforms have not been immune from accidents. In 1988 the Piper Alpha disaster resulted in loss of life after fire and explosions aboard an offshore oil and gas platform. Attempts to improve safety standards resulted from the report by Lord Cullen in the inquiry into the disaster (see: The Public Inquiry into the Piper Alpha Disaster, Department of Energy, Cm. 1310 HMSO, 1990). The Offshore Safety Act 1992 was enacted to provide better standards of safety in the industry (also see: Offshore Safety (Protection Against Victimisation) Act 1992).

The Shetland tanker accident in January 1993 prompted the government to introduce a voluntary code of conduct for ships operating around the United Kingdom's coastline. This code was endorsed by the International Maritime Organisation in July 1993. There are a number of statutory requirements under the Merchant Shipping Act 1988 that require owners of ships to take all reasonable steps to ensure that the ship is operated in a safe manner.

Oil exploration is licensed under the Petroleum (Production) Act 1934. The regulation of pipelines is provided by the Petroleum and Submarine Pipelines Act 1975. Authorisation must be obtained from the Secretary of State to operate a system of pipe-lines in 'controlled waters', namely United Kingdom territorial waters and those adjacent to the seas under the Continental Shelf Act 1964. The exploration for hard minerals such as manganese, nickel, cobalt, copper, phosphorous and molybdenum is regulated under the Deep Sea Mining (Temporary Provisions) Act 1981.

Civil liability arising from oil pollution from ships

Civil liability may arise under international law from liability under industry agreements and where relevant under the national law of the state. In the case of international law, Article 235 of the United Nations Convention on the Law of the Sea requires states to ensure that there is prompt and adequate compensation or other relief available in respect of damage caused by pollution of the marine environment. Cooperation between states is a cornerstone of the enforceability of the convention. Forms of compulsory insurance are favoured as the most appropriate international response to oil pollution, although individual states may develop their own system. There is a 1969 International Convention on Civil Liability for

Oil Pollution Damage, which came into force in 1975, to ensure that compulsory insurance would provide adequate redress against shipowners. In the United Kingdom the Merchant Shipping (Oil Pollution) Act 1971 implements the main provisions of the 1969 convention. Amendments to the various protocols of the convention are implemented under Schedule 4 to the Merchant Shipping Act 1988.

Liability may be attributed for the costs of preventative measures and for the costs of any reasonable pollution prevention operations, as a result of any discharges or escapes. There is strict liability for the damage caused by any discharge or the escape of oil. Once an owner has incurred liability under the Act he must set up a compensation fund. The value of the fund is assessed on the tonnage of the vessel and amounts may be paid from the fund for compensation. There is a limit on the amount of compensation payable, set at the amount of the fund. Liability beyond this depends on proving that the escape or discharge was the fault of the owner.

In addition to liability because of the convention or liability agreements, there is common law liability for damage caused by the carriage of harmful substances. This is an area of law that draws on the general principles of civil liability, such as trespass, public and private nuisance, negligence and the rule in *Rylands* v *Fletcher* discussed in previous chapters.

Conclusions

The Marine and Coastal Access Act 2009 is a significant and timely initiative to provide coherent policies and a unified approach to the marine environment. Managing the oceans as a sustainable resource is a challenge that will continue into the next century. Eliminating marine pollution and stopping waste discharges into the sea involves high costs and demands political action. The global nature of the problem means that international law must be engaged as well as the law of the nation state. International law, and this is replicated in national law, makes a distinction between oceans and watercourses. The reality is that land-based pollution provides much of the waste that pollutes marine life. Is there not a case as advocated by Freestone and Salman[17] to incorporate the two systems of managing oceans and managing waterways if the aim is to protect and preserve different ecosystems? Tackling the problem of waste in all its forms and from all sources is a matter of great importance. The disposal of waste is problematic whether on land or at sea. There is an unenviable choice between the costs of land and sea disposal and the relative safety of each. Marine disposal is often less costly but the benefits of a cleaner marine environment must be properly assessed in balancing decisions. Marine pollution must be considered at the global and national levels. It is likely that marine disposal will remain a preferred option to other means of disposal. It may appear to be the best practicable environmental option. The absorptive capacity of the marine environment to sustain current levels of waste disposal is, however, in doubt. Exploiting natural resources will one day demand a higher price than we may fully realise.

---

[17] Freestone and Salman, 'Ocean and freshwater resources' in D. Bodansky, Jutta Brunée and Ellen Hey (eds), *The Oxford Handbook of International Environmental Law* Oxford: Oxford University Press, 2006, p. 360.

Sustainable development in the context of marine and coastal systems is based on a number of supporting principles:

- the use of the best possible scientific information;
- where there is uncertainty and potentially serious risks exists precautionary action may be necessary;
- ecological impacts must be considered particularly where resources are non-renewable or effects may be irreversible;
- cost implications should be brought home directly to the people responsible – the 'polluter pays' principle.

The discussion in this chapter serves to illustrate the considerable uncertainty that surrounds our knowledge about marine ecosystems and the protection of marine organisms. In truth we have hardly started to grapple with the challenge of ensuring the sustainability of our oceans.

Further reading

R.S.K. Barnes and R.N. Hughes, *An Introduction to Marine Ecology* 3rd edition, London: Blackwell Scientific Publications, 1988.

R. Barnes, D. Freestone and D. Ong (eds), *The Law of the Sea: The Role of the Law of the Sea Convention* Leiden: Martinus Nijhoff, 2005.

J.H. Bates, *United Kingdom Marine Pollution Law* Lloyd's of London Press Ltd, 1995.

J.H. Bates and C. Benson, *Marine Environment Law* Lloyd's of London Press Ltd, 1993.

R.B. Clark, *Marine Pollution* Oxford: Clarendon Press, 1989.

K. Clayton and T. O'Riordan, Coastal processes and Management. In D. Bodansky, J. Brunée and E. Hey (eds), *The Oxford Handbook of International Environmental Law* Oxford: OUP, 2006.

W. Douglas, 'Environmental problems and the oceans: the need for international controls' 1 *Environment Law* 149 (1971).

D. Freestone and S.M.A. Salman, 'Ocean and freshwater resources' in D. Bodansky, Jutta Brunee and Ellen Hey (eds), *The Oxford Handbook of International Environmental Law* Oxford: Oxford University Press, 2006.

A. Grant and T. Jickells, 'Marine and estuarine pollution' in T. O'Riordan *Environmental Science for Environmental Management*, Harlow, Essex: Longman, 1995.

W. Howarth, *Water Pollution Law* London: Shaw and Sons, 1988.

S. Marr, *The Precautionary Principle in the Law of the Sea – Modern Decision-Making in International Law* London: London University Press, 2003.

P. Sands, *Principles of International Environmental Law* Cambridge: Cambridge University Press, 2003.

Reports

Cabinet Office, Prime Minister's Strategy Unit, Marine Environment (2004).

Convention on Civil Liability for Oil Pollution Damage 1969.

Defra, *Net Benefits: A Sustainable and Profitable Future for UK fishing* Defra London, 2004.

Defra Policy documents associated with the new Marine and Coastal Access Act 2009.

Royal Commission on Pollution 25th Report Turning the Tide: Addressing the Impacts of Fisheries on the Marine Environment Cm 6392 December, 2004.

United Nations Economic Commission for Europe (UNECE), Policies for Integrated Water Management E/ECE/1084 (1985).

UNEP and GPA *The State of the Marine Environment. Trends and Processes* UNEP/Earthprint, 2006.

The Government's White Paper, Review of Radioactive Waste Management Policy (Cm 2919, HMSO, July 1995).

Visit **http://www.mylawchamber.co.uk/mceldowney** to access key issue checklists and practice exam questions to test yourself on this chapter.

14 Air quality and pollution in an era of climate change

Introduction

The law relating to atmospheric pollution and air quality is the subject of this chapter. The atmosphere provides essential gases for aerobic respiration and photosynthesis and contains a large and important pool of compounds for some biogeochemical cycles, e.g. carbon, nitrogen and oxygen. The balance of gases in the atmosphere supports life as we know it on this planet. Good air quality whether at work or home is essential for human health. A range of medical problems such as asthma and bronchitis are aggravated and possibly induced by poor air quality. Indeed, a recent study has suggested that some childhood asthma may be linked to foetal exposure to traffic emissions.[1] Asthma, in particular, is one of the fastest growing diseases in the United Kingdom. It is estimated that 20 per cent of children may be suffering from this complaint. Not only gaseous pollutants are implicated in having significant health effects, but also particulate matter emitted from traffic and industry. For example, human exposure to particulate matter of different sizes and composition has been implicated in increasing the risk of cardiovascular disease.[2]

Poor air quality can also have an effect on animal and plant life. Long-term effects of poor air quality can change the quality of water and soil. Taken together, these effects can substantially alter ecosystem health. Atmospheric pollution may also damage the fabric of buildings, e.g. through the action of acid rain. Atmospheric pollution is not solely linked to low-level effects but can have significant impacts on the upper atmosphere, for example through ozone depletion. Air pollution also contributes to global warming, with potential for serious and long-term impacts to the environment, agriculture, climate and sea level that are not easily reversed or predicted. In an influential report from the Royal Commission on Pollution,[3] it is estimated that carbon dioxide emissions from road transport in the United Kingdom will increase significantly over the next 25 years unless abatement measures are

---

[1] Perera, F., Tang, W-y, Herbstman, J., Tang, D., Levin, L., Miller, R. and Ho, S-m (2009) Relation of DNA methylation of 5'-CpG Island of $ACSL_3$ to transplacental exposure to airborne polycyclic aromatic hydrocarbons and childhood asthma. *PLoS ONE* **14**.

[2] Polichetti, G., Cocco, S., Spinali, A., Trimarco, V. and Nunziata, A. (2009) 'The effects of particulate matter (PM_{10}, $PM_{2.5}$ and PM_1) on the cardiovascular system'. *Toxicology* Vol. 261, pp. 1–8.

[3] Royal Commission on Environmental Pollution, 18th Report *Transport and the Environment*, 1994, p. 40.

taken. Our economic development at present is far from sustainable. As Kiss and Shelton have explained:

> The introduction of pollutants into the atmosphere creates multiple effects, because the air is essentially a place of transit; gases or particles remain there temporarily and manifest many of their impacts only after returning to the soil, plants, marine waters, lakes or rivers. Poisonous air also directly damages living creatures and objects.[4]

The link between controls over atmospheric emissions and air quality raises difficult issues for industry, transport and electricity generation. It would be wrong, however, to think of air pollution as solely a consequence of the industrial revolution: agriculture is also an important source of emissions. The arrangements intended to control atmospheric pollution involves measures to manage industrial emissions through such mechanisms as integrated pollution prevention and control, and measures that set environmental standards for air quality. The atmosphere is fluid and dynamic and certainly does not recognise boundaries between countries. It is, therefore, important to understand the significant role of both European and national law in protecting air quality and how they must work together. The role of international law is also key in addressing the transboundary and sometimes global nature of atmospheric pollution and in managing its effective control.

LAW IN CONTEXT

Air pollution and human health

There are many examples of the major consequences of atmospheric pollution. In the United Kingdom in the 1950s, smogs in London were due to the combination of domestic coal fires and industrial pollution. It is estimated that up to 8,000 people died as a result of the smog. Traffic fumes trapped at ground level during December 1991 produced excessively high levels of nitrogen dioxide in London. The atmospheric concentration of nitrogen dioxide reached 423 ppb (more than twice the limit) and raised the death rate by 10 per cent, equivalent to 160 extra deaths. The build-up of photochemical smog at ground level continues to be a major problem in urban environments. Rural areas are not immune to air quality problems. Not only do high ozone concentrations occur in periods of warm weather in cities, but they also occur in rural areas. Indeed rural ozone levels can be higher than those in cities. World events have highlighted the potentially acute affect of industrial releases to the atmosphere. The discharge of 30–40 tonnes of methylisocyanate to the air after a disaster at a chemical plant in Bhopal, India in December 1984 resulted in 3,300 deaths and 200,000 injuries, many of them serious (for example, causing blindness). The explosion and fire at the Chernobyl nuclear reactor in 1986 released 50–100 million curies of radioactivity into the atmosphere. The plume of radionuclides (287 million curies of radioisotopes) from the reactor spread over large areas of Eastern and Western Europe 7–10 days after the accident; up to 400 million people were exposed to radiation and agricultural and

➡

[4] A. Kiss and D. Shelton, *Guide to International Environmental Law* Martinus Nijhoff Publishers, 2007, p. 160.

environmental systems were contaminated. Such an incident highlights the fact that atmospheric pollution does not recognise national boundaries. The natural and built environments also suffer substantial consequences from atmospheric pollution. Sulphur dioxide and nitrogen oxides are emitted from power plants, from other industry and from traffic. These gases dissolve in rainwater, producing acid rain which causes substantial environmental harm to freshwater habitats, forests and woodlands through acidification, as well as considerable damage to historic monuments. Acid rain travels across national boundaries in the same way as other types of atmospheric contaminants. Air pollution, then, requires action, not only in the individual state, but also by the European Community and through international law.

In the United Kingdom there has been an increase in the awareness of pollutants after a landmark High Court case (likely to be appealed). The case focused on the impact of contaminants from the clean-up of a redundant steelworks in Corby. A class action, meaning that all the 18 complainants who alleged that there was a credible link between exposure to airborne contaminants and birth defects, took a civil claim against Corby Council for negligence and public nuisance. The birth defects were evidenced by deformed hands or feet. In the High Court in July 2009 it was held that the Council had been extensively negligent.[5] The case is a landmark of its type because of the way science was accepted by the court in evidence. This reinforces the need for a proper priority to be given to air pollution because of the potential harm to human health.

Climate change in an era of economic transformation

The consequences of some types of atmospheric pollution go far beyond national or even regional boundaries and have their impact on a global scale. Thus the production of greenhouse gases, e.g. carbon dioxide and methane that result in climate change, and the production of chlorofluorocarbons and other compounds that deplete the stratospheric ozone layer, can only be successfully controlled at an international level. The magnitude of the threat posed by climate change cannot be overstated. This, together with the uncertainty that surrounds predictions of the speed and extent of warming and sea-level rise, makes long-term strategic planning to reduce the worst impacts very difficult. Even moderate predictions of the effects of climate change on the environment, agriculture, water resources, societies and economies point to a radical change in our world and the way we live. Even so, achieving a political and economic consensus to tackle global gas emission over the past two decades has been slow and has often had poor outcomes. Since this is a global threat, it is important that responses should be achieved through a global consensus. A global response cannot be avoided. This is clearly illustrated by a current problem: although western economies have been slowly addressing reductions in greenhouse emissions through improvements in technology, any reduction in emissions has been more than compensated for by greenhouse gases produced by the new economies of China and India. Thus there is no net reduction across the

[5] ENDS Report 415, August 2009, p. 20.

world: indeed, rather, a rise in emissions. This may have the depressing effect of destabilising economic growth everywhere as the costs of climate change exceed economic growth. There is also an imperative from the perspective of good governance and the rule of law. The grant of economic aid to developing economies is often linked by donor organisations to sustainable development strategies and also to the development of new processes for addressing pollution control. The policy and the operation of a sustainable development strategy for new economic growth is an opportunity to recalibrate responses to climate change. This is costly but in the interests of the global economy and security.

There are a number of distinctive contributions to the debate on climate change. First, there is the science of climate change and, second, the economic analysis that argues on a cost–benefit basis that it is more cost-effective to act now than delay acting in the future. The scientific evidence for climate change is well established but it is still contested by a few scientific groups. Admittedly many more scientists favour the interpretation that global warming and resulting climate change are human-made and stem from greenhouse gas pollutants, primarily CO_2 emissions. So the scientific community are largely united in the claim that scientific evidence exists for climate change. The proof, however, is always subject to interpretation and there are some who doubt that the scientific evidence is conclusive. This leaves open some room for manoeuvre for policy-makers and more than anything else this has caused delay and a slower response to the problem than many would see as desirable. There is also some difficulty in calculating the timescale. Predicting climate change is difficult and assumptions that climate change will build incrementally may not necessarily prove accurate. Some recent evidence suggests that there is a tipping point where climate change may speed up and at a certain critical point may be difficult or impossible to reverse. The reliance on science and scientific evidence lies at the heart of many policy and legal decisions on the environment. The absence of scientific consensus for many years and the difficulty of predicting the future pathway of climate change have all contributed to uncertainty and slowed our response.

The second source of analysis of climate change is drawn from an economic scrutiny of the costs of its likely impacts. The familiar lack of consensus among scientists about the evidence for climate change is also apparent among economists about the effects of climate change on the economy of the world. The United Kingdom Treasury commissioned a Report on the *Economics of Climate Change* in 2006 by Stern, and this has led the way to outline the case for immediate action rather than any postponement or delay.

The scientific analysis of climate change

Science provides an important way to understand the causes of global warming and its impact. Global warming is one of the biggest environmental problems facing the world today. Greenhouse gases in the atmosphere are transparent to short-wave radiation from the sun but absorb long-wave terrestrial radiation which would otherwise escape to space. The energy trapped within the atmosphere acts to warm it and long-wave radiation is re-radiated to the earth from the atmosphere, warming the surface. The main gases that contribute to the greenhouse effect are carbon dioxide, methane, nitrous oxide and various chlorofluorocarbons (CFCs). Low-level ozone and water vapour can also contribute to the effect. This, of course, is a natural process and is essential for maintaining the earth's temperature above freezing. Concern arises because the concentrations of greenhouse gases have been increasing in recent years. This is primarily due to humans' activities, in particular the burning of fossil fuels for energy production and deforestation by burning to clear land for agriculture. Forest burning not only adds directly to the carbon dioxide in the atmosphere, but also removes an important sink for CO_2: that is, the loss of trees reduces CO_2 use in photosynthesis and incorporation in plant material.

Predictions have been made that if the production of greenhouse gases goes unchecked, then CO_2 levels will be double those prior to the industrial revolution by the 2030s. This would result in a global temperature rise of 2–5 °C. There is a variety of models predicting the impact of this on changes in temperature and rainfall patterns with latitude and region. For example, several of the models indicate that important areas of grain production in North America and Russia will become warmer and drier, significantly reducing the yield in these important areas of food production. Much of Africa is also likely to become substantially drier, with a significant reduction in agricultural production. In contrast, some predictions suggest that the UK will become wetter. Recent models indicate that the UK and northern Europe are likely to become colder, owing to changes in the Gulf Stream induced by global warming. Regional changes in precipitation, snow and glacier melt and evapotranspiration – the process by which water is lost to the atmosphere from land, fresh and sea water and from plants – have important implications for river flow and water resources. This will affect a variety of activities, including agriculture, groundwater levels, drinking water availability and river management (flooding, erosion and sedimentation). Not only will there be changes in the pattern of precipitation and temperature across the globe, but also the frequency and intensity of storms will be changed, probably increasing. Climate change will also result in habitat loss and there will be a substantial reduction in biodiversity, with as many as 40 per cent of species on the earth becoming extinct.

Global warming will also cause a rise in sea level. This is for two reasons. First, melting ice on land will contribute to sea-level rise and, second, thermal warming of surface water will increase the volume of sea water. The predictions for the increase in sea level vary considerably. For example, values for sea-level rise predicted for the year 2100 range from 20–165 cm to 3.5 m. The higher predictions for sea-level rise would see as many as 200 million people permanently displaced from coastal regions. Taking the lower prediction, this still means that sea level will be 20 to 100 cm higher than at present by 2030. Even this increase in sea level means that low-lying land is at risk from flooding. The Caribbean and Pacific coral islands, major tropical and subtropical river deltas such as the Nile delta of Egypt, the Ganges–Brahmaputra–Meghna delta of Bangladesh and the Mississippi delta of the USA are all at risk of inundation under even this moderate scenario. The Netherlands is also vulnerable unless coastal defences are significantly raised and reinforced, as are low-lying areas in the UK. Many of these areas are densely populated and have high agricultural or industrial productivity. The economic burden of strengthening existing coastal defences or developing new ones will be immense. The sea-level changes will be gradual, but storms will undoubtedly result in periodic flooding of low-lying and vulnerable areas, inevitably leading to loss of life and considerable agricultural and commercial damage. It should not be forgotten that sea-level rises will also have an impact on coastal habitats. There will be changes in the pattern of coastal erosion and ingress by sea water into terrestrial habitats and groundwater, an important source of drinking water in many countries. Vulnerable coastal habitats such as marshes and swamps will be damaged, with the probability of species loss. Even the productivity, diversity and density of sea-water species are likely to be affected by warmer seas.

LAW IN CONTEXT

Direct effects of raised levels of atmospheric CO_2

Our concern about greenhouse gas emissions has largely focused on climate change but this is not the only effect that might be significant and have unforeseen consequences. There are two impacts that are worthy of mention here. Increased concentrations of carbon dioxide in the atmosphere have a direct effect on crop productivity. This varies with the biochemical pathway by which plants fix carbon dioxide during photosynthesis. Plants designated C3 plants – primarily temperate species such as wheat, rye, rice, barley, legumes, most grasses and forest species – increase their photosynthetic efficiency with carbon dioxide concentration (to a maximum of 1000 ppm carbon dioxide) increasing yields by 10–50 per cent. In contrast, C4 plants – e.g. corn, sugar cane, maize, millet, sorghum – are unlikely to show any net benefit from higher concentrations of carbon dioxide in the atmosphere. Increased carbon dioxide concentrations in the atmosphere may raise the efficiency of water use in plants through a reduction of transpiration through stomata (inducing partial closure of stomata), thus increasing their resistance to water stress. These effects have not been demonstrated beyond experimental systems. The balance between the effect of climate change on agricultural yields and any improvements in yield that may accrue from raised CO_2 is unknown. The impact of climate change and elevated CO_2 on non-agricultural plants in terrestrial ecosystems is also difficult to predict, but may be large.

The second is ocean acidification. Increased uptake of CO_2 from the atmosphere by surface waters of oceans has already reduced the overall pH of oceans from 8.16 to 8.05, and the process is continuing. Ocean acidification is likely to have profound effects on ocean biodiversity and productivity. Among the most vulnerable organisms to acidification are the tropical and subtropical corals, and even cold water corals may be affected. Corals are some of the most productive and diverse habitats on earth. In addition other calcifying organisms, i.e. organisms that have calcareous material as part of their body, crucially including a variety of phytoplankton and zooplankton, will be severely affected. Any reduction in phytoplankton and zooplankton populations will have a significant impact on fish and other sea animals, since they are a major food source for these organisms. The impact on the diversity and productivity of our oceans is unpredictable but will probably be considerable and long-lived.

We are, then, embarking on a global experiment the outcome of which is difficult to predict. There is no doubt, even if CO_2 emissions are extensively limited over the next few years, that we are committed to global climate change and to other perhaps unforeseen consequences. The issue at hand is whether we can limit the extent of the damage; we can no longer avoid it, but we may be able to go some way to reducing impacts to manageable levels. Clearly, no one country can address such a global problem. It is being addressed at an international level through international conventions.

Responses to climate change

There have been a number of responses to climate change that have been confronted by the problem of the application of national or regional solutions to a global phenomenon. Moreover, as we have seen, the scientific evidence for human-made global warming through greenhouse gas emission has often been strongly contested until relatively recently. This has partly been because of the high economic and political costs involved in tackling climate change. Until recently the market economy and its expansion has been driven forward as a mechanism for continued growth and social development. The era of 'light touch' regulation facilitated economic and global expansion of many financial and industrial markets. Such economic forces are difficult to withstand and many countries, including the USA, were largely in denial that the problems of climate change existed. The economic reality has now changed as has governments' response to managing greenhouse gas emissions, which is beginning to evolve beyond denial. That is not to say that action had not been taken previously, but there were some highly polluting countries, e.g. USA and China, not fully engaged in developing solutions. To date, the climate change debate has been characterised by the need for local, transboundary and global solutions. Given the global nature of the problem, a key response is found in the regulation of atmospheric pollution under international law. This is critical to successfully controlling climate change and indeed other global and regional effects that arise from atmospheric pollution.

International law responses to transboundary pollution

International law has sought to recognise that gaseous pollutants, including greenhouse gas emissions, have transboundary effects. The Trail Smelter case set out the principles on gaseous emissions under customary international law. In brief, the facts of the case related to the external effects of a Canadian mining company who caused pollution but the impact was felt on an adjoining logging company situated ten miles away across the border in the United States of America.

CASE STUDY

Facts of transboundary pollution case: *United States* v *Canada* 3 RIAA 1907 (1941), The Trail Smelter case

A Canadian mining company operated a zinc and lead smelter. The company was situated on the Columbia River at Trail in British Columbia. The emissions from the company contained large quantifies of sulphur dioxide that came from 400-foot chimneys at the smelter. The impact of the emissions damaged wheat and oats, trees used for logging and various pastures that were 10 miles south of the smelter in the US State of Washington. The dispute was taken up by the US government against the Canadian government and went through two arbitrations. The International Joint Commission set up by the United States and Canada awarded $428,000 compensation to the United States, based on damage to forests and pastures, and also required additional monitoring of the smelter.

The essential finding is that no state has the right to use or permit the use of its territory so as to cause fumes or injury on the territory of another. It is clear that the finding is subject to a number of caveats:

- The difficulties of proving cause and effect. This must satisfy the test of providing 'clear and convincing evidence'. In the Trail Smelter case there was a clear link between the smelter and the alleged harm. In many industrial situations tracing harm is more difficult although modern technology has come into practical effect. The latest monitoring techniques can trace most gaseous pollutants back to their source. Europe has had a Programme for the Monitoring and Evaluation of Long-Range Transmission of Air Pollutants in Europe (EMEP) since 1977.

- Difficulties in assessing the balance between states. Every country exports and imports pollution at some level and this makes it difficult to balance any resultant harm between states. Assessing the balance is further complicated by the regional nature of some problems, making the transboundary issue of secondary importance.

- The principle of compensating for transboundary harm is based on present harm rather than a projected assessment of future harm. Prevention and standard-setting are intertwined but it is difficult to provide a satisfactory basis to assess potential future harm and act accordingly.

- The assessment of serious harm is difficult especially if the areas affected are wild and natural habitats that have no monetary or economic value attached to them. The ownership of land or wilderness may also pose a difficulty.

- Legal and juridical controls are subject to proof, evidence and quantum of damages. This may limit the effective use of legal rules, especially when the parties that conduct the dispute are mainly national governments. This gives rise to a political overlay that influences what is to be disputed and what is not. Many countries may not engage with the process as there may be reluctance to accept the nature of the problem.

- Private companies or organisations may also seek redress in national courts. This suggests that the legal rules have a part to play in transboundary pollution. Their use is, of course, tied to their effectiveness. The use of national courts, however, needs re-examination in the context of the numerous treaties that negotiate how transboundary disputes are best examined.

The Trail Smelter case is a significant decision in terms of providing the opportunity for legal redress under international law. Its limits reflect market forces, political indecision, and a variety of evidential issues associated with legal evidence and proof.

■ The 1979 Geneva Convention on Long-Range Transboundary Air Pollution

This convention was agreed as part of the UN Economic Commission for Europe (UNECE). The aim was to create a set of framework controls over air pollution that had their impact across quite distant countries. The 1979 Convention came into force in 1983 and has a number of characteristics:

- no liability is provided throughout its provisions;
- the aim of the convention is to act in a preventative way;

- the main effect of the treaty was to engage countries in mutual agreements and cooperation. These involved European states as well as Canada and the USA.

The convention highlights how air pollution and its remediation is at its heart a political question and requires the political system of each country to engage with the problem. The treaty reflects this reality through its approach – flexible and intended to develop cooperation between states. Setting limits on air pollution is a primary responsibility of the convention, which attempts to base control on the use of the best technology available to reduce, prevent and contain pollution. This is a sensible approach, as strategies aimed at prevention and reduction are linked to economic costs and feasibility. The need for transparency over the quantification of such costs is a major step in setting incentives to prevent pollution in the first place. The convention provides a good foundation on which to build, as it engages with stakeholders and creates a generally agreed statement of intent on which to build future strategies. Its critics see this as weak and ineffective because of the lack of sanctions and penalties and in the generality of its scope. This misses the point of the convention, which is intended to lead to further research, create general collaboration and exchange information. Consequently there are five protocols that relate to different aspects of air pollution that have been created under the convention since 1979.

Sulphur dioxide reduction

The first protocol on the reduction of sulphur dioxide, a key gas in the formation of acid rain (see above) was agreed in 1985[6] and later replaced in 1994 by a new potocol in Oslo with a revised set of targets.[7] The 1985 Protocol was intended to offer a 30 per cent flat-rate reduction in sulphur dioxide emissions. The UK and another three high polluting states declined to sign and objected to the flat-rate reduction. They also claimed the timetable was unrealistic. The 1994 Protocol adopted a different approach and set targets for each country with a more realistic aim of a 20 per cent reduction based on 1980 levels by 2010.

The operation of the new protocols has seen a reduction of sulphur dioxide emissions, arising in particular from the use of gas-fuelled electricity generation. The use of gas for electricity generation has an uncertain future in the UK, as there are doubts about the stability of gas supplies, given the increasing dependence on importing gas from abroad. The government has decided to opt for new generation nuclear- and coal-powered generation stations. Coal burning may increase sulphur dioxide emissions and it will be interesting to see how the UK continues to control emissions.

Nitrous dioxide

A second protocol under the Geneva Convention applies to nitrous oxide, and was concluded in 1988 in Sofia. This protocol follows the practice of setting levels of emissions that were to be reached by 1994. Further protocols have followed covering organic pollutants and heavy metals.[8]

[6] Protocol to LRTAP on the Reduction of Sulphur Emissions Helsinki, 8 July 1985 27 ILM 707 (1988).
[7] Protocol to LRTAP on Further Reduction of Sulphur Emissions Oslo, 14 June 1994 33 ILM 540 (1994).
[8] Protocols on Long-Range Transboundary Air Pollution Concerning the Control of Emissions of Volatile Organic Compounds or their Transboundary Fluxes, Geneva, 18 November 1991 31 ILM 568 (1992); Protocol to LRTP on Heavy Metals Aarhus, 24 June 1998; Protocol to LRTP on Persistent Organic Pollutants, Aarhus 24 June 1998; Protocol to LRTP to Abate Acidification, Euthrophication and Ground level Ozone Gothenburg, 30 November 1999.

■ The Vienna Convention for the Protection of the Ozone Layer 1985

In 1985 in Vienna, the Vienna Convention for the Protection of the Ozone Layer was concluded. This took place after protracted and detailed negotiations that lasted four years. The model adopted was to follow the Geneva Convention and build on consensus and cooperation. Its aims were to create a focused framework that would support protection of the ozone layer.

LAW IN CONTEXT

Ozone layer

The ozone layer in the stratosphere, some 50 km above the earth's surface, is produced from oxygen by the energy in sunlight. In normal conditions stratospheric ozone is in a dynamic equilibrium, continually produced and destroyed by natural chemical reactions. A number of polluting gases, however, also catalyse the destruction of ozone. Particularly problematic in this respect are the chlorofluorocarbons (CFCs), which have a variety of applications, such as refrigerants and flame retardants. The latter are present in common products, such as furniture, e.g. sofas. These compounds contain carbon, chlorine, fluorine and hydrogen. Sunlight in the upper atmosphere breaks off chlorine atoms from CFCs and it is these that react with ozone, catalysing its conversion back to oxygen and resulting in the depletion of the ozone layer. The number of chlorine atoms in CFCs and the longevity of the CFC are used to calculate the Ozone Depleting Potential (ODP) of the CFC. The ODP is compared against that of CFC-11, the commonest type of CFC. In fact the impact of a CFC on ozone is not only related to its ODP but also dependent on the quantity produced. Ozone depletion has been particularly marked in the southern hemisphere, with a 'hole' in the ozone layer developing in the spring each year and extending from Antarctica to parts of Australia. In the northern hemisphere the effect has been a general thinning of the ozone layer. Stratospheric ozone depletion results in increased levels of ultraviolet radiation reaching earth. This substantially raises the risk of human skin cancers and eye cataracts in both animals and humans. Consequences for plants are uncertain, but there is the beginning of evidence that amphibians may be severely affected.

In recognition of the problems caused by CFCs, they were originally substituted by hydrogen fluorocarbons (HCFCs), which were thought to be less polluting. It is now clear that these molecules also have ozone-depleting potential and in turn they are being phased out. CFCs and HCFCs are good examples of pollutants that may have more than one serious impact. Both CFCs and HCFCs are greenhouse gases and are responsible for up to 10 per cent of global warming. The Montreal Protocol has resulted in the elimination of CFCs, halons, methyl chloroform and carbon tetrachloride, and the phased reduction of HCFC production. As a consequence, there are the first signs that the ozone layer is beginning to recover or, at least, not being depleted as rapidly as before. It will, however, take many more decades before the ozone layer recovers fully.

The Vienna Convention broke new ground in adopting the precautionary principle and in the assumption that adverse effects of gaseous pollutants included greenhouse warming. The Vienna Convention then gave rise, two years later, to the Montreal Protocol and this added various measures such as a ban on CFCs and related substances. Funds were agreed for the compensation needed to meet the demands set by the protocol. Account was also taken of the needs of poorer nations in terms of implementing the ban. The Montreal Protocol was far-sighted as, at the time of the Montreal Protocol in 1987, there was considerable scientific uncertainty surrounding global warming and climate change. The predictions of the rate and extent of ozone depletion were also uncertain and, in fact, the severity of the problem was greater than initially thought so that more robust action has been implemented. There are now international treaty arrangements attached to the Montreal Protocol. This has resulted in 2007 of the banning of up to 96 chemicals with Ozone Depleting Potential (see Law in context, above).

It is difficult to asses whether the Montreal Protocol has achieved what it intended. Kiss and Shelton suggest that the protocol has achieved some success:

> International efforts to protect the ozone layer have had substantial impact. By 1995, global production of the most significant ozone-depleted substances, the CFCs, was down 76% from the peak of 1988. Several countries and regions advanced beyond the agreements. The EU announced a phase-out of HCFCs by 2015, five years before it is legally required to do so.[9]

Challenges and aspirations

The threat posed by climate change goes beyond traditional debates about protecting and enhancing the environment. Our economic development is entwined with the production of greenhouse gases from industrial, agricultural, transport and domestic sources. New technologies and products will inevitably also contribute to the burden of greenhouse gases. This much is now realised and generally accepted. The problem is, of course, global, highly complex and technical. The chain of causation is large and permeates every part of human activities, from power generation to animal husbandry; from crop production, logging and deforestation for agricultural production to manufacturing; and finally to waste disposal. The life cycle of every product, i.e. its manufacture, use and disposal, has a carbon footprint and contributes to global warming. The impacts of global warming are well rehearsed and cover changes in natural habitats and impacts on human health and welfare that are fully examined in the Stern Review in terms of their economic impact.[10] Food and water shortages owing to changes in weather conditions show how delicate and vulnerable humans' survival on the planet really is. Climate change will inevitably hold severe consequences for food production and the availability of water. Other impacts may be less well known: for example, it is likely that certain human diseases, such as malaria, may spread. Indeed, this effect will not be limited to human diseases but will extend to animal and plant diseases, not only in agricultural systems but also in natural habitats. These impacts will feed into economies through higher costs. There will be additional expenses of higher energy costs brought by necessary changes in energy generation; higher insurance costs because of the increased frequency of storms; and higher food bills because of crop failures and food shortages.

---

[9] A. Kiss and D. Shelton, *Guide to International Environmental Law* Martinus Nijhoff Publishers, 2007, p. 169.
[10] N. Stern, *Stern Review on the Economics of Climate Change* HM Treasury, 2007.

It is clear that climate change is not a legal problem alone but a problem that crosses socio-economic boundaries and goes beyond legal controls. Important political choices that will have a crucial impact on the well-being of future generations have to be made and acted on.

The steps taken to directly address the problem of climate change began in 1988. The Framework Convention on Climate Change was established by the World Meteorological Organization (WMO) and the United Nations Environmental Panel through the creation of an Intergovernmental Panel on Climate Change (IPCC) in 1988. The First Report of the IPCC in 1990 provided an early assessment of the probable causes and effects of climate change and was soon followed up by the 1992 Rio Conference where the UN Framework Convention on Climate Change was agreed. Over 50 countries agreed and ratified the convention, which came into force in March 1994. The United Kingdom and the EU were included in the agreement which marked a step in the direction of accepting the need for global action to address climate change. The convention was a 'mapping exercise' that set the foundations for building a future environmental strategy to counter climate change. There was also acceptance that while there was a common interest in global solutions there had to be recognition of regional differences, especially related to social and economic development. A framework of principles and objectives has been settled under the convention to stabilise greenhouse gases while allowing sustainable development. There are also principles of cooperation and for the development of an international economic system. There is little doubt that Rio has set the direction for the future consideration of global issues, which does not use enforcement but rather builds on the strategies of compromise, consensus and cooperation. The main weakness of Rio has undoubtedly been the lack of enforceable norms, namely legally applied principles. This, however, should not obscure the fact that included in the toolbox of devices to foster sustainable development and counter climate change under the convention is the idea of setting specific emission targets, with the theoretical possibility of returning emissions to those of 1990. There is also a separation of responsibilities between developing and developed countries with the general commitments set according to the economic and social burdens of each country.

Judging the Rio agreement solely on the basis of lack of enforcement overlooks the very real progress made under the convention. While it may have left freedom for countries to adapt at their own pace, it also insured recognition of climate change and its potential significance for the future.

The Kyoto Protocol

The Kyoto Protocol came about in 1997 and was put into force in 2005. Its main achievement was to take forward from the Rio agreement the process of setting of specific targets for greenhouse gases. The United States found the negotiations very demanding, since there was a general agreement by the majority that the targets should be enforceable and forward-looking. After prolonged and difficult discussions a number of targets were agreed relating to various greenhouse gases. These were:

- carbon dioxide
- nitrous oxide
- hydroflurocarbons

- perflurocarbons
- methane
- ground-level ozone.

On average the Kyoto Protocol required a 5 per cent reduction on 1990 levels of greenhouse gases set out in a timetable from 2008 to 2013. The Rio agreement had insisted on a form of differentiation between countries reflecting different economic circumstances. The Kyoto Protocol takes this approach in the sharing of responsibilities. This means that countries may cooperate and combine their emissions for the purposes of meeting the protocol. A number of articles reflect this:

- *Article 4 – Aggregating Emissions.* Two or more parties may aggregate their emissions, provided that within their group of countries the overall limit assigned to that group has not been exceeded. This permits individual countries to exceed their limits set by the quota, provided they do not exceed the combined limit.
- *Article 6 – Joint Implementation.* Credit support may be granted to reduce green house emissions. Examples include support for energy efficiency or the transfer of clean technology.
- *Articles 4 and 17.* This is intended to enable countries with significant surplus emissions reduction to sell their surplus to other countries or create a deficit which can form a stockpile. Such a stockpile might be used to meet any future excess or if there are future reductions in targets.
- *Article 12.* As various developing countries do not fall under the requirements of reduction targets there was a need to provide incentives. Those countries that form Annex 1 countries where targets are required receive credits for helping developing countries use clean technologies that meet certified emission reductions. Carbon trading is an attempt across all sectors to reduce overall carbon emissions.

The Kyoto Protocol also includes various devices to generate carbon sinks, a way to remove carbon from the atmosphere and store it in non-gaseous form. Simply explained, this means a credit for every tonne of carbon that is stored through trees or forest management schemes. The credit allows payments to offset the high costs of carbon emissions. There is no exact science in the calculation of the amounts saved but estimates may be used to offset carbon targets. Since 2006, there has been a Compliance Committee for the Kyoto Protocol. This provides some enforcement of the protocol and monitors problems with compliance. In addition, there is a Facilitative Branch designed to give advice and assistance to the parties.

It must be remembered that the Kyoto Protocol breaks new ground in addressing issues that go to the heart of sustainable development in a way that confronts market forces intended to deliver growth and development. This is not easy. The United Nations Secretariat is aware of how international carbon emissions markets are susceptible to manipulation by the vested interests of countries. Carbon allowances are difficult to operate and compliance is measured when comparing the emissions to the allowances granted. There are real economic and political challenges in achieving conformity. The failure of the United States to be a party to the Kyoto Protocol has had a major impact on the working of the protocol and has considerably weakened its effectiveness. The regulation of the Kyoto Protocol leaves much to be desired.

The second meeting of the parties to the United Nations Framework Convention on Climate Change took place in Bali in Indonesia in December, 2007. A major change in the global emissions since Kyoto is that China has jumped ahead of the USA to become the largest polluter; consequently this has to be factored into the working of the protocol. The reluctance and objections from the United States, however, remained an obstacle until relatively recently. The role of the USA under President Obama, who has acknowledged the significance of climate change, is expected to be far more constructive and to engage more fully with the development and implementation of future targets on carbon emissions. The new negotiations mean that focus is being put on tackling carbon emissions through scientific development. Innovative designs of new technologies for carbon capture have produced encouraging results. Existing protocols on marine dumping have been amended to accommodate new ways of dumping carbon in storage areas under the sea. This should, however, be viewed with some caution. It would be wrong to expect new technologies to be the sole contributor to the control of greenhouse gas emissions; ultimately there will have to be unavoidable changes in the way we all live. It is not surprising that the European Union has become active in providing an answer to climate change through their role as a party to international convention.

European and UK responses to climate change through emissions trading

One of the important impacts of Kyoto is to encourage cooperation among countries. Consequently the EU has ratified the convention and the protocol. The EU has responded through world-wide initiatives, including the Vienna Convention on the Protection of the Ozone layer (see above). Regulation 2037/2000/EC is the EU ban on substances that deplete the ozone layer.

The EU solution is to aggregate reductions in greenhouse gases to 8 per cent of the 1990 levels by 2008–12. There is an Emissions Trading Directive (2003/87/EC) and an allocation of targets to be met among some of the most polluting states. The EU countries have developed an allocation that is part of a European Climate Change Programme, begun in 2000 and revised in 2005. This has resulted in a large number of directives that address the key elements of implementing cleaner energy, more efficient use of energy and the use of alternative fuels, including biofuels.[11]

The European emissions-trading system

Since the EU had expanded to 27 countries by 2007 the operation of an EU Emissions Trading System (ETS) has become crucial. The system is found in Directive 2003/87/EC consolidated 2009/29/EC and applies to all six of the greenhouse gases controlled under the Kyoto Protocol (see above). There are a vast number of installations from oil refineries to

---

[11] Directive on an Emissions Trading Scheme 2003/87/EC and reporting and monitoring obligations 2004/156/EC repealed by 2007/589/EC. Joint implementation and clean development mechanisms credits under the Emissions Trading Scheme 2004/101/EC. Directive on EU greenhouse gas emissions and Kyoto Protocol Decision 280/2004 and implemented 2005/166/EC. Directive promoting cogeneration of heat and electricity 2004/8/EC. Directive in the promotion of renewable energy 2001/77/EC. Directive on biofuels for transport 2003/30/EC. Directive on the energy performance of buildings 2002/91/EC and a revised Directive on energy and efficiency and energy services 2006/32/EC.

steelworks affected by the directive. This is likely to increase in the coming years as more processes are incorporated. The elements of ETS are as follows:

- Installations subject to the directive are covered by a permit that is itself subject to conditions, inspection and monitoring systems.

- The permit falls under Integrated Pollution Prevention and Control IPPC arrangements and to date priority has been given to CO_2.

- Each member state has an allocated allowance based on the overall strategic plan. The National Allocation Plan is detailed and contains reference to the installations covered, and entitlements.

- The system of trading is based around the principles that installations that are below their allocated level may trade their allowance with those that exceed their allocation. There is a trading period and set rules on the limits of its operation.

- An installation that fails to meet requirements and is unable to pay for an allowance is liable to a fine for each excess tonne of CO_2 emitted.

The United Kingdom has adopted the arrangements under the Greenhouse Gas Emissions Trading Scheme Regulations 2005. The implementation of the trading scheme consists of a number of phases: Phase 1 between 1 January 2005 and 31 December 2007; Phase II from 1 January 2008 to 31 December 2012; and Phase III between 2013 and 2020.

The scheme has had many problems. The first period from 2005 to 2007 was marked by legal challenges and disputes.[12] The emissions target was fairly modest. It was based on individual member state caps and set as an EU cap of 6,542 m.t. CO_2 (m.t. is a metric ton or 1,000 kg). The outcome was that this cap was easily met, with only four member states exceeding their allocations – Italy, Spain, Slovenia and the United Kingdom. In the United Kingdom the allocation was 245 m.t. CO_2, which amounted to an 8 per cent reduction in emissions. The scheme works in individual member states on the basis of a National Allocation Plan linked to a trading scheme. The National Allocation Plan is drawn up by each member state and allowances are apportioned to each industrial installation. Industry is consulted and the final plan has to be agreed with the commission. The Trading Scheme allows installations that will meet their targets to trade their emissions allowance with installations that may exceed their targets. The allowances are underpinned by fines for installations that exceed their allowances. The details are set out in the Greenhouse Gas Emissions Trading Scheme Regulations 2005, as amended. The strategy adopted by many member states was to protect their heavy CO_2 installations by allocating excess allowances. In the United Kingdom coal-fired generation installations received this form of protection through the use of historic emissions levels to allocate allowances. Member states under Phase I were allowed to auction 5 per cent of their national allocation. The United Kingdom in common with many other member states did not auction any allowances. As an inevitable consequence of this type of action by member states, the trading scheme did not work very efficiently. Effectively, member states distorted the market by allocating excess allowances to protect their highly polluting installations. There was a great deal of price volatility in the trading scheme and there were unforeseen fluctuations in price caused by external factors, such as a warmer winter resulting in less demand for electricity generation. In the United

---

[12] See: Case T-178/05 *United Kingdom* v *Commission* [2006] Env LR 26.

Kingdom there are 900 sites participating in the scheme at present. This accounts for about 50 per cent of UK CO_2 emissions.

Phase II of the scheme began on 1 January 2008 and will end in December 2012. There is a revised EU-wide cap that is 10 per cent below the cap set in Phase I. The total cap of the United Kingdom is 246 m.t. CO_2 annually. There is an increase in the number of installations and this time only the power sector has been allocated allowances to allow the continuation of electricity generation. The United Kingdom can buy allowances from other participants in the EU member states. The amount of allowances open to auction is 7 per cent of the total. The Operation of Phase II is intended to be tighter and more efficient than Phase I.

In reviewing the scheme, the Environmental Audit Committee of the House of Commons concluded that:[13]

- the national caps across the EU were too unambitious;

- the UK method of allocating allowances was unsatisfactory;

- the 10 per cent limit set on auctioning allowances under Phase II was too restrictive and the UK should have chosen more than 7 per cent of allowances to be open to auction;

- The UK limit on the use of project credits generated by emissions reduction projects outside the EU was set too high.

Assessing the scheme is difficult as the aim is to reduce CO_2 emissions in a cost-effective and efficient way. The use of trading mechanisms is in theory intended to ensure cost-effective incentives that favour low-carbon or carbon-neutral installations. Emissions trading emanates from the Kyoto Protocol but it is also directed at valuable investment by developing countries in green technologies that foster low CO_2 emissions. Reducing the CO_2 emissions in this way is intended to meet Kyoto standards. The National Audit Office note how difficult it is to evaluate the scheme:

> Assessing the impact of the Scheme by reference to the overall cap set and outturn performance is insufficient, as it fails to take account of the range of economic factors and other policy instruments which may affect companies' operational and investment decisions and resulting performance.[14]

Assessing the success of the scheme after it has been operational is difficult, as very often the forecasts for emission reductions were made on the assumption that the status quo would continue rather than there would be any radical change. The manipulation of the market had considerable consequences. Thus the emissions after Phase I were significantly below the EU cap of 6,542 m.t. CO_2 coming in at 6,093 m.t. CO_2. This is still an increase before Phase 1. It is unclear if the current arrangements under Phase II will bring in any real drop in emissions. The first data only became available late in 2009. Phase III of the trading scheme will operate from 2013 to 2020. There is ongoing consultation from November 2006 on the scheme with a revised directive ratified by the European Union Parliament on 17 December 2008.[15] This was intended to strengthen the EU's negotiation at the Copenhagen meeting in late 2009 (considered in more detail below).

---

[13] House of Commons Environmental Audit Committee (2007), *The EU Emissions Trading Scheme: Lessons for the Future. Second Report of the Session 2006–07 HC 70.*
[14] NAO, European Union Emissions Trading Scheme London: NAO, March 2009, para. 10.
[15] Directive 2008/101/EC amending Directive 2003/87/EC.

Air pollution and air quality

■ EU responses to air pollution

The EU reaction to air pollution problems also illustrate the need to address international developments. Essentially, key changes in the EUs response to air pollution took place from the mid-1980s with the EC's Sixth Environmental Action Programme. The fact that air quality and health were interrelated was identified in this programme, together with the acknowledgment that existing standards would be unlikely to meet safe environmental health levels. Unacceptable risks to health set the main focus of the EU strategy, and environmental health objectives were also embedded in the Clean Air for Europe Programme, which set the scene for technical and policy objectives to be combined. The outcome of these developments was a new Air Quality Directive in 2005.[16]

There are a number of strands to EU strategy to improve air quality. Primarily these are either to target specific areas (e.g. industrial, transport) for attention and set emissions controls, or to adopt product standards and identify dangerous pollutants for specific control.[17] There are various framework directives that address air quality and Clean Air for Europe,[18] which is likely to result in a new directive in 2009/10. The key elements of the framework directive are setting specific levels for various emissions[19] and also ensuring that there is adequate monitoring and public availability of information at local authority levels. The United Kingdom's Environment Agency is central to the UK's ability to meet EU air quality obligations. The agency provides an overarching support for local government as well as monitoring implementation strategies.

One innovative policy was introduced in 2001 under the National Emissions Ceilings Directive 2001/81/EC: this sets upper limits on member states emissions and obliges member states to draw up action programmes on air quality. The United Kingdom adopted the EU requirements under the National Emission Ceiling Regulations 2002. Another innovation is the adoption in the EU of the Large Combustion Plants Directive 2001/80/EC for large industrial works. The directive stipulates emissions levels for sulphur dioxide, nitrogen oxide and ammonia. This is relevant to large industrial power stations as well as refineries and steelworks. There are also various directives to ensure that process standards are met under the Best Available Technology (BAT) system.[20] Perhaps the area where the most noticeable

---

[16] COM (2005) 447.

[17] Directive 1994/63/EC on the Control of Volatile Organic Compounds (VOC); Directive 1996/61/EC concerning integrated pollution, prevention and control (IPPC) providing best available techniques; Directive 1996/62/EC on ambient air quality assessment and management; Directive 1998/69/EC providing measures to be taken against air pollution from vehicle emissions; Directive 1999/13/EC in the limitation of emissions of VOCs due to the use of organic solvents in certain prescribed activities and installations; Directive 1999/32/EC relating to the reduction of the sulphur content of certain liquefied fuels; Directive 2000/76/EC on waste incineration; Directive 2001/80/EC on the limitations on emissions from certain pollutants from large combustion plants; Directive 2001/81/EC on national emission ceilings for certain atmospheric pollutants.

[18] Directive 96/62/EC.

[19] NOx, S02, Pb and PM10 are covered in Directive 99/30/EC and benzene and carbon monoxide Directive 2000/69/EC; ozone Directive 2002/03/EC and arsenic, cadmium, mercury, nickel, polycyclic aromatic hydrocarbons Directive 2004/107/EC see Consolidation Directive 2008/50/EC.

[20] IPPC Directive 96/61/EC.

changes have been achieved is on vehicle emissions, which have been generally well controlled.[21] Even so there is a continuing need to reduce air pollution and improve fuel economy. There are proposals to improve on the current levels of transport emissions and develop strategies for environmentally friendly motor vehicles.

■ The United Kingdom's air quality strategy and response to atmospheric pollution

The United Kingdom responses to air quality have largely been reactive. Smoke control, a legacy of the nineteenth century had created clean air legislation in the 1960s and 1970s. The move from coal fires to central heating was accompanied by schemes to enforce clean air in cities and towns. Strategic air policy came under the Environment Act 1995. The Act addressed future air quality through setting standards and measuring pollution levels. The link between good health and good air quality was well established. The rise in pollution during the summer months increased the outbreaks of asthma and related diseases. The industrial base of the United Kingdom's economy was also being changed. The production of electricity from nuclear and gas-fired generation stations marked the move away from coal. The development of new technology and the technological revolution of IT and the growth in financial services coincided with a shift from old industries, often highly polluting and labour-intensive, to new industries with cleaner technology. Monitoring air pollution in major cities and towns provided useful data on which to build an air quality strategy. In 1994 the Royal Commission on Environmental Pollution published an influential report[22] recognising that transport was a major contributor to air pollution. Techniques to mitigate the impact of road and air transport systems were considered essential to minimise the damaging effects of pollution.

Since then there have been a number of steps in the direction of improving air quality. This is in line with Kyoto and also the various European Union directives on Air Quality. Since 1995 under section 80 of the Environment Act 1995, the Secretary of State is under a duty to maintain and improve on a National Air Quality Strategy. The current version was produced in 2007 and provides obligations on local authorities to undertake reviews, monitoring and take action in their own particular locality. There are the detailed Air Quality (England) Regulations 2000 that have been amended and currently there are the Air Quality Standards Regulations 2007. These regulations provide standards laid down in EU law for acceptable limits and also set targets. There are general duties to monitor and apply standards.

It is important to note that pre-existing air quality strategies and objectives may be found as part of the powers contained in various pieces of legislation. The Clean Air Act 1993 gives local authorities powers to declare a smoke control area and this includes the ability to set emissions standards from chimneys. This is a long-standing response to the smog and pollution of the early industrial revolution.

---

[21] Directive 70/220/EEC and also 88/77/EEC. There are a number of directives relevant to the quality of build, the roadworthiness of motor vehicles and sulphur content of petrol and diesel, Directive 98/70/EC.

[22] Eighteenth Report of the Royal Commission on Pollution: *Transport and the Environment* Cm. 2674 (October 1994).

Legislative powers also include traffic management and planning powers. The Transport Act 2000 provides another set of air quality rules as part of local transport plans. The aim is for each local authority to draw up its own policies for the promotion of public transport, for charging road users and for the use of park-and-ride schemes as part of the Road Traffic Reduction Act 1997; there are duties on local authorities to set regulations on traffic schemes, including pedestrianised areas and traffic reduction measures. The latter is contained in Highways (Traffic Calming) Regulations 1999 which allow narrow entrances into built-up areas. There are wide powers under land-use planning, including Planning Policy Guidance 13 on Transport and also Planning Policy Statement 6 on Planning and Town Centres. Finally, there are various controls set on motor vehicles and their emissions. The Motor Vehicles (Type Approval) (Great Britain) Regulations 1994 set out standards for motor vehicles and their use. The Road Vehicle (Construction and Use) (Amendment) Regulations 2003 include standards for exhausts, including catalytic converters, unleaded petrol and emissions levels that are checked through MOT systems of quality assurance for each motor vehicle in use. There is also the possibility of monitoring vehicle emissions through random tests and road-side checks. Carbon monoxide and smoke exhaust must be at a certain specified standard.

As a result of a private member's Bill, the Climate Change and Sustainable Energy Act 2006 was passed, addressing the need for energy efficiency in buildings, the operation of micro Combined Heat and Power (CHP) systems and also micro-generation of electricity. There are also plans to introduce into every household in the United Kingdom energy meters, with the aim of encouraging savings. There is a raft of building regulations associated with the Home Information Packs Scheme (HIPS) designed to provide potential buyers with advice on the energy efficiency of houses. The shortfalls in any energy-efficiency measures are intended to be made up by sellers who are encouraged to insulate and obtain good energy ratings. Energy companies are under a legal obligation to pay a fair price for the purchase of electricity from micro-generation systems. Heat loss from buildings is now subject to higher thermal performance values than previously. There is a Government Standard Assessment Procedure (SAP) rating that is a compulsory part of building regulations and part of the process of evaluating and assessing thermal energy ratings for every dwelling. Taken together, the legislation may help improve the energy efficiency of buildings, which will in turn reduce greenhouse gas emissions produced during electricity generation and the production of heat.

Addressing the need for fuel-efficient vehicles and air pollution reduction in towns and cities will continue to challenge policy-makers for the rest of the twenty-first century. A major challenge as indicated above is the issue of energy resources. The United Kingdom's response is contained in the Government White Paper: *Meeting the Energy Challenge: A White Paper on Nuclear Power*.[23] The government's strategy is to build new nuclear power stations that will enable it to meet the competitive energy market and protect the United Kingdom from any market volatility in gas supplies. Linked to this strategy are continued commitments to renewable energy, the adoption of new technology for coal including, Carbon Capture and Storage strategies. The aim is to ensure that there is an adequate energy mix (Table 14.1) that will also address the CO_2 emission targets of a 26 to 32 per cent cut by 2020 reaching 60 per cent by 2050. Achieving such targets will require extensive adjustments in meeting energy requirements at a time when there is a need to build around 30 to 35 GW of new electricity-generating capacity.

[23] Cm 7296 (January, 2008) Department for Business, Enterprise and Regulatory Reform.

Table 14.1 UK targets for renewable energy

UK component	Renewable energy target	Date
Energy	15%	2020
Transport	5.75% energy content for diesel and petrol	31 December 2010
	10% from road and rail transport	2020
Electricity	30% renewable sources	2013–2014
	20% renewable	2020

Source: NAO Report, *Renewable Energy: Options for Scrutiny* (July 2008). See also the Government's Renewable Energy Strategy, which implements the Renewable Energy Directive (2009/28/EC).

In reality the measures described above cannot alone address climate change; a more holistic approach is needed. This issue is addressed in the Climate Change Act 2008.

The Climate Change Act 2008

The Climate Change Act 2008 takes air standards strategy into a new era. The focus on climate change is an important shift of emphasis in terms of air quality and CO_2 emissions. It provides legally binding duties on carbon budgeting in line with the post-Kyoto era. This gives the United Kingdom a statutory framework within which to build responses to climate change. The Act looks past the failures of Kyoto to make a meaningful impact among the major industrial countries. The best way to view the Climate Change Act 2008 is as a scoping exercise providing an arena for government policy to be developed as the details of future international agreements emerge, but also as part of independent government policy-making. The 2008 Act builds on the Stern Review[24] where a leading economist calculated that an annual commitment of 1 per cent of GDP might be required in order implement an adequate response to controlling and mitigating the effect of climate change. This is in contrast to inaction which was calculated by Stern as likely to cost from 5 to 20 per cent of GDP, depending on the severity of the impacts. The likelihood of inaction appears to be lower, as major countries including the United States have begun to accept the need for action to combat climate change. There has been a renewed interest in scientific data that is beginning to resolve uncertainties and develop improved models of the possible outcomes of global warming. There are some predictions that the global climate might reach a tipping point from which recovery will be very difficult. Doubts remain over the reliablity of the data on climate change.

The Climate Change Act 2008 adopts an economic approach to climate change. By making climate change central to the UK whole economy, it builds responses that go beyond the narrow confines of a single Whitehall department, or that are relegated to the general umbrella of 'the environment' but rather into strategies that transverse government departments and policies. The 2008 Act sets targets to be reached by the year 2020 and by 2050. The aim is to produce regular mitigation strategies setting out proposals and policies linked to timescales and budgets with a reporting loop back to Parliament. There is a newly established Committee on Climate Change with a new central government department, the Department of Energy and Climate Change. The new department combines energy and climate change into a single department consistent with the climate change strategy. The Committee on Climate Change is required to advise on carbon budget levels. Controversially included are international aviation and shipping, but although this had been originally excluded, it is now

---

[24] N. Stern, *Economic Impacts of Climate Change* London: Cabinet Office, 2006.

included as part of future strategy. For the interim the budgeting may take account of aviation and shipping as part of conforming to international practice. The Act makes important connections between energy and economic, social and fiscal considerations as part of a more holistic approach to climate change than in the past. There are suggestions that perhaps environmental taxes may be used to secure compliance with the targets but this is left to the government's discretion. Remaining within the Act is the basic tool kit set after Kyoto, namely setting caps and allowing a trade in emissions. There is an overall objective of an 80 per cent reduction of greenhouse gas emissions set against the 1990 baseline over the period of the Act. Realistically this takes account of the changes in industrial development in Britain since 1990 and the movement of large polluting industries to other countries. Some scientific views are that temperature changes are set to rise notwithstanding the targets set.

The Climate Change Act 2008 is in line with the European Union Emissions Trading Scheme and Kyoto Protocols. It creates a large United Kingdom carbon account that is based around emissions levels and greenhouse gas levels. The newly created Committee on Climate Change is there to advise and assist the process which is largely in the discretion of the Secretary of State. This includes laying before Parliament:

- an annual statement of UK emissions and details of the carbon account;
- five-yearly statements setting out the budgetary periods, containing details of the carbon account;
- and in 2050 a final statement setting out the economic record and carbon account.

There is also a five-yearly reporting duty that requires the UK to assess the risks from climate change for the United Kingdom. There is a requirement to provide supplementary reports, setting out objectives and policies and how this impacts on government strategy and programmes.

The role of the Committee on Climate Change is advisory. Its reports must be considered by the government and new regulations must be first taken to the committee for review and advice. The committee also has a role, although somewhat indirectly, in the risk assessment and impact reports. Each of the statements, i.e. the annual, five-yearly and final statements, also require the committee's input. Despite these inputs from the committee, the political controls are very much at the apex of the decision-making process. This limits the extent of the committee's actual powers, which may be regarded as influential but not determinative of issues. Setting duties on the government to consult with the Committee on Climate Change, however, may be more important than at first considered. The committee has a duty to report to Parliament and as a result Parliament is given a very wide remit. Through parliamentary debate it would be possible for Parliament to make a considerable contribution to the government's climate change strategy and the system of compliance. This may also have the consequence of reducing the potential for judicial review. Parliamentary oversight over policy-making is seen as preferable to judicial control over administrative decision-making.[25] Implicit in the Climate Change Act 2008 is a suggestion of pragmatism based on parliamentary dialogue. The Act is not explicit in the acceptance of 'cap and trade', namely the Kyoto principle of allowing the market to lead the discipline of applying a carbon cap. The Act does, however, recognise the emissions-trading arrangements as part of the EU system. There is no mention of the auctioning of allowances or the prices to be paid. This is set to continue under Treasury control and within the annual Finance Bill.

[25] See: Mark Stallworthy, 'Legislating against climate change: a UK perspective on a Sisyphean challenge' (2009) 73(3) *Modern Law Review* 412–62.

The Climate Change Act 2008 will need to be evaluated over the next few years. It is remarkable in adopting an economic-based approach to controlling greenhouse gas emissions and insisting on transparency, accountability and effectiveness as the pillars of the legislation. There are many unanswered questions as to whether or not the Act will be effective, particularly in the light of Parliament's central role and government's duties to report. One of the criteria to judge the legislation is its educative value, and the creation of the Committee on Climate Change may provide a new dimension to the way science and advice informs policy-making in this important issue of how to predict and prevent climate change.

There are also signs that new initiatives to promote green energy carry electoral advantages. One recent example is the Green Energy (Definition and Promotion) Act 2009. The Act's aims are to define and promote 'green energy' and support micro-generation strategies as part of the planning system. Under a broader scope for Permitted Development Rights, allowing alterations to houses without a formal planning application to be made, it is possible to install a domestic wind turbine or an air source heat pump without the formalities of having to seek planning permission.[26] Another example is the Fuel Poverty Bill, building on the framework set out in the Warm Homes and Energy Conservation Act 2000. The Bill sought to identify and remediate housing vulnerable to poor energy conservation by 2010. Then, by 2016, extend to the remaining households the requirement of raising the energy conservation, linked to programmes to improve energy efficiency and reduce high fuel costs.[27]

Conclusions

The next steps: Copenhagen 2009 and beyond

The Kyoto period set to meet targets expires in 2012 and further action is essential beyond this period. Since Kyoto, there have been further conferences and discussions. In December 2007, the Bali Conference included China, a fast-developing nation responsible for the largest emission of greenhouse emissions, largely because of the use of coal-fired power stations. The United States continued to prove reluctant to contribute to negotiations but there was a large measure of agreement that 'deep cuts' are required in global emissions. These cuts are focused on developed countries, but also include required action by developing countries. The Bali Conference failed to specify the nature of the cuts and left the position unclear until the next climate conference in 2009.

The need for a more substantial climate change agreement arises from scientific concerns that climate change is not abating but is speeding up. There is increasing evidence that variations in extreme weather conditions are more widespread than in the past and that the presence of greenhouse gases is a more critical factor influencing climate than was previously assumed. There is a pressing need for a new agreement. There is also a perception that the need for action is more urgent than at first thought. There was a *Fourth Assessment Report of the Intergovernmental Panel on Climate Change* in 2007, which reflected a growing scientific consensus that the impact of climate change and acidification on the marine ecosystem will be more rapid and far-reaching than previously assumed. Setting targets for 2050 at 50 per cent reduction now appears to be inadequate and a more realistic target is at 80 per cent.

[26] House of Commons Library Research Paper 09/41 6 May 2009 *Green Energy (Definition and Promotion) Bill 2008–9.*

[27] House of Commons Library Research Paper 09/2517 March 2009 *Fuel Poverty Bill Bill 11 of 2008–09.*

There are widespread economic and industrial consequences, not least for future developing countries. In fact, the global recession and the economic downturn probably offers a good opportunity as the industrial base is downsizing, leading to reductions in carbon emissions.

There were a number of key aims set for the UN Summit at Copenhagen in December 2009. These included:

- a new global agreement to prevent climate change and it was hoped that this would be inclusive of the United States;

- the Carbon Trading mechanism agreed at Kyoto might be improved and timetabling should include financial aid for poorer countries to meet the demands of a new climate change commitment.

The creation of a new protocol on climate change is most likely to build on the Kyoto arrangements. The use of carbon trading, based on trading allowances might also be considered in the context of the effective use of taxation. A carbon tax might in the end become more attractive than carbon trading. It is simpler to operate and brings transparency in its collection and application. There is also a great opportunity through International Monetary Fund (IMF) or World Bank loans to make loan conditions apply that give incentives to carbon reduction. The debate over the best strategy is likely to spill beyond 2010 before an agreement is finally reached.[28] In the end the Copenhagen conference was unsuccessful in extending Kyoto targets and ended in some disarray. There was, however, a brief Copenhagen Accord agreed including the United States and China as signatories. This recognises that the increases in global temperature should be limited to 2°C.

Further reading

D. Freestone and C. Streck (eds) *Legal Aspects of Implementing the Kyoto Protocol Mechanisms: Making Kyoto Work* Oxford: Oxford University Press, 2005.

A. Gore, *An Inconvenient Truth* Emmaus, PA: Rodale, 2006.

D. Helm, *Climate Change Policy* Oxford: Oxford University Press, 2005.

G. Monbiot, *Heat: How to Stop the Planet from Burning* Cambridge MA: South End Press, 2007.

N. Stern, Review (2006) The Economics of Climate Change London: HM 1979 Treasury, 2006.

T. Williamson and L. Murley (eds), *The Clean Air Revolution 1952–2052* Brighton London: NSCA, 2003.

---

[28] 'The Rough Guide to Copenhagen's Risks' ENDS Report 410, March 2009, pp. 24–32.

Visit **http://www.mylawchamber.co.uk/mceldowney** to access key issue checklists and practice exam questions to test yourself on this chapter.

15 Noise and control

Introduction

Almost every aspect of modern-day living brings us into contact with noise: so much so that it is now a well-recognised pollutant. Excess noise may not only cause considerable discomfit but in excess can damage health. In recent years noise from industry, road transport and airplanes has significantly increased especially in congested urban areas. Historically noise pollution was primarily linked to the workplace either in traditional heavy industries such as steel, shipbuilding or in light manufacturing. Noise at work has been controlled by strict health and safety legislation but this falls outside the remit of this book. It has now been recognised that domestic noise is also a chronic problem and can be regarded as an environmental issue. Domestic noise attracts a significant number of complaints each year.[1] In the mid-1990s there were equal numbers of complaints about industrial and domestic noise. Since 2000 there has been a step change with the number of domestic complaints about noise far exceeding those about industrial noise. In our everyday life, high street traffic or living near large urban conurbations brings an acute awareness of noise as an irritation and annoyance. The problem has significant impacts beyond this, however, with prolonged exposure to noise potentially causing severe hearing damage. Moreover, there is a body of medical evidence that also recognises that noise is harmful to human health in other ways. Two recent government reports published by the Department of Environment, Food and Rural Affairs (Defra) and the Department of Health (DoH) concluded that many aspects of general ill health may be related to noise, including cardiovascular effects, sleep disturbance and the cognitive development of children.[2] There is even evidence of behavioural changes in birds because of noise pollution. In urban areas some common songbirds are singing during the relative quiet of the night rather than competing with the noise of morning.

Control of noise is, undoubtedly, an important aspect of environmental protection and coincides with a public-health approach to noise. Environmental health officers are the recipients of complaints about noise. Local control of noise through the statutory nuisance powers of local authorities has been the historical approach to noise and its abatement. The control of noise pollution has also involved standard-setting through the definition of permissible noise levels. This includes standards for processes or manufacturing as well as

[1] See: The Chartered Institute for Environmental Health for statistics.
[2] ENDS Report, 9 July 2009.

finished products. There is less tolerance of noise than in the past, clearly illustrated by the increasing number of complaints, and a growing trend in favour of approaching noise regulation through prevention and cure. This proactive approach involves noise mapping and establishing quiet zones.

In this chapter the legal remedies and controls on noise will be examined. How is noise measured? What techniques can be used to reduce noise and minimise the risk to health? Limits on noise are also set to protect the environment and ensure that human activity is compatible with enjoyment of the environment. Setting such noise standards for products or particular activities also requires effective enforcement measures. Airport and transport noise are also considerable problems and we will consider their control through the use of Noise Action Plans. Linked to noise pollution is greater public awareness, and litigation in this area has become more common than in the past.[3]

Measuring noise and creating Noise Action Plans

Regulating noise has shifted perceptibly from the nineteenth-century approach of statutory nuisance to the modern approach of setting standards on products, in the workplace as part of health and safety, and providing protection against noisy neighbours. Human stress is often related to noise from transport, with the twenty-first century witnessing a marked increase in noise from high-speed railways, road traffic and aircraft movements. There are other significant sources of noise that come with economic activity, including large construction projects and manufacturing processes. Complaints about noise are often only a small part of the overall picture, as many complaints are never made officially. Defining and measuring noise is, however, somewhat complicated (see Law in context, below).

LAW IN CONTEXT

Measuring and defining noise

There is no satisfactory overriding legal definition of noise. Directive 2002/49/EC defines noise as 'unwanted or harmful outdoor sound created by human activities, including noise emitted by means of transport, road traffic, rail traffic and noise from sites of industrial activity'. This excludes many common sources of domestic noise such as neighbour noise, noise at the workplace, noise inside transport or military operations. While this is unsatisfactory, the law does have an important role. Instead of providing a workable definition of noise, the law has focused on the means to control noise and has recognised difficulties of measuring noise. In 1963 the Wilson Committee made a useful contribution when it defined noise as 'sound which is undesired by the recipient' (see: Noise, Cmnd 2056, 1963).

---

[3] A good example is the action taken by a group of Councils to oppose the expansion of Heathrow through the use of a Judicial Review in August 2009. See ENDS Report 395, December 2007, pp. 30–3, and Greenpeace UK, 6 August 2009.

Table 15.1 Noise levels and different sounds

Decibels (db)	Sound
0	Threshold of hearing
10	Leaves rustling
30	Quiet bedroom at night
40	Average living room
50	Living room with distant traffic noise
60	Busy office
70	Conversational speech
75	Major road with heavy traffic
88	Heavy lorry on busy road
90 +	Potential loss of hearing from prolonged exposure
100	House near airport
125	Jet aircraft taking off
140	Threshold of pain

Sources: Adapted from C.S. Kerse, *The Law Relating to Noise* London: Oyez, 1975. D. Van Wynsberghe, C.R. Noback and R. Carola, *Human Anatomy and Physiology* Third edition, New York: McGraw Hill 1995.

Noise is measured in decibels (db) (Table 15.1), but objective measurements of noise do not equate with the nuisance noise may cause. It is commonly agreed that the polluting nature of noise has both objective and subjective elements. The objective element provides some basic criteria for the measurement of noise. The subjective element (see: *Gaunt* v *Fynney* (1872) 8 Ch App 8) implied in noise pollution is that the noise is unwanted. This unwanted element makes legal definition difficult. Relevant considerations as to whether noise is unwanted may include questions of excess use or whether the use is reasonable or necessary. We experience a variety of noise levels in everyday life. The human ear is surprisingly sensitive to noise. It can detect approximately a one-decibel change in sound intensity. Prolonged exposure to noise above 90 db may cause damage to hearing, though the level where harm to human health may occur may vary according to the duration of exposure and the sensitivity of the individual.

There have been attempts to limit noise levels for various activities through international agreements and the European Community. International law, however, has only a limited role in noise pollution but there are a number of relevant international conventions. The Working Environment (Air Pollution, Noise and Vibration) Convention 1977 deals with noise and working conditions and was developed as part of the work of the International Labour Organisation. There are also a number of conventions on aircraft noise, including the International Civil Aviation Convention of 1947. Emissions standards arise from the 1979 Convention on Long-Range Transboundary Air Pollution and Noise Pollution may form one of the quality standards near residential property. The Stockholm Action Plan in 1972 acknowledged the significance of noise as part of its overarching but non-binding plan. Significantly noise is claimed as an important part of human rights' jurisprudence of the European Convention on Human Rights. It is considered as pertinent to the protection of human rights involving privacy and the right to a peaceful enjoyment of home life.[4] Several important cases have claimed this right although much of the detail of any protection is devolved to the member state's regulatory system.

The EU has made considerable progress in developing strategies to address noise. The Directive on Environmental Noise (Directive 2002/49/EC), which has been incorporated into UK law in the Environmental Noise (England) Regulations 2006 (SI 2006/2238) (and amended by SI 2008/375), makes significant progress in noise control. It includes a requirement for strategic noise maps, as well as detailed regulations for airports. Every five years, at least, noise plans should be revised and there should be a reassessment of noise levels when a major development occurs. The 2006 regulations have recently been supplemented by the Environmental Noise (England) (Amendment) Regulations 2009 (SI 2009/1610). The first noise mapping exercise was completed at the end of 2007. The next initiative is to extend this assessment and manage environmental noise in the light of the mapping exercises, the so called END initiative. The aims are to determine our exposure to environmental noise from road traffic, aircraft and industry and to provide better public information. Importantly, the initiative is focused on setting identifiable quiet areas between 30 September 2007 and 30 September 2012. This also involves mechanisms for reviewing and revising quiet areas. There is also guidance on the monitoring and recording of noise levels. Future strategy will involve updating and consolidating END through consultation and negotiations.

The next step is to draft Noise Action Plans and Defra has an ongoing consultation process as part of the preparation for and implementation of the plans. The first round to 2007 has already been completed for agglomerations. There are two remaining draft action plans:

- the second outside the agglomerations is for major roads;
- the third applies to major railways.

It is noticeable that none of the above plans applies to airports. There are specific regulations that apply to airports and these identify the competent authorities and the relevant airport operators. Many airport operators have already published their plans, linked to a consultation process. In recent years, there have been heightened concerns that aircraft noise at night is incompatible with human rights and this has given rise to a number of test cases.

Noise can be regarded as part of our subjective sense of what may be considered enjoyable and pleasurable or disagreeable and objectionable. There is a balance to be struck between acceptable and unacceptable noise levels, which may vary with individual and inevitably involves compromises. For example, the environmental case for wind turbine farms as a means of producing sustainable and environmentally friendly energy has to be offset by the objections over unacceptable levels of noise in farming communities and wilderness areas. The tensions between acceptable and unacceptable noise levels will undoubtedly continue.

It is possible to set out a working definition of noise generally derived from EU law (Directive 2002/49/EC) (see discussion in Law in context, p. 341):

> Environmental noise is defined as unwanted or harmful outdoor sound created by human activities, including noise emitted by means of transport, road, rail or air traffic, and from sites of industrial activity.

---

[4] Examples include: *Hatton* v *United Kingdom* Application 36022/97 (2003) 37 EHRR 611.

The EU strategy for controlling noise pollution has four main objectives:

- Monitoring by member states of the environmental problems associated with noise. This is intended to involve the development of strategic noise maps for major centres of noise such as roads, railways, airports. Daytime and night-time noise are to be addressed separately.

- Informing and consulting the public. Following the principles of the Aarhus Convention, the idea is to provide noise measurements to the public together with information on how to mitigate noise and cope with its effects. This may also involve planning control that sets standards for noise reduction measures in building construction. This is a practical way of limiting the effects of noise by ensuring that buildings are well insulated and conform to best practice in building design. The Building Regulations 1991 (SI 1991/2768) apply here and set norms for the construction of flats, semi-detached houses or terraced properties.

- Addressing local noise. This objective is intended to assist local authorities in drawing up action plans to reduce noise and to maintain good quality noise controls whenever possible.

- Development of a long-term EU strategy and setting objectives for the future, in particular to ensure that noise reduction is addressed at source. The development of strategy objectives is intended to help in the preparation of legislation.

Currently the 2002 Directive 2002/30/EC provides for limits or reductions in the noise-related activities at airports within the EU. The United Kingdom Noise Act 1996 has been revised and updated to take account of this EU development, which is consistent with a Neighbourhood Noise Strategy 2008 (see below).

The best way to understand the law on noise is to consider controls under two broad categories. Public law control includes the role of local authorities, while private law remedies allow the citizen to pursue remedies in the courts. There is a greater awareness of noise than in the past and consequently the Human Rights Act 1998 has also become important. Noise complaints formed a number of legal challenges arising from a human rights perspective on noise.

Public law controls and noise pollution

The haphazard development of the law in this area indicates the difficulty in legally defining noise pollution and providing a coherent strategy for control. Initially, local authority by-laws and local Acts of Parliament provided a miscellaneous number of rules and regulations on noise. The first major legislative attempt to bring order to this confusion was the Noise Abatement Act 1960. The Act codified existing local authority powers. Part III of the Control of Pollution Act 1974 introduced further changes to the law, with further consolidation by the Environmental Protection Act 1990 (hereinafter the EPA). There also have been some amendments to the Control of Pollution Act 1974 and the Environment Protection Act 1990 from the Noise and Statutory Nuisance Act 1993 that covers construction sites and work-related noise. The Noise Act 1996, which does not extend to Scotland, provides a more specific approach to the control of noise at night. The approach includes detection, prevention and remedies through abatement or warning notices.

It is also noteworthy that noise is a relevant issue under planning law. Some planning authorities have included the control of noise when drawing up their statutory plans. The use and imposition of planning conditions, which used to apply under section 106 of the Town and Country Planning Act 1990 but has now been amended and replaced by section 46 of the Planning and Compulsory Purchase Act 2004, may lessen the necessity to impose the stricter noise condition found in the EPA. The use of development control for many large-scale developments may require close liaison between environmental health, planning, transport and local authorities. The first wide-ranging guide to planning and noise was issued in October 1994 by the Department of Environment (see the still in force PPG24 Planning and Noise HMSO, 1994). The aims of the guidance are to provide planners and developers alongside local communities with some degree of certainty about the particular type of developments that are acceptable or those in which special measure may be required to mitigate the impact of noise.[5] The guidance provides an important contribution to the debate about noise by setting out noise bands to assist local authorities in determining applications within residential areas. There have been unsuccessful attempts by the Royal Commission on Environmental Pollution[6] to introduce a system of acceptable day and night noise. PPG24 is an attempt at compromise through planning policy, although there is a gradual shift to replace PPG with Planning Policy Statements (PPSs).

Nuisance

The use of a remedy in nuisance[7] may be valuable in tackling environmental noise problems. The most common and useful form of nuisance is a statutory nuisance, which may provide a local authority with sufficient powers to serve an abatement notice. This is a useful remedy and allows enforcement powers to be combined with the remedy. Statutory nuisances have a legislative history that can be traced back through the Control of Pollution Act 1974, the Public Health Act 1936 and the Nuisance Removal and Disease Prevention Act 1846. There are a number of statutory nuisances relevant to noise. Section 79(1)(g) and (6) of the EPA 1990 make it a statutory nuisance to emit noise from premises that is prejudicial to health or a nuisance. Normally the power to take action to stop the nuisance is given to the local authority, but there are specific procedures to be used when action is taken by an aggrieved citizen. The local authority has powers to serve a notice on the owner or occupier of premises to stop noise from the premises (section 80 of the EPA). This is subject to an appeal procedure. An aggrieved citizen may make a complaint about nuisance caused by noise to the magistrates under section 82 of the EPA. This procedure may result in an abatement notice if the magistrates are satisfied that the nuisance exists or, though temporarily abated, is likely to recur on the same premises. This procedure is available against the person causing the noise or the occupier or owner of the premises.

---

[5] See: *R v Kennet District Council, ex parte Somerfield Property Co. Ltd* [1999] JPL 361.

[6] See: 18th Report of the Royal Commission on Environmental Pollution; *Transport and the Environment* Cm 2674 (1994).

[7] B.S. Markesinis, 'Negligence, nuisance and affirmative duties of action' (1989) 105 LQR 104. For an historical oversight see: Brenner, 'Nuisance law and the industrial revolution' 3 (1974) *Journal LS* 403; J.P.S. McLaren, 'The common law nuisance actions and the environmental battle – well-tempered swords or broken reeds?' 10 (1972) *Osgoode Hall LJ* 505.

A further example of a statutory nuisance is provided in section 2 of the Noise and Statutory Nuisance Act 1993, which amends section 79 of the EPA. Under this section it is a statutory nuisance for noise to be emitted from or be caused by a vehicle, machinery or equipment in a street. There are also powers to allow a local authority officer to enter, open or remove a vehicle or machinery or equipment in a street to abate the nuisance arising from street noise. The 1993 Act also extends powers of the local authority by empowering local authorities to impose charges on premises for the recovery of expenses incurred in abating nuisance under Part III of the EPA. The Environment Act 1995 provides a further extension of the framework for nuisance control under Part III of the Environmental Protection Act 1990 in England and Wales to Scotland.

One difficulty, often caused by changes in this area of law, is that recent legislation may overturn regulations currently in operation to provide abatement notices or other forms of relief to aggrieved citizens suffering noise pollution. The House of Lords has recently accepted that enforcement notices made under legislation prior to the EPA 1990 will remain valid even though the EPA repealed many of the statutory powers under earlier legislation.[8]

Noise abatement zones

The statutory arrangements for noise abatement zones are in Part III of the Control of Pollution Act 1974. The general guidance is from the EC Environmental Noise Directive. This has been supplemented by Part III of the Environmental Protection Act 1990 and the Noise and Statutory Nuisance Act 1993. This provides local authorities with the powers to designate an area or part of an area as a noise abatement zone. There are inspection powers whereby the local authority is under a clear legal duty to inspect an area from time to time (section 57(b) of the Control of Pollution Act 1974). There are comprehensive powers for procedures to draw up noise abatement zones under the Noise and Statutory Nuisance Act 1993 and the Noise Act 1996. These include serving notice on each owner advertising the noise abatement zone. There are also procedures for taking objections, which include receiving written objections within six weeks and proposing the order after considering all the relevant objections. The implications of making a noise abatement order are that the local authority is required to measure noise levels from premises within the area designated in the order (see the Noise and Statutory Nuisance Act 1993). Records of measurements must be kept (see below) and copies of such records forwarded to the occupier or owner of premises. There is an appeal system (see the Statutory Nuisance (Appeals) Regulations 1990, amended by the Statutory Nuisance (Appeals) Regulations 1995 SI 1995/2644) to the Secretary of State. The main sanction for exceeding noise levels and breaching a noise abatement zone order is a court order. It is also a criminal offence.

The designation of a noise abatement zone requires the local authority to measure the noise levels and record these details in a Noise Level Register. This register must contain various details for each of the premises within the zone. Details of the address, particulars of noise and the dates on which each entry are made must be recorded.

Local authorities have a number of other powers available to them in respect of noise. They can make noise level determinations for new buildings. The Local Government Act 2000 requires local authorities to address how to improve the economic, social and environmental

---

[8] *Aitken* v *South Hams District Council* [1994] 3 All ER 400.

well-being of their area and, as part of this responsibility, to address noise pollution. This includes the use of community agendas together with setting noise strategies. Local authorities have a number of powers to support the strategy. They may make use of a noise abatement notice on individual premises. Permitted noise levels must be recorded in the Noise Level Register, which sets out the acceptable noise level for the building. There are procedures for appeal and the serving of notice on the occupier or owner of premises. Local authorities may also make a noise reduction notice which may specify the time of day, particular days and the duration of the required noise reduction. There are appeal procedures in respect of such a notice.

Noise controls over transport, aircraft and airports

There are a variety of special provisions introduced to deal with specific noise problems. For example, construction site noise (see sections 60 and 61 of the Control of Pollution Act 1974) provides for the regulation of construction site noise and the serving of a notice subject to the correct procedures. Traffic noise falls under section 1 of the Road Traffic Regulation Act 1984. Controls may be placed on traffic flows and there are powers for the restriction and regulation of heavy vehicles. For example, access to town centres or routes through built-up areas or where there are schools and children playing may be restricted. Vehicle noise is regulated under the Road Traffic Act 1988 and the Road Vehicles (Construction and Use) Regulations 1986 (SI No. 1078) and also Motor Vehicles (EC Type Approval) Regulations 1998 (SI 1998/2051). It is an offence to exceed the limits on noise prescribed by the regulations. Under the Noise and Statutory Nuisance Act 1993 (discussed below), it is a statutory nuisance to emit a noise from machinery, vehicle or equipment in a street. The Highways Noise Payments and Moveable Homes (England) Regulations 2000 (SI 2000/2887) provide that residents living in mobile homes subjected to excessive traffic noise, including road works, may be entitled to compensation from local authorities.

Aircraft noise is the subject of specific regulation. Section 76 of the Civil Aviation Act 1982 exempts actions for trespass or nuisance in respect of the flight of aircraft over property. This exemption takes account of a number of factors such as the height of the aircraft, weather conditions and the ordinary circumstances of air travel (such as authorised flight paths) and that the aircraft is not flown in a dangerous manner. Also exempt under the Air Navigation Order (see Air Navigation Order SI 1989/2004), made under the Civil Aviation Act 1982, are the conditions under which noise and vibration may be caused by aircraft on aerodromes. In the case of aircraft taking off and landing, regulations are provided under the Air Navigation (General) Regulations 1981 (SI No. 1981/57). The aircraft must satisfy certain safety requirements to come within the exemption of liability.

Outside the exemption there may be liability arising from the operation of aircraft. For example, section 76(2) of the Civil Aviation Act 1982 provides strict liability where items fall from the aircraft when taking off or landing or while in flight. This may also cover damage caused by sonic boom. Aircraft engine noise is regulated by the Air Navigation (Noise Certification) Order 1990 (SI No. 1514). This order takes account of various EC directives (see Directive 80/51/EEC and 83/206/EEC). Airport noise is controlled by a mixture of regulatory powers. The Secretary of State and the Civil Aviation Authority have various powers under the Civil Aviation Act 1982. These powers are of a miscellaneous variety in terms of the proper management of airports. Section 63 of the Airports Act 1986 provides powers to make by-laws for the control of aircraft operations and limits on the noise and vibration coming from the airport. The licensing functions of the Civil Aviation Authority may also include aerodromes. Licensing air operators also provides a means to achieve standards of performance (see the Air Navigation (Aeroplane and Aeroplane Engine Emissions of Unburned Hydrocarbons) Order SI 1988/1994). A general duty exists to minimise, as far as it may be practicable, the effects on the environment of noise, vibration, atmospheric pollution or any other cause attributable to the civil aviation use of aircraft (see section 68(3) of the Civil Aviation Act 1982).

Noise and airports form a discrete area of the law and engender strong feelings that have resulted in human rights challenges over night flights (see Case study, below). Any proposed expansion of airports or increased numbers of flights is always controversial, with problems from noise pollution often a key issue.

CASE STUDY

Night flights and human rights

In *Hatton* v *United Kindom* (2003) the residents living near Heathrow airport complained about night flights. Their action in the European Court of Human Rights argued under Article 8 of the European Convention on Human Rights that disturbed nights of sleep and other inconvenience breached their right to respect for their home and family life. Previously claims in nuisance and statute had failed in the UK courts. Initial success came from a finding that Article 8 applied and it was breached by night flights. Damages were payable and this was estimated to be as substantial as over £2 billion. The case attracted a great deal of academic and practitioner attention. Cases involving the application of Article 8 to environmental law were trumpeted as a new departure in environmental law, giving the litigant potential for expanding the role of courts in monitoring environmental obligations. The United Kingdom, however, appealed successfully. The Grand Chamber deferred to the economic necessities of the United Kingdom's government appeal. The degree of harm suffered was not severe and it was for the United Kingdom government to regulate night flights rather than the strict application of Article 8. Although it was conceded that Article 8 was breached, it was accepted that unless there was some manifest illegality the Grand Chamber did not see any point in intervening. Consequently the applicants lost their case. As a consequence, the potential to make use of Article 8 in such cases has been severely reduced although there remains a possibility of using Article 8 where appropriate. This still leaves the possibility of judicial review over procedural matters such as failure to consult widely or to consider objections to any government policy. The prediction of increased air travel and its likely doubling effect by 2020 of the traffic in and out of major airports makes the issue of noise a matter of great public concern. Nuisance remains an important part of the control and regulation of noise. In *Dennis* v *Ministry of Defence*[9] a nuisance claim alongside a human rights challenge was used to object to the noise from an RAF training airfield where low-level flights were undertaken. Damages by way of compensation was payable, though the flights continued.

[9] [2003] 2 EGLR 121.

Currently there is considerable debate over the future expansion of Heathrow and the building of a third runway. The debate has focused on the need for extra capacity and the problem of noise pollution. The Department of Trade has issued a consultation paper, *Adding Capacity at Heathrow: Decisions Following Consultation*.[10] The paper addresses the government's desire to go ahead with a third runway and assumes that this will meet noise limits as follows:

> Air traffic movements on a three-runway airport would need to be limited in the early years in order to keep within the 127 sq km noise contour. Estimates suggest that the airport could, in 2020, operate at around 605,000 ATMs with a 57-dBA noise contour of 126.7 sq km with further increases at ATMs over time as older, noisier aircraft are retired.

In considering the next steps, it is clear that planning law will apply to any application that BAA (the private sector owner) of the airport will make. It is likely that the planning application will come under the new Planning Act 2008, which is due to come into force in spring 2010. On such a major planning matter the new Infrastructure Planning Commission is likely to be used and will probably coincide with a National Policy Statement on the Third Runway. It is not certain that this will be the procedure adopted as there is currently no national policy statement for aviation.[11]

Noise from construction works and industrial sites

Local authorities have powers to address the problem of noise from construction works under the Control of Pollution Act 1974 sections 59A, 60 and 61. These powers permit controls over the way work is carried out, including the type of machinery and plant that are in use and the times they can be used. The powers are widely drawn and may also be applied to DIY work. There are strong enforcement powers that include possible criminal offences. There are a series of consents issued by the local authority to enable certain types of work to be undertaken.

Generally speaking, industrial sites that emit noise pollution fall under the Pollution Prevention Control Regime. The Environment Agency may issue guidance and set standards for companies to comply with. Noise should not be loud enough to give reasonable cause for annoyance to neighbours or persons living in the vicinity of the installations. There is an expectation that noise management plans are in place to ensure that the conditions or permits are fulfilled. Workers who are engaged in construction or industrial work come within the protection of health and safety rules, including the Noise at Work Regulations (1989 SI 1989/1790). The planning system is expected to consider the site of industrial or manufacturing installations and take account of reducing noise pollution to those who are locally resident.

Building regulations must conform to adequate standards of noise control in their construction and design. Part E, Schedule 1 to the Building Regulations 2000 (SI 2000/ 2531) applies and this provides standards of construction for different types of housing to prevent noise pollution.

---

[10] See: DFT, *Adding Capacity at Heathrow: Decisions Following Consultation* January 2009.

[11] For a detailed analysis of the third runway proposal, including background history and likely environmental impact see: House of Commons Library Research Paper 09/11 *Expansion of Heathrow Airport* (4 February 2009).

Noise and neighbours

The Noise and Statutory Nuisance Act 1993, a private member's Bill, came into force on 5 January 1994. The 1993 Act provides local authorities with powers to investigate and deal with noise nuisances that arise in streets. Noise emitted from a vehicle, machinery or equipment in the street may be a statutory nuisance. One important addition in noise control is the intrusive impact of burglar alarms. The 1993 Act reinforces controls contained under sections 91 and 92 of the Control of Pollution Act 1974 in respect of rights of entry to premises to silence audible alarms. Abatement notices may be more conveniently served by fixing the notice to the vehicle, premises, machinery or equipment. The hours at which loudspeakers may be used in the street are also prescribed under section 7 of the 1993 Act, which amends section 62 of the Control of Pollution Act 1974. Given the increase in noise complaints by neighbours, there has recently been the use of mediation services by local authorities to address noise from children, DIY work and music. In addition, the Crime and Disorder Act 1998 creates the opportunity for antisocial behaviour orders to be served on individuals who cause or are likely to cause harassment, alarm and distress. They may be used in cases of excessive noisiness. Orders may be sought by local authorities, with the advice and consultation of the chief police officer for the area. The use of such orders, known as ASBOs, is controversial and creates a heightened sense of unease as the powers of the state are being harnessed to address private-party disputes over issues such as noise. In addition section 42 of the Anti-social Behaviour Act 2003 provides local authorities with additional powers to regulate night noise.

The Housing Act 1986 provides comprehensive powers for private landlords to evict noisy tenants. This may include the seizure of noisy equipment, and the assistance of local authorities is provided in terms of evidence and enforcement. There is also a licensing system for public entertainment undertaken by local authorities. This is provided for in Schedule 1 to the Local Government (Miscellaneous Provisions) Act 1982. It applies automatically to indoor events, with the exception of music associated with religious places or functions. The Department of Environment Working Party (see: Neighbouring Noise Working Party, Review of the Effectiveness of Neighbour Noise Controls (Department of Environment, 1995) has recommended new powers and a new offence of night-time disturbance, including confiscation powers to deal with the increasing problems of neighbourhood noise.

EC Directive 2000/14/EC, adopted in 2000, applies to the use of equipment outdoors. The United Kingdom introduced the Noise Emissions in the Environment by Equipment for Use Outdoors Regulations 2001 (SI 2001/1701) and amended by SI 2001/1803). These regulations are under the Vehicle Certification Agency and are based on equipment standards that apply to the marketing of any equipment for outdoor use as well as the use of the equipment.

Private law remedies

The citizen may rely on the powers of the local authority discussed above. It is also possible to take a private action for nuisance. The plaintiff must show on the balance of probabilities the existence of the noise that constitutes the nuisance. The courts may consider a variety of issues such as the nature of the locality, the duration of the noise, the harm suffered by the plaintiff, the social and economic consequences of the defendant's actions, the state of mind of the defendant and the effects of noise on the plaintiff. Concluding whether there is a nuisance and setting damages or granting an injunction to stop the nuisance requires a careful balance of the issues in dispute. Individual action by a citizen may not be as effective as group action taken on behalf of a group of local residents (see: *Gillingham Borough Council* v *Medway (Chatham) Dock Company Ltd* [1992] 3 WLR 449).

Conclusions

Noise is fast becoming one of the worst effects of modern-day living. Schemes for proper noise insulation are becoming more common and there are grants available for noise installation to reduce aircraft noise and traffic noise. There are limited compensation schemes available under the Land Compensation Act 1973 in respect of highways or road schemes built after 17 October 1969. Highway authorities may undertake works to mitigate the consequences of traffic improvements or the building or updating of highways. The question of noise pollution is also a matter of public awareness and perception. Cost-effective measures to provide a sensible policy for noise reduction appears more attractive than attempts to control noise pollution. Van Wynsberghe estimates that 'some environmental noises are twice as intense as they were in the 1960s' and this intensity is expected to double every 10 years.[12] The future of strategies for noise reduction lies in greater awareness of the risks to health from noise pollution and greater sensitivity to the needs of others. Aircraft and rail transport are two areas where noise is likely to remain a key factor for the development and use of new technology. Wind turbines also show signs of causing a growing irritation as a source of noise pollution. Modern-day life leads to many noises and disturbances that go beyond public health concerns alone. The culture of rights gives rise to claims against noise polluters that would in the past be ignored. Taking account of noise sets one of the major challenges of the twenty-first century for environmental protection.

Further reading

Generally the Defra website provides a useful source for information on noise regulations and controls. It is also a useful source for up-to-date information on the latest consultation papers and also European Union initiatives. See: *http://www.defra.gov.uk/environment/noise*.

M. Adams and F. McManus, *Noise and Noise Law: A Practical Approach* Chichester: Wiley Chancery, 1994.

C.S. Kerse, *The Law Relating to Noise* London: Oyez, 1975.

R. Malcolm and J. Ponting, *Statutory Nuisance: Law and Practice* Oxford: Oxford University Press, 2002.

R. McCracken *et al.*, *Statutory Nuisance* London: Butterworths, 2001.

[12] D. Van Wynsberghe, C.R. Noback and R. Carola, *Human Anatomy and Physiology* Third edition, McGraw Hill Inc, New York, 1995, p. 514.

F. McManus and T. Burns, 'The impact of EC Law on noise law in the United Kingdom' in J. Holder (ed.), *The Impact of EC Environmental Law in the United Kingdom* Chichester: Wiley, 1997.

C.N. Penn, *Noise Control* London: Shaw and Sons, 2002.

D. Van Wynsberghe, C.R. Noback and R. Carola, *Human Anatomy and Physiology* 3rd edition, New York: McGraw Hill Inc, 1995.

Reports

Final Report of the Parliamentary Committee on the Problem of Noise (Wilson Committee) Cmnd 2056 1963.

Annual report of the Institution of Environmental Officers.

Neighbouring Noise Working Party, Review of the Effectiveness of Neighbour Noise Controls (Department of Environment, 1995).

Visit **http://www.mylawchamber.co.uk/mceldowney** to access key issue checklists and practice exam questions to test yourself on this chapter.

16 Environmental law: mapping the future?

Introduction

Since the beginning of the twenty-first century increases in oil prices and the gradual acceptance of climate change has forced the environment further up the legal, economic, social and political agenda. Science has played a fundamental role in beginning to unravel the future of global change and our manifold impacts on the environment. Today the environmental agenda is shaped through an essential collaboration between scientific and non-science disciplines. The emergence of China and India, as important industrialised regions of the new global economy has drawn attention to the importance of global collaboration on environmental matters and the role of international law and regulation in protecting the environment. Lessons from the development of EU and United Kingdom environmental law are important to share and the opportunity for the new economies to learn from the mistakes of western economic growth and development should not be missed.

The future directions of environmental law have always been resistant to easy prediction, as environmental law has tended to evolve in an organic way. Historically environmental law grew out of a response to problems of pollution and the demands of improving public health. This evolutionary process has continued. It has responded to new developments in science and technology, and scientific research has provided a more evaluative basis for environmental law. The European Union has had major influence in shaping the environmental law of the United Kingdom. As a consequence of these influences environmental law has begun to become less reactive and more proactive in environmental protection. One reason for a more proactive approach is that the techniques now available to environmental lawyers to help address environmental problems has widened and diversified. Environmental lawyers continue to draw on distinct areas of the law such as criminal law, the law of property, contract and tort as well as planning and administrative law – but the whole is greater than the parts and environmental law has its own language and legal rules. Human rights and the environment has added a fresh and dynamic dimension to environmental law especially when environmental rights are considered. As well as changes in the law, there is also a much more holistic approach to the environment than in the past and a growing realisation of our reliance on the environment and its often scarce resources.

Environmental law has also a fundamental place in what is termed socio-legal studies. This provides both an empirical base as well as an analytical framework for the study of environmental law. The focus is not only on legal institutions and how they work but also on the impact of law and how attitudes to the environment may be shaped by environmental laws. Environmental law now has a firm root as part of socio-legal studies. Less clear is how to ensure the important role of science, particularly well-informed sound science, is recognised and how it can be used effectively and communicated to the general public. Within the breadth of socio-legal studies globalisation is recognised and embraced, no less so in environmental law, with the immense geographical distribution of resources setting sustainable development at the top of the international as well as national agenda for environmental law.

It is clear that environmental law can adapt and face new environmental challenges. There is a sense that environmental law as a discipline may fit the description of a 'genuinely scientific social science of law'.[1] Elevating environmental law to take a pivotal place in the curriculum will take some time. The possibility, however, that such a specialised field will provide a more theoretical, but at the same time evidence-based approach to law than hitherto,[2] is being considered by many writers (see Chapter 8).

The processes of globalisation[3] and the challenges of climate change offer a suitable context and a means of overviewing achievements, strengths and weaknesses. There has been a gradual recognition that managing scarce resources, including natural habitats and nature conservation strategies, contribute to protecting the planet and to sustainability. Managing industrial processes and developments, especially in the newly developed economies, requires careful adjudication to ensure that past mistakes are not repeated. This is a timely moment to entertain questions about the future of environmental law amidst a global economic downturn. We have the opportunity to make decisions for the future as part of a sustainable financial and economic strategy that must prioritise the environment and scarce environmental resources. It is equally a time to ensure that an analytical framework for the study of environmental law should be fostered that locates environmental rights, ethics and values as central to the debate on sustainable development. In an age of financial and economic turbulence, there is a significant role for the study of environmental law to fulfil. It must provide analysis and ideas that go to ensure that economic criteria do not outweigh the needs of the environment. Recognising science as an ally in this ambition will draw legal scholars into new and exciting challenges. The transnational dimension of environmental law itself offers a rare opportunity to engage in comparative evaluations, including examining the effectiveness and efficiency of law for the protection of the environment.

Studying environmental law: issues and perspectives

Studying environmental law involves many strategies.[4] Environmental law cases are heard before the ordinary courts, though the development of planning law and public inquiries has been an example of a growing specialist system away from ordinary administrative law.

---

[1] See. W. Twinning, *General Jurisprudence* Cambridge: Cambridge University Press, 2009, p. 264.
[2] Consider the development of the law of restitution and how the subject has been shaped and influenced by leading academic writers.
[3] J. Stiglitz, *Globalisation and Its Discontents* New York: WW Norton, London: Allen Lane, 2004.
[4] See: E. Fisher, B. Lange, E. Scotford, C. Carlane, 'Maturity and methodology: starting a debate about environmental scholarship' (2009) J Env L 213.

There is no dedicated environmental law court; even though a strong case has been made for one, it was rejected by the government. It is also clear that environmental law draws on specific and technical statutory provisions, such as public health legislation and statutes on the control of pollution. The ability to interpret and understand complex statutory enactments is greatly helped by the accompanying explanatory notes and guides to the legislation. The House of Commons Library Research Papers are another useful way of discovering aspects of environmental law and policy.

In recent years environmental law has been subject to new and significant developments that reflect changing attitudes to environmental matters among policy-makers and politicians. Generalisations about these changes are dangerous and apt to oversimplify or rely on a selective reading of patterns of development.[5] It is helpful to try and understand environmental law by trying to trace both historical and contemporary developments. The 1970s provided a legislative framework that was aimed at pollution control and, through 'command and control' styles of regulation, attempted to prohibit or restrict environmentally harmful activities or substances. Standard-setting and target limits on emissions, together with penalties to ensure that standards were observed, were frequently involved. At this time science and law were conjoined in an enterprise of risk assessment and prescribing what was safe and ultimately sustainable. The adoption of best available technology was prevalent, with instructions on processes and procedures. The approach also favoured licenses and permits as well as recognition that safety standards allowed 'sound science' a stake in establishing, evaluating and policing their observance. The approach taken was also in keeping with a relatively soft regulatory approach to state intervention. By maintaining acceptable environmental standards, the market economy was considered to be sustainable and forms of self-regulation were adopted to ensure that outcome was in line with industry best practice. Included in the scope of regulatory activities were the main stakeholders, the various levels of central and local government and a proliferation of agencies. It was an approach that found favour in the major industrialised economies.

The 1980s represented a new ideological shift from centralised state-focused regulation to a market-led orientation. The costs of regulation in terms of jobs and market share became an issue as emerging economies began to dominate the market beyond the boundaries of the more tightly regulated western economies. This shift in workforce practices to new economic regions in Asia, India and Africa was argued to be a direct result of the command–control form of regulation with its heavy costs on business and industry. Direct regulation of many processes found less favour with governments, while a more market-driven solution to reduce economic costs became the preferred option. Privatisation strategies, particularly involving the public utilities, including energy and water, revealed uneconomic practices, poor investment and high business costs – that were rapidly passed to consumers in the newly competitive sectors.

Industry and business successfully complained that the costs of environmental regulation were too high and unfairly targeted on industry rather than consumers or end-users. The adoption by the European Union of a number of economic instruments targeted on environmental protection became commonly used. In the United Kingdom, such economic instruments operated alongside the more traditional command and control systems.

[5] Neil Gunningham, 'Environment law, regulation and governance: shifting architectures' (2009) *Journal of Environmental Law* 179.

Various taxation strategies were introduced. Particularly important are the Aggregates Levy (2002), Landfill Tax (1996) and Climate Change Levy (2000) as examples of their kind.[6] In the 1990s they were added to by an air passenger duty. In 1999 a peak was reached with environmental tax receipts reaching 3.6 per cent of GDP. Since then the average environmental tax has been around 2 per cent of GDP. The current forecast is that environmental taxes should achieve values over £470,480 million annually. The greatest yields, currently, are from the aggregates levy, the landfill tax and the climate change levy. The role of taxation in protecting the environment is important, as taxation sets responsibilities for citizens across the nation and may set an agenda for behavioural changes that foster good environmental behaviour and practice. Studying environmental law connects with the wide variety of techniques available, including the policy and political implications of different rules and norms. For example, one curiosity of taxation is that very few environmental taxes are hypothecated – meaning that the tax yield goes to protecting the environment. Many policy-makers do not favour hypothecated taxes as they do not have an impact on the wider economy. There is also the paradox, as Bell has pointed out, that if the measure of the success for environmental taxes is changing behaviour, then their tax-raising function is greatly diminished.[7] The 2002 Treasury Report identified a number of objectives contained in environmental taxation. These include tackling climate change, improving waste management and regenerating British towns and cities as well as protecting the British countryside and natural resources. Measures that might well be introduced were suggested in the Institute of Fiscal Studies Report in 2006 and include charges for road users; greater use of a carbon tax and a tax on the use of plastics, including carrier bags. Energy-related taxes are likely to dominate the current millennium as the struggle to make wiser use of fossil fuels continues.

In addition to the taxation strategy to tackle environmental problems, the 1990s witnessed a wide variety of voluntary agreements and codes of practice, as industry sought to persuade government that self-regulation would work more efficiently than traditional command and control systems. There is a growing sophistication in the way the environment is being tackled. Passing many environmental costs on to the end-user is a common strategy organised around the 'polluter pays' principle. Another strategy was to incorporate into decision-making systems-operating standards and cost–benefit risk assessment. This form of regulation (often called meta-regulation) encapsulates a related discipline of regulatory design and agency regulation including inspection, reporting and inquiry. Linked to the audit culture of financial risk management are environmental issues associated with corporate government. Engaging industry and business through flexible regulatory instruments that appear to be self-regulation but are driven by firm penalties is set out in the recent Hampton and Macrory reviews of regulation, the latter being mainly focused on the use of criminal sanctions.[8]

---

[6] HM Treasury, *Tax and the Environment; using economic instruments* Pre-budget Report 2002 London, 2002. Andrew Leicester, *The UK Tax System and the Environment* IFS London, 2006 See: Barbara E. Bell 'Environmental Taxation' in (2008) *VAT Digest* 1.

[7] See Bell, pp. 3–4.

[8] Philip Hampton, *Reducing Administrative Burdens: Effective Inspection and Enforcement Final Report* London: HM Treasury, 2005; J. Black, 'Tensions in the regulatory state' (2007) *Public Law* 58 at p. 66; R. Macrory, *Regulatory Justice: Sanctioning in a Post-Hampton World: A Consultation Document* London: Cabinet Office, May 2006 and *Regulatory Justice: Making Sanctions Effective* London: Cabinet Office, November 2006.

The success or failure of one style of regulation over another is difficult to evaluate accurately. Limited empirical studies have been undertaken to examine the claims and counter-claims of different styles of regulation. In an institutional context the evaluation of regulatory agencies is also a critical issue. Public opinion has increasingly questioned the reliability and values of science and the effectiveness of environmental regulation. Heightened public interest in the environment is not confined to environmental crisis that is industrially or commercially driven. Managing domestic flooding caused by seasonal high rainfall or periods of drought are both examples of public concern. Public awareness of science and public access to environmental information have fuelled the activities of pressure groups who lobby for environmental causes. Greenpeace secured 'victory' in a notable environmental campaign against BP and Shell when they sought to dismantle and dispose at sea the Brent Spar oil rig. The World Development Movement secured success in campaigning in the courts over Pergau Dam in Malaysia and there are countless examples of smaller lobbying causes, often locally led, against road building, electricity generators, and enlargement of airports. In fact the role of pressure groups and campaigns includes shaping and informing public opinion itself.[9] There is clearly a moment when environmental issues may set the agenda of policy-making. The Stern Report and the admission that environmental issues can set the agenda in terms of policy have given rise to Gunningham's analysis that new regulation is a form of 'new environmental governance'.[10] This suggests that legal rules and analysis in environmental law must work collaboratively with new disciplines and that the stewardship of natural resources requires sharing analytical tools and techniques.

Such changes appear to provide environmental law with its own conceptual framework and distinct contribution to the way legal rules are framed. Legal rules tend to rely on detection after the event of their breach. Courts provide an examination of what has occurred and only rarely evaluate future risks. This is anathema to environmental law, which must attempt to predict outcomes and take steps in anticipation of risks. Principles such as 'the polluter pays' and the 'precautionary principle', techniques such as 'eco-labelling' and the development of environmental impact assessment and integrated pollution control are examples of the distinct contribution environmental law is making to the general development of new concepts in law. Environmental lawyers place reliance on scientific data and methodology in measuring and understanding anthropogenic impacts on the environment and to provide monitoring techniques. Science is used to help predict outcomes and deal with the impact of humans' activities on the environment. Scientists will increasingly need to understand the impact of legal rules on the environment. Evolving legal rules to serve the needs of the scientist presents one of the formidable challenges for the future.

At international, European and national level, environmental policies are being shaped, albeit belatedly, that begin to take account of the challenges to the environment in the twenty-first century. In 1992 the UN Earth Summit drew attention to the need for international action to tackle global problems such as climate change, and biodiversity and forest loss. This highlights the fact that humans' environmental impacts do not recognise national boundaries and action is required on an international basis. Even so since the UN Earth Summit, globalised responses to environmental change have struggled to be effective. The

---

[9] See: W. Maloney and G. Jordan, 'Participation and the environment' (1995) *Contemporary Political Studies*, pp. 1137–53.
[10] N. Gunningham *op. cit.*, fn. 4.

end of the last century saw the realisation that environmental protection and conservation rests heavily on the implementation of policies such as clean technology, waste minimisation and sustainable development.[11] The lessons for future generations are summarised by Tolba:

> Concern for the environment is as old as human civilisation. History abounds with examples of the wide variations in human understanding of the environment and in our ability to maintain it in a healthy condition. Those societies that managed to provide their material, cultural and spiritual needs in a sustainable manner were those that succeeded in reconciling their needs and aspirations with the maintenance of a viable environment. Whenever the outer limits of the physical environment were exceeded, civilizations declined or even vanished.[12]

Sustainable development and environmental rights

A crucial part of the future strategy for the environment continues to be sustainable development, as defined by the Brundland Commission in 1987, to meet 'the needs of the present without compromising the ability of future generations to meet their own needs'. In the United Kingdom this has been translated into a number of initiatives, some institutional such as the establishment of the Environment Agency in 1995.[13] Concerns about climate change and biodiversity are among future priorities for sustainable development[14] together with:

- a high priority to the definition of environmental objectives and targets;
- publication of a set of indicators in areas such as air quality, water quality, land, wildlife and habitats and the impacts on these of social and economic change;
- education about the environment, including the views of consideration of the government's Sustainable Development Commission;
- priority to improve relationships between industry and government;
- clarify the need for environmental regulation and the use of fiscal instruments, including taxation of pollution;
- set the agenda and priorities for sustainable development;
- to provide advice and make recommendations on actions to achieve sustainable development;
- to promote strong economic development in harmony with true stewardship of the environment.

Allied to the desire to adopt sustainable development strategies, there is also a growing sense of the significance of environmental rights. This is partly as a result of a better informed public because of access to environmental information. There is also a traditional conflict

---

[11] In January 1994 the United Kingdom Government embarked on a national strategy for sustainable development (see: This Common Inheritance UK Annual Report Cmd 2822 HMSO, 1995).

[12] For a retrospective look see Mostafa Tolba, *et al.*, *The World Environment 1972–1992* Chapman and Hall, 1992, pp. 804–5.

[13] The UK Annual Report on *This Common Inheritance* (see: Cmd 2822, (1995 HMSO), has noted that the common theme in the sustainable development strategy adopted by the government for the environment has been 'to establish more specific targets and objectives, together with quantified indicators of progress' for different parts of the environment (see: Sustainable Development: The UK Strategy (HMSO, 1994).

[14] There are a number of key elements in this strategy (see: Cmd 2822 HMSO, 1995, pp. 9–38).

between individual private property law and collective public values. It is clear from the discussion in previous chapters (see Chapters 6 and 8) that there remains considerable potential for human rights derived from the Human Rights Act 1998 to trickle down into environmental issues. This is not as simple as it may first appear. Human rights may help drive environmental protection but environmental protection is not the same as human rights. The balance between private individual rights – such as the various freedoms under Article 10, freedom of expression and the right to assemble peacefully under Article 11 – are examples of how rights may help determine how protests are managed. While the individual right to respect for home life (Article 8) may provide a protection against extreme pollution, its potential to do so has only been reluctantly recognised by the courts.

In the future, there is likely to be consideration of how far collective rights may be expressly defined and applied beyond the existing Human Rights Framework set by the European Convention on Human Rights. To date the signs are that this step has not been fully endorsed. The European Union has not favoured this approach and while Article 4 of the 1995 Draft International Covenant on Environment and Development for the World Conservation Union states that 'environmental protection and respect for human rights and fundamental freedoms are interdependent', little real progress has been made in that direction.[15] Reconciling human rights, such as 'protecting the quality of the environment' contained in the EC Treaty, and free trade even when it is expected to be sustainable, is not easy. The likely outcome is that as fossil fuels become increasingly costly and scarce, and as climate change rises up the political agenda, environmental rights tied to human development will have to be addressed. Business and industry as well as the financial sector will have to become accustomed to managing the transition to a low-carbon economy in a way that is sympathetic to rights and human development.

The future of environmental law, regulation and policy-making

On 22 July 2002, the Parliament and Council of the EU adopted the Sixth Community Action Program, extending over a ten-year period, to promote ways of adopting into public and private matters general environmental policy. The priorities are climate change, nature and biodiversity, environment, health and the quality of life. We have already seen in Chapter 8 how much of environmental law has come under different influences from each sector, which are outlined in Part II of the book. Since 2002, two aspects of globalisation have emerged as defining issues for the new millennium. The first is global warming linked to climate change. The second is financial and how global finance might address problems related to global warming.

There are various objectives, techniques and strategies in environmental law (see Chapter 8). It is clear that setting objectives and adopting strategies for the environment is a multi-disciplined task. Monitoring how environmental laws are obeyed is the first step. This is an evolutionary process whereby learning how procedures and processes work will help ensure a better understanding of regulation and law. Ensuring adequate enforcement of

[15] Also see the Ksentini Report (1994) undertaken by the UN Special Rapporteur on Human Rights and the Environment.

environmental law at national and European Community level sets immense challenges for the future of environmental law. It is also essential to set priorities that make environmental enforcement an essential value in society.

In the chapters in Part I of this book we examined the variety of techniques and institutions that are involved in attempts to resolve environmental problems. Concepts such as Best Practicable Means or Best Practicable Environmental Option have become common in the articulation of principles of environmental law. As the Tenth Report of the Royal Commission *Tackling Pollution – Experience and Prospects*[16] explained, the terms, Best Practicable Means or Best Practicable Environmental Option, must inevitably involve the control of different sectors of the environment to minimise damage overall. In its widest context it involves a consideration of the financial implications in the calculation of the best practicable means to deal with environmental pollution. Section 7 of the Environmental Protection Act 1991 takes this concept further with the Best Available Techniques Not Entailing Excessive Costs (BATNECC). This formulation considers what is economically possible, what is environmentally practical and what is legally achievable within the legal powers available. BATNECC has been adopted at national, European and international levels. The concept of Best Practical Environmental Option (BPEO) developed by the Royal Commission on Pollution[17] provides opportunities to set emission standards for specific proscribed processes and substances. Other important techniques available include Integrated Pollution Control (IPC) and Environmental Impact Assessment (EIA). These are likely to dominate environmental law and science in the twenty-first century.

The greatest challenge is to place in a legal framework the development of scientific and technological responses to pollution control. In particular, emphasis should be placed on:

- the development of appropriate, perhaps continuous, monitoring procedures on discharges, together with regular and effective monitoring of the receiving environment. This must be achieved within a realistic economic framework;

- improved methods for assessing potential harm arising from a pollutant (or mixture of pollutants) to organisms and the environment;

- the development and application of waste minimisation and clean technologies (i.e. the prevention of waste);

- limiting damage to the environment to the greatest extent achievable, subject to reasonable cost;

- designing strategies that achieve a true balance between environmental and resource protection and economic and social development in the application of the sustainable development principle.

Setting standards is often controversial and may appear haphazard. There are many examples of different forms of standard-setting such as emissions controls, or design standards such as eco-labelling. Standard-setting will inevitably be influenced by the sensitivity of monitoring equipment, but should be based more properly on a scientific assessment of the risk and hazard to the environment. The techniques of predicting outcomes and consequences from existing data and information remain complex. Risk assessment techniques and mathematical

---

[16] Cmnd 9149, 1984.
[17] Fifth Report Cmnd 6371.

modelling procedures attempt to establish predictive and quantitative assessments of the likely impact of humans' activities on the local and global environment. It is on these predictions that future policies and regulations may be developed.

Scientists may have yet another role to perform in environmental monitoring: that is, determining the probable source of a pollutant incident. Evaluating who is responsible for environmental damage may involve a degree of scientific detective work, but may not necessarily provide solutions as to how to clean up the environment or prevent harm in the future. The principle that 'the polluter pays' may simply result in clean-up costs being borne by the end-user who is able to pass costs on to the consumer. Thus a notional environmental 'overhead' may be built into pricing mechanisms. This does not provide long-term benefits for the environment. Scientists must also contribute to environmental management by meeting the challenge inherent in the development of economic remediation and restoration techniques.[18]

In addition to the scientific challenges there are challenges to how management issues should be addressed. Environmental management techniques have adapted to accommodating a more problem-focused and policy-driven approach to the environment. Public education and forging interrelations between science and industry, government and law are an intrinsic part of the work of the environmental scientist today. Scientists may be able to determine the extent of 'harm' to the environment and suggest procedures to limit, control or ameliorate the harmful effects. This knowledge is, however, only truly valuable if it is used to inform industry, policy-makers and the public realistically and fully. The creation of the Environment Agency and the Scottish Environment Protection Agency under the Environment Act 1995, and the European Environment Agency reflect public demands for standard-setting and auditing of the environment, demands that must ultimately be met by scientists.

Finally there are challenges in ensuring that financial instruments take account of a low-carbon economy. Benjamin Richardson[19] argues that government intervention will be required to ensure that global warming is addressed by the financial sector. Significant issues will arise after 2012 when the current Kyoto Protocol expires. Richardson observes that insufficient account has been taken in the financial services markets and a low-carbon footprint might be of benefit to investors. Addressing the financial issues associated with environmental responsibilities is essential and policy-makers who are wedded to sustainable development face an inevitable question of how to reconcile financial instruments with environmental protection.

Conclusions

Policy-makers and politicians must face the important challenges that arise from many of the environmental problems highlighted in this book. All aspects of human activity, from agriculture to industry and urbanisation, impinge on the environment in which we live. Environmental problems transcend national, European and international boundaries and

[18] See: Jenny Steele, 'Remedies and remediation: foundational issues in environmental liability' [1995] 58 *Modern Law Review* 615.

[19] Benjamin J. Richardson, 'Climate finance and its governance: moving to a low carbon economy through socially responsible financing?' (2009) *International and Comparative Law Quarterly* 597.

legal systems. The global economy and the use of natural and energy resources must be confronted at every level, both local and global. The implementation of policies for sustainable development must measure the foreseen benefits as well as the detriments of humans' activities, and attempt to predict unforeseen effects. Sustainable development must secure the best use of the world's resources measured in long-term as well as short-term strategies. Proactive rather than reactive policy-making must be found in economic and scientific instruments that are sanctioned by law. Finally, environmental laws must take account of the consequences of scientific and technological achievements and the unpredictable nature of human endeavour. Where market failures and financial crisis may fit various models and solutions, environmental law, regulation and governance may not find it easy to remedy failures in environmental protection that lead to irreversible changes to the natural world with significance for all humanity.

Further reading

S. Baughen, *International Trade and the Protection of the Environment* London: Routledge-Cavendish, 2007.

D. Bornstein, *How to Change the World: Social Entrepreneurs and the Power of New Ideas* Oxford: Oxford University Press, 2004.

J. Diamond, *Collapse: How Societies Choose to Fail or Succeed* New York: Viking Penguin, 2005.

M. Everson and E. Vos (eds), *Uncertain Risks Regulated* London: Routledge-Cavendish Press, 2009.

J. Fenger and C.J. Tjell (eds), *Air Pollution* London: The Royal Society of Chemistry, 2009.

A. Gilpin, *Environmental Impact Assessment* Cambridge: Cambridge University Press, 1995.

N. Gunningham, R. Kagan and D. Thornton, *Shades of Green: Business, Regulation and Environment* California: Stanford University Press, 2003.

R.M. Harrison (ed.), *Introduction to Pollution Science* London: The Royal Society of Chemistry, 2006.

R.M. Harrison and R. Hester (eds), *Air Quality in Urban Environments* London: The Royal Society of Chemistry, 2009.

R.E. Hester and R.M. Harrison (eds), *Biodiversity Under Threat* London: The Royal Society of Chemistry, 2007.

J. Holder and M. Lee, *Environmental Protection, Law and Policy* 2nd edition Cambridge: Cambridge University Press, 2007.

R. Lazarus, *The Making of Environmental Law* Chicago Ill: University of Chicago Press, 2004.

A.M. Mannion and S.R. Bowlby *Environmental Issues in the 1990s* London: John Wiley, 1992.

C. Mungall and D. McLaren (eds), *Planet Under Stress* Oxford University Press, 1990.

T. O'Riordan (ed.), *Environmental Science for Environmental Management* London: Longman, 1995.

D. Pearce and Edward B. Barbier, *Blueprint for a Sustainable Economy* London; Earthscan, 2000.

T. Pogge, 'A critique of the capability approach' in H. Brighouse and I. Robeyns (eds), *Measuring Justice: Primary Goods and Capabilities* Cambridge: Cambridge University Press, 2009.

B.J. Rochardson and S. Wood (eds), *Environmental Law for Sustainability* Oxford: Hart Publishers, 2006.

P. Rogers, K.F. Jalal and J.A. Boyd, *An Introduction to Sustainable Development* London: Earthscan, 2007.

A. Sen, *The Idea of Justice* London: Penguin, 2009.

J. Stiglitz, *Globalisation and Its Discontents* New York: WW Norton, London: Allen Lane, 2004.

M. Tolba *et al.*, *The World Environment 1972–1992* London: Chapman and Hall, 1992.

United Nations, *Agenda 21: The United Nation's Programme of Action from Rio* United Nations, 1992.

UNDP, *Human Development Report 1992* Oxford: Oxford University Press, 1992.

World Bank, *World Development Report 1992* Oxford: Oxford University Press, 1992.

World Commission on Environment and Development, *Our Common Future* Oxford: Oxford University Press, 1987.

Bibliography

Listed below are a number of useful sources for the study of environmental law, including EU environmental law.

Ackerman, B.A. and Stewart, R.B. 'Reforming Environmental Law' (1986), Stanford Law Review 1333.

Adams, M. and McManus, F. *Noise and Noise Law: A Practical Approach*, Chichester: Wiley Chancery, 1994.

Adams, W.M. *Future Nature* new edition revised, London: Earthscan, 2003.

Adler, J. 'Environmental Impact Assessment: The inadequacies of English Law' (1993) 5 JEL 203.

Akehurst, M. *A Modern Introduction to International Law*, 3rd edition, London: George Allen and Unwin, 1977.

Alder, J. and Wilkinson, D. *Environmental Law and Ethics*, London: Macmillan, 1999.

Alexander, K. et al., *Global Governance of Financial Systems*, Oxford: Oxford University Press, 2006.

Anderson, M. and Galizzi, P. (eds.) *International Environmental Law in National Courts*, London BIICL, 2002.

Archer, C. *The European Union*, London: Routledge, 2008.

Armstrong, M., Cowan, S. and Vickers, J. *Regulatory Reform*, MIT: Cambridge, 1998.

Arthurs, H. *'Without the Law': Administrative Justice and Legal Pluralism in Nineteenth Century England*, Toronto: University of Toronto Press, 1985.

Ashby, E. and Anderson, M. *The politics of Clean Air*, Oxford: OUP, 1981.

Attfield, R. *The Ethics of the Global Environment*, Edinburgh Studies in World Ethics, Edinburgh: Edinburgh University Press, 1999.

Ayres, I. and Braithwaite, J. *Responsive Regulation: Transcending the Deregulation Debate*, Oxford University Press, New York, 1992.

Bailey, R., *Earth Report 2000* London: McGraw-Hill, 2000.

Baldwin, R. (ed.) *Law and Uncertainty: Risks and Legal Processes*, London: Kluwer Law International, 1997.

Baldwin, R., Scott, C. and Hood, C., *A Reader on Regulation*, Oxford: Oxford University Press, 1998.

Baldwin, R. (ed.) *Regulation in Question: The Growing Agenda*, London: London School of Economics, 1995.

Baldwin, R. and Black, J. 'Really Responsive Regulation' (2008) 71 *Modern Law Review* 59–64.

Barnes, R. *Property Rights and Natural Resources*, Oxford: Hart Publishing, 2007.

Barnes, R.S.K. and Hughes, R.N. *An Introduction to Marine Ecology*, London: Blackwell Scientific Publications, 1988.

Barnes, R., Freestone, D. and Ong, D., (eds.) *The Law of the Sea: The Role of the Law of the Sea Convention*, Leiden: Martinus Nijhoff, 2005.

Barry, J. *Environment and Social Theory*, London: Routledge, 1999.

Bateman, I.J. 'Environmental Impact Assessment, Cost-Benefit Analysis and the Valuation of Environmental Impacts' in Petts, J., (ed.) *Handbook of Environmental Impact Assessment: vol. 1 Process, Methods and Potential*, Oxford: Blackwell, 1999.

Bates, J.H. *United Kingdom Marine Pollution Law*, Lloyd's of London Press Ltd. 1995.

Bates, J.H. and Benson, C. *Marine Environment Law*, Lloyd's of London Press Ltd. 1993.

Baughen, S. *International Trade and the Protection of the Environment*, Routledge-Cavendish, 2007.

Beck, U. *Risk Society: Towards a New Modernity*, London: Sage, 1992.

Beckerman, W. 'Sustainable Development: Is It a Useful Concept?' (1994) *Environmental Values* 3(3) 191–209.

Begon, M., Harper, J.L. and Townsend, C.R. *Ecology. Individuals, Populations and Communities*. 3rd edition. Blackwell, 1996.

Bel, G. and Fageda, X. 'Why do Local Governments Privatise Public Services? A Survey of Empirical Studies' (2007) 33(4) *Local Government Studies* 517–34.

Bell, S. and McGillivray, D. *Environmental Law*, 3rd edition, Oxford: Oxford University Press, 2008.

Bernascovi, N. et al., *Environment and Trade: A Guide to WTO Jurisprudence* London: Earthscan, 2006.

Bernauer, T. *Genes, Trade, and Regulation: The Seeds of Conflict in Food Biotechnology*, Princeton: Princeton University, 2003.

Besley, T. and Coate, S., 'Centralized versus decentralized provision of local public goods: a political economy analysis' *National Bureau of Economic Research Working Paper* (1999) No. 784.

Birnie, P. and Boyle, A. *International Law and the Environment*, 2nd edition, Oxford: Oxford University Press, 2003.

Black, J. 'Regulation as Facilitation: Negotiating the Genetic Revolution' (1998) 61 *Modern Law Review* 621.

Black, J. 'The Emergence of Risk Based Regulation and the New Public Risk Management in the UK' (2005) *Public Law* 512.

Bodansky, A. 'The United Nations Framework Convention on Climate Change: A Commentary' (1993) 18 *Yale Journal of International Law* 451–558.

Bodansky, D., Brunnée, J. and Hey, E. (eds.) *The Oxford Handbook of International Environmental Law*, Oxford: Oxford University Press, 2007.

Bornstein, D. *How to Change the World: Social Entrepreneurs and the Power of New Ideas*, Oxford: Oxford University Press, 2004.

Booth, W.H. and Renshaw, J.B.C. *Smoke prevention and fuel economy*, London: Earthscan, 1911.

Bosselman, E.P. and Tarlock, A.D. 'The influence of Ecologcal Science on American Law' (1994) 69 Chichago-Kent L Rev. 847.

Boyle, A. and Anderson, M.R. (eds.) *Human Rights Approaches to Environmental Protection*, Oxford: Oxford University Press, 1996.

Boyle, A. and Freestone, D. (eds.) *International Law and Sustainable Development*, Oxford: Oxford University Press, 1999.

Boyne, G.A. 'The determinants of variations on local service contracting – garbage in, garbage out?' (1998) 34(1) *Urban Affairs Review* 150–63.

Brandl, E. and Bungert, H. 'Constitutional Entrenchment of Environmental Protection: A Comparative Analysis of Experiences Abroad' (1992) 16(1) *Harvard Environmental Law Review* 1–100.

Brown, E.D. 'The Conventional Law of the Environment' 13 *Natural Resources Journal* 203 (1973).

Bryson, B. (ed.) *Seeing Further: The Story of Science and the Royal Society*, London: The Royal Society, 2010.

Buclet, N. and others *Municipal Waste Management in European Policy: Between Harmonisation and Subsidiarity*, London, London University Press, 2002.

Bullard, R.D. *The Quest for Environmental Justice: Human Rights and the Politics of Pollution*, University of California, UCLA Press 2005.

Burnett, J. *Plenty and Want: A Social History of Food in England from 1815 to the Present Day*, 2nd edition, London: Routledge, 1989.

Caddell, R. 'Biodiversity Loss and the Prospects for International Cooperation: EU Law and the Conservation of Migratory Species of Wild Animals' (2008) 8 *The Yearbook of European Environmental Law* 218–264.

Cassese, A. *International law in a Divided World*, Oxford: Clarendon, 1990.

Clapp, B.W. *An Environmental History of Britain*, London: Longman, 1994.

Cave, M. and Baldwin, R. *Understanding Regulation*, Oxford: Oxford University Press, 1999.

Clark, R.B. *Marine Pollution*, Oxford: Clarendon Press, 1989.

Chandler, T.J. *Climate of London*, London: Hutchinson, 1965.

Clapp, B.W. *An Environmental History of Britain*, London: Longman, 1994.

Cohen, R. *Global Diasporas*, London: University College Press, 1999.

Coleman, J. 'Environmental Barriers to Trade and EC Law' (1993) 2(11) EELR 295.

Comte, F. and Kramer, L. (eds.) *Environmental Crime in Europe: Rules of Sanctions*, Gronigen: Europa, 2004.

Cook, K. 'The Natural Environment and Rural Communities Act 2006' (2006) 8(4) Env.L.R. 292.

Coyle, S. and Morrow, K. *The Philosophical Foundations of Environmental Law: Property, Rights and Nature*, Oxford: Hart Publishing, 2004.

Craig, P. and de Burca, G. (eds.) *The Evolution of EC Law*, Oxford: Oxford University Press, 1999.

Cullingworth, B. and Nadin, V. *Town and Country Planning in Britain*, 13th edition, London: Routledge, 2002.

Cranor, C.F. *Regulating Toxic Substances: A Philosophy of Science and Law* New York, Oxford: Oxford University Press, 1993.

Daintith, T. (ed.) *Law as an Instrument of Economic Policy: Comparative and Critical Approaches*, Berlin: W de Gruyter, 1988.

Davies, P.G.G. *European Union Environmental Law*, Ashgate: London, 2004.

de Sadeleer, N. *Environmental Principles*, Oxford: Oxford University Press, 2005.

Denhardt, R.B. and Denhardt, J.V. 'The New Public Management: serving rather than steering' (2000) *Public Administration Review* 60(6) 549–59.

Diamond, J. *Collapse: How Societies Choose to Fail or Succeed*, New York, Viking Penguin, 2005.

DiMento, J. *The Global Environment and International Law*, University of Texas Press, 2003.

Dobson, A. *Justice and the Environment*, Oxford: Oxford University Press 1998.

Dodansky, D., 'The Legitimacy of International Governance: A coming challenge for International Environmental Law', (1999) 93 Am. J. Int'l L. 614.

Douglas, W. 'Environmental Problems and the Oceans: The Need for International Controls', 1 *Environment Law* 149 (1971).

Duxbury, R. Telling and Duxbury's Planning Law and Procedure, 13th edition, London: Butterworths, 2006.

Ebbesson, J., *Compatibility of International and national Environmental Law*, London, The Hague, Boston: Kluwer Law International, 1996.

Elworthy, S. and Holder, J. *Environmental Protection: Text and Materials*, London: Butterworths, 1997.

Elworthy, S. 'Finding the causes of events or preventing "state of affairs"? Designation of nitrate vulnerable zones' [1998] JEL 92.

Evans, E.J. *The Forging of the Modern State Early Industrial Britain 1783–1870*, London: Longman, 1996.

Everson, M. and Vos, E. (eds.) *Uncertain Risks Regulated*, Routledge Cavendish Press, 2009.

Freestone, D. and Salman, S.M.A. 'Ocean and Freshwater Resources' in Bodansky, D., Bruneé, J. and Hey, E. (eds.) *The Oxford Handbook of International Environmental Law*, Oxford: Oxford University Press, 2006.

Freestone, D. and Streck, C. (eds.) *Legal Aspects of Implementing the Kyoto Protocol Mechanisms: Making Kyoto Work*, Oxford: Oxford University Press, 2005.

French, R. 'The Changing Nature of Environmental Protection: Recent developments Regarding Trade and the Environment in the European Union and the World Trade Organization' (2000) XLVII *Netherlands International Law Review* 1.

Gearty, C. (ed.) *European Civil Liberties and the European Convention on Human Rights*, London: Martinus Nijhoff Publishers, 1997.

Ghai, Y. (ed.) *Autonomy and Ethnicity*, Cambridge: Cambridge University Press, 2000.

Giddens, A. *Modernity and Self-Identity: Self and Society in the Late Modern Age*, London: Polity Press, 1990.

Giddens, A. *Beyond Left and Right*, Cambridge: Polity Press, 1994.

Giddens, A. *The Third Way*, Cambridge: Polity Press, 1998.

Gilpin, A. *Environmental Impact Assessment*, Cambridge: Cambridge University Press, 1995.

Gore, A. *An Inconvenient Truth*, Emmaus, Penn Rodale, 2006.

Gouldon, A. and Murphy, J. *Regulatory Realities. The Implementation and Impact of Industrial Environmental Regulation*, London: Earthscan Publications Ltd, 1998.

Gormley, L. 'Free Movement of Goods and the Environment' in Holder, J. (ed.) The Impact of EC Environment Law in the UK (1997) 289.

Grant, A. and Jickells, T. 'Marine and estuarine pollution' in O'Riordan, T. *Environmental Science for Environmental Management*, Essex Longman, 1995.

Grant, W. *Pressure Groups, Politics and Democracy in Britain*, London: Philip Allan, 1989.

Grant, W. 'Insider and Outsider Pressure Groups' (January, 1990) *Social Studies Review* pp. 10–15.

Grant, W., Matthews, D. and Newell, P. *The Effectiveness of European Union Environmental Policy*, London: Macmillan 2000.

Gray, N.F. *Drinking Water Quality: Problems and Solutions*, London: John Wiley, 1994.

Gunningham, N. and Grabosky, P. *Smart Regulation: Designing Environmental Policy*, Oxford: Clarendon Press, 1998.

Gunningham, N., Kagan R. and Thornton, D. *Shades of Green: Business, Regulation and Environment*, Stanford University Press, California, 2003.

Gunningham, N. and Sinclair, D. 'Policy instrument choices and diffuse source pollution' (2005) 17 JEL 51.

Haack, S. *Defending Science*, Amherst, New York: Prometheus Books, 2007.

Hancock, J. *Environmental Human Rights: Power, Ethics and Law*, Aldershot: Ashgate, 2003.

Hardin, G. 'The Tragedy of the Commons' 162 (1968) *Science* 1243.

Harremoës, P. et al. (eds.) *The Precautionary Principle in the 20th Century: Late Lessons from Early Warnings*, London: Earthscan, 2001.

Harris, G. *Seeking Sustainability in an Age of Complexity*, Cambridge: Cambridge University Press, 2007.

Harrison, R.M. (ed.) *Pollution: Causes, Effects and Control*, London: The Royal Society of Chemistry, 2001.

Harrison, R.M. (ed.) *Introduction to Pollution Science*, London: The Royal Society of Chemistry, 2006.

Harrison, R.M. and Hester, R. (eds.) *Biodiversity under Threat*, London: The Royal Society of Chemistry, 2007.

Harvey, G. *The Killing of the Countryside*, London: Jonathan Cape, 1997.

Haslem, S.M. *River Pollution an Ecological Perspective*, London: John Wiley & Sons, 1990.

Havemann, P. 'Modernity, Commodification and Social Citizenship' (1997) 1(1) *Yearbook of New Zealand Jurisprudence* 17.

Hawke, N. *Environmental Policy: Implementation and Enforcement*, London: Ashgate, 2002.

Hawkins, R. and Shaw, H. *The Practical Guide to Waste Management law*, London: Thomas Telford, 2004.

Hayward, T. *Constitutional Environmental Rights*, Oxford: Oxford University Press, 2005.

Heftz, A. and Warner, M. 'Privatization and its reverse: explaining the dynamics of the government contracting process' (2004) 14(2) *Journal of Public Administration Research and Theory* 171–90.

Helm, D. *Environmental Policy: Objectives, Instruments and Implementation*, Oxford: Oxford University Press, 2000.

Hilson, C. *Regulating Pollution: A UK and EC Perspective*, Oxford: Hart.

Holder, J. 'New Age: Rediscovering Natural Law' (2000) 53 *Current Legal Problems* 151.

Holder, J. *Environmental Asessment: The Regulation of Decision Making*, Oxford: Oxford University Press, 2004.

Holder, J. and Lee, M. *Environmental Protection: Text and Materials*, Cambridge: Cambridge University Press, 2007.

Holder, J. and McGillivray, D. (eds.) *Taking Stock of Environmental Assessment*, London: Routledge-Cavendish, 2007.

Horan, N.J. *Biological Wastewater Treatment Systems. Theory and Operation*, London: John Wiley & Sons, 1990.

Howarth, W. *Water Pollution Law*, London: Shaw and Sons, 1988.

Howarth, W. 'Environmental Human Rights and Parliamentary Democracy' (2002) 14 *Journal of Environmental Law*, pp. 353–89.

Howarth, W. and McGillivray, D. *Water Pollution and Water Quality Laws*, London: Crayford: Shaw and Sons, 2001.

Hunt, M. *Using Human Rights Law in English Courts*, Oxford: Hart Publishing 1998.

Ilbery, B. *The Geography of Rural Change*, Essex: Longman, 1998.

Jacobs, M. *The Green Economy*, London: Pluto, 1991.

Jans, J. and Vedder, H. *European Environmental Law*, Gronigen: Europa, 2007.

Jasanoff, S. *The Fifth Branch: Science Advisers as Policymakers*, Cambridge, Mass. Harvard, 1990.

Jewell, T. and Steele, J. (eds.) *Law in Environmental Decision Making*, Oxford: Clarendon Press, 1998.

Jones, B., Palmer, J. and Sydenham, A. *Countryside Law*, 4th edition, Crayford: Shaw and Sons, 2004.

Kelsey, J. *The New Zealand Experiment*, Auckland: Auckland University Press, 1995.

Kinnersley, D. *Coming Clean: The Politics of Water and the Environment*, London: Harmondsworth, Penguin, 1994.

Kiss, A. and Shelton, D. *Manual of European Environmental Law* 2nd edition, Cambridge: Cambridge University Press, 1997.

Kiss, A. and Shelton, D. *Guide to International Environmental Law*, Martinus Nijhoff Publishers: Leiden and Boston, 2007.

Klonk, C. *Science and the Perception of* Nature, Yale: Yale University Press, 1996.

Ksentini Report, *Human Rights and the Environment* UN Doc. E/CN.4/Sub.2/1994/9, 6 July 1994.

Kramer, L. *EC Environmental Law*, 5th edition, London: Sweet and Maxwell, 2003.

Lawrence, D. and Lee, R. 'Permitting uncertainty: owners, occupiers and responsibility for remediation' (2003) 66 *Modern Law Review* 261.

Lazarus, R.J. *The Making of Environmental Law*, University of Chicago Press: Chicago, 2004.

Lee, M. *EU Environmental Law*, Hart: Oxford, 2005.

Lee, M. 'What is private nuisance?' 119 *Law Quarterly Review* 298.

Leicester, A. *The UK Tax System and the Environment*, London: Institute for Fiscal Studies 2006.

Lombourg, B. *The Skeptical Environmentalist*, Cambridge: Cambridge University Press, 2001.

Malcolm, R. and Ponting, J. *Statutory Nuisance: Law and Practice*, Oxford: Oxford University Press, 2002.

Malthus, T. *Essay on the Principle of Population*, London: 1798 reprinted Pelican edition, London, 1970.

Mannion, A.M. and Bowlby, S.R. *Environmental Issues in the 1990s*, London: John Wiley, 1992.

Markham, A. *A Brief History of Pollution*, London: Earthscan, 1994.

Marr, S. *The Precautionary Principle in the Law of the Sea – Modern Decision-Making in International Law*, London: London University Press, 2003.

Marren, P. *Nature Conservation: A Review of the Conservation of Wildlife in Britain 1950–2001*, London: Harper Collins, 2002.

Martins, S.W. *Farmers, Landlords and Landscapes: Rural Britain 1720–1870*, Cheshire: Windgather Press, 2004.

Mason, C.F. *Biology of Freshwater Pollution*, 3rd edition, Longman Scientific & Technical, 1995.

Merrills, J.G. 'Environmental Protection and Human Rights: Conceptual Aspects' in Boyle, A.E. and Anderson, M. (eds.) *Human Rights Approaches to Environmental Protection*, Oxford: Clarendon Press, 1996.

Miller, C. *Environmental Rights – Critical Perspectives*, London: Routledge, 1998.

Monbiot, G. *Heat: How to Stop the Planet from Burning*, Cambridge Mass.: South End Press, 2007.

Moore, V. *A Practical Approach to Planning Law*, 9th edition, Oxford: Oxford University Press, 2005.

Moser, C.A. *Social Conditions in England and Wales*, Oxford: Clarendon Press, 1958.

Mungall, C. and McLaren, D. (eds.) *Planet Under Stress*, Oxford: Oxford University Press, 1990.

MacNeil, M., Sargent, N. and Swan, P. (eds.) *Law, Regulation and Governance*, Oxford: Oxford University Press, 2003.

Macrory, R. (ed.) *Reflections on 30 years of EU Environmental Law: A High Level of Protection?*, Gronigen: Europa, 2005.

Macrory, R., Havercroft, I. and Purdy, R. *Principles of European Environmental Law*, Gronigen: Europa, 2004.

Macrory, R. (ed.) *Principles of European Environmental Law*, London: Europa, 2004.

Macrory, R. *Regulatory Justice: Making Sanctions Effective*, London Cabinet Office, 2006.

Macrory, R. 'Regulating in a Risky Environment' [2001] *Current Legal Problems* 619.

Macrory, R. *Modernising Justice: Regulation and the Role of an Environmental Tribunal*, March 2003, Centre for Law and the Environment. Faculty of Laws, University College, London (available through Defra).

Macrory, R. *The Environmental Justice Report*, Environmental Law Foundation, 2004 (available through Defra).

McAuslan, P. *Ideologies of Planning Law*, Oxford: Pergamon Press, 1980.

McCormick, J. *Environmental Policy in the European Union*, London: Palgrave, 2001.

McCracken, R. et al., *Statutory Nuisance*, London: Butterworths, 2001.

McEldowney, J.F. and McEldowney, S. *Environment and the Law*, Essex: Longman, 1996.

McEldowney, J.F. and McEldowney, S. *Environmental Law and Regulation*, London and Oxford: Blackstone and Oxford University Press, 2001.

McManus, F. and Burns, T. 'The impact of EC Law on Noise law in the United Kingdom' in Holder, J. (ed.) *The Impact of EC Environmental Law in the United Kingdom*, Chichester: Wiley, p. 15, 1997.

McNeill, J. *Something New Under the Sun: An environmental history of the twentieth century*, London: Penguin, 2000.

Nagle, J.C. and Ruhl, J.B. *The Law of Biodiversity and Ecosystems Management*, 2nd edition, New York: New York Foundation Press, 2006.

O'Brien, M. *Making Better Environmental Decisions*, Cambridge: MIT Press, 2000.

O'Riordan, T. (ed.) *Environmental Science for Environmental Management*, London: Longman, 1995.

O'Riordan, T. (ed.) *Ecotaxation*, London: Earthscan Publications, 1997.

Orwin, C.S. and Whetham, E.H. *History of British Agriculture 1846–1914*, 2nd edition, Harlow: Longman, 1971.

Overton, M. *Agricultural Revolution in England: The Transformation of the agrarian economy 1500–1850*, 5th edition, Cambridge: Cambridge University Press, 2006.

Parpworth, N., Thompson, K. and Jones, B. 'Environmental Offences: utilising civil penalties' (2005) JPL 560.

Pearce, D. and Barbier, E.B. *Blueprint for a Sustainable Economy*, London; Earthscan, 2000.

Penn, C.N. *Noise Control*, London: Shaw and Sons, 2002.

Pigou, A.C. *Wealth and Welfare*, 1912.

Pitchtel, J. *Waste Management Practices: Municipal, Hazardous and Industrial*, London: Taylor and Francis, 2005.

Pogge, T. *World Poverty and Human Rights: Cosmopolitan Responsibilities and Reforms*, Cambridge and Malden: Polity Press, Blackwell, 2002.

Pontin, B. 'Integrated Pollution control in Victorian Britain: rethinking progress within the history of environmental law' (2007) 19 *Journal of Environmental Law* 173.

Ponting, C. *A Green History of the World*, London: Sinclair-Stevenson, 1991.

Porritt, J. *Seeing Green: The Politics of Ecology Explained*, Oxford: Blackwell: 1984.

Porritt, J. *Capitalism*, London: Earthscan, 2005.

Porter, R. *Enlightenment, Britain and the creation of the Modern World*, London: Penguin Books, 2000.

Rackham, O. *The History of the Countryside*, London: Orion, 2000.

Redclift, M. and Woodgate, G. (eds.) *The International Handbook of Environmental Sociology*, Cheltenham: Edward Elgar Publishing, 1997.

Reid, C. *Nature Conservation Law*, 2nd edition, Edinburgh: W. Green, 2002.

Reid, C. Regulation in a Changing World: Review and revision of environmental permits (2008) *Cambridge Law Journal* 126.

Revez, R., Sands, P. and Stewart, R.B. *Environmental Law, The Economy and Sustainable Development*, Cambridge: Cambridge University Press, 2000.

Richardson, B.J. and Wood, S. *Environmental Law for Sustainability: A Reader*, Oxford: Hart Publishing, 2006.

Richardson, B.J. *Socially Responsible Investment Law: Regulating Unseen Polluters*, Oxford: Oxford University Press, 2008.

Richardson, B.J. et al. (eds.) *Climate Law and Developing Countries: Legal and Policy Challenges for the World Economy*, Cheltenham: Edward Elgar Publishing, 2009.

Richardson, G., Ogus, A. and Barrows, P. *Policing Pollution*, Oxford: Oxford University Press, 1983.

Robertson, D. and Kellow, A. *Globalisation and the Environment. Risk Assessment and the WTO*, London: Routledge, 2001.

Rogers, P.P., Jalal, K.F. and Boyd, J.A. *An Introduction to Sustainable Development*, London: Earthscan, 2008.

Ross, A. 'The UK approach to delivering sustainable development in government: a case study in joined-up working' (2005) 17 JEL 27.

Rycroft, R.W. and Kash, D.E. *The Complexity Challenge: Technological Innovation for the 21st Century*, London: Pinter, 1999.

Sackville, R. 'Mega-Litigation: towards a new approach' (2008) *Civil Justice Quarterly* 244.

Sands, P. *Principles of International Environmental Law*, 2nd edition, Cambridge: Cambridge University Press, 2003.

Sands, P. *Lawless World*, London: Penguin, 2006.

Sands, P. *Lawless World: America and the Making and Breaking of Global* Rules, London: Penguin, 2005.

Scott, C. 'Accountability in the Regulatory State' (2000) 27 *Journal of Law and Society* 38–60.

Scott, J. *EC Environmental Law*, London: Sweet and Maxwell, 1998.

Sen, A. *The Idea of Justice*, London: Penguin, 2009.

Shaw, M. *International Law*, 4th edition, Cambridge: Cambridge University Press, 1997.

Shaw, N. and Owen, J.S. *The Smoke Problem of Great Cities*, London; Constable, 1925.

Shelton, D. 'Environmental Rights' in Alston, P. *People's Rights*, Oxford: Oxford University Press, 2001.

Smout, T. *Nature Contested*, Edinburgh: Edinburgh University Press, 2000.

Somsen, H. (ed.) *The Regulatory Challenge of Biotechnology*, Cheltenham: Edward Elgar Publishing, 2007.

Somsen, H. (ed.) *The Yearbook of European Environmental Law*, Oxford: Oxford University Press, 2000.

Stallworthy, M. *Sustainability, Land Use and the Environment*, London: Cavendish, 2002.

Stallworthy, M. 'Whether Environmental Human Rights?' (2005) 7 *Environmental Law Review* 12–33.

Steele, J. *Risks and Legal Theory*, Oxford: Hart Publishing, 2004.

Stern, N. *The Economics of Climate Change*, London: HM Treasury, 2006.

Stiglitz, J. *Globalisation and Its Discontents*, New York: WW Norton, London: Allen Lane, 2004.

Sunstein, C. *Risk and Reason*, Cambridge: Cambridge University Press, 2002.

Sunstein, C. *Laws of Fear: Beyond the Precautionary Principle*, Cambridge: Cambridge University Press, 2005.

Snyder, F. (ed.) *The Europeanisation of Law*, Oxford: Hart Publishing, 2000.

Therivel, R. *Strategic Environmental Assessment in Action*, London: Earthscan, 2004.

Thornton, J. and Beckwith, S. *Environmental Law*, 2nd edition, London: Sweet and Maxwell, 2004.

Tolba, M. et al., *The World Environment 1972–1992*, London: Chapman and Hall, 1992.

Tromans, S. and Turrell-Clarke, R. *Contaminated Land*, 2nd edition, London: Sweet and Maxwell, 2008.

Tromans, S. 'EC Waste Law – A Complete Mess?' (2001) 13(2) JEL 133.

Van Wynsberghe, D., Noback, C.R. and Carola, R. *Human Anatomy and Physiology*, 3rd edition, New York: McGraw Hill Inc, 1995.

Vogel, D. *National Styles of Regulation*, Cornell, USA: Cornell University Press, 1986.

Vogler, J. *The Global Commons: A Regime Analysis*, Chichester: Wiley, 1995.

Wadsworth, R. and Treweek, J. *Geographical Information Systems for Ecology*, Essex: Longman, 1999.

Waldron, J. (ed.) *Theories of Rights*, Oxford: Oxford University Press, 1984.

Waldron, J. *The Law, Theory and Practice in British Politics*, London: Routledge, 1990.

Waldron, J. 'A Rights-Based Critique of Constitutional Rights' (1993) 13 *Oxford Journal of Legal Studies* 18.

Walls, M., Maculey, M., and Anderson, S. 'Private markets, contracts and government provision. What explains the organization of local waste and recycling markets?' (2005) 40(5) *Urban Affairs Review* 590–613.

Warren, L. 'Global climate change: A Stern response' (2007) Env.L.Rev. 77.

White, F. and Hollingsworth, K. *Audit, Accountability and Government*, Oxford: Oxford University Press, 1999.

Wilkinson, D. *Environment and Law*, London: Routledge, 2002.

Wilkinson, H. 'Subsidiarity and EC Environmental Policy: Taking People's Concerns Seriously' (1994) 6(1) JEL 85.

Williamson, T. *The Transformation of Rural England: Farming and the Landscape 1700–1870*, Exeter, University of Exeter Press, 2003.

Williamson, T. and Murley, L. (eds.) *The Clean Air Revolution 1952–2052*, Brighton: NSCA, 2003.

Winichokoff, D., Jasanoff, S., Busch, L., Grove-White,R. and Wynne, B. 'Adjudicating the GN Food wars: science, risk and democracy in world trade law' (2005) 20 *Yale Journal of International Law* 81.

Winter, G. 'Perspectives for Environmental Law-Entering the Fourth Phase', *Journal of Environmental Law* vol. 1 no. 1 p. 42.

Wohl, A.S. *Endangered Lives; Public Health in Victorian Britain*, London: J.M. Dent and Sons Ltd, 1983.

A.S. Wohl, *The Eternal Slum: Housing and Social Policy in Victorian England* London: Edward Arnold, 1977.

Wood, C. *Environmental Impact Assessment: A comparative Review*, 2nd edition, London: Pearson, 2002.

Woods, M. and Macrory, R. *Environmental Civil Penalties – A More Proportionate Response to Breach?*, London: UCL, 2003.

Woolf, M. *Why Globalisation Works*, Yale University, 2004.

Woolf, S., White, A. and Stanley, N. *Principles of Environmental Law*, 3rd edition, Cavendish London, 2002.

Woolley, J. et al., *Environmental Law*, Oxford: OUP, 2000.

Zillman, D., et al. (eds.), *Human Rights in Natural resource Development*, Oxford: Oxford University Press, 2002.

Zweigert, K. and Kotz, H. *An Introduction to Comparative Law*, 2nd edition, Oxford: Clarendon Press, 1994.

Government Reports

OECD, *Report of the OECD Workshop on Environmental Hazard/Risk Assessment.* Environment Monograph no 105. (OECD, 1995).

OECD, *OECD Guidelines for the Testing of Chemicals, Plus the 9th Addendum.* (OECD, 1998).

OFWAT, *Paying for Quality: The Political Perspective* (OFWAT, 1993).

OFWAT, *Paying For Water: A Time for Decisions* (OFWAT, 1991).

OFWAT, *Future Charges for Water and Sewerage Services: The Outcome of the Periodic Review* (OFWAT, 1994).

PPG24 *Planning and Noise* (HMSO, 1994).

Report of the Noise Review Working Party (HMSO, 1990).

Royal Commission on Environmental Pollution, 16th Report *Freshwater Quality* June, 1992 (Cm 1966) (HMSO, 1992).

Royal Commission on Environmental Pollution, 21st Report *Environmental Pollution on Setting Environmental Standards* Cm 4053 (October 1998) (HMSO, 1998).

Rural England Cm 3016 (HMSO, 1995).

Stewart, M., 'Modelling sewage treatment costs' Office of Water Services Research Paper No.4 January 1994.

Stewart, M., 'Modelling water costs' Office of Water Services Research Paper no 2 and Warwick Economic Working Paper No.9416, 1994.

Stewart,M., 'Modelling water costs' Office of Water Services Research Paper No.3 January 1994.

The Government's White Paper, *Review of Radioactive Waste Management Policy* (Cm 2919) (HMSO, 1995).

This Common Inheritance Cm 1200 (HMSO, 1990).

UK Annual Report *This Common Inheritance* Cm 2822 (HMSO, 1995).

UK Groundwater Forum, *Groundwater in the UK A strategic Study* UK Groundwater Resources, June, 1995.

UK.Sustainable Development: the United Kingdom Strategy (HMSO, 1994).

UNDP, *Human Development Report 1992* (Oxford University Press, 1992).

United Nations Economic Commission for Europe (UNECE), *Policies for Integrated Water Management* E/ECE/1084 (1985).

United Nations, *Agenda 21: The United Nation's Programme of Action from Rio* (United Nations, 1992).

Waste Strategy for England 2007 Cm 7086.

WHO *Guidelines for Drinking-water Quality.* Vol. 2 pp. 290–292. (World Health Organisation, 1984).

WHO Health Hazards from Nitrates in Drinking-Water. (World Health Organisation, 1985).

World Commission on Environment and Development, *Our Common Future* Oxford: Oxford university Press, 1987.

World Bank, World Development Report 1992 (Oxford University Press, 1992).

Selected websites

Useful sites

You will find the European Environmental Law Network provides up-to-date information and discussion at *www.asser.nl/default.aspx?site_id=7.*

The International Environmental Law Research Guide gives access to a wealth of information and databases, see *www.ll.georgetown.edu/guides/InternationalEnvironmentalLaw.cfm.*

The International Union for Conservation of Nature, founded in 1948, is also a useful information source, see *www.iucn.org/* as is the United Nations Environmental Programme (UNEP) at *www.unep.org.*

There are also a variety of organisations that are important for environmental law such as the World Trade Organization at *www.wto.org*.

The *www.worldtradelaw.net* is also a useful source for world trade law.

The Organisation for Economic Co-operation and Development (OECD), which supports sustainable economic growth internationally, provides material relevant to environmental law, see *www.oecd.org*.

Europe and European Union matters are covered at *http://europa.eu/index_en.htm*.

ENDS (Environmental Data Services Reports)
www.ends.co.uk/index.htm

EU sources and institutions
www.europa.eu.int/eur-lex/en/index.htm
www.europa.eu.int/comm./environment/index_en.htm

European Environmental Law Homepage
www.eel.nl

UK sources and government bodies/departments
www.open.gov.uk
www.defra.gov.uk

www.defra.gov.uk/environment/climatechange/uk/ukcccp/index.htm
www.rcep.org.uk

Environment Agency
www.environment-agency.gov.uk

Centre for Corporate Accountability
www.corporateaccountability.org

International Law and related sources

Climate Change Convention Secretariat
www.unfcc.int

Commission on Sustainable Development
www.un.org/esa/dsd/csd/csd_aboucsd.shtml

Judgements of the ICJ
www.icj-cij.org

International Maritime Organisation
www.imo.org/

World Bank
www.worldbank.org/

World Trade
www.worldtradelaw.net

World Trade Organisation
www.wto.org/

American Society of International Law
www.eisil.org

Index

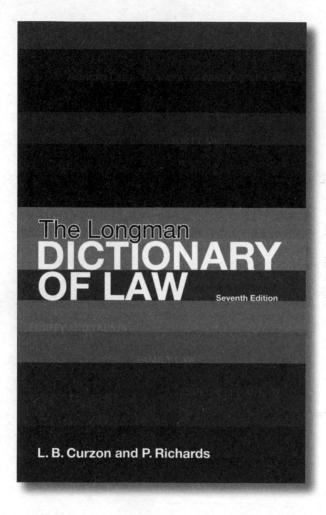